THE PROPHECIES

OF

THE PROPHET EZEKIEL

ELUCIDATED.

BY

E. W. HENGSTENBERG, D.D.,
PROFESSOR OF THEOLOGY, BERLIN.

𝕮𝖗𝖆𝖓𝖘𝖑𝖆𝖙𝖊𝖉 𝖇𝖞
A. C. MURPHY, A.M., AND J. G. MURPHY, LL.D.

Wipf & Stock
PUBLISHERS
Eugene, Oregon

Wipf and Stock Publishers
199 W 8th Ave, Suite 3
Eugene, OR 97401

The Prophecies of the Prophet Ezekiel Elucidated
By Hengstenberg, E. W.
ISBN: 1-59752-173-6
Publication date 5/5/2005
Previously published by T. & T. Clark, 1869

THE AUTHOR'S PREFACE.

THERE are two kinds of commentaries on Holy Scripture—those that are more adapted for perusal, and those that are more suitable for reference. Both are necessary, and it would not be desirable that either should exclude the other. The present work belongs to the former class. The progress in it is rapid, and the whole is designed to give the reader a clear view of the reality of Ezekiel, and in this grand prophetical figure to bring before his mind at the same time the nature of prophecy in general.

The time is no longer distant when every pastor worthy of his calling will make it a rule of life to read his chapter daily, as in the original text of the New Testament, so also in that of the Old Testament. The exposition of Scripture must meet such a laudable custom, which is formed even in education. There is a want of such expositions of the books of the Old Testament, as truly correspond with the requirements of the clerical office. The author has here earnestly aimed at this object. How far he has succeeded it is not for him to judge, but for those for whom he has written. It will depend very much on this, whether he has succeeded in edifying without going out of his proper sphere by the introduction of ascetic considerations.

The present work, however, is not designed solely for the clergy. It will also meet the desire awakening among the educated laity to penetrate more deeply into Scripture. There are many who would rather take from the first than the second hand, whom the annotated Bibles do not satisfy, the authors of which cannot do otherwise than repeat in a convenient form what others have said before them. The text is here so arranged throughout, that it presents no difficulties or hindrances to those who are not acquainted with the original language of Scripture. Everything verbal is referred to the notes, and even in these is treated only so far as the Lexicon and Grammar do not suffice.

The author has throughout compared Luther's version with his own. Though the time has not come for an improvement of this imperishable work, yet it appears not unsuitable even now to gather stones for a building fitted for better times, for which much more may certainly be done by individual labour than by commissions.

Ezekiel prophesied in a time of great decision, in a time of the "iniquity of the end," in which sin was ripe, and with it punishment. He is exactly the prophet for our times. Whosoever penetrates into him will be deeply stirred by his earnestness, and will feel himself impelled to exert all his powers, that the crisis on which we have entered may be brought to a prosperous issue. At the same time, however, if it should please God to bring great sifting judgments upon us, to pull down what He has built up, and to root out what He has planted, we may gain from Him an immoveable confidence in the final victory of the kingdom of God, who kills and makes alive, wounds and heals, and who, after He has sent the darkest cloud, at length remembers His covenant, and displays His shining bow.

[It is only necessary to add to the Author's Preface, that mere citations from Luther's version are omitted, as not necessary for the English reader, and that the two parts of the original work are here combined, so that the reader has the whole Commentary on Ezekiel, with the Appendix, in one volume. The theologian may not agree with every opinion advanced in this volume; but he will find it one of the freshest and most edifying productions of the esteemed author.—TR.]

CONTENTS.

	PAGE
THE FIRST CYCLE (Chap. i.–vii.),	1
THE SECOND CYCLE (Chap. viii.–xix.),	68
THE THIRD CYCLE (Chap. xx.–xxiii.),	167
THE FOURTH CYCLE (Chap. xxiv.),	207
FOREIGN NATIONS (Chap. xxv.–xxxii.)—	
The Ammonites,	218
Moab,	220
Edom,	221
The Philistines,	222
Tyre and Sidon,	223
Egypt,	250
Conclusion to Chap. i.–xxxii. (Chap. xxxiii. 1–20),	288
WORDS OF COMFORT (Chap. xxxiii. 21–xxxix.),	292
RESTORATION (Chap. xl.–xlviii.),	347
RETROSPECT,	493

APPENDIX.

THE CHERUBIM,	499

THE PROPHECIES OF EZEKIEL.

THE FIRST CYCLE.

CHAPTERS I.–VII.

HE first cycle of the predictions of the prophet embraces ch. i.–vii. A sublime vision forms the introduction. To this prophetic discourses are appended which serve to explain the vision. At the close in ch. vii. a song.

In ch. i. 1–3 the introduction. Ver. 1. And it came to pass in the thirtieth year, in the fourth month, on the fifth day, as I was among the captives by the river Chebar, the heavens were opened, and I saw visions of God. 2. On the fifth day of the month (in the said year), which was the fifth year of King Jehoiachin's captivity, 3. The word of the Lord came to Ezekiel, the son of Buzi, the priest, in the land of the Chaldeans, by the river Chebar; and the hand of the Lord was there upon him.

The book begins with an *and*. This must necessarily connect it with an earlier book, as the book of Joshua, by a like beginning, is connected with the Pentateuch, the book of Judges with Joshua, the books of Samuel, as also the book of Ruth, with that of Judges. In general, Ezekiel, by beginning with an *and*, presents itself as one link of a chain of sacred books, as the book of Esther, beginning in the same way, is joined only in general to the preceding sacred literature; but in particular it is connected with Jeremiah, as appears from the fact that throughout it is fastened *par excellence* to this link of the prophetic chain. Shortly before the appearance of Ezekiel, Jeremiah had addressed a missive to the exiles. This formed, as it were, the programme of the agency which Ezekiel developed under him.

The "thirtieth year," in which the first appearance of the prophet took place, can only be the year of the prophet's life. This was just the year which was of peculiar significance to the man of priestly family—the man who in every reference presents himself as the priest among the prophets. The Levites' time of service generally began, according to Num. viii. 24, with the twenty-fifth year. According to Num. iv. 29, 30, however, it was not till thirty that they entered on the performance of those services which required the full vigour of manhood (the carrying of the sanctuary in the passage through the wilderness); compare *Beiträge*, iii. p. 392 f. According to the theological exposition of this passage, to which also the entrance of the Baptist and of Christ upon office after the completion of the thirtieth year points back, Ezekiel recognises it as significant that he was called to the prophetical office just in the thirtieth year (probably near the completion of it), which made amends, as it were, for the service in the temple of which he was deprived. As Ezekiel here at thirty sees heaven opened by a river, so Jesus in Matt. iii. 16, compared with Luke iii. 21. The general era is indicated in ver. 2, and for this very reason the reference here can only be to the year of the prophet's life. The fifth year of the captivity of Jehoiachin was the most important objective mark of time for those who were then led into captivity, among whom Ezekiel had to labour. Another era running parallel to it must have been indicated more exactly; the prophet would not have left his reader to conjecture here. There is no general era of which every one must at once have thought. Of an era of Nabopolassar there is otherwise no trace in Scripture. That the month and day belong not to the year of the prophet's life, but to that of the objective era, the captivity of Jehoiachin, is shown by the repetition of the phrase "in the fifth month" in ver. 2, which was necessary to remove any uncertainty in the reference.

The appearance of Ezekiel is fixed by definite relations of time, and the knowledge of these relations forms the key to the understanding of his prophecies. Ch. xxvii.-xxix. of Jeremiah especially afford us insight into them. These chapters belong to one another. They describe the reaction of Jeremiah against the political agitation that was leading the people away from their true objects, and which was called forth by the formation of a great anti-Chaldaic coalition. In the conflict with this enemy Ezekiel stepped to the side of Jeremiah: not policy, but penitence, is the common watchword.

According to Jer. xxvii., ambassadors from the kings of Edom, Moab, Ammon, Tyre, and Sidon had come to Jerusalem in the reign of Zedekiah to draw the king into a confederacy against the Chaldeans. We have here five of the seven nations whom Ezekiel in ch. xxv. f. threatens with destruction by the Chaldeans, in opposition to the foolish hopes which had just been reposed in them. The Egyptians also are there named, who were evidently the mainstay of the whole coalition; and the Philistines, who were connected with the Egyptian race. That the hopes and intrigues extended themselves still further, that the eye was fixed even upon the distant Sheba or Meroe, which stood in close relation to Egypt, and not less on the distant Asiatic Elam, from which, after the lapse of the seventy years' Chaldean servitude fore-ordained by God, the overthrow of Babylon undoubtedly proceeded, we learn from Ezek. viii. and xxiii.,—passages which place before our eyes the whole magnitude of the political infatuation by which Judah was seized, the whole fearfulness of her apostasy from God, who had so clearly marked out other ways for her, so that the coalition was directed no less against her than against the king of Babylon. They wished to attain deliverance without God, yea, against God.

The twenty-seventh chapter of Jeremiah begins with the words: "In the beginning of the reign of Jehoiakim the son of Josiah." Ver. 3 shows that it is not the elder Jehoiakim who is meant, but he who revives again in Zedekiah, who, according to 2 Kings xxiv. 9, " did that which was evil in the sight of the Lord, according to all that his father had done." This typical usage of speech, which is largely diffused through the Scripture, the expositors could not comprehend. We have the key to it in that very passage of the book of Kings.

In view of the political agitation called forth by the embassy, Jeremiah exhorts to humiliation under the mighty hand of God: " Hearken not ye to your prophets, nor to your diviners, nor to your dreams, nor to your enchanters, nor to your sorcerers, who speak unto you, saying, Ye shall not serve the king of Babylon. . . . Hearken not unto them: serve the king of Babylon, and live; wherefore should this city be laid waste?"

According to Jer. xxviii., in the fourth year of Zedekiah, in the fifth month—eleven months, therefore, before the appearance of Ezekiel—the "prophet" Hananiah announces to the prophet Jeremiah, in the name of the Lord, that the yoke of the king of Babylon shall be broken. After the lapse of two years the Lord will bring back to Jerusalem all the vessels of the temple that Nebuchadnezzar took away, and also King Jehoiachin, and all the captives. Jeremiah answers in the name of the Lord: "The wooden yoke I break, and make instead thereof an iron yoke." By the popular intrigues their position will only be rendered more difficult. Jeremiah announces death to the false prophet; and this follows in the same year, in the seventh month, nine months before the appearance of Ezekiel.

The twenty-ninth chapter enters still more closely into the relations of Ezekiel. It contains a letter of Jeremiah to the captives. He warns them in ver. 8: "Let not your prophets and your diviners, that be in the midst of you, deceive you; neither hearken to your dreams which ye cause to be dreamed. For they prophesy falsely unto you in my name: I have not sent them, saith the Lord." "Which ye cause to be dreamed:" the false prophets prophesied to order; they flattered the then ruling humour of the people. Jeremiah shows the captives that the unalterably fixed seventy years of the Babylonian servitude, of which only eleven had then elapsed, must first run their full course. He seeks to lead them to repentance and to faith; as this was the legitimate course to pursue, in order to return home after patiently awaiting the period of their punishment. So far from thinking already of the return of the exiles to Jerusalem, the heaviest judgments still stand over Jerusalem, and those who remain there.

We learn from this chapter that the *false* prophets and the *true* prophets in Jerusalem were in correspondence with the exiles: bane and antidote proceeded from thence. It is no less evident also from this, that those in exile sought to exercise an influence upon the state of things in the fatherland. The false prophet Shemaiah sends an accusation against Jeremiah to the priest, who had the superintendence in the temple.

In ver. 21 Jeremiah announces that the false prophets of the captivity, Ahab and Zedekiah, shall be given into the hand of Nebuchadnezzar king of Babylon, and be slain by him. From this we learn that the commotions among the exiles were of a serious character. In vers. 24–32 he foretells destruction to another false prophet, Shemaiah already mentioned, to whom he gives the derisive surname of "Dreamer."[1]

In ch. xxix. 23 the prophet compares the behaviour of the false prophets among the exiles to adultery. "They commit adultery," he says, "with their neighbours' wives." Graf says, "They appear to have been guilty also of immoral conduct in private life." But this is quite foreign to the present connection. An abridged comparison is made. Spiritual adultery appears under the phrases of corporeal.

It was high time for the Lord to raise up among the exiles themselves a counterforce against such adulterous behaviour. This was accomplished by the calling of Ezekiel.

Like all the names of the canonical prophets, that of Ezekiel is not that which he had borne from his youth, but an official title which he had received at the beginning of his calling. It means not, "whom God strengthens," which according to the form it cannot signify, but, "God is, or becomes strong; he in relation to whom God is strong." We have the root of the name in Jer. xx. 7: "Thou art stronger than I, and hast prevailed." The explanation is here given in ch. i. 3, "And the hand of the Lord was upon him;" but especially in iii. 14, "And the hand of the Lord was strong upon me." It was God's becoming strong upon the prophet that made him strong in the sight of an apostate and disobedient people, made his face hard against their face, and his forehead against their forehead (iii. 8),—made his forehead harder than flint, so that he had no fear of them.

The heavens are opened to the prophet, and he sees visions

[1] The name is formed from the 1st plur. fut., like the name Nimrod, which the tyrant of the olden time received from the watchword *Rebellemus*, which he with his comrades employed. Nechalami means, a native of the place where dreaming has become a watchword.

of God.[1] Visions of God are, in the first place, visions which proceed from God, as in the prophecy of Balaam (Num. xxiv. 4) the vision of the Almighty is the vision which goes forth from the Almighty. Divine visions stand opposed to the visions of one's own heart, the vain fancies of false prophets, who say, "I have dreamed, I have dreamed; and it is only the deceit of their own heart" (Jer. xxiii. 25, 26). Visions which proceed from God are, however, as such, at the same time visions which have God for their object; there can only be seen in them that which has been taken into connection with God, which belongs to the sphere of Elohim, which embraces all that is divine (1 Sam. xxviii. 13). In this respect, so far as the language refers to heavenly images, the sight of which is the result of the opening of heaven, we may compare 2 Kings vi. 17: "And the Lord opened the eyes of the young man; and he saw: and, behold, the mountain was full of horses and chariots of fire round about Elisha;" and Matt. iii. 16: "And, lo, the heavens were opened unto him, and he saw the Spirit of God descending like a dove." The Spirit of God in the form of a dove is in this respect an illustrative example of the visions of God.

Ver. 4. And I looked, and, behold, a whirlwind came out of the north, a great cloud, and a fire infolding itself, and a brightness[2] was about it, and out of the midst of it was as the colour of shining brass, out of the midst of the fire.

This verse points, in the first place, to that which forms the principal feature in the visions of God—the appearance of God in His angry majesty. This is followed by the description of the cherubim and the wheels, which are *also* comprehended among the visions of God. Vers. 27, 28 return to the appearance of God, and carry out in reference to it what is here only alluded to.

The storm represents a severe visitation of the people, to whom the mission of all the prophets is directed, and of whom we must therefore also here think, as we have before us the consecration of a prophet to his office. The winds are in

---

[1] מַרְאָה, what is seen, ὅραμα, is not essentially distinguished from חִזָּיוֹן, view—what one views.

[2] Luther's translation, "which shone everywhere around," assigns the brightness to the *fire*, instead of the whole appearance.

Scripture the customary symbols of the judgments, the storms of sufferings and trials decreed by God. Job, the type of the Israelitish people, says of God in ch. ix. 17, "He breaketh me with a tempest, and multiplieth my wounds without cause." In the often falsely interpreted passage, 1 Kings xix. 11, "The great and strong wind rending the mountains, and breaking in pieces the rocks before the Lord," signifies the storm of trials and calamities which went over the church and her representative the prophet. Jeremiah announces in ch. iv. 11, 12 that a strong wind shall come upon the people of God, and explains it thus: "I will give sentence against them."

Storm! With this one word the prophet places himself in rugged opposition to the false prophets who proclaimed with one mouth serene tranquillity—$\gamma a \lambda \eta \nu \eta$ $\mu \epsilon \gamma a \lambda \eta$, Matt. viii. 26—and deals a great blow to the joyous hopes they had excited.

The storm comes out of the *north.* This is among the prophets the region pregnant with fate, the quarter from which the Asiatic world-powers—namely, the Chaldeans—were wont to break into the holy land. "I will bring evil from the north, and a great destruction," God says by Jeremiah (ch. iv. 6). Exactly parallel to the storm out of the north here is the seething-pot coming from the north, which the prophet (ch. i. 13) sees likewise on his first calling. The seething-pot there signifies the war-fire coming from the north. In the exposition of the symbol given by the Lord, it is said (vers. 14, 15), "Out of the north an evil shall break forth upon all the inhabitants of the land. For, lo, I will call all the families of the kingdoms of the north; and they shall come, and they shall set every one his throne at the entering of the gates of Jerusalem." According to the intimate relation between Jeremiah and Ezekiel, this interpretation serves likewise for the latter.

Hitzig objects: "It is clear that passages like Jer. i. 14 do not apply here; for it is Jehovah, not Nebuchadnezzar, that appears, and the latter would have come from the south to the scene of action." But Nebuchadnezzar, the servant of the Lord, and Jehovah form no opposition; much rather the word holds here, "They come out of distant lands, the Lord and the instruments of His wrath, to lay waste the whole earth;" and with the Asiatic world-kingdoms, when the inundation of the holy land is in hand, it is not the site of the capital city that is regarded, but the quarter out of which the invasion took place. This proceeded from the north, from Syria, because the eastern side of the holy land was covered by the vast, trackless wilderness of Arabia Deserta.

The coalition which gave occasion to the appearance of Ezekiel was directed against the north. The storm out of the north drives all the sanguine hopes which were founded on this coalition like withered leaves before it.

Next to the storm comes a "great cloud." The clouds with which, or in the company of which, the Lord comes, are in Scripture the adumbration of judgment; comp. my comm. on Rev. i. 7. Storm and cloud appear conjoined as here in Nah. i. 3: "The Lord hath His way in the whirlwind and in the storm, and the clouds are the dust of His feet."

All was in expectation of the sun soon about to break forth clearly in the political heavens, and of the healing under His wings (Mal. iv. 2). The prophet cannot chime in with this jubilee. He sees the heavens covered with black clouds as with a pall.

The third symbol of wrath, the close infolding fire, is from Ex. ix. 24. There it falls upon the Egyptians; here it is directed against the degenerate people of God. As they have become conformed to the Egyptians in their practices, they need not wonder if also the fate of the Egyptians befalls them. They have not, in fact, desired otherwise. Or should their God, like the false gods of the heathen, have a blind love for His people? In that case He could not be righteous (Deut. xxxii. 4) (Luther, pious), *i.e.* so constituted as He should be, as corresponds with the nature of the true God, who as such recompenses to every one according to his works, without regarding such wretched things as circumcision and ceremonies. Deut. iv. 24 gives the interpretation of the symbol. There "God is a consuming fire, even a jealous God." The fire signifies the energy of His punitive justice. Of this, in its relation to the degenerate covenant people, it is already said in Deut. xxxii. 22: "For a fire is kindled in mine anger, and shall burn unto the lowest hell, and shall consume the earth with her increase, and set on fire the foundations of the mountains."

The future appeared to the people to be full of light; the prophet bears down without remorse on these foolish hopes, and sets before the view scorching flames which leave nothing but a heap of ashes behind.

The prophet views first the storm, the cloud, the fire, then the symbol of the glory of God. In existing circumstances, it was not of so much import that God appeared in general, as in what character He appeared; and this character is represented by storm, cloud, and fire. This was a powerful stroke against the illusions, the dreams of a gracious God, and of an immediately impending future of prosperity.

These illusions, however, are only the perversions of a deep truth; and to this truth the prophet assigns rightful place in the words, "and a brightness was about it." These words occur again in ver. 27. After this is the clear brightness which surrounds the at first *threatening* appearance of God, the emblem of that grace of God which stands in the background of judgment, pointing to the times of refreshing that shall come to the people of God, when judgment has first done its work upon them. The contrast of the false prophets and of the true is not that of deliverance and judgment, but that of deliverance without punishment and without repentance, and of the deliverance which after judgment falls to the lot of the penitent people—of a bare gospel, crying, Peace, peace, when there is no peace, and of the law and the gospel, each in its own time. A prophet who proclaimed only punishment, would be no less false than one who presents to view nothing but peace. Law and gospel, each in its entire fulness—this is, even to this very day, the token of the true servant of God.

The *it* refers to the whole of the appearance—storm, cloud, fire.[1] The *brightness* has first of all only a subordinate import. To this points the pronoun in the phrase, "out of the midst of it," going back at once to the more remote *fire*, which, as it were, ignores the preceding clause, "and brightness was about it." To remove every uncertainty and ambiguity, it is further added at the close, "out of the midst of the fire." At first

---

[1] The masc. suff. is intentionally put (the masc. pron. in ver. 28 also refers to the whole of the appearance); for if the femin. suff. had been put, we should have held by the reference to the next preceding noun. It would have been natural also to think of the brightness issuing from the fire itself (comp. v. 13), whereas in fact the brightness is different from the fire, and presents a contrast to it.

nothing stands in view but storm, cloud, fire. The brightness gleams only out of the far distance. But here already reference must be made to it. For it is necessary that it should be known, if storm, cloud, fire, are to exercise their proper effect "Merciful and gracious, long-suffering, and abundant in goodness and truth" (Ex. xxxiv. 6): this must stand before our eyes, if the sorrow called forth by sin is to bring with it the healthful fruit of righteousness.

Out of the midst of the fire an appearance went forth, " to look upon like *chasmal*," shining brass. "To look upon:" this indicates that it is not realities that are here spoken of, but only the imperfect *forms* of realities. That he indicates this so pointedly and continually, that he opposes so resolutely the bare realism which refuses to know anything of the distinction between thought and its dress, is one of the peculiarities of Ezekiel. Expressions like these—the appearance, the likeness, even the appearance of the likeness (ver. 28)—continually recur, for the purpose of guarding against that bare realism which, while it assumes the air of vindicating the interests of faith against a "false spiritualism," is at the same time nothing else than weakness in the exposition of Scripture. *Chasmal*, with which in ch. viii. 2 זהר, brightness, is joined by way of explanation, which is used in Dan. xii. 3 of the brightness of heaven, the LXX. render by *electrum*, a metal distinguished for its brightness, consisting of gold mixed with a fifth part of silver. It here portrays the kernel of the personality of God—His holiness, that is, His absoluteness, His unconditioned seclusion from all earthly, and in general creaturely nature— His incomparable glory.[1]

After, therefore, the leading point in the appearance has been brought forward first in outline, the prophet proceeds to the description of that which still remained to be seen, to return afterwards to the main subject. The impression which ver. 4 is fitted to make is indicated in the words of James, "Behold, the Judge standeth before the door." From this the exhortation naturally flows, "Repent, that the Judge may be gracious to you, and that the sun may appear after the cloud."

Vers. 5-14. *The Cherubim.*—God in His wrath—this was the real import of ver. 4. To increase the feeling of terror, it

[1] Compare my comm. on Ps. xxii. 4, Rev. iv. 8.

is here made prominent that this God who appears for judgment is the Almighty, the God of the spirits of all flesh, whom all that lives on earth serves, and who can bring it into the field against His people, against whom all coalitions are impotent, who alone says with entire right, "There is none that can deliver out of my hand."

The *name* of the cherubim appears later in Ezekiel for the first time in ch. ix. 3. On independent grounds the description should go side by side with that of the cherubim in the tabernacle of testimony. It is only by degrees that we perceive that the beings here described are identical with the cherubim there spoken of.

What the beings which the prophet here portrays had to signify, could not be doubtful to the intelligent mind. The four living creatures with the faces, which denote the leading classes of animals on earth, can only be the ideal combination of all that lives on earth—" the living (creature) under the God of Israel," as is said in ch. x. 20.

The appearance of the cherubim is not in itself terrible. The thought that all that lives on the earth serves God, may, in some circumstances, be very comforting. To Him who sits upon the cherubim, who alone is God over all the kingdoms of the earth, Hezekiah lifted up his eyes, according to Isa. xxxvii. 16, when he was oppressed by the power of Assyria. The appearance here assumes the threatening aspect from its connection with that which precedes in ver. 4, and from the fact that the living creatures go forth out of the fire, and are thus destined for a mission of wrath. The reality corresponding to the figure of the living creatures issuing out of the fire is the invasion of the Chaldeans, connected with the dispersion of all hopes founded on the anti-Chaldaic coalition.

Of the living creatures there are four, and they have each four faces and four wings, because four is the signature of the earth. The human form prevails among them, because man takes absolutely the first place among the living. From man they derive the face on the principal side—that turned towards the east—the upright gait, and the hands. The three other classes are represented each by one of the four faces. Then from the cattle they have the likeness of the soles of their feet, and from the birds their wings.

Ver. 5. "And I saw out of the midst thereof (of the fire) the likeness of four living creatures. And this was their appearance; they had the likeness of men. 6. And every one had four faces, and every one of them had four wings. 7. And their feet were straight feet; and the sole of their feet was like the sole of a calf's foot; and they sparkled like the colour of glowing brass. 8. And a man's hand was under their wings on their four sides; and they four had their faces and their wings. 9. Their wings were joined one to another; they turned not when they went; they went every one straight forward. 10. As for the likeness of their faces, they four had the face of a man and the face of a lion on the right side; and they four had the face of a bull on the left side; they four also had the face of an eagle.[1] 11. And (such are) their faces: and their wings were divided above;[2] each had two joined with one another, and two covered their bodies. 12. And they went every one straight forward: whither the spirit was to go they went; they turned not when they went. 13. As for the likeness of the living creatures, their appearance was like burning coals of fire, like the appearance of torches: the fire went along among the living creatures; and the fire was bright, and out of the fire went forth lightning. 14. And the living creatures ran and returned as the appearance of flashing fire."

The first part of the delineation, vers. 5-8, takes a general survey of the appearance of the cherubim; the second part, vers. 9-14, describes more particularly the wings and faces already brought forward in the survey. Ver. 8*b* turns from the hands, which were last mentioned in the survey—where after the upper parts, the faces and the wings, followed the lowest part, the feet—back to the wings and faces. After the words, "And they four had their faces and their wings," it might have been expected that the closer description would have begun with

---

[1] Luther's translation, "Their faces on the right side of the four were like a man and a lion, but on the left side of the four their faces were like an ox and an eagle," changes the four-sidedness of the appearance into a two-sidedness, removes the front and back, and leaves only the right and left.

[2] Luther's translation, "And their faces and wings were divided above," refers to the faces what only suits the wings.

the faces. It begins, however, with the wings, because in flying these rose above the faces. Still they are only so far described in ver. 9a as this holds good; and the description then passes over at once to the faces, the proper description of the wings following only in ver. 11. In ver. 12 the kind and manner of their movement are next described. In vers. 13 and 14 so much is brought forward as belonged to the cherubim, not generally, but only in relation to the matter in hand, in harmony with the threatening character of the whole appearance.

Straight feet, without bending of the knee, are in ver. 7 attributed to the cherubim, as distinguished from the animal foot.[1] The sole of the foot like that of a calf, "round and like itself all over, while the human foot is drawn out in length," is explained by the design of giving a part in the group to the cattle represented in it through the cherubim. The placing of the calf here shows that the ox in ver. 10 comes into consideration only as the representative of the cattle, and was all the more necessary as the ox in the olden time was so often regarded in other points of view; for example, as the symbol of the power of nature, which did not here come into consideration. The placing of the calf, with which these views were not connected, is designed to remove all extraneous notions. The case is similar where, in Rev. iv. 7, the eagle is described as *a flying one*, to indicate that it is brought into view simply and solely as the representative of the *birds*. The shining or scintillating is literally affirmed of the cherubim in general, not of their feet in particular.[2] Still, what is here affirmed of the cherubim refers, in point of fact, to the feet in particular: "And they were (there, on the soles of the feet) sparkling." A general affirmative would not suit here. John thus conceived the words in the Apocalypse, ch. i. 15, where it is said of Christ appearing for judgment, "And His *feet* like unto shining brass (Germ. light-brass), as if they burned in a fur-

---

[1] The living creatures are through the whole verse treated as masculine, as also already in להם at the close of ver. 6. This is explained by the fact that the proper name Cherubim, standing in the background, is masculine, and the whole appearance of the cherubim here is human. It is properly said, "straight foot." The numerical plurality is contracted into the ideal unity of the foot.

[2] The mascul. מצצים can refer only to the cherubim, not to the feet.

nace." In Dan. x. 6 it is said of Michael, "And his arms and his *feet* like in colour to shining brass." *Shining brass* is the same as glowing brass.¹ The sparkling or scintillating of the feet like glowing brass has nothing whatever to do with the nature of the cherubim, as little as the flaming sword in Gen. iii. It refers to the special mission in hand, which is one of wrath. It stands in like connection with the fire and lightning, which in ver. 13 are attributed to the entire appearance of the cherubim, with the element of fire in the appearance of the Lord Himself in ver. 4 and ver. 27.

In ver. 8 it is said literally, "its human hand," or, "its hand of a man."² The discourse is of *its* hand, not of their hands, in consequence of the ideal comprehension of the quaternity of the cherubim in the unity of the cherub—the living creature, which elsewhere also occurs along with the cherubim (Ps. xviii. 11; Ezek. ix. 3, x. 4).

The words, "And they four had their faces and their wings," only repeat, as has been remarked, what was already said in ver. 6, to indicate the return from the feet and hands to the upper parts, which are to be more exactly described.

As the wings in ver. 9 only come into consideration beforehand in so far as they rise above the face, so of the four wings which each cherub possessed according to ver. 6, only the one pair is regarded which was employed in flying; from which it is to be noted that the prophet, who describes only what is seen, sees the living creatures in motion, according to ver. 14. This pair of wings is stretched upwards, so that the one wing stands over against the other, and is in so far "joined" to it. This one pair of wings is immediately under the "vault" by which heaven is imaged, in harmony with Gen. i. 20, according to which the birds fly above the earth to the vault of heaven.

The second part turns from the wings to the faces. In relation to these it is first noted, that as, according to ver. 6, there were four of them, they did not need to turn in their

---

¹ It is properly called light (adj.) brass. But this is the same as glowing brass, because the light is represented as lighter than the dark, as the sharp is lighter than the blunt. Comp. my comm. on Rev. i. 15. נחשת does not mean shining, but sparkling—*scintillantes*.

² According to ch. x. 8, the singular ידו is to be read. The Masoretic alteration, the plural, arises, as usual, from misunderstanding.

movement, inasmuch as, in whatever direction they went, one face was always directed forwards. By this the thought is expressed that the creature is in all directions ready for the service of God; that He can very easily summon it to that place where He wishes to employ it for blessing or for punishment.

In ver. 10 the faces are then individually named. That the cherub is the representation of the living creation, appears very clearly from this designation of the faces. The combination of man, lion, ox, and eagle can only be explained in this way; as also the order of succession and the bearing towards the east. At the head the man's face stands; and this must be on the east side, which as the principal side, and as we always turn to the east when it is intended to mark the quarters of the heavens, needed no closer designation. The eagle, as the representative of the birds, takes the hindmost place. To the right, or southwards, Ps. lxxxix. 13 (Eng. 12), is the lion, the representative of all wild animals, to which the pre-eminence among the brute creation had been already accorded, from the fact that the name of "living creature," by which the animate was distinguished from the inanimate creation, is in Gen. i. appropriated specially to them, in contrast with those other classes in which the power of life was less energetic. Not without reason is the lion held among all nations as the king of beasts in general, not merely of wild beasts. In Job xxviii. 8 the wild beasts are called sons of haughtiness or of pride. To the left, or northwards, is the ox, the representative of the cattle.

We have here the most exact correspondence with Gen. i., except that here, where the object was to bring forward the living creation in great outlines, the fishes and the small land animals are disregarded. The order is quite the same, except that in the creation the progress is from the lower to the higher, whereas here the reverse order holds. First, after the swarm of the sea, the fowls come into existence. (That this is omitted in the cherubim, goes hand in hand with the fact that it was the lowest part of creation in Gen. i.) The wild beast holds in Gen. i. also the pre-eminence above the cattle. In the decree of God in ver. 24, the cattle stand foremost because of their special usefulness to men, but in the execution of it the wild beast is placed at the head. Man forms the crown of the whole.

The phrase "and (such are) their faces" serves as the conclusion to the subject of the faces, and forms the transition to that which still remained after ver. 9 to be said of the wings. Two wings, the same which were already named there, are represented as *divided,* in contrast with the other two, which were closed upon the body. The same two wings are also represented as joined together, because they stand freely over against one another, in contrast with the other two, which are separated from one another by the body.

Wings are allotted to the cherubim in general, to suit the class of birds represented in the group. But besides this, two of these wings serve to exhibit the connection between the earth and the heaven represented by the vault,—a connection which is necessary, that heaven and earth may be presented as parts of one whole, the creation of God, over which He is enthroned, and whose powers are all at His bidding, for blessing or for punishment (Job xxxvii. 13). The wings are all the better fitted to exhibit this connection, as the fowls represented by them come into closest proximity with heaven, on which account they are also called "the fowls of heaven" (Ps. viii. 9). The idea of a *carrying* of the vault upon the wings of the cherubim must be entirely abandoned. Wings are not of themselves fitted for this, and here all the less so, as they serve for flying, and are occasionally *lowered* (ver. 24). The object is only to give the medium of the connection, or a *figuration* of it.

"Divided"—namely, from the body. "Above," in contrast with the wings that covered the body. "Each had two which were joined with one (cherub)," two standing upright, which reached forth to those of another cherub, whilst also the wings of this one stretched upward.[1] We must distinguish what is here said from what is said in ver. 9. It was there said that the upper wings were joined with *one another.*

What has been already said in the particular description of ver. 9 is made prominent once more in ver. 12, with an important additional statement, which assigns the *cause* of the movement: "Whither the spirit was to go, they went." Whither the impulse standing under God's direction was to go, they went without any difficulty: no behind and no before;

---

[1] The second איש as well as the first, and also the איש in ver. 12, can only refer to the cherub.

every way stands open to them. Woe to him, therefore, against whom God in His wrath directs them; and this is, alas, the first thought, as the mission here is one of wrath, but also weal to him who is in favour with God.

The moving cause is the *Spirit*, the life-breath of God, who dwells within the creature, and leads it, according to the laws which He prescribes for it, to the ends which He places before it. God is the "God of the spirits of all flesh" (Num. xvi. 22). It is implied in this, that the creature in itself cannot and need not be the object of love, of trust, and of fear. The Spirit of God appears already in the history of the creation as the animating power in the universe. The spirit here is the spirit dwelling within the creatures. That the spirit is first of all the spirit of the living, is shown in ver. 21. That this spirit immanent in the creatures is, however, only an effluence of the Spirit of God, and stands therefore under the unconditional direction of Him who bends the hearts of kings like the waterbrooks, appears from vers. 20, 21, according to which the same spirit is in the beasts and in the wheels, in the living creatures and in the powers of nature.

Vers. 13 and 14 do not refer to the nature of the living creature in itself, but to its present mission, which is one of wrath. The fire, representing wrath and vengeance, appears separated from the cherubim themselves; it runs among the cherubim; they are, as it were, dipt in fire. "All things," remarks Grotius, "pointed to vengeance after the long patience of God"—*omnia post longam patientiam Dei ad ultionem spectabant.* The fire here must be regarded in the same light as the fire in ver. 4 and in ver. 7. In ver. 4 the fire goes hand in hand with the other symbols of the wrath of God, the storm and the cloud. In other circumstances, if the mission were friendly, the cherubim would appear wholly enveloped in light; they would *shine forth* with the God enthroned above them (Ps. xciv. 1). In itself the fire might also be directed against the *enemies* of the people of God, as formerly the fire in the pillar of cloud (Ex. xiv. 24); it might indicate the vengeance impending over them. But that it is here directed against the covenant people, that God has turned Himself into a fierce enemy against them (Job xxx. 21), appears from ver. 4, where the fire comes out of the north, the home of the world-power, not goes to the north. For now the watchword is: "Upon those who are near me will I sanctify myself;" "You only do I know of all nations of the earth, therefore will I visit upon you all your sins;" "Judgment must begin at the house of God."

The living creature runs to and fro, showing the energy of the impulse of wrath proceeding from God and filling them, which cannot rest a moment, nor abide the time when they shall be let loose. Woe to him on whom they then come! Something of this "flashing of lightning" Ezekiel might have already perceived with the natural eye among the Chaldeans.

Vers. 15–21. *The Wheels.*—These wheels represent the powers of nature. They do not *bear* the cherubim, but they stand independently *beside* them, although they occupy the lower place, the cherubim the upper. Not only do the wheels move as in a chariot, but also the cherubim move, and in such a way indeed that their movement is the primary and original one, while that of the wheels only goes along with it (vers. 14, 19). That they move simultaneously with the cherubim, arises, according to ver. 21, from this, that the spirit of the living creature is in the wheels. Externally, therefore, they are not inseparably joined with the living creature, but both obey one and the same impelling power. The local subordination to the cherubim finds its explanation only in the fact that wheels usually occupy the lowest place in a vehicle. If the powers of nature, on account of their weight, were thus viewed under the figure of a wheel in motion, this place must here have been allotted to the wheel. The whole was designed to make a single impression, to represent a kind of vehicle, in which the Lord occupied the place of the charioteer, the living creature the place of the chariot, under which are the powers of nature represented by the wheels, which are really co-ordinate with the living creature. The thought is this, that all powers as well as beings of nature serve God when He appears for judgment. This must fill men's hearts with fear and trembling before Him. Among the powers of nature, fire comes *here* particularly into consideration, just as man does among the living creatures. "He burnt up their city" (Matt. xxii. 7). These words bring out the idea. It is out of the wheels that the fire is taken in ch. x. 2 for the destruction of Jerusalem. That the powers of nature, however, serve God's purposes also in a wider extent, appears, for example, from the hail with which the Egyptians, and also the Canaanites, are visited, and from the lightning and storm in the history of Job.

Ver. 15. And I saw the living creatures, and, behold, a wheel upon the earth by the living creatures with their four faces.¹ 16. The appearance of the wheels and their work were like unto the colour of the chrysolite: and they four had one likeness: and their appearance and their work were as it were a wheel in the midst of a wheel. 17. When they went, they went upon their four sides; they turned not when they went. 18. And their felloes, they were high and terrible; and their felloes were full of eyes round about them four. 19. And when the living creatures went, the wheels went beside them; and when the living creatures were lifted up from the earth, the wheels were lifted up. 20. Whither the spirit willed to go, they went; if the spirit willed to go thither, then the wheels were lifted up beside them: for the spirit of the living creature was in the wheels. 21. When those went, they went; and when they stood, they stood; and when they were lifted up from the earth, the wheels were lifted up by the side of them: for the spirit of the living creature was in the wheels.

The appearance of the wheels is, according to ver. 16, like that of jasper or chrysolite. By this the glory of the powers of nature is indicated, as it is exhibited, for example, in a conflagration. In Ex. xxviii. 20 the jasper occurs among the precious stones in the breastplate of the high priest. In Dan. x. 6 the body of Michael is like jasper, his face like lightning, his eyes like torches of fire. There also glory and grandeur are signified by the jasper.

The wheels are not ordinary wheels, according to the second half of ver. 16, but double wheels, one set into the other. On what account it is so we learn from ver. 17, " that they might go on all sides without turning round." It is not hereby intended to take into consideration the physical possibility, but only to fix the eye upon the thought that the powers of nature,

---

¹ Luther, "And it was to look upon as four wheels." He has been led astray by the sing. suff. in מַרְאֵיהֶן. This belongs to the cherub as collective, so that there were thus of course four wheels. Comp. x. 9, where this is expressly affirmed (1 Kings vii. 30).

no less than the living creatures, promptly obey God whithersoever He sends them.

In ver. 18 the wheels are alternately treated as masculine and feminine. The height and dreadfulness ascribed to the felloes of the wheels correspond to their comparison with the chrysolite. The fact that the felloes are full of eyes points to this, that the power of nature is no blind force, that it is employed in the service of God's providence, that all over it the stamp of reason is impressed. It is this very thing which makes the power of nature terrible to him whose enemy is God. The eyes on the felloes of the wheels give them direction, lead them onwards into the most secret lurking-places of the enemies of God. The words in ver. 20, "For the spirit of the living creature was in the wheels," account for the simultaneous movement of the wheels and cherubim. Then only, however, are they appropriate if the meaning be this: "One and the same spirit worked in the living creatures and in the wheels." The unity of the *spiritus rector* effected the harmony.[1]

The description begins neither from above, from him that sits upon the vehicle, nor from below, from the wheels, but in the middle, with the living creatures, corresponding to the chariot. This is explained by the fact that the living creatures are peculiarly concerned in the present case. The writer is treating of the Chaldean catastrophe, the inevitable approach of which, to those who were seized with a political bewilderment, must be borne in mind. But the reference to Him who guides the whole goes before (in ver. 4) the description of details. That He is the Alpha and the Omega is brought to view in this, that He forms the opening and the close.

Vers. 22-25. *The vault.*—In the representation of Jehovah, who draws near for judgment to His unfaithful people as the God of the universe, whose hand no one can escape, *heaven* must not be left out of account. It is this that appears all through the Old Testament as the most illustrious proof of the greatness of God; it is presented in the language as the plural, the heavens, in contrast with the poor earth standing in the

---

[1] The explanation "breath of life," or "living soul," gives an improper sense here and in ver. 21, as the writer treats of the ground of the simultaneousness of the movement. Also חיה cannot otherwise stand here than in ver. 22, where it signifies the living—the living creatures.

singular; it is the heavens pre-eminently which, according to Ps. xix., "declare the glory of God." God is frequently called the God of heaven, to indicate His omnipotence. The Almighty is still more frequently called the God of hosts, *i.e.* the God whom the powers of heaven serve, than He who sits enthroned upon the cherubim, which designates Him by the proofs of His omnipotence in the earthly creatures. Heaven, then, is here presented in the great panorama of the universe—which, next to the vision of the new temple, is the noblest ornament of the prophecies of Ezekiel—as a *vault*, the word which in Gen. i. is consecrated to the description of heaven, and is never otherwise used except for this (comp. Ps. xix. 1 and Dan. xii. 3). To the words, "as the colour of the terrible crystal," correspond here the words in Daniel, "They shall shine as the brightness of the vault," and in Ps. cl. 1 the designation of the vault as the *mighty*. Beneath the vault are the cherubim, the representatives of the earthly creation; yet not that which is beneath alone, but that which is above, is in the vault here the same that is elsewhere in the heaven. The latter appears always as the place of God's throne, as here the throne of God stands upon the vault.

Ver. 22. And over the heads of the living creature was the likeness of a vault, as the colour of the terrible crystal, stretched forth over their heads above. 23. And under the vault, their wings standing upright, the one toward the other: every one of them had, besides, two which covered their bodies. 24. And when they went I heard the voice of their wings, like the voice of many waters, like the voice of the Almighty, a voice of roaring like the voice of a host: when they stood, they let down their wings. 25. And there was a voice over the vault which was above their head: when they stood, they let down their wings.

Ex. xxiv. 10 forms the foundation of ver. 22: "And they saw the God of Israel; and under His feet was there like a work of shining sapphire, and like heaven itself in clearness." There already we have in an appearance of God the same image of heaven. The crystal is noted as *terrible*, because it excites awe by its splendour, in which that of the Creator is reflected. Dreadfulness had been already, in ver. 18, attributed to the wheels, the powers of nature. To the comparison of the latter with the chrysolite the comparison of heaven here with crystal corresponds. Everywhere in the creation the glory of the Creator shines forth upon us. Heaven is represented as "stretched out"[1] over above the heads of the living creatures. We have here merely an "over," not that the heads carried it. The heads are at no time immediately under the firmament; for the wings rose over the heads, according to vers. 19, 23.

Under the vault, according to ver. 23, is the one pair of wings standing upright. It is this which serves for flying, in contrast with the other, which covers the body, because the creaturely is not worthy to appear unveiled before the eyes of the Thrice Holy. The tips of the wings reach upwards to the vault. Carrying is not to be thought of. Wings are not suited for this; and here particularly carrying would be out of place, because the wings, according to ver. 24, make a loud noise, and are therefore in free motion; further, because, according to what follows, the wings are let down upon occasion. They carry the heaven just as little as the wheels the chariot. The local proximity serves here, as there, only to indicate the connection between the several provinces of creation—is meant to present the creation as a uniform whole.[2]

The wings, the noise of which, according to ver. 24, Ezekiel hears, can naturally only be those standing upright, for it is for the very purpose of flying that they stand upright. The flapping of the wings shows, in harmony with ver. 14, that the living creatures long to fulfil their mission, that the time of this fulfilment is thus drawing near. Light is thrown upon the similes which are used to represent the loudness of the sounding of their wings, if the cherubim be recognised as the representation of the whole living creation upon earth. All the sounding of the creatures upon earth appears here gathered into one vast tone. The sounding was terrible to those who

---

[1] *Stretched out;* this is the standing expression in reference to the relation of heaven to earth. Isa. xl. 22, "That stretcheth out the heaven as a curtain;" xlii. 5, xliv. 24; Jer. x. 12.

[2] The repetition of the words, "one had two which covered it," is meant to indicate that, besides the outstretched wings, each *single* cherub had two which covered the body. Without the repetition the sense might be that each had only one. The word *every one* is therefore expressed.

recognised the import of the present mission of the cherubim. The noise is first compared to the noise of many waters, to which Isaiah in ch. xvii. 12, 13 compares the tumult of the heathen world-power, Assyria, as it presses against Israel; then to the voice of the Almighty, the thunder. Comp. Rev. xix. 6, where the voice of the church, included with the cherubim, is likened to the voice of "mighty thunderings:" "And I heard as it were the voice of a great multitude, and as the voice of many waters, and as the voice of mighty thunderings, saying, Alleluia! for the Lord God, the Omnipotent, reigneth." In Rev. xiv. 2, also, the voice of the church is likened to the voice of many waters, and to the voice of thunder. To the voice of roaring, like the voice of a host,[1] here, corresponds the "voice of a great multitude" in Rev. xix. 6. The distinction therefore is only this, that what forms the end here is there removed to the beginning.

Ver. 25 passes over to Him who is enthroned above the whole appearance, to whom everything in it is subjected, and serves His purposes. A voice issues from the vault, which still for a time checks the impetuosity of the instruments of the divine vengeance. He from whom the voice proceeds is then further described in vers. 26, 27. As to the connection with the previous verse, the standing still of the cherubim, and the letting down of their wings, which had been spoken of there, is here carried back to its ground. In form the prophet speaks in general: "When they stand, they let them down;" but he draws the general out of the particular, which he just now perceives; so that these words stand in the background: "Whilst they stood, they let them down." "The vault which was over their head" leaves no doubt as to the signification of the cherubim: the heaven arches itself over the head of the earthly creatures. Cocceius has already correctly given the essential burden of the voice: "The sovereignty of God, by which He restrains the nations and bids them be at peace."

Vers. 26–29. *The highest Object in the Appearance.*—The end here falls back upon the beginning in ver. 4; what is there indicated is here developed.

---

[1] המלה elsewhere only in Jer. xi. 16. There the "great tumult" represents the *tumultus bellicus Chaldæorum*, which even here also is mainly signified by the appearance of the cherubim.

Ver. 26. And above the vault that was over their head was the likeness of a throne, as the appearance of a sapphire stone; and upon the likeness of the throne was the likeness as the appearance of a man above upon it. 27. And I saw as the colour of shining brass, as the appearance of fire which was enfolded round about: from the appearance of his loins and upward, and from the appearance of his loins and downward, I saw as it were the appearance of fire; and it had brightness round about.[1] 28. As the appearance of the bow that is in the cloud in the day of rain, so was the appearance of the brightness round about. This was the appearance of the likeness of the glory of the Lord. And I saw, and fell upon my face, and heard the voice of one that spake.

Here, at the very height of the appearance, are accumulated indications of the fact that the forms which the prophet beholds are not adequate for their object, but are only meant to bring it, as far as may be, home to the human understanding. Had the prophet made this mistake, he would have come in conflict with the Mosaic commandment, "Thou shalt not make unto thee any image, nor any likeness," which is directed against those representations of the Divine Being that lay claim to be adequate to exhaust the fulness of their object, and represent it, of which adoration is then the immediate sequel.

That God should present Himself in human form (ver. 26) is explained by Gen. i., according to which, among all created things which might supply the substratum for the vision of the Eternal, if He is to be seen at all, man alone bears the image of God, and is a type of the appearance of God in the flesh. Dan. vii. 13 is parallel, where one "like a son of man" appears in the clouds of heaven.

That the sapphire is brought forward on account of its heaven-like colour is shown by Ex. xxiv. 10, where the whiteness, or the clear shining of the sapphire, stands in connection with the purity of heaven. The heaven-like colour of the throne indicates the infinite eminence of God's dominion over the earth, with its impotence, sin, and unrighteousness.

[1] Luther, "From his loins, above them and below them, I saw as it were fire shining round and round." Thereby *chasmal*, fire, and brightness, which are entirely distinct from one another, are completely confounded.

On *chasmal*, shining brass, in ver. 27, see ver. 4; according to ch. viii. 2, it is to be explained thus: "From the appearance of the loins upward" it looked like shining brass. This supplementary statement follows quite of itself, as in the sequel the region from the loins downward is expressly connected with the fire. At first it is said that He who sat upon the throne presented a double appearance; then the regions of each of these appearances are more exactly indicated.

The shining brass indicates the invariable character of God's personality—His holiness in the scriptural sense, *i.e.* His nature separated from everything creaturely—His absoluteness, through which He has His measure in Himself alone, and never can be meted by a human standard: "My thoughts are not your thoughts, neither are your ways my ways," etc. (Isa. lv. 8, 9.) The lower parts are allotted to the fire, the avenging wrath of God, because this bears only an accidental character —is only made prominent in present circumstances; in other circumstances, other sides of the divine nature will appear. The attribute of God indicated by the fire is derived from that indicated by the shining brass: God's absoluteness must, when it meets with daring opposition, go forth against it raging and destroying. The attribute indicated by the fire receives also from that indicated by the shining brass its exact determination: the Holy, the Absolute One can never be angry like man, who is determined by his lower passionate impulses. As soon as repentance shows itself, compassion steps into the place of wrath: "I will not execute the fierceness of mine anger, I will not utterly destroy Ephraim; for I am God, and not man, the Holy One in the midst of thee, and I will not enter into the city;" I am not like the children of men, as they wander up and down in the cities, who can be sorely offended once, but can never be softened to reconciliation (Hos. xi. 9). It certainly appears, on the other side, in the determination which the wrath of God receives from His holiness, that He bears the character of the most absolute energy, has in Him nothing of human slackness, does not stop short even of the destruction of that which opposes itself, when He meets with headstrong obduracy, so that it is a fearful thing to fall into the hands of the living God.

The fire is more closely described as " a house round about

it," as encompassed about, in order to indicate the extent of its burning; comp. Gen. xv. 17, where God appears to Abram in the form of a fiery *furnace:* correspondent is the enfolded fire of ver. 4. 2 Thess. i. 8, 9 is a New Testament parallel passage: there Christ is revealed from heaven in flaming fire, to take vengeance upon those who know not God, and obey not the gospel. As the fire is there directed against those who despise the gospel, so here against those who despise the law.

The "brightness round about" the appearance of God, of which the close of ver. 27 speaks, is more exactly described in ver. 28. Accordingly it signifies here, as in the outline of ver. 4, out of which the words are first transferred, to connect it with the detailed statement of the following verse, the grace that will follow the wrath, as formerly in the flood, where it was represented by the shining of the rainbow.

The words, "as the appearance ... of the brightness round about" (ver. 28), give the exacter description of the brightness with allusion to Gen. ix. 13. The rainbow, according to its proper institution, is not the symbol of grace in general, but of grace returning after wrath. The wrath is here indicated by גשם, violent rain. In the fire and the rainbow we have the two fundamental elements of the prophecy of Ezekiel, first judgment, and then grace. Grotius has given the idea here quite correctly: "The divine judgments, however severe they may be, shall not, however, obliterate the memory of the covenant made with Abraham, Isaac, and Jacob." Fire and the rainbow are here equally applied to the church. It is otherwise in Rev. iv. 3, x. 1. There the fire of the divine wrath is directed against the enemies of the church; the rainbow round about the throne (in ch. x. 1 about the head of Christ) points to this, that judgment is to the church an act of grace. But here also grace is hidden behind judgment. The fire has to convey its precise import to the rainbow. The latter points not merely to that which is to follow *after* judgment: it teaches us to recognise even in relentless judgment an act of grace to the church.

The words, "This is the appearance of the likeness of the glory of the Lord," apply to the whole of the appearance of God, as it was described in vers. 27 and 28, and conclude this description. The words, "And I saw, and fell on my face," depict next the impression which this appearance made upon the prophet: he falls down before the majesty of an angry God. The address of God which follows gives the explanation of His appearance, and the commentary upon it.

The vision places before the eyes of the prophet the character of the proximate future of the people of God. It indicates that this people, who yielded themselves up to fond dreams —who, like the ten tribes of old, in foolish blindness, and in complete misapprehension of the signs of the times, said, "The bricks are fallen down, and we will build with hewn stones; the sycamores are cut down, and we will change them into cedars" (Isa. ix. 10)—are on the eve of a grievous judgment. Hereby the general character of his mission was already indicated to the prophet. He was to dissipate illusions, to proclaim judgment, to appear as a stern preacher of repentance. The great hardships, also, which he had to endure lay already bound up in the vision. The people who have incurred severe divine judgment cannot be willing to receive the servant of God; the preaching of repentance must create exasperation among the impenitent. What might have been already inferred from the vision, will be now brought forward expressly in words.

First, a prefatory narrative. Ch. ii. 1: "And he said unto me, Son of man, stand upon thy feet, and I will speak unto thee. 2. And the Spirit entered into me when He spake unto me, and set me upon my feet; and I heard Him that spake unto me."

"Son of man:" so he calls him, remarks Rashi, that his spirit might not be puffed up by this vision. But such an acceptation *isolates* this passage. "Son of man:" so the Lord *customarily* addresses our prophet more than eighty times; as an address to the prophets it occurs elsewhere only in Dan. viii. 17: and it is manifest that all these passages must be regarded from one point of view. The difficulty of Ezekiel's commission consisted in this, that he was sent as a child of man to the children of men; so that a multitude of weak objections were raised: "What knowest thou that we do not know?" "Thou boilest also with water," etc. The address as son of man admits the difficulty; but then we are referred to this, that behind the son of man another stands who possesses all that is wanting to the son of man, so that he dare not despair, nor dare any one gainsay his word, or lay hands upon him. To the present address, "Thou son of man," correspond the words of ver. 4, "And thou shalt say unto them, Thus saith the Lord Jehovah." When the designation is thus conceived, it necessarily connects itself with the "Son of man" as self-designation of Christ, which occurs especially in expressions that refer to His rejection, humiliation, and sufferings. There is also admitted what lies before the eyes, but at the same time there is a reference to the divine background of his manifestation. In Dan. vii. 13 it is said of Christ, "And, behold, one *like* a son of man came with the clouds of heaven,"—a man, and yet not a man. This word, "*like* a son of man," applies also in a certain sense to Ezekiel. He has not, like the Messiah, a divine nature along with the human; but yet there is in him, as in every true servant of God, along with the human side of his existence, a divine. He is an angel of the Lord of hosts (Hag. i. 13): who hears him, hears God; and who is ashamed of him shall receive the judgment of God.

The spirit who sets the prophet upon his feet is the same spirit that was operative in the living creatures and in the wheels (ch. i. 20, 21). It is not the "spiritual equipment of the prophet" that is treated of, but only the spirit of life that raises up again him who has fallen down "as dead" (Rev. i. 7). 1 Kings x. 5 is parallel, where the queen of Sheba was so struck with astonishment at Solomon, that there was no more spirit in her.

Vers. 3–7. The prophet is armed against the contradiction that was to be expected from the people. Ver. 3. And he said unto me, Son of man, I send thee unto the children of Israel, to heathen nations, to the rebellious, who have rebelled against me: they and their fathers have transgressed against me even unto this very day. 4. And they are children of hard face and stiff heart: I send thee unto them; and thou shalt say unto them, Thus saith the Lord Jehovah. 5. And they may hear or forbear; for they are a house of stubbornness, and they shall know that there hath been a prophet among them. 6. And thou, son of man, be not afraid of them, neither be afraid of their words, for rebels and thorns are with thee, and thou dwellest among scorpions: be not afraid of their words, nor be dismayed at their looks, because they are a house of stubbornness. 7.

And thou shalt speak my words unto them, whether they will hear or forbear; for they are stubbornness itself.

They to whom the prophet is sent are in ver. 3 described first according to that which they ought to be—sons of Israel, the man of faith, who wrestled in prayer with God and man and prevailed; then according to that which they in reality are, —a microcosm, as it were, of the whole heathen world, whose religion and manners are reflected in them. " To heathen nations :" this goes beyond even Isa. i. 21, where degenerate Israel is described as a heathen nation. " Of hard face and stiff heart " (ver. 4) : this is in itself no fault; it may be, in certain cases, great praise (iii. 8, 9; Isa. l. 7); it becomes blame only through its connection with ver. 3. Accordingly we must think of stedfastness and resolute bearing in rebellion against God. To have a character for ungodliness, to be complete in this, is the very worst reproach, as it is the highest praise to have a character for the fear of God, and to be complete in this. In ver. 5 we must supply out of ver. 4, " Thou shalt announce to them the word of God." That this must be supplied, appears also from the definitive repetition of it in ver. 7. The words " or forbear " are to be considered as *accented*. That this latter case also is taken into view, is proved by the words, " for they are a house of stubbornness," an obstinate company. The words, " and they shall know "—that is, they shall then know "that there hath been a prophet among them" —bring into view what will befall them in the latter case. If they do not give ear to the prophet—which, from the character ascribed to them in ver. 4, is very much to be feared—they will perceive his prophetic mission in the fulfilment of his threats of punishment; so that this will in no case be in vain: he will at all events in the long-run receive his due from them. In ver. 6 the literal expression " rebels " comes first; then follow two figurative ones, thorns and scorpions. Such conjunction of literal and figurative expressions is very common, *e.g.* Ps. xxvii. 1, " The Lord is my light and my salvation." The scorpions are here a metaphorical designation for evil men; in 1 Kings xii. 11, for evil *punishments*. Prosaic expositors have there substituted for them whips with stings in them. The words, " for they are a house of stubbornness," do not give a reason for fearlessness, but explain why he is exhorted to it. " They are stubbornness" (ver. 7): this is represented as incorporate in them. "Stubbornness" is put emphatically here for the "house of stubbornness" in ver. 6; comp. ver. 8, xliv. 6.

Ch. ii. 8–iii. 3. The prophet swallows a book, the archetype, as it were, of the book which is here presented, the seed from which it springs,—related to it as the heavenly archetype of the tabernacle, which Moses is shown upon the mount, to the tabernacle itself. Jer. xv. 16 forms the groundwork: "I found Thy words, and ate them; and Thy words were unto me the joy and rejoicing of my heart: for Thy name was called upon me, O Lord God of hosts." The idea there only hinted at is here amplified into a symbolic act, in which we are not indeed to think of any outward process of nature, and which in this respect serves as a finger-post to the later symbolic actions of the prophet. The fundamental thought is, that Ezekiel is no prophet out of his own heart. He only publishes what he has received from above. Is the burden peculiarly sorrowful? That is not to be ascribed to the son of man, but it comes from Him who stands behind him. Instead of murmuring against the poor instrument that has received so stern a commission, let them repent. We have here an important passage concerning the relation which the believer has to sustain to holy Scripture—a warning against all capricious treatment of it—an injunction that everything be received as it is given, because what is despised descends on the head of the despiser. As our passage rests upon Jeremiah, so the "book" in Rev. v. 1, and the "little book" in Rev. x. 2, point back to the book before us.

Ch. ii. 8. And thou, son of man, hear what I say unto thee: Be not thou rebellious like the house of rebellion: open thy mouth, and eat what I give thee. 9. And I looked, and, behold, a hand was sent unto me; and, lo, a roll of a book was therein;[1] 10. And he spread it out before me: and it was written before and behind: and therein were written lamentations, and mourning, and woe. Ch. iii. 1. And he said unto me, Son of man, eat what thou findest; eat this roll, and go speak unto the house of Israel. 2. And I opened my mouth, and he caused me to

[1] Luther, "which had a letter folded up." The suff. in בּוֹ stands for the neut. "therein." יָד is always femin.

eat that roll. 3. And he said unto me, Son of man, thou shalt cause thy belly to eat this roll which I give thee, and fill thy bowels with it. And I ate; and it was in my mouth as honey for sweetness.

The exhortation, "Be not rebellious," in ch. ii. 8 presupposes that the contents of the book have something revolting to the prophet. This finds place in a twofold way. In the first place, he is one of his own people; and the lamentations, and mourning, and woe, in ver. 10, strike his own flesh, so that on this account he has "great heaviness and continual sorrow in his heart" (Rom. ix. 9). Ah, how sorely he wished that the bitter cup might pass away from his people, that the Lord might promise peace to his people! Then, again, he must be prepared for persecution, on account of the mournful burden of his prophecy. The people desire such as cry, Peace, peace, when there is no peace, and prophesy to them of wine and strong drink. Just now they are lulled into fond dreams, and will rise exasperated against him who frightens them out of these, and places the naked reality before their eyes, more especially as he has an inner ally in their conscience hardly hushed to rest. The book is unfolded before the prophet, according to ver. 10, before it is handed to him to swallow: he must undertake his mission with a clear consciousness of its difficulty. The roll of the book is written upon before and behind. The fulness of the contents, which are immediately afterwards described as very sorrowful, is so great, that the front side, which was usually alone written upon, does not suffice. "Eat what thou findest"[1] (ch. iii. 1): what the Lord says to His disciples with regard to their ordinary food, "Eat what is set before you," holds good also with regard to the divine revelation. This arbitrary disposition of mind, which instead of the word "what I find" puts "what I may," is of evil.

The words point to this, that the prophet has arrived at his prediction without his own motion, and that those who on this account rebel against him, who must accept what is presented to him, are on a false track. "And it was in my mouth as honey for sweetness" (ver. 3); as the word of the living God, which as such is sweet as honey and the honeycomb (Ps.

[1] According to the fundamental passage in Jeremiah, we must not interpret "attainest."

xix. 10), even when it is of the most painful import. That this is mainly the ground of the sweetness, appears from the fundamental passage, Jer. xv. 16 : "*for* Thy name is called upon me, Jehovah, God of hosts." It is infinitely sweet and lovely to be the organ and the spokesman of the Most High. The nature of the words themselves, however, comes next into consideration. Even the most grievous divine truths have to the spiritually-minded man a joyous and refreshing aspect. The proclamation of judgment, even when it falls upon our-- selves, carries us into the depths of the divine righteousness, and thus provides nourishment for our soul. Then also grace is hidden behind judgment; athwart the cloud the rainbow gleams. Better to be condemned by God than comforted by the world. For He who smites can also heal, and will heal, if His proclamation of judgment, and the judgment itself, be met by penitence; while, on the other hand, the comfort of the world is vain.

Vers. 4–9. God will endow His servant with unconquerable courage in the face of the people's stubbornness. This is a great comfort for one who had to stand alone against a rebellious people, not *once* only, but through a whole long life. He who has to contend against public opinion is lost, if he have not a fast hold upon Omnipotence; and he is a fool who, without such support, undertakes this warfare, the costs of which will certainly be required. He who has not God decidedly upon his side, must of necessity make terms with the majority.

Ver. 4. And He said to me, Son of man, go, get thee to the house of Israel, and speak with my words unto them. 5. For thou art sent not to a people of deep speech, and heavy tongue, unto the house of Israel. 6. Not to many peoples of deep speech, and heavy tongue, whose words thou understandest not: surely, had I sent thee to them, they would have hearkened unto thee. 7. And the house of Israel will not hearken unto thee; for they will not hearken unto me: for all the house of Israel are stiff of neck and hard of heart. 8. Behold, I make thy face strong against their face, and thy forehead strong against their forehead. 9. As diamond, harder than flint, I make thy forehead: thou shalt not fear them, nor be dismayed before them, because they are a house of rebellion.

The ground for accepting the commission given in ver. 4 is not probably concluded in ver. 5, but goes on to the end of the section: "*for* I will be with thee," although thy mission is a very difficult one, far harder than if it were directed to the heathen. "Unto the house of Israel," for "if thou art sent to the house of Israel." The contrast is between the outer hindrance which diversity of speech presents, and the inner hindrance which arises from the opposition of the heart—from this, that "they *would* not" (Matt. xxiii. 37). The outer difficulties are overcome when the cordial desire for mutual understanding exists on both sides. "Deep," in relation to the lip or speech (the expression is derived from Isa. xxxiii. 19), and "heavy," or difficult in relation to the tongue, are those whose speech is hard to be understood. Along with difference of speech goes difference in the circle of ideas, which among the Jews presented the most manifold points of connection with the activity of God's servants, while these were entirely wanting among the Gentiles. What Hävernick adduces, however, is not to the purpose: "dulness of sense, want of spiritual susceptibility for what is higher and divine." This lies on the side of the *Jews*. When it is said in ver. 6, that the spiritual susceptibility of the Gentiles would break through the outward difficu.:ies, in case the mission of the prophet were directed to them,[1] this is in harmony with the history of Naaman the Syrian, and of Jonah, in the Old Testament; in the New Testament, with the history of the Canaanitish woman, whom Jesus seeks out, while He must conceal Himself from the Jews, and of the Gentile centurion (Matt. viii. 10-12). It certainly follows from the susceptibility of the Gentiles here made prominent, that salvation shall be yet one day offered to them in an effectual way, since God wills not the death of the sinner,

[1] אִם לֹא asseverates. "Had I sent thee to them" corresponds to "does he reproach that panteth after me" (Ps. lvii. 3). The interpretation, "But to them (namely, to Israel) I send thee, they will understand thee, but the house of Israel will not want to understand thee," fails in this respect, that to "hearken to" any one can never be said of the mere outward understanding. It rather indicates assent. Against Hitzig's interpretation, "But I send thee to those, those should hearken unto thee," it is decisive that the words *those* and *should* are not precisely indicated in the text. הֵמָּה is most naturally referred to those who have been described in what goes immediately before.

but that he should repent and live. Just so, we expect, after what is here said of the hard-heartedness of the Jews, that in the lapse of time a great sifting and separating will take place among them. "They will not hearken unto thee, for they will not hearken unto me" (ver. 7): we have here not merely an *as*, but a *because*. Disobedience to the prophet springs from disobedience to God. The New Testament parallels are, Matt. x. 24, 25, John xv. 20, 21. In vers. 8 and 9 follows the peculiar thought of the passage, the promise of God's sure support against the anticipated opposition. It is not said, "Fear not, and be not dismayed," but, "Thou shalt not fear." It is not an admonition, but a promise. The strength of the Almighty passes over to the poor son of man.

Ch. iii. 10-15. The raising up is followed by the letting down. The prophet has been in the spirit, and in this condition has seen visions of God. He now returns out of the ecstasy into the condition of ordinary consciousness, and remains therein seven days : so long did the relaxation last which followed the extreme strain. It is said of Daniel in ch. viii. 27, after he had seen a high vision : " And I Daniel was sick several days : afterward I rose up, and did the king's business." The same holds good of Ezekiel also, according to ver. 16; only with this difference, that Ezekiel the prophet, after recovering strength, has to execute the business of the heavenly King, while Daniel the statesman attends to the service of the earthly king. The local change took place only in the region of the subjective. It was thus that the prophet had been at the river Chebar (ch. i. 1, and especially iii. 23, x. 22), as Daniel in ch. viii. 2 was by the river of Ulai; and in another vision, according to ch. x. 4, at the great river Hiddekel, the Tigris. The prophet is removed to the Chebar, because there he is far from the mass of men, and is invited to great thoughts by the rushing of the water. That he was there only in a vision, is manifest from this, that "the Spirit took me away" (vers. 12, 14). If it was the Spirit that bore him away, it must have been the Spirit also that had borne him thither. Compare ch. viii. 3, where the Spirit carries the prophet to Jerusalem " in the visions of God;" ch. xi. 1, where the Spirit brings him to the east gate of the temple;

ch. xi. 24, where the Spirit takes him up and brings him back from Jerusalem to the land of the Chaldeans, and where it is expressly added that this took place " in the vision, in the Spirit of God." We must accustom ourselves to measure the prophets, who are not for nothing called seers and spectators, by their own rule.

Ver. 10. And he said to me, Son of man, all my words which I shall speak to thee receive in thine heart, and hear them with thine ears. 11. And go, get thee to the exiles, to the children of thy people, and speak to them, and say, Thus saith the Lord Jehovah, Let them now hear, or let them forbear. 12. And the Spirit lifted me up, and I heard behind me the voice of a great rushing: Blessed be the glory of the Lord from His place. 13. And the voice[1] of the wings of the living creatures which beat upon one another, and the voice of the wheels beside them, and the noise of a great rushing. 14. And the Spirit lifted me up, and took me, and I went bitterly, in the glow of my spirit; and the hand of the Lord was strong upon me. 15. And I came to the exiles at Tel-abib,[2] who sit there by the river Chebar, and there where they sit,[3] and I sat there astonished among them seven days.

Vers. 10 and 11 close the intercourse with the prophet, and draw the conclusion; *in short.* It is said, " which I shall speak," not " which I speak," for the prophet had not till now received any special message for the people. " Receive them in thine heart, and hear them with thine ears:" all fruitful discourse must be first preceded by hearing. The ear is the spiritual ear, by which alone God's words can be understood, and thus not different from the heart—the *hysteron proteron* only apparent: comp. the " uncircumcised in heart and ears "

---

[1] Luther, " And *there was* a rushing," forgetting the dependence upon " I heard " in ver. 12.

[2] Luther, " where the sheaves stood in the month Abib." Tel-abib, hill of corn-ears, was the dwelling-place of the prophet.

[3] Luther, " and seated myself by them that sat there." He follows the marginal reading, or Masoretic conjecture, וָאֵשֵׁב, " and I sat," which arises from misapprehension. The authentic reading is אֲשֶׁר, with אֶל to be supplied from the foregoing, " and there where they sat." The words signify more exactly, that he came into the midst of them; comp. " in their midst," in contrast with the solitude of his cell, where he had seen the vision.

(Acts vii. 5); and, "The heart of this people is waxed gross, and their ears are dull of hearing" (Acts xxviii. 27). There also the ear is the spiritual ear. That this is wanting to many who have bodily ears, is indicated by the words, "Who hath ears to hear, let him hear." The Spirit[1] lifts the prophet up, in order to restore him to his usual circumstances. We learn this from ver. 14, where " the Spirit lifted me up" is repeated, after mention has been made of a hearing which is imparted to the prophet at the moment of his departure. The appearance of God ensues solely on the prophet's account, to communicate to him the mission which is shadowed forth by the character of the appearance. It is therefore natural that, simultaneously with the return of the prophet to his usual circumstances, the "glory of God," the symbol of the divine presence, is withdrawn. Gen. xviii. 33 is typical of the present proceeding: "And the Lord went His way, as soon as He had left communing with Abraham; and Abraham returned to his place." The prophet hears the voice of a great rushing *behind* him: the face of the departing prophet is turned in the direction of his journey. The " great rushing," the loud cry, "Blessed be the glory of the Lord from His place," proceeds from the living creatures, the cherubim, to whom elsewhere also such laudations of God are attributed, because their presence is a real praise of God (Rev. iv. 9). Correspondingly in Ps. xix. the *declaration* of God's glory is ascribed to the heavens, as it has made itself known in them. "From His place" is equivalent to "who now leaves his place."[2] The praise which is presented to the Lord on His departure from the place points to this, that the glory of the Lord is made known by His presence in the place—that the appearance serves great and holy purposes, important to the world of man. The wings of the cherubim, in ver. 13, struck one another in flying. The pair of wings is meant, which are described in ch. i. as standing upright and connected, in distinction from the two wings cover-

---

[1] That רוח is spirit, appears from the parallel passage xi. 24, for it is there explained by רוח אלהים; also from ch. viii. 3, where "hand" and "wind" would not harmonize; and ii. 2.

[2] ממקומו occurs nineteen times, and always stands for one who leaves his place. The יצא, going forth (Isa. xxvi. 21; Mic. i. 3), is here left out in poetic brevity; comp. the ממלאה, ch. xii. 19.

ing the body. The prophet betakes himself to his place, bitter, and in the glow of his spirit. "Bitter" is used here not in the sense of grief ("in the glow of my spirit" shows that sympathy with the people is not to be thought of), but in the sense of holy irritation,[1] called forth as it was by that which the Lord had said about the hardness and rebelliousness of the people, and no less also by the punishment of them represented in the vision, which presupposes the revolting magnitude of their offence. This holy irritation is quite characteristic of Ezekiel, in contrast with the prevailing elegiac turn of Jeremiah. Compare, for example, the prophecy of the sword in ch. xxi. 8 f., which some expositors have represented as a "battle song." "In the glow of my spirit," that is, inflamed with wrath. The wrath is directed against the sins of the covenant people. The inner glow has been kindled at the fire in which the whole appearance of God is bathed. Comp. Jer. vi. 11 : "And I am so full of the glow of the Lord, that I cannot endure it; I pour it out upon the children abroad, and upon the assembly of the young men : man and also woman shall be fallen upon, the aged and he that is full of days." Further (Jer. xv. 17) : "And I sat not in the assembly of the mockers, nor rejoiced : because of Thy hand I sat alone ; for Thou hadst filled me with *indignation*." The indignation there, corresponding to the glow of spirit here, is directed against the apostasy of the people. This indignation is not regarded as human weakness, but rather is represented as the work of God's hand, derived from His influence. The servant of God who does not feel it, must suffer on that account. It is in harmony with Jeremiah that the prophet here is indignant, and full of that glow of the spirit which springs from this, that the hand of the Lord was strong upon him, the divine influence mighty in him. Were this not so, he would live and let live ; he would occupy a friendly attitude towards the sin and the apostasy of his people. The prophet, according to ver. 15, sits seven days astonished in the midst of his companions. The subject of his astonishment is the threatening future of his people. The demeanour of the prophet was a mute sermon. All marked that something extraordinary must have occurred with him. Probably also he permitted them to see him, while otherwise remaining in

[1] Hab. i. 6 ; Judg. xviii. 25 ; 2 Sam. xvii. 8.

deep silence. Ezra ix. 3, ·4 may serve as commentary to the "astonished:" "And when I heard this word I rent my clothes, and tore the hair from my head and beard, and sat down astonished. Then were assembled to me all that trembled at the words of the God of Israel, and the transgression of the captives; and I sat astonished till the evening sacrifice."

Ch. iii. 16–21. At the end of the seven days the divine revelations begin again. First of all here Ezekiel is a *watchman* appointed by God; he is not a prophet after his own heart, but he *must* speak; he has a high duty, and woe to him if he do not discharge it. Everything aims at this, that he place the dignity of his call before the people's eyes. He is to rebuke the wicked, that they may repent, and so be delivered from the judgments of God; to warn the righteous, that they may not through apostasy incur the judgments of God. Let each one, then, take heed how he hears. He has to do not with the mere son of man, but in the son of man with God, who is omnipotent to destroy and to save.

Ver. 16. And it came to pass at the end of seven days, that the word of the Lord came to me, saying, 17. Son of man, I gave thee as a watchman to the house of Israel: and thou shalt hear a word out of my mouth, and warn them from me. 18. When I say to the wicked, Thou shalt die; and thou warnest him not, and speakest not to warn the wicked of his wicked way, so as to save his life; then shall he, the wicked, die because of his iniquity; but his blood will I require at thy hand. 19. But if thou warn the wicked, and he turn not from his wickedness and from his wicked way, he shall die because of his iniquity; but thou hast delivered thy soul. 20. And when the righteous turns from his righteousness, and does unrighteousness, and I lay a stumbling-block before him, he shall die: if thou hast not warned him, because of his sin shall he die, and all his righteousness which he hath done shall not be regarded; but his blood will I require at thy hand. 21. And if thou hast warned him, the righteous, that the righteous sin not, and he does not sin, then he shall live, for he has been warned; and thou hast delivered thy soul.

Ezekiel is placed, according to ver. 17, as a *watchman* over the people. Already in Isa. lvi. 10 the leading personages appear under the figure of watchmen, who, stationed on a lofty tower, give the signal of alarm when danger approaches: "His watchmen are blind: they are all ignorant." So in Jer. vi. 17: "And I set watchmen over you, 'Attend the sound of the trumpet;' and they say, 'We will not attend.'" The wicked in ver. 18, as also the righteous in the following passage, is not a single individual, but an ideal person—the species personified. In those immoral times the extent of the wicked almost coincided with that of the people. The righteous formed only a little company, and they had also many interests in common with the wicked: through the prevalence of unrighteousness their love had grown cold. Public preaching is meant, not the particular cure of souls, with which the prophet was not entrusted, as his mission was to the whole of the people. The prophecies of Ezekiel have a national import throughout. He has never to do with individuals as such. If the prophet neglects his duty, that does not help the wicked; he dies because of his iniquity; he has Moses verily. Where the public ministry does not do its duty, holy Scripture is still at hand, and it is each one's fault if he be not called to repentance by the voice of this. But in such a case Gen. ix. 5 is fulfilled upon the unfaithful servant of God, according to which God will require the soul of the man from him who sheddeth blood. Who sheddeth blood: this is not merely restricted to ordinary murderers. It covers all those who in any way, by act or neglect, trifle with the life of their neighbours, especially those who are not faithful in the discharge of the divine office of the ministry appointed for life and salvation. Thou art every moment in danger of becoming a murderer, and undergoing the judgment of the murderer: this is an effectual spur to every one who is entrusted with the office of the public ministry. The righteous in ver. 20 does not necessarily form a personal contrast to the wicked in ver. 18. The same person may be described as wicked in regard to his present state, and as righteous in regard to his destiny and his better past. The people to whom the mission of the prophet was directed were at the same time wicked and righteous, as Isaiah comprehends both in the words, "How is the faithful city, full of right, become an harlot! righteousness dwelt in her, and now murderers." It belongs, however, to the nature of the covenant people that the character of righteousness was never wholly lost to them, even regarded in their present state, so that they might be described by the name of the upright (Num. xxiii. 21). There is always among them an election in which this character is prominently presented; and also the entire national life, as long as the covenant endures, is interwoven with elements which do not appear in the national life of the heathen. Even in the greatest decline there is always to be found in this case (Matt. xxiii. 38) a background of righteousness. To lay a stumbling-block before any one is equivalent to exposing him to danger, according to Jer. vi. 21. The stumbling-block in the time of the prophet was the impending danger of destruction from the Chaldeans. "All his righteousness," properly his acts of righteousness. These are the good works of pious forefathers, from Abraham, Isaac, and Jacob down, and particularly those of the time of David, as being the proper golden age (Ps. cxxxii. 1).

Ch. iii. 22-27. We have here the explanation of the word Nabi, prophet, which signifies one who has divine communications; also the explanation of the name Ezekiel, which indicates a man who is under the absolute influence of God. The prophet is not a prophet out of his own heart, nor after the will of the people; but speaks only when, and because, the Lord opens his mouth. Woe, then, to him (this is the practical point of view) who will not hear him when he speaks: he neglects it at his own peril.

Ver. 22. And the hand of the Lord was there upon me; and he said to me, Arise, go forth into the valley, and I will there talk with thee. 23. And I arose, and went forth into the valley: and, behold, the glory of the Lord stood there, as the glory which I saw by the river Chebar: and I fell on my face. 24. And the Spirit came upon me, and set me on my feet; and he spoke to me, and said to me, Go, shut thyself within thy house. 25. And thou, son of man, behold, they lay bands upon thee, and bind thee with them, and thou shalt not go out among them. 26. And I will make thy tongue cleave to thy mouth, and thou shalt be dumb, and shalt not be to them a reprover; for they are a house of rebellion. 27. And when I speak with thee, I will open thy mouth, and thou shalt say to them, Thus saith the Lord Jehovah, Whoso heareth, let him hear; and whoso forbeareth, let him forbear: for they are a house of rebellion.

The valley in ver. 22, in contrast with the *hill* of corn, the city set upon an hill, as the name Tel-abib already shows, is the plain beside the river Chebar. The reason why the prophet is to go thither is, as previously when he was at Chebar, the solitude which is better suited for the divine appearance and communication. But that here also it was in the *spirit* that he betook himself to the valley, we conclude from his previous presence at Chebar, which upon ascertained grounds can only have belonged to the region of the spirit, but especially from this, that we have here to do with a paroxysm which presupposes inwardness. The universal rule is, that isolation is the condition of the receipt of divine communications. God makes Himself known to the mind only when it has been entirely withdrawn from worldly influences. We must be in the valley; but we may be in the bustling town, and yet in the valley. In ver. 23 the *glory* of the Lord is mentioned, to indicate that the Lord revealed Himself afresh to the prophet in the full majesty of His nature, accompanied with the cherubim, etc. This new appearance is to give to the prophet and to the people a new impression of the dignity of his mission. It served very well to form a counterpoise to the poor son of man, who presented so agreeable a pretext for ungodliness. The words, "And they were offended in Him" (Matt. xiii. 57), passed over from the prophet to Christ the Son of man. How the ungodly loved to separate between God and the men whom He chose for His instruments, and to set aside the latter under the pretext that they, too, were men like all the rest, we learn from Isa. vii. 13, where the prophet upbraids the godless Ahaz, after he had declined the proffered sign, with having *now* insulted not merely man, but also God, who had just offered to show manifestly that He Himself stood behind the man.

The prophet is to shut himself within his house (ver. 24), in contrast with the *in publicum prodire*, the public appearance as preacher. The naked thought is in ver. 25: Let them do what they will with thee; thou shalt not appear as preacher, unless thou hast received a special commission from me. The case, which is indeed merely suppositious, is brought forward in the form of one actually occurring, or in regard to the vision it is actual. The last words, "but thou shalt not go out to them," show the object of the binding with bands. They break into the closed house, and bind the recusant, to bring him into their assembly, in the expectation that he will there speak; but he is to offer the utmost resistance, and God will not suffer him to speak. Those who think the binding is to *hinder* the prophet in speaking, do manifest violence to the words. The words, "for they are a house of rebellion," in ver. 26, point, in passing, and out of connection with the leading thought, to this, that the people are unworthy of any preacher of repentance, since they have already set at nought so many warnings.

Ch. iv.—Ch. ii. and iii. are intended to place before the eyes of the people in manifold forms the dignity of the mission of Ezekiel, to fill them with a sense of the responsibility which sprang out of this mission to them. They have to do not with a mere son of man—they have to do with God in the prophet; and woe to them if they do not obey His voice. Upon the accrediting of the messenger follows then the first communication of the message. The sore judgment which is to discharge itself upon Jerusalem is announced, in harmony with the appearance in ch. i., which already portrays the approach of God for judgment. The prophets are throughout "counsellors;" they announce the future everywhere only in the interest of the soul's salvation. The moral is this: Renounce utterly your sanguine hopes, your political illusions; the only way to salvation is through repentance, which can no longer indeed avert judgment from all, though it may cause the individual to find a gracious God, and also God's grace after judgment again to return to the people. Worthy of note is the unbounded confidence of the prophet in the announcement of the disaster, whilst the political aspects were still so favourable, and the most sagacious politicians so full of hopes for the future. This confidence, confirmed by all that followed, can only be derived from a divine principle; and he who rightly weighs this fact will not be tempted to criticise the predictions of the prophet in detail, or to doubt whether he had not afterwards given them a precision derived from the issue, such as they did not originally possess,— a doubt which is at the same time an offence against the honesty and integrity which everywhere bears witness for itself in the prophet, and can only proceed from such as measure the man of God by the standard of their own want of trustworthiness.

The line of thought, viewed apart from its symbolic form, is this: The prophet announces the close siege of the city (vers. 1-3, and ver. 7); shows that this is the merited punishment for an apostasy of the people of 390 years, and especially culminating in the last 40 years (vers. 4-6); describes their condition during the siege as one of famine and trouble (vers. 8-11, and vers. 16, 17); and shows that the siege will end in exile (vers. 12-15).

In vers. 1-3 the prophet receives the command to portray the siege of the city. Ver. 1. "And thou, son of man, take thee a tile, and lay it before thee, and portray upon it a city, Jerusalem. 2. And lay siege against it, and build towers against it, and raise a rampart against it, and set the camp against it, and place battering-rams against it round about. 3. And take thee an iron pan, and make it for an iron wall between thee and between the city; and set thy face against it, and let it be besieged, and thou shalt press hard upon it. This is a sign for the house of Israel."

In ver. 1 the prophet at first receives only the charge to portray a city. The more exact direction comes afterwards. Jerusalem, the last of all the cities of the earth to be thought of, if it is to be besieged by the Lord! After Jerusalem, we are to suppose, as it were, a note of exclamation. How far must it have gone, how completely must it have degenerated, when the Lord proposes to deal thus with it! To the title belongs merely the picture of the city. That which is mentioned in ver. 2 is not figured on the tile, but is applied to the city represented by it. "And lay siege[1] against it" (ver. 2): how the prophet is to give or lay siege against "it," Jerusalem, which was represented by the tile, is shown by what follows, which stands related to this as the special to the general.[2]

---

[1] מצור, siege; comp. ver. 7.

[2] דיק denotes the besieging tower. The word, occurring in the time of the exile, is no doubt taken from the Aramaic, and is probably the Chaldaic *term. techn.* For this Isaiah in ch. xxiii. 13 has בחינים. The word occurs always in the sing., and denotes not the single tower, but the whole of the besieging towers, to which the "round about" in Jer. lii. 4 leads.

Here it is already clear that the symbolic action belongs to the subjective; by which it is also explained that the prophet reports only the divine command, without mentioning the execution. Externally taken, the action would have made a very feeble impression, as the corresponding means of representation were wanting to the prophet, and the arrangements for besieging a city represented on a single tile must have appeared very insignificant. It is not to be forgotten that the prophet in Tel-abib, a small obscure place, had only a handful of exiles around him; whereas his mission, like that of all prophets, was to the whole of Israel, including the great mass still residing in their native land. Whence it follows that with him literary activity was the thing of chief importance; quite otherwise than with Jeremiah, who prophesied at the centre of the nation. For the purpose of literary activity, however, it was of no consequence whether the symbolic action was external or not. In what follows, invincible difficulties stand in the way of the external exhibition. The symbolic actions of Ezekiel are only vividly drawn pictures, intended to make an indelible impression on the imagination. The prophets, according to the two aspects of their calling, as mediators between God and the people, alternately represent God and the people in their symbolic actions. In ver. 3 the prophet takes the place of God. This we learn from the fact that he is to besiege the city. But the besieger can be no other than the Lord, whose instrument the Chaldeans are. The *pan*, which the prophet is to place as an iron wall between himself and the city, is the embodiment of the utterance, Isa. lix. 2, " Your iniquities have separated between you and your God;" and the passage must remain unintelligible if we do not refer to this key. In the pan, the only thing to be observed is that it is *iron*, and not the dark colour, which must have been noted, if the eye was to be fixed upon it. The pan here has nothing to do with the iron pot of Jeremiah in ch. i. 13. The " practical secondary object " also of the pan to prepare hot cakes (ver. 12), is only an invention of the expositors, whose fancy has been excessively busy in this chapter. "Against it :" this refers to the city, not to the pan. In the first part of the verse is the refusal of divine aid, which could not fail the city—which Isaiah (ch. xxix. 1) designates as " Ariel, the lion of God, the city where David dwelt "—if it had not by its sins driven Him away from it who was formerly known in its palaces as a refuge (Ps. xlviii. 3); in the second part it is said that God Himself is the assailant.

In vers. 4–6, the guilt by which Jerusalem brought this visitation on itself. Ver. 4. " And thou, lie upon thy left side, and lay the iniquity of the house of Israel upon it: during the number of the days that thou shalt lie upon it, thou shalt take their iniquity on thee. 5. And I have given thee the years of their iniquity, according to the number of days, three hundred and ninety days; and thou shalt take on thee the iniquity of the house of Israel. 6. And when thou hast accomplished these, thou shalt next lie on thy right side, and take on thee the iniquity of the house of Judah forty days: a day for each year have I given thee."

In this new turn of the symbolic action the prophet takes the place of Israel. He lies 390 days on his left side, and thus represents the punishment which Israel has to bear for his guilt of 390 years. To take iniquity upon him (not bear: this the word never means), means always to answer for it, to suffer punishment for it. The substitution is here, however, purely symbolic, not real, as in the servant of the Lord, Isa. liii. That the prophet takes the iniquity upon himself, is here only a representation of the punishment falling upon Israel. The left side comes in here as the less noble. The right side is reserved for the symbolic representation of the heaviest guilt—the wicked opposition of the people to the last attempt for their deliverance. That an external symbolic action is not here intended, is as clear as day. Those who assert the contrary may make the trial to lie 390 days unmoved on the left side, and in this situation also act as besieger (ver. 7), prepare bread (ver. 9), and bake cakes (ver. 12). And what would have come out of this certainly enormous effort! The situation would have had a laughable effect, and the prophet would soon have become a sport for children. Its purely internal nature is also proved by ver. 9, according to which the whole time amounts to 390 days. The 40 days of lying on the right side must thus have been included in the 390 days of lying on the left, which is impossible in an external exhibition. Three hundred and ninety days on the left side, 40 days on the right, and yet only 390 in all: this is the riddle, the solution of which is only possible if the purely internal nature of the process be acknowledged. Figures of thought are tractable and not exclusive, as bodily actions are. The coincidence of the 40 days with the close of the 390 is also demanded by the case itself, as the 390 years extend to the time of the siege of Jerusalem, and thus no space remains after them for the 40 years.

The lying of the prophet is a figure of the wretched condition of the people during the time of the siege described vers. 1–3. As the siege of Jerusalem is to be represented, the ten tribes come into account only so far as they are part of collective Israel, which in the time of the prophet only continued to exist in Judah, which must bear the punishment for the common guilt; comp. on ch. xxiii. 45, where the same view is presented. Judah answers not for foreign guilt, but on it comes to maturity the common guilt of the two houses, of the whole house of Israel, which is now represented by Judah alone. For the ten tribes were at that time, so far as they were carried into exile (those who remained in the land were included in Judah), branches cut off, that could only again come into account if they were grafted anew into the vine.

The starting-point for the 390 years we have in 2 Chron. xii. 1, compared with 2 Chron. xi. 17. In the first three years of Rehoboam a fresh theocratic zeal awoke in Judah, to which the God-fearing from the ten tribes had attached themselves: " They walked in the way of David and Solomon three years." But at the end of these three years, in the great mass of the people, this zeal that had arisen from opposition to the revolt of the ten tribes appeared as a fire of straw: " And it came to pass, when Rehoboam had established the kingdom, and had strengthened himself, he forsook the law of the Lord, *and all Israel with him.*" This is the fatal year of falling into sin for the whole nation. In the ten tribes this fall coincided with the beginning of Jeroboam's reign. But all Israel first became rebellious three years later. Thenceforth the corruption forms a continuous whole, that suffers only partial and imperfect interruptions. This long period of revolt must now be requited,— requited first by the hard and tedious siege of the capital, on which the punishment must concentrate itself, as the sin had concentrated itself in it.

The computation of the 390 years is very simple. "All the years of the kings of Judah," says Vitringa,[1] "from the foundation of the temple, or the fourth year of Solomon, to the destruction of the state under Zedekiah the last king, computed according to the numbers in the books of Kings, give the sum of 430 years and six months. This number of years agrees remarkably with the 390 days of Ezekiel, during which he is to bear the iniquity of Israel (ch. iv. 9). For these days stand symbolically for so many years, during which the Jews renounced the true worship, beginning with the fourth year of Rehoboam, in which Judah and Israel *began* to revolt from God. If from the 430 years be taken the 37 years of Solomon, after the foundation of the temple, and the three years of Rehoboam, there remain 390."

The 390 days corresponding to the 390 years refer only to the duration of the guilt of Israel: they are not to indicate the proper duration of the siege, but only in general to point to this, that it will be tedious. This is clear from the 40 days for the 40 years in ver. 6, which can only be referred to the guilt. The siege also lasted longer than 390 days. It began on the tenth day of the tenth month of the ninth year of Zedekiah, and lasted till the ninth day of the second month in the eleventh year.

The contrast of the house of Judah in ver. 6, to the house of Israel in ver. 4, is not that of Judah and the ten tribes, but of Judah and the whole people: the house of Israel is indeed immediately before (ver. 3) employed to designate the whole of the people that was represented by Judah in the time of the prophet. There are three hundred and ninety years of the common guilt, then 40 years (of these 390) of special guilt; the despising of the grace of God in the awakening of Josiah the king, of whom it is said, " Like unto him was there no king before him, that turned to the Lord with all his heart, and with all his soul, and with all his might" (2 Kings xxiii. 25), and the failure of the last attempt, which was made by Jeremiah. The beginning of the 40 years is the thirteenth year of Josiah, in which Jeremiah, shortly after the beginning of the reformation of Josiah (2 Chron. xxxiv. 3), first appeared

---

[1] In the admirable and hitherto unexcelled *hypotyposis historiæ et chronol. sacræ*, that well deserves a republication, p. 31.

as prophet. Forty years: so long the activity of Jeremiah lasted, until the destruction of the city.[1]

In ver. 7, the prophet again takes the same position as in ver. 3. Standing in the place of Jehovah, he besieges Jerusalem. "And thou shalt set thy face to the siege of Jerusalem, and thine arm shall be uncovered, and thou shalt prophesy against it." The uncovered, outstretched arm, not resting in the bosom, belongs to the bold combatant. The prophecy is made by this very gesture, which announces the siege begun. The recumbent posture is not suited to action, and we have here an irreconcilable contradiction, if the symbolic action be regarded as external. The verse is the mere resumption of vers. 1–3, to indicate that the activity of the prophet there presented is not removed by what is related in vers. 4–6. After this object has been attained, the prophet in ver. 8 f. again connects with ver. 6 and further developes what the people have to suffer in the siege. The two parts which the prophet has to represent are related as action and passion.

In vers. 8–11 we have the terrors of the siege. Ver. 8. "And, behold, I lay bands upon thee, and thou shalt not turn thee from the one side to the other, till thou hast ended the days of thy siege. 9. And thou, take thee wheat, and barley, and beans, and lentiles, and millet, and spelt, and put them in a vessel, and make thee bread of it for the number of the days that thou shalt lie upon thy side; three hundred and ninety days shalt thou eat it. 10. And thy meat which thou shalt eat, shalt thou eat by weight, twenty shekels a day: from time to time shalt thou eat it. 11. And water by measure thou shalt drink, the sixth part of an hin: from time to time shalt thou drink it."

The prophet in ver. 8 again represents the people. The bands which the Lord lays on him are to restrain him from every movement. This represents the restraint of the besieged, the futility of all attempts to attain to a freer movement. That the prophet here plays a passive part, that the days of the siege are the days in which he is besieged, appears from the mention of the side, which comes into consideration, according to vers. 4–6, only in representing the suffering of the people. The co-ordinate action of lying on the right side is here, as in ver. 9, abstracted; or rather, the distinction of right and left is en-

[1] Michaelis, *bibl. Hebr. præf. ad Jer.* § 4.

tirely abandoned. In ver. 9 the idea is, that the inhabitants of Jerusalem are put on short allowance. The articles of food are considered in themselves quite good. The point of importance is, that they are put into *one* vessel. This shows that they have only a little of each, that they must take all together. Not the quality of the food, but the small quantity, is contemplated in ver. 10.[1] To eat bread by weight and not be satisfied, is among the punishments of the rebellious people (Lev. xxvi. 26). From time to time, not at the call of hunger, but at stated times, that are to be measured, that the life may scarcely be preserved.

In vers. 12-15 is a new condition. In the foregoing the scarcity of the food, here the impurity. The first refers to the siege, the second to the condition after the siege—the sojourn of the exiles in the heathen land. We must not rest in the external Levitical impurity, but also ascend to that which is thereby signified. The moral impurity of the heathen world was in its gross form hard to bear, even for those who in their native land had sat very loose to the commands of God. Ver. 12. And the barley cakes which thou shalt eat, these shalt thou bake with man's dung before their eyes. 13. And the Lord said, Even thus shall the children of Israel eat their bread unclean among the heathen, whither I will drive them. 14. And I said, Ah Lord Jehovah! behold, my soul has not been polluted; and carrion, or that which is torn, I have not eaten from my youth up until now; and loathsome flesh has not come into my mouth. 15. And he said unto me, Lo, I have given thee cow's dung for man's dung, and thou shalt prepare thy bread thereon.

That the man's dung (ver. 12), which appears in Deut. xxiii. 13-15 as in the highest degree unclean, is not to be mingled with the food, but to serve for fuel, is evident from the expression *thereon* in ver. 15. The barley cakes here have nothing whatever to do with the pot in ver. 9. This is gone. Vers. 13 and 14 serve to enhance the horror of the approaching condition. The concession only sets the disagreeableness of the condition in a clearer light.

[1] חטין with the Chaldaic ending only here: in barley and lentiles we have the Hebrew plural. The explanation probably lies in this, that wheat was the usual fare among the exiles. Hence the Chaldaic form appears.

In vers. 16 and 17 the conclusion returns to the main thought—that which they have to suffer in the siege itself. Ver. 16. And he said unto me, Son of man, behold, I will break the staff of bread in Jerusalem : and they shall eat bread by weight, and in trouble ; and they shall drink water by measure, and with astonishment : 17. That they may want bread and water, and be astonished one with another, and pine away in their iniquity.

Allusion is here made to Lev. xxvi. 26, "When I have broken for you the staff of bread;" and ver. 39, "And they that are left of you shall pine away in their iniquity." The *trouble* concerns itself chiefly with the question, What shall we eat ? what shall we drink ? The *astonishment* has the state of despair for its object.

Ch. v. The prophet predicts first the destruction of Jerusalem by a new symbolic action, vers. 1-4; and then describes it in vers. 5-17 in the usual prophetic style, which, according to ver. 12, is to be regarded as the interpretation of the symbolic action. The action rests on Isa. vii. 20 : "In that day shall the Lord shave with a razor hired beyond the Euphrates, with the king of Assyria, the head and the hair of the feet; and also the beard will He take away." The body represents here the people ; the hair denotes the men ; the beard, the princes with the king at their head—the beard being regarded in the East as the ornament of man. The place which the king of Assyria has there, the king of Babylon takes here : the present possessor of the world-monarchy beyond the river, he is to carry into complete fulfilment the prophecy of Isaiah that is here only repeated. This prophecy, occasioned by the inconsiderate alliance which Ahab wished to form with the trans-Euphratean world-power, places before the eyes the whole of the sufferings which this power will inflict on Judah. That the king of Assyria represents the whole of this world-power is expressly said in it, as he is first named after the mention of the trans-Euphratean power. Isaiah never expects a catastrophe of so vast importance from Assyria in its historical isolation. He is rather opposed to those who were afraid of this power. In him it is always Babylon that completes the work for which Assyria only prepares. Comp. ch. xxxix.

External execution has here also its difficulties. To shave himself with a sword on head and beard, so that not a hair remains, is certainly a very difficult task, especially for a man of great abstraction, who is not wont to be clever at such manipulations. And then in the external execution it would slide into the laughable, and prevent any serious impression. That we have here only a vividly expressed figure before us, is obvious also from ver. 2. There the reality behind the figure protrudes itself: the language refers to the days of the siege, the circumstances of Jerusalem. In an external representation, figure and reality would be quite at variance.

Ver. 1. And thou, son of man, take thee a sharp sword, take thee a barber's razor, and let it pass over thy head and thy chin: and take thee a balance of weight, and divide the hair. 2. A third part thou shalt burn in the flame within the city, when the days of the siege are fulfilled; and thou shalt take a third part, and smite about it (Jerusalem) with the sword; and a third part thou shalt scatter to the wind: and I will draw out a sword after them. 3. And thou shalt take thence a few in number, and bind them in thy skirt. 4. And thou shalt take of them again, and cast them into the midst of the fire, and burn them in the fire: therefrom shall a fire come forth unto all the house of Israel.

The sword in ver. 1 must be taken in the proper sense, since it is added that it is to do the work of a razor, and thus cannot be itself a razor; and immediately in ver. 2 stands the sword in the proper sense. The sword represents here, first of all, the avenging sword of God (Deut. xxxii. 41), the punishment to be awarded by Him. The sword of Nebuchadnezzar comes here into view only as the visible form of the sword of God, as it is also said in the fundamental passage of Isaiah, "The Lord will shave." The prophet depicts throughout in his symbolic actions only the doing of God, or the doing and suffering of the people. In ch. iv. also, where the prophet besieges Jerusalem, Nebuchadnezzar comes into view only in the second place. It is God who says in ver. 2, "I will draw out the sword after them." The balance of weight is a balance provided with weights. The balance has already appeared in Isa. xxviii. 17 as a symbol of the divine righteousness measuring the punishment. Ever according to the result of the weighing are the hairs assigned to their respective destinies. Chr. B. Michaelis says briefly and well: "The razor is the divine vengeance, the balance its equity; the hairs are the Jews, the parting the punishment assigned to each." It is the common fate of all (ver. 2) to be separated from the body politic, but the modes of separation are various. The flame,[1] according to the words, "When the days of the siege are fulfilled,"[2] can only be the fire of Jerusalem burned by the enemy. Ver. 12, where the first third consists of those who perish within the city by pestilence and famine *during* the siege, is reconciled with our passage by the assumption that the flame consumes the dead bodies, so that the two passages are to be completed from one another. The flame belongs to the symbol, because this only, not pestilence or famine, suits the figure of the hair; but the completion must be carried out in the usual prophetical style, otherwise misunderstanding is likely to arise. Plague and famine play also elsewhere too important a part in the threatenings of the prophet against Jerusalem to be here practically neglected. That the flame consumes only the corpses of those who had formerly died, follows besides from this, that the first place is assigned to this third. The second third consists of those who fall around the city in the sallies in search for food, and in the attempts to escape. The sword, as distinguished from the flame and the wind, denotes here the death decreed of God by the hand of the foe, and so is taken more strictly than in ver. 1, where it is the general symbol for the divine vengeance. As the first third is given to the flame, the second to the sword, so is the third given to the wind: it consists of the fugitives, especially the captives, who are scattered to the four winds. With the dispersion, however, the business is not yet finished. God's sword—His vengeance—follows them even in the dispersion. The fundamental passage here is Lev. xxvi. 33: "And I will scatter you among the heathen, and draw out the sword after you." "Thence" (ver. 3), from the last third. "A few in number," those who are spared by the sword at the end of ver. 2. The binding of the few remaining hairs in the skirt denotes the tender care that the Lord takes of the rem-

---

[1] אוּר, flame, not fire, distinguished from fire, Isa. l. 11.

[2] That it can only be explained thus, appears from Jer. xxv. 12: "And it shall come to pass, when seventy years are full," that is, are finished.

nant of His people, and that He will gather them from their dispersion, and restore them to their home. "And thou shalt take of them again, and cast them into the fire" (ver. 4): this presupposes that even among the remnant that at first, as God's care shows, were come to a better mind, corruption will afterwards break out, so that God's vengeance will once more manifest itself in a fearful manner. But this vengeance does not affect the whole remnant: "of them," it is said. This presupposes that, along with these objects of the divine judgment, there is an *election* that does *not* fall under the divine judgment. This election, however, is numerically inconsiderable—a mere minority, a "little flock." This is shown by the words, "Therefrom (that is, from them; the numerical majority is combined into an ideal unity with reference to the uniting bond of the evil disposition by which they are connected) shall a fire come forth into all the house of Israel." *The party is so numerous, that the vengeance which falls upon them* overtakes *the people* as such.

We have here the announcement of a second annihilating judgment which, after the Chaldean, will fall upon the people restored by the grace of God,—the outline of that which, after the infliction of the Chaldean judgment, Zechariah in ch. v., and especially in ch. xi.—the strictly classical passage—further expands, whom Malachi also after the exile follows; and, at the same time, the intimation of a little flock which is not affected by this new national judgment,—an intimation which likewise finds its expression in Zechariah. In this announcement Ezekiel has been preceded by Isaiah, the central prophet, in whom all sides of the announcement of the future are either unfolded or exhibited in germ. He says, in the remarkable outline of the fate of God's people in ch. vi., after he has predicted the first great catastrophe, as it took effect in the destruction of the city by the Chaldeans and the removal of the people: "And yet in the land shall be a tenth, but it again shall be consumed, like the terebinth and the oak, in the falling of which a shoot remains of it, and its shoot is a holy seed." These are predictions at which we must fold our hands. They contain the doom of the attempt of Hitzig to release himself from the troublesome predictions of Ezekiel, the fulfilment of which falls in his lifetime, by the assumption that the prophet has a copy of the history ascribed to him as prophecy.

The fire is here not merely a symbol of the divine wrath: it indicates that in this catastrophe, as in the first, the divine wrath will appear also in material fire, as actually took place in the Roman conquest. We need not separate the fire here from the flame in ver. 2.

With ver. 5 begins the further development in plain language of the thought contained in the description of the symbolic action, or rather in the communication of the command (for the execution is here also not described, because the action belongs to the sphere of thought, in which there is no difference between command and execution). Their punishment and their guilt are placed before the eyes of the people.

Ver. 5. Thus saith the Lord Jehovah, This is Jerusalem: in the midst of the nations I placed her, and round about her the countries. 6. And she opposed my judgments worse than the heathen, and my statutes than the countries that are round about her; for they have refused my judgments, and in my statutes they have not walked. 7. Therefore thus saith the Lord Jehovah, Because ye raged more than the heathen who are round about you, ye walked not in my statutes, and did not after the judgments of the heathen that are round about you. 8. Therefore thus saith the Lord Jehovah, Behold I, even I, am against thee, and will execute judgments in the midst of thee in the eyes of the heathen. 9. And I will do in thee that which I have not done, and the like of which I will no more do, because of all thine abominations. 10. Therefore the fathers shall eat the sons in thy midst, and the sons the fathers: and I will execute judgments in thee, and will scatter the whole remnant of thee to all the winds. 11. Therefore, as I live, saith the Lord Jehovah, Surely, because thou hast defiled my sanctuary with all thy detestable things, and with all thy abominations, I will also diminish thee; and my eye shall not spare, and I also will not pity. 12. A third part of thee shall die with the pestilence, and with famine shall they perish in thy midst; and a third part shall fall by the sword round about thee; and a third part I will scatter to all the winds; and I will draw out a sword after them. 13. And my anger shall be accomplished, and I will cause my fury to rest upon them, and I will be comforted: and they shall know that I the LORD have spoken in my zeal, when I accomplish my fury in them.

14. And I will give thee for desolation, and for reproach among the heathen that are round about thee, in the eyes of all that pass by. 15. And she shall be a reproach and a taunt, a warning and an astonishment, to the heathen that are round about thee, when I execute judgments upon thee in anger and in fury, and in furious rebukes. I the LORD have spoken it. 16. When I send the evil arrows of famine upon them, which are for destruction, which I will send to destroy you: and I will increase the famine upon you, and break your staff of bread. 17. And I will send upon you famine and evil beasts, and they shall bereave thee; and pestilence and blood shall pass over thee; and I will bring a sword upon thee. I the LORD have spoken it.

Jerusalem is the central point of the nations and countries: not geographically—this never occurs in Scripture, and would not come into account for the purpose of the prophet—but theologically. It is the model people prepared of God by His revelation, the community of the "righteous" founded by Him, Jeshurun, that it might shed its light on the surrounding heathen darkness, redound to the glory of its God, and attract men to Him. Moses says (Deut. iv. 5, 6) to Israel, "Behold, I have taught you statutes and judgments, as the Lord my God commanded me, that ye should do so in the land into which ye will come. Keep therefore, and do them: for this is your wisdom and understanding among all nations, when they shall hear all these statutes, that they must say, Ah, what a wise and understanding people is this, and a glorious nation!" In Isa. xlii. 19 they appear as the messenger whom the Lord sends—His mission amid the heathen world. Corresponding with this is that which Christ says of the community of the New Testament, the legitimate successor of Jerusalem: "Ye are the light of the world. A city cannot be hid that is set on a hill" (Matt. v. 14). So also Peter says, "That ye should show forth the virtues of Him who has called you out of darkness into His marvellous light." With ver. 6, where Jerusalem is upbraided because things are worse with her than among the heathen, is to be compared 1 Cor. v. 1: "It is reported that there is fornication among you, such as the heathen cannot name." The words in ver. 7, "because ye raged more than the heathen," refer to the beginning of the second Psalm, where the raging of the heathen against the Lord, their fierce rebellion, is described. In ch. xi. 12 they are thus upbraided: "and have done after the judgments of the heathen that are round about you." Here the reproach is different: they are degraded in their manners far below the heathen; compare ver. 6, according to which they are worse than the heathen. This verse confirms the negation. The passage is important, because it sets out from the view that the heathen have a law written in the heart, from which laudable judgments proceed (Rom. ii. 14, 15). "In the eyes of the heathen" (ver. 8), among whom the name of the true God is disgraced by the bad conduct of its confessors (Rom. ii. 24); so that He must vindicate His honour by exemplary punishment. The words in ver. 9, "and the like of which I will no more do," yield no comfort for degenerate Christianity. The divine righteousness remains always equally energetic. Like guilt must draw like punishment after it; and the responsibility is still weightier under the New Testament. Only this is said, that the judgment on degenerate Israel will present peculiarities which will not be found elsewhere: it will be unique in its kind, unparalleled in the world's history. All great judgments and all great graces have peculiarities in which they are unique. "I will also diminish thee" (ver. 11): the fundamental passage is Deut. iv. 2 (xiii. 1), "Ye shall not add to this word which I command you, and ye shall not diminish from it." They have diminished, they have taken His own from God by the transgression of His commandments; so will God also take from them that which He has promised to give them. The diminishing on the part of Israel has shown itself chiefly in this, that against the most emphatic injunctions and threatenings of God they have defiled His sanctuary by idols. It is not merely of the idols we have to think, which were actually found in the temple. According to the Old Testament view — as it appears, for example, in Lev. xvi.—the temple is the ideal dwelling-place of Israel, and all sins, wheresoever committed, take place there: comp. on ch. viii. The anger is fulfilled (ver. 13) when it displays itself in its fullest power. Thereby is the bearer of it comforted: he receives his satisfaction in the vengeance, because he destroys the violator of his honour, and thereby vindicates his rights against him. Vengeance, unlawful in the finite, is legitimate in the absolute personality. A god who does not avenge himself is an idol. We have here a combination of the Chaldean and the Roman catastrophe in one form of terror. The warrant for this assumption lies in vers. 3, 4. It would be absurd to speak here of "a Jewish idea." History has long shown that it refers to a terrible reality. It would be no less absurd to wish to talk of a difference between the O. and N. T. For the terrors depicted by Ezekiel extend to the times of the N. T., and Jesus announces equally fearful judgments on Jerusalem. "And they shall know that I the Lord have spoken it." What the son of man has spoken in the name of God, and for which he has become a mockery and a song in the streets, this is proved to be the word of God by the coincidence of the event with the announcement. The mocking of the son of man comes on the head of the ungodly. In ver. 15 there is a sudden turn from the simple description to the address as it appears in ver. 14. "Round about thee"—about them. The sentence, "I the Lord have spoken it," at the close, calls upon us anew to turn away the eye from the son of man. The arrows in ver. 16 are taken from Deut. xxxii. 23, 42. In ver. 17, besides famine, pestilence, and blood, "evil beasts" also are threatened, in allusion to Lev. xxvi. 22, "I will send wild beasts among you, which shall rob you of your children." The wild beasts threatened by the law here present themselves in human form; wild beasts, in the ordinary sense, could have no place in the *capital.* We may compare Isa. lvi. 9, Jer. xii. 9, where the wild beasts are undeniably the heathen. The designation of brutalized men, who have no breath from God, as beasts, is deeply rooted in Scripture.

Ch. vi. We have here the continuation of ch. v., the further elucidation of the two symbolic actions in ch. iv. and ch. v. 1-4. The chapter falls into two sections. First, vers. 1-10:—

Ver. 1. And the word of the LORD came unto me, saying, 2. Son of man, set thy face towards the mountains of Israel, and prophesy to them, 3. And say, Ye mountains of Israel, hear the word of the Lord Jehovah; Thus saith the Lord Jehovah to the mountains and to the hills, to the rivers and to the valleys, Behold, I, even I, bring a sword upon you, and destroy your high places. 4. And your altars shall be wasted, and your sun-pillars broken; and I will cast down your slain men before your abominations. 5. And I will lay the corpses of the children of Israel before their abominations, and scatter your bones around your altars. 6. In all your dwelling-places the cities shall be laid waste, and the high places desolated; that your altars may be laid waste and become guilty, and your abominations broken and laid aside, and your sun-pillars cut down, and your works abolished. 7. And the slain shall fall in the midst of you; and ye shall know that I am the LORD. 8. And I will leave you a remnant, so that ye shall have some that have escaped from the sword among the heathen, when ye are scattered in the countries. 9. And they that escape of you shall remember me among the heathen whither they are carried captive, when I have broken their whorish heart, which has departed from me, and their eyes, which go a whoring after their detestable things: and they shall loathe themselves in their own eyes, for the evils which they have done in all their abominations. 10. And they shall know that I am the LORD; not in vain have I said that I would do this evil unto them.

The mountains of Israel (ver. 2) denote the whole land, the characteristic of which is to be mountainous (Deut. xi. 12). The mountains, generally the prominent points, in the highland of Canaan, come necessarily into the foreground. The valleys appear as an appendage to these. The prophet before had a special view to Jerusalem, now to the whole land. On ver. 3 compare Lev. xxvi. 30, "And I will destroy your high places, and cut down your sun-pillars, and cast your carcases upon the carcases of your idols." "Before your abominations" (ver. 4), your idols, properly your filthy things, your idols that are as worthless as the filth, your dirt-gods. "The cities and the high places" (ver. 6) are in themselves innocent. That which takes place in them is only intended to destroy the offences that exist in these regions, the idol altars, and so on. The altars are *guilty*, because, by the destruction to which they are doomed, they are convicted of the false pretension to be true places of divine worship. "Your works" include that which is narrated in detail. In the idols and so on are the products of the sinful action of God's people destroyed, which they have erected in scorn of Him. Ver. 7 reverts to vers. 4, 5, to connect therewith the thought that the event will serve to prove the sole Godhead of Jehovah, against whom the idols are not able to protect their worshippers. *The slain* embraces the multitude of the slain in one ideal person. Vers. 8-10 are not intended to mitigate the judgment, which in this connection would be unsuitable. They serve rather to place in a clear light the heavy guilt of the people. When, the intoxication over, the punishment has come on, the remnant will themselves, with deep shame and bitter pain, confess the sins of the people, and the sole deity of Him who announced to them by the prophets their downfall on account of these sins. The words "And I will leave a remnant" (ver. 8; comp. Rom. ix. 27, xi. 5) have no independent meaning, but lead on to what follows—to the thought that the eyes of the people themselves will hereafter be opened to their own heavy evils. When once, in the course of events, the bandage falls off with which their eyes are now covered, they will perceive with astonishment whither they have been going.[1] To loathe their face (ver. 9) is to be a loathing to themselves. The face stands often for the person which it represents. "Not in vain" (ver. 10): the Lord would have spoken in vain, or to no purpose, if the event had not corresponded with the utterance. By the correspondence of utterance and event, they know that He who has spoken by the son of man is Jehovah—is God in the fullest sense.

Ver. 11. Thus saith the Lord Jehovah, Smite with thy hand, and stamp with thy foot, and say, Alas for all the evil abominations of the house of Israel! which will fall by the sword, by famine, and by pestilence. 12. He that is far off shall die of the pestilence; and he that is near shall fall by the sword; and he that remains and is preserved shall die by the famine: and I will accomplish my fury upon them. 13. And ye shall know that I am the LORD, when their slain are among their detestable things round about their altars, upon every

---

[1] נשברתי in ver. 9 means properly, "I was broken." This stands for "I have broken for myself." The passivity goes over from those whose heart is broken, as it were, to him by whom and in whose interest it has been broken. Allusion is made to the broken heart of David after his adultery with Bathsheba (Ps. li. 12), the rather because here also mention is made of the whorish heart and eyes (2 Sam. xi. 2). Analogous are נעתר, properly "be entreated," then "obtain by prayer," such an entreaty as attains its object (1 Sam. xx. 6); נענה, properly "receive answer," then "give answer" (ch. xiv. 4, 7).

high hill, on all the tops of the mountains, and under every green tree, and under every thick oak, there where they offered sweet savour to all their detestable idols. 14. And I will stretch out my hand upon them, and make the land a waste and a desert more than the wilderness of Diblathah, in all their dwelling-places; and they shall know that I am the LORD.

"Smite with thy hand" (ver. 11): to be compared is Num. xxiv. 10, "And Balak's anger was kindled against Balaam, and he smote his hands together." The clapping of hands, in general a gesture of highly excited emotion, which may be of various kinds, is there, according to the existing circumstances, a symbolic "Away with you." "Flee thee" gives the real import in ver. 11. Jer. xv. 1 serves for elucidation: "Though Moses and Samuel stood before me, I could have no heart to this people: cast them out of my sight, and let them go forth." "Stamp with thy foot," a gesture of the impatience that cannot wait for the time when it will be otherwise, when the sinful action will be followed by the suffering that is inseparably connected with it. To be compared is ch. xxv. 6, where, as here, the smiting with the hand and the stamping with the foot are connected. "He that is far off" from the foe, separated from him by the walls of the city. "He that remains" from the pestilence, and is "preserved" from the sword, which cannot reach him on account of the protecting walls. "More than the wilderness of Diblathah" (ver. 14). Diblathah, or Diblathaim, the Moabitish city, whose desolation is announced by Jeremiah (ch. xlviii. 22), lay on the border of the great wilderness of *Arabia Deserta*, which is here named after it.[1]

Ch. vii. We have here the close of the whole cycle, which rises as such to a lyrical grandeur; as also the second cycle, in ch. xix., terminates in a song. This solemn close corresponds with the solemn introduction in ch. i. The subject is here also the destruction which will come upon the sinful covenant people. Heavy blows are here dealt against the hopes placed in the anti-Chaldaic coalition.

Ver. 1. And the word of the LORD came unto me, saying, 2. And thou, son of man, thus saith the Lord Jehovah of the

[1] Compare Graf on Jeremiah at the place quoted.

land of Israel, An end, the end is come upon the four borders of the land. 3. Now is the end upon thee, and I will send my anger upon thee, and judge thee according to thy ways, and lay on thee all thine abominations. 4. And my eye shall not spare thee, nor will I pity: I will lay thy ways upon thee, and thy abominations shall be in the midst of thee; and ye shall know that I am the LORD.

"Thy abominations shall be in the midst of thee" (ver. 4), —namely, in their punishment. Sin has an active and a passive history. When the latter begins, that which was before the object of gratification becomes the object of terror.

Ver. 5. Thus saith the Lord Jehovah, A grievous evil, behold, it comes. 6. An end is come, the end is come: it awakes against thee; behold, it is come.[1] 7. The lot is come unto thee,[2] who dwellest in the land: the time is come, the day is near, tumult, and not the shout[3] of the mountains. 8. Now shortly will I pour out my fury upon thee, and accomplish my anger upon thee, and judge thee according to thy ways, and lay on thee all thy abominations. 9. And my eye shall not spare, nor will I pity: according to thy ways will I lay upon thee, and thy abominations shall be in the midst of thee; and ye shall know that I, the LORD, do smite. 10. Behold the day, behold, it is come; the lot is gone forth; the rod hath blossomed; pride hath budded. 11. Violence is risen into a rod of wickedness: not of them, nor of their tumult, nor of them and them; nor is there wailing among them.

"An evil" (ver. 5), so bad that they have enough of it. The character of the terrible lies not in the unity, but in this, that the *one* evil is so bad. There is something sarcastic in the *one*. "Tumult, and not joyful shout of the mountains" (ver. 7). The shout of joy is ascribed to the mountains, because it is mostly heard on them, and indeed not accidentally, but because it is called forth through them. It is said in Ps. lxxxix. 13, "Tabor and Hermon shall rejoice in thy name"—over it, over

---

[1] באה refers to the grievous evil identical with the end in ver. 5.

[2] Luther, "It rises already, and therefore breaks over thee." צפירה, properly "ring," then "crown," here used of the lot as completed in itself, probably an expression which Ezekiel took from his Chaldaic circumstances, by which he denoted the *ineluctabile fatum*.

[3] הידד=הד, "joyful cry," as of the vintager or the conqueror.

the deeds of thy glory that are done in them. This mute gladness of the mountains themselves comes to its expression in the acclaim of men. In the place of such joyful acclaim will come the tumult—the piercing cry of those who, struck by grievous misfortune, seek deliverance. The blossoming rod in ver. 10 is that of the Chaldean supremacy. The figure is borrowed from Num. xvii. 2, 3, where the prosperity of the priestly office is indicated by the budding and blossoming rod of Aaron. Hence also is the *budding*. The pride belongs also to the Chaldeans. Its budding signifies that a favourable issue is secured to it. The rod of wickedness in ver. 11 is the Chaldean despotism. " Not of them nor of their tumult or noise," forms the counterpart to the political frenzy which had at present seized the Jews, and in which they expected to have the reins in their hands, and make some figure in the history of the world. The poor fools! In place of action, the suffering will come too soon. They will simply have to suffer whatever comes upon them, without being able to exercise any independent influence on the progress of events, however loudly they may now cry or strenuously endeavour. "Nor of them and them," that is, of them, how much soever they may hold up their heads.[1] It throws contempt on the *we* which they had continually in their mouths, and repeated with great emphasis: We, we shall do everything; I am a Jew. It is said, Jer. xxx. 21, " And their mighty (collective) shall be of themselves, and their governor shall proceed from their midst." And in Zech. x. 4, " Out of him the corner, out of him the nail, out of him the battle-bow, out of him will go forth every governor together." This is no doubt guaranteed to the people of God, and imparted to them in due time. But the rebellious generation of the present have lost the privilege of the people of God; they must leave the initiative to the world, and are reduced to mere passivity. The expansion of " nor is their wailing among them"[2] we have in ch. xxiv. 15 f. The calamity will be so terrible, stroke will so come upon stroke, that lamentation will be forgotten in deep despair. It is the highest degree of pain, when the capacity to complain expires.

Ver. 12. The time is come, the day draweth nigh: let not

---

[1] Comp. הם הם, " they, and once more they," Isa. lvii. 6.
[2] Comp. Mic. ii. 4.

the buyer rejoice, nor the seller mourn; for wrath is upon all the tumult thereof. 13. For the seller shall not return to that which is sold, and their life is still among the living: for the vision is touching the whole tumult thereof; it shall not return; and many a one in his iniquity will not preserve his life. 14. They blow the trumpet, and make all ready; but none goeth to the battle: for my wrath is upon all the tumult thereof. 15. The sword is without, and the pestilence and the famine within: he that is in the field shall die with the sword; and him that is in the city famine and pestilence shall devour. 16. And they that escape of them shall escape, and shall be on the mountains like doves of the valleys, all of them mourning, every one for his iniquity. 17. All hands shall be feeble, and all knees shall go into water. 18. And they shall gird on sackcloth, and horror shall cover them; and shame shall be upon all faces, and baldness upon all their heads.

The buyer gains nothing (ver. 12), and whosoever is compelled to sell loses nothing, for all comes into the enemy's hand. "Their tumult," their multitude, that makes so much noise for nothing; an allusion to Ps. xxxix. 7, "Only in vain they make a noise; they gather, and know not who shall seize it." Ver. 13 gives at once the reason of the words, "Wrath is upon all their tumult." As the catastrophe is national, it is a matter of indifference to the seller that he has sold: he will in no case return to that which he has sold, so that he should regard it with pain, for the whole land is stripped of its inhabitants. It may, however, happen that he shall lose his life, and he has to count it good fortune if this does not take place, so that the thing sold cannot under any circumstances be a source of pain to him.[1] Instead of the *wrath* in the foregoing verse, stands here the *vision* in a like sense, for the vision has the wrath for its object. None goeth to the battle (ver. 14), because all are either already carried off, or seized with deadly fear; all hands weak, and all knees trembling (ver. 17), many powerless from famine and sickness (ver. 16). The mountains in ver. 16 come into account as the place of refuge for the fugitive (Ps. xi. 1; Matt. xxiv. 16); the doves only on account of their plain-

---

[1] איש, not "every one;" this would not suit the foregoing—*universal* slaughter is also never announced by Ezekiel; but "one." It implies that this case also occurs along with the other, that one remains in life.

tive tones, their melancholy cooing; doves of the valleys, in whose cliffs they build their nests. The water is, in ver. 17, a figure of dissolution going on everywhere; the knees are so relaxed that they are become as water.[1] On all their heads is baldness (ver. 18), because they have plucked off the hair in their deep grief (Ezra ix. 3).

Ver. 19. They shall cast their silver in the streets, and their gold shall be for uncleanness: their silver and their gold shall not be able to deliver them in the day of the wrath of the LORD; they shall not satisfy their souls, nor fill their bowels, because it is the stumbling-block of their iniquity. 20. And his glorious ornament he has set for pride; and they made the images of their abominations and detestable idols of it: therefore have I laid it on them for uncleanness. 21. And I will give it into the hand of strangers for a prey, and to the wicked of the earth for a spoil; and they shall pollute her. 22. And my face will I turn from them, and they shall pollute my secret; and the violent shall enter into her, and defile her.

"They shall cast their silver and gold on the streets" (ver. 19), to give to the rapacity of the enemy no point of attraction by which to endanger their persons; for rapacity goes hand in hand with bloodthirstiness. That this is the cause of their casting it away, is obvious from the following: "Their gold shall be for uncleanness," detested as an unclean thing, because life is endangered by it. The gold and silver cannot deliver them, because the cruel foes whom the Lord sends against them, aim at their lives (Isa. xiii. 17); it cannot at all be the means of satisfying their hunger, because there is nothing to buy—the gold has lost all its value. The ground of this curse that rests on their gold and silver, of this practical exhibition of their worthlessness, is found in the words, "because it is the stumbling-block of their iniquity." Stumbling-block is occasion for stumbling. The addition "of their iniquity" (comp. ver. 14) shows that a spiritual stumbling is here spoken of; that is, the possession of gold and silver gave them occasion for stumbling, or for sinning—tempted them to commit iniquity. How far, is shown in ver. 20. Israel has perverted his glorious

---

[1] הלך with the accusative of that which anything becomes, to become anything; comp. Joel iii. 18, "**The hills shall go into milk**" for "they shall turn into milk."

ornament, the gold and silver wherewith his God has furnished and adorned him, in the interest of his pride (ver. 20). From this proceeds, in fact, his tendency to idolatry, which in Isa. ii. 8, 9, 20-22, is regarded in the light of pride. Idolatry proceeds from the principle of independence in religious matters. Israel will have the initiative in matters of religion, make gods for himself, not submit himself in humility to the God of revelation, not serve Him as He is, and as He has made Himself known to him, and in the way prescribed by Him. All idolatry is at bottom egoism, the apotheosis of self, that sets up its god out of itself—first makes and then adores. They shall pollute her (ver. 21)—Zion or Jerusalem. Israel is profaned, secularized in his very centre, with all his shamefully abused possessions, because he has separated himself from his God, on whom his holiness depended. He is become profane in his conduct, and now is profaned also in his experience; he has spiritually rent asunder the partition between him and the strangers, and now in punishment this partition is also materially destroyed. "My secret" (ver. 22): according to the connection, this can refer only to his treasures. These are, so long as the people remain true to their God, placed under his protection and guarantee. All the means of Israel, as long as he is worthy of his name, are, as it were, the treasure of the Lord. Now that he has fallen from his God, this higher consecration of his means is taken away; it is secularized.[1]

Ver. 23. Make the chain; for the land is full of bloody crimes, and the city is full of violence. 24. And I will bring the worst of the heathen, and they shall seize their houses: and I will make the pride of the strong to cease; and they who consecrate them shall be defiled. 25. Destruction cometh; and they shall seek peace, and it shall not be. 26. Mischief shall come upon mischief, message shall be upon message; and they shall seek a vision from the prophet: and the law shall perish from the priest, and counsels from the elders. 27. The king shall mourn, and the prince shall clothe himself with astonishment, and the hands of the people of the land shall be

[1] Even in reference to the glory of Tyre occurs, in Isa. xxiii. 9, the חלל, because, so long as its iniquity was not yet full, it was, as it were, a sanctuary. The suffix in מהם refers to the Israelites; the subject of חללו is the enemy; the suffixes in בה and חלליה refer to the city.

troubled: I will do unto them according to their ways, and judge them according to their judgments; and they shall know that I am the LORD.

The chain which the prophet is to make (ver. 23) (an undeniable example of a purely internal symbolic action; or will they make the prophet a smith, as they made him a cook in ch. xxiv.?) points to this, that Israel the transgressor is to be instantly cast into chains and bands, and thus prefigures the misery of the future; comp. vers. 10–16, like to which is Ps. cvii., composed after the return from the exile, where Israel appears in his misery under the figure of a people fettered in dark prisons, of an incarcerated company. "I will make the pride of the strong to cease" (ver. 24): the fundamental passage is Lev. xxvi. 19, where, in the threatening against the rebellious people, it is said, "I will break the pride of your power." "And they who consecrate them shall be defiled:" to be compared is Isa. xliii. 26, 27, "Thy first father (the high priest) hath sinned, and thy intercessors have transgressed against me. Therefore will I profane the princes of the sanctuary, and give Jacob to the curse, and Israel to reproach." With the approaching destruction of the sanctuary are the priests also, who can no longer officiate, desecrated, and thus the means of expiation are withdrawn from Israel. Jeremiah, in ch. xxxiii., meets with the word of promise a deep trouble of the people, that which must have been called forth here by the threatening of the prophet: the temple, changed into a den of robbers by the guilt of the people, was to be destroyed. On the existence of the temple depended that of the Levitical priesthood; and if this went to the ground because an unsubstantial shadow, where would then be the forgiveness of sins, which in the law (for ex. Lev. xvi.) was connected with the mediation of the Levitical priesthood? Ezekiel points only to the cloud; Jeremiah opens the view to the sun concealed behind the cloud. "Destruction cometh" (ver. 25); properly contraction, in contrast with the expansion which is connected with all joyful prosperity. Such expansion is founded in the nature of the people of God: comp. Gen. xxviii. 14; Isa. liv. 3, "Thou shalt break forth right and left, and thy seed shall inherit the heathen;" and where the expansion gives place to the contraction, the state of restriction and diminution, it is a mournful anomaly, which can have its ground only in this, that the people of God have degenerated, and become unfaithful to their call. "They shall seek a vision from the prophet" (ver. 26): from their prophets, who hitherto have presented the future to them in rosy colours, and to whom the heavens have been full of music. Now they make a lamentable figure; they are stricken on the mouth by the event. "The law shall perish from the priest." The law comes into consideration in this connection in a peculiar respect. The priests before the catastrophe had so explained the law, that the people were lulled into a false security. They had given a one-sided prominence to the election of the people, and the lofty promises made to them, without referring to the conditions on which the election depended, or the severe threatenings in case of infidelity. Now they no longer venture to come forth with such interpretations of the law that turned the grace of God into lasciviousness. Events compel them no further to do violence to the law, as Zephaniah reproaches the priests, ch. iii. 4 (comp. Jer. ii. 8; Ezek. xxii. 26). "Judge them according to their judgments" (ver. 27)—corresponding to their deeds. "And they shall know that I am the Lord:" this knowledge, which they despised, is now forced upon them. In their downfall they must acknowledge it. With these words recurring in Ezekiel like a refrain, the first cycle of his prophecies closes.

THE SECOND CYCLE.

CHAPTERS VIII.-XIX.

HE second cycle (ch. viii.-xix.) is separated from the first by an interval of a year and two months. The date is here the sixth year after the captivity of Jehoiachin, the sixth month, the fifth day, about five years before the destruction of Jerusalem. A vision here also forms the introduction, a song the close in ch. xix., in the midst of prophetic discourses that elucidate the vision, obviate objections, and form a bridge between it and the mind. The historical starting-point and the tendency also are similar. The prophet here also strives against the political dreams, represents the destruction as inevitable, and points to repentance as the only way of safety.

The vision is here far more comprehensive than in the first cycle. It occupies four whole chapters. It gives a complete representation of the sins of the people; and here accordingly is unfolded what in the first vision is only indicated concerning the punishment. Common to both visions is the delineation of the theophany itself, and in particular the description of the cherubim. The former delineation is supplemented by that here given only in details.

Ch. viii. contains the exposition of the guilt—the delineation of the four abominations of Jerusalem; ch. ix., the first punishment—Jerusalem filled with dead bodies; ch. x., the second punishment—Jerusalem burnt; ch. xi. 1-12, the third—God's vengeance follows the survivors of the catastrophe. The close consists of comfort for the captives, who are already in exile with Ezekiel, and on whom the inhabitants of Jerusalem proudly look down; of these will God Himself take care, after the total disappointment of all human hopes (vers. 13-21). The prophet then sees still (vers. 22, 23) how the glory of the Lord leaves the temple; and then the ecstasy comes to an end (vers. 24, 25).

Ch. viii. 1. And it came to pass in the sixth year, the sixth month, on the fifth day, I sat in my house, and the elders of Judah sat before me, and the hand of the Lord Jehovah fell there upon me. 2. And I beheld, and lo a form to look upon as fire : from the loins downward, to look upon as fire; and from the loins upward, to look upon as brightness, as the look of shining brass. 3. And he stretched out the form of a hand, and took me by a lock of my head ; and the Spirit lifted me up between the earth and the heaven, and brought me to Jerusalem, in the visions of God, to the door of the gate of the inner court[1] that looketh towards the north ; where was the seat of the image of jealousy which provoketh to jealousy. 4. And, behold, there was the glory of the God of Israel, like the vision that I saw in the valley. 5. And he said to me, Son of man, lift up thine eyes toward the north. And I lifted my eyes toward the north, and behold northward at the gate of the altar this image of jealousy at the entrance. 6. And he said unto me, Son of man, seest thou what they do ? The great abomination, that the house of Israel here committeth, that they should go far off from my sanctuary ? And thou shalt yet again see great abominations.

The elders of Judah sit before the prophet (ver. 1). An exciting political report is current, perhaps that of the coalition formed between Elam and Media (ch. viii. 15-17) ;[2] and the elders come to the prophet in the hope of receiving from him, under this change of affairs, a reversal of the former threatenings against Jerusalem, and a confirmation of their pleasing dreams, which they cannot well enjoy, so long as they have the prophet against them (comp. on ch. xx. 1). The fire in ver. 2 first draws the attention of the prophet to it, because this stood in connection with present circumstances, whereas the brightness depicts the essence of God, which is ever the same. The fire was antecedently destructive of all the fond hopes of the people (comp. on ch. i. 4, 27). " And He stretched out : " the subject can only be the same who is spoken of in ver. 2—

---

[1] Luther, " to the inner gate." But Michaelis rightly remarks : הַפְּנִימִית, femininum, neque cum Petach neque cum Schaar mascul., sed cum subintellecto חָצֵר, quod commune est, convenit. In ver. 16 חָצֵר is added. It is characteristic of Ezekiel the priest, that he says " the inner " briefly for " the inner court."

[2] M. Niebuhr, History of Assyria and Babylon, p. 212.

the Lord, to whom the hand already belongs in ver. 1. If the hand be the hand of God, *ruach* can only denote Spirit, power, not wind. For the wind suits not the hand of God, but the Spirit perfectly, which is active even through the hand, as also in ver. 1 the Spirit of God acts on the prophet through the hand. In fact, the hand is only a symbol of the energetic Spirit. The addition, "in the visions of God" (comp. ch. i. 1), prevents the thing from being carried into the sphere of the external. "Where was the seat of the image of jealousy which provoketh to jealousy." The latter words indicate in what sense the prophet speaks of the image of jealousy, inasmuch as it provokes to jealousy the jealous, the energetic God, who as such gives not His honour to another, and calls forth His reaction against the wrong done to His honour. That the words only serve for explanation appears from ver. 5, where, after the explanation here given, the image of jealousy stands alone. From the north the punishment was to come (ch. i. 4). Thus the image of jealousy had its right place there. It was an actual summons to the north to send forth its avenging hosts. This leads us at once to see, that we here find ourselves on a purely ideal ground, —that the realistic interpretation of that which the prophet observes in the temple, and the attempt to draw therefrom historical conclusions concerning the then state of the temple, are altogether perverse. Several other grounds also speak for the ideality: for ex., the phrase "every one in his chamber" (ver. 12), where the reality suddenly breaks forth; further, the expression "in the dark" itself, thus not in a public place; the circumstance that Ezekiel must first break a door for himself (ver. 8); the 70 men in ver. 11, and the 25 in ver. 16,—a formal representation of the people, that in so official a manner, though certainly not at that time, did homage to idols in the temple; and so on. Even beforehand it cannot be imagined that the vision was a simple copy of The reality. This would contradict its very nature throughout. It is intended to present the thing in its deeper reality, as it cannot be seen with the eye of flesh. The temple was the ideal dwelling-place of the people. This is an idea that is widely spread Through the Old Testament.[1] In Lev. xvi. all the sins of the people appear to

---

[1] Comp. *Christol.* Part ii. p. 599 f.; further, my comm. on Ps. xxiii. 6, xxvii. 4, lxxxiv. 5, and on John ii. 19.

be committed in the temple, the "tent of meeting," in which the sinners dwelt with the holy God. It is there said, in ver. 16: "And he (the high priest) shall expiate the sanctuary from the impurities of the children of Israel, and from their transgressions in all their sins: and so shall he do for the tent of meeting, that dwelleth among them in the midst of their impurities." Because in a spiritual sense all the children of Israel dwell in the sanctuary, this will be polluted by every sin. In Amos ix. 1 the altar in Jerusalem appears as the place of transgression; there the prophet sees all the abominations of Israel and Judah laid down. The altar was the place where the people of the two kingdoms were to lay down the embodied expression of their pious feelings. There lay, in point of fact, the fruits of the counterpart of these feelings; there was heaped up the unexpiated iniquity of the whole people. In the place of transgression appears the Lord to glorify Himself in the downfall of those who had not glorified Him by their life. So, then, here also, all that was extant in the land of an idolatrous character is united in a single figure, and placed in the temple, to cry thence to God and call forth His vengeance. This being so, we must in the further investigation rise above the image of jealousy. It is an ideal concentration of all superstitious dealing in Israel—a confluence of all the several forms of idols, the gods of the nations of the earth, that are the work of man, which are in 2 Chron. xxxii. 19 set over against the God of Israel. In the great importance which is attached to politics in the prophecies of Ezekiel, we must besides pay less regard to an idolatry that sprang from a confusion of the religious impulse, than to a homage which was offered to the world-powers, in order to attain to safety by their aid without God, or even against God. This homage went back at length to the heathen gods, because these were the ruling powers in the popular life. The comparison of ch. xxiii. will leave no doubt in reference to the correctness of this remark. It is possible that the image of jealousy has a still more special political import—that the northward direction refers not merely to the punishment to be expected, but also to the sin already committed. Then would the image of jealousy refer to the political adulteries of Jerusalem with the northern power of Babylon, against which they alternately conspired, and then again sought to gain it over; as Zedekiah, in the same year in which he had treated with the kings of Edom, Moab, and others, concerning a common undertaking against Babel, suddenly made off again to Babylon (Jer. li. 59).[1] That the seat of the image of jealousy was in the north, is here mentioned by anticipation, to give the reason why the prophet is transported thither. The proper description of the image of jealousy follows only in ver. 5. "The image of jealousy that provoketh to jealousy" points to Deut. xxxii. 16, "They moved Him to jealousy with strange gods, with abominations they provoked Him." To the position towards the north, so far as it refers to the punishment to be expected, corresponds there the sentence, "And I will provoke them to jealousy by not a people" (ver. 21). "The gate of the altar" (ver. 5): it is so called because it led from the outer to the inner court, in which the altar stood. The prophet stands in the outer court, immediately at the door of the inner, and of course the northern one. At hand in the outer court, in the direction of the north, stands the image of jealousy. The removal in ver. 6 can only refer to those who were mentioned immediately before: to be removed can only mean, "that they be removed." The right interpretation would not have been missed, had the import of the temple, as the place where the people dwell spiritually with the Lord, been duly recognised. By their idolatry, their adulterous intercourse with the world-powers, they have made themselves unworthy of dwelling with the Lord. They must be cast out of the sanctuary, the place of blessing and of grace, as formerly Adam, in consequence of his fall, was driven out of Paradise. The idea is the dissolution of the covenant, the abandonment to the world.

Ver. 7. And he brought me to the door of the court; and I looked, and behold a hole in the wall. 8. And he said unto me, Son of man, break through the wall; and I broke through the wall, and behold a door. 9. And he said unto me, Go in, and see the wicked abominations that they do here. 10. And I went in and saw; and, behold, every form of moving thing, and abominable beasts, and all the detestable things of the house of Israel, portrayed upon the wall round about. 11. And seventy men of the elders of the house of Israel, and Jaazaniah son of Shaphan, standing in their midst, stood before them, and

[1] Niebuhr, p. 211.

every man had his censer in his hand; and the prayer of the cloud of incense went up. 12. And he said unto me, Seest thou, son of man, what the elders of the house of Israel do in the dark, every man in his image-chambers? for they say, The Lord seeth us not; the Lord hath forsaken the land. 13. And he said unto me, Still further shalt thou see great abominations that they do.

The door of the court (ver. 7) is the chief door, the eastern. Thither is the prophet transported from the northern one (ver. 3). The hole which the prophet here sees is identical with that which he is to dig (ver. 8). He sees here, as it were, the model. The idea which lies at the base of the symbolic representation comes out in ver. 12. It is, that superstition, as a work of darkness, was driven into secret places. Just here it appears quite clear that the transportation to the temple has a purely ideal meaning. It is equally plain, however, that the superstition here spoken of has a political character—that the question is about political combinations. For then only does the secret movement explain itself: they do not wish yet to break openly with Babylon. A purely religious aberration would not have needed to hide itself in darkness: it had nothing to fear at that time. The wall, according to ver. 8, must first be broken through to reach the door. We see clearly from this that we are not in the region of reality. If the wall was before the door, how, then, did the idolaters enter? If there was an entrance for these, why must the prophet break open an entrance for himself? Our passage shows that under Zedekiah the temple itself was free from superstitious abominations. The same appears also from ch. xxiii. 38. There the prophet reproaches the inhabitants of Jerusalem, because they, after sullying themselves with idolatry outside the temple, visited the temple, as if nothing had happened. The animal-worship to which, according to ver. 10, the rulers of the people devoted themselves, is peculiar in all antiquity to Egypt only, and so characteristic of it that the mention of it is equivalent to the express naming of Egypt. We must antecedently expect a certain participation in Egyptian idolatry in the Jews of that day, according to the political relations of the past. With the political fraternizations the religious went hand in hand. Religion was a power so far governing the whole life, that, for ex., an embassy sent to Egypt could not avoid participating in the idolatry of the day. Dan. iii. brings to our view the close relationship of politics and religion. But Egypt appears in ch. xxiii. 19-21, 27, as the chief power by which Judah sought aid against the Chaldeans. It is there also expressly said, that with the political dependence was also connected the participation in the worship (vers. 7, 30, 37). But even the political dependence on Egypt itself, the seeking of help in it, may be regarded in the light of a participation in its superstition, inasmuch as its gods were the powers governing the life. He that trusted in Egypt trusted in its gods—which are already in the Pentateuch placed in inseparable connection with it (Ex. xii. 12)—and substituted for the honour of the eternal God the figure of an ox that eateth grass. This is certainly the chief point. The more rarely occurring external participation in Egyptian idolatry is only a single consequence of this whole unnatural relation. "Moving thing" is all that moves on the earth; comp. Gen. ix. 3, "every moving thing that liveth." The limitation to the smaller animals lies, where it finds place, not in the word itself, but in this, that the greater animals are specially named along with it. So here also the moving thing is the generic name. Along with this are the cattle named as the most prominent species in the genus. The animal-worship must, according to its principle, have been specially directed to the most useful animals. "Abomination" stands in apposition to cattle, and forms with it a kind of compound—abomination cattle. The cattle become an abomination, because the honour belonging to the Creator is assigned to them (Rom. i. 23). Everything created, however good it may be in itself, becomes an abomination as soon as it stands with man beside, or quite above, God. "All the detestable things of the house of Israel:" this means especially the idols, which belong to the same category with those expressly named. Only the land animals are here expressly named, whereas in the prohibition of the Egyptian animal-worship in Deut. iv. 17, 18, mention is made also of fowls and aquatic animals. But at all events only the Egyptain gods come into account. *The detestable*, properly the filthy, *stercorei*, a designation of idols particularly natural to Ezekiel, refers everywhere to Lev. xxvi. 30. The filthy is a designation peculiarly suitable to animal-gods, the filthy ones of Egypt (Ex. xxiv. 7). "The filthy" also occurs especially of the Egyptian gods in Deut. xxix. 17, the only place in the books of Moses where the word is found, except Ex. xxvi. 30. "Portrayed upon the wall:" Moses in Deut. iv. 17, 18 speaks of artificial representations of animals as the object of worship. "The seventy of the elders of Israel" (ver. 11) are from Ex. xxiv. 1, 9, Num. xi. 16, 24. As they there, as a chosen part, represent the whole of the elders, the men in authority, so also here. In ver. 12 the elders of the house of Israel are spoken of in general. The idea is, that the leaning to Egyptian customs, the trust in the shadow of Egypt (Isa. xxx. 22), is in the strict sense a national sin. If the state as such had abandoned itself to dependence on Egypt, and thereby committed a felony, it renounced the God of the spirits of all flesh, and called down His vengeance upon itself. "And Jaazaniah son of Shaphan standing in their midst:" Shaphan occurs in 2 Kings xxii. 3, 10 as chancellor under Josiah. His son, who is probably invested with the same office, was no doubt the soul of the negotiations with Egypt. The prophet introduces the historical personality into this ideal company partly on this account, partly on account of his ominous name, The Lord hears, who was to come down on the head of these worshippers of beasts, and who pronounced judgment on their whole procedure. "Before them"—the pictures of animals. "And the prayer[1] of the cloud of incense went up." The cloud of incense is called prayer, because it was an embodied prayer; comp. on Ps. cxli. 2, Rev. v. 8, viii. 3, 4, where we have the interpretation of the symbol, "The incense is the prayers of saints." They say by the incense before those miserable figures, "Deliver me, for thou art my god" (Isa. xliv. 17). Here it is obvious that the prophet has before him not merely the direct participation in Egyptian idolatry. This was certainly not so general. Already Cocceius perceived the right meaning. He thus gives the real import: "The people of Israel relied at that time on the aid of the Egyptians, and looked to them as to their Saviour." The words, "in the dark, every man in his image-chamber" (ver. 12), point to this, that

---

[1] עתר, not incense, scent,—a meaning that rests on no ground whatever.

revolt from Babylon, undertaken in concert with Egypt, was not at that time officially proclaimed—that it was still a secret, though a public one. Their inner apartments appear as image-chambers, because they deceive themselves in their inmost hearts with Egyptian fancies, which here find their external representation in the Egyptian figures on the walls. In ch. xxiii. 14 the earlier Chaldean sympathies appear also in the objective form of pictures. They point to their justification of their shameless course in the words, "The Lord seeth us not, the Lord hath forsaken His land." By these words they wish to refer the guilt to God. As He does nothing for them, they must help themselves as well as they can. Where punishment coincides with a defective sense of sin, revolt from God is the necessary consequence.

Ver. 14. And he brought me to the door of the gate of the Lord's house, which was toward the north; and, behold, the women sat there weeping for Tammuz. 15. And he said unto me, Seest thou, son of man? Still further shalt thou see greater abominations than these.

That the prophet is led to the north gate points to this, that the worship which is here treated of springs from the north. This suits Adonis, already recognised by Jerome in Tammuz, whose worship had its chief seat in Byblos, a city of northern Phœnicia, between Tripolis and Berytus, to which also the very characteristic mark of the weeping women leads. The real import is the seeking of political aid among the Phœnicians, who, according to the discussions on ch. i., belonged to the anti-Chaldaic coalition. "Abominations greater than these" (ver. 15): in the previous passages it was merely, "Thou shalt still further see great abominations." The gradation leads us to understand that the prophet here comes to the sin which stood at present in its full bloom. It was probably the project of a league with Medo-Persia which filled their minds with new hopes, and had called forth the new inquiry of the elders. The excitement was so much the greater, because the exiles were the appropriate agents for this alliance, as in general the Diaspora afforded a proper instrument for effecting the then far-reaching political combinations. We have only to think of the connection which even now subsists among the Jews of all countries.

Ver. 16. And he brought me into the inner court of the Lord's house; and, behold, at the door of the temple of the Lord, between the porch and the altar, about five and twenty men, whose backs were toward the temple of the Lord, and their faces towards the east; and they worshipped the sun toward the east. 17. And he said unto me, Hast thou seen, O son of man? Is it too little for the house of Judah to do the abominations which they have here done? that they have filled the land with violence, that they now still further provoke me to anger; and, lo, they put the vine-branch to their nose. 18. Therefore will I also deal in fury: my eye shall not spare, nor will I pity; and they shall cry in my ears with a loud voice, and I will not hear them.

The five and twenty in ver. 16 are, according to ch. xi. 1, princes of the people. We have here, as in the seventy, an ideal representation of the ruling powers, so composed that for every one of the twelve tribes of which Israel ideally consisted, two men were counted, and one over as president. It is here said *about* twenty-five, in contradistinction to the seventy without the *about* in ver. 11. There the number had a definite basis in the Mosaic books; here this is wanting. This very *about* decides against the assumption that the twenty-five were the chiefs of the twenty-four classes of priests, with the high priest at their head. In this case the number would be sharply defined. Against the priests speaks also the political character of the whole scene, which becomes particularly evident by comparison with ch. xxiii., and by reference to the historical starting-point of the prophecies of Ezekiel, a great insurrection against the Chaldean monarchy. Moreover, it had never been really a fact that the whole priesthood, as one man, had given themselves over to idolatry. To this is added the impossibility of separating the twenty-five here from the twenty-five in ch. xi. We have here the transgression, there the punishment. In ch. ix. the latter was represented only in regard to the seventy. The place between the porch and the altar, immediately at the entrance of the court of the priests, on which especially the interpretation of the twenty-five by the priests was based, was also the appropriate one for the civic representatives in solemn supplications. As the priests stand there, according to Joel ii. 17, to be in close proximity with the people in whose name they appear, so here the highest officebearers of the people come as near the altar as was lawful for them, to show their contempt for the God of Israel. The Jews think they have behaved unbecomingly toward the altar. This is not ill devised, and goes further in the direction indicated by Ezekiel. The prophet has in view a new aspect of the political superstition of the people. It was a national sin; and so, along with the former representation of the people, consisting of seventy elders, a new one is here formed consisting of twenty-five princes. We learn more exactly the nature of this political superstition from the mention of the *sun* as the object of worship, and especially from the close of ver. 17, where a rite of the Medo-Persian religion is undeniably spoken of. If any one turned attention to the confederates against the Chaldeans, he must have thought above all of those whom Isaiah had already named as the destroyers of the in his time only dawning Chaldean empire, the Medo-Persians. "As the power," it was remarked in the *Christology*, "which will subvert the Babylonian monarchy, appear the Medes in Isa. xiii. 17. In ch. xxi. 2 Elam is named along with Madai, by which, in the usage of Isaiah, Persia is designated. This power, and at its head the conqueror from the east, Koresh, will, according to the announcement of Isaiah, bring salvation to Judah; through it will he gain a restoration to his native land." The revolt might here shelter itself under the appearance of piety: the word of God itself seemed to point to alliance with the Persians, and to invite to the same. As Babylon, according to Isa. xxxix., Ezek. xvi. and xxiii., and other accounts, conspired against Assyria a long time before it was able to overthrow it, so it is to be supposed that the Medo-Persian power first attained its object after many previous unsuccessful attempts. But we are distinctly assured of this by Ezekiel in ch. xxxii. 24, 25. There appear the Elamites, " who caused their terror in the land of the living," among the nations who were discomfited by the Chaldeans, without doubt in consequence of the coalition, which we here see in the act of formation. In Jeremiah, ch. xxv. 25, the kings of Media and Elam are named in the first year of Nebuchadnezzar among those who are to drink the cup of wrath. In the face of the fulfilment of this former prophecy, Jeremiah threatens, in the beginning of the reign of

Zedekiah (ch. xlix. 34 f.), that the Lord will break the bow of Elam, without doubt in reference to the political hopes which were at this time placed in Elam. Graf says on this passage: "Elam's power also is broken; the enemies, the instruments of the divine anger, surprise it, and before their terrible annihilating sword it flees to all nations: its land becomes subject to a foreign power. But yet once more is Elam restored." Jeremiah plays no empty trick. He must have had a real cause for threatening destruction to Elam. The predictions of the prophets are "counsels" (Isa. xli. 28). After a full historical investigation, M. Niebuhr says in the *History of Assyria and Babylon*, p. 212: "A successful war of Nebuchadnezzar with Elam, between the ninth and twentieth years of his reign, is certain." The twenty-five stand not in the inner court, but at the door of it. That they appear in the temple of Jehovah, implies that they wish to maintain externally their relation to the Lord. But that they turn their back to the sanctuary of the Lord and their face to the sun, shows that in their political course they count the Lord for nothing; and, on the contrary, place their hope in the worshippers of the sun. The worship of the stars and the elements was, as Herodotus testified, peculiar to the Medo-Persian religion. They had no gods of wood and stone, no image-worship like the Egyptians. The chief object of their veneration was, along with fire, the sun. Hyde, *De Religione Persarum*, p. 305, gives from the ruins of Persepolis a copy of a scene—the king of Persia as he stands worshipping before the fire and the sun. The sun is here to be regarded more exactly as the rising sun. We have a reference to the Persian worship of the rising sun in Isa. xli. 2, "who awakened from the sunrise;" and xlvi. 11, "who calls from the sunrise an eagle." The name Koresh itself, according to the Greek writers, signifies the *sun*. The Persian king was regarded as an incarnation of the sun-god. In that sculpture in Persepolis, the spirit of the king moves before the sun, from which it proceeds and to which it returns.[1] In ver. 17 it is said that Judah is already

---

[1] We must beware of misunderstanding the anomalous form משתחויתם as it occurs directly in Ezekiel, of whom the abnormal is a characteristic peculiarity. The form is a *quid pro quo*, but so is the practice signified by it. Lightfoot says, *vox miro modo formata, ad miram abo-*

sufficiently burdened with "the abominations which they have done, that they have filled the land with violence," so that it is really not the time to provoke God further by these new abominations. *Here:* this refers to sins with which they, the house of Judah, and especially their princes (for the *violence* points to these), have already filled the land, which have thus been committed abroad outside the temple. But yet they were, as the *here* shows, committed in the temple. For the temple is, in a spiritual sense, the dwelling of the Israelites, and all that they did took place there. In what the new transgression consists, by which they provoke God, is intimated in the words, "They put the vine-branch to the nose." That it belongs to the religious department, in contrast with the former sins, which moved in the moral region, appears from the phrase "to provoke me" in its reference to Deut. xxxii. 16, "They vex Him with strange gods, with abominations they provoke Him." The vine-branch[1] held before corresponds here with the worship of the sun in ver. 16. The vine-stock is the pre-eminent product of the sun, and so to the sun-worshippers the chief object of thanksgiving and prayer, the most suitable representative of all for which thanks are due to the sun. The Persian sun-worshipper, according to Strabo and others, held in his hand a bunch of shoots, called Barsom, when praying to the sun, and

minationem efficacius exprimendam. The regular form would be the participle משתחוים. But the prophet, by inserting ת, gives a criticism of their proceeding. To be compared is Ex. xxiv. 1, "And he said unto Moses, Come up unto the Lord, thou and Aaron, and seventy of the elders of Israel; and worship ye afar off." Further, Deut. xi. 16, "Take heed that your heart be not deceived, and ye turn aside and serve other gods, and worship them, and the Lord's wrath be kindled against you." The last passage is especially to the point. The ת serves the purpose of a quotation, that is, they worship; whereas it is said in the law of God, Ye shall not worship. You may declare this to be a mere play; but this does not at all alter the fact.

[1] זמורה means only vine-stock, nothing else, and so occurs in ch. xv. 2. Every other explanation is thus to be rejected as arbitrary. The word never means shoot in general. Even according to its derivation, it suits only the vine-stock, to which alone it applies in use. The verb is used of the pruning of the vineyard. The noun, properly pruning, points to the care which the vine needs, if it is to thrive and bear fruit—the καθαίρει of John xv. 2. Of the requital, which is brought in here by an arbitrary interpretation of זמרתם, mention is first made in ver. 18.

applied it to the mouth when uttering prayer. This quite agrees with the rite here. For the vine-branch here needs not be a single rod, and the nose is derisively mentioned in place of the mouth, according to the leaning to irony and sarcasm which appears so often in the prophets when they oppose and chastise superstitious folly.

Ch. ix. From the sin the prophet turns to the punishment. The announcement of this begins in this section with the slaying of the sinful inhabitants of the city, and then in the following chapter we have the destruction of the city itself. The scene is the following: At the command of the Lord, who will punish the revolt of His people, appear the ministers of His righteousness, six in number, and in their midst "a man clothed in linen," the former with weapons of destruction, the latter with an inkhorn. They come (the scene is the temple) near the brazen altar: thence the glory of the Lord went towards them from the most holy place to the threshold of the temple. It gives to the man clothed in linen the order to protect the pious, to the others the order to destroy the ungodly without mercy. These orders are executed.

Ver. 1. And he called in my ears with a loud voice, saying, The visitations of the city draw near,[1] and let every man have his destroying weapon in his hand. 2. And, behold, six men came by the way of the upper gate, which lies toward the north, and each had his breaking weapon in his hand; and one man was in their midst clothed in linen, and an inkhorn upon his loins: and they came and stood beside the brazen altar. 3. And the glory of the God of Israel went up from the cherub, on which it was, to the threshold of the house; and he called to the man clothed in linen, who had the inkhorn at his loins. 4. And the Lord said unto him, Pass through the midst of the city, through Jerusalem, and set a mark upon the foreheads of the men that sigh and that groan for all the abominations that are done in the midst of it. 5. And to those he said in my ears, Pass through

---

[1] Luther, "cause to come near." But קרבו is usually the perfect in Kal, and occurs in ch. xii. 23, xlii. 14. As imperative it is found only once, Isa. xli. 25. For treating it as the perfect, the fundamental passage Hos. ix. 7 speaks, "The days of *visitation* are come."

F

the city after him, and smite; let not your eyes[1] spare, nor have ye pity. 6. Old and young, and maiden and child, and women, slay to destruction; and any man upon whom is the mark touch not; and begin at my sanctuary. And they began at the old men that were before the house. 7. And he said unto them, Defile the house, and fill the courts with the slain: go ye forth. And they went forth, and slew in the city. 8. And it came to pass, when they had slain them, and I was left, then fell I on my face, and cried, and said, Ah Lord Jehovah! wilt thou destroy all the remnant of Israel, when thou pourest out thy fury upon Jerusalem? 9. And he said unto me, The iniquity of the house of Israel and Judah is exceedingly great, and the land is filled with blood, and the city filled with perversity: for they say, The Lord hath forsaken the land, and the Lord seeth not. 10. And I also, my eye shall not spare, nor will I pity; their way I have laid upon their own head. 11. And, behold, the man clothed in linen, who had the inkhorn at his loins, returned word, saying, I have done as thou hast commanded me.

"He called" (ver. 1)—He who had formerly spoken—the Lord (comp. ver. 4). The loud voice corresponds to the greatness of the abominations that cry to God. God speaks to the ministers of His vengeance, and announces to them that now it is time to go to work. The visitation in itself may also be used in a good sense: that it is here penal, lies in the connection with the foregoing, according to which Jerusalem can only be the object of the divine anger, and also in the summons, founded on the actual state of things, to the ministers of God to provide themselves with destructive weapons. The six men in ver. 2 can only be angels in human form, which they must assume to be visible to the prophet. For only thus do they suit as the retinue of the man clothed in linen, who on sure grounds can be no other than the angel of the Lord, and whom we never see accompanied with any other retinue than that of the lower angels; comp. for ex. Zech. i. 11 f. and Josh. v. 14, where the angel of the Lord designates himself as the

---

[1] עַל stands for אֶל. The reading attested by manuscripts is עֵינֵיכֶם, for which the marginal reading gives the singular. It is to be rejected as explanatory. The eyes are combined into an ideal unity, and so the verb may stand in the singular. The Masoretes could not understand this.

Prince of the host of the Lord. The men come from the north, because the earthly foes were to come thence, whom the proper factors, the heavenly powers, employ as their instruments (comp. ch. i. 4; Jer. i. 14). That the man clothed in linen is the angel of the Lord, appears from Dan. x. 5, xii. 6, 7, where Michael, the angel of the Lord (comp. *Beiträge*, i. p. 166, and the comm. on ch. xii. of Revelation), is designated in the same way,—a remarkable coincidence between the two prophets of the exile. But the thing itself shows that the man clothed in linen is no other than the angel of the Lord. The clothing is that of the earthly high priest. All the different pieces of raiment of the earthly high priest are, according to Lev. xvi. 4, 23, of linen: hence is explained also the plural, linen garments. The earthly high priest cannot be here intended. But the Antitype of the same, the heavenly High Priest and Intercessor, is the Angel of the Lord, the Angel of the covenant (Mal. iii. 1), who in Zech. i. 12 makes intercession for the covenant people, and to whom the Lord answers with good and comfortable words. The high priest appears in Zech. iii. as a type of Christ, and a figure of the angel of the Lord (comp. the *Christol.* on the passage). But we have to regard the man clothed in linen not alone as appointed to the work of delivering the pious—not as standing in opposition to the six ministers of righteousness. The protection of the pious is his privilege; but the work of vengeance also stands under his control. The six are to be regarded as absolutely subordinate to him, executing the work of destruction only by his order and under his authority. We must regard this as antecedently probable, because the angel of the Lord is elsewhere represented as the leading personage in the great judgments of God, which are executed in the interest of the kingdom of God. It was he, for ex., who, as the "destroying angel," smote the first-born of Egypt (Ex. xii. 23, compared with vers. 12, 13). Especially *here* the number seven leads to the intimate connection of the man clothed in linen with the six. The former also appears at the altar, so that he thus belongs to the eagles, who gather where the carcase is, comes in the midst of the rest, who follow after him. In ch. x. 2, 7, the man clothed in linen is expressly declared to be he who executes the judgments of the Lord: the burning of the city proceeds from him, and this is inseparably connected with the slaying of the guilty inhabitants. According to ver. 5 *here,* " pass through the city *after him,*" *the* angels in the work of destruction are the retinue of *the* angel. In ver. 11, after the completion of the work of destruction, the man clothed in linen says, " I have done as Thou hast commanded me." Accordingly, the order for destruction is especially addressed to him. The man clothed in linen has an inkhorn on his loins : the Orientals to this day often carry the inkhorn in the girdle at the side. The use to be made of the inkhorn we learn from ver. 4. It serves to mark the foreheads of the elect. It is a question whether it is intended at the same time for inscribing them in the book of life, which is first mentioned in Ex. xxxii. 32 (comp. Ps. lxix. 28, and on Rev. xx. 12). This is indeed probable, especially on account of the fundamental passage, Isa. iv. 3, " Every one that is written for life in Jerusalem." Accordingly the inscription in the book of life is to be regarded as the original act, the marking on the forehead as the consequence. The ministers of vengeance " came and stood by the brazen altar." The brazen altar is the altar of burnt-offering. This is the place of transgression. There lies accumulated the unexpiated iniquity of the whole people, instead of the rich treasure of faith and love that should lie there embodied in offering. The ministers of God appear in the place of transgression, to glorify Him in the fall of those who would not glorify Him by their life. In the one or the other way He must necessarily come to His right and to His honour in them. The delineation of sin also, in ch. viii., involves the principle that, ideally taken, all the sins of the people are committed in the temple. The fundamental passage is Amos ix. The Lord appears on the point of punishing the sins of Israel upon the altar, on which they are heaped up. The angels *stand* beside the desecrated altar, awaiting the beck and command of God. He whose spiritual eye was opened to see them standing there, could only look with deep horror on the people, filled with joyful hopes of the future. According to ver. 3, the glory of God moves from the most holy place, where it sat over *the* cherub, the ideal unity of the cherubim, to the gate of the sanctuary, near which the altar stood, to give orders to His ministers standing at the altar. First in ver. 4, the order is issued to the man clothed in linen, to make a sign on the forehead of the men who are the objects of sparing mercy, because they have kept themselves free from the community of corruption. By the *sign* one is separated from the mass. This may be done according to circumstances, either for honour or dishonour, for salvation or for destruction. In Ps. lxxviii. 41 the marking is dishonouring. To mark, stands there as the Latin *notare*, for to dishonour: here, where the mass is devoted to destruction, the marking is one that honours and saves. The marking takes place on the *forehead*, the place where the sign is most easily seen. The sign on the forehead here, the symbolic expression of the truth that God in great judgments holds the sheltering hand of His grace over His own, that He " knoweth how to deliver the godly out of temptations" (2 Pet. ii. 9), corresponds to the sprinkling with blood of the door-posts of those who are to be spared in the judgment upon Egypt in Ex. xii., where Grotius justly remarks, " He marks the foreheads, not the door-posts, as formerly in Egypt, because the act of deliverance was to be wrought, not for whole families, but for individuals, and indeed the elect." At that time stood house against house, people against people; now the great separation is to be among the people themselves. We have here the fundamental passage for the sealing of the elect on their foreheads in Rev. vii. 2, 3. The marking secures not against any share in the divine judgments; this would not correspond with the nature of the divine righteousness, as even the elect are in many ways affected with the prevailing corruption (comp. Isa. vi. 5): it secures only against being swept away with the wicked (Ps. xxviii. 3), against an evil death, and all that would stand in contradiction with the rule that " all things work together for good to them that love God" (Rom. viii. 28). We have an example of the fulfilment of this symbolic prophecy in Jeremiah, whose life was preserved in the taking of the city. A personal application of the general truth here expressed we have in that which the Lord by Jeremiah says to the God-fearing Ebed-melech (ch. xxxix. 16-18), " Behold, I will bring my words upon this city for evil, and not for good; and they shall be before thee in that day. But I will deliver thee in that day; ... and thou shalt have thy life for a prey, because thou hast trusted in me." So also is it said to Baruch in Jer. xlv. 5, " Behold, I will bring evil upon all flesh; but thy soul will I give unto thee for a prey, in all places whither thou goest." The " old men" in ver. 6, which forms the fundamental passage for 1 Pet. iv. 17, " Judgment must begin at the house of God," are the seventy elders in ch. viii. 11. The sanctuary, often elsewhere the dwelling-place of the whole people, appears here specially as the dwelling-place of their representatives: on the other hand, the mass of the people is assigned to the city, which, however, forms no counterpart to the temple, but is, as it were, a chapel of ease to it. In ver. 7, in the words, " Defile the house, and fill the courts with the slain," that which has already taken place is approved in the form of an order, to connect it with the actual order, " Go ye forth." The expression has the air of military abruptness. The uncleanness of the human corpse is, according to the law, especially great (Num. xix. 11), much greater than that of the animal carcase (Lev. xi. 24). It is here peculiarly great, as it concerns those who perish amidst their sins. The house is defiled by the corpses, which are heaped in its courts. Nothing is said, either here or in ver. 6, of any being slain in the house. The prophet, in ver. 8, does not express his own feeling, but speaks from the soul of those upon whom the judgment of God has fallen, and appears as their representative: only on this supposition, for which there is abundance of analogy, is his speech conceivable. The remnant is the remnant in full that was left, after the Assyrian and the former Chaldean visitation. The small election, consisting of those marked, is overlooked. But the exiles come not into account, according to the view of those whom the prophet represents. The inhabitants of Jerusalem regarded themselves as the whole of Israel, and the exiles as a cut off and rejected branch of the vine (ch. xi. 15).[1] In the divine answer in ver. 9, which turns away the complaint by reference to the greatness of the people's guilt, Israel is the whole, Judah the part, in which the whole at that time alone continued to exist. For the ten tribes, as branches cut off, come not into account: they could attain again to significance only by renewed connection with the vine, which was prepared by the exile of Judah, and partly accomplished. The fearful

---

[1] נשׁארי is the 3 perf., with א inserted, which here takes the place of a noun: a he-remained-over.

extent of the moral declension is referred to this, that they say, "The Lord hath forsaken the land, and the Lord seeth not." On this Michaelis remarks: "The source of all transgression is the denial of the providence of God." To this denial they have attained, inasmuch as, from defect in the acknowledgment of their sins, they can discover no reason in their misfortunes; rather must they see in them, as they are, witnesses against the power and good-will of their God. The man clothed in linen says, in ver. 11, "I have done as Thou hast commanded me"— in both respects, the destruction and the preservation. The first comes pre-eminently into account. For only destruction is mentioned in the immediate context. We have here the transition from the slaying of the citizens to the destruction of the city, of which the following chapter treats. Our verse forms the close of the former work.

Ch. x. The following is the arrangement of this chapter, which exhibits the second act of the divine righteousness. He that sits on the throne commands the man clothed in linen to take fire out of the midst of the wheels of the cherubim, and scatter it over the city (vers. 1, 2). In vers. 3-5 it is parenthetically related concerning the position which the cherubim and the glory of the Lord then took, that the latter then prefigured the approaching departure from the temple, and the cherubim already prepared themselves for this. In vers. 6, 7 is the partial execution of the command: the man in linen places himself by the wheels, and a cherub takes fire from the midst, and hands it to him: he takes it, and goes out. In vers. 8-14, the observations which the prophet made on this occasion in regard to the cherubim and the wheels. In vers. 15-19, the advance of the glory of the Lord with the cherubim and the wheels, the removal of which is the preliminary condition of the scattering of the fire over the city, to the passage out of the temple. In vers. 20-22, the remark that the cherubim which the prophet here saw in the temple, present themselves as identical in every respect with "the living creature" which he had seen before at the river Chebar.

Ver. 1. And I looked, and, behold, in the vault which was above the head of the cherubim appeared something like a sapphire-stone, as the appearance of the likeness of a throne above them. 2. And he said unto the man clothed in linen as follows, Go in between the whirl under the cherub, and fill thy hollow hands with coals of fire from between the cherubim, and scatter them over the city. And he went in before my eyes.

The glory of the Lord is in ver. 1 again over the cherubim, from which it had separated itself. As this separation served only a quite definite purpose, it was unnecessary to remark that it ceased as soon as this purpose was effected. That it retired to its original place is even here indirectly affirmed. First, in ver. 4, the glory of the Lord raises itself anew from the cherubim (comp. ver. 18). Concerning the vault, see on i. 22, 25; the throne, i. 26.[1] "He said" (ver. 2),—namely, He that sitteth on the throne (comp. i. 26). Maius observes: "God the Father sitting on the throne to the Son, to whom He has given full power to execute judgment" (John v. 27). The repeated "And he said," which we have given by "as follows," is designed to turn the attention to the important statement. The fire is here not a symbolic designation of the anger of God, but elementary fire, for the firing and burning of the city are to be represented. The *wheels* are a symbol of the powers of nature, among which fire holds a prominent place. The ultimate cause of the burning of the city (this is the fundamental idea) is not earthly, but heavenly, and hence the folly of hoping and working for its preservation. The command proceeds from Him who sits on the throne to His angel: the fire is only the instrumental means in the hand of the latter, who takes it, and scatters it over the city. Four potencies are engaged in the destruction of the city,—He who sits on the throne, the man clothed in linen, the fire, and the cherub who hands it to the angel. The former two are absolutely ruling, the latter two absolutely ministering. It might at first sight appear that the man clothed in linen does not here come into account in the aspect which is figured by his raiment. He wears this as the heavenly high priest, the representative of the church with God. Thus it appears that the designation is only suitable in such acts as are for the safety of the church; whereas the present act is an annihilating judgment. But on a profounder view the destruction serves for safety, as it is the

[1] אל for על, as not unfrequently in Ezekiel (ii. 10, xi. 11).

necessary prerequisite of it. The Lord must first in judgment wash away the defilement of the daughter of Zion (Isa. iv. 4), before He can draw nigh to her in salvation. The removal of the dross is also placed in the light of grace in Isa. i. 25, 26; also in Mal. iii. 2, 3. By the *whirl* are the wheels designated on account of the weight of their movement, according to ver. 13. The words "from between the cherubim" imply that the cherubim also have their part in the wheels. The city was indeed to be burned by men, who are included under the cherubim. According to ver. 7, the cherub presents the fire to the man clothed in linen.[1]

Vers. 3-5 interrupt the connection, as they refer to the position which the glory of the Lord with the cherubim at that time took, and to the remarkable phenomena which accompanied both. Ver. 3. And the cherubim stood on the right side of the house when the man went in; and the cloud filled the inner court. 4. And the glory of the Lord was lifted from the cherub upon the threshold of the house; and the house was filled with the cloud, and the court was full of the brightness of the Lord's glory. 5. And the sound of the cherubim's wings was heard even to the outer court, as the voice of the Almighty God when he speaketh.

"Right side of the house" (ver. 3): on the south side of it. The cloud belongs to the divine glory throned above the cherubim. It is the companion of the fire. Its coming out so strongly, pressing forth from the temple in the inner court, and filling it, indicate that God will soon manifest Himself in His character of a consuming fire, a jealous God (Deut. iv. 24). The heavenly fire manifests itself in face of the preparation for kindling the material fire, which is only a reflection of the heavenly. The movement of the glory of the Lord from the cherub to the threshold of the house (ver. 4) indicates that He will soon leave the house altogether, and corresponds with the preparations for kindling the material fire, which may then first break forth when the glory of the Lord has wholly left

---

[1] בא is here and in ver. 3 not "come," but "go." We have here a very striking parallel to Dan. i. 1, where the expedition of Nebuchadnezzar begins in the third year of Jehoiakim, on which in the fourth year the taking of Jerusalem follows, with which the seven years of the Babylonish servitude begin in Jeremiah.

the house. The glory of the Lord in ver. 18 again unites itself with the cherub, but only to carry out the purpose here already figuratively indicated. Cloud and brightness are inseparably connected. The brightness is that of the fire, which signifies the absolute energy of God, here especially the energy of His punitive justice; and the cloud is either the thundercloud, from which the brightness or the fire proceeds, or is formed by the smoke of the fire (comp. Isa. iv. 5). We need not therefore assign the cloud specially to the temple, and the brightness to the court; but both cloud and brightness belong first to the temple, and pass over thence into the court. The very decided manifestation of the fire-nature of God is a presage with respect to the material fire which will consume the rebellious city. Already in Isa. vi. 4 the filling of the house with smoke prefigures the destructive judgment breaking in upon the backsliding covenant people; see further on Rev. xv. 8. The cherubim also make ready (ver. 5) for departure, the near approach of which they know from this, that the glory of the Lord, of which they are the inseparable companions, moves in preparation to the threshold of the house, and then from this, that the fiery nature of God makes itself so decidedly manifest. "The voice of the Almighty God when He speaks" is the thunder. That the sound of the wing-stroke of the cherubim may be compared with this on account of its violence, is evidence of itself; if the cherub is the concentration of all created life on earth, then its sound is the concentration of all sound on earth.

Ver. 6. And it came to pass, when he commanded the man clothed in linen, saying, Take fire from between the whirl, from between the cherubim, then he went in, and stood beside the wheel. 7. And the cherub stretched forth his hand from between the cherubim unto the fire that was between the cherubim, and took and gave it into the hands of him who was clothed in linen; and he took it, and went out.

The prophet here returns to the narrative begun in vers. 1 and 2, which was interrupted by the account of an appearance running parallel with that described there. "Beside the wheel" (ver. 6): the wheel is the ideal combination of the wheels, as the cherub stands collectively for the cherubim. The cherub hands the fire (ver. 6); the earth serves as an instrument for heaven. Those who burned the city were immediately the Chaldeans, who are included under the cherubim; but behind them stood another. The burning is no further delineated: it lies beyond xi. 23, where first the glory of the Lord wholly departs from the city; and the prophet could not describe it, as he was, according to ver. 24, at this time removed from Jerusalem.

The action proceeding from the cherubim along with the wheels leads the prophet to enter more fully into the description of them. Ver. 8. And there appeared in the cherubim the form of a man's hand under their wings. 9. And I looked, and, behold, four wheels by the cherubim, one wheel by the one cherub, and one wheel by the one cherub; and the appearance of the wheels was like a chrysolite. 10. And their appearance, all four were of one likeness, as if the wheel were in the midst of the wheel. 11. When they went, they went upon their four sides; they turned not as they went, for whither the head turned they went after it; they turned not as they went. 12. And their whole flesh, and their backs, and their hands, and their wings, and the wheels, were full of eyes round about; all four had their wheels. 13. The wheels were called the whirl in my ears. 14. And every one had four faces: the face of the one the face of a cherub, and the face of the second the face of a man, and the third the face of a lion, and the fourth the face of an eagle.

First in ver. 8 it is said of the cherubim that they had hands, because the hand was brought into action in ver. 7. Then follows in vers. 9-13 the description of the wheels, because the fire is taken from them. The description of the wheel agrees in the main with ch. i. The most essential additions are presented in ver. 12, where, to the former statement that the wheels were full of eyes, it is added that the cherubim also were covered with eyes; and in ver. 13, which gives the interpretation of the symbol of the wheels. The head in ver. 11 can only be the head among the wheels. A reference to the cherubim must have been more distinctly marked. Head stands also frequently in impersonal things for the upmost, highest, or most excellent; and thus here it can only be the wheel which had the direction for the time, and which the others should follow. If, for ex., the mission goes to the south, the wheel facing that way carries the others with it, without requiring to make any turn. The wheels were so arranged that they could follow in all directions, without turning, the *primus motor*, the directing wheel. Ver. 12 also refers to the wheels; only here, to the statement that the wheels were full of eyes (i. 18), it is premised, that the signature of the divine providence was impressed on the cherubim also. It did not need to be more particularly mentioned that at the beginning the cherubim, and not the wheels, were spoken of, as the expression "their flesh" applies only to the cherubim, and not to the wheels. "The whirl:" so are the wheels, and the powers of nature expressed by them, designated in ver. 13, on account of the great momentum residing in them. As the cherubs, the representatives of living beings, come here into view chiefly on the human side, so the wheels, the symbols of the powers of nature, in the fire. After the description of that which came specially into view in the cherubim with its appendage for the present occasion, follow now in ver. 14 the *faces* of the cherubim, because these served to disclose their nature, as in the wheels the name *whirl* applied to them in ver. 13. Of the four faces of each, only that is precisely described which formed the front and presented itself first to the beholder. As in the cherubim a predominating significance of the ox nowhere appears, neither in reference to the form nor the idea, the ground of the face of the ox (ch. i. 10), being here designated as the face of the cherub, can only lie in this, that this face was presented to the prophet's eye in the position in which he stood. The ground will lie in ch. x. 8, compared with ch. viii. 3 and i. 10.

The cherubim move, and this gives occasion to the prophet to describe in general the way and manner of their movement. Ver. 15. And the cherubim were lifted up. This is the living creature that I saw at the river Chebar. 16. And when the cherubim went, the wheels went by them; and when the cherubim lifted up their wings to mount up from the earth, the wheels also turned not away from them. 17. When they stand, these stand; and when they lift themselves up, these lift themselves up with them, for the spirit of the living creature is in them. 18. And the glory of the LORD went away from the threshold of the house, and stood over the cherubim.

19. And the cherubim lifted up their wings, and mounted up from the earth before my eyes; when they went out, and the wheels beside them, and stood[1] at the door of the east gate of the house of the LORD, and the glory of the God of Israel was over them above.

The statement, "The cherubim lifted themselves up," in ver. 15—comp. the preparation for this in ver. 5—is again taken up in ver. 19, after it has been described in the interval how the cherubim usually moved. "This is the living creature that I saw at the river Chebar:" there it was also the instrument by which he was lifted up. On ver. 17, "for the spirit of the living creature was in them," comp. i. 20. The prerequisite of the departure of the cherubim is the return of the glory of the Lord (ver. 18), which had betaken itself, according to ver. 4, to the threshold of the house, as it were pointing out the way in which it was presently to go. That the glory of the Lord retires from the temple in several stages (xi. 23, the glory of the Lord with the cherubim wholly leaves the temple and city), should teach us, according to Grotius, "that the temple will be wholly deprived of the divine protection." Parallel in sentiment is Hos. v. 15, "I will go and return to my place, till they become guilty and seek my face: in their need they will seek me early."

At the close is now again expressed the relation of the cherubim to "the living creature" in ch. i. Ver. 20. This is the living creature that I saw under the God of Israel at the river Chebar, and I knew that they were cherubim. 21. Every one had four faces, and every one four wings, and the similitude of a man's hands under their wings. 22. And the likeness of their faces, these are the faces which I saw at the river Chebar, their appearance and themselves: they went every one according to his face.

"The living creature under the God of Israel" (ver. 20): this designation of the cherubim leaves no doubt that they are a representation of living creatures on the earth. "And I knew that they were cherubim." Mich. says: "Those living creatures signify the same as the cherubim in the temple and

---

[1] The subject of ויעמד is the whole of the appearance, cherub and wheels with the Lord enthroned above them. The singular points to the unity in the multiplicity.

over the ark." The name of the cherubim was not employed in the first description. Only in the second is prominence given to the identity of the living creatures, making at first an independent appearance with the well-known cherubim. Ver. 21 is not an idle repetition, but gives prominence to the fact that, in proof of the identity of the cherubim here with the living creatures in ch. i., the number four was common to the faces, etc., of both; comp. ver. 22, where the comparison is carried out. The words "their appearance and themselves" in ver. 22 are dependent on "I saw," to wit, at that time I saw their appearance and themselves: they were wholly the same, not merely in their external appearance, but also in their essence.

Ch. xi. In vers. 1–12, the third element of the punishment of ungodly Jerusalem,—the vengeance which follows those who save their lives in the taking of the city, especially the ungodly nobles, who by their corrupt counsels had hastened its fall. In vers. 13–21, the comfort in face of the threatening destruction, in the background of which stands the admonition not to make common cause with those devoted to inevitable destruction, and thereby involve themselves in their fate. If the present Zion be thus doomed to perish, if all plans are futile which are directed to its preservation, yet is not Zion therefore lost. The Israel of God continues among the exiles. Among them even in their banishment will God's presence be made known; and in His time He will bring them back to the holy land, restore the sanctuary, and give them, instead of a stony heart, a heart of flesh. In vers. 22–25, the close of the vision.

Ver. 1. And the spirit lifted me up, and brought me unto the front gate of the LORD's house, which looketh eastward: and behold at the door of the gate five and twenty men; and I saw in their midst Jaazaniah the son of Azur, and Pelatiah the son of Benaiah, princes of the people. 2. And he said unto me, Son of man, these are the men who devise mischief, and give wicked counsel in this city; 3. Who say, It is not near to build houses: they are the caldron, and we are the flesh. 4. Therefore prophesy against them, prophesy, son of man. 5. And the Spirit of the Lord fell upon me, and said unto me, Say; Thus saith the Lord, Thus have ye said, O house of Israel; and that which riseth up in your mind I know. 6. Ye have multiplied your slain in the city, and filled its streets with the slain. 7. Therefore thus saith the Lord Jehovah, Your slain whom ye have laid in the midst of it, they are the flesh, and it is the caldron; and one shall bring you forth[1] out of the midst of it. 8. Ye have feared a sword; and a sword will I bring upon you, saith the Lord Jehovah. 9. And I will bring you out of the midst thereof, and give you into the hand of strangers, and execute judgments among you. 10. By the sword ye shall fall, in the border of Israel will I judge you; and ye shall know that I am the LORD. 11. This shall not be the caldron for you, and ye shall not be the flesh in the midst of it; in the border of Israel will I judge you. 12. And ye shall know that I am the LORD, who have not walked in my statutes, nor executed my judgments; and ye have done after the judgments of the heathen that are round about you.

The five and twenty in ch. viii. 16 here return; there the transgression, here the punishment. The latter was carried out in ch. ix. only in reference to the seventy of ch. viii. 11. An essential element was wanting also in regard to the punishment. The divine vengeance was to come out not merely in the death of the sinful inhabitants within the city, and in the burning of the city; it was to display itself also in those who escaped with life in the taking of the city: comp. ch. v. 2, where it is said, in reference to those who are preserved alive in the catastrophe of the city, "The sword will I draw out after them." As the representatives of those who suffer punishment in this way appear here the same five and twenty nobles whom the prophet causes to symbolize the sin of the people in ch. viii., the designation of two among the five and twenty, and so indirectly of the whole, as princes of the people in ver. 1, shows clearly that priests are not meant, but only respectable citizens. In what follows also they appear as mere statesmen. And the fate which is here predicted for them corresponds exactly with that which, according to history, befell the nobles of the people, the most distinguished officers of Zedekiah. From the east, the region to which they turned in adoration, and whence they had sought help (ch. viii. 16), shall the avenging power come. Hence the double designation of the gate—the "front," and "which looketh eastward." In the names of the men them-

[1] הוֹצִיא, either infinitive or 3 perf., "one shall bring forth."

selves, and their fathers, we have the concentration of these thoughts: all is full of music with them. God-hears, the son of the helper, and God-helps, the son of God-builds—these are fit names for men who promise salvation without repentance, the direct opposite of that which the name of Jeremiah, God-casts-down, presents. They were probably real nobles of that time, whose counsels had weight with the king; but on account of their significance he gives their names precisely, whereas he might otherwise have named others as well. Jaazaniah is here, by the name of his father, distinguished from him of ch. viii. 11. The more threatening the contraction of the political sky, the stronger would be the tendency, by the choice of a name promising salvation for their children, to repel anxiety and soothe the conscience, which presented to view the opposite of this name. "He said" (ver. 2): he who stands so constantly before the eyes of the prophets, that they often introduce him speaking without any previous notice. "The men who devise mischief or evil:" their plans of resistance, formed in perverse opposition to the will of God, so repeatedly and emphatically announced by Jeremiah; their political intrigues, where repentance ought to have been exhibited, bring incalculable death and destruction (ver. 6). "It is not time to build houses" (ver. 3): Jeremiah had written to the exiles excited by political hopes (ch. xxix. 5), "Build ye houses, and dwell in them; and plant vineyards, and eat." This, they think, cannot at all events apply to the inhabitants of Jerusalem. They first negative the building of houses which exile implies, and then affirm that they will maintain themselves in their present possession. The words may also be taken interrogatively; and then the princes, in the face of the destruction threatened by the men of God, would say, Is it not nigh to build houses? the time soon comes when Jerusalem shall be extended beyond its present boundary; comp. Isa. ix. 10, where the inhabitants of Samaria, after suffering heavy losses, say, "The bricks are fallen, but we will build with hewn stones." But it is not the most natural way to view it as a question, and hence the note of interrogation should not in that case have been wanting. The name Benaiah would certainly in that case suit still better. "It is the caldron, and we are the flesh:" this denotes their inseparable connection with the city, from which no man shall sever them, nothing remove them. The interpretation, We shall soon be baked by the fire of war, is refuted by ver. 7, according to which the sense can only be, that they expect to remain in the city. Son of man: this comes in ver. 4 with a certain irony. The concealed elevation of the prophet is not recognised by the many above his apparent lowliness, but it appears afterwards above the head of these. The pierced, in ver. 6, are those about to be slain by the Chaldeans, or, according to the point of view assumed, already slain. They are, by their evil counsels (ver. 2), the authors of their own death. Their word, "It is the caldron, and we are the flesh," is, according to ver. 7, to receive by the sequel a certain but a terrible confirmation. "Your slain, whom ye have laid in the midst of it:" they were the real murderers, because by their impious devices they brought in the Chaldeans. "One shall bring you forth:" this is, in the first place, opposed to their hope of remaining in the city; they shall rather be brought forth. Then in the following words it is added, that this bringing forth takes place not in a friendly sense, but only to prolong their suffering. God's avenging sword pursues the exiles. Ver. 8. From fear of the sword (of the king of Babylon), they had kindled the fire of rebellion, and pushed their resistance to the utmost, when he advanced to punish this rebellion; but the very effort they make for fear of the sword will bring the sword upon them, which they would have escaped by humble submission under the mighty hand of God, as Jeremiah had predicted. The king of Egypt will not deliver them, with the whole confederacy that has gathered around him as its centre. On vers. 10, 11 we may comp. 2 Kings xxv. 18-21. After the capture of the city the most distinguished officers and notables were brought to Riblah on the Orontes, at the north end of Cœlesyria, before Nebuchadnezzar, and there put to death by his command. The king of Babylon, it is said (Jer. xxxix. 6, lii. 10), slew all the princes of Judah at Riblah. Behind the king of Babylon the Lord is concealed, whose servant Jeremiah declares Nebuchadnezzar to be (ch. xxv. 9). The prophecy cannot be framed after the event: Ezekiel laid his book before his contemporaries, who had the power to control him. And the guarantee for the predictions, which were fulfilled in the lifetime of the prophet, lies in those which were fulfilled long after his death.

But the confidence with which Ezekiel predicts the downfall of the confederacy is a sufficient proof that there is a supernatural element in his prophecy; and if this must be admitted, we can make no further objection to the details. To pronounce these to be afterwards introduced by the prophet, is to degrade him into a deceiver. " And ye shall know that I am the Lord " (ver. 12): they know from the fate that befalls them, that He who is called Jehovah is Jehovah in reality, the possessor of true Godhead, because He has announced this fate to them beforehand by His prophets. Had the confederacy taken effect, which was impossible, they would have concluded with justice, that the God in whose name the true prophets spoke, merely arrogated to Himself the Godhead. It is lamentable if we must gain the knowledge of God by our own destruction,—if He in whom we live, and move, and are, is first recognised by the strokes which break our own head. The knowledge has here, moreover, no moral import. It is a mere passive knowledge, forced upon the ungodly, unconnected with repentance.

Ver. 13. And it came to pass, when I prophesied, that Pelatiah the son of Benaiah died: and I fell upon my face, and cried with a loud voice, and said, Ah Lord Jehovah! dost thou make an end of the remnant of Israel? 14. And the word of the LORD came unto me, saying, 15. Son of man, thy brethren, thy brethren are the men of thy ransom, and all the house of Israel, all of them to whom the inhabitants of Jerusalem have said, Get ye far from the LORD; unto us is this land given for a possession.[1] 16. Therefore say, Thus saith the Lord Jehovah, Though I have cast them far off among the heathen, and scattered them among the countries, yet I will be to them a sanctuary for a little in the countries whither they come. 17. Therefore say, Thus saith the Lord Jehovah, And I will gather you from the nations, and assemble you out of the countries where ye were scattered, and give you the land of Israel. 18. And they shall come thither, and remove all its detestable things, and all its abominations, from it. 19.

---

[1] Luther, "Thou son of man, thy brothers and near friends, and the whole house of Israel, who still dwell in Jerusalem, say to one another, Those have fled far from the Lord, but we have the land in possession." The sense of the whole verse is missed.

And I will give them one heart, and put a new spirit within you; and I will take the heart of stone out of their flesh, and give them a heart of flesh; 20. That they may walk in my statutes, and keep my judgments, and do them: and they shall be my people, and I will be their God. 21. And when their heart walks after the heart of their detestable things and abominations, I will lay their way upon their own heads, saith the Lord Jehovah.[1]

The event of ver. 13 belongs to the world not of reality, but of vision, and affords the measure for judging of many other events occurring in Ezekiel; for ex., the death of his wife. What was hitherto predicted as future, this now suddenly appears in the form of a fact entering into the present. The transition is the easier, when we reflect that the previous announcement of the future as future does not spring from a subjective foreboding, but rests upon inspiration, and thus bears with it an absolute assurance. That out of the number of the five and twenty men collectively devoted to death, precisely Pelatiah the son of Benaiah must die, to prefigure the fate awaiting all, is explained by his name, according to which with him, as it were, all salvation for Judah fell to the ground. In Pelatiah perished, as the lamentation of the prophet shows, as it were, the remnant of Israel, if, according to the view of the inhabitants, the capital was deemed the proper seat of Israel, and the exiles were regarded as cast-off and withered branches. That this view was false, however, the prophet will teach in the sequel. The prophet, when he falls down and cries, "Ah, Lord, dost Thou make an end of the remnant of Israel?" does not give expression merely to his personal feelings, but changes his place in a strange way (compare a series of similar cases in the prophets; *Christol.* i. p. 490 f.), and appears as the representative of the current view, to give occasion for its rectification. He himself could not possibly, according to Jer. xxiv., be involved in the view which he here brings to light. He plays the part of the inhabitant of Jerusalem. The brethren of the prophets (ver. 15), true brethren, who are so not merely in the flesh, but also in the spirit, represent the Israelites already carried into exile, whom Jeremiah in ch. xxiv. had characterized as the better part of the people—as

[1] A fuller elucidation of this section in the *Christol.* ii. p. 534 f.

those to whom the future of the kingdom of God belongs; while he announces that those who remained in Jerusalem, notwithstanding their high pretensions, are doomed to destruction. The contrast is naturally such in every particular. If this were not acknowledged, Jeremiah would be no true Israelite. According to ch. ix., even in Jerusalem there is an election, which is the object of the Lord's sheltering protection, although they cannot prevent the downfall of the corrupt city. And according to ch. xiv. there is also much refuse among the exiles. The difference, so far as it exists, is explained by this, that the Chaldeans, who were well acquainted with the internal state of the Jews, had, in the captivity under Jehoiachin, removed chiefly the holders of the Israelitish principle, because they saw in them the national strength of the people. Moreover, the godly met death willingly and joyfully, as it was, according to the announcement of Jeremiah, the portal of life; whereas the ungodly did their utmost to remain in their country, in the hope that things would soon take a turn for the better. "The men of thy ransom"—those whom thou art bound to ransom. This alludes to Lev. xxv. 25, where to the relative of an impoverished man the right is given to redeem in his favour his estate that has been sold. In point of fact, the men of his ransom are those for whom the prophet has to be answerable—whom he has to represent with God. The ground on which he is to interest himself only in them is added in the words, "and (they are) all the house of Israel," from which that rebellious mass in Jerusalem, according to the word of the Mosaic law, "that soul is cut off from his people," is, notwithstanding its high claims, excluded. We have here the parallel to Ps. lxxiii. 1, "God is only good to Israel, to such as are clean of heart," in opposition to a merely seeming Israel,—the fundamental passage for John i. 47, where Jesus speaks of those who are Israelites indeed, and thus, as Luther says, "divides the people into two parts;" and also for Rom. ii. 28, 29, and ix. 6. In the distinction of appearance and reality among God's people, Jeremiah was before Ezekiel, since in ch. vii. 4 he addresses the people in Jerusalem thus: "Trust ye not in lying words, saying, The temple of the Lord, the temple of the Lord, the temple of the Lord are these"—the inhabitants of Jerusalem. The temple of the Lord, which comes into account not as an external building, but as the community of the living God (1 Tim. iii. 15; 1 Cor. iii. 9), corresponds to Israel here. It is a false pretension of the inhabitant of Jerusalem to be the temple of the Lord: the necessary requisite is wanting in them, the circumcision of the heart, its purification from ungodly movements, which is the indispensable condition of the dwelling of God among His people. The words, "unto whom the inhabitants of Jerusalem have said, Get ye far from the Lord, unto us is this land given for a possession," refer to a strange delusion by which the inhabitants of Jerusalem are held captive. Even those excluded from Israel dispute with the true Israelites every claim to be Israel. This they do, because they estimate the grace of God according to the external event of the moment. The exiles, they think, are condemned of God; but on *their* way God has impressed His seal, inasmuch as He has left them in their native land, where they expect soon to reach the summit. Thereby they show how inexperienced they are in the ways of God, how far they are from having the heart of true Israelites, how little they deserve that the prophet should take an interest in them. Can they prosper who have severed themselves so decidedly from the brotherhood of the pious? In opposition to this exclusive judgment of the inhabitants of Jerusalem, the Lord promises the exiles first, that He will Himself be their sanctuary during the comparatively short period of their banishment.[1] The essence of the sanctuary is the presence of the Lord among His people. This is evident even from the name which the external sanctuary bore in its oldest form, "the tent of meeting," the place where God met with His people. See other proofs on Ps. lxxiii. 17, John ii. 19. This essence remains also to the exiles, while the citizens of the capital possess only the empty shell of the external sanctuary, to which is wanting the proper substance, the real presence of the Lord, "with His help and grace." The sanctuary stands in Isa. viii. 14, as here, in a purely spiritual sense. There Jehovah is for a sanctuary to the God-fearing; He gladdens them by His presence in the midst of them. The Lord made Himself known to the exiles as the sanctuary, by furnishing our prophet, for example, with His spirit and

---

[1] As מקדש is the stat. absol., מעט can only be an adverb. It stands, "often of time, a little, a short time."

His power, so that he could officiate as a true priest, notwithstanding his local separation from the external sanctuary: then by that which took place in and through Daniel, by the circumcision of their heart, etc. But even the inferior privilege of which they are deprived, to which "for a little" points, is not removal for ever: in the near future will they receive again the form in addition to the essence of the sanctuary. The new speech of the Lord in ver. 17 begins with *and*, to represent it as the continuation of the former, to which it would have been immediately annexed, had not this portion of the comforting announcement to be introduced by a new asseveration, which is here the more necessary, as it treats of matters which, estimated by a human standard, were impossible. Ver. 19 promises, instead of the stony heart, a heart of flesh, soft and susceptible of the impressions of divine grace. The promise is essentially Messianic, although a beginning of its fulfilment is already to be recognised in the period immediately after the return from the exile. With the promise goes (ver. 21) a threatening hand in hand, and in this the whole terminates in a remarkable way; but woe to the hypocrites and rebels among them! Even among the new covenant people is a gloomy declension, a new carcase, which summons again the eagles. Their heart walks after the heart of their idols: the idols are in themselves dead, the mere reflexes and images of the popular spirit; yet even as such they exercise an enormous power over individuals. What power has mammon now as a Jewish national god over Jewish minds, although he is in himself a mere shadow!

Ver. 22. And the cherubim lifted up their wings, and the wheels beside them; and the glory of the God of Israel was over them above. 23. And the glory of the Lord went up from the midst of the city, and stood upon the mountain which is on the east of the city. 24. And a spirit took me up, and brought me to the Chaldeans, to the captivity in vision by the Spirit of God: and the vision that I had seen went up from me. 25. And I spake to the captivity all the words of the Lord which he showed me.—In vers. 22, 23, the departure of the glory of the Lord from the temple and the city, that are doomed to ruin. This could only come down upon it when God had withdrawn His presence (Hos. v. 15, "I will go and return to my place"). *Here* the glory of the Lord does not *immediately* betake itself to its place: it stands first on the Mount of Olives, to conduct the approaching siege of Jerusalem, and preside over its destruction. In Zech. xiv. 4 also the Mount of Olives appears as a military post, which the Lord as general assumes. On the Mount of Olives the Saviour announces the destruction of Jerusalem (Matt. xxiv. 3). The Mount of Olives, 2556 feet high, 175 feet higher than Zion, 416 feet higher than the valley of the Kidron, is the masterpoint in reference to Jerusalem, which is overlooked from it in its whole extent. The vision goes up (ver. 24); it returns, as it were, to Him who gave it: comp. Acts x. 16, where the vessel that had presented itself in the vision of Peter is again received up into heaven.

Ch. xii. Now begin the amplifications, the marginal notes, so to speak, on the great text in ch. viii.-xi., which extend to ch. xix., and there terminate in a song, corresponding to the song in the first group in ch. vii. The approaching catastrophe of Jerusalem forms the central point throughout. The prophet is inexhaustible in the announcement of this, as the false patriotism was inexhaustible in its announcements of salvation.

In ch. xii. 1-16, the lamentable fate which will overtake the inhabitants of Jerusalem, and the king at their head; in vers. 17-20, the desolation of the land; in vers. 21-28, the immediate fulfilment of the threat of punishment. Vers. 1-16 are, by the repeated sentence, "And the word of the Lord came unto me," divided into two parts, in the first of which we have the order for the symbolic action and its execution; in the second, ver. 8 f., the interpretation.

Ver. 1. And the word of the Lord came unto me, saying, 2. Son of man, thou dwellest in the midst of a rebellious house; who have eyes to see, and see not; they have ears to hear, and hear not: for they are a rebellious house. 3. And thou, son of man, make thee baggage of the emigrant, and remove by day before their eyes, and thou shalt remove from thy place to another place before their eyes; it may be they will consider, for they are a house of rebellion. 4. And thou shalt bring forth thy baggage, as baggage of the emigrant, by day in their eyes; and thou shalt depart at even in their sight, like the removals of the emigrant. 5. In their sight dig for thee through the wall, and carry out the baggage thereby. 6. In their eyes shalt thou bear upon thy shoulder, in the dark shalt thou carry it forth : thou shalt cover thy face, and thou shalt not see the land; for I have set thee for a sign to the house of Israel. 7. And I did so, as I was commanded: I brought forth my baggage by day, as baggage of the emigrant, and in the evening I digged through the wall with my hand: I brought it forth in the dark; I bare on my shoulder in their eyes.

The people, according to vers. 2, 3, are blinded by their political passions: the word of Moses (Deut. xxix. 3), " And the Lord hath not given you a heart to perceive, and eyes to see, and ears to hear" (Michaelis: " God gave not, because ye would not" (Matt. xxiii. 37)), has been verified anew in them. Therefore must the truth be set before their eyes in rough, palpable, overpowering reality, if it is to find entrance to their minds, and succeed in emancipating them from those dreams of the future which are preventing their repentance. The central figure among these is the king at Jerusalem, with whom, therefore, the palpable exhibition of the real future has chiefly to do. The repeated " before their eyes," in ver. 3, stands in relation with the sentence, " who have eyes, and see not," in ver. 2. The greater the weakness of their eyes, the more conspicuous must be the exhibition of the truth. " For they are a rebellious house :" so that the most powerful means of conviction are needed. The people proved themselves to be a rebellious house by this, that they could dream of salvation for Jerusalem, although their sins, calling down the divine vengeance, according to the infallible law of God, lay open to the day, and the Holy Spirit of God had announced by Jeremiah this vengeance in the most emphatic and persistent manner. To be compared is the word of Stephen to the Jews in Acts vii. 51, " Ye stiffnecked, ye do always resist the Holy Ghost." The symbolic action belongs here also, no doubt, to the department of the internal. The presumption is in favour of this in Ezekiel still more than in the other prophets (comp. on ch. iv.). In the small circle of his immediate auditory, the chief thing was at all events the written description, and for this it was of no consequence whether the action were external or not. The remark, that "a sign that was not performed would have had no meaning," does not apply, as the plastic visibility to which alone it refers remains even in the internal conception: the design is to throw into the imagination a reality instead of an empty figure of the future. For the internal speaks the analogy of the symbolic action in vers. 16–20, which was scarcely to be exhibited in an outward form. Of importance is, further, ver. 7. If we assume an external procedure, the wall there can only be the city wall of Tel-abib. Even if this place had a wall, yet it was certainly so built, that a single individual could not at once break a hole of the size of a man. The difficulty is increased by this, that the prophet accomplished the thing with the bare hand, without tools, to avoid a disturbance, which might call the attention of the enemy. Exile in particular is set forth in the symbolic threat of punishment to Jerusalem, because it is designed to reconcile the exiles with their condition, who, as we learn from Jer. xxix., envied their brethren remaining at home, and were excited by hopes of an early return, and plans for its accomplishment. If the exile of Jerusalem is at hand, the envy ceases, the occasion for political intrigues vanishes: they will be contented with their lot, and direct their whole effort to be reconciled with God. The prophet represents, in the symbolic action, first in general the destiny of the people in Jerusalem— the exile of all those who were not already swept away by the sword, famine, or pestilence (vers. 11, 16); then specially the destiny of the king, who will endeavour to escape by night from Jerusalem (ver. 12). This double-sidedness of the symbolic action can only be learned from the *interpretation*, beginning with ver. 8, which moreover, in the same manner as the interpretation of the parables of the Lord in the New Testament is at the same time a reconstruction, imparts several details which did not appear in the symbolic action, as the frustration of the king's flight, his capture, his being blinded, and carried to Babylon. "The baggage of the emigrant"[1] is the equipment which is made by one who enters on a journey never to return. With the baggage the prophet, according to ver. 4, departs by day, and brings it to the wall, for so far all might be public. What took place within the city the enemy saw not: when the

[1] גֹּלָה, the emigrant, is the ideal unification of the emigrants.

darkness comes on, he breaks a hole through the wall, and carries the baggage through it. " Like the removals of the emigrant :" in the costume and with the manner of emigrants. Kimchi, " with a bag on the shoulder and a staff in the hand ;" others, " sad and with drooping head." Both are to be combined. By the wall, in ver. 5, can only be understood the wall of the city, not that of the house. The prophet has already left the house with the baggage: he breaks through the city wall only in the evening, because the enemy are beyond it, whose prying eyes he can only escape in the dark. The wall in ver. 12 means the city wall. According to ver. 6, the prophet is to cover his face. The face is covered either not to be seen (2 Sam. xv. 30; Jer. xiv. 3), or not to see, to avoid a painful sight, here that of the beloved native land. The latter holds here and in ver. 12, where this end comes out still more clearly. To the expression, " Thou shalt cover thy face, and shalt not see the land"—that is, that thou mayest not see the land—corresponds Jer. ix. 19, " We are greatly confounded, for we have forsaken the land." " I have set thee for a wonder to the house of Israel :" that which was extraordinary, exciting wonder in the conduct of the prophet, which could not be explained from his personal relations, led them to seek the key in the relations of the people. The wonder is, as such, at the same time a *sign*.

The interpretation now follows in the second paragraph. Ver. 8. And in the morning came the word of the Lord unto me, saying, 9. Son of man, hath not the house of Israel, the rebellious house, said unto thee, What doest thou? 10. Say unto them, Thus saith the Lord Jehovah, The prince is this burden on Jerusalem, and all the house of Israel that are among them. 11. Say, I am your wonder: as I have done, so shall it be done unto them; as exiles they shall go into captivity. 12. And the prince who is among them shall bear upon the shoulder in the dark, and shall go out:[1] they shall break through the wall to carry out (the baggage) thereby: he shall cover his face, that he see not the land with his eye. 13. And I will spread my net upon him, and he shall be taken in my snare; and I will bring him to Babylon, to the land of the Chaldeans, and he shall not see it, and there he shall die. 14. And all his help round about him, and all his squadrons, I

---

[1] The ו in ויצא serves to give prominence to the dark moment.

will scatter to every wind, and a sword I will draw out after them. 15. And they shall know that I am the LORD, when I scatter them among the heathen, and disperse them in the countries. 16. And of them I will leave men of number (few) from the sword, from the famine and from the pestilence, that they may declare all their abominations among the heathen whither they come; and they shall know that I am the LORD.

The symbolic action announcing misfortune applies, according to ver. 10, first to the prince in Jerusalem, and then to the inhabitants, and prefigures the conduct and the fortune of both. *Burden:* this is a prophetical expression, especially consecrated by Isaiah in his ten *burdens* (ch. xiii.-xxiii.), to express a threatening message, and the misfortune itself announced therein. The prince in Jerusalem is himself the burden: prince and burden, as it were, coincide; because the burden is of a crushing character, the prince wholly falls into misfortune, which leaves nothing of him remaining. The Hebrew name of the *prince* signifies one on whom something is laid, who is burdened. The burden is the government, which he bears, as it were, on his shoulder (Isa. vi. 6). Here the prince, instead of the usual burden, receives another far more oppressive: he is burdened with the load of misfortune. Along with the king is named, as bearer of the burden, "all the house of Israel *that are among them.*"[1] This addition was necessary, inasmuch as there was another house of Israel still (ch. xi. 15). Here the house of Israel came into account only in so far as it existed among the inhabitants of Jerusalem. Ver. 11 carries out first the second part of ver. 10—unfolds the prophetic import of the symbol in reference to the whole people. Ver. 12 then returns to the chief object, the prince. The latter will be still in a third sense one burdened; he will bear his baggage in the night. And shall any hope be placed on such a poor baggage-bearer! His own land he may not (ver. 13) see in the grief of departure, and the heathen land he *cannot* see although he comes to it. The latter is a riddle, which history was the first to solve. Zedekiah was blinded before he reached Babylon. The historical commentary on the announcement, so far as Zedekiah is concerned, we have in 2 Kings xxv., Jer. xxxix. 1 f. and

---

[1] Instead of "which is therein," it properly is, "who are in the midst of them." The suffix refers to Jerusalem or its inhabitants.

lii. Zedekiah fled by night from the city (Jer. xxxix. 4, lii. 7), but was caught by the Chaldeans in the neighbourhood of Jericho, brought to Riblah before the king of Babylon, there blinded and sent in chains to Babylon, where he died in prison. The announcement in ver. 16 takes place not so much by words as rather by the event, as in Ps. xix. 1 mention is made of a practical announcement. It is made by the heavy sufferings which they have to bear, and the misery of their whole condition; thus in the same way in which the Jews, after the betrayal of Jesus, have announced the sins of their fathers among the heathen. Only in this view is the sentence, "and they shall know that I am the Lord," apposite, which refers also to their destiny. Ver. 15 shows that those who shall know this are not the heathen, but the Jews. The reference to the agents themselves is also the only one suitable to the conclusion. In regard to the Jews, these words recur as a refrain in Ezekiel.

Ver. 17–20. A close siege will be followed by the desolation of the country. The prophet pours cold water on the heated fancies of the exiles, who expected an approaching miraculous renewal of their native land, in contrast with the desolation of the land of the Chaldeans, which they thought was approaching. Ver. 17. And the word of the Lord came unto me, saying, 18. Son of man, eat thy bread with quaking, and drink thy water with trembling and with care. 19. And thou shalt say to the people of the land, Thus saith the Lord Jehovah of the inhabitants of Jerusalem in the land of Israel, They shall eat their bread with care, and drink their water with astonishment, that her land may be astonished from the fulness thereof, for the violence of all who dwell in it. 20. And the inhabited cities shall be laid waste, and the land shall be desolate, and ye shall know that I am the LORD.

The prophet represents in ver. 18 the condition of the inhabitants of Jerusalem in the approaching siege. This second symbolic action can scarcely be reduced to outward exhibition. If such were intended, it must have been stated how often, or how long, or under what precise circumstances, or in what position the prophet should so act. That a single act is not intended, is manifest from the phrase, *thy* bread, *thy* water. The people of the land in ver. 19 are those dwelling in Chaldea, in opposition to the inhabitants of Jerusalem. "Her land"—the land of Jerusalem. "May be astonished:" the astonishment of the inhabitants goes before the astonishment or desolation of the land, and has this for its object. "From the fulness thereof;" so that it loses its fulness of men, animals, fruits, etc., and nothing is left but the bare ground—a *tohu vabohu*.

Vers. 21-28. The incredulous doubt of the fulfilment of his threatening prophecy, the prophet opposes by the announcement made in the name of God that it will certainly be fulfilled, and that in the immediate future. The same thought is treated in two paragraphs, vers. 21-25 and vers. 26-28.

Ver. 21. And the word of the Lord came unto me, saying, 22. Son of man, what is that proverb ye have in the land of Israel, saying, The days are prolonged, and every vision faileth? 23. Therefore say unto them, Thus saith the Lord Jehovah, I will make this proverb to cease, and they shall no more use it in Israel; but speak unto them, The days are at hand, and the word of every vision. 24. For there shall be no more any vain vision or smooth divination within the house of Israel. 25. For I the LORD will speak the word that I shall speak; and it shall be done, it shall be no more prolonged: for in your days, O rebellious house, will I speak a word, and do it, saith the Lord Jehovah. 26. And the word of the Lord came unto me, saying, 27. Son of man, behold, the house of Israel say, The vision that he seeth is for many days, and he prophesieth of the times that are far off. 28. Therefore say unto them, Thus saith the Lord Jehovah, none of my words shall be prolonged any more: for I will speak a word, and it shall be done, saith the Lord Jehovah.

The prophet in ver. 22 opposes an opinion which had been formed in the land of Israel, and thence had penetrated to the exiles. It had been expressed in a pointed sentence, a proverb in a wider sense, according to which it embraces everything that has a poetical character, and straightway became popular as a watchword, which was taken up on every occasion against the true prophet, a parole of the ungodly. The announcement of the fall of the city and temple given long ago by Jeremiah had, as it appears, given occasion to this saying. As the fulfilment crept on so slowly, it was concluded that the prediction of the true prophets would come to nothing. That the expression, the days are prolonged, goes further than the words imply —conveys, in fact, a doubt of the fulfilment—appears from the parallel sentence, "and every vision faileth." There is yet a long time to the fulfilment: this is a jeering expression for its total failure. An end is made to the proverb by the force of facts (ver. 23). When the fulfilment of the predictions comes upon their head, the jeer will stick in their throat. "And the word of every vision"—the contents of every prediction. According to the connection with vers. 1–20, the visions are meant which represent destruction and downfall. The prophet therefore finds it unnecessary to be more definite, because only visions of this sort are real visions, in contrast with the false visions in ver. 24. "Word of every vision" implies that all that the true prophets have predicted will be completely fulfilled, in contrast with a mere partial fulfilment; contrary to the opinion that it will not be quite so bad, that the prophets have exaggerated, that some abatement of their words may be made. In ver. 24 the true predictions pass into fulfilment; for false prophecy or smooth divination,[1] flattering and fair-speaking, which is even as such unworthy of the name of prophecy—*prophecy* and *roughness*, these go hand in hand among a sinful people—is so confounded by the event, that no one any longer ventures to come forward with it. In ver. 25 the false predictions are confounded because the true are fulfilled. Ver. 27 is distinguished from the foregoing only by this, that it treats of the announcements of Ezekiel in particular, whereas the foregoing treated of true prophecy in general. The doubt also here refers to any fulfilment whatever, although in form it is only deferred to a remote period. The address "son of man" shows that it was at that time popular to degrade prophecy quite rationalistically into the region of the subjective. It admits what lies before the eyes; but then a mighty counterpoise is given in ver. 28 by the word, "Thus saith the Lord." The announcement of the prophet has passed into fulfilment in a terrible manner. Scarcely five years elapsed when Jerusalem with its temple lay in ruins; and those who had filled their belly with the east wind of their proud hopes of

---

[1] Literally, "divination of the smooth," that has the character of smoothness, corresponding to deceit in the vision of falsehood in ch. xiii. 6, 7.

the future, were either lost or envied the dead. Humanly taken, these were certainly in a sense much more prudent and sharpwitted than the true prophets; but the Spirit of God made the eyes of the latter clear.

Ch. xiii. In the endeavour to remove the hindrances which opposed the reception of the important contents of the vision in ch. viii. 11 into the minds of the people, the prophet here comes to the false prophets, who in Jerusalem and among the exiles (comp. Jer. xxix.) announced salvation without repentance, grace without judgment. He describes them in the first section as bad daubers, in the second (ver. 17 f.) as women on account of their feebleness. The introduction to this rebuke of the false prophets is already found in ch. xii. 24, where the prophet announces that all deceitful vision and flattering divination will be overturned by the events of the future. In another respect also this chapter stands in connection with the foregoing section. To the recommendation there of the true prophecy, corresponds here the warning against the false. We have here the parallel to the classical passage of Jeremiah against the false prophets (ch. xxiii. 9 f.). The false prophecy, against which the prophet contends, continues substantially to exist in the church of the New Testament. There, through all ages, along with the true theology, descends a false theology, which in varying forms divests God of the energy of His righteousness, and presents to view salvation without genuine renewal of heart, without washing away the defilement of the daughter of Zion by the sternness of judgments.

Ver. 1. And the word of the Lord came unto me, saying, 2. Son of man, prophesy unto the prophets of Israel, who prophesy, and say unto the prophets out of their own hearts, Hear ye the word of the Lord. 3. Thus saith the Lord Jehovah, Woe unto the foolish prophets, that walk after their own spirit, and after that which they see not! 4. Like foxes in the ruins are thy prophets, O Israel. 5. Ye have not gone up into the breaches, nor built up a wall round the house of Israel, to stand in the war in the day of the Lord. 6. They behold deceit and lying divination, who say, Thus saith the LORD, though the LORD hath not sent them, and expect the confirmation of the word. 7. Have ye not seen a deceitful vision, and spoken a lying divination, when ye say, Thus saith the Lord, although I have not spoken? 8. Therefore thus saith the Lord Jehovah, Because ye speak deceit, and see a lie, therefore, behold, I am upon you, saith the Lord Jehovah. 9. And my hand shall be upon the prophets that see deceit, and divine a lie: they shall not be in the community of my people, neither shall they be written in the writing of the house of Israel, neither shall they enter into the land of Israel; and ye shall know that I am the Lord Jehovah. 10. Because, even because they have led my people astray, saying, Peace, and there is no peace; and one builds a wall, and, lo, they daub it with absurdity. 11. Say unto those who daub with absurdity, that it shall fall: there shall be an overflowing shower, and ye hailstones shall fall; and a stormy wind thou shalt rend. 12. Lo, when the wall is fallen, shall it not be said unto you, Where is the daubing wherewith ye have daubed? 13. Therefore thus saith the Lord Jehovah, And I will send a stormy wind in my fury, and there shall be an overflowing shower in my wrath, and hailstones in fury to consume. 14. And I will break down the wall that ye have daubed with absurdity, and cast it to the earth, and the foundation thereof shall be discovered, and it (Jerusalem[1]) shall fall, and ye shall be consumed in the midst thereof; and ye shall know that I am the LORD. 15. And I will accomplish my fury upon the wall, and upon those who daub it with absurdity; and will say to you, The wall is not, neither are they who daub it. 16. The prophets of Israel, who prophesy concerning Jerusalem, and see for it a vision of peace, and there is no peace, saith the Lord Jehovah.

The prophet is first commanded, in ver. 1, to prophesy against the "prophets of Israel." This is explained by the fact that the false prophets had at that time absolutely the upper hand, and demeaned themselves simply as the prophets. Jeremiah in Jerusalem, and Ezekiel among the exiles, stood as individuals over against a great multitude; and not only so, but the false prophets alone had public recognition as "prophets of Israel," at least in the capital; while the true prophets were regarded as peculiar, and had the government and the

[1] Luther, "and it shall fall," referred to the wall, to which, however, the following words, "in the midst thereof," do not suit.

spirit of the age and the people absolutely against them. "Who prophesy:" this points back to the word "prophesy." Prophecy against " prophecy"—the prophecy from above against the " prophecy" from beneath: this is the perpetual order in the kingdom of God. When the powers of falsehood puff themselves up, then the truth must enter the lists. The prophets of Israel are then more exactly designated as prophets out of their own hearts—those who follow the inclinations of their hearts, and give these out as divine revelations. To these the prophet shall announce the true word of God, that proves itself to be such by its harmony with the eternal law of God, and the conscience corresponding thereto. What Jesus says, " If any man will do His will," etc., holds also in reference to the true prophets. The foxes come into regard in ver. 4, as " the dangerous foes and destroyers of the coverts," as a zoologist calls them. Thus they stand already in ch. ii. 15 of the Song of Songs; and in Luke xiii. 31, 32, the Lord calls Herod a fox, as the destroyer of God's people. The foxes nowhere come into regard for their craft, as in heathen antiquity. The foxes here correspond to the ravening wolves in Matt. vii. 15, and the grievous wolves in Acts xx. 29, representing false teachers. "Ruins" are a favourite resort of foxes. So also the spiritual foxes: the false teachers flourish the better, the more degraded the condition of the people. At no time were the false prophets rifer than in the last days of the Jewish state. The " breach" in ver. 5 is the sinful condition of the people, which withdraws from them the grace of God, and opens the way to all hostile powers. To enter the breach, and withal draw a wall round the people of God, is to preach repentance, which alone can give security against the wrath to come. To walk in the spirit of repentance, which must take its beginning from the preacher of repentance himself—this is to stand or be stedfast in the war in the day of the Lord. The day of the Lord is the time of decision, the crisis, the arrival of the judgment. The hostile power is sin. When this gains the upper hand, the crisis has a fatal issue. From the proposed combat against this destructive power, the false prophets withdrew themselves as miserable deserters; nay, as traitors, they lent a helping hand to the enemy, and looked upon it as the proper business of their lives to counteract the true warriors. The question in ver. 7 is a question of conscience. If there be any shred of truth still in the false prophets, they must answer in the affirmative. The false prophets, according to ver. 9, shall not come into the land of Israel, either because they shall perish in the downfall of Jerusalem, or they shall be smitten by the avenging hand of God in exile. "And ye shall know that I am the Lord Jehovah:" the knowledge is such as even the ungodly cannot shake off, being forced upon them by the event. On the downfall of the false prophets, over whom the avenging hand of God prevails, it will be known that He who speaks by Ezekiel is God in the fullest sense. The strong expression of causality by "because, even because," in ver. 10, is taken from Lev. xxvi. 43. The building of the wall by the people denotes the political activity whereby they sought to raise themselves up—the effort made by the coalition. The false prophets daubed this wall; they gave to the impious and ungodly movement of the people, that was condemned by the word of the true prophets, the appearance of a higher sanction, and confirmed them in it. The wall is a spiritual one; and so the absurdity suits it as a spiritual mortar. The attempt to put, instead of the spiritual, a material mortar, has arisen only from the so often observable want of capacity in expositors to understand the interchange of figure and reality. Nothing can be more absurd than to announce safety to a people living in sin, and to promise success to counsels that are in open contradiction to the revealed counsels of God.[1] Ver. 11 forms the ground for the close of the sermon on the mount (Matt. vii. 25, 27). "Thou wilt rend" is, in accordance with the address to the hailstones, an address to God, as ver 13 shows. "To rend asunder something hitherto closed, is the same as to open, that the enclosed may burst forth." Shower, hail, stormy wind, denote the Chaldean catastrophe, the approach of which the people, by their political

---

[1] The meaning "absurd, unreasonable," is ascertained for תפל, and there is no reason to exchange it for the not sufficiently ascertained meaning "lime," especially as תפל and תפלה occur in the sense of absurdity in Lam. ii. 14 and Jer. xxiii. 13, expressly in reference to the false prophets. Lime also would scarcely suit, as a designation of the bad quality of the mortar must be expected, as even Luther acknowledged, who translates "loose lime." The absurdity is here the mortar, exactly as in Isa. v. 18 the deceit is the cord.

intrigues, instead of preventing, only invite. In the falling of the wall (ver. 12) God Himself appears as theologian; and those miserable false theologians, who have misused His name, come into deep disgrace. The foundation of the wall is discovered (ver. 14); it is overturned to the very ground. "It falls"—that is, Jerusalem. With the political intrigues designated by the wall, which were intended to stand between the city and its foes as a partition wall (Eph. ii. 14), falls also the city; and with the city go down also the false prophets, who madly impressed the seal of God on their bad measures. "And will say unto you" (ver. 15): we have here the triumphant contempt which God heaps upon the false prophets who have misused His name, and made it a covert for their wickedness. And shall a man hearken at present to those whose disgrace will so soon be manifest? Ver. 16 is in apposition with the closing words of ver. 15.

In vers. 17-23 we have the effeminate movement of the false prophets. Ver. 17. And thou, son of man, set thy face against the daughters of thy people, who prophesy out of their own heart; and prophesy thou against them, 18. And say, Thus saith the Lord Jehovah, Woe to those who sew cushions to all joints of my hands,[1] and make kerchiefs upon the head of every rank, to hunt souls! Ye hunt souls among my people, and ye make souls alive for you. 19. And ye profane me among my people for handfuls of barley, and for pieces of bread, that ye may slay souls that should not die, and make souls alive that should not live, by your lying to my people that hearken to a lie. 20. Wherefore thus saith the Lord Jehovah, Behold, I am against your cushions, where ye hunt the souls as birds; and I will tear them from your arms, and let the souls free, where ye hunt the souls as birds. 21. And I will tear your kerchiefs, and deliver my people out of your hand, and they shall be no more in your hand for a prey; and ye shall know that I am the LORD. 22. Because ye trouble the heart of the righteous with falsehood, whom I have not troubled, and strengthen the hands of the wicked, that he should not return from his wicked way and be kept in life; 23. Therefore ye shall no more see deceit, nor divine divination: and I will

---

[1] Luther, "under the arms of the people," whereas the text speaks of the hands of God.

deliver my people out of your hand; and ye shall know that I am the LORD.

It is one of the many occidentalisms and prosaisms of our exegesis, if we refer to ordinary women what is here said of the effeminate nature and movement of the "prophets." The masculine pronouns designedly interspersed point the other way, of which no less than three occur in vers. 19 and 20. By this the prophet all but expressly says that he has to do with women in men's clothes. Further, only three or four real prophetesses occur in all the Old Testament—Miriam, Deborah, Huldah, and perhaps also the wife of Isaiah; but a false prophetess is nowhere mentioned. But even if one such had appeared here and there, so serious a punishment would have been out of place. The prophet is directed to fix his eye upon the properly national wickedness. What the prophet here ascribes to the prophesying women as characteristic, belonged also to the false prophets, whose whole endeavour was to ingratiate themselves with the people, and flatter the spirit of the age (Mic. iii. 5); and to them Micah opposes himself as a *man* (ch. iii. 8, "But I am full of power by the Spirit of the LORD, and of judgment, and of *manhood*, to declare unto Jacob his transgression, and to Israel his sin"). *Effeminate is all accommodation theology.* In Rev. ii. 20 the false teaching which would blend heathenism with the church, instead of meeting it with a manful resistance, appears as the woman Jezebel. "All joints of my hands" (ver. 18); so that my, that is, the Lord's hands, cannot sharply grasp any one. It is the nature of all accommodation theology to set aside, as in general all that is inconvenient to the old Adam and gives him pain, so especially the energy of the requiring and punishing divine righteousness—the *severity* of God (Rom. xi. 22). Where Ezekiel puts the cushions, there we put perhaps the icy glove. Besides the cushions for the hands of the Lord, which in their natural state touch many very ungently, as surely as our God is a jealous God, a consuming fire, visiting the iniquity of the fathers upon the children unto the third and fourth generation, they make also for the same purpose kerchiefs for the heads of their penitents, that the hand of God may not touch them ungently; and indeed for heads or people (persons are represented by the head, as the part that comes in the way of the descending hand must before all be secured, especially as the stroke, when it smites here, has fatal effect) of every rank, always according to the greatness of the reward to be expected —the greatest for the king. The higher any one is placed, more zealously do they endeavour to clear his conscience, as Jesuits before the Jesuits, differing from their successors in this, that the latter had in view the interest and maintenance of the church, while the former only served their own appetites. Souls must perish by such false theology, which brings ruin on the land and the people, as God, notwithstanding these endeavours to conceal His true form, remains what He is. Yet this troubles them not: they make their own souls alive by the destructive deadly hurt; they procure for themselves earthly fortune and well-being. Certainly they also at last come to an end with terror, as truly as God lives, who is a revenger of blood, and cannot let those go unpunished who misuse His name. The words, " The souls ye hunt among my people, and souls for you ye make alive," besides the explanation given, admit of another: they make the souls for themselves, living for their own interest,[1] and even thereby hand them over to death. They profane God among the people (ver. 19), inasmuch as they assign Him a friendly position towards sin; and this they do for filthy lucre (Tit. i. 11), and to fill their own belly (Rom. xvi. 18). While they thus lead the people away from repentance, they cause the death of those who, according to the will of God, should return and live, and provide for themselves a pleasant life at their cost, as it were, for the price of their blood. The souls who should not live are, according to the explanation of ver. 18 given in the first place, those of these public betrayers. According to others, the killing and making alive refer to the prophetic announcement of death and life. The false prophets set death before the pious—for ex. a Jeremiah (comp. Jer. xxix., xxvi. 7)—and life before the ungodly. With the words, " While ye lie to my people, that hearken to a lie," is to be compared Mic. ii. 11, " If a man walking with wind and falsehood lie, 'I will prophesy unto thee of wine and strong drink,' he would be the prophet of this people." This delight of the people in falsehood lessens not the guilt of the false prophets, but at the same

[1] Tremellius: *quum utile vobis futurum sit, eis pronunciate vitam.*

time demonstrates the ruin of the people to be deserved. The cushions in ver. 20 denote the effeminate doctrines concerning God that strip Him of His righteousness. God destroys the cushions by the events, the great impending facts, in which the energy of His righteousness displays itself. "Where ye hunt the souls:" the cushions are, as it were, the ground on which the hunt takes place. "As birds:" the hunters are more precisely defined as fowlers; comp. Ps. cxxiv. 7, "Our soul is escaped as a bird out of the snare of the fowler; the snare is broken, and we are escaped." "And I will tear them from your arms:" the arms are those of the fowlers, from whose power the poor souls are torn, after their miserable theology has been annihilated by facts. They hunt the souls as birds; but God at length makes an end of this shameful hunt (Hab. i. 15), when He actually appears in His true form and lets the souls free. "Because ye trouble the heart of the righteous" (ver. 22): an example of such a righteous one is Jeremiah, against whom the false prophets kindled the fire of persecution.

Ch. xiv. 1–11. Without repentance there is no salvation for the exiles, in whom also the evil spirit is still active, nor for the whole people. Let us not make demands on the true prophets which they cannot fulfil, with an appeal to the false prophets. These shall perish along with the sinful people who are led astray by their responses. Only by punishment is a faithful people of God raised up, on whom His grace may unfold itself.

This word of God is occasioned by the visits of the elders of the people to the prophet. The object of their visit we learn partly from the answer here, partly from ch. xx. 1. They wish to make an experiment, whether they cannot obtain a more favourable answer through the prophet, whose fearfully threatening announcement they have heard not without shuddering. They ask, "Has the Lord, then, forgotten to be gracious? Has He in wrath shut up His tender mercy?" Of repentance there was not a word. They appealed to grace, although they were the children of wrath. The inquirers are not to be regarded as representatives of the whole of the exiles, but, as the nature of the thing and the answer show, representatives of those who only outwardly fear God, but inwardly serve the spirit of the world and the age. The truly God-fearing community humbled themselves under the mighty hand of God, and submitted to the order prescribed by the prophet. The answer goes only as far as ver. 11. Beyond this there is found no more reference to the proposal of the elders. That no great importance is to be attached to this, we learn even from the significant brevity with which the visit is mentioned.

Ver. 1. Then came men of the elders of Israel unto me, and sat before me. 2. And the word of the LORD came unto me, saying, 3. Son of man, these men have set up their abominations in their heart, and put the stumbling-block of their iniquity before their face: should I be inquired of at all by them?[1] 4. Therefore speak with them, and say unto them, Thus saith the Lord Jehovah, Every man of the house of Israel that setteth up his abominations in his heart, and putteth the stumbling-block of his iniquity before his face, and cometh to the prophet, should I the LORD answer him thereby, after the multitude of his abominations?[2] 5. That I may take the house of Israel in their own heart, who are estranged from me through all their abominations. 6. Therefore say unto the house of Israel, Thus saith the Lord Jehovah, Repent, and turn from your abominations, and from all your detestable idols turn away your faces. 7. For every man of the house of Israel, or of the strangers that sojourn in Israel, who separateth himself from me, and setteth up his abominations in his heart, and putteth the stumbling-block of his iniquity before his face, and cometh to the prophet to inquire of him in me, should I the LORD answer him in myself? 8. And I will set my face against that man, and destroy him, for a sign and for proverbs, and will cut him off from the midst of my people; and ye shall know that I am the LORD. 9. And if the prophet

---

[1] The foregoing infinitive, אִדְּרֹשׁ, gives a sharp emphasis to the question. The sharper the inspection, the more its impossibility comes to the light.

[2] Luther, "So will I the Lord answer the same, as he hath deserved by his gross idolatry;" contrary to ver. 3, where every answer is refused (the external notation of the question there makes it here unnecessary); comp. also ver. 9.

be deceived and speak a word, I the LORD have deceived that prophet; and I will stretch out my hand upon him, and will destroy him from the midst of my people Israel. 10. And they shall take upon them their iniquity: as the iniquity of the inquirer, so shall the iniquity of the prophet be; 11. That the house of Israel may go no more astray from me, nor be polluted any more by all their transgressions; and they shall be my people, and I will be their God, saith the Lord Jehovah.

"The stumbling-block of their iniquity" (ver. 3): the idols which bring them to ruin, involve them in iniquity and its punishment. "Thereby"[1] (ver. 4)—as it is with him. The more precise explanation follows, "after the multitude of their abominations." The question in ver. 4 is in the sense of a negative—I will not answer; and this negative has its ground in ver. 5. God leaves sinners without answer or help, that they may come to a knowledge of their sin. "To take in the heart," is to touch the conscience. "Turn" (ver. 6)—the sense and heart (ver. 3). "To inquire of him in me" (ver. 7): the question goes only in the first instance to the prophet, who is simply the medium: He to whom it is really addressed is Jehovah; and therefore the meaning is, to inquire of *me* through him. "Should I the Lord answer him in myself?" so that the answer actually comes from me. Whosoever acknowledges that Jehovah is the background of prophecy—that the prophets give no reply of themselves, but as they are moved by the Holy Spirit (2 Pet. i. 20, 21)—he will not expect this. "In:" this designates the department in which the question and answer move. "For a sign and for a proverb" (ver. 8): an exemplary punishment. Ver. 9 meets the objection that the other prophets besides Jeremiah and Ezekiel announce salvation, and that these take up a doubtful and singular position over against the great chorus of their colleagues, who have also the Spirit of God. The deception proceeds originally from indwelling sin (Jas. i. 14), otherwise it could not be the object of punishment; but in the development of sin God has no inactive part: He knows how to regulate things, that sin attains to its full development and maturity, and brings punishment along with it (Rom. i. 26).

---

[1] The marginal reading בא, that comes, has only arisen from a misunderstanding.

He takes care that there can be no standing still, no halting at an intermediate stage: He makes the occasions and removes the hindrances. There is scarcely a notable fall into sin, in which this activity of God does not display itself in a terrible manner. Those miserable men, who themselves lie under the destiny of God, are led by Him whither they will not, and hasten to meet the judgment, cannot possibly exchange one staff for another. Whosoever will cite them as authority against the true prophets, or make demands from these on the ground of their utterances, is a poor fool. "The speaking of the word" receives a precise definition, from the petition which is offered for a *favourable* answer. To take iniquity upon one's self (ver. 10) is to repent. Grotius says, "Both shall equally suffer punishment, those who buy prophecies and those who sell." Both suffer deserved punishment, because they are not concerned in their hearts to learn the truth, but only follow their own hearts' lusts, and endeavour to make God serviceable to these. The answer to this deep humiliation of God is given to them by their own humiliation. In ver. 11 the object of punishment extends over the deceiver and the deceived. It serves to purify the people of God. For the particular sinful generation, it flows from the principle of retribution; but for the whole of the community of God, a purpose of mercy lies at the ground of the exercise of this retribution. The prophet here clearly opens up the view to the light which shines behind the darkness.

Ch. xiv. 12-23. The deep corruption of Jerusalem inevitably draws on its destruction. The righteous in Jerusalem are so few, that exemption cannot be claimed on their account (vers. 12-21). How great is the debasement of its inhabitants, we may see even in their remnant (vers. 22, 23). The prophet encounters a thought which Abraham uttered in view of the determined destruction of Sodom and Gomorrah (Gen. xviii.), and thus destroys a false ground of security, a hindrance to the full effect of the great vision in ch. viii.-xi., for which all that is in ch. xii.-xix. serves to prepare the way. The corruption of Jerusalem was so great, that God could not grant it exemption on account of the few righteous. No reference to the visit of the elders in ver. 1 is here to be discovered. And the significant way in which this visit is mentioned shows that even for that section it was not of paramount importance, and only gave the outward impulse to the discussion of a point, the mention of which serves the purpose which the prophet has throughout before him in ch. xii.-xix.

Ver. 12. And the word of the LORD came unto me, saying, 13. Son of man, if a land sin against me to commit a trespass, and I stretch out my hand upon it, and break for it the staff of bread, and send upon it famine, and cut off from it man and beast: 14. And there be these three men in the midst of it, Noah, Daniel, and Job, they shall deliver their own souls by their righteousness, saith the Lord Jehovah. 15. If I cause evil beasts to pass through the land, and they bereave it, and it become desolate, without any one passing through because of the beasts: 16. Were these three men in the midst of it, as I live, saith the Lord Jehovah, they shall deliver neither sons nor daughters; they alone shall be delivered, but the land shall be desolate. 17. Or if I bring a sword upon that land, and say, A sword shall go through the land, and I cut off from it man and beast: 18. And these three men are in the midst of it, as I live, saith the Lord Jehovah, they shall deliver neither sons nor daughters; for they alone shall be delivered. 19. Or if I send a pestilence into that land, and pour out my fury upon it with blood, to cut off from it man and beast; 20. And Noah, Daniel, and Job are in the midst of it, as I live, saith the Lord Jehovah, they shall deliver neither son nor daughter; they shall by their righteousness deliver their own soul. 21. For thus saith the Lord Jehovah, How much more shall I send my four sore judgments, sword, and famine, and evil beasts, and pestilence upon Jerusalem, to cut off from it man and beast. 22. And, behold, therein shall be left a remnant escaped that are brought forth, sons and daughters; behold, they shall come forth unto you, and ye shall see their way and their doings,[1] and shall be comforted concerning the evil that I have brought upon Jerusalem, all that I have brought upon it. 23. And they shall comfort you, when ye see their way and their doings: and ye shall know that I have not

---

[1] Luther, "that ye shall see how it goes with them," contrary to what is added, "their doings," according to which the way is to be taken in the sense of the walk, not the lot.

done without cause all that I have done in it, saith the Lord Jehovah.

Instead of the three mentioned in ver. 14 stand Moses and Samuel in the fundamental passage, Jer. xv. 1, who, along with their personal righteousness, come into consideration there on account of their effectual intercession. The relations in which Job appears in the book named after him are throughout those of the patriarchal time. Daniel is designedly placed in the middle of the two primeval personages to glorify him, as it were to canonize him, just as he appears in ch. xxviii. 3, by an apparently undesigned accident, as the pinnacle of human wisdom, to bring out his eminence in this respect in the community of God. What is intended here, appears from the character of those by whom he is enclosed on both sides. Of Noah it is said at the head of the narrative relating to him in Gen. vi. 9, "Noah was a just man, and blameless among his contemporaries: Noah walked with God." And of Job it is likewise said at the head of ch. i., " There was a man in the land of Uz, whose name was Job; and that man was blameless and upright, and fearing God, and far from evil." Thus the righteousness and the walking with God must be what are regarded also in Daniel. The connection also leads us to the same result. Only the walking with God and the righteousness could possibly suspend a judgment which followed on account of ungodliness and unrighteousness. The reference to Gen. xviii. also leads to the same result. It is the righteous, who may be in Sodom, that awaken the consideration of Abraham in reference to its decreed destruction. Our announcement belongs, according to ch. viii. 1, compared with ch. xx., to the sixth year after the captivity of Jehoiachin. About fourteen years before, in the fourth year of Jehoiakim, Daniel as a youth was carried into exile. The fervour of his righteousness and piety was already observed, according to Dan. i., during the three years of his preparation for the royal service. Immediately after the end of this period of preparation, Daniel gave a conspicuous proof of his walking with God in the interpretation of Nebuchadnezzar's dream (Dan. ii. 1). The occurrence also in ch. iii., in which Daniel made confession to God at the risk of his life, and received testimony from God in his miraculous deliverance, belonged probably to the earlier period of

Nebuchadnezzar: the golden image which he set up was a monument of the lofty flight which the Chaldean power had taken in the beginning of the reign of Nebuchadnezzar, from the first to the eighth year of his reign,[1] before the formation of the great coalition, which brought all again into peril. Such clear proofs of the righteousness and piety of Daniel—proofs that were not confined to the narrow limits of a private circle, but displayed themselves on the theatre of the world, must have been historically extant in the time of our prophecy. For Ezekiel would otherwise have made himself and Daniel ridiculous by placing him beside the grand figures of Noah and Job. We have here a solid basis for the historical character of the book of Daniel. It is of importance also to put our passage in connection with ch. xxviii. 3. The connection of eminent piety and righteousness with eminent wisdom is exactly the characteristic of the personality of Daniel, as it appears in his book. The coincidence is so much the greater, as the wisdom of Daniel appears in ch. xxviii. to be such as to deal with sacred things, to understand all mysteries. " Evil beasts" (ver. 15), in the usual sense or in human form (v. 17). The expression "with blood" (ver. 19) points, as in ch. v. 17, to this, that the pestilence is to be placed in the like point of view as the sword in ver. 17—namely, that of punishment. The four visitations of God, which are here introduced each with an *if*, should actually come, as had been repeatedly predicted, unitedly upon the degenerate covenant people, upon the desecrated land of the Lord. The prophet, however, treats the matter first in general, without regard to the existing relations, that the emotion called forth by the sight of the latter may not have a disturbing influence. The transition from the merely hypothetical to the actual follows in ver. 21. The *for* at the beginning points to the ground of the discussion instituted, shows that it is no mere idle commonplace. "How much more" must the general standard of the divine judgments manifest itself before all in the servant, who knows his master's will, and yet does what is worthy of stripes! "You only have I known of all the families of the earth; therefore I will visit upon you all your iniquities," says Amos. In the same relation with the people of the Old Testament stand here

[1] Niebuhr, *History of Asshur and Babel*, pp. 206–11.

he Christian nations, only that in them the responsibility appears enhanced. The evil beasts must stand here in the figurative sense, as the lions in ch. xix. 2; for only wild beasts in human form can be employed against Jerusalem, the walled city, and were employed against it. The comfort in ver. 22 lies in the justification of the ways of God. The central part of the pain was, that they were gone astray from their God. Should not the Judge of all the earth do right? Should He slay the righteous with the wicked, so that it fared with the righteous as with the wicked (Gen. xviii. 25)? Knowledge of the greatness and depth of sin—this forms the chief foundation of the theodicy. This knowledge they shall gain here in the pitiful figures of those who, after the destruction of Jerusalem, shall find their way to them, as the surviving monuments of its shame. These miserable men shall be a living apologetic, and as such *comfort* the exiles, inasmuch as they put to silence the most painful of all lamentations—namely, " Where is our God?"

Ch. xv. Israel the vine of the Lord—this was an occasion of false security, a shield which was held up against the prophet's threat of punishment, with an appeal probably to Ps. lxxx., the classic passage, where Israel appears under the developed image of the vine.[1] The contradiction runs thus: Israel by his guilt is no longer a true vine; he is become mere wood, and the barren wood must be burned.

Ver. 1. And the word of the Lord came unto me, saying, 2. Son of man, what is the wood of the vine more than any tree, the vine-branch which is among the trees of the forest? 3. Shall wood be taken thereof to make any work? Or will a man take a pin of it to hang any vessel thereon? 4. Behold, it is cast into the fire for fuel; both its ends the fire consumes, and its middle is scorched. Is it fit for any work? 5. Behold, when it was whole, it was not made into any work; much less, when the fire hath consumed it, and it is scorched, shall it be made into any work. 6. Therefore thus saith the Lord Jehovah, As the wood of the vine among the trees of the forest, which I have given to the fire for fuel, so will I

[1] Compare, in reference to the other passages of the O. T., my comm. on Isa. xv. 1.

give the inhabitants of Jerusalem. 7. And I will set my face against them; they came out of the fire, and the fire shall consume them: and ye shall know that I am the LORD, when I set my face against them. 8. And I will make the land a desolation, because they have committed a trespass, saith the Lord Jehovah.

"What is the wood of the vine more than any tree?" (ver. 2;) what advantage has it over any other tree? The vine is nobler than the other trees, because it yields the most precious fruit. If it, however, degenerate, bear either no fruit or bad grapes (Isa. v. 2), and thus come into account merely for its wood, it has no advantage at all over the other trees. "The vine-shoot, which is[1] among the trees of the wood," is the vine which corresponds with the forest-trees in barrenness, as it is mere wood. It is not the wild vine that is meant.[2] This would not suit here. As the degenerate vine denotes Israel, so the trees of the wood the remaining nations, and the heathen nations, as there is none else besides Israel. In ver. 2 the dead vine is no better than the trees of the forest; in ver. 3 it is even worse. One can make nothing of it, while the wood of the other trees serves for many uses. The application is this: a people or an individual, to whom God makes Himself known, and who turns His grace into lasciviousness, sinks far beneath those who have not known God (Heb. vi. 4-8). A heathen nation may have still much good and a future; degenerate Israel, that dwells at present in Jerusalem (this limitation is given by ver. 6 and by the nature of the thing), is utterly miserable, and must perish without remedy. The vine is Israel from the first, as the vineyard in Isa. v. and Matt. xxi. 33; and the relation of vers. 1-5 to vers. 6-8 would be understood incorrectly, if it were thus defined: first the relation of the unfruitful natural vine to the other trees, then the application to Israel. The correct relation is this: in vers. 6-8 it is expressly said that vers. 1-5 is a parable, and that by the vine Israel is there

---

[1] היה; the masculine is used, because the vine, according to the foregoing, comes into account only for its wood. It does not bear fruit. The masc. also in vers. 3-5 refers to the wood of the vine.

[2] The wild vine, which never occurs in Scripture, cannot be denoted by זמורה. The name itself, from זמר, to cleanse (Lev. xxv. 3, 4), points to the vine as a cultivated plant (comp. Isa. xv. 2).

to be understood. That this relation is to be so understood, appears very clearly from ver. 4, in which is presented that which does not suit the natural vine. The phrase "it is cast" leads us to a historical situation. The process of burning has already *begun* in the withered vine of Israel. Only a little of its ancient glory remains. How could anything come of such a people? How could it have a future? What has already taken place in the beginning of the end? The wrath of God already entered into activity will not rest until it has completed its work. Hitherto, as has been remarked, there has been an interchange of figure and reality: Israel appeared under the form of a degenerate vine. In ver. 6 figure and reality are separated. "Which I give to the fire for fuel:" the Lord of nature has so constituted the vine, that, when it withers, it is fit for nothing but to be burned. "Out of the fire are they come" (ver. 7): the fire of the divine wrath has already wrought great desolations under Jehoiakim and Jehoiachin.

Ch. xvi. We have here one of the grandest prophecies of Ezekiel, to which ch. xxiii. forms the parallel. The prophet surveys in the Spirit of God the whole of the development of Israel, the past and the future. First, vers. 1–34, the sin of Israel. The inserted description of the benefits of God only sets this sin in its true light, as in Deut. xxxii. "Let us love Him, because He has first loved us:" whosoever disregards this, must be fundamentally bad. In the very second verse it is said, "Cause Jerusalem to know her sins;" and ver. 3 points to this, that the people in their very first beginnings bore a root of sin in themselves. In the previous section Israel appeared as an unfruitful vine. What was then presupposed is here proved. In the second part, vers. 35–52, follows Israel's punishment; in the third, vers. 53–63, his forgiveness.

Grotius says, the whole chapter has a wonderful emphasis, while it admirably carries out the similitude of adultery. The figure of adultery is the special physiognomy of the section. What otherwise distinguishes it, the thought that salvation comes to us of grace and pure love, stands in close connection with this figure. The professed adulteress is, by her conduct, completely excluded from salvation. Whosoever took in the import of this section, all his political hopes were burned to a heap of ashes. Jerusalem presented herself to him as a detestable adulteress, that cannot escape the punishment so richly deserved, as surely as a righteous God exists, who can bestow salvation not in the way of political intrigue, but only after punishment by the grace of the merciful God; and that may no longer haughtily look down upon the heathen, but must be content if she only receive mercy along with them.

The first part (vers. 1-34) falls into three divisions: first, Israel's misery, in a moral sense (ver. 3), in respect of his condition (vers. 4, 5); then God's compassionate love, whereby He is concerned for the miserable (vers. 6-14); finally, Israel's shameful ingratitude (vers. 15-34). Vers. 3-5 forms *the introduction* to the description of God's benefits; they were a people of sinful tendency (ver. 3), fallen into deep misery (vers. 4, 5). And yet God was concerned for them. What an incentive to true returning love, and what culpability if the love was repaid with ingratitude!

Ver. 1. And the word of the LORD came unto me, saying, 2. Son of man, cause Jerusalem to know her abominations, 3. And say, Thus saith the Lord Jehovah unto Jerusalem, Thy descent and birth is of the land of the Canaanite; thy father was an Amorite, and thy mother a Hittite. 4. And thy birth, in the day when thou wast born thy navel was not cut, nor wast thou washed with water for purification: thou wast not rubbed with salt nor rolled in swaddling-bands. 5. No eye pitied thee, to do any of these things for thee to have compassion on thee; and thou wast cast out on the open field in loathing of thy soul in the day when thou wast born.

Although descended from the patriarchs, Israel from his first beginning, according to ver. 3, has rather the nature of his heathenish native land than that of his pious ancestors. There is here an abridged comparison: thou art not otherwise constituted than if thou wert descended from the Canaanites. The passages of the Old Testament in which the degenerate community of God are designated as heathen, uncircumcised, or specially as Canaanites or some other heathen people, are discussed in the *Christology* on Zech. xiv. 2. The naming of the Canaanites here was the more natural, as Israel in ancient times was in many ways under the direct influence of this corrupt heathen people. The Amorites and the Hittites are two chief Canaanitish tribes, that elsewhere also often represent the whole of the Canaanites; the Amorites already, in Gen. xv. 16, where they specially represent the Canaanitish people in their sinfulness. The proof of the evil disposition dwelling in the people from their first origin, lies in the miserable condition into which they fell in Egypt, which, according to the Old Testament doctrine of retributive divine justice, can only be regarded in the light of punishment, and must be so regarded, according to the scattered indications of the books of Moses concerning the deep corruption of the Israelites before Moses, and their participation in the idolatry of Egypt. A distinct intimation that the suffering in Egypt is to be regarded in the light of a judgment, is found in Gen. xv. 13, 14 : "And they shall serve them, and these shall oppress them four hundred years; and *also* the people whom they shall serve will I judge." The time of Israel's birth, in ver. 4, is when in Egypt they passed from a family to a nation, and thereby drew the envy and persecution of the Egyptians upon them. We have here also an abridged comparison : the beginnings were as miserable as those of a child, etc. Rubbings with salt were practised in ancient times with infants, according to Galen, to make the skin tighter and firmer. According to that which follows, all refers to the external condition of Israel, the period of suffering in Egypt, not to their moral state. There is a connection with ver. 3, so far as the misery was, as it were, the reflection of the moral state there described. Precisely because this was so, is the mercy of God brought more prominently into view, who delivered His people from their deserved suffering. The real subject of ver. 5 is the relentless cruelty of the Egyptians. " With contempt (or loathing) of thy soul :" the soul of Israel is his life : the existence of Israel as a people was the object of loathing to the Egyptians, who endeavoured to annihilate them, not otherwise than as one casts a helpless infant on the open field. The figure of the child is so much the more suitable, as Moses, the type of his people, was actually exposed, and by the providence of God delivered from threatening death. We may not explain : " with contempt of thy life, as it is *all the same* to the people whether thou perish or not." The direct aim was the downfall, the destruction of the national existence at its very birth.

It is now explained how God's grace was concerned for this sinful and miserable people. Ver. 6. And I passed by thee, and saw thee trampled in thy blood, and said unto thee in thy blood, Live; and said unto thee in thy blood, Live. 7. I made thee myriads,[1] like the bud of the field; and thou didst increase, and wax great, and camest to complete ornament: the breasts were fashioned, and thy hair was grown, but thou wast naked and bare. 8. And I passed by thee, and saw thee, and, behold, thy time was the time of love; and I spread my skirt over thee, and covered thy nakedness; and I sware unto thee, and entered into a covenant with thee, saith the Lord Jehovah, and thou becamest mine. 9. And I washed thee with water, and cleansed away thy blood from thee, and anointed thee with oil. 10. And I clothed thee with broidered work, and shod thee with badger's skin, and bound thee with fine linen, and covered thee with silk.[2] 11. And I decked thee with ornament, and put bracelets on thy hands, and a chain on thy neck. 12. And I put a ring on thy nose,[3] and drops in thine ears, and a beautiful crown upon thy head. 13. And thou wast decked with gold and silver, and thy raiment was of fine linen, and silk, and broidered work: fine flour, and honey and oil, thou didst eat; and wast exceedingly fair, and didst prosper into a kingdom. 14. And thy name went forth among the heathen for thy beauty, because it was perfect through my ornature which I put upon thee, saith the Lord Jehovah.

"Trampled," in ver. 6, is not merely exposed to trampling, but actually trampled upon; as surely as Israel in Egypt was actually a trampled people, upon whom the Egyptians trod. *This* child was able to survive such trampling. The words, "And I said unto thee in thy blood, Live," are repeated, to fix the attention of the ungrateful people, and impress them on their conscience. Ver. 7 does not abandon the allegory, but it

---

[1] רבבה is not one myriad, but the myriad denotes the numerical measure. It is an ideal unity, which includes in itself a multitude of actual myriads.

[2] Luther, "I gave thee fine linen clothes and silken veils." But the *binding* refers to the head; and ver. 13 shows that silken *clothes* are to be understood, along with the party-coloured.

[3] Luther, "and gave thee a hair-band on thy forehead." He could not understand the nose-ring, or he has intentionally set it aside, as foreign to German customs.

refers to an ideal child, that comes to view in a multiplicity of single existences. The words, "myriads—wax great," refer to Ex. i. 12, "And as they afflicted them, so they multiplied and broke forth." "And camest to complete ornament:" the beauty is figuratively designated as an ornament: the people were adorned with beauty. "And thou wast naked and bare." Grotius, "This signifies the misery of the people in Egypt." The blessing of God going forth under the cross caused the vigorous growth and prosperity of the people; but their external condition was still miserable, and all external conditions of national existence were wanting. In ver. 8 is the closing of the covenant with the people, as it began with the calling of Moses at Sinai, and attained to its conclusion during the sojourn of the people there. The covering with the skirt of the mantle is the figurative designation for taking under protection (Ruth iii. 9). In connection with this stands here the covering of the nakedness, which indicates the want of protection and help. "Saith the Lord Jehovah:" What grace, when the Holy and Almighty One condescends to enter into covenant with so sinful and miserable a people! The washing with water and anointing with oil (ver. 9) signify the translation from the low and miserable Egyptian condition to a higher and better. Spiritual benefits are not to be thought of. As the blood formerly signified the external misery of the people in Egypt, so also, by the washing with water, can only be understood the removal of the external misery. The prophet adheres to the palpable benefits of God, which even the ungodly, whose conscience he wishes to reach, must have recognised as such. Ver. 10 f. refer specially to the flourishing period of the people under David and Solomon. The "beautiful crown" in ver. 12 belongs, according to ver. 13, to the kingdom of Israel. The royal splendour passed from David and Solomon over to the whole people. These bore the beautiful crown, as representatives of the people.

Next follows in two paragraphs the way in which Israel repaid the great grace of God. Ver. 15. And thou didst trust in thy beauty, and didst play the harlot on thy name, and pouredst out thy fornications on every one that passed by: his be it. 16. And thou tookest of thy garments, and deckedst thy high places with divers colours, and playedst the harlot with them:[1] the like shall not come nor happen.[2] 17. And thou tookest thy fair jewels of my gold and of my silver which I had given thee, and madest for thee images of men, and playedst the harlot with them. 18. And thou tookest thy broidered garments, and coveredst them; and didst set my oil and my incense before them. 19. And my bread which I gave thee, fine flour, and oil, and honey, I gave thee to eat, and thou didst set it before them for a sweet savour: and thus it was, saith the Lord Jehovah. 20. And thou tookest thy sons and thy daughters, whom thou hadst borne to me, and didst offer them to them to devour. Were thy whoredoms too little? 21. And thou didst slay my sons, and gavest them to pass them through (the fire) for them. 22. And in all thy abominations and thy whoredoms thou didst not remember the days of thy youth, when thou wast naked and bare, and wast trampled in thy blood.

"Thou didst trust in thy beauty" (ver. 15)—thoughtest to be allowed to do everything on this account. Hand in hand with this goes, "Thou whoredst on thy name:" the name is, as it were, the foundation of the whoredom; in reliance on thy renown acquired by thy beauty (ver. 14), which thou acknowledgedst not to be a divine endowment, and regardedst as a licence for ungoverned wantonness. The divine gifts, as soon as they cease to be regarded as such, inevitably become a snare. The heart, which they have rendered haughty, becomes the sport of all lusts and passions. "His be it" are the words of the adulteress; that is, to him will I yield myself. "High places with divers colours," fitted up with garments (ver. 16), can only be idol-temples, as they are fitted up for domestic use. The words " shall not come nor happen" denote an unprecedented shamelessness. Everything that exceeds the usual measure has in it aspects in which it is unique in its kind. "Images of men" (ver. 17): so are the idols designated, in accordance with the representation of Israel as an adulteress. "My oil and my incense:" what God has given remains His

---

[1] Luther, "and playedst thine harlotry *thereon*." But the masculine suffix is rather to be referred to the paramours, ver. 15, who are the object of the whoredom. על as אל in vers. 26, 28.

[2] Luther, "as never happened, nor will happen." But באות always denotes the future. It is here plural of the fem. standing for the neut. In יהיה the neut. is denoted by the masc.

even after He has given it, and may not be alienated. "Were thy whoredoms too little?" (ver. 20), so that thou must add murderous to thy adulterous practices.¹ The sacrifice of children appears in Ezekiel as a new aggravated crime in addition to idolatry (xxiii. 37, xx. 26). "Pass through" (ver. 21), that is, to pass through the fire (xx. 31). That the consequence of this passing through was death, appears from the foregoing words, "Thou didst slay them," and also from the phrase "to devour" in ver. 20. The passing through was the mode of slaying, and the devouring was the consequence of it. The idols were thought to be present in the fire.²

In the second part of the representation of the ingratitude the aggravation of the apostasy is described, as it coincided with the times of national misfortune, of oppression under the world-powers. Thenceforward the apostasy was truly national. Misfortune always makes worse, if not better. Merely formal is the distinction, that formerly the paramours were pre-eminently the idols themselves, now the idolatrous nations, in whom Israel seeks the help that was denied of God in righteous judgment. Ver. 23. And it came to pass, after all thy wickedness; Woe, woe unto thee, saith the Lord Jehovah. 24. And thou didst build for thee a vault, and madest for thee high places in every street. 25. At every crossway thou didst build thy high place, and didst abhor thy beauty,³ and didst spread out thy feet to every passer-by, and didst multiply thy whoredoms. 26. And thou didst whore with the sons of Egypt, thy neighbours, great of flesh, and multiply thy whoredoms to provoke me. 27. And, behold, I stretched out my hand over thee, and diminished thy statute, and delivered thee to the soul of thy haters, the daughters of the Philistines, who were ashamed of thy lewd way. 28. And thou didst whore with the sons of Asshur, because thou wast not satisfied; and though thou didst whore with them, thou wast not satisfied. 29. And thou multipliedst thy whoredoms unto the land of Canaan toward Chaldea, and yet with this thou wast not satisfied. 30. How

---

¹ מעט with מן always means too little; properly, little from some person or thing.

² The suffix in להם, vers. 20, 21, refers to the idols.

³ Luther, "madest a thing only to be abhorred." The verb means in Piel always to abhor, never to make to be abhorred.

withered is thy heart, saith the Lord Jehovah, when thou doest all these things, the work of a whorish imperious woman. 31. When thou didst build thy vault at every crossway, and madest thy high place in every street, thou wast not like the harlot, since thou scornedst hire. 32. The woman that committeth adultery under her husband receiveth strangers. 33. They give gifts to all whores, and thou givest thy gifts to all thy lovers, and hirest them, that they may come unto thee on every side for thy whoredoms. 34. And there is in thee the contrary of the women in thy whoredoms, and after thee they follow not for whoredom, and thou givest a hire, and no hire is given unto thee, and so thou art the contrary.

The "vault" in ver. 24 is a place raised by art for the practice of idolatry. The natural heights are too far from the people hungering after idols. They wish to plant idolatry in the city thoroughfare, and so build for themselves artificial heights. We must distinguish between the thought and its clothing. The thought is, that the objects of idolatry became the prime impulse of the popular life, by which is to be understood much less religious than political adultery, though both went hand in hand. "Thou abhorrest thy beauty" (ver. 25): whosoever abandons it to another must esteem it very little, —must, as it were, conceive a hatred against it. The beauty is the national honour, a noble boon bestowed by God, which not to esteem but to prostitute is a sign of deep degeneracy and alienation from God. This is a disgrace which, as the Jews, so also the Germans formerly, brought upon themselves in large measure, and into which they will soon enough sink back, if they do not gain a firm hold on God, and a clear and certain view of the boon bestowed upon them by Him. "Every passer-by:" at an earlier period Israel stood, by the situation of their country, which admitted no isolation, in manifold intercourse with the world (ver. 15); but in the time which the prophet has in view they lay in the middle of the contending world-powers, the Asiatic and the African, and were thus in their intervening territory tempted by the force of circumstances to adultery with powerful neighbours, if they did not wish honestly to turn to the Almighty God, the only one who could deliver them from this dire necessity, and did deliver them when they, as under Hezekiah, were disposed to do so.

"Great of flesh" (ver. 25): this it was that provoked their adulterous desires. In reality, great of flesh means great of power. Here it is very clear that the immediate object of adultery is not the idols in the usual sense, but the world-powers —that the adultery bears essentially a political character: the idols only stand in the second place, in so far as he that pays homage to a people is constrained at the same time to do reverence to their national gods, as we may plainly see from Dan. iii. As here this self-interested political alliance, so in Isa. xxiii. 17, 18, the commercial alliance is designated as adultery. "I diminished thy statute" (ver. 27): this is that which comes to the woman of right, whom the husband must nourish and clothe, according to the determination of the law. This means all the benefits which the Lord has promised in the law to His people in case of fidelity, and according to ver. 9, so richly secured in their later times. These are here *diminished* as a punishment; the people sink lower and lower in consequence of their adultery with the world-power, as we may follow out through their history from Ahaz onward, who first entered into this adulterous connection with the world-powers (2 Kings xvi. 7). The Philistines, who were always at hand when Israel had to suffer from the great world-powers, are specially named, because it was a great disgrace to be compelled to suffer from this petty neighbouring people, and not to be a match for their power. The daughters of the Philistines are the Philistine cities or small states. They are presented as daughters or wives, because Judah also appears as a wife. That the Philistines were, as it were in heart, ashamed of Israel on account of their moral degradation, is the key to the fact that this heathen nation, not knowing the living God or His revealed word, should have gained the supremacy over Israel. If the political adultery with the African world-power procures not the desired result—security against the Asiatic—if Egypt proves a broken reed, they make the attempt with the Asiatic world-power, with the Assyrians themselves (ver. 28). The words, "and thou wast not satisfied," introduce that which follows. As they turn to the Assyrians, because the adulterous connection with Egypt yields not the desired result, they turn on the same ground from the Assyrians to the Babylonians—to the aid which Asia itself appears to present against Asia. How the Jews, through connection with Babylon before it had attained the world-sovereignty, sought to deliver themselves from the danger threatening from Assyria, ch. xxxix. of Isaiah gives some hints, which are completed by his predictions directed against Babylon; and we find a more definite disclosure on the subject in ch. xxiii. For the understanding of the disputed predictions of Isaiah the declarations of Ezekiel concerning the relation of Judah to Babylon during the time of the Assyrian dominion are of the greatest importance. The starting-point of the attack is the want of insight into the historical relations existing in the time of Isaiah. The doubts lie here, as in the Scripture generally, only on the surface. But even by this new adultery Judah was not satisfied (ver. 29), as appears from this, that they had returned even now, in the time when Ezekiel prophesied, to their old lovers the Egyptians. They had, as Isaiah so emphatically predicted, to suffer still more heavily from their old friends the Chaldeans than from the Assyrians, against whom they sought their aid. Chaldea is designated as a land of Canaan, because it was a second Canaan, a land of shopkeepers, a political Canaan, like that commonly so called,—a mercantile people, regarding its own interest alone, whose friendship was only a disguised selfishness. To the land of Canaan here corresponds the designation of Babylon as a "city of merchants" in ch. xvii. 4. He is a fool who seeks real love in such a people, and founds the hope of his safety on connection with them. A withered heart (ver. 30) that has lost sap and power (Ps. xxxii. 4) is the heritage of those who seek in the world what God alone can secure. Hope always disappointed is the enemy of life.[1] "Imperious:" to be ungovernable is a disgrace for a wife, who from God and by right is "under the husband," and the sure forerunner of the ruin which is now meeting all those who boast of the "free spirit." The word means properly potent; but to be potent in relation to God is the highest impotence, as surely as freedom consists in this only, to serve God. That in which Israel is unlike ordinary harlots, is that, whereas they prostitute themselves for hire, she despises the harlot's hire (ver. 31). The thought is, that Israel casts herself at the feet of the world-

---

[1] The form לבה, not otherwise occurring, stands intentionally in the singular—an effeminate heart.

powers, without any political advantage being secured or even claimed by her, content if she can even secure bare existence. This thought is again carried out in vers. 32-34. Ver. 32 forms only the introduction to this amplification. The wife is Israel. "Under her husband"—while she stands under her husband, and is bound to be devoted to him.

In vers. 35-52, the *punishment*. Ver. 35. Wherefore, O harlot, hear the word of the LORD. 36. Thus saith the Lord Jehovah, Because thy brass was wasted, and thy nakedness uncovered by thy whoredoms with thy lovers, and with all thy horrible abominations, and for the blood[1] of thy sons, whom thou hast given unto them; 37. Therefore, behold, I will gather all thy lovers, with whom thou hast been pleased,[2] and all whom thou lovedst, with all whom thou hatedst; and I will gather them against thee round about, and will discover thy nakedness unto them, and they shall see all thy nakedness. 38. And I will judge thee with the judgments of adulteresses, and of those who shed blood; and I will give thee blood of fury and jealousy. 39. And I will give thee into their hand, and they shall throw down thy vault, and break down thy high places: and they shall strip thee of thy clothes, and take away thy costly jewels, and leave thee sitting naked and bare. 40. And they shall bring up a company against thee, and cast at thee with stones, and hew thee with their swords. 41. And they shall burn thy houses with fire, and execute judgments upon thee in the sight of many women; and I will make thee rest from being a harlot, and thou shalt not give a hire any more. 42. And I will make my fury against thee rest, and my jealousy shall depart from thee; and I will be quiet, and no more be angry. 43. Because thou didst not remember the days of thy youth, and didst rage against me in all this,[3] I also give thee thy way upon thy head, saith the Lord Jehovah; and thou shalt not commit this lewdness above all thy abominations.[4]

---

[1] Properly "as the blood," corresponding to it, in righteous retribution for the shedding of it.

[2] Luther, "with whom thou hast taken pleasure," *commixta es*, without warrant from the text.

[3] Luther, "but provoked me with all this," which רגן with ל cannot possibly signify.

[4] Luther, "although I have not therewith done after the vice in thy

44. Behold, every part shall sing over thee, saying, As is the mother, so is her daughter. 45. Thou art thy mother's daughter, that loathes her husband and her children; and thou art the sister of thy sisters,[1] who loathed their husbands and their children: your mother was a Hittite, and your father an Amorite. 46. And thy elder sister is Samaria, she and her daughters, that dwell at thy left; and thy sister younger than thou, that dwelleth at thy right, is Sodom and her daughters. 47. And thou hast not walked after their ways, nor done after their abominations: it wanted a little, and thou behavedst more corruptly than they in all thy ways. 48. As I live, saith the Lord Jehovah, Sodom thy sister hath not done, she or her daughters, as thou hast done, thou and thy daughters. 49. Behold, this was the iniquity of Sodom thy sister: pride and abundance of everything, and quiet security, were to her and her daughters; and the hand of the wretched and the needy she did not take. 50. And they were haughty, and committed abomination before me; and I took them away when I saw it. 51. And Samaria hath not committed half of thy sins; and thou didst multiply thy abominations more than they, and didst justify thy sisters by all thy abominations which thou didst. 52. Thou also take thy shame, who didst judge thy sisters; by thy sins, wherein thou hast behaved more abominably than they, they are become more righteous than thou; and also be thou confounded, and take thy shame upon thee, because thou hast justified thy sisters.

The brass (ver. 36) represents metal in general, namely, coined metal. Brass here stands as the metal usually employed for money, as in Isa. xlvi. 6, where it is said of the idolaters, "They lavish gold out of the bag"—gold, as the most precious. That the Jews, at least those in exile, as well as classic antiquity, had copper money, follows even from our passage, and is confirmed by Matt. x. 9, Mark xii. 41, where brass occurs

abominations." עשיתי is, however, an unusual form of the 2 fem., for which the Masoretes here, as in זכרתי, substitute the usual one.

[1] It is literally "of thy sister;" but the sister is an ideal person, the sisterhood, that is here presented in two sisters. Thus the singular stands also in ver. 51, where the Masoretes wish to substitute in place of the singular the plural, the vowels of which stand under the text. The assumption of an unusual plural form is to be rejected. The plural, signifying the real multiplicity, appears in place of the ideal unity in ver. 22.

directly for money. The paramours are, according to what follows, pre-eminently the world-powers themselves. Along with them are named, in the second place, the heathen gods, whose worship was a consequence of political dependence. The penal uncovering of the nakedness (ver. 37) is the righteous retribution for licentiousness. The latter denotes the shameful prostitution and self-degradation of the people of God, who went a-begging in the world; the former the shameful external misery into which they fell through the world-powers, to whom they had devoted themselves. The lovers are, according to the foregoing, Assyria and Babylon. The haters are the surrounding nations, who were always lying in wait for the occasion. "With the judgments of adulteresses and murderers" (ver. 38): adultery and murder are, according to the law, punished with death, and must thus also occasion death in the immediate exercise of the divine judgment. Israel had made himself guilty of murder by the worship of Moloch. The blood of fury and jealousy is that which is shed in fury and jealousy. Into this blood Jerusalem went, as it were, wholly: she was wholly transformed into blood. The blood of fury is the punishment for the murder that in human relations calls forth fierce revenge: the blood of jealousy is the retribution for adultery that in human relations awakens the spirit of jealousy. "They leave thee naked and bare" (ver. 39), as thou wast before the Lord had mercy on thee (ver. 7). The unfaithful use of the gifts of God inevitably brings on their loss. God cannot be mocked. Ver. 40. As the local community is called together against the ordinary adulteress, to execute upon her the penalty of stoning (comp. Deut. xxii. 24, where this punishment is expressly prescribed in reference to the betrothed maiden who has broken her troth; whereas in the case of married women the law speaks only of the punishment of death in general), so there assemble against adulterous Israel, as it were, an assembly of nations, and execute upon it the penalty of stoning with slinging engines. As murderers are usually executed by the sword, so is murderous Israel hewn down by the enemy with the sword. These are the judgments of the adulteresses and murderers (ver. 38). "And execute judgments upon thee in the sight of many women" (ver. 41): the many women are the many nations. There is an allusion to Deut. xiii. 16, according to which a city in Israel that serves other gods shall be burned with fire, after its inhabitants had been extirpated by the sword. This command closes a prediction of the fate which should befall Israel in case of its apostasy. " Thou shalt not give a hire any more" (vers. 33, 34), because thou wilt have no more lovers; wilt, on the whole, after the dissolution of thy national independence, be no more in a condition which admits of impure intercourse with the world-powers. The jealousy ceases (ver. 42), because it has found its satisfaction in their punishment, and exhausted itself therein, as the fire ceases when it has consumed its fuel. " And didst rage against me in all these" (ver. 43)—notwithstanding all the benefits which thou didst receive from me. The starting-point of adultery with the world and its gods was anger against the true God, who had diminished His benefits to Israel (ver. 27). Instead of recognising therein a deserved punishment, Israel sees an unjust neglect, " falls into anger, and curses his God and his king" (Isa. viii. 21), and seeks in others what he refuses. The visitation which, instead of leading to repentance, brings on a complete apostasy, has for its consequence the completion of the judgment. " Thou shalt not commit this lewdness above all thy abominations." Lewdness and abomination are not in themselves different: the thought is, that the measure of the lewdness and abomination is now full— that it is time for punishment to enter into the place of sin. " As the mother, so the daughter," runs the poetic sentence, according to ver. 44. As Israel became like the original inhabitants of Canaan in her manners, so also in her fate, which had already been realized when this sentence was composed. That the mother is the people of Canaan, into whose footsteps Israel had entered, appears from a reference to ver. 3, and as expressly affirmed in ver. 45. The spiritual mother of Israel, the daughter of Canaan, abhorred her husband, the one true God, who according to Gen. i. 26 created all men after His image, gives to all life, and breath, and all things (Acts xvii. 25), in whom all men live, and move, and have their being (ver. 28), and who even on this account has a claim on the devoted love of all men; whereas she preferred to Him other gods, the work of men's hands, and abhorred her children, inasmuch as she sacrificed them to the gods in the fire (ver. 20; comp. Lev.

xviii. 21, 24, where it is expressly said that the sacrifice of children offered to Moloch was a native custom among the nations, whom the Lord drove out before Israel (Deut. xii. 30, 31)). The sisters, to whom, along with the mother, Israel, now perpetuated only in Judah, has become like in transgression, and shall be like in punishment, are, according to ver. 46, Samaria and Sodom. These in particular are selected out of the mass of nations, because Sodom was notorious before all others as the greatest sinner, and Samaria stood nearest to Jerusalem. It is said, "who loathed their husbands," because the one true God, who is the lawful husband to the sisters as to the mother, was another in relation to Sodom and in relation to Samaria: there Elohim, the Godhead; here Jehovah, the historically revealed, the covenant God. Samaria is called in ver. 46 the elder sister of Judah, because the northern kingdom embracing the ten tribes was the greater; Sodom the younger, because her territory was smaller than that of Judah. The *daughters* denote the daughter-cities, and point to this, that Samaria and Sodom come into regard not as single cities, but as centres of a great whole. That Sodom was the chief city of the Jordan valley, appears from the whole account in Gen. xviii. and xix., especially from this, that there the trial was instituted, and also from ch. xiv. 21, where the king of Sodom alone treats with Abraham concerning the spoil. Wherever the cities of the Jordan valley are enumerated, Sodom stands at the head. Jerusalem has, according to ver. 47, not been contented with walking in the ways of Sodom and Gomorrah: she has pursued a course that was still worse. The prefixed *almost*[1] serves for modification, points to this, that the sentence has only a partial truth. This truth rests on the statement, Luke xii. 48: "Unto whomsoever much is given, of him shall much be required; and unto whom much is committed, of him they will ask the more." Judah trespassed against God, who was revealed in her midst in manifold ways. Judah was worse than Sodom: this thought recurs also in the N. T. (Matt. xi. 24). The deepest gulfs of evil open up first in those to whom God has made Himself known, and who have hardened their heart against His revelation. The sin of Sodom

[1] כמעט, only a little, wanted a little. מע according to the Arab. *only*.

and its punishment are laid down in vers. 49, 50, that Israel may set herself right as to what she is, and what she has to expect. The prosperity and comfort of existence are connected with pride, in so far as in the mind, like the rich man in the Gospel, she entered wholly into these conditions, so that they became marks of character in her, and ceased to be external and accessory. "When I saw it:" this points to Gen. xviii. 21. God conducts the inspection by His angels. Judah justifies her sisters (ver. 51), inasmuch as they in reference to her appear as innocent. Her sins weigh heavier than even those of Samaria, because much richer means of grace were bestowed on her. She had before her the temple and the pure worship of God, the sovereignty of the family of David, from which pious kings might and often did descend, the legitimate priesthood, a greater wealth of prophetic gifts, and a longer time for repentance. "Who didst judge thy sisters"[1] (ver. 52): Judah had concurred from the heart in the divine judgment on Sodom and Samaria, and exalted herself above them on this account, as the Pharisee in the Gospel. In the condemnation of her sisters she had condemned herself (Rom. ii. 1). Jerusalem has "justified" her sisters, inasmuch as she has behaved worse than they, and so retributive punishment must overtake her also.

Vers. 53-63.[2] We have here the forgiveness. This is imparted to Jerusalem not for herself alone, but in common with those whom she resembled, both in her sin and her punishment. If Judah is destitute no less than they of any glory before God, if she can obtain redemption only through grace, it is natural that the redemption is not limited to her, but that God, who has mercy upon all His works, extends it also to the others. As righteousness from works goes hand in hand with the limitation to the Jews, so righteousness from above with an extension far beyond these limits (Rom. xi. 32).

Ver. 53. And I shall turn back to their captivity, to the captivity of Sodom and her daughters, and to the captivity of Samaria and her daughters, and to thy most miserable cap-

---

[1] We are not to explain, "which (the shame) thou didst award to thy sisters." The verb does not occur elsewhere in this sense, and "*thy* shame" then makes a difficulty.

[2] Comp. on this section, *Christology*, ii. p. 547 f.

tivity in the midst of them. 54. That thou mayest take on thee thy disgrace, and be ashamed of all that thou hast done, when thou comfortest them. 55. And thy sisters, Sodom and her daughters, shall return to their former state, and Samaria and her daughters shall return to their former state, and thou with thy daughters shalt return to thy former state. 56. And was not thy sister Sodom slandered by thy mouth in the day of thy pride? 57. Before thy wickedness was discovered, as (was the case) in the time of the disgrace of the daughters of Aram and all who were round about her, the daughters of the Philistines, who despise thee round about. 58. Thy lewdness and thy abominations thou hast taken upon thee, saith the LORD. 59. For thus saith the Lord Jehovah, And I will do with thee as thou hast done, who hast despised the oath to break the covenant. 60. And I will remember my covenant with thee in the days of thy youth, and will establish unto thee an everlasting covenant. 61. And thou shalt remember thy ways and be ashamed, when thou shalt receive thy sisters, those greater than thyself, and those less than thyself; and I shall give them unto thee for daughters, and not by thy covenant. 62. And I will establish my covenant with thee; and thou shalt know that I am the LORD: 63. That thou mayest remember, and be ashamed, and no more open thy mouth because of thy shame, when I cover for thee all that thou hast done, saith the Lord Jehovah.

To return to the captivity (ver. 53), is to have compassion on the miserable.[1] The captivity cannot be taken in a strict sense, as Sodom and the other cities of the Jordan valley were not carried away captive, but utterly destroyed. The word misery itself is taken from another land, the genus being named after the chief species. Sodom represents the collective heathen world standing in like relations with her. That

---

[1] Comp. my comm. on Ps. xiv. 7; *Contributions to the Introd. to the O. T.*, ii. p. 104 f. שׁוּב שְׁבוּת is to be distinguished from הֵשִׁיב שְׁבוּת, to restore the captivity (Jer. xlix. 6). This is the *consequence* of returning to the captivity, or the miserable. That שׁוּב may also signify to bring back or restore, it has been sought to prove from Nah. ii. 3, but incorrectly. The Lord there turns back to the loftiness of Jacob, which gives the *ground* of his return. Jacob is at the same time Israel, and as such endowed with a higher dignity, that of the church of God, which may be obscured by its sin, but never destroyed. שְׁבִית and שְׁבוּת signify in this

great crushing judgments will fall upon the whole heathen world no less than on Sodom itself, is the uniform announcement of the prophets, also of Ezekiel, in ch. xxv. and xxvi.; so that the remark, that " Sodom is not the type of heathendom on this account, because heathendom does not need to be restored," is not to the point. The representative character of Sodom lies in the nature of the thing. If God pities the most notorious sinners among the heathen, how should He not pity all? And it is confirmed by ch. xlvii. 18, where the sea introduced in place of Sodom is a symbol of the world dead in sins. Sodom also stands frequently elsewhere in the O. T. as a representative of deep corruption (Deut. xxxii. 32; Isa. i. 10; Jer. xxiii. 14). But all doubt is excluded by ver. 61. There the representative character of Sodom is expressly affirmed. Yet we may not exclude even Sodom itself from salvation. The special references to it are too strong for this (comp. especially vers. 49, 50). Ch. B. Michaelis says, " As Samaria and Jerusalem, so must Sodom also, it appears, be taken literally." As a restoration of the city is not to be thought of, its inhabitants swept away by the judgment can only be the object of salvation; and we have here an allusion to a continuance of the arrangements of grace after death for those for whom on earth salvation did not attain to its highest completion, the Old Testament basis for 1 Pet. iii. 20, 21, iv. 6, especially for the latter passage; also for Matt. xii. 41, 42, a passage that indeed only indirectly leads to the same result. " And to thy most miserable captivity in the midst of them :" Jerusalem has behaved worse than Sodom and Samaria; therefore must she suffer more severely than they. She experiences for the same reason also not a separate forgiveness, placing her above her sisters, but is only favoured among her sisters with an equal participation in the same redemption. There is here no difference; all have sinned and come short of glory before God, and are justified

phrase always the captivity as a state, and not the multitude of the captives. The fundamental passage is Deut. xxx. 3, " And the LORD thy God will return to thy captivity." That the allusion to this passage may be as literal as possible, Ezekiel puts first the there occurring form שבית, and afterwards that which was current in his own time, שבות. The assimilating Masoretes have removed this distinction: Thy misery's misery, that is, thy highest misery, a captivity of the captivity, such as displays itself amidst the captivity as a captivity.

freely by His grace (Rom. iii. 23): God has in like manner included all among the disobedient, that He might have mercy on all. Parallel is Isa. xix. 23, 24. There, in the Messianic times, Egypt with Assyria serves the Lord, and Israel is the third in their covenant—" a blessing in the midst of the land." Both there and here, in vers. 54, 61, Israel appears as the point from which the blessing passes over to the other nations, who were strangers to the commonwealth of Israel. It is, however, not accidental, that Israel here, as in Isaiah, takes only the third place. There lies in this a hint that the heathen world will sooner attain to salvation, and a preparation for Rom. xi. 25. This hint, however, in reference to the precedence of the heathen in realizing salvation, receives a limitation and restriction in vers. 54, 61. According to this, salvation comes first from an election out of the Jews to the Gentiles, and then returns from the Gentiles to the Jews. This process of the proclamation and acceptance of salvation Isaiah has already presented in sharper definiteness in the closing chapter of his predictions. Ver. 54 is to be explained by ver. 61. Accordingly, the comfort (Isa. xl. 1) consists in the announcement of the gospel, the comforting truth, to the sisters: The Lord returns to thy captivity. To receive this mission to the heathen is a high honour; and this office she fulfils with deep shame, on account of her former apostasy, for which she deserved something far different from this distinction. The prophet, in ver. 55, clings to the thought of restoration to her former better position (Acts iii. 21). But the restoration is here, as in Job, at the same time elevation to a stage of existence far surpassing the former. Ver. 61 shows that the salvation of Sodom and Samaria consists in admission into the kingdom of God, and participation in all the blessings of this kingdom. " Was not Sodom a talk[1] in thy mouth?" so that thou couldst not cease to spread the report of her shameful deeds and her terrible downfall, but ever again didst revert to this record out of the foretime. This her former haughty pride Israel will remember with deep shame, when she becomes like Sodom in sin and punishment, and a partaker with Sodom of the same undeserved mercy. The wickedness of Jerusalem was discovered (ver. 57) by her punishment. By that which she

[1] שְׁמוּעָה is knowledge, nothing more.

suffered she learned what she had done, and the delusions of her pride vanished: she no longer spoke of Sodom with a "God, I thank thee," but laid her hand upon her own heart. The daughters of Aram are the Aramaic cities and tribes. These come not into regard as the destroying powers—were the instruments of the divine vengeance to be named, Assyria and Babylon would rather be cited—but as borderers mocking at the calamity coming from another quarter. The genus to this species are "all who were round about her," that is, about thee (comp. v. 5, 6; Dan. ix. 16; Mic. v. 6). As a second species of this genus, are then named the daughters of the Philistines, who were especially distinguished among the mockers around by their hatred. This disgrace, which came upon Israel in the time of her calamity, was the just recompense for the arrogance with which she looked down upon Sodom in the time of her prosperity. "Thy lewdness and thy abominations thou hast taken upon thee" (ver. 58): this point of transition to salvation cannot be allowed to thee more than to Sodom and Samaria. "For thus saith the Lord Jehovah, And I will do" (ver. 59): first attention is drawn anew to this, that not the son of man as such speaks, but the Lord, who is concealed behind him, that thus threatening and the preaching of salvation may have the most solid ground. Then, by beginning with *and*, it is intimated that this is a continuation of what goes before. *The oath* is the swearing to the covenant on the part of God (Deut. xxix. 11, 12). After the announcement of punishment to the rebellious people in Lev. xxvi. 42, God had promised that He would be mindful of His covenant. Deep shame takes hold on Israel (ver. 61), that notwithstanding her deep sinfulness, she was deemed worthy to enter into a motherly relation to the heathen world, to receive them into herself into the kingdom of God, which was the highest honour that could be put upon her. That this honour is not imparted to the whole people, but only to the election (especially represented by the apostolate), is said not here, but elsewhere in the O. T., and even by Ezekiel himself, in the most emphatic manner (comp. for ex. ch. iv. 4). It was here intimated in ver. 53. In regard to the greater and lesser sisters, Cocceius aptly remarks: "The plural shows that what was said of Samaria and Sodom, refers not to them alone, but to all nations, great and small." The heathen nations that were to be received by her intervention into the kingdom of God appear as *daughters* of Jerusalem already in the Song of Songs, on which our chapter is manifestly dependent (comp. my comm. on ch. i. 5). Jerusalem *receives* the heathen nations, takes possession of them as her property, belonging to her, and Jehovah *gives* them to her as daughters. Sisters they were before; and even on this it depends that they are given to her for daughters. According to Gen. i., which teaches the descent of all men from one pair, the whole human race forms a great family. Accordingly, the kingdom of God can only for a time be limited to a single people, and the limiting must be the means of unlimiting. All Christian nations are in fact daughters of Jerusalem, as surely as they are built upon the foundation of the apostles and prophets (Eph. ii. 20). Parallel in import is Isa. ii. 3, where, in the day of salvation, many peoples go to the mountain of the Lord that is established on the top of the mountains, and say, " Come, and let us go up to the mountain of the Lord, to the house of the God of Jacob; and He will teach us of His ways, and we will walk in His paths : for out of Zion shall go forth the law, and the word of the Lord from Jerusalem." The short hint conveyed in the words, " and not by thy covenant," receives light from ver. 59. It means, accordingly, not by thy keeping of covenant, not because the fulfilment of thy covenant obligations gave thee any claim. The covenant may, so far as Israel's obligation is concerned, be called his covenant; so far as Jehovah's promise is contemplated, it is God's covenant. It is expressly said in ver. 60, that on the divine side the new blessing is rooted in the old covenant relation, so that we cannot say, " Thy covenant means the former reciprocal one." The covenant that is to be established (ver. 62), can only be the so-called *new* covenant of Jer. xxxi. 31, the more intimate relation into which God is about to enter with Zion, the supremely intimate nature of which is evinced by this among other things, that it draws the heathen more powerfully to it. The *knowing* is here practical. As formerly by punishment, so now by grace, Zion knows that her God is in the fullest sense God. The higher the benefit, the deeper is the shame (ver. 63) that she has fallen so disgracefully from a God so essentially good.

Ch. xvii. The predominant practical tendency of this chapter, is to strike down the vain hopes that were founded on the alliance of Zedekiah with Egypt, that the people may attain to salvation by the way of repentance. The prophet, however, does not stop with the annihilation of earthly hopes. At the close he points to the glorious exaltation of the kingdom of David, which the Lord will bring to pass at the end of days. Whosoever laid up this promise in his heart, would thereby be delivered from the region of vain political hopes and intrigues. The saying of Augustine applies here: "That which thou seekest is; but it is not where thou seekest it." The central point of the hopes of the future was the person of the king. God, they thought, cannot let him fall, without reversing the glorious promises that He had made to the house of David. To all outward appearance, the hopes of the house of David are buried with Zedekiah. The prophet, on the contrary, teaches that Zedekiah will find what his deeds deserve, and yet God will at length, when all seems to be lost, gloriously fulfil His promise to the house of David. The prophecy falls into three paragraphs: the parable representing the emptiness of all earthly hopes of the future; its exposition, ver. 11 f.; the salvation from above, ver. 22 f.

Ver. 1. And the word of the LORD came unto me, saying, 2. Son of man, put forth a riddle, and speak a parable unto the house of Israel; 3. And say, Thus saith the Lord Jehovah, The great eagle, with great wings, with long quills, full of feathers, which had divers colours, came unto Lebanon, and took the leafy crown of the cedar. 4. The top of its young twigs he plucked off, and brought it to the land of Canaan; in a city of merchants he set it. 5. And he took of the seed of the land, and put it in a seed field: he took it to many waters, and set it as a willow tree. 6. And it sprouted, and became a spreading vine of low stature, whose branches should turn towards him, and its roots be under him: and it became a vine, and sent out branches and shot forth sprigs. 7. And there was a great eagle, with great wings and many feathers; and, behold, this vine hungered in its roots after him, and sent forth its branches towards him, that he might water it from the beds where it was planted. 8. In a good field by many waters was it planted, that it might send out leaves and bear fruit, and become a goodly vine. 9. Say thou, Thus saith the Lord Jehovah, Shall it prosper? Shall he not pull up the roots thereof, and cut off the fruit thereof, that it wither? In all the verdure of its shoots i' shall wither; and not by a great arm or many people will it be taken away with its roots. 10. And, behold, it is planted: shall it prosper? Shall it not utterly wither when the east wind toucheth it? It shall wither on the beds of its shoots.

The great eagle (ver. 3) is the king of Babylon, who is among the kings what the eagle is among the birds: in the composition of the cherubim, the eagle represents the whole class of birds. The greatness of the wings and of the quills denotes the extension of his dominion: comp. Isa. viii. 8, where the outstretched wings of the king of Assyria cover the entire holy land. The thickness of the feathers denotes the great multitude of his subjects; the divers colours, the multiplicity of the nations. In the carrying out of this symbol, the mountain chain which on the north separated the heathen country from the abode of God's people, is employed now as a figure of the native kingdom (comp. *Christol.* on Zech. xi. 1), now as a figure of the heathen monarchy (comp. my comm. on ch. iv. 8 of the Song of Songs),—a double meaning, which was yielded by the intervening position of Lebanon. The cedar on Lebanon is the house of David: comp. Dan. iv. 8, 9, where Nebuchadnezzar appears as a great and strong tree, and Ezek. xxxi. 3 f., where Assyria is designated as a cedar on Lebanon. The leafy crown[1] of the cedar is the then royal court, which was carried away by Nebuchadnezzar, and whose constituent parts are described in 2 Kings xxiv. 14. To the leafy crown here corresponds, in the exposition, ver. 12, the king of Jerusalem with her princes. The top of the young twigs of the cedar, in ver. 4, is different from the leafy crown in ver. 3. While the latter designates the whole court, the former refers to him who is specially concerned, king Jehoiachin, who is the more aptly compared with a twig, as he was a youth when carried captive. The country of the Chaldeans cannot here be called Canaan, that is, *a merchant's land;* nor can Babylon be called *a city of traders,* in the usual sense. This would be a designation that,

---

[1] צַמֶּרֶת, properly the wool of the tree, the top, where the foliage is rankest.

irrespective of its being not at all characteristic, would not meet the case in point. That which is intended is rather the Chaldean diplomacy, the policy of the interests that were thus pursued, just as we speak of political negotiations and international intrigues. From this policy originated the removal of Jehoiachin to Babylon. Self-interest is the point of comparison between politics and trade. This community of principle also explains how both politics and trade are represented in Scripture under the figure of adultery, the self-seeking, that conceals itself under the appearance of love (comp. my comm. on Rev. xiv. 8, xvii. 2); the self-seeking policy, Nah. iii. 4; the trade, Isa. xxiii. 15 f. It was, as it were, a profitable stroke of business, that Jehoiachin, who was favourable to Egypt, should be removed to Babylon, and a creature of the king of Babylon set up in his stead, whose fidelity he might count upon, because he had the legitimate sovereign in his custody, and could make use of him according to circumstances. The king of Babylon " took of the seed of the land" (ver. 5), in opposition to the appointment of a foreign regent; Zedekiah, whom the Chaldeans appointed, was of the old native royal family (2 Kings xxiv. 17; here ver. 13). The Chaldean policy preferred such a one, in order to secure the sympathies of the people. The " field of seed" in which the new king was planted, is a fertile soil, in opposition to a barren region. It refers, besides the fertility, to the advantageous situation of the promised land in a commercial aspect, on the highway of the world's commerce by land and by water, to which the blessing of Jacob had pointed (Gen. xlix. 13); and likewise the blessing of Moses (Deut. xxxiii. 19).[1] " He took it to many waters." Waters, in the symbolic style of Scripture, signify the sources of nourishment (comp. on Ps. cvii. 33; Rev. xvii. 1, 2). " Set it as a willow :" set the new king, so that in a spiritual sense he was a willow, resembled this in fresh bloom (comp. the figure of the tree planted by the water-brooks in Ps. i.). The following figure of the vine is not here in contradiction with that of the willow. The two figures present different aspects. The subject in ver. 6 is not the willow tree, but the king. The new king (ver. 6) is a vine, not a cedar, as the earlier inde-

[1] קח is abbreviated from לקח. The abbreviation is intended to point to the previous ויקח, and to resume this. Mich. *accepit* inquam.

pendent family of David. "Spreading," so that it grew luxuriantly indeed, but in breadth, not in height, which is still more definitely shown by the addition "of low stature." Its (Zedekiah's) roots should be under him—should not be withdrawn from dependence on the king of Babylon. The words, "And it (the vine *in spe*) became a vine, and sent out branches and shot forth sprigs," prepare for what follows. From the prosperity of the new kingdom arose the arrogance which led to the attempt to shake off the yoke of Babylon. The second great eagle (ver. 7) is the king of Egypt, the African world-power. It also has great wings, an extended dominion, and is rich in feathers—has a numerous population under it; but the other is *the* great, this only *a* great eagle; and it wants the "divers colours," the multitude of nations united under its sway. This kingdom is not a composite one, extending over a wide surface of nations, like the Asiatic, whose sovereign called himself king of kings, but a homogeneous one. The vine, the kingdom of Judah, " hungers" or longs after the second eagle, or the king of Egypt; and this hunger belongs especially to its roots,[1] which particularly need strengthening, and in which the defect of the new kingdom displayed itself. The *watering* appears to allude to the Nile, the symbol of Egypt and its king, which waters Egypt, led by the trenches into the fields (comp. Jer. ii. 18). The words "from its beds," the bed where it was planted, belong to the phrase, " it hungered and sent out." The planting bed is Canaan, where the king is planted by the Chaldeans, and is thereby bound to obey him,—a thought which is carried out further in ver. 8. In ver. 8 we have the good design of the king of Babylon, and of God, who makes use of him as His instrument. Only from mischievous ingratitude could Zedekiah seek to attach himself to the king of Egypt. Hitherto the motive to judgment; in ver. 9 the judgment itself,—a judgment pronounced not by the son of man, but by Him who speaks and it is done. In the words, " Shall he not pull up the roots thereof?" the subject is the king of Babylon. The roots signify the national existence; the fruit the produce of the land, or the collective gain. The vine becomes

[1] These stand in the so-called relative accusative, which limits more strictly the sphere.

dry[1] in all its sprouting leaves: these signify all that by which a prosperous national life is displayed. "Not by a great arm or many people will it be taken away with its roots." According to Jer. xxxiv., Nebuchadnezzar led a numerous army to Jerusalem; but there was no need of so great preparations. If a nation have God for its enemy, one can chase a thousand of them, and two can put ten thousand to flight (Deut. xxxii. 30; comp. Lev. xxvi. 8). The Egyptians were quite passive (comp. ver. 17). The taking away with the roots[2] signifies the total abolition of the national existence. The destructive east wind, in ver. 10, signifies the king of Babylon.

Then follows, in vers. 11-21, the exposition of the parable. Ver. 11. And the word of the LORD came unto me, saying, 12. Say now to the house of rebellion, Know ye not what this is? Say, Behold, the king of Babylon came to Jerusalem, and took its king, and its princes, and brought them to him to Babylon. 13. And he took of the king's seed, and made a covenant with him, and took an oath of him; and he took the mighty of the land: 14. That it might be a base kingdom, that it might not lift itself up, that his covenant might be kept and might stand. 15. And he rebelled against him in sending his ambassadors into Egypt, that they might give him horses and much people. Shall he prosper? shall he escape that doeth such things? and should he break the covenant, and escape? 16. As I live, saith the Lord Jehovah, in the place of the king that made him king, whose oath he despised, and whose covenant he brake, he shall die with him in the midst of Babylon. 17. Neither shall Pharaoh with mighty army and great company act with him in war, by casting up a mount, and building a fort, to cut off many souls. 18. And he has despised the oath, to break the covenant, and, behold, he gave his hand, and all this he did, he shall not escape. 19. Therefore thus saith the Lord Jehovah, As I live, mine oath that he despised, and my covenant that he broke, this will I lay upon his head. 20. And I will spread my net over him, and he shall be taken in my snare; and I will bring him to Babylon, and plead with him there for his trespass which he hath com-

---

[1] חָיָבֵשׁ refers to the vine, as in ver. 10.
[2] Job xxviii. 9, ἐκ ῥιζῶν; Mark xi. 20; comp. Matt. iii. 10, Luke iii. 9, where the axe lies at the root of the trees.

mitted against me. 21. And all his fugitives[1] with all his squadrons shall fall by the sword, and they that remain shall be scattered towards all winds: and ye shall know that I the Lord have spoken it.

"The house of rebellion" (ver. 12), the rebellious company, should have been led by the parable and its exposition to submission to the destiny of God. "He took the mighty of the land" (ver. 13): the noblest of the land were, according to 2 Kings xxiv. 15, carried away with Jehoiachin to Babel. Nebuchadnezzar retained them as hostages for the fidelity of Zedekiah, but especially to weaken the power of the vassal-kingdom (ver. 14). "With him" (ver. 17): this is most simply referred to the rebel king. Pharaoh will not render him the expected powerful aid against the Chaldeans; he will leave his protégé in the lurch, when he is hard pressed by his enemies. That the Chaldeans need no great military force against Jerusalem, is manifest here from this, that the Egyptians, against whom alone it could be necessary, come not to its aid with any force. Egypt was already at that time worm-eaten; which the Spirit of God showed to His prophets, while the world went no further than the surface.

In vers. 22-24, the promise.[2] Ver. 22. Thus saith the Lord Jehovah, And I will take of the leafy crown of the high cedar, and set it; I will crop off from the top of his young twigs a tender one, and plant it on a mountain high and eminent. 23. On the high mountain of Israel will I plant it; and it shall put forth branches, and bear fruit, and become a goodly cedar: and under it shall dwell all fowl of every wing;[3] in the shadow of its branches shall they dwell. 24. And all the trees of the field shall know that I the LORD have brought down the high tree, have exalted the low tree, have dried up the green tree, and made the dry tree to flourish; I the LORD have spoken and done it.

The beginning of the discourse of God with *and*—"And I will take"—points out that this procedure of God is the con-

---

[1] An allusion to מברחיו, his elect, *quid pro quo*.
[2] *Christol.* ii. p. 475 f.
[3] That we must explain "fowl of every wing" by as many as have wings, is obvious from the parallel passage, xxxix. 4, 17, and the fundamental passage, Gen. vii. 14.

tinuation of a former one—His destructive interposition against the house of David, according to the saying, "I kill, and I heal." The doubled emphasis on *I* points out that the procedure here announced has the warrant of success in the person of the speaker. This *I* is of powerful import, as the speaker is no other than "the Lord Jehovah," the Almighty, the purely absolute Being, whom no created thing can resist. This *I* forms the counterpart to the present weak and barren attempt to maintain the house of David in its dignity. When all these political intrigues are shattered, the Lord takes the matter in hand—the same who defeated these human schemes of deliverance. The *cedar* is here, as before, the house of David. The tenderness of the twig points to this, that the branch of David will present itself at first small and obscure, in accordance with the announcement of the earlier prophets, that the Messiah will appear in the time of the deepest humiliation of the house of David, rise from the fallen tabernacle of David (Amos ix. 11), a rod out of the stem of Jesse (Isa. xi. 1), a root out of a dry ground (Isa. liii. 2). The mountain high and eminent, on which the tender twig is planted, is the symbol of a mighty kingdom. The high mountain of Israel, in ver. 23, forms the more exact description of the mountain high and eminent. It means, according to ch. xx. 40, Mount Zion, which is here, however, viewed not according to its natural height, in respect to which it stands far behind Lebanon, which appeared in ver. 3 as the symbol of the kingdom of God, but according to its spiritual height, which already existed in the times of the O. T., according to Ps. xlviii. 3, "Beautiful for its height, the joy of the whole earth, is Mount Zion, the city of the great King" (Ps. lxviii. 17), but first attains to its full import in the Messianic times; comp. Mic. iv. 1, Isa. ii. 2, according to which in that time, " at the end of days," the mountain of the Lord's house shall be established on the top of the mountains, and exalted above the hills.[1] In point of fact, Mount Zion signifies the kingdom to be raised to the supremacy over the world-kingdoms. Yet we must expect that, when the fulfilment of our prophecy begins, the kingdom of God will have

---

[1] Cocceius: *qui ut altior erat omnibus montibus in toto mundo, quia domus Dei tantum in illo erat, ita longe altior futurus erat, quum Rex regum in eo manifestaretur.*

its seat on the natural Zion; and so in fact it happened. The branches, which the shoot puts forth, signify the extension of the sovereignty of that great descendant of David; the fruits which it bears (comp. Isa. xi. 1, " a branch out of its roots shall bear fruit"), signify the saving operations that come from Him. The words, " and become a goodly cedar," show that the cedar with its leafy crown, in ver. 22, existed only in an ideal sense, and had entirely disappeared from the common reality. With the new shoot it entered again into this with imposing effect. To represent powerful ruling families under the form of an overshadowing tree, is a figure particularly acceptable in the Chaldean period, and probably borrowed from the Chaldees (xxxi. 3 f.; Dan. iv. 7, 8). Matt. xiii. 32 rests on our passage. The trees of the field (ver. 24) are, in the symbolic style of Scripture, the princes and the mighty ones of the earth (in Rev. vii. 1). The high tree is the worldly dominion. The humiliation of this is implied in the exaltation of the house of David, announced in the previous verse: when all the fowls dwell under that cedar, there remains no more room for the worldly dominion. The low tree is David, or the family of David, that attains to its exaltation in the Messiah. With the fact of the exaltation is given its accomplishment by Jehovah, as surely as the family of David stands under the protection of Jehovah. The green tree is the world-monarchy that flourished luxuriantly at the time when this prophecy was published; comp. Dan. iv. 8, 9, where it is said in the description of Nebuchadnezzar's dream, " The tree was great and strong, and its height reached unto heaven, and the sight thereof to the end of the whole earth; its leaf was fair, and its fruit much," etc. In the exposition (ver. 19) it is said, " Thou art the tree, O king;" while the tree of David's race was already almost dried up, and according to the announcement of the prophet, should soon be altogether dried up.

The exposition of the symbol is not added here, for the same reason that a prediction against Babylon is wanting in Ezekiel, whereas the whole of the predictions of Jeremiah culminate in this. The prophet spoke in the country of the Chaldees; and that they kept an observant eye on the predictions in Israel, is plain, among other passages, from Jer. xxix. 21, 22.

Caution in regard to the surrounding heathen is also observable in the whole book of Ecclesiastes.

The words, "I the Lord speak and do," oppose to the visible, in which the promise is devoid of all ground, the person of the promiser. Experience has shown that this power concealed behind the visible is of infinitely more importance than the visible, that is so imposing. Babylon, and with it the whole series of the old world-powers, are dried up; David flourishes and bears fruit, and under the shadow of his offshoot the fowls of the heaven dwell.

Ch. xviii. A hindrance to the salutary effect of the announcement of judgment in ch. viii.-xi., a shield which was held up against the implied demand for a radical conversion, lay in the fancy that the Lord visits the sins of the fathers upon the present generation. Accordingly, repentance was represented as fruitless. This fancy, resting on the misinterpretation of Ex. xx. 5, xxxiv. 7, has its proper starting-point in a mistake about personal sinfulness: instead of this true cause of the divine judgments, a false one is substituted. The prophet, on the contrary, follows out the principle, that every one receives what his own deeds deserve; that not foreign sins involve in the judgments of God, not even personal ones, if they be penitently abandoned (vers. 21-29). Therefore let a man return to God (vers. 30-32). The repeated enumeration of the actions in which the essence of righteousness consists, shows how the people came to refer the guilt to the fathers, and murmur against God, who punished them for guilt not their own, rather than against their own sin. The human heart is prone to place righteousness in external forms and ceremonies. In these they were exact. While the prophet holds up before them the mirror of true righteousness, he shows them that there is a simple solution of the problem, in which the guilt falls not on the side of God, but on their own head, and in which repentance is represented not as fruitless, but as salutary, and absolutely necessary.

First, in vers. 1-3, the ungodly proverb, and the declaration that it shall be no more heard in Israel; then, in ver. 4, the thesis by which, while it establishes personal accountability, the misunderstanding must be destroyed. After this, the carrying out into details. Ver. 1. And the word of the Lord came unto me, saying, 2. What is for you, that ye use this proverb in the land of Israel, saying, The fathers ate sour grapes, and the children's teeth are set on edge? 3. As I live, saith the Lord Jehovah, ye shall not use this proverb any more in Israel. 4. Behold, all souls are mine; as the soul of the father, so also the soul of the son is mine: the soul that sinneth, it shall die.

The dictum of the people mentioned in ver. 2 occurs before in Jer. xxxi. 29. It has been shown in my *Contributions* (*Beiträge*), iii. p. 544 f., that the passages of the law that lie at the foundation of this dictum contain no such doctrine; that, according to the uniform doctrine of the Holy Scripture, no man is punished but for his own guilt; that only the ungodly son is involved in the punishment of the fathers; that Ezekiel comes forward here simply as the expositor, not the amender, of the law. The Lord asserts, in ver. 3, that such a proverb shall no more be heard in Israel. He does not forbid it, but He declares that He Himself will expel it from them; comp. the passage cited from Jeremiah. The cause of its cessation is the severity of the divine judgments. When these come on, the fig-leaves fall off, the slumbering conscience awakens, and cries out, It is I and my sins. There is a multitude of philosophemes and theological dogmas that are only possible in certain times, and sneak away in confusion when the thunders of the divine judgment begin to roll. In ver. 4, the antithesis to the thesis of the people. "The souls are mine"—belong to me. God would surrender His property, if He permitted souls, whether individuals or whole generations, to suffer punishment for the guilt of others. In the likeness of God, on which the sentence "All souls are mine" rests, lies the principle that souls cannot be degraded into servile instruments—that each can only be treated according to his works. "The soul of the son as that of the father:" in reference to the proverb, son and father represent at the same time the earlier and the later generation.

Now follows the carrying out into detail. First (vers. 5-9), true righteousness—which exhibits itself in the fulfilment of the commandments of God—and salvation are inseparably connected. In the more exact designation of righteousness—which was necessary, because so many gave themselves over in this respect to false imaginations, from which the fancy that men suffer for the extraneous sins of their fathers originated—such sins are especially made prominent as were at that time in vogue.

Ver. 5. And if a man be just, and do judgment and righteousness, 6. And eat not upon the mountains, nor lift up his eyes to the abominations of the house of Israel, nor defile his neighbour's wife, nor come near to a menstruous woman, 7. And do not oppress any, restore his pledge for debt,[1] do not commit robbery, give his bread to the hungry, and cover the naked with a garment; 8. If he give not on usury, nor take increase, turn his hand from iniquity, execute true judgment between man and man, 9. Walk in my statutes, and keep my judgments, to do the truth; he is just, he shall surely live, saith the Lord Jehovah.

In ver. 6, out of the first table the command, Thou shalt have no other gods before me—the mountains as the places of the idolatrous nature-worship; out of the second, Thou shalt not commit adultery. The prohibition of impurities in the married state is included in the latter, which is directed against unbridled lust, that bows not to the ordinance of God. The pledge, in ver. 7, is more exactly defined by reference to the legal decisions in Ex. xxii. 25, Deut. xxiv. 6, 10 f., as something which is necessary to the existence of the poor man. The truth, in ver. 9, is the real righteousness in opposition to the show of it, with which so many deceive themselves and others.

Vers. 10-13. On the contrary, if a righteous man have an unrighteous son, he will come short of salvation, and his father's righteousness will not avail him.

Ver. 10. And if he beget a violent son, who sheds blood, and doeth to his brother[2] any of those things, 11. And he

[1] חוב is the accusative of restriction.
[2] אח, in regard to his brother, in relation to him. That אח must have the usual meaning of brother, is shown by ver. 18. Among the characteristics of the son in the first member, the violations of the commandments of the second table are specially regarded. Fellow-men, and especially fellow-Israelites, are expressly designated in the law as friends and brothers, to show that the violation of love towards them is unnatural and penal. מאחד, one or other, as Lev. iv. 2. Luther, "or does this thing once," omitting the brother.

doeth not all those things, for he eateth upon the mountains, and defileth his neighbour's wife, 12. He oppresseth the poor and needy, committeth robbery, restoreth not the pledge, and lifteth up his eyes to the abominations, and practiseth that which is detestable, 13. Giveth forth on usury, and taketh increase, should he live? He shall not live: he hath done all these abominations; he shall be put to death; his blood shall be upon him.

"Of these things" (ver. 10)—the things that are characterized as ungodly in the previous verses. "And he doeth not all those things" that are enumerated in vers. 6-9 as necessary qualifications of the righteous, and are practised by his father. "His blood shall be upon him" (ver. 13): he is the author of his own misfortune; he must ascribe it to himself.

Vers. 14-20. Again, if this unrighteous man have a righteous son, the unrighteousness of his father will not injure him, and salvation will return to him. Ver. 14. And, lo, he hath begotten a son, and he seeth all his father's sins which he hath done, and seeth them,[1] and doeth not the like; 15. He eateth not upon the mountains, nor lifteth up his eyes to the abominations of the house of Israel, and defileth not his neighbour's wife; 16. And oppresseth no one, taketh no pledge, and committeth no robbery; giveth his bread to the hungry, and covereth the naked with a garment; 17. Turneth away his hand from the poor, taketh not usury or increase, executeth my judgments, walketh in my statutes: he shall not die for the iniquity of his father, he shall surely live. 18. His father, because he cruelly oppressed, committed robbery on his brother, and did that which is not good among his people, lo, he died in his iniquity. 19. And ye say, Why doth not the son partake in the iniquity of the father? And the son hath done judgment and righteousness, hath kept my statutes and done them : he shall surely live. 20. The soul that sinneth, it shall die. The son shall not partake in the iniquity of the father, and the father shall not partake in the iniquity of the son; the righteousness of the righteous shall be upon him, and the wickedness of the wicked shall be upon him.

[1] Luther, "and feareth." The reading is to be pointed as before. The Masoretes wish to read ויראה, thinking that the full form suits the emphasis.

"And seeth them:" this is in ver. 14 emphatically repeated, to show that the seeing of the sins of his father in their terrible odiousness, and of the punishments inseparably connected with them, serves as a warning to him. Vers. 19 and 20 refer the special to the general, the individual case to the rule. It is a mere variation, if the question as to the "why" is put in the mouth of the people. The thought is thus only introduced in a more animated way, as much as to say, And will ye know why the son takes not upon him the iniquity of the father, as I say? The close of the amplification returns to the general thesis of ver. 4. "And the father shall not take upon him the iniquity of the son," no more than the father suffers for the iniquity of the son.

Vers. 21-29. So far from the sins of his fathers excluding from salvation, not even his own do this, if they be penitently forsaken. Ver. 21. And the wicked, if he turn from all his sins that he hath committed, and keep all my statutes, and do judgment and righteousness, he shall surely live, he shall not die. 22. All his transgressions that he hath committed shall not be mentioned unto him: in his righteousness that he hath done he shall live. 23. Have I any pleasure at all in the death of the wicked? saith the Lord Jehovah: if he return from his way,[1] should he not live? 24. And when the righteous turneth away from his righteousness, and committeth iniquity, and doeth according to all the abominations that the wicked doeth, should he live? All his righteousness that he hath done shall not be mentioned: in his perfidy that he hath practised, and in his sin that he hath sinned, therein he shall die. 25. And ye say, The way of the Lord is not equal. Hear now, O house of Israel, Should not my way be equal? Are not your ways unequal? 26. When the righteous turneth away from his righteousness, and committeth iniquity, and dieth therein, for his iniquity that he hath done he dieth. 27. And if the wicked turn away from his wickedness that he hath committed, and do judgment and righteousness, he shall save his soul alive. 28. And he seeth and turneth away from all his transgressions that he hath committed, he shall surely live, he shall not die. 29. And the house of Israel saith, The way of the LORD is not

---

[1] Luther, "and not rather that he turn from his nature, and live." "From his way:" for this the Masoretes read, "from his ways."

equal. Are not my ways equal, O house of Israel? Are not your ways unequal?[1]

They asserted (ver. 25) that the ways of God were not right—properly, not weighed in the balance of righteousness (Job xxxi. 6)—but regulated by caprice. This assertion proceeded from defective consciousness of sin, that could find no other key to suffering than this, that it was decreed unrighteously, on account of the sins of the fathers. The prophet points to this, that the guilt lies on their side. If they only sincerely return to God, they will no more have cause to complain of Him.

In vers. 30-32 the practical result: Turn ye, so shall ye attain to salvation. Ver. 30. Therefore will I judge you, O house of Israel, every one according to his ways, saith the Lord Jehovah. Return ye, and turn from all your transgressions, and let not iniquity be your ruin. 31. Cast away from you all your transgressions whereby ye have transgressed, and make you a new heart and a new spirit; and why will ye die, O house of Israel? 32. For I have no pleasure in the death of the dead, saith the Lord Jehovah; turn ye, then, and live.

"And turn" (ver. 30)—heart and senses (comp. xiv. 6). "And let not iniquity be your ruin:" provide that iniquity involve you not in the judgment of God, and occasion your fall. "Make you a new heart" (ver. 31): only God can do this, which the O. T. teaches no less emphatically than the N. (Ps. li.; Ezek. xi. 19.) But it does not come, unless the human will move to meet it; comp. Matt. xxiii. 37, "And ye would not." Hence the act is ascribed to man also. "The dead," in ver. 32, is one given over to certain death, who is already as good as dead.

Ch. xix. A song here forms the close of the whole cycle from ch. viii., as in ch. vii. at the close of that beginning with ch. i. The song first laments the miserable fate that awaits the kingdom (vers. 1-9); then the sad lot of the people, who sink back into the state in which they were formerly in the journey through the wilderness.

[1] The singular, יכן, at the close, is explained by this, that the actual plurality of the way is compressed into the ideal unity of the walk.

The lament concerning the princes goes at once to the facts, that were matter of history at the time when these words were spoken,—the carrying away of Jehoahaz into Egypt (vers. 1-4), and that of Jehoiachin to Babylon (vers. 5-9). But as prophecy deals not with the purely past, and the parallel lamentation concerning the people refers to the future, we must assume that the prophet regards those facts of the past as types of that which will befall the present Zedekiah; so that we have to suppose a break after ver. 9, or a "Whoso readeth, let him understand;" "Who hath ears to hear, let him hear." Quite analogous is ch. xxxi., where the fall of the king of Assyria is presented as a type of that of the king of Egypt: there also the history is a concealed prophecy. Only in this way also is explained the strange circumstance, that Jehoahaz and Jehoiachin are arranged one immediately after the other; and Jehoiakim, standing historically between them, is omitted. Though he was a more important personage than either, and reigned much longer, and though his reign presented abundant matter for lamentation, as the beginning of the Chaldean servitude and the first taking of Jerusalem fall in it; and even a second, occasioned by his revolt, in which the king himself lost his life, took place under him; yet he belonged not to this connection, as the carrying away of Zedekiah into a heathen land, and specially into Babylon, is to be foreshadowed.

Ver. 1. And take thou up a lamentation for the princes of Israel, 2. And say, How is thy mother a lioness? she lay down among lions, among ravening lions she reared her whelps. 3. And she brought up one of her whelps, and he became a ravening lion, and learned to catch the prey: he devoured men. 4. And the heathen heard of him: he was taken in their pit; and they brought him with rings to the land of Egypt. 5. And she saw that she had waited; her hope was lost: and she took another of her whelps; she made him a ravenous lion. 6. And he walked in the midst of the lions; he became a ravenous lion, and learned to catch the prey: he devoured men. 7. And he knew his widows, and laid waste their cities; and the land was desolate, and its fulness, through the noise of his roaring. 8. And the heathen gave against him round about from the provinces, and spread their net over him:

he was taken in their pit. 9. And they put him in ward in rings, and brought him to the king of Babylon: they brought him into the nets,[1] that his voice should no more be heard on the mountains of Israel.

The " how" (ver. 2) is an exclamation of surprise (comp. xvi. 30) at the former glory, which, as this glory is now vanished, is in reality a bitter lamentation. The address is to the man Judah, the people of the present. The mother is the people in itself. The people appears as a lioness on the ground of Gen. xlix. 9, to which passage the couching in particular refers (comp. Num. xxiii. 24, xxiv. 9; Isa. xxix. 1), because it was a royal people, of equal birth with other independent and powerful nations, as this royal nature was historically displayed, especially in the times of David and Solomon. The highest development of this lion-nature, the true verification of Gen. xlix. 9, 10, first came to pass in the future, in the appearance of the Messiah, the Lion of the tribe of Judah (Rev. v. 5). Before, however, this highest development could take place, the people must first sink so deep as to resemble a worm rather than a lion. For in the kingdom of God the way is *per ardua ad astra:* there is no state of exaltation without the corresponding state of humiliation. The whelps of the mother are the sons of the king of Israel. The bringing up of these among lions points to the fact that the kingdom of Israel was of equal birth with the mighty kingdoms of the heathen world. In ver. 3 the figure of the lion is otherwise applied. The ignoble side of the lion-nature is here brought to view. The distance, however, is not very great: there is a close connection between the two sides. By the constitution of human nature, arrogance is inseparably connected with high rank, and therewith a rude barbarity towards all who stand in the way of self-will. He only who walks with God can escape this natural consequence; and the walk of faith is not the attainment of every man. It should, however, be the attainment of every man among the people of God; and where it fails, and the corrupt nature unfolds itself without resistance,

---

[1] Luther, " and they kept him." מְצוֹדָה is not "hold" (against this are the plural, and the mention of Babylon in the foregoing passage), but net (Eccles. ix. 12; comp. here xii. 13, xxxii. 3). For the taking of so dangerous a wild beast many nets were necessary.

there the vengeance of God takes effect. Jehoahaz proved to be a barbarous tyrant toward his own subjects; whereas, according to its constitution, the kingdom of Israel should exhibit a heroic power against the enemies of the people of God. For this reason he was punished. To the mother here corresponds, in 2 Kings xxiii. 30, the people of the land, who, after Josiah fell in the battle with the Egyptians, made Jehoahaz king. To that which is said here concerning his disposition, corresponds 2 Kings xxiii. 32, " And he did that which was evil in the sight of the LORD, according to all that his fathers had done." On ver. 4, Chr. B. Michaelis says: " There is an allusion to the custom, when the news arrives that a lion or other savage beast is committing mischief, of assembling on all sides to seize and slay it." The *ring* lays on the wild beast the necessity of following whither it will not (comp. 2 Kings xix. 28). In reality, the fetters correspond to the ring. 2 Kings xxiii. 33, 34 gives the historical commentary : " And Pharaoh-Necho fettered him at Riblah, in the land of Hamath, . . . and took him and brought him to Egypt, and he died there."

In ver. 5 f. the second type of the fate awaiting Zedekiah is still more definite than the first, because Zedekiah, like Jehoiachin, was also to be carried away to Babylon. The co-operation of the people in the elevation of Jehoiachin to the throne is not mentioned in the narrative, as it is expressly in the case of Jehoahaz. But respect to the wishes of the people is implied in his being the son of Jehoiakim. " And she saw that she had waited, her hope was lost :" that is, while she waited, namely, for the return of Jehoahaz from Egypt. Jehoiachin also (ver. 6) exposed the bad side of the lion-nature. In accordance with our passage, it is said of him (2 Kings xxiv. 9), notwithstanding his reign of only a few months, " he did that which was evil in the sight of the Lord, according to all that his father had done." The *knowing* in ver. 7 denotes the practising of brutalities. *His*, that is, the king's widows, are the widows whom he, as king, was bound to protect. *His* widows are at the same time their, the people's, widows, the wretched and suffering, the *personæ miserabiles*. The subject is the king as a lion, as a hard and cruel man. There is an abridged comparison here : he acts towards the wretched, whom he was called on to protect, as one who injures a widow confided to his protection. The fulness of the land is that which lives and moves in it. The lion roars when he is about to rend; and this rending is to be added to the roar, as only thus the effect ascribed to the roar is explained. "Gave against him" (ver. 8): what they gave is not said. It is to be supplied from the connection—every one his gift, his contribution, to make him harmless. The provinces are the surrounding countries, as parts of the Chaldean empire; comp. 2 Kings xxiv. 2, according to which the Syrians, Ammonites, and Moabites were summoned against Jehoiakim, the father of Jehoiachin. Ver. 9*b* returns to ver. 8*b*, to give prominence to the object of the whole procedure.

While the first part of the elegy refers to the kingdom, the second describes the existing condition of the people. It appears in the close of the 80th Psalm under the figure of a choice vine that is now wasted. Ver. 10. Thy mother, it seems to thee, is like a vine planted by the waters: she was fruitful and full of branches from many waters. 11. And she had strong rods for sceptres of rulers, and her growth was high above the clouds; and she was conspicuous in her height, in the fulness of her branches. 12. And she was torn out in fury, cast to the earth, and the east wind dried up her fruit; and her strong rods were broken and dried up, fire consumed them. 13. And now she is planted in the wilderness, in a land of drought and thirst. 14. And fire went out of the rod of her branches, consumed her fruit; and there was not in her a strong rod, a sceptre for ruling. This is a lamentation, and shall be for a lamentation.

The people of the present are addressed in ver. 10. His mother is the people in itself. The phrase, "it seems to thee," properly, in thy idea or likeness,[1] points to this, that what is here said of the mother, the comparison with the vine to be utterly destroyed, applies pre-eminently to the people of the present, and calls out to them, *tua res agitur*, is equivalent to the saying, "Verily I say unto you, this generation shall not pass till all these things come to pass." The many waters signify the divine blessing which ruled over Israel, the rich influx of grace. Ver. 11 refers especially to the glorious condition of the people in the time of David and Solomon, under

[1] דָּם = דְּמוּת; comp. ἐν παραβολῇ, Heb. xi. 19.

whom Israel became a world-power like Assyria, of whom the same is said in ch. xxxi. 3.[1] The east wind (ver. 2) is a figure of the divine judgment to be executed by the Chaldeans. The fire denotes the same divine judgment in its destroying character.[2] The wilderness (ver. 13) denotes the misery of the state of exile, in which the passing of Israel through the wilderness in the olden time repeated itself. Such a wilderness may even be in the midst of a cultivated land. The fire in ver. 14 goes out from the chief stem of the branches: it does not take its rise from the Chaldees, but proceeds from the royal family itself, which by its crimes called down the divine vengeance. The fruit denotes the prosperity of the people. The prophet here dwells on that which Israel receives in the way of her works. She falls into utter destruction, until, with the appearance of the Messiah, through God's unmerited grace, a new beginning is made, and the word is heard, " I am the true vine." They who stop the ear against the word abide in death, to which they are doomed by their works. The lamentation is (properly was, with prophetic anticipation of the future) for a lamentation: it is not the fancy of a gloomy seer, but the prediction of a lamentation, which will actually flow in a thousand voices from the mouth of the people. What Ezekiel here pronounces, the people will too soon be compelled to repeat after him. His lamentation is, as it were, the sowing, out of which a rich harvest of lamentation grows. At present the sky is full of joyous music to the people; but very soon it will be said: " My harp is turned to mourning, and my flute to the voice of weeping."

---

[1] עבות, " clouds," gradually loses its plural meaning. From this Ezekiel has formed the new plural עבותים, which is found in him only in this meaning (*Christol.* iii. p. 457). It is properly, " over between the clouds." It grows through between the clouds, and out above them. The suffix in קומתו refers to the royal family, the collection of the ruling rods; and this is also the subject in וירא. This is properly, they were seen, they appeared, displayed themselves openly, shone in the eyes of all.

[2] The strong rod is the collection of the strong rods or branches, that became sceptres of rulers in ver. 11. This explains the construction with the plural. The suffix in אכלתהו refers not to the vine, but to the strong rod. The misfortune of the king, however, was at the same time that of the people.

THE THIRD AND FOURTH CYCLES.

THE THIRD.—CHAPTERS XX.-XXIII.

We have here the third cycle. The prophet takes occasion for a new beginning, from the visit of men from the elders of the people. These are here, as in ch. xiv. 1, representatives, not of the totality of the exiles, but of the great mass of those only externally fearing God, but internally addicted to the spirit of the world and the age. The embassy had probably a special occasion in the circumstances of the time, in a favourable turn which the affairs of the coalition had taken. They wish to obtain confirmation of their joyful hopes from the mouth of the prophet. As long as he remains in the former position, things do not stand well with them. The prominent question is not about salvation in general, but whether there can be salvation without judgment and without repentance—salvation for the people as they now are. They do not consider that a total revolution must take place in them, if they are to be capable of salvation.

The direct answer to the embassy is contained in ch. xx.; the further details are given in ch. xxi.-xxiii. In ch. xx. the prophet sets their sins before Israel till ver. 20. The description has four paragraphs: Israel in Egypt—the first station in the wilderness—the second station—Israel in Canaan. With a people so obstinately persevering in their sins, from their origin, through all times down to the present, God must hold a great reckoning, which is at the same time a purification (vers. 30-39). Yet the judgment will be followed by grace for those who are purified thereby (vers. 40-44).

Ver. 1. And it came to pass in the seventh year, in the fifth month, on the tenth day, came men of the elders of Israel to inquire of the LORD; and they sat before me. 2. And the word of the LORD came unto me, saying, 3. Son of man, speak unto the elders of Israel, and say unto them, Thus saith the Lord Jehovah, Are ye come to inquire of me? As I live, saith the Lord Jehovah, I will not be inquired of by you. 4. Wilt thou judge them, wilt thou judge them, son of man? Make known to them the abominations of their fathers.

The question, repeated in the liveliness of emotion, "Wilt thou judge them?" is a question of impatience, to which things go too slowly, and shows how little right they have to look for grace, or expect a pleasing answer. The son of man cannot go soon enough for the Lord to the work of judgment and punishment for sin, which is here alone announced, and is to be executed in His name. Those who wish to have another answer, must repent beforehand. The summons to make known to them the sins of their fathers, points to this, that the evil is deep-seated, and a radical cure is to be desired, which can only be effected by a judgment of inflexible rigour.

First, Israel's sins in Egypt. God made Himself known to Israel in Egypt by wonders and signs; said to them, in fact, "I am your God," and held out to them the land of promise. But they requited His kindness with ingratitude; yet God brought them out of Egypt. Ver. 5. And say unto them, Thus saith the Lord Jehovah, In the day when I chose Israel, and lifted up my hand to the seed of the house of Jacob, and made myself known to them in the land of Egypt, and lifted up my hand to them, saying, I am the LORD your God; 6. In that day I lifted up my hand to them, to bring them out of the land of Egypt into the land which I had espied for them, flowing with milk and honey, which is an ornament for all lands. 7. And I said unto them, Cast away every man the idols of his eyes, and defile not yourselves with the abominations of Egypt: I am the LORD your God. 8. And they rebelled against me, and would not hearken unto me: they did not cast away every man the idols of his eyes, nor forsake the abominations of Egypt; and I said, I will pour out my fury upon them, I will accomplish my anger upon them in the midst of the land of Egypt. 9. And I did it for my name's sake, that it should not be polluted before the heathen among whom they were, in whose sight I made myself known to them, to lead them out of the land of Egypt.

There can be no doubt that the lifting up of the hand in vers. 5 and 6 is the gesture of the oath; for so it undeniably occurs in ver. 15, ver. 28, and in the fundamental passage, Ex. vi. 8. Now in the last the oath refers solely to the leading out of Egypt, and to this we must here also adhere. The hand is here lifted up beforehand, to warrant this assurance. The expressions, "I made myself known to them," and "I said, I am the Lord your God," serve only to bring the oath impressively before their minds. It takes place, as it were, while the hand is lifted up to this oath, to give a practical foundation for faith in it. Both refer to the wonders and signs in Egypt. By these God made Himself known to His people, and said to them, "I am the Lord your God;" comp. Ex. vi. 2, according to which, God by these facts made Himself known by His name Jehovah. "Into the land which I had espied for them:" God, as it were, spied out this land for them, sought it out with the greatest care as the best. No gift of God without obligation (ver. 7). How should they not truly serve Him who had exerted Himself so signally for them? The words, "I am the Lord your God," point to the ground of obligation. In ver. 8 we are told how badly the people in Egypt responded to His call. History does not expressly mention such a revolt of the people in Egypt; yet we are led indirectly to this by the statements of the books of Moses concerning the perpetual tendency of the people in the wilderness to the customs of Egypt. To this belongs, for ex., the making of the golden calf, in which there is an imitation of the Egyptian worship of the brute; further, Lev. xvii. 7, according to which Israel in the wilderness served he-goats. The worship of a deity under the form of a he-goat was peculiar to Egypt; Lev. xviii. 3, where the people are admonished: "After the doings of the land of Egypt, wherein ye dwelt, shall ye not do." That the Israelites generally served idols in Egypt, is attested by Josh. xxiv. 14; and this being so, it is to be expected beforehand that this inclination would not immediately cease after the true God had made Himself known to them. The murmuring also of the people in Egypt against Moses and Aaron (Ex. v. 21), implies an under-current of Egyptian tendencies. "And I did" (ver. 9): namely, what I did—the well-known fact to be afterwards more exactly defined, that I, notwithstanding their infidelity, led them out of Egypt. The ground which determines God to this—respect for His name, His honour—is further amplified in Num. xiv. 13–16.¹ God's name and call would be desecrated, degraded into the sphere of impotence and falsehood, if He did not perform what He had proposed.

Vers. 10–17. The sin of the first generation of Israel in the wilderness. Ver. 10. And I led them forth out of the land of Egypt, and brought them into the wilderness. 11. And I gave them my statutes, and showed them my judgments, by which, if a man do them, he shall live. 12. And also my sabbaths I gave them, to be a sign between me and them, that they might know that I the LORD do sanctify them. 13. And the house of Israel rebelled against me in the wilderness; they walked not in my statutes, and they despised my judgments, by which a man lives, if he do them; and my sabbaths they greatly polluted; and I said I would pour out my fury upon them in the wilderness, to consume them. 14. And I did it for my name's sake, that it should not be polluted before the heathen, in whose sight I led them out. 15. And also I lifted up my hand to them in the wilderness, that I would not bring them into the land which I had given them, flowing with milk and honey, which is an ornament for all lands. 16. Because they despised my judgments, and walked not in my statutes, and polluted my sabbaths; for their heart went after their abominations. 17. And my eye spared them that I should not destroy them, and I did not make an end of them in the wilderness.

The precepts which God gave His people bring (ver. 11) life and salvation with them to him who does them. What grace in God, who gives such precepts! what a summons to true obedience! These precepts also imply before all things, that they shall confess their sins, and seek forgiveness in the blood of atonement. This is required by the laws concerning the sin-offerings, which in the Mosaic law form the root of all other offerings; the passover, which so strictly requires us to strive after the forgiveness of sins, and connects all salvation with it and the great day of atonement. The Sabbath, instituted by God, and altogether peculiar to Israel (ver. 12), is a weekly recurring confession of God to His people, and of the people to their God,—a sign that God sanctifies this people,

¹ החל, infinitive in *Niphal*, from חלל (comp. vii. 24).

and separates them from the mass of other nations as His own people. How careful must they be to keep holy an institution so rich in grace! Whosoever violates it, transgresses against his existence. "My Sabbaths they greatly polluted" (ver. 13): history records nothing of an external violation of the Sabbath during the journey through the wilderness. Num. xv. 32 f., where the man who gathered wood on the Sabbath was brought before the congregation, and stoned by them after formal sentence, is rather a proof that in this respect they were not wanting in zeal. But the prophet, in accordance with Isa. lviii. 13, 14, and with Moses himself, who commanded to *sanctify* the Sabbath, to consecrate it in every respect to God, and withdraw it wholly from the region of self-interest, of personal sinful inclination, according to which the festival cannot possibly be observed with indolent repose, forms a deeper and more spiritual idea of the Sabbath. "Thou shalt cease from thy doing, that God may have His work in thee:" in this sense the truly God-fearing only can celebrate the Sabbath; so that all that in the books of Moses attests the want of true godliness among the people in the wilderness, involves at the same time the charge of desecrating the Sabbath. For His name's sake God destroys not the people (ver. 14); but He excludes the present generation from the possession of Canaan, in just retribution for that which they have practised against Him. To this just retribution points the "and I also." It depends on the will of every one what position he will take towards God; but he must be prepared for this, that his act will be attended with a corresponding divine act. That the lifting up of the hand here has the import of an oath, is shown by Num. xiv. 28–30; Ps. cvi. 26, "And He lifted up His hand to them, that He would overthrow them in the wilderness." Ver. 17 reverts to ver. 14. Although the present generation was condemned to perish, God did not give over the whole people to the destruction they deserved.

In vers. 18–26 are the sins of the second generation in the journey through the wilderness. Ver. 18. And I said unto their children in the wilderness, Walk ye not in the statutes of your fathers, neither observe their judgments, nor defile yourselves with their abominations. 19. I am the LORD your God: walk in my statutes, and keep my judgments, and do them;

20. And hallow my sabbaths, and they shall be a sign between me and you, that it may be known that I am the Lord your God. 21. And the children rebelled against me: they walked not in my statutes, neither kept my judgments to do them, by which the man that does them lives; and they polluted my sabbaths: and I said, I would pour out my fury upon them, to accomplish my anger upon them in the wilderness. 22. And I turned back my hand, and did it for my name's sake, that it should not be polluted before the heathen, in whose sight I led them forth. 23. I also lifted up my hand unto them in the wilderness, to scatter them among the heathen, and disperse them in the countries; 24. Because they did not execute my judgments, and despised my statutes, and polluted my sabbaths, and their eyes were after their fathers' abominations. 25. And I also gave them statutes that were not good, and judgments whereby they should not live. 26. And I polluted them by their own gifts, in that they caused all to pass through that openeth the womb, that I might lay them desolate, that they might know that I am the LORD.

To the "*children*" (ver. 18) belongs, among other things, the whole second law-giving, with its impressive admonitions, as it was promulgated in Arboth-Moab, and is recorded in Deuteronomy. God, for His name's sake, has not destroyed the apostate generation in the wilderness (vers. 21, 22); but He has in just retribution, before the entrance into the promised land, set before their eyes the impending dispersion among the heathen (vers. 23, 24). The prophet refers to the passages in the books of Moses, in which the exile was held out in prospect to apostate Israel, as Deut. xxviii., xxx. 1. In vers. 25, 26, a second retribution. We may compare here Rom. i. 24, according to which God, in just retribution for their revolt, gave over the heathen to vile affections; Acts vii. 42, where it is traced back to God, that the heathen served the host of heaven; and 2 Thess. ii. 11, where God sends the apostates strong delusions. God has so constituted human nature, that revolt from Him must be followed by total darkness and disorder; that no moderation in error and sin, no standing still at the middle point, is possible; that the man, however willing he might be to stand still, must, against his will, sink from step to step. Revolt from God is the crime, excess in error and moral degradation the merited doom, from which all would willingly escape if this were in their power. Grotius writes: " I have taken from them the understanding, that in despising my laws they may make for themselves hard and death-bearing laws." By way of example, the custom of sacrificing children is mentioned in ver. 26. " I polluted them" (ver. 26): this means, according to ver. 25, not as older expositors and Hävernick, evacuating the sense, explain, I declared them unclean, treated them as such; but that to God, who governs even in the evolution of sin, is attributed the polluting itself, which takes place according to a law beyond their power. " By their offerings," which they presented to their idols, with the hope of obtaining, through their purification, forgiveness of sins and salvation. Wherein these gifts consisted, is intimated in the words, " in that they caused all to pass through." " To cause to pass through" the fire (ver. 31; comp. xvi. 21, xxiii. 37), is the current phrase for sacrificing children which were offered to Moloch. Into such a detestable custom did God in His righteous judgment permit them to fall, that the merited punishment might come upon them (" that I might lay them desolate"), by which they learn that their paternal God, whom they set at nought, is God in the full sense, whom to forsake is at once to fall into misery. That the presentation of children as sacrifices was already common in the time of Moses, is plain from Num. xviii. 21, Deut. xviii. 10.

In vers. 27-29, the continuance of the revolt from the Lord during the sojourn in Canaan. Ver. 27. Therefore, son of man, speak to the house of Israel, and say unto them, Thus saith the Lord Jehovah, Yet in this your fathers blasphemed me, in dealing treacherously with me. 28. And I brought them to the land, which I lifted up my hand to give them; and they saw every high hill, and every thick-leaved tree, and offered there their sacrifices, and presented there the provocation of their offering, and there made their sweet savour, and there poured out their drink-offerings. 29. And I said unto them, What is the high place whereunto ye go? And the name thereof is called High Place unto this day.

" Therefore" (ver. 27)—since ye are a people so utterly corrupt. " Yet in this your fathers blasphemed me :" every revolt from God, every departure from His commands, is a practical blasphemy, a denial of His righteousness and omnipotence; for where these are vividly realized, there a man will love God with all his heart, and not deviate a step from His commandments. The stricter designation of blasphemy follows in ver. 28, after it was designated in general, at the close of ver. 27, in the words, " in dealing treacherously with me." "The provocation of their offering" (ver. 28)—the offerings to idols, whereby they provoked the anger of God; comp. Deut. xxxii. 16, 17, " They provoked Him to jealousy with strange (gods); with abominations they made Him indignant. They sacrificed to lords which were not God, to gods whom they knew not." God says to them in the tone of reproach (1 Kings ix. 13), " What is the high place whereunto ye go?" (ver. 29) : how can ye, instead of seeking me in my true sanctuary, turn to these miserable places, with their miserable gods? And yet these are named high places unto this day, in the sense of sanctuaries, and with the notion that they have something peculiar about them.

In vers. 30–38, the punishment. Ver. 30. Therefore say unto the house of Israel, Thus saith the Lord Jehovah, Are ye polluted in the way of your fathers, and do ye go a whoring after their abominations? 31. And when ye offer your gifts, when ye make your sons pass through the fire, ye pollute yourselves with all your abominations unto this day: and shall I be inquired of by you, O house of Israel? As I live, saith the Lord Jehovah, I will not be inquired of by you. 32. And that which cometh into your mind shall not be at all, when ye say, We shall be as the heathen, as the families of the countries, to serve wood and stone. 33. As I live, saith the Lord Jehovah, Surely with a mighty hand, and with outstretched arm, and with fury poured out, will I rule over you. 34. And I will lead you out from the peoples, and gather you out of the countries wherein ye were scattered, with a mighty hand, and with an outstretched arm, and with fury poured out. 35. And I will bring you into the wilderness of the peoples, and there will I plead with you face to face. 36. So as I pleaded with your fathers in the wilderness of the land of Egypt, will I plead with you, saith the Lord Jehovah. 37. And I will cause you to pass under the staff, and bring you into the bond of the covenant. 38. And I will purge out from you the rebels and the transgressors against me: I will lead them forth out of the land of their sojourning, and into the land of Israel he shall not come; and ye shall know that I am the LORD.

First, in vers. 30, 31, the refusal of the grace sought; then from ver. 32 on, the announcement of the continued punishment. The heathen stood under the divine long-suffering (Rom. iii. 25); not so Israel, to whom God had so gloriously made Himself known. Wherein the heathen may prosper, therein Israel must decline. The designation of the heathen gods as wood and stone, alone sufficient to counteract the strange notion which attributed a real existence to the heathen gods, is taken from Deut. iv. 28, xxviii. 36. "Will I rule over you" (ver. 33): for the friendly and gracious government of God they have given Him little thanks, and have wickedly withdrawn from Him. As God, however, must come to His sovereign rights, so His sovereignty now assumes a terrible form. The prophet speaks, in vers. 34, 35, to those who are already in exile, who can therefore no more be threatened with removal into exile. To those who fancied that with the removal into exile the judicial activity of God was already closed, and the dawn of the day of grace was immediately approaching, He announces a new phase of this judicial activity, similar to that which first came over Israel in the wilderness. If they are really led out of the former state into the new one, in which they underlie a second judgment, *formally* they are led into the wilderness, which here designates a state similar to that in which Israel was formerly in the wilderness. The wilderness is designated as "the wilderness of the peoples," in contradistinction to the former wilderness, where was only the howling of wild beasts (Deut. xxxii. 10), lions, serpents, and the like (Deut. viii. 15; Isa. xxx. 6). The new wilderness is one in which Israel is in the midst of the peoples, and can therefore be no ordinary wilderness, for wilderness and peoples exclude one another. It must rather be a symbolic or typical designation of the state of punishment and purification. The interchange of type and thing is in ver. 36 separated. From the defect of historical notices concerning the state of the exiles, we cannot show the fulfilment of this prophetic announcement. It is natural, however, to suppose that the part taken by the exiles in the political intrigues of the home country brought upon them also severe sufferings. A short time before, Jeremiah, in ch. xxix. 21, 22, predicted to Ahab and Zedekiah, the false prophets of the exile, who incited the people by their predictions against the Chaldean government, the downfall by Nebuchadnezzar. Besides, the threatening is conditional. Its fulfilment might be prevented by sincere repentance. Very many would take to heart this earnest warning of the prophet, and be thereby delivered from a participation in the threatened punishment. The staff in ver. 37 is the shepherd's staff, from the government of which they had withdrawn (Lev. xxvii. 32; Mic. vii. 14). By the decree of punishment they are brought to submit themselves again to this staff. By chastisement also they are brought into "the bond of the covenant," necessitated to yield to the conditions of the covenant, the laws of God; whereas they were heretofore without bond or bond, brothers of the free spirit (Isa. xlvi. 12). "Let the wicked be favoured, yet will he not learn righteousness; in the land of uprightness he will deal unjustly, and regard not the majesty of the Lord" (Isa. xxvi. 10). As once in the wilderness judgment was held on the generation that came out of Egypt, and the greater part was condemned not to enter Canaan (Num. xiv. 28–30), so shall it be also in the exile. The dreams of those who announce that Jerusalem will not fall, but rather in the briefest space all the exiles after the immediately approaching fall of the Chaldean monarchy shall return thither in vast numbers (Jer. xxviii. 1-4), will come to a miserable end. From the land of their sojourning (that is, the state of exile) they shall be brought out, not, as they think, to return home, but to meet with an overwhelming punishment. "He shall not come:" the rebels are here collected into one ideal person. "They shall know that I am the Lord:" this is the painful experience that will sooner or later force itself upon all those who despise salvation.

In vers. 39–44, the promise. Ver. 39. And ye, O house of Israel, thus saith the Lord Jehovah, Go ye, serve every one his idols, and hereafter surely ye will hearken unto me; and pollute ye no more my holy name with your gifts and your abominations. 40. For in my holy mountain, in the high mountain of Israel, saith the Lord Jehovah, there shall all the house of Israel, all of them in the land, serve me: there will

I accept them, and there will I require your heave-offerings, and the first-fruits of your oblations, with all your holy things. 41. I will accept you as a sweet savour, when I shall lead you out from the peoples, and gather you out of the countries wherein ye have been scattered; and I will be sanctified on you before the heathen. 42. And ye shall know that I am the Lord, when I bring you into the land of Israel, the land which I lifted up my hand to give to your fathers. 43. And there shall ye remember your ways, and all your doings, wherein ye have been defiled; and ye shall loathe yourselves in your own sight for all your evils that ye have committed. 44. And ye shall know that I am the Lord, when I deal with you for my name's sake, not according to your evil ways and your corrupt doings, O house of Israel, saith the Lord Jehovah.

Though they now do what they cannot leave off (ver. 39), the Lord regards it with calm equanimity, because He knows that a time comes when, penetrated by the severity of the divine judgment, they will return to Him.[1] They wished, however, at present to adhere to that which the future will reject of itself with contempt. The first fulfilment took place in the time immediately after the exile; to the last Paul refers in Rom. xi. 25. The proper author of the great change here announced in the temper and tendency of the people is God, who gives them a new spirit, and takes away the stony heart (ch. xi. 19). Yet they must and will do their own part (ch. xviii. 31): they must leave off their wicked opposition to the Holy Spirit (Acts vii. 51), and their sad unwillingness (Matt. xxiii. 37). Therein, along with the severity of the crushing divine judgments, will the love of God work, which displays itself gloriously in their redemption from their deliverance from the exile onwards, but above all in Christ. "Pollute ye no more my holy name:" every form of idolatry among the people of God was a desecration of the name of God, when the impotent and the abominable were preferred. "The height of the mountain of Israel" (ver. 40) is a spiritual mountain (comp. xvii. 23). "As a sweet savour will I accept you" (ver. 41): the people consecrating themselves anew to the Lord, appear as an acceptable offering. The practical explanation of this accept-

---

[1] אם לא is a particle of swearing. The preterite stands in place of the future, because the future is regarded as the present.

ance is, that God brings them back, and *sanctifies* or glorifies Himself among them before the heathen by the acts of His redeeming grace. To loathe in one's sight (ver. 43), is to become oneself an object of loathing (ch. vi. 9).

Ch. xxi. In vivid terms the prophet now places before the eyes of the people, captivated by foolish hopes, a figure of the fall of the city and kingdom, which formed the bright points of their hopes. The endeavour is everywhere visible, to obtain by the clearness of the description a representation of the reality not yet existing, but already germinating, and in this way to withdraw the people from their delusions, and make penitence take the place of politics.

The prophet first, in vers. 1–5, brings before the people in a riddle the catastrophe awaiting the mother country, to which all their longing was directed. Ver. 1. And the word of the Lord came unto me, saying, 2. Son of man, set thy face towards the right, and drop towards the south, and prophesy against the forest of the south field. 3. And say to the forest of the south, Hear the word of the LORD. Thus saith the Lord Jehovah, Behold, I will kindle a fire in thee, and it will devour every green tree in thee, and every dry tree: the flaming flame shall not be quenched, and all faces from south to north shall be scorched thereby. 4. And all flesh shall see that I the LORD have kindled it; it shall not be quenched. 5. And I said, Ah Lord Jehovah, they say of me, Doth he not speak parables?

Judea appears as the south land (ver. 2), from the standpoint of the exile. It is usual with the prophets to designate Chaldea, and in general the world-monarchy in inner Asia, as the north country, wherein the geographical situation is not so much regarded as the circumstance that the armies of this power entered the land from the north through Syria, and the captives were also carried away to the north. The forest in its density is a figure for the people. It is designated as the forest of the field, in opposition to that of the mountain, because it is here treated of a people of culture. The destruction of a people under the figure of a forest on fire appears already in Isa. ix. 18. "Green tree and dry tree" (ver. 3) are, according to the exposition in vers. 8, 9, the righteous and the unrighteous (comp. Luke xxiii. 31). The *faces* represent, as often, the whole persons. This is the noble material which the fire has to consume. Even its non-extinction (ver. 4) shows that the Lord kindled the fire. If we see that all human plans and devices, even the most promising, come to nothing, we are led to the confession that we have to do with personal omnipotence and righteousness, against which the battle is unavailing. The riddle is easy to solve, and the prophet has to do with a sharp-witted people; but the hearers *will* not understand (ver. 5), because the truth is unpleasant to them, and retire with a certain irony behind the difficulty of the form, and make as if they did not understand. To take away this miserable excuse from them, to punish them for their ironical hardness of hearing, he expresses the same in clear and plain terms in the following passage.

Ver. 6. And the word of the LORD came unto me, saying, 7. Son of man, set thy face toward Jerusalem, and drop toward the holy places, and prophesy against the land of Israel. 8. And say to the land of Israel, Thus saith the LORD, Behold, I am on thee, and will draw my sword out of its sheath, and will cut off from thee the righteous and the wicked. 9. Because I cut off from thee the righteous and the wicked, therefore shall my sword go forth out of its sheath on all flesh from south to north. 10. And all flesh shall know that I the LORD have drawn my sword out of its sheath: it shall not return. 11. And thou, son of man, sigh with the breaking of thy loins, and with bitterness shalt thou sigh before their eyes. 12. And it shall be, when they say unto thee, Wherefore sighest thou? then thou shalt say, For the tidings, because it cometh; and every heart shall melt, and all hands shall be feeble, and every spirit shall faint, and all knees shall dissolve into water: behold, it is come, and has happened, saith the Lord Jehovah.

"Drop toward the holy places" (ver. 7): to drop (comp. ver. 2) is a term of art to denote the prophetic utterance, taken from Deut. xxxii. 2, to which passage the word, wherever it occurs, points as definitely as an express citation. Moses there compares his word, the primeval form of all prophecy, with a fruitful rain, though it is a sharp discourse of punishment and repentance, and holds forth the crushing judgments of God. The salutary effect is the point of comparison. What is bitter to the mouth is wholesome to the heart. The word of God in all its parts, even there where it is sharper than a two-edged sword, is like the quickening rain. Of the *holy place* (the plural refers to the glory of the one sanctuary) as a *building* the prophet does not speak in the following words. All applies there to the people. The holy place here, as often (comp. especially Jer. vii. 4), can only be regarded as the spiritual abode of the people. The catastrophe, according to ver. 8, comes upon the righteous and the wicked. This is not in contradiction with ch. ix. 4, according to which the righteous, amidst the impending catastrophe, are the object of the protecting and sustaining activity of God. For if two suffer the same, yet it is not the same. To those who love God must *all things* be for the best (Rom. viii. 28). "From north to south" (ver. 9), from Dan to Beersheba, in the whole compass of the Jewish territory (comp. ver. 3). In the sentence, "it shall not return" (ver. 10), the subject is, according to ver. 4, not misfortune in its divine determination, but misfortune generally. That God has drawn the sword, will appear from the futility of all attempts to turn away the sword or the misfortune. The prophet laments in ver. 11 not from his own soul, but as representative of Israel.[1] Michaelis writes, "Because thou art set as a type of the future misfortune of the Jews." The loins of him are said to be broken whom acute pain robs of all power and strength. The *tidings* in ver. 12 is the account of the accomplished misfortune which the prophet, representing his people, wrapt into the future, has already received. All knees are dissolved as water, or into water, so that they become water, like water in laxity and incoherence. The prophet represents in his own person this future condition of the people.

Vers. 13–22. The figure already indicated in vers. 8–12, of the avenging sword of God, is here unfolded: we have here, so to speak, a sacred sword and battle song. Ver. 13. And the word of the Lord came unto me, saying, 14. Son of man, prophesy and say, Thus saith the Lord, Say, A sword, a sword is sharpened, and also furbished. 15. For slaughter to slay is it sharpened, and it is furbished that it may flash: or shall we rejoice over the rod of my son, despising every tree? 16. And he gave it to be furbished, that he might hold it with the

[1] Comp. Mic. i. 8; Isa. xx. 3, 4, xxi. 3, 4; *Christol.* i. 490 f.

palm: this sword is sharpened and furbished, that he may give it into the hand of the slayer. 17. Cry and howl, son of man; for it shall be upon my people, it shall be upon all the princes of Israel: they shall be devoted to the sword with my people: therefore smite upon the thigh. 18. For it is a trial, and how? Should the despising rod not be? saith the Lord Jehovah. 19. And thou, son of man, prophesy, and smite palm on palm, and the sword shall be doubled threefold: it is the sword of the slain, the sword of a slain man of the great, that pierces into them. 20. That the heart may faint, and the stumblings be multiplied at all their gates, I give the weight[1] of the sword: ah! it is made to flash, sharpened for slaughter. 21. Unite thyself, go to the right, give heed, go to the left, whither thy face is set. 22. And I also will smite my palm upon my palm, and make my fury rest: I the Lord have spoken.

"And also furbished" (ver. 14), so that with its terrible flash it dazzles the eyes of those against whom it is drawn. "The rod of the son, which despises all wood" (ver. 15), is the punishment hanging over Israel, which exceeds all other punishments in rigour, according to the law that is set forth in Luke xii. 47: every one is judged according to the measure of grace which he has received. This rod, says the Lord, is truly no object of joy.[2] The joy is the counterpart to the sighing in ver. 12; comp. ver. 17, "Have I not had cause enough to call thee to sighing, or shall we rejoice?" etc. "We"—I and thou—comes out from the soul of the people itself. For the emotion here applies not to the representative, but to those whose lot and mood are represented. The Lord first Himself takes the sharpened and polished sword into His hand (ver. 16), and then hands it over to the instruments of His punitive justice. In ver. 17 also the prophet is not to express his personal compassion, but to foreshadow the expression of those on whom the judgment fell. The words "for (it is) a trial" point with the utmost brevity to the character of the impending time, which presented itself in rosy hues to the politically excited people. Trial is a terrible word to a people that suffers the deepest calamities. When the trial comes, nothing remains undisclosed, nothing

---

[1] The sense of this word, occurring only here, can be determined only by the context.

[2] שוש with the accusative of the object of joy (Isa. xxxv. 1).

unrequited; every varnish disappears, and all glitter vanishes. With a view to the sanguine imaginations by which the people sought to banish the thought of the hardness of the times, the prophet then asks, "And how? Should the despising rod (the punishment that far outstrips all other punishments, ver. 15) not be?" And the answer to this question he gives in the names of God, which utter a loud *no* to these illusions. Clapping the hands (ver. 19) is a gesture of lively excited feeling, which may be of various kinds (2 Kings xi. 12; Job xxvii. 23), and is here the prognostic of an impending energetic action. The sword shall be doubled for the third time, three times doubled,—a combination of two different designations of the earnestness and energy of the divine punishment. That it is the sword of the slain points to this, that many shall thereby fall; that it is the sword of one slain of the great, of a slain one who is great, indicates that it rages not merely in the lower regions, but ascends to the highest (comp. ver. 30). The stumblings before the gates (ver. 20), at which in the sallies the fiercest conflict burns, are the heaps of the fallen over which a man stumbles. In ver. 21 the address is to the sword. "Unite thyself" alludes to the thrice doubled sword in ver. 19. In reality, the terrible weight is designated with which the divine judgment falls on him whom it is to strike. "Go to the right," "go to the left," intimates that the sphere of the judgment to be executed has wide dimensions; it embraces not merely Judea, but a whole group of peoples. "Give heed" corresponds to "unite thyself," and implies that the sword must and will do its part earnestly and zealously. The sword will perform the said actions, whither its face is set, where only God orders it to rage for merited punishment. "And I also" (ver. 22): this looks back to ver. 19, where God commands the *prophet* to smite on the hands. The fury *rests* when it reaches the object to which it is directed (ver. 13).

Vers. 23-37. Judah, who thinks himself above all the peoples, first incurs the divine vengeance, yet not to perpetual ruin; Ammon, that mocked at his calamity, shall follow him therein, but not resemble him in his restoration. The beginning is here also fearfully threatening, sharply cutting off all hope; yet, at the end, a ray of promise falls upon the chilly night.

Ver. 23. And the word of the LORD came unto me, saying, 24. And thou, son of man, appoint thee two ways, that the sword of the king of Babylon may come: they both shall come out of one land, and form a hand, form it at the head of the way to a city. 25. Thou shalt appoint a way, that the sword may come to Rabbah of the sons of Ammon, and to Judah in Jerusalem the fortified. 26. For the king of Babylon stands at the mother of the way, at the head of the two ways, to use divinations: shakes the arrows, consults the teraphim, inspects the liver. 27. In his right hand is the divination, Jerusalem, to place battering-rams, to open the mouth in the slaughter, to lift up the voice with the war-cry, to place rams at the gates, to cast a mount, to build towers. 28. And it is to them a treacherous divination in their eyes, that was sworn with an oath to them; and he calls to remembrance iniquity, that he may be taken.

Ver. 24. The action belongs here also only to the inner world. The external representation would descend into the puerile. Because the matter belongs to the internal, the mere command suffices; the execution is not mentioned. We have here the outline that is carried out in what follows. According to it, two ways are parted, not from home, from Babylon; the parting commences at a determinate point, at which the prophet in the very beginning is placed, because the decision is there made. The *hand*, or the guide, points to the end of the way, which cannot always pursue its end on account of the difficulties presented by the country, and indicates the direction only for a short distance. The city is still undefined; the definition follows in ver. 25. " In Jerusalem" (ver. 25): this shows that Judah has his essence in Jerusalem. Materially, Jerusalem lay in Judah; spiritually, Judah in Jerusalem. " The fortified:" this points out how far Judah lay in Jerusalem. It is the beating heart of the land, and therefore is fortified in the strongest manner. The historical presupposition is, that Ammon no less than Judah has incurred the anger of the king of Babylon. With Judah it belonged to the same anti-Chaldaic coalition; and it is antecedently settled that it, no less than Judah, had to expect the vengeance of the king of Babylon. It lay somewhat nearer Chaldea than Jerusalem, and hence the human probability was that the judgment would commence there. But the prophet learns the contrary by divine revelation. By the providence of God, who turns the hearts of men as the water-brooks, it comes to pass that judgment begins at the house of God. The mother of the way (ver. 26) is the main road, from which two by-roads, the daughters, branch off. That there are here two, is asserted in what follows, at the head of the *two* ways. What is said of divination is only dress taken from the manner in which decisions were usually made among the Chaldeans. The thought is simply that, in the providence of God, who is here to be conceived as standing behind the divination, which is in itself utterly delusive, according to vers. 28 and 34, and bending it to his own objects, the king will first march against Jerusalem, lulling itself asleep with delusive hopes. The practice of soothsaying, which here includes the interpretation of signs, is the general; the three different species follow. The teraphim are intermediate gods, serving for the investigation of the future.[1] "In his right hand is the divination, Jerusalem" (ver. 27)—is handled with the right hand: he has the decision spiritually therein; is determined in his actions by the decision given for Jerusalem through the divination in its three forms, or at least in the most weighty of them. The placing of the battering-rams is followed by the cry accompanying them; it is then taken up again, and with it the other directly practical measures are connected. The slaughter-cry of the besiegers is called slaughter, because the slaughter is virtually contained in it. The inhabitants of Jerusalem (ver. 28) foreboded not, in their blindness, what was before them. They repelled every thought of the impending destruction, as if the question was only about delusive soothsaying (the true prophets they degraded to miserable soothsayers; the false, who promised them good fortune, they elevated into true prophets); whereas it was in truth about a fixed and irrevocable decree of God,[2] which is made known to them anew by His servant the prophet, the son of man, behind whom the Almighty stands. In this manner Judah brings to remembrance the iniquity, to atone for which by sincere repentance was his immediate duty.

[1] *Christol.* on Hos. iii. 4, Zech. x. 2.
[2] The sworn of the oath is that which is sworn to by oath, as the announcement of destruction in Ezekiel is mostly introduced by the formula, "As I live."

Ver. 29 shows that Israel is spoken of in the words, "and he calls to remembrance."

Vers. 29-37. We have here the second paragraph of the section, connected with the first not merely by the formula, "And the word of the Lord came unto me, saying," but by the placing of Judah over against Ammon. The beginning here again is threatening. In the course of the prophecy, however, reference is made to the glorious resurrection of Israel after the judgments, whereas Ammon is doomed by them to utter perdition.

Ver. 29. Therefore thus saith the Lord Jehovah, Because ye bring your iniquity to remembrance, since your transgressions are discovered, and your sins are seen in all your doings; because ye are come to remembrance, ye shall be taken with the palm. 30. And thou, slain wicked one, prince of Israel, whose day comes at the time of the iniquity of the end: 31. Thus saith the Lord Jehovah, Remove the head-band, and take off the crown: this is not this; to exalt the low, and abase the high. 32. Overturn, overturn, overturn will I make it: this also is not, until he come whose right it is; to him I give it. 33. And thou, son of man, prophesy and say, Thus saith the Lord Jehovah of the children of Ammon and of their reproach: and thou shalt say, A sword, a sword is drawn to slay, furbished sufficiently,[1] in order to flash. 34. While they see vanity for thee, while they divine a lie to thee, to set thee on the necks of the slain among the wicked, whose day is come in the time of the iniquity of the end. 35. Return (thy sword) into its sheath: in the place where thou wast created, in the land of thy origin will I judge thee. 36. And I will pour out my anger upon thee; the fire of my indignation I will blow upon thee, and I will give thee into the hand of burning men skilful to destroy. 37. Thou shalt be for fuel to the fire; thy blood shall be in the midst of the land: thou shalt not be remembered; for I the Lord have spoken it.

They bring their iniquity to remembrance (ver. 29) by this, that they continue their sinful life in the face of judgment. The *palm* is that of the minister of the divine vengeance.

---

[1] Luther, "that it shall consume." להכיל (comp. xxiii. 32) means properly embracing, filling up the whole sphere of a polished sword. Luther has derived the form from אכל, to consume.

The king, in ver. 30,[1] includes the people under him, and comes forward as their representative. It is not implied in this, that he shall personally and individually submit to the sword, which would be in contradiction with ch. xii. 13, according to which he shall come to Babylon, but not see it. This can be the less thought of, as the sword in the foregoing passage is God's sword of vengeance, the symbol of His punitive justice. The "iniquity of the end" is the iniquity that brings on the end, the catastrophe, by which the measure will at length be made full. The iniquity of the end for Zedekiah was resistance to the faithful counsel of Jeremiah. The infinitive in ver. 31 denotes the mere action, without stating from whom it proceeds. Ideally regarded, the king bears, as the representative of the whole people, along with the crown, the *head-band*, or priestly cap.[2] The two are closely connected. The crown without the band is an empty show. The forgiveness of sins, which was secured by the mediation of the high priest, whose dignity was overthrown with the fall of the sanctuary, forms the foundation of all the royal blessings of God. In the Messiah, in whom the kingdom attained to its full reality, a real union of the kingly and priestly offices is to take place (Zech. vi.), which were practically divided under the Old Testament on account of human weakness. "This is not this:" by this an entire revolution of the existing state of things is signified. This is also intimated by the abasing of the high, and the exalting of the low.[3] In a general overthrow the low is exalted, even by the fact that it becomes like the high, who are involved in the same downfall. The people have in their procedure turned the lowest into the highest; and in just retribution, the same takes place in their experience. All is levelled. The threefold repetition of *overturning*, or destruction, in ver. 32, points to its completeness. "An overturning I make *it*"—the existing state of things, or even the land.

---

[1] On vers. 30–32 more extended discussions are given in *Christol.* ii. p. 562 f.

[2] מצנפת is only used for the diadem of the high priest, and stands for this in the Pentateuch, which Ezekiel closely follows no less than eleven times.

[3] שפלה is masc., with ה unaccented, which here only serves to make the form fuller and more sonorous.

"This also," the new state of things produced by the destruction, "is not," has no permanence. Overthrow follows on overthrow, as on the Chaldean period soon follows the Persian, and so on, till at length the Messiah comes, brings all into order, and founds a state of unchangeable duration. The Messiah is designated as He "whose right it is." The right is God's, according to Deut. i. 17; and this right He gives to the Messiah, as His representative on earth, that He may uphold it there, and make an end of the reign of wrong, according to Ps. lxxii. 1, to which passage there is a pointed reference.[1]

The children of Ammon (ver. 33) represent the world-power hostile to the kingdom of God. Yet the representative is not taken accidentally out of the multitude of the heathen peoples hostile to the kingdom of God; but the prophet takes occasion from the circumstances of the time. Ammon had at that time, no less than Judah, incurred the anger of the Chaldeans; and so it was natural to exemplify in him the general truth; the more natural, because the vengeance was first to fall on Judah, while Ammon appeared to come out of the affair with high shoes, and mocked Judah, who had to pay the score. "Their reproach"—the insults which they heaped upon Judah. The prophet foresees that the Ammonites, on the approach of danger, will withdraw from the coalition (comp. Lam. i. 2), and on the catastrophe of Jerusalem give free course to their ancient hatred against Judah. Judah exchanges the prophecy that was unfavourable to him for the divination (ver. 28), and by this fatal exchange falls: Ammon exchanges (ver. 34) the divination favourable to him for the prophecy, and thereby prepares himself at all events for the downfall. The *necks* of the slain are specially prominent, because they have there received the death-stroke. All the resistance of Ammon is vain (ver. 35), for they have God for their foe. The prophet sees before his eyes how they draw the sword to guard against

---

[1] At the same time to the prophecy concerning Shiloh, the peaceful, to whom the peoples shall adhere, in Gen. xlix. 10. The letters of this word form the beginnings of the words in Ezekiel (*Christol.* i. 99). "To whom I give it;" properly, and I give it. The suffix refers to the right. The fundamental passage (Ps. lxxii. 1) requires this reference. The person to whom it is given being known from the context, needs no closer designation.

the foe. This explains the phrase "return into its sheath," without express mention of the sword. We have here the fundamental passage for Matt. xxvi. 52. "Burning men" (ver. 36) are those who are filled with glowing anger. "Thou shalt not be remembered" (ver. 37). From the times of the Maccabees, the Ammonites and Moabites have quite disappeared out of history.

Ch. xxii. In amplification of ch. xxi. 29, the prophet depicts in three paragraphs the sins of Judah, by which the judgment depicted in the preceding passage is brought on, and thereby confirms the conviction that it is inevitable.

Ver. 1. And the word of the Lord came unto me, saying, 2. And thou, son of man, wilt thou judge, wilt thou judge the city of blood? and make known to her all her abominations. 3. And say, Thus saith the Lord Jehovah, A city that sheddeth blood in the midst of it, that its time may come, and maketh idols over itself for defilement. 4. In thy blood which thou hast shed thou art become guilty; and in thy abominations which thou hast made thou art defiled; and thou hast brought nigh thy days, and art come to thy years: therefore I give thee for a reproach to the heathen, and for a mocking to all lands. 5. They that are nigh, and those that are far from thee, shall mock at thee, thou unclean of name and full of confusion. 6. Behold, the princes of Judah are every one according to his arm in thee, to shed blood. 7. Father and mother they lightly esteem in thee; with the stranger they deal by oppression in thy midst; the widow and the orphan they vex in thee. 8. My sanctuaries thou hast despised, and hast profaned my sabbaths. 9. Men of slander were in thee, to shed blood; and in thee they ate upon the mountains; they committed lewdness in thy midst. 10. In thee one uncovers a father's nakedness; in thee they humble her that is unclean in her separation. 11. And one commits abomination with his neighbour's wife; and another lewdly defiles his daughter-in-law; and another in thee humbleth his sister, his father's daughter. 12. In thee they take a gift to shed blood; usury and increase thou takest, and overreachest thy neighbour with oppression, and forgettest me, saith the Lord Jehovah. 13. And, behold, I smite my palm at thy gain, which thou hast made, and at thy blood which is in thy midst. 14. Will thy heart be stedfast or thy hands be strong in the days when I shall deal with thee? I the LORD have spoken, and will do it. 15. And I will scatter thee among the heathen, and disperse thee in the countries, and consume thy filthiness out of thee. 16. And thou shalt be profaned in thee before the eyes of the heathen, and thou shalt know that I am the LORD.

The question in ver. 2, " Wilt thou judge, judge?" is here, as in ch. xx. 4, an expression of the impatience to which the son of man is too slow. "Wilt thou judge?" is, in fact, the same as, Judge thou; and with this agrees the addition "make known." "Over itself for defilement" (ver. 3): to heap upon itself defilement with its consequences. The days and years in ver. 4 are those of decision, of the crisis, which she brings on by her violent dealing: for as a man drives, so it goes. The mocking in ver. 5 suits the destiny; and to this refer also the "unclean of name," on account of her ignominious walk (comp. xxiii. 10), and the "full of confusion," unrest and tumult, as they are the companions of the accomplished catastrophe.[1] According to ver. 6, the arm, not the right, is the *measure* with the great. The Sabbaths in ver. 8 are related to the sanctuaries as the part to the whole. The idea of the sanctuary is as broad as that of the religion of Israel. All that the Holy One has instituted, consecrated, and commanded, is a sanctuary for His people. The moral prescriptions also belong thereto. The *despising* takes place in many ways. All belongs to this, which in the sequel is enumerated in detail,— every violation of the commands of God, every kind of indifference, every homage to a false religion. The desecration of the Sabbath does not consist merely in breaking the external rest: all sins in thought, word, or deed are a breach of the Sabbath (comp. Isa. lviii. 13, 14; and here, ch. xx. 21). Instead of "men of *slander*" (ver. 9), it is properly "men of the *slanderer*." The slanderer appears as an ideal person, to whom belong the individual slanderers. *Malignant* slanderers are meant, who bring false charges, by which life is endangered. The eating on the mountains, the seats of idolatry, belongs to the department of the first table. The prophet is prone to interweave with one

---

[1] מהומה, as penal evil, also Deut. xxviii. 20; comp. Deut. vii. 23, 2 Chron. xv. 5, and especially here, vii. 7.

another the sins against the two tables, and in fact they proceed from one source, and the distinction of religion and morals is a fiction contrary to experience. He that is not true to his God cannot love his neighbour. The lewdness with the stepmother (ver. 10) points to Lev. xx. 11 (comp. 1 Cor. v. 1). The prophet says not, in ver. 11, that the transgressions named are common in Jerusalem, but only that such cases occur there. Where individuals go so far, the moral atmosphere must be generally corrupt. The hand in ver. 13 is the penal one. Along with the gain, it strikes the blood, that is, blood-guiltiness.[1] The heart fails them, the hands sink down powerless by the side (ver. 14), when God's vengeance for such wickedness comes upon them. The removal of the uncleanness of Jerusalem (ver. 15) is effected by the extirpation of the sinful inhabitants. Jerusalem has desecrated the sanctuaries of the Lord (ver. 8); therefore shall it also be desecrated for a requital (ver. 16). It has wickedly insulted the dignity of God; for this it must suffer the loss of its own dignity. "In thee," so that thou must experience in thyself the desecration, whereas before thou didst send it forth from thee. Such things always return to him from whom they proceed.

Vers. 17–22. Corrupt Israel must be molten in the fire of the divine judgment. 17. And the word of the LORD came unto me, saying, 18. Son of man, the house of Israel is to me become dross: they are all brass, and tin, and iron, and lead, in the midst of the furnace; they are the dross of silver. 19. Therefore thus saith the Lord Jehovah, Because ye are all become dross, therefore, behold, I will gather you into the midst of Jerusalem. 20. As a man gathereth silver, and brass, and iron, and lead, and tin into the furnace, that he may blow the fire upon it, to melt them; so will I gather in my anger and in my fury, and lay you down and melt you. 21. And I will gather you, and blow upon you the fire of my wrath; and ye shall be melted in the midst thereof. 22. As silver is melted in the midst of the furnace, so shall ye be melted in the midst thereof; and ye shall know that I the LORD have poured out my fury upon you.

"Dross" (ver. 18), properly waste, inferior metal, which is mingled with the precious. In the spiritual department the

[1] היו, a plural of quantity: much of which is under thee.

silver may become altogether dross. The *furnace* is Jerusalem, according to its destination to serve for a smelting-pot. Dross of silver, is silver that has become dross. They are all gathered into Jerusalem (ver. 19), as the people far and wide, under the pressure of the foe, seek refuge in the fortified city. In the whole section the judgment is regarded not in the light of purification, but in that of destruction; as Ezekiel usually considers the population of Jerusalem as an ungodly multitude doomed to be extirpated.

Vers. 23-31. In this third section the judgment is represented as inevitable, because the corruption pervades all ranks of the people. Ver. 23. And the word of the LORD came unto me, saying, 24. Son of man, say unto her, Thou art a land that is not cleansed, that has no rain in the day of indignation. 25. The conspiracy of her prophets is in her midst, like a roaring lion ravening the prey: they devour souls, they take treasure and precious things, they multiply her widows in her midst. 26. Her priests violate my law, and profane my sanctuaries: they distinguish not between holy and profane, and they discern not between the unclean and the clean,[1] and they hide their eyes from my sabbaths; and I am profaned in their midst. 27. Her princes in her midst are like wolves ravening the prey, to shed blood, to destroy souls, and to make gain. 28. And her prophets daub them with absurdity, seeing vanity and divining a lie unto them, saying, Thus saith the Lord Jehovah, when Jehovah hath not spoken. 29. The people of the land exercise oppression and commit robbery, and vex the poor and needy, and oppress the stranger without right. 30. And I sought for a man among them that built up the wall, and stood in the breach before me for the land, that I might not destroy it; and I found none. 31. Therefore I pour out my indignation upon them; I consume them with the fury of my wrath: their own way I lay upon their heads, saith the Lord Jehovah.

A land that has no rain in the day of indignation (ver. 24), is a land that in the outburst of the divine judgment finds no grace; and simply, as the connection shows, because its impurity is not removed. The rain in the day of indignation would be a benefit. It would quench the flame of the divine

[1] " Know" in a judicial sense, that is, pass sentence.

indignation. To the indignation, the full energy of which is here called forth by the uncleanness, may be applied that which is said in the Song of Songs (viii. 7) of the fire of love: "Many waters cannot quench love, neither can the rivers drown it." The false prophets (ver. 25), who have got the upper hand so far that the true cannot prevail beside them, but that they alone count as prophets, rob the goods and devour the souls, in so far as they stand by to help forward the robbing and murdering acts of the great (ver. 27), and sharpen not, but rather soothe their conscience by saying, Peace, peace, when there is no peace. Thus they are accomplices in the robbing and murdering course of the great, who have them in their pay. They deport themselves as smooth and peaceful men, and present themselves as men of tenderness, in contrast with the rough preachers of repentance, the true prophets; but when examined in the light, they are thieves and murderers. To this they are as it were *sworn*. That the words are to be so understood, is shown by their relation to ver. 27, where the same is said of the nobles, and by repetition in ver. 28, which serves to explain the sense. The moral principle that is in keeping with the inclination of the people is charged upon the priests, who endeavour by a violent interpretation to bring it into harmony with the law of God. "And profane my sanctuaries:" these include all that is commanded of God; comp. xxii. 8. To the distinguishing between holy and profane, clean and unclean, corresponds, in the fundamental passage, Lev. x. 11, "And to teach the children of Israel all the statutes which the Lord hath spoken unto them." The law of the Sabbath is given as an example. This they rob of its deep spiritual import, and limit it to the external rest, as if it were given for animals, and not for men, who are to serve God in spirit; comp. on. xxii. 8. Because they thus let down the commandments of God to the level of man, and make them minister to human inclination, God Himself is desecrated by them: in place of the dread and holy God, who visits the iniquity of the fathers upon the children, appears a lax and sin-favouring god, who creates no one, and is glad if any one will only acknowledge him, and is thankful for every bow that is made to him. The princes (ver. 27), the political authorities and officials, resemble the wolves in their ravenous bloodthirstiness, for the satisfaction of which the party-spirit of the times affords them a welcome occasion. The false prophets recur once more, in ver. 28, as abettors of the nobles, to whom they hold out deliverance, and thereby confirm them in their shameful course, instead of vehemently testifying against their sins, and setting before them the judgments of God. On daubing with absurdity, see ch. xiii. 10. In ver. 29, after the three orders of shepherds follow the people. What is meant by building a wall and mounting a breach (ver. 30), we learn from ch. xiii. 5. Jeremiah, by his powerful preaching of repentance, presented himself as such a public deliverer; but they despised him, and he could gain no position. The man alone is nothing. The position must be added, and the people must gather around him. One " against whom every man contends" cannot avert the judgment of God; he can only accelerate it.

Ch. xxiii. We have here the closing passage of ch. xx.–xxiii.,—an extended survey of the whole historical development of Israel, the result of which is the inevitableness of the judgment from which the elders had sought deliverance. Israel and Judah appear, in keeping with ch. xvi., under the figure of two harlots, to whose rebellious course an end must at length be put.

In vers. 1–4 the introduction, which affords the preliminary acquaintance with the two evil characters. Ver. 1. And the word of the LORD came unto me, saying, 2. Son of man, there were two women, daughters of one mother. 3. And they committed whoredom in Egypt; in their youth they committed whoredom: there were their breasts pressed, and there they handled their virgin bosoms. 4. And their names were Oholah the great, and Oholibah her sister; and they became mine, and bare sons and daughters: and their names were Samaria Oholah, and Jerusalem Oholibah.

The mother in ver. 2 is the people in general. The prophet makes the bipartition of the people not to begin with the separation of the kingdoms, but to be already extant in Egypt, in harmony with the blessing of Jacob (Gen. xlix.), in which the two tribes of Judah and Ephraim stand out absolutely before the others, and appear as two independent powers. In ver. 3 we have the participation in Egyptian customs, in the idolatry and moral corruption of Egypt in the former times, which is attested in so many ways in the books of Moses. "In their youth:" this points to the corruption that manifested itself in the very beginning of their existence. "Their virgin bosoms:" at that time Israel was still unmarried: the marriage with Jehovah took place when the covenant was made at Sinai. But she was even at that time betrothed. This is proved by what God had done to the patriarchs, and by the circumcision to which they had submitted; and hence their unchaste conduct fell under the judgment of Deut. xxii. 23 f. Their business was to prepare themselves as a pure virgin for marriage. The great, in ver. 4, is the elder, according to the usage of the language. This refers to the precedence of Joseph in Egypt, who was crowned among his brethren (Gen. xlix. 26); to that of Ephraim in the time of Joshua and the judges; and to that of Benjamin, belonging to the ten tribes, in the time of Saul. Judah attained the supremacy at a very late period in the time of David. These relations are treated of at full length in Ps. lxxviii. The elder sister is called Oholah, her tent, that can call a tent her own, that has a house of her own, an independent existence. The tent, without further distinction, can only be the dwelling. Similar is the name of Esau's wife, Oholibamah (Gen. xxxvi. 2)—my tent is high, I have a high tent. The younger sister is called Oholibah, my tent is in her; Jehovah being speaker. The name refers to the advantage which Judah had on the separation of the kingdoms, in the possession of the true sanctuary. At the close of the introduction the well-known historical names are given, along with the significant names formed by the prophet.

Vers. 5-10 now treat of Oholah, her adultery with Assyria, and the punishment, the instrument of which was the same people which she had made the object of her impure love. Ver. 5. And Oholah played the harlot under me, and doted on her lovers, on Assyria, her neighbour, 6. Clothed in purple, captains and rulers, all of them comely young men, knights riding upon horses. 7. And she bestowed her whoredoms upon them, all of them the choice of the sons of Assyria; and with all on whom she doted, with all their abominations was she defiled. 8. And she left not her whoredoms with Egypt;

for they lay with her in her youth, and handled her virgin bosom, and poured out their whoredoms upon her. 9. Wherefore I delivered her into the hand of her lovers, into the hands of the sons of Assyria, on whom she doted. 10. These uncovered her nakedness; they took her sons and daughters, and herself they slew with the sword, and she became a name among women; and they executed judgment upon her.

"Played the harlot under me" (ver. 5): this is to be explained by Hos. iv. 12, where it is said directly of the people of the ten tribes, "And they have gone a whoring from under their God." The woman is under the man (Rom. vii. 2); and if she in this state have to do with another, she incurs the judgment. "Her neighbour;" that is, who or when they are come into her neighbourhood.² The neighbours recur in ver. 12. The opposite we have in ver. 14: there the far are cherished. We have here the ground which tempted Oholah to become unfaithful to her God. It lay in this, that the paramour Assyria came into her neighbourhood, and placed his grandeur before her. Therein lay the temptation to sue for his favour to ward off injury. The adultery has here not so much a religious as a political import. The paramour, on whose account Israel forsakes his God, is Assyria itself, not its god, though they endeavoured, no doubt from fear of the people, to make friends of its gods also. The historical situation, which the prophet has here before his eye, is thus represented in the *Christology*, i. p. 190, on the ground of the predictions of the Israelitish prophet Hosea: "The people, sorely oppressed by Assyria, seek now to obtain help from Egypt against Assyria, now to be on friendly terms with the latter." Thus the situation is precisely described in Hos. vii. 11, "They call to Egypt; they go to Assyria." What threatened Israel was, according to Hos. viii. 10, "the burden of the king of princes," the king of Assyria (ver. 9). This they endeavoured to avert partly by their adulterous arts, partly by appealing to the king of Egypt. "Assyria alone is the king *combatant*, Hos. v. 13, x. 6." This was the great sin of Israel, that in their political oppression they sought help in man, even in their oppressors, instead of turning with heartfelt confidence to their God, the only one to whom to surrender oneself unconditionally is not

¹ קרובים takes the place of a whole sentence.

to degrade oneself. Ver. 6 describes with a touch of irony how Oholah fell into this unfortunate connection with Assyria. The thought is, that her eyes and heart were blinded and captivated by the power of Assyria. That, however, is named which strikes the eye of a worldly-minded woman. Ver. 7 points to this, that their idols are inseparable from the world-powers, as powers beyond and above them, but themselves made objective and quite incorporated with them, so that to defile herself with the Assyrians is at the same time to defile herself with their idols (comp. ver. 30). Besides Assyria, Oholah played the harlot also with Egypt (ver. 8), that land into the shameful spiritual slavery of which she had already fallen in former times (ver. 3). With this compare 2 Kings xvii. 4, according to which Hoshea, the last king of Israel, brought on the final catastrophe by refusing the tribute to the king of Assyria, in reliance on Egypt. This was only one out of many acts which Ezekiel here includes. The uncovering of the nakedness (ver. 10) denotes the ignominious treatment which Israel must suffer from Assyria, as a punishment for her revolt to Egypt. Oholah is slain with the sword: the proper substance of the people, the men fit for service, fell in the war, while the weaker portion was carried into exile. "She became a name among women," famous among the nations by the exemplary punishment which she suffered.

In vers. 11–35, Oholibah or Jerusalem. First, in vers. 11–21, her guilt. 11. And her sister Oholibah saw (this), and she corrupted her lust still more than she, and her whoredoms more than the whoredoms of her sister. 12. She doted on the sons of Assyria, captains and rulers, her neighbours, clothed in splendour, knights riding on horses, all of them comely young men. 13. And I saw that she was defiled: one way was to both of them. 14. And she added to her whoredoms; and she saw men portrayed upon the wall, images of the Chaldeans, drawn in ruddle, 15. Girt with girdles on their loins, waving turbans on their heads, all of them looking like knights, the likeness of the sons of Babylon, the Chaldeans in the land of their birth. 16. And she doted on them for that which her eyes saw, and sent messengers unto them to Chaldea. 17. And the sons of Babylon came to her into a bed of love, and defiled her with their whoredom; and she was defiled with them, and her soul was estranged from them. 18. And she uncovered her whoredoms, and uncovered her nakedness: and my soul was estranged from her, as my soul was estranged from her sister. 19. And she multiplied her whoredoms, remembering the days of her youth, when she played the harlot in the land of Egypt. 20. And she doted upon her paramours, whose flesh is the flesh of asses, and their issue the issue of horses. 21. And thou didst visit the lewdness of thy youth, when a man of Egypt handled thy bosom, on account of the breasts of thy youth.

"And her sister saw" (ver. 11) the shameful course of Oholah, and the divine vengeance. Already should the first have filled her with deep loathing and abhorrence. Instead of this, she behaved still worse: according to what follows, her adultery was multiplied still more: she did not rest with those near, but sent also to those far away. The seeing of God (ver. 13) holds out a bad prospect. We expect that it will not fare better with Oholibah than with her sister, unless she repent in time. In ver. 14 f. we have her impure intercourse with the Chaldeans. This passage is important for the history. That the Chaldeans, before they attained the supremacy, and while they were under the sway of Assyria, sought an alliance with Judah in the war against Assyria, is shown by the embassy of Merodach Baladan to Hezekiah (2 Kings xx., Isa. xxxix.; comp. Gesenius on the passage). According to our passage, however, attempts must have been made by Judah also to form a connection with the Chaldeans, and certainly at the time when the Assyrian monarchy still existed; and the initiative in regard to the whole relation must have been taken by Judah, and consequently before the embassy of Merodach Baladan. For the occasion for the adulterous intercourse is here stated to be this, that Oholibah sees Chaldeans portrayed on the wall. This implies that she had not yet seen living Chaldeans. In form it belongs only to the dress which Ezekiel takes from that which he observed among the Chaldeans around him. There such wall-pictures for the glorification of the people and their victories were found; whereas in Jerusalem they certainly were not in existence. The real meaning, however, can only be this, that Judah, in distinction from the relation to Assyria, which arose from the fact that Assyria came into the land (ver. 12), sought a connection with the Chaldeans, on the mere report of their military valour. The images on the walls are, in fact, the fancy forms, raised up by hearsay, of the Chaldeans, as a brave and aspiring power, in which help might be found against the old oppressor Assyria. The representation in ver. 14 refers to the Chaldeans themselves, and not to their idols; as, according to that which history relates of Hezekiah, the Chaldeans themselves, and not their idols, were the object of idolatrous reliance.[1] "Drawn in ruddle:" red is the most suitable colour for men of war. The girdle (ver. 15) is the war-girdle (Isa. v. 27). "In the land of their birth" forms the contrast to the Assyrians, whom they had come to see in their own land. There seems to be an allusion to Gen. xi. 28, where Ur of the Chaldees (to which Babylon of the Chaldeans here corresponds) is designated as the native land of Abraham's family. The native land of the Chaldees is at the same time that of Israel. The original blood-relationship might perhaps have come to utterance in this political intercourse. The messengers (ver. 16) whom Jerusalem sent to Chaldea, were probably the occasion of the embassy sent from the Chaldeans, according to Isaiah and 2 Kings, who were to take a view of the resources of the power proposing an alliance. It is antecedently probable that not Babylon, but the weaker power, took the initiative. This visiting of the remote Chaldeans was a denial of the power and will of God to help His people. Had their eyes been open, they would have perceived, that if the proposal took effect, it could only end in a change of masters. In this view Isaiah had already anticipated our prophet. As the sending to Egypt, so the proposed treaty with the Chaldeans was the object of vehement prophetic rebuke. "And her soul was estranged from them" (ver. 17); properly, disjointed from those to whom she had grown, as it were, a limb; the opposite of the expression, "My soul is fast bound to your daughter" (Gen. xxxiv. 8). Having attained the supremacy, the Chaldeans turned the rough side out, cast off the mask under which their selfishness had concealed itself,

---

[1] The form כַּשְׂדָּיִים, instead of כַּשְׂדִּים, which was usual in Palestine, is a Chaldaizing one: in Daniel the singular is כַּשְׂדָּי, the plur. כַּשְׂדָּאִין. In ver. 15 is the usual Heb. form, which the Masoretes wish to place here also. Similar changes occur elsewhere also in Ezekiel.

and now the vague desires of the deluded Jerusalem ceased. Estrangement—this is the usual end of impure love, of selfishness disguised in love. According to ver. 18, the matter does not end with this, that she does not find the expected satisfaction in the adulterous intercourse with Chaldea of long continuance; by her shameless and disgraceful devotion to those unworthy associates, she has estranged from herself the only true Friend in heaven and on earth. But now, instead of returning with penitence and regret to the Friend of her youth, and entreating His forgiveness, she follows after new adulterers (ver. 19): when she became wearied of the Chaldeans, she turned again to the Egyptians, her former adulterers; comp. ver. 3. The paramours (ver. 20)—a derisive term, as it is elsewhere used only of concubines—corresponds to the adulterers in ver. 5. As there the adulterers are the Assyrians, so here the Egyptians, to whom the *her* refers. The nations with which Jerusalem enters into impure intercourse appear now as a unity, and again as a plurality. The real import of the words, "their flesh," and so on, is the great propensity of the Egyptians to enter into impure political intercourse; so that Jerusalem may there expect full satisfaction for her adulterous lust. The falling power of Egypt sought to provide a prop for itself by diplomatic art. Asses and horses come into view as particularly lecherous animals. The *flesh* is named, because the lechery has its seat there. Jehoiakim, Jehoiachin, Zedekiah, all three met their downfall by conspiring with the Egyptians against the Chaldeans. The sudden transition to the address in ver. 21 is explained by this, that the prophet has here before his eyes the actual state of affairs. "And thou didst visit the lewdness of thy youth:" the falling back into the old sin is, as it were, a visit which is paid to that which ought to be hated and avoided. The words, "when a man of Egypt handled," and so on, refer to the attempt of the Egyptians to draw the people in their first beginnings into the Egyptian unity, and so to nationalize them,—an attempt to which the youth of the people furnished the occasion. That the attempt went before and along with the cruel measures of which history speaks, we cannot doubt. This lay in the nature of things. History also presents several traces of the more friendly disposition of the Egyptians; for ex., the conduct of the Egyptian king's daughter to Moses, and the gifts of the Egyptians to the departing Israelites.

In vers. 22–35, the transgression of Oholibah is followed by her punishment. Ver. 22. Therefore, Oholibah, thus saith the Lord Jehovah, Behold, I will awaken thy lovers against thee, from whom thy soul is estranged, and I will bring them upon thee from every side; 23. The sons of Babylon, and all the Chaldeans; Pekod, and Shoa, and Koa, all the sons of Assyria with them: comely young men, captains and rulers all of them; knights and counsellors, riding on horses all of them. 24. And they shall come against thee with sabre,[1] chariot, and wheel, and with a multitude of nations; target, and shield, and helmet they shall set against thee round about: and I will set judgment before them, and they shall judge thee with their judgments. 25. And I will set my jealousy upon thee, and they shall deal with thee in fury: thy nose and thine ears they shall take away, and thy remnant shall fall by the sword: they shall take thy sons and thy daughters, and thy remnant shall be consumed with fire. 26. And they shall strip thee of thy clothes, and take away thy fair jewels. 27. And I will make thy lewdness to cease from thee, and thy whoredom from the land of Egypt; and thou shalt not lift up thine eyes to them, nor remember Egypt any more. 28. For thus saith the Lord Jehovah, Behold, I will deliver thee into the hands of those whom thou hatest, into the hand of those from whom thy soul is estranged. 29. And they shall deal with thee in hatred, and shall take away all thy earning, and leave thee naked and bare; and the nakedness of thy whoring, and thy lewdness, and thy whoredoms, shall be uncovered. 30. This shall be done unto thee for thy whoring after the heathen, because thou art polluted with their abominations. 31. In the way of thy sister thou hast walked, and I give her cup into thy hand. 32. Thus saith the Lord Jehovah, The cup of thy sister shalt thou drink, the deep and the wide: thou shalt be a scoff and a mockery of large measure. 33. Thou shalt be filled with drunkenness and sorrow; the cup of wasting and desolation shalt thou drink, the cup of thy sister Samaria. 34. And thou shalt drink it,

---

[1] הֶגֶן, here only, is without doubt a designation, taken from the Chaldean military language, of the offensive weapons with which they fought from the chariot. The swords in ch. xxxviii. 4 correspond.

and suck it out; and thou shalt break the sherds thereof, and pluck off thy breasts: for I have spoken it, saith the Lord Jehovah. 35. Therefore thus saith the Lord Jehovah, Because thou hast forgotten me, and cast me behind thy back,[1] therefore take thou also upon thee thy lewdness and thy whoredoms.

Ver. 22. "From whom thy soul is estranged"—the Chaldeans (ver. 17). Pekod (supremacy), Shoa (the chief[2]), and Koa (of uncertain meaning), are titles of Chaldee dignitaries. There is a sarcasm in the use of these names. They were in all mouths formerly in the time of adultery. Now they would gladly be rid of Pekod and the rest. He has brought them into trouble. Along with the Chaldeans appear also the old lovers, the Assyrians again, now their vassals. These "comely young men," formerly so beloved, shall now make the clear day dark to them. "I will set judgment before them" (ver. 24): God chooses them as judges in His cause, and entrusts them with the execution of justice. "Thy nose and thine ears they shall take away" (ver. 25): what nose and ears are for a woman, that for a people is their military strength, the bloom of the nation. When this is annihilated, a people has lost its beauty. That the words must refer to this, is shown by those immediately adjoining, and giving the explanation, "thy remnant shall fall by the sword." Zion has various forms of existence, and therefore a manifold remnant. The first remnant refers to the fighting men, who, so to speak, shall fall by the sword to the last man—the falling of the remnant presupposes the falling of all the rest; the second remnant refers to Zion as a city, the houses, all of which shall be destroyed by fire. In ver. 26, the plunder. The sin ceases (ver. 27) with the annihilation of the sinner. The whoredom ceases "from the land of Egypt," to which hitherto her wanton course was directed. "The nakedness of thy whoring" (ver. 29): as long as all went well, this nakedness was covered. The shamefulness of her conduct did not come to the light. In that which she suffers, what she has done will be manifest to all the world. The cup in ver. 32 is the figure of the destiny.

---

[1] גַּו, a later form for גֵּו.
[2] In Job xxxiv. 19, in opposition to the small, דַּל.

The "mockery of large measure"[1] corresponds to the cup of wide compass—the greatness of the mockery to the greatness of the calamity, that called forth the mockery so much the more, the greater the pretensions of the Jews, who conducted themselves as the people to whom was secured the universal supremacy, who had always in their mouth the saying, "My enemies shall fall, but I shall tread on their high places." "The cup of wasting and desolation" (ver. 33): thy destiny will be to be waste and desolate. "And suck it out" (ver. 34): this means that she shall fully empty the cup, that her calamity shall be complete, that there shall be no cessation until she has come to the last drop. "Thou shalt break the sherds thereof," as one who, having taken a very bad potion in ill-humour, shatters the vessel. "Pluck off thy breasts" thereon —on the sherds: the attempt, arising from the utmost abhorrence of her sad destiny, to deliver herself, only leads to new misfortune. We find a historical illustration of this in the treatment they gave Gedaliah, the Chaldean governor of those who were left in the country after the taking of the city, for which they were compelled to suffer (Jer. xli.).

In the conclusion the prophet joins the two women together. First, in vers. 36-45, the figure of their sin. Ver. 36. And the LORD said unto me, Son of man, wilt thou judge Oholah and Oholibah, and show them their abominations? 37. For they have committed adultery, and blood is in their hands, and with their abominations they have committed adultery; and also their sons whom they bare unto me, they passed through for them for food. 38. This, moreover, they did to me: they defiled my sanctuary in that day, and profaned my sabbaths. 39. And when they sacrificed their sons to their abominations, they came in that day into my sanctuary to profane it; and, lo, thus have they done in the midst of my house. 40. And also because they sent to men coming from afar, unto whom a messenger was sent; and, lo, they came, for whom thou didst wash thyself, paint thine eyes, and put on ornaments. 41. And thou sattest upon a stately bed, and a table was laid before it; and mine incense and mine oil thou didst set upon it. 42. And the voice of a secure murmur is in her, and to men of the multitude of men are brought Sabean topers from the

[1] Literally, greatness in regard to holding, capacious; comp. xxi. 33.

wilderness; and they put bracelets on their hands, and a beautiful crown upon their heads. 43. And I said, Are adulteries to the faded? Shall adulteries be still committed even with *her*? 44. And one comes to her, as one comes to a harlot: so come they to Oholah and to Oholibah, the women of lewdness. 45. And righteous men, they shall judge them with the judgment of adulteresses, and with the judgment of those who shed blood; for they are adulteresses, and blood is in their hands.

"Wilt thou judge?" (ver. 36; comp. xx. 4, xxii. 2.) The double transgression, adultery and murder, is first briefly stated in ver. 37, and then further amplified: the adultery refers to the idolatry; the murder to the sacrifices of children, which they offered to their idols (comp. xx. 31). The defiling of the sanctuary of God, which appears in ver. 38 as a second crime, which they lay upon themselves, takes place, according to ver. 39, in this way, that they enter it polluted with idolatrous abominations. In like manner follows also the profanation of the Sabbath. The idolater can keep no Sabbath; and if he keeps it externally, he profanes it. The essence of the Sabbath is to be wrapt up in God; and this cannot be where the heart clings to idols. "In that day:" this points to the unseemly coincidence of the two movements. Oholah also made herself guilty of defiling the sanctuary, when she gave up the external connection with the temple in Jerusalem. For she continues in the service of Jehovah, and in the claim to His grace. Ideally also they have recourse to the sanctuary of God.[1] But it is possible, too, that the prophet from ver. 36 has in view only the time after the destruction of the kingdom of the ten tribes, when the sanctuary in Jerusalem again became common to the whole nation. In ver. 40 the prophet passes from religious to political adultery. He censures the forming of adulterous connections, even with the far distant, in opposition to the near (vers. 5, 11), as the visiting of the Chaldeans, who are mentioned in ver. 16, and of the Sabeans, ver. 42. The washing, painting, and adorning signify that Jerusalem uses every means to make herself agreeable to her lovers, the world-powers. Already, in ch. lvii. 9, Isaiah rebukes the faithless Zion: "And thou lookest to the king in

[1] Comp. *Christol.* on Amos ix. 1.

oil (perfumed), and increasest thy scents, and sendest thy messengers far away, and sendest them down to hell;" without doubt referring specially to the mission to the Chaldeans against the Assyrians, as it, along with that to the Egyptians and Sabeans, took place at the instigation of the nobles in the time of Hezekiah. The prophet first addresses the two sisters;[1] then he passes to the singular, because the transgression here mentioned fell as a charge especially on Jerusalem. The board or the table, in ver. 41, is furnished with meats and drinks. Eating and drinking play an important part in adultery, either in the usual or the spiritual sense. "Upon it:" this can only refer to the bed.[2] This is made fragrant by the incense and the oil. Religious ceremonies are not here spoken of. We find ourselves in the region of political idolatry, which in the latest times of the people, from the days of Ahaz and Hezekiah, far outweighed that of religion. The corresponding reality consists in the rich gifts by which Judah endeavoured to purchase the favour of the heathen sovereigns; comp. Isa. xxx. 6. The secure murmur (ver. 42) arises from the noisy and self-confident intercourse of the adulterers with the adulteresses, from the festivals which were held for the sealing of political friendship. Among the adulterers are found, besides many others from all the world (this refers to the great anti-Assyrian coalition in the time of Hezekiah), Sabean topers[3] also from the wilderness, loose barbarians, who are not too vile for her. "In her:" here the personification is abandoned. The bracelets and the golden crowns are the gifts which the adulterers from afar give; comp. xvi. 11, Gen. xxiv. 22, where likewise gifts from the man to the woman are spoken of. The author refers to political connections with Ethiopia, whose capital was Seba or Meroe. In the time of Hezekiah, Tirhakah king of Kush, or Ethiopia, marched to raise the siege of Jerusalem when beleaguered by Sennacherib king of Assyria (Isa. xxxvii. 9; 2 Kings

---

[1] *And* (this also is of importance, or comes into consideration) "that they send," for "and they even sent." The future denotes the often repeated action in the past.

[2] שִׁלְחָן is always, and so in our verse, masculine.

[3] The form is a mixed one, that signifies both Sabeans and topers: סוֹבָאִים instead of סְבָאִים, Isa. xlv. 14, as the Masoretes wish to read.

xix. 9); and Isa. xlv. 14 also implies the seeking of help from the Sabeans or inhabitants of Meroe in the time of Isaiah: "Thus saith the Lord, The labour of Egypt, and the merchandise of Cush and the Sabeans, men of stature, shall go over unto thee, and be thine: they shall go after thee; in chains they shall go over, and they shall fall down unto thee to beseech thee; only in thee is God, and there is no God beside." We have here the opposite of the ignominious dependence on Egypt and Ethiopia, which is connected with it, especially Meroe, as it existed in the time of the prophet. To such a subordinate relation Isaiah points also in ch. xliii. 3: the future will show that Israel, through his God, stands higher than Egypt and Sheba, to whom he once ignominiously yielded. The object of Sennacherib's expedition was, as M. v. Niebuhr (*History of Assyria and Babylon*, p. 171 f.) has shown, the breaking up of a great coalition, which threatened the Assyrian dominion in Syria, and not merely the subjugation of the small kingdom of Judah. Trusting to this coalition, Hezekiah had rebelled against Assyria. The arrival of Tirhakah, remarks Niebuhr, at the bottom of which lay probably an alliance with the native Egyptian princes, is a movement that can only be explained by the seeking of aid on the part of Hezekiah. This seeking of aid from the Sabeans went hand in hand with that from the Chaldeans, which was before mentioned by the prophet. These were the two extreme ends of the coalition against Assyria. In regard to these relations we may compare also Isa. xviii. There the intelligence of the glorious deliverance which the Lord has secured to His people against Assyria is brought to Kush, in proof that this country was at that time connected with Judah by a close community of political interests. Judea had looked for aid to Ethiopia, instead of which Kush is taken into the community of the salvation secured to Judah by his God. "To the inveterate are adulteries?" (ver. 43): Shall her adulteries go on still further? "Shall adulteries be still committed even with her?"[1] The thought is, that the Lord cannot possibly suffer this, that He must at length make an end of such a course;

---

[1] The reading of the text is יִזְנֶה. The Masoretic reading יִזְנוּ is a good interpretation. Comp. בָּאוּ, ver. 44.

comp. ver. 45. It may seem strange that in ver. 44 (as also in ver. 45), along with Oholibah, Oholah also appears still in the present pursuing her adulterous course. The solution, however, is, that after the fall of the kingdom of the ten tribes, Oholah still continued to exist in close community with Oholibah. That Judah, to which no inconsiderable number of the citizens of the former kingdom of the ten tribes had attached themselves (comp. 2 Chron. xxxv. 18), thenceforward represents the collective nation, is shown by the name Israel which was now assumed by it. The righteous men in ver. 45 are the Chaldeans. They are righteous, according to their mission as ministers of the divine vengeance; whereby it is not excluded that they, in regard to their motive, are evil, and themselves liable to the divine vengeance. The heathen tyrant also, in Isa. xlix. 24, is designated as righteous. The blood refers to the sacrificing of children; comp. ver. 37.

In vers. 46–49, the punishment to which the last verse of the foregoing section had conducted. Ver. 46. For thus saith the Lord Jehovah, Bring up against them a company, and give them to maltreatment and spoiling. 47. And the company shall cast stones upon them, and cleave them with their swords: they shall slay their sons and their daughters, and burn their houses with fire. 48. And I will cause lewdness to cease out of the land; and all women shall be warned, and shall not do after their lewdness. 49. And they shall requite your lewdness upon you, and the sins of your abominations ye shall take upon you: and ye shall know that I am the Lord.

In ver. 46 the prophet is first addressed. What shall happen is, as it were, wrought by him, as the power which gave the prophecy produces also the fulfilment; in the prophecy also, ideally considered, the fulfilment is already present. The *community* denotes usually the congregation of Israel. As this has failed to do its duty, reacting against the crime, as once happened in the war against Benjamin (Judg. xx.), so stands here the community of the heathen, which God summons to execute His vengeance. The women in ver. 48 are the nations to whom the execution decreed against Israel shall serve for a warning and deterring example. "The sins of your abominations" (ver. 49)—those committed in commerce with them.

THE FOURTH CYCLE.—CHAPTER XXIV.

As all the prophecies of Ezekiel are arranged chronologically, this embraces ch. xxv. as well as ch. xxiv. For the next chronological date is found in ch. xxvi. 1. The starting-point is the beginning of the siege of Jerusalem, descried in spirit by Ezekiel: comp. with ch. xxiv. 1, 2, 2 Kings xxv. 1, Jer. lii. 4, xxxix. 1 f., Zech. viii. 19. This event first gives occasion to the prophet's closing threatening against Judah, which is much shorter than the previous one, because the opening thunders of the divine judgment themselves now speak. From the chief criminal Judah, with whom the judgment of God must begin, the prophet then turns to the accomplices, the heathen members of the coalition, where he takes an ideal standpoint, and presupposes as already present what had been predicted, ch. xxiv., in reference to Judah.

The announcement of the judgment on Judah falls into two symbolic actions taking place internally. The first parable, that of the caldron, denotes the destiny of the people; the second, the death of the prophet's wife, represents how they will be affected thereby, the facts and the disposition called forth thereby. Ver. 1. And the word of the LORD came unto me in the ninth year, in the tenth month, in the tenth of the month, saying, 2. Son of man, write thee the name of the day, this same day: the king of Babylon moves towards Jerusalem this same day. 3. And utter against the house of rebellion a parable; and say unto them, Thus saith the Lord Jehovah, Set on a pot, set it on, and pour water into it: 4. Gather its pieces into it, every good piece, thigh and shoulder; fill it with the choice of the bones. 5. Take the choice of the flock, and also the wood-pile of the bones under it; let it boil and boil,[1] so that its bones be sodden in the midst of it. 6. Therefore thus saith the Lord Jehovah, Woe to the city of blood, the pot whose rust is in it, and whose rust is not gone out of it! empty it[2] piece for piece; no lot falls upon it. 7. For her blood is

---
[1] Properly, "cook its cookery."
[2] Properly, "bring it out," namely according to its flesh pieces, which belong to the consistency of the pot, as the inhabitants denoted by them to that of the city; so that to bring it out is in reality to bring them out

in the midst of her; on the bare rock has she laid it; she poured it not upon the earth, to cover it with dust. 8. That I might raise up fury, take vengeance, I set her blood upon the bare rock, that it should not be covered. 9. Therefore thus saith the Lord Jehovah, Woe to the city of blood! I will also make the wood-pile great. 10. Heap on wood, kindle the fire, make ready the flesh, and put in the spice, and let the bones be burnt. 11. And set it empty upon its coals, that it may be hot, and its brass may burn, and its impurity in it may be melted, and its rust be finished. 12. She has been wearied with labours, and her much rust went not out of her; her rust into the fire. 13. In thy filthiness is lewdness: because I purged thee, and thou wast not purged, thou shalt no more be purged from thy filthiness, until I cause my fury to rest upon thee. 14. I the LORD have spoken: it shall come, and I will do it; I will neither spare nor repent: according to thy ways, and according to thy doings, shall they judge thee, saith the Lord Jehovah.

The prophet is to write down the day (ver. 2), as a man does with remarkable days, in order not to forget the date. The object, to make use of this afterwards in proof of his prophetic office, needed to be more definitely noticed. That he knew in spirit the event of the day, presents itself to the prophet as so natural, that he makes nothing more of it. The action which the prophet is to take is in ver. 3 expressly described as a parable,—a description which occurs nowhere of an externally accomplished action. Ver. 5 also does not permit us to think of such an action, according to which a whole number of sheep are to be put into the caldron. If the first symbolic action belongs to the department of the inner, the same holds good obviously of the second, which is closely connected with the first. A wife of Ezekiel has no more actually died, than he has actually set on a caldron. The caldron is Jerusalem. The flesh and the bones, that are put therein, are the Jews, the ordinary inhabitants of the city, and the fugitives from the country; the fire is the fire of war. Water is poured into the caldron, because in the first place only the inhabitants are regarded, not the city as such. Afterwards, where the caldron only is intended, it is set on empty (ver. 11). The bones, in ver. 4, in contradistinction to the pieces of flesh, are those who lend support to the body of the state—the authorities, with the king at their head. The wood-pile of the bones in ver. 5 is a wood-pile that is adapted to a cooking process, in which bones also are to be cooked. With ver. 6 begins the interpretation of the parable, yet so that with it the further development of it goes hand in hand. The rust in the pot signifies the sin of Jerusalem. The pieces are cast out after they are burned (ver. 10). This destiny, to be burned and then cast out, comes upon all without distinction, and so there is no way, in regard to the pot or its contents, by which a man might go off free. In ver. 7 we have the cause of this judgment: deeds of murder are done in Jerusalem boldly and without abhorrence, by which we are to understand the numerous judicial murders which were perpetrated by the party who had at that time seized the helm of the state, the party of the external alliances against which all were indignant, who in the name of the God of Israel raised a protest against this adulterous movement. An example of such judicial murder is the prophet Urijah (Jer. xxvi. 20 f.). She has not covered her sins, therefore will they not be covered by the Lord (ver. 8). Forgiveness of sins is not for the *peccata voluntaria*—for those which, according to Num. xv. 31, are perpetrated with a high hand, with bold disregard of the covenant and the command of God. They are punished with extinction. The fate of Sodom is a type of this. The address in ver. 10 is directed to the prophet. It is intended first of all to represent symbolically, in the region of the purely internal, what was immediately to enter into realization. "Put in the spice," lay on spice, that the flesh may be savoury for the foe or for the devouring sword. The prophet is once again sarcastic. "And let the bones be burned:" the fire shall be so strong, that even the most powerful cannot resist its violence. On the destruction of the inhabitants, figured by flesh and bones, follows in ver. 11 the destruction of the city itself, figured by the caldron. "She has been wearied with labours" (ver. 12): the pot, Jerusalem, is wearied of the severe labour which the true servants of the Lord have undergone, to remove the rust, the sin from her, so that they are compelled to say, "I have laboured in vain, I have spent my strength for nought and in vain" (Isa. xlix. 4). Hence the last means must be applied to remove the rust, the fire, by which with the rust the pot also is destroyed. The impurity has increased to lewdness (ver. 13), inasmuch as the earnest endeavours of God to purify Jerusalem, as by the mission of His servant Jeremiah, are rudely repelled: comp. 2 Chron. xxxvi. 15, 16. God makes no longer trial, therefore, of such purification, the term of which is run out (Jer. xiii. 27): He now discharges upon it His fury, that thereby the purification may be effected, which is identical with destruction, and of which Isaiah prophesied, ch. iv. 4.

Vers. 15-24. The thought here is, a time of immeasurable sorrow draws nigh to the people. This alone, and not penitence or impenitence, is here spoken of. The prophet will annihilate the last remnant of sanguine hope. Ver. 15. And the word of the Lord came unto me, saying, 16. Son of man, behold, I take from thee the delight of thine eyes with a stroke; and thou shalt not lament nor weep, neither shall thy tears fall. 17. Groan, be still,[1] make no mourning for the dead, bind the tire of thine head upon thee, and put thy shoes upon thy feet, and cover not thy beard, and eat not the bread of men. 18. And I spake unto the people in the morning, and in the evening my wife died; and I did in the morning as I was commanded. 19. And the people said to me, Wilt thou not tell us what these things are to us? for thou doest it. 20. And I said unto them, The word of the LORD came unto me, saying, 21. Say to the house of Israel, Thus saith the Lord Jehovah, Behold, I will profane my sanctuary, the pride of your strength, the delight of your eyes, and the pity of your soul;[2] and your sons and your daughters whom ye have left shall fall by the sword. 22. And ye shall do as I have done; ye shall not cover your beard, nor eat the bread of men. 23. And your tire shall be on your heads, and shoes on your feet: ye shall not mourn nor weep; and ye shall pine away in your iniquities, and groan every man to his brother. 24. And Ezekiel is unto you a wonder; according to all that he hath done, shall ye do: when this cometh, ye shall know that I am the Lord.

On ver. 16 it has been erroneously remarked by the older

---

[1] Luther, "Secretly *mayest* thou sigh." But not a concession, but a command, is meant. The passage speaks also not of a secret, but of a *low* groaning.

[2] The sympathy of the soul,—an object which, when it suffers, draws the soul that is inwardly united with it into a state of sympathy.

expositors: "The miserable death of the Jewish church is prefigured, which was, as it were, a spouse of God." The prophet is the type of the people, the wife the counterpart of all that was dear and precious to the people,—namely, the temple, in which all else was included. They shall not weep for the downfall of it, because they shall be wholly taken up with the pain of their own misery. There is a degree of suffering where sympathy ceases in those who are not deeply founded in God (and of such it is here treated), because they are swallowed up with dull and deep despair. "Groan, be still" (ver. 17): the prophet is to groan low, in order to represent the dull pain no longer capable of any lively sensation. "Mourning for the dead"—the solemn mourning, which is appointed in cases of death.[1] This is the general; the following are the several acts of which mourning usually consisted. The tire is not specially the priestly bonnet, against which ver. 23 decides, but the head-dress that was commonly worn. This was taken off in mourning, in order to scatter ashes on the head (Isa. lxi. 3). It belonged to mourning also, that a man should walk barefooted (2 Sam. xv. 30). The covering of the beard occurs as a sign of mourning in Lev. xiii. 45 and Mic. iii. 7. The beard is thus regarded as an ornament of a man. If a sign were required "that a man wishes not to speak," the beard would certainly not be mentioned. *Bread of men* is the *ordinary* food (in such circumstances, in cases of death). The thought in both verses is, not that the existing public misfortune is so great, that the pain of the individual on account of the heaviest personal loss is thereby overpowered; but the prophet, as the following clearly shows, appears merely as a holy actor—he prefigures a future state of the people. This confirms to us what we had already concluded from the analogy of the parable of the caldron, that the occurrence is not external, but that we have to do with a mere figure; so that it is questionable whether Ezekiel had a wife at all: the contrary, at all events, cannot be proved from this occurrence. A moral relation like marriage cannot be degraded to a mere mode of representation. Were Ezekiel's wife, the delight of his eyes, actually dead, it would be unnatural if he, suppressing

---

[1] מתים is the relative accusative; or we may read both words as a kind of *nomen compositum*.

all tenderer feeling, had used this occurrence only as an outward representation of the impression which the existing great misfortune should make on the people. It would be strange also, if God had lowered His servant the prophet so far into a mere instrument of His plan, that He took from him his wife on no other ground than to give him occasion for a mimetic representation of the future state of the people. If we have only a vividly drawn figure before us, these thoughts vanish away. If the married relation of the prophet be only a mode of representation, the thoughts fall away that refer to a real marriage. The prophet, according to ver. 18, imparts the received divine command immediately on the same morning when he received it, or after the night, to the people. On the following morning he appears with the already announced actions before the people, informing them that in the evening his wife died, which is a fact, but a symbolic fact, belonging to the holy phantasy. Even the manner in which the people, according to ver. 19, receive the action of the prophet, scarcely gives rise to the thought of the existence of the actual fact. For otherwise the people would not have been so readily convinced of the symbolic character of his proceeding. The words, "For thou doest it," express the conviction that the prophet here is regarded purely in his official character, and not as a private individual. To him whom such a calamity has struck as the loss of a beloved wife, no one will so speak, even if he were a prophet. They say not that the action of the prophet is so peculiar, that it transcends his private relations; but they express the conviction that what the prophet does, irrespective of its peculiarity, even because he does it, must be significant for the future of the people. This shows that no event had transpired in which the private character of the prophet came into the foreground. The sanctuary comes into view in ver. 21 as the dwelling-place of the whole people. In its profanation is included the dissolving of the whole covenant relation, the removal of everything sublime and glorious, that had flown from that covenant relation, of all that was valuable and dear to the people. The general conception is demanded by the fundamental passage, Lev. xxvi. 19, where by "the pride of power" is meant all the glory of Israel. Then also by ver. 25, where in place of the sanctuary here all that is glorious appears. The sons and the daughters are here related to the sanctuary, as the part to the whole. The sons and the daughters are not those of individuals, but of the people as a whole. The house of Israel, not the exiles in particular, are addressed. In point of fact, it is as much as to say, your countrymen. "Ye shall pine away in your iniquities:" with this comp. ch. iv. 17, Lev. xxvi. 39; what is there threatened to the people in case of rebellion, now passes into terrible fulfilment. "And Ezekiel is unto you a wonder" (ver. 24): the type is designated as a wonder, because it must draw wonder to itself, as the exact representation of the future state of things. "When it cometh, ye shall know that I am the Lord Jehovah," because by my servant I have placed before your eyes the image of the future in lines so clear and sharp.

In vers. 25-27, the close of this discourse, and at the same time of the whole national announcement of the prophet before the execution of the judgment. Ver. 25. And thou, son of man, surely in the day when I take from them their stronghold, their proud joy, the delight of their eyes and the desire of their soul, their sons and their daughters; 26. In that day, he that is escaped shall come unto thee, to cause thine ears to hear. 27. In that day shall thy mouth be opened with him that is escaped, and thou shalt speak, and be no more dumb: and thou shalt be a wonder unto them; and they shall know that I am the LORD.

"In the day" (ver. 25) is the same as "at the time." The "stronghold of the people" is, according to ver. 21, the temple, to which the sons and daughters belong as a part to the whole. "From them," regarded as the whole people. The people lose their all, when they lose their sons and daughters. "He that is escaped" (ver. 26) is, as in Gen. xiv. 13, an ideal person, and includes in reality a plurality in itself—the whole host of those carried away after the destruction of Jerusalem, who were directed to the dwelling-place of the prophet, or passed it. To gain the foundation for the new appearance of the prophet, the mere *rumour* of the taking of Jerusalem and the destruction of the temple was not sufficient: it was necessary that eye-witnesses should come, who by their arrival, and by the vivid report of personal experience, might call forth a profound emotion of the heart. The prophet is dumb (ver. 27), because now nothing more can be done—the die is cast. Ch. xxiv. is to be regarded as a farewell. Hence its brevity. Formerly Israel might still have been brought to reason. Now Nebuchadnezzar stands before the gates. Formerly sin was active: now the passive history of sin has made its commencement. A new period for prophetic utterance came when the misfortune was realized. This was first to prepare the soil. The prophet can only speak " with him that is escaped," in accordance with the news which he will bring; comp. ch. xxxiii. 21, where that which is here announced is accomplished. Yet the dumbness only refers to domestic relations. In the very time of his silence regarding these, the predictions of the prophet regarding foreign nations are unfolded. " And thou shalt be a wonder unto them." When the eye-witnesses (the escaped) report that all has happened as the Lord proclaimed by Ezekiel, he will be to them an object of wonder; they will recognise the Lord concealed behind the Son of man, and be seized with the feeling of His real Godhead. This result of the message of the fugitives was a necessary foundation for the new appearance of the prophet.

FOREIGN NATIONS.

CHAPTERS XXV.-XXXII.

CHAPTER XXV.

E have here the second part of the discourse of the prophet, beginning in ch. xxiv. All the prophecies of Ezekiel are chronologically determined. Hence the date in ch. xxiv. 1 applies to this also.

What was predicted in ch. xxiv. regarding the immediate future of Judah is here presupposed as already accomplished; so that the point of view is ideal. Judgment must begin at the house of God, but it does not stop there; it passes over thence to the heathen members of the coalition, especially to the tribes related by race to Judah: Ammon (vers. 1-7), Moab (vers. 8-11), Edom (vers. 12-14)—who will smart for their hostile, mischief-loving demonstrations at the destruction of Judah,—and lastly the Philistines (vers. 15-17). When the prophet has grouped together these small border tribes, he afterwards announces the judgment of God in several predictions to the nations of the world that had taken part in the coalition—Tyre and Egypt.

The nations threatened with destruction are seven in all. The seven are divided into four and three. The confederate nations besides Judah were properly only six; but to gain the number seven, and consequently the three, the prophet subjoins to the lengthened predictions against Tyre a brief one against Sidon, which indeed is also expressly mentioned along with Tyre in the enumeration of the members of the coalition (Jer. xxvii. 3).

The absence of a prophetic menace against the Chaldeans must surprise us the more, as Jeremiah, Ezekiel's predecessor, had announced their destruction in the review of the approaching judgments of God in ch. xxv. ("And the king of Sheshach," by a sort of anagram for Babel, "shall drink after them"), and had closed his book with a lengthened proclamation against Babylon. Among the personal relations of Ezekiel, the reason can perhaps only lie in this, that he prophesied in the midst of the Chaldeans. A reason for braving the danger did not present itself. Jeremiah had treated exhaustively of this matter; and Ezekiel, while he took up again the other announcements of his predecessor, as good as pointed expressly to this particular topic. Then the prophecy against Tyre is indirectly at the same time a prophecy against Babylon; and this perhaps explains its comparative fulness. That which is uttered against the city in which the trade of the world culminated, holds good also of the city in which the dominion of the world was centred, which the prophet already in ch. xvii. 4 had, in reference to Tyre, designated as the city of the merchants—of the political *negotiations*.

These prophecies against foreign nations serve to extend the range of vision—to give, through the insertion of the special judgment on Judah in the greater whole of the divine judgments, a deeper impression of its import, and to arouse to sincere conversion to God, who walks solemnly along, judging the nations; and who, as He is rich in judgment, must be rich also in mercy—as He is mighty to destroy, must be mighty also to deliver. Whosoever thus received an insight into the whole of the divine judicial acts, must have been thereby powerfully drawn from politics to repentance. Whosoever should not turn with his whole heart to a God who, while His people lie low, walks victoriously over the high places of the earth, and even thereby shows that the humiliation of His people is the merited punishment of their sins, is not a contradiction of His power, but a testimony to it. We have in these prophecies against foreign nations the preparation for the later direct announcement of salvation for Israel, with which the prophet wished then to come forward, when judgment had completed its course. These prophecies present themselves as forerunners of cheering intelligence also, in so far as the downfall of the heathen powers here announced is throughout total and definitive, whereas hope is still left to Israel even in the deepest misery. This view is expressly opened up in ch. xxviii. 25, 26. This also is very consolatory to Israel, that among the causes of the divine judgments on the heathen world, the wrong done to Israel occupies so important a place (ch. xxv. 3, 8, 12, 15). How could God leave a people in misery whose cause He makes His own, even when they pine in misery, and regarding whom He says, "What ye have done to the least of these, ye have done to me?"

From the point of view from which Ezekiel regards the destinies of the nations, it is plain that he turns his attention chiefly to the judicial activity of God in regard to the heathen, and looks away from the future proofs of His mercy and compassion towards them. How rich and deep was Ezekiel's knowledge of this appears, for ex., from ch. xvi.

We have here not perhaps a separate book of the prophecies of Ezekiel against foreign nations; but the chronological principle ruling the whole collection is here also applicable. The prophecies against foreign nations are inserted here simply because they mostly took place at that very time, between the last announcement of the downfall of Judah, with which the beginning of the announcement against the heathen nations in ch. xxv. is combined into one prophetic discourse, and the announcement of salvation delivered after the downfall was completed. But with the chronological order is connected an order of nature. The prophecies which refer to one of the two great nations, Tyre and Egypt, are not to be separated from one another, and yet are to be chronologically arranged among themselves. The prophecy against Tyre in ch. xxvi. 1 belongs to a somewhat later point than the first prophecy against Egypt in ch. xxix. 1. The chief power in the coalition must form the close, and is formally separated from the foregoing by the closing formula in ch. xxviii. 25, 26. And to the prophecies against Egypt, which fall between the last threat against Judah and the promise, is added by way of appendix, to bring all that relates to Egypt together, a prophecy in ch. xxix. 17 f., which was delivered some time after the promise to Judah, and which, in strict adherence to chronological order, would form the last part of the whole book. The two prophecies in ch. xxxii. 1 and xxxii. 17 also are of somewhat later date than the beginning of the predictions of promise (ch. xxxiii. 21).

The proclamation of the judgment against the four heathen nations, that were always filled with envy and hatred, around Israel, begins with the three whose guilt was enhanced by their relationship. At the head stand in ch. xxv. 1-7 the Ammonites. They belonged, with Judah, to the anti-Chaldaic coalition; comp. ch. xxi. 20 f. The avenging march of the king of Babylon was directed first against Judah, according to the same passage, and now the neighbouring nations were busied in separating their cause from that of Judah (Lam. i. 2); and in place of friendship came the old enmity, which, as the prophet, after the example of Obadiah and other prophets, foresees, was to be particularly active in the impending catastrophe of Judah. According to 2 Kings xxiv. 2, Ammonites and Moabites, in fact, took part in the expedition of Nebuchadnezzar against Jerusalem. That the Ammonites here open the series is to be explained either from this, that their hostility against Judah was peculiarly intense, or from the fact that among the combined nations they dwelt nearest the Chaldeans. In ch. xxi. 19 also, Ammon appears next to Israel as the immediate object of the Chaldean vengeance.

Ver. 1. And the word of the Lord came unto me, saying, 2. Son of man, set thy face against the sons of Ammon, and prophesy against them; 3. And say unto the sons of Ammon, Hear the word of the Lord Jehovah; Thus saith the Lord Jehovah, Because thou saidst, Aha, against my sanctuary, because it was profaned; and against the land of Israel, because it was wasted; and against the house of Judah, because they went into captivity; 4. Therefore, behold, I will deliver thee to the sons of the east for a possession, and they shall set their houses in thee, and make their dwellings in thee: they shall eat thy fruit, and they shall drink thy milk. 5. And I will give Rabbah for a stall for camels, and the sons of Ammon a couching-place of sheep; and ye shall know that I am the LORD. 6. For thus saith the Lord Jehovah, Because thou clappest the hand, and stampest with the foot, and rejoicest with all thy despite of soul over the land of Israel; 7. Therefore, behold, I will stretch out my hand against thee, and give thee for food[1] to the heathen; and cut thee off from the

---

[1] Luther, after the *Keri*, "for a spoil." For בג the Masoretes wish to read בז, spoil, which, like all the *Keris*, is a mere conjecture. But בג in Persian,

nations, and destroy thee out of the lands: I will extirpate thee; and thou shalt know that I am the LORD.

The sons of the east, in ver. 4, are not the proper instruments of the judgment. These are, as in Judah, so also in the whole system of prophecies against the foreign nations, the Chaldeans, as surely as all these nations were the members of the anti-Chaldaic coalition, who oppose themselves in vain to the scourge which the Lord has sent upon them. The sons of the east—an old designation borrowed from the books of Moses for the Arabians, who appear under the latter name first in Isa. xiii. 20—are rather the vultures that fall upon the carcases of the people, those who always appear where fire and sword have wasted a country, and overspread it with their flocks, in which character they appear also in the passage quoted from Isaiah. The sons of the east do nothing more than take possession of the land that has been already desolated. Among the number of the nations over whom the judgment by the Chaldeans passes, appear the Ammonites already in Jer. xxv. 21, xxvii. 3, xlix. 1 f. In Ezekiel also (ch. xxi.) the king of Babylon considers whether he shall direct his avenging activity first against the Ammonites or against Jerusalem; and the decision falling upon the latter refers only to the order of time. That which the prophet first expressly says of Tyre, ch. xxvi. 7, "Behold, I bring Nebuchadnezzar king of Babylon from the north, the king of kings," refers in reality to all the seven kings of the coalition. That it is first uttered of Tyre, corresponds to the richer unfolding of the prophetic discourse, as it generally appears where the prophet comes to this principal nation, which in its grandeur was best fitted to bring into view the thought of the vanity of human glory. The more exact designation of

allotted portion, food, is confirmed by פתבג, mouth-portion, Dan. i. 5, xi. 26, and particularly suits ver. 4, "They shall eat thy fruit and drink thy milk," and still better the following, which speaks of total annihilation. The conjecture בז was rendered natural by the fact that בג, probably connected with the Greek φάγειν, does not occur elsewhere in the Old Testament, and also by ch. xxvi. 5, where Tyre becomes a spoil (בז) for the heathen, which is an intentional variation of our passage. The coincidence in the use of a Persian word not elsewhere occurring in the whole Old Testament, is one of the many indications of the contemporaneousness of Ezekiel and Daniel.

the instrument of the divine vengeance appears also there first in the development, and indeed at the very commencement of it. In the introduction there (vers. 2–5), the general tenor of the proclamation against the four neighbouring nations continues. The old Ammonitis, the ruin of which began in the time of Nebuchadnezzar, and continued thenceforward without interruption, is abandoned to the Bedouin Arabs unto this day. Rabbah (ver. 5) is the old capital of the Ammonites, to whose name, the Populous, the stall for camels forms a melancholy contrast. Camel and wilderness go inseparably together. The clapping of the hands, in ver. 6, is the gesture of highly excited feeling. On the stamping with the foot, comp. vi. 11.

After Ammon follows, in vers. 8–11, the brother people Moab. Ver. 8. Thus saith the Lord Jehovah, Because Moab and Seir say, Behold, like all the heathen is the house of Judah; 9. Therefore, behold, I will open the shoulder of Moab from the cities, from his cities at his end, the beauty of the land, Beth-jeshimoth, Baal-meon, and unto Kiriathaim, 10. To the sons of the east, with the sons of Ammon; and I will give it for a possession, that the sons of Ammon may be no more remembered among the heathen. 11. And on Moab will I execute judgments, and they shall know that I am the LORD.

Mention is already by anticipation made of Seir and Edom in ver. 8, along with Moab (the prophet treats of him fully in ver. 12 f.), to guard against the thought that the guilt here mentioned is peculiar to Moab, to indicate that it belongs to Moab only as a part of the surrounding heathendom. The guilt consists in the denial of the true deity of the God of Israel, for only on this ground could Israel be placed on the same level with all other nations. The pretence for this denial they take from the misery of Israel, which they derive not from their guilt, but from the feebleness of their God, and discern therein a palpable proof against His true and full deity. Their God Jehovah, the absolutely pure Being, the primeval ground of all things, the absolutely certain Helper of His people, is a mere fancy: otherwise must they soar above, and not sink beneath. This full deity, against whose historically extant evidences they rashly close their eyes, they must now discover by their own destruction. The transgression is seemingly small; but it is that by which the nations perish even to the present day. As each takes its stand towards God, who is historically revealed in His church, so is its destiny measured out. The lot which fell upon Moab and his confederates, on account of guilt comparatively so light, which it did not enter into his mind to regard as such, is a warning-cry which should not be unheard. The shoulder in ver. 9 is named as the place where blows and sword-strokes are most easily applied. It is "opened," when it is made accessible to these. The "cities" appear as strongholds. In these the opening begins, and then proceeds unhindered to the other parts of the country. The strong forts lie naturally at the "end" of the land, its border. Before "the beauty of the land" "I open" is to be repeated. What follows individualizes the beauty, as the best parts are named. "And unto Kiriathaim:" this was the outermost among the radiant points of the land. Ver. 10 declares to whom it is opened. "I give it," both Moab and Ammon, that form together a national unity, in which the Ammonites, as in Judg. xi. 12 f., form the prominent part; for which reason in the words, "that the sons of Ammon be no more remembered," these alone are named. According to ver. 11, through the judgments under which with Ammon Moab also falls (the latter is connected, as in guilt with Edom, so in punishment with Ammon), it is forced to acknowledge the true deity of Jehovah, which it did not willingly accept.

In vers. 12-14, Edom. Ver. 12. Thus saith the Lord Jehovah, Because Edom is busy in taking vengeance on the house of Judah, and they have been guilty and have taken vengeance on them; 13. Therefore thus saith the Lord Jehovah, And I will stretch out my hand upon Edom, and cut off from it man and beast, and make it a desert from Teman; and unto Dedan they shall fall by the sword. 14. And I will lay my vengeance on Edom through my people Israel: and they shall do in Edom according to my anger and according to my fury; and they shall know my vengeance, saith the Lord Jehovah.

Edom is guilty in the Chaldean catastrophe (ver. 12), because he seizes the occasion to avenge himself on Judah for former injustice. This involves the historically established principle, that Edom brought upon himself by his own conduct, what he formerly, particularly under David, suffered from Judah. For only on this supposition was the revenge sinful. "And I will stretch out:" the *and* connects this with the foregoing threatenings against Ammon and Moab, and points out the proceeding against Edom as one link of a chain. Teman, a district in the southern part of Edom; Dedan in the northern. If the destruction sets out from Teman, and extends to Dedan, it embraces the whole country. "Through my people Israel" (ver. 14): these are the proper authors, the Chaldeans only their instruments; as in the second part of Isaiah, what Cyrus shall do to the Chaldeans is referred to Israel (ch. xlv. 4), and in Jeremiah Nebuchadnezzar appears as the servant of the God who rules in Israel. The immediate instruments of the divine judgments here threatened in all the seven prophecies against foreign nations are the Chaldeans, as the prophet himself had already expressly said in regard to the Ammonites, who stand at their head. But to Israel is the work of vengeance ascribed so much the more, because afterwards, in the time of the appearance of Christ, he was to come forward without a substitute warring and conquering again the heathen world. Comp. Amos ix. 11, 12; Obad. 17 f.; Jer. xlix. 20, where this final victory of the people of God over the heathen world is, even as here, individually applied to Edom.

In vers. 15–17, the Philistines. The fundamental passage here is Jer. xlvii. There the Philistines are flooded with a great flood from the north, the symbol of the Asiatic world-power. Ver. 15. Thus saith the Lord Jehovah, Because the Philistines are busy with vengeance, and avenge themselves with despite of their whole soul,[1] for a destruction of perpetual hatred; 16. Therefore thus saith the Lord Jehovah; Behold, I stretch out my hand upon the Philistines, and cut off the Kerethim, and destroy the remnant at the haven of the sea. 17. And I will take on them great vengeance with rebukes of fury; and they shall know that I am the LORD, when I lay my vengeance upon them.

[1] Literally, in soul; so that the soul, the seat of the affections, is active therein; in contrast with a contempt which has its seat prominently only on their lips.

The destruction of perpetual hatred (ver. 15) is that which grows out of perpetual hatred. "And cut off the Kerethim" (ver. 16): the name Philistines signifies probably the emigrants, in accordance with the accounts of the books of Moses concerning their migration from the regions on the Black Sea, from Colchis, and the adjacent Pontic Cappadocia, Kaphtor. By the side of this name goes, of substantially like signification for the same people, Kerethim, extirpated—those who were forced to leave their native land. These Kerethim are now to become Kerethim a second time; their name shall verify itself anew. The destruction of the remnant points to this, that they shall be destroyed to the last man, as in fact the Philistines have utterly disappeared. It is the great privilege of the people of God, that how heavy soever the judgments of God may be upon them, never will it be said of them, I will destroy the remnant.

CHAPTERS XXVI.–XXVIII.

These chapters describe the fall of Tyre and Sidon. First the prophecy against Tyre in ch. xxvi. Then the lamentation over Tyre in ch. xxvii. In ch. xxviii. 1–10 the fall of the prince of Tyre; in vers. 11–19 the lamentation over him. In vers. 20–24 the prophecy concerning Sidon. In vers. 25, 26, before the fall of the chief power in the coalition, Egypt, we have the close of the prophecies concerning the neighbouring nations.

The prophet has good reason to be so full in his announcement against Tyre. Along with Babylon and Egypt, Tyre was then the most glorious concentration of the worldly power. In the queen of the sea the thought of the vanity of all worldly power was strikingly exemplified. Hand in hand with this thought goes, in Ezekiel, that of the indestructibleness of the kingdom of God. The design to raise the light of the kingdom of God through the shade of the world, appears manifestly at the close of the whole in ch. xxviii. 25, 26, and even before at the close of ch. xxvi. The prophet wishes to prevent the despondency which the contemplation of the world shining in its glory may so easily call forth in the people of God groaning under the cross.

The prophecy in ch. xxvi. has four clauses: the destruction of Tyre in outline, vers. 2–6; the detail, vers. 7–14; the lamentation of the princes of the sea over Tyre, vers. 15–18; and the epilogue, in which Tyre in its total downfall is contrasted with Zion in its glorious resurrection, vers. 19–21.

Ver. 1. And it came to pass in the eleventh year, in the first of the month, the word of the LORD came unto me, saying. In the date the month is wanting. This omission of the month indicates here, as in ch. xxxii. 17, that it is to be taken from the last previous date, that is, from ch. xxiv. 1. Accordingly it is the tenth month. The prominence given to the similarity of the month leads to the similarity of the situation: there the day of the opening of the siege of Jerusalem, here that of the opening of the siege of Tyre. In the same month in which Tyre a few years before had rejoiced, must she now lament. When Ezekiel uttered this prophecy, the proclamation against Jerusalem in ch. xxiv. was already fulfilled by the conquest of it which took place in the fourth month of the eleventh year (Jer. xxxix. 2). Already came the change to its heathen rival Tyre, who had rejoiced in the downfall of Jerusalem, thinking that she would come off free, and gain by its fall.

Ver. 2. Son of man, because Tyre saith against Jerusalem, Aha, broken is the gate of the peoples;[1] it is turned to me;[2] I will be replenished, she is laid waste. 3. Therefore thus saith the Lord Jehovah; Behold, I am against thee, Tyre, and I will bring up many nations upon thee, as if I brought up the sea with its waves. 4. And they shall destroy the walls of Tyre, and break down her towers: and I will sweep away her dust from her, and make her a bare rock. 5. A place for spreading a net shall she be in the midst of the sea: for I have spoken it, saith the Lord Jehovah; and she shall become a spoil to the heathen. 6. And her daughters which are in the field shall be slain by the sword; and they shall know that I am the LORD.

---

[1] Luther, "The gates of the peoples are broken." But the sing. of the verb shows that the plur. of the noun denotes here, as often, one gate.

[2] Luther, "It is turned." But the fem. refers obviously to the gate: this, or in fact the prerogative of being the gathering point of the nations, is gone over to Tyre.

The general thought in ver. 2 is this: the world triumphs over the church, when the latter suffers a heavy overthrow and is visited by the judgments of her God; but its laughter will be changed into howling. Both Jerusalem and Tyre laid claim to be the world-city,—the one because she regarded the true religion as the highest good, the other because she considered material gain and earthly riches as alone real. By the taking of Jerusalem the process seemed to be decided in favour of Tyre, and she exulted in this decision. In the Messianic announcements, the homage of Tyre to Jerusalem, and its incorporation into the kingdom of God, were expressly celebrated. In Ps. xlv. 13 it is said, " The daughter of Tyre shall entreat thee with a gift, the rich among the people." In Ps. lxxxvii. 4, " I proclaim Rahab and Babylon as my confessors; behold Philistia, and Tyre, with Kush, (of these it is said,) This was born there." Tyre, in the future, will in Jerusalem be born again to a new life. In Isa. xxiii., Tyre, after she has been made tender by the judgments of God, consecrates herself, and all that she has, to the Lord. Without doubt these bold hopes of Zion were known in Tyre, and caused much bad blood in the proud queen of the sea. Already they seemed to be proved by facts to be vain fancies. Zion lay low, and Tyre stood upright, and believed that in the heart of the seas she might despise the world-conqueror, especially as Assyria had already assailed her in vain. " The gate of the peoples:" so is Jerusalem named, on account of the influx of the nations, which was destined for her in the future. Comp. especially the expression, " All nations shall flow into it" (Isa. ii. 2 ; Mic. iv. 1), not without a connecting point in the present, as Jerusalem was at all times a magnet for the God-seeking hearts among the heathen. " It is turned to me:" namely, the gate of the peoples. Tyre considers herself the heiress of Jerusalem. The fall of the spiritual centre presents to view the enhanced importance of the secular. " As if I brought up the sea with its waves:" so we must interpret ver. 3 according to ver. 19. The " many nations," according to ver. 7, gather around Nebuchadnezzar as their leader. Tyre, the insular (Scripture knows no other;[1] and that this alone can be meant here, is proved even

---

[1] Only by a wrong interpretation has Hävernick found a notice of Palætyrus in Hos. ix. 13.

by the contrast of the daughters in the field, ver. 6, and her situation on a rock), sinks back (ver. 4) into her original state: all that was added by man vanishes—there remains only the bare, naked rock in the sea; all glorious array, wherewith she was adorned, disappears as a dream on awaking. The daughters of Tyre in the field (ver. 6) are the cities dependent on her on the mainland, perhaps the so-called Palætyrus in particular, the suburb of the insular Tyre, standing on the shore. The field forms the contrast to the rock of the insular Tyre, on which was neither sowing nor planting.

The survey of the fate of Tyre is now followed by the detailed description of its siege and capture by Nebuchadnezzar. In so full a description of the siege, the casting up of a mound is nowhere mentioned. This shows that such already existed before Nebuchadnezzar undertook the siege. This is also antecedently probable. Great accumulations by the Tyrians themselves are expressly mentioned in history. Tyre was pre-eminently a merchant city. The possible disadvantages in war of the connection with the mainland might the less outweigh the great and permanent advantages for trade, as the mound might be so easily cut through in case of danger.

Ver. 7. For thus saith the Lord Jehovah, Behold, I bring upon Tyre Nebuchadrezzar[1] king of Babylon from the north, a king of kings, with horse, and with chariot, and with riders, and company, and much people. 8. Thy daughters in the field he will slay with the sword, and set a tower against thee, and cast up a wall against thee, and lift up the buckler against thee. 9. And the destruction[2] of his engine he shall set against thy walls, and break down thy towers with his swords.[3] 10. From the abundance of his horses, their dust shall cover thee: at the sound of the rider, and the wheel, and the chariot, thy walls shall shake, when he entereth into thy gates, like the entrance into a broken city. 11. With the hoofs of his horses he shall tread all thy streets: thy people shall he slay with the

---

[1] This comes nearer the native form. Abroad the r was softened into n (Niebuhr, p. 41).

[2] מחי, destruction (comp. 2 Kings xxi. 13), in connection with יחץ, corresponds to יחץ; that is, he will destroy thy walls with his engines.

[3] Luther, "his weapons." There is no ground, however, for taking חרב in other than the usual sense of sword.

sword, and thy strong pillars shall come down to the earth. 12. And they shall plunder thy riches, and despoil thy merchandise, and break down thy walls, and pull down thy fair houses,[1] and lay thy stones, and thy timbers, and thy dust, in the midst of the water. 13. And I will cause the noise of thy songs to cease; and the sound of thy harps shall be no more heard. 14. And I will make thee a bare rock: a spreading-place of nets shalt thou be; thou shalt be built no more: for I the Lord have spoken it, saith the Lord Jehovah.

The riders, along with the horses and chariots (ver. 7), are the chariot-warriors; comp. ver. 10. The words, "Thy daughters in the field he will slay with the sword," are repeated in ver. 8 and ver. 6, to indicate that we have here the filling up of what was there given in outline. By the connection with a distinct personality already present on the scene they receive a new import. The swords in ver. 9, which slay the defenders, are at the same time the means of destroying the towers. The wheels and the chariots are distinguished in ver. 10: the chariots themselves also rattle. The falling of the "strong pillars" (ver. 11) has its special import in this, that these pillars were symbols of the power and glory of Tyre, as the image erected by Nebuchadnezzar (Dan. iii.) was a symbol of the glory of the Chaldean empire. The first place among these pillars was taken by those of Hercules (Herod. ii. 44), who, as even his name indicates, properly the Merchant, was exactly the objective I of the Tyrians.[2] Ver. 14 returns as a refrain to vers. 4, 5. According to Isa. xxiii. 15-18, Tyre, seventy years after her fall by the Chaldeans, returns to prosperity, "whores" or trades "with all the kingdoms of the earth," and consecrates herself, and all her gains, to the true God. A contradiction does not arise here; but the one prophet is to be completed from the other. Ezekiel does not touch on the *lucidum intervallum* celebrated by Isaiah, because, in regard to the heathen nations in general, his eye is directed only to the side of wrath, which alone served his purpose. Isaiah obtains from him the completion, that a *lucidum intervallum* only is

---

[1] Concerning חמד and חמדה—never longing, pleasure, but always the beautiful, or beauty—comp. *Christol.* on Hag. ii. 7. The fair houses here correspond to the palaces of Tyre destroyed by the Chaldeans (Isa. xxiii. 13).

[2] Compare רבלה, ver. 12.

meant, that the restored Tyre will not understand the time of her visitation, and that the neglect of the light will bring on a deeper darkness. It is not to be overlooked, however, that the restoration in Isaiah is only partial. Tyre is, in him, after the lapse of the seventy years of Chaldean supremacy, certainly again an important merchant city, but not a merchant power.

In vers. 15–18 the impression which the fall of Tyre will make on its confederates. Ver. 15. Thus saith the Lord Jehovah to Tyre, Shall not the isles shake at the sound of thy fall, when the wounded cry, and slaughter is made in thy midst? 16. And all the princes of the sea shall come down from their thrones, and lay aside their robes, and put off their broidered garments: they shall clothe themselves with trembling, sit on the earth and tremble at every moment, and be amazed at thee. 17. And they shall take up a lamentation for thee, and say to thee, How art thou destroyed, that art inhabited from the seas, the renowned city, which wast strong in the sea, she and her inhabitants, which cause terror to all her inhabitants! 18. Now shall the isles [1] tremble in the day of thy fall, and the isles that are in the sea shall be troubled at thy departure.

The islands shake in ver. 15, not exactly on account of any immediate danger which accrued to them from the fall of Tyre, but because now nothing any more in all the world appears to be secure. The fall of Tyre is an impressive sermon on the vanity of all earthly things, the transitory nature of all glory that has its foundation only in the earth. "That art inhabited from the seas" (ver. 17)—out of the seas: this is exactly the aspect that especially interests those princes of the seas standing in connection with Tyre, the conflux from the colonies, and other seaports in the mother city and central place. "She and her inhabitants, who caused their terror to all her inhabitants:" Tyre had a twofold class of inhabitants, like Jerusalem, whose inhabitants were in a certain sense all the inhabitants of the land: first, the inhabitants in the strict sense—the citizens; then her connections in the colonies and in other seaports more or less dependent on Tyre, who at all events, ideally taken, dwelt in Tyre, because the roots of their existence were there; on which account they often be-

---

[1] Intentionally stands first the Chaldee form אִין.

took themselves thither and made their abode there for a time: they flowed into and out of the central state. The inhabitants in the one sense were the terror of the inhabitants in the other sense. They must bow before them, and obey their commands. The departure in ver. 18 is the end.

In the epilogue, vers. 19-21, the contrast of Tyre in its irretrievable destruction, and Zion in its joyful resurrection. Ver. 19. Thus saith the Lord Jehovah, When I shall make thee a desolate city, like the cities that are not inhabited; when I bring up the deep upon thee, and many waters cover thee; 20. And I bring thee down with them that go down into the pit, to the perpetual people, and cause thee to dwell in the land of the deep, in waste lands of old with those that go down to the pit, that thou sit not; then shall I set beauty in the land of the living; 21. I will make thee a terror, and thou shalt be no more; and thou shalt be sought, and no more found for ever, saith the Lord Jehovah.

In ver. 19 the city, in ver. 20 the inhabitants, ruins above, a terrible wilderness beneath, in the desolate places of Sheol, the land of death-darkness without order (Job x. 22). Then, in contrast with both, Zion gloriously risen from her fall. He who has such a hope may well be patient with the scorn of Tyre (ver. 2), and answer it with a simple *respice finem*. With respect to Zion the mere indication suffices, the reference to the fact that on the ruin of Tyre on the earth there is a place of glory. It is only necessary to mark the place for the announcement of salvation hereafter to be unfolded. With "Then shall I set" begins the apodosis. On the relation of the words, inserted with enigmatical brevity, to Zion there can be the less doubt, when the fundamental passage in Isa. xxiv. 16 is considered. There also the beauty denotes the glory of Israel rising out of a heavy divine visitation. The flood in ver. 19 is ideal, the overflowing of the nations; comp. ver. 3, where the comparison, here abridged, is expanded. The perpetual people (ver. 20) are those who from primeval times have been in hell—its ancestral guests, so to speak—to whom all others, and among them the inhabitants of Tyre, go down, especially the "heroes of eternity," or antiquity, who perished in the deluge (Gen. vi. 4). "That thou sit not:" to sit is the opposite of lying down. The land of the living points to Ps. xxvii. 13, where the singer, or Israel, expresses the assurance that he will see the goodness of the Lord in the land of the living, and forms the contrast to Sheol, the land of the dead, to which in the foregoing the inhabitants of Tyre are assigned. The prophet has, in regard to Tyre, comprised in vers. 19–21 what was historically realized by degrees, and has now become a completed fact for many centuries. The truth of his announcement consists in this, that the first taking of Tyre by Nebuchadnezzar was the beginning of the end, the germ of its downfall, that it never again attained to its ancient greatness, but rather step by step reached its total overthrow, although, in harmony with the prophecy of Isaiah, an apparent improvement in its condition occasionally took place. No human eye could discern that precisely this moment was of decisive importance for the whole future of the city. Rationalism has made the assertion that Tyre was not taken by Nebuchadnezzar. On the contrary, this one thing is sufficient, that Ezekiel makes the communication a long time after the decision to prepare a collection of his prophecies was formed. Had it not been fulfilled, the prophet by the very communication would have exposed himself to the judgment pronounced in Deut. xviii. 22. We have a clear evidence of the fulfilment further on, in ch. xxix. 17–21.[1]

Ch. xxvii. We have here the lamentation over the fall of Tyre, announced in the foregoing chapter. First, its present glory is presented at full length to the view, vers. 1–25; then its fall, the importance of which can only be understood from the knowledge of its glory. We must profoundly know the *gloria mundi*, if we are to take to heart the *sic transit gloria mundi*. In vers. 3–9, the splendour of the city and the state; in vers. 10, 11, its admirable state of defence; in vers. 12–25, its world-wide trade. And all this to disappear without a trace !

Ver. 1. And the word of the LORD came unto me, saying, 2. And thou, son of man, take up a lamentation over Tyre; 3. And say to Tyre, that dwells at the entrances of the sea, that

[1] The full demonstration of the fulfilment is given in my treatise, *De rebus Tyriorum*, with which comp. Hävernick, *Comm.*; Movers, *Phœnicians*, ii. 1, pp. 428, 48 f., 61 f.; Niebuhr, *Hist. of Ass. and Babylon*, p. 216

trades with the nations in many isles, Thus saith the Lord Jehovah, O Tyre, thou sayest, I am perfect in beauty. 4. In the heart of the sea is thy border, thy builders have perfected thy beauty. 5. Of the cypresses of Shenir they have built for thee all thy boards; they have taken cedars of Lebanon to make the mast for thee. 6. Of the oaks of Bashan have they made thine oars; thy benches they have made of ivory, inlaid in larch from the isles of Chittim. 7. Embroidered byssus from Egypt was thy outspreading, to be a banner for thee; purple and crimson from the isles of Elishah was thy covering. 8. The inhabitants of Zidon and Arvad were thy rowers; thy wise men, O Tyre, were in thee: they were thy pilots. 9. The ancients of Gebal and its wise men were in thee, repairing thy chinks; all the ships of the sea and their mariners were in thee to carry on thy merchandise.

"In the entrances of the sea" (ver. 3), in a place from which the sea is easily accessible on all sides, in the centre of the civilised world, as the entrance of the city in Judg. i. 24, 25, is the entrance to the city. That others may easily come to it is not in the words, although it is the necessary consequence of what is said, but that it may easily come to all others, in harmony with the following, where Tyre appears throughout as active, as one who visits the nations for trade. Tyre lies, according to ver. 4, as it were in the heart, in the midst of the sea, because in its favourable situation all seas are easily accessible to it. In connection with this favourable situation in the heart of the sea, whose treasures flow into it from all sides, so that it already has what in Isa. lx. 5 is presented as the future of Zion—" The abundance of the sea shall be turned unto thee: the wealth of the Gentiles shall come unto thee,"—stands the perfect beauty which is ascribed to Tyre in the second half verse. This refers not merely to the city as such, in its buildings, but, as the following shows, to the whole state. In ver. 5 f. the state of Tyre appears under the figure of a splendid ship. By the ship, where many are together, and have a common object, danger, profit, and loss, are communities usually denoted in the symbolic language of Scripture. In the passage lying at the ground of the present one (Ps. xlviii. 8), where, in the celebration of a defeat which the Lord on behalf of His kingdom has sent on the hostile heathen, it is said, " By the east wind Thou breakest the ships of Tarshish;" in Isa. xxxiii. 21 and Rev. viii. 9 the ships signify states. Elsewhere the church appears under the symbol of a ship; comp. on John vi. 24, 25. In the Tyrian state, the representation by the symbol of a ship was the more natural, as it was a maritime power: the capital lay like a ship in the midst of the sea, and was surrounded with a forest of masts. The materials that are employed for the state ship are the most precious of which the city was built, especially the most costly articles which commerce brought to it, on which account several of the articles here mentioned are wanting in the later description of the trade. Shenir (ver. 5) is, according to Deut. iii. 9, the old Amoritish name of Hermon, which, as unusual, was specially adapted for the lofty prophetic style,[1] but is employed here perhaps also, because it suited the Canaanites, to whom the Tyrians belonged. " Of ivory inlaid in larch" (ver. 6): it is literally, ivory, daughter of the larch-trees. By daughter is meant the subordinate relation. The solid material is wood; the ivory serves only for inlaying. " The isles of Chittim:" Cyprus and the surrounding islands and coasts. " The outspreading" (ver. 7) is, as the addition " to be a banner for thee" shows, the unfurled flag; comp. Isa. xxxiii. 23, " they spread a banner." The sail, which some thought must be here introduced, is not mentioned, because this ship does not move, but remains in its place, and only sends out the smaller ships from it (ver. 9). The thought in vers. 8 and 9a is, that the powers of the other Phœnician cities are for the good of the Tyrian state; but the prerogatives of supremacy remain in the chief state, and the bearers of the highest offices proceed from it. " All the ships of the sea and their mariners were in thee, to carry on thy merchandise" (9b): the ships and seamen of the Tyrians are meant, with their colonies, to whom the ships in this description belong, which alone are represented as active in it. The ships of other nations, which, in comparison with those of Tyre, come not into view, are disregarded. All the ships of Tyre are, as it were, in this giant ship, as the jolly-boats in an ordinary large ship, and are sent thence, as occasion requires, on their particular errand.

In vers. 10, 11, the military fortification of Tyre. The figure of the ship is omitted here, where walls and towers are

[1] Comp. my comment on iv. 8 of the Song of Songs.

spoken of, and is only resumed in ver. 26, on the transition from the description of the splendour to that of the destruction. Ver. 10. Paras, and Lud, and Phut, were in thy force, thy men of war: shield and helmet, they hanged in thee; they set forth thy beauty. 11. The sons of Arvad and thy force were on thy walls round about, and bold champions in thy towers: their shields they hanged upon thy walls round about: they completed thy beauty.

In ver. 10, the foreign mercenaries, who had their fixed quarters in Tyre, and were sent from it on external expeditions; at their head the Persians from inner Asia, who stood related to Tyre, probably even then in connection with the anti-Chaldaic coalition, the first germ of their later victorious lifting of the shield against the Chaldean empire: comp. on ch. viii. 16, xxxii. 24. Then the African nations Lud and Phut. These were the most remote among the countries from which Tyre drew its mercenaries. "They set forth thy beauty:" Grotius says, It was honourable to thee to have so many nations in thy service. In apposition to the foreign mercenaries appear those from Aradus (ver. 11), the garrison forces from the other Phœnician cities. But along with these, Tyre has also a native force; and this is mentioned in the third place. The sons of Arvad and thy force are related to one another, as in ver. 8 the inhabitants of Zidon and thy wise men. Towers and walls are only relied on in Phœnician warfare. "Bold champions:" this term not occurring elsewhere, is probably the Tyrian designation of a choice troop. The hanging of the weapons on the walls serves as an external symbol of self-defence. The words, "They completed thy beauty," refer to ver. 3, where Tyre piques itself on its perfect beauty; and ver. 4, where the prophet says, "Thy builders completed thy beauty."

In vers. 12-25, to complete the representation of the glory of Tyre, we have the description of its trade, which begins and ends with Tarshish, the chief place of trade, but otherwise moves quite freely, and aims neither at completeness nor at geographical order. The attempt to force the latter upon the picture has done material injury to the representation.

Ver. 12. Tarshish traded with thee on account of the fulness of thy wealth :[1] silver, iron, tin, and lead, they gave thee for sale. 13. Javan, Tubal, and Meshech, they traded with thee: souls of men and vessels of brass they gave thee for wares. 14. From the house of Togarmah they gave horses, and riders, and mules to thee for sale. 15. The sons of Dedan traded with thee: many isles bartered with thee: ivory and ebony they returned thee for a gift. 16. Aram traded with thee on account of the abundance of thy works: carbuncle, purple, and embroidery, and byssus, and precious things,[2] and rubies, they gave thee for sale. 17. Judah and the land of Israel, they traded with thee: wheat of Minnith, and dainties, and honey, and oil, and balm, they gave thee for wares. 18. Damascus traded with thee on account of the abundance of thy works, the abundance of thy wealth, in wine of Helbon and bright wool. 19. Vedan and Javan gave thee yarn: wrought iron,[3] cassia, and cinnamon, were among thy wares. 20. Dedan traded with thee in broad coverings for riding. 21. Arabia and all the princes of Kedar, they bartered with thee: in lambs, and rams, and he-goats, in these they bartered with thee. 22. The merchants of Sheba and Raamah traded with thee: the chief of all spices, and all precious stones and gold, they gave thee for sale. 23. Haran, and Kanneh, and Eden, the merchants of Sheba, Asshur, and Kilmad, traded with thee. 24. They traded with thee in ornaments, mantles of purple and embroidery, and in treasures[4] of damask, bound with cords, and fastened in thy market. 25. The ships of Tarshish visit thee, thy wares: and thou becamest full, and very glorious, in the heart of the sea.

Tarshish in ver. 12 is Tartessus in Spain, Javan (ver. 13) Greece; in connection with which, notwithstanding the local

[1] Luther, "Thou hast had thy trade on the sea:" setting aside the ships of Tarshish, for which in ver. 25 also he puts ships of the sea.

[2] Luther, "velvet." By derivation the word signifies *excelsa*. It is best explained by precious things or precious stones. This meaning suits also in Job xxviii. 18 and Prov. xxiv. 7. " For the fool, wisdom is ramoth :" an individualizing designation of a good unattainable by him.

[3] Luther, " Dan, and Javan, and Mehusal, brought iron-work to thy markets ;" instead of Vedan, Dan, and Meussal, falsely, as a proper name.

[4] Luther, " costly chests." There is no reason for omitting the ascertained meaning, treasures.

distance, on account of the similarity of the wares, Meshech and Tubal, the Moschi and Tibareni on the border of the Black Sea.[1] Togarmah in ver. 14 is probably Armenia. As Scripture knows only one Dedan, the Arabic, Dedan in ver. 15 cannot be different from Dedan in ver. 20. The "many isles" here have nothing geographically to do with Dedan. The prophet was probably unable to define them exactly. The Dedanites with their caravans appear as representatives of the inland trade. The same products, however, were imported into Tyre by sea, and thus came from "the isles," the islands and coasts. "They returned thee for a gift:" all trade is a return. "On account of the abundance of thy works" (ver. 16)—thy works of art. The abundance in these is that which enticed Aram to trade. What Tyre offers is only indicated in a brief allusion: the prophet is full only in respect of the imported goods, because the conflux of these to Tyre constitutes the glory of the city, and thus gives the ground for picturing the depth of its fall. The point of view to which the prophet keeps in the whole picture, is exactly given in the words of the close: "And thou becamest full and very glorious in the heart of the sea." Accordingly, what Tyre exported comes out only as an allusion in passing. That Tyre was so full and honoured, while Zion became ever poorer and poorer, and sank into misery —this was a stone of stumbling to the people of God. The prophet removes the stumbling-stone when he points to the end. There all fulness and glory are vanished from Tyre, for ever vanished, buried in the depth of the sea; and, on the contrary, Zion begins to bloom.[2] Minnith in ver. 17 is the name of a place in the transjordanic region (Judg. xi. 33). For the nobler gifts, which the land of Israel could offer, Tyre had no taste. Damascus, included under Aram, ver. 16, occurs again expressly in ver. 18, because it was a chief place of trade for Tyre. Along with works of art from Tyre, which were already mentioned in ver. 16, is noticed here the abundance of all riches as a motive for Damascus to enter into relations of trade with Tyre. This proves that the trade of Tyre was no

[1] Niebuhr, p. 135.
[2] The ב in בנפך might be wanting, according to ver. 12 and ver. 19. It is not needful to think of a meaning deviating from these parallels. Properly, in rubies; so that the works furnished by them consisted in these.

mere barter—that it also paid for wares with money; for this especially is to be understood by riches. Helbon, a place in Antilibanus, where even now the vine is largely cultivated. Vedan, in ver. 19, cannot be determined, and was probably known to the prophet himself only by name. Javan is always Greece, and occurred before in ver. 13. The second half-verse says nothing of the origin of the wares. Goods must have been brought in of which the prophet knew not the origin. Among Greek commodities, yarn only is mentioned here; others are named in ver. 13. Dedan, mentioned before in ver. 15, recurs once more in ver. 20, to complete by a new commodity the splendid warerooms of Tyre. All that flowed into Tyre interests the prophet more than the order in the enumeration of the places whence it came. Sheba, mentioned before in ver. 22, recurs in ver. 23, where it was intended to give at the close a collection of the most diverse regions, and bring to view the extent of the Tyrian trade. This alone is the object of the prophet. He writes as little from the view of a minister of commerce, as Isaiah in ch. iii. from that of a milliner. The succession of places is then only "highly disorderly and surprising," when we measure the prophet by a false standard. Excessive order would not suit the prophet. Concerning Kilmad, Ezekiel himself had perhaps no more exact information to give than concerning Vedan. He knew only one thing for certain, that there was a Kilmad, and that Tyre had commercial relations with it; and this only concerns us here. Ornaments (ver. 24), properly perfections, is the general, which is then followed by the special. "Bound with cords, and fastened:" Ezekiel describes the bales of such stuffs probably according to his own view. "The ships of Tarshish visit thee, thy wares" (ver. 25): these were the special object of the visit. But while they fetched, they also carried—comp. ver. 12, to which the close of the whole section returns,—and that which they brought comes here specially into view, as the second part of the verse shows. The ships of Tarshish come so far into view as they contribute to this, that Tyre becomes full and glorious.

Hitherto is the delineation of the glory of Tyre, which has no other object than to bring to the light the depth of its fall, and indelibly impress upon the mind the vanity of all earthly things. "The glory of the lands must come to dust and ashes:" this is now exemplified in Tyre in vers. 26-36, the greatness of which had been so long for Israel a riddle and a stumbling-stone, that still stood upright, when Zion already lay in ruins. Jeremiah had already struck up his song: "How sits the city so solitary, that was full of people! She is become as a widow: a princess among the nations, and a queen in the provinces, she must now serve." We have here a plaster for the wound, which this lamentation of Jeremiah describes.

Ver. 26. Thy rowers have brought thee into great waters; the east wind[1] hath broken thee in the heart of the seas. 27. Thy riches and thy merchandise, thy wares,[2] thy mariners and thy pilots, the repairers of thy chinks, and those who dealt in thy wares, and all thy men of war that are in thee, and all thy company[3] which is in thy midst, shall fall into the heart of the sea in the day of thy fall. 28. At the sound of the cry of thy pilots the borders shall shake. 29. And all that handle the oar, the mariners, and all the pilots of the sea, shall come down from their ships: they shall stand upon the land. 30. And they shall make their voice heard over thee, and cry bitterly, and cast dust upon their head: they shall strew themselves with ashes. 31. And they shall shave themselves bald for thee, and gird themselves with sackcloth, and weep for thee in bitterness of soul with a bitter wailing. 32. And in their wailing they shall take up a lamentation[4] for thee, and lament over thee, Who is like Tyre, like one that is destroyed[5] amidst the sea? 33. When thy merchandise went out from

---

[1] Luther, "And thy mariners have conveyed for thee upon great waters but an east wind." But it is not said, they have brought *for thee*, but *thee*.

[2] Luther, "thy wares, buyers, traders." He overlooked that the first three words refer to the goods, and then a double triad of persons follows.

[3] It is literally, "and in or on thy great multitude," so that the falling consists in the multitude. ב occurs several times in this way in Genesis, for ex. ix. 10.

[4] Luther, after a wrong reading, "their children also shall lament thee." נִי is contracted from נְהִי, Jer. ix. 17, 18; comp. נֶה, Ezek. vii. 11. The reading "their sons" is only a bad conjecture. Not their sons—they themselves lament.

[5] דֻמָּה is not the participle, but the past tense in *Pual*, that here, as often the past tense—for ex. הֻלְלָה, ch. xxvi. 17—stands in the place of the participle.

the seas, thou satisfiedst many people: with the abundance of thy riches and thy wares thou didst enrich the kings of the earth. 34. In the time when thou art broken from the sea in the depths of the waters,[1] thy wares and all thy company in thy midst shall fall. 35. All the inhabitants of the isles shall be astonished at thee, and thy kings shall shudder, they shall be troubled in face. 36. The merchants among the people shall hiss at thee; thou shalt be a terror, and shalt not be for ever.

In ver. 26, Tyre appears again, as in vers. 4–9, under the figure of a ship, and her fall as a shipwreck. The many waters are a figure of great dangers and sufferings (Ps. xlii. 8). The east wind—this in particular, as the most violent in Palestine—signifies the storm of dangers. The fundamental passage is Ps. xlviii. 8. "In the heart of the sea:" this recurs from ver. 25. The earlier state of glory now changes into its grave. According to ver. 29, the catastrophe is regarded by all seafaring men standing in close relation with Tyre as a common one. They lament over the fall of Tyre, because nothing more is certain in the whole world, if even the queen of the sea must fall. They are so overwhelmed with terror, that they leave the uncertain sea, as the fall of Tyre shows, and betake themselves to the land. No one is like Tyre (ver. 30), in the combination of former unexampled glory and present total destruction. The point of departure for the wares of Tyre is the sea (ver. 33), whence they are exported into the havens of all the world. The satisfying denotes the appeasing of desire. The wares are those, the importation of which into Tyre was described in vers. 12–25. Tyre is (ver. 34) broken from the seas, from which formerly its wares came (ver. 33), in the depth of the waters, as a sunken ship, and with it are its wares drowned in the deep. Formerly the sympathy of friends, but in ver. 36 the scorn of the rivals and the envious.

---

[1] Luther, "but *now* art thou plunged from the sea in the deepest waters." Other expositors also take עֵת for an accus. of time now. But it does not so occur elsewhere. According to all parallel passages, נִשְׁבֶּרֶת must give the more exact definition of the time—at the time when. From the contrast with ver. 33 also, the chief emphasis must lie on the loss of the wares: the destruction of Tyre itself can only be regarded as its conditioning cause.

Ch. xxviii. The city of Tyre is here followed by the *prince of Tyre*, the prophecy concerning him (vers. 1-10), and the lamentation over him (vers. 11-19). The new point of most importance here is the emphatic indication of the *guilt* by which the catastrophe was brought upon Tyre. The king of Tyre forms not the contrast to the city, but its complement. The prophet had the more reason to bring him forward in its fall, as he thus obtains a counterpart to the glorious rise of the kingdom of Israel in Christ.

Ver. 1. And the word of the LORD came unto me, saying, 2. Son of man, say unto the prince of Tyre, Thus saith the Lord Jehovah, Because thy heart is lifted up, and thou sayest, I am God, in the seat of God I sit in the heart of the sea; and thou art man, and not God, and settest thy heart as the heart of God: 3. Behold, thou art wiser than Daniel; no secret have they hid from thee. 4. By thy wisdom and thy understanding thou hast gotten thee riches, and hast gotten gold and silver in thy treasures: 5. By the greatness of thy wisdom, by thy traffic, hast thou increased thy riches, and thy heart is glad through thy riches: 6. Therefore thus saith the Lord Jehovah, Because thou settest thy heart as the heart of God; 7. Therefore, behold, I will bring on thee strangers, the violent of the heathen; and they shall draw their swords against the beauty of thy wisdom, and defile thy brightness. 8. They shall bring thee down to the pit, and thou shalt die the death of the slain in the heart of the seas. 9. Wilt thou say, I am God, before thy slayer? and thou art man, and not God, in the hand of him who defileth thee. 10. The death of the uncircumcised shalt thou die by the hand of strangers: for I have spoken it, saith the Lord Jehovah.

The seat of God (ver. 2) is a seat which, in its absolute inaccessibleness, is like the seat of God in heaven.[1] He sets or makes his mind like the mind of God; he has so pushed himself into the height, that in his folly he arrogates to himself what God claims to Himself by right. It belongs to the nature of God, to be and to have all from Himself; to the nature of man, to derive all from the fulness of God. If man imagines himself to subsist as God in himself, this is the

---

[1] Grotius: *sic ut Deus ab omni injuria tutus est in arce cœlesti, sic me defendit mare.*

greatest of all perversities, which cannot remain unpunished, because God does not give His glory to another. The fundamental passage is Isa. xiv. 14, where the king of Babylon compares himself with the Most High. The general divine name, Elohim, the Godhead, stands as usual, where there is a contrast of man and God, of earth and heaven. Hand in hand with the charge that he likens himself with God, goes in ver. 3 the reproach that he counts himself wiser than Daniel. Denying the authenticity of Daniel, Bernstein was right in declaring this passage and ch. xiv. 14 to have been interpolated after the composition of the book of Daniel, in which, however, no one has been able to follow him. We find here, as in ch. xiv. 14, the most remarkable harmony with the book of Daniel. The prophet would have made himself and Daniel ridiculous, if the latter had not given such proofs of a wisdom surpassing all that was ordinary, as his book presents. To declare himself wiser than Daniel, is at once to transcend the stage of man, and make himself equal with God. The prophet presumes it to be acknowledged that Daniel stands on the highest stage of wisdom attainable by man. This rests on a fact by which the pre-eminence of Daniel above all other wise men was proved—that recorded in Dan. ii., where Daniel performs what all the wise men of Babylon could not perform, what they had designated as exceeding human power. Comp. ch. ii. 10, 11, where they say, "There is not a man upon earth who could tell what the king asks; there is none who can tell it except the holy gods, who dwell not with men." Daniel's wisdom must have been generally known and acknowledged, especially among the Jews in the Chaldean exile, for whom in the first instance Ezekiel wrote: for Ezekiel presupposes that the king of Tyre knew of Daniel, and certainly as one whom no other but himself excelled in wisdom; so that Daniel can be no mere Jewish celebrity, but must have proved his wisdom on the theatre of the world, as is recorded of him in the book of Daniel. But Ezekiel ascribes to Daniel not merely wisdom, but even a special kind of it, that to which nothing hidden was dark. This very kind of wisdom meets us in the book of Daniel. The king of Babylon says of Daniel in ch. iv. 6, "I know that the spirit of the holy gods is in thee, and no secret troubleth thee." Daniel had appeared as one from whom no secret was hidden in the very beginning of his career, and thereby laid the foundation of his prominent position. He performed in secret wisdom what all the Chaldean wise men could not do. It is said in ch. ii. 19, "Then was the secret revealed unto Daniel in a night vision." Finally, from the contrast with the prince of Tyre, who had to prove his wisdom on the theatre of the world (comp. ver. 5, where the wisdom is immediately connected with the trade), we expect that Daniel also was no *solitary* sage, that he exercised his wisdom in *great public circumstances*. In harmony with this, Daniel appears in the book named after him, as the *statesman* among the prophets. He holds from his youth, contemporary with the king of Tyre, the highest civic offices in the Chaldean empire. He was, in particular, placed at the head of all the Chaldean wise men, who exercised so important an influence on public affairs; comp. ch. ii. 48, 49. Whosoever, in the investigation of the authenticity of the book of Daniel, declines to go thoroughly into the facts presented here and in ch. xiv. 14, thereby shows that he is devoid of purely scientific interest, a slave to dogmatic preconceptions, and determined not by facts, but by leanings. The violent among the heathen (ver. 7), so violent that the others beside them do not come into view, are the Chaldeans, the then world-conquerors; so active, that what others undertook against them, only aimed at repelling the violence. "Defile thy brightness"—which was hitherto a sanctuary bestowed on him by God, and stood under His protection. He himself has first defiled it, because he ascribed to himself what belonged to God. Now he is also desecrated as a punishment. The cruelly estranged brightness was dragged through the mire. "Thou shalt die the death of the slain" (ver. 8): it is literally the deaths, as is also said in ver. 10 of the death of the king. The king, the central personage, the animating breath of the whole people, as the king is called in Lam. iv. 20, dies as it were many deaths—dies in each of his slain subjects. In the same respect it is said in ch. xxix. 5 of Pharaoh, "Thou shalt not be gathered nor heaped up." Already in Gen. xiv. 10 it was said of the kings of Sodom and Gomorrah, that they fell into the slime-pits, which befell them only in their subjects, while as individuals they remained alive. The foolish thoughts of pride, which creep into men only in good fortune, will vanish from the king (ver. 9) when he stands helpless before his slayer, when he is in the hand of him who defiles him; comp. ver. 7. Thus will it be manifest that he is man, and not God. "The death of the uncircumcised shalt thou die" (ver. 10): the circumcision of the flesh is, according to the law, a symbol of the circumcision of the heart (Lev. xxvi. 41; Deut. x. 16, xxx. 6). On this account, in Ezekiel, the uncircumcised stand at once for the men of unclean heart, the ungodly and the wicked (xxxi. 18, xxxii. 19), the uncircumcised in heart and ears (Acts vii. 51; comp. Ezek. xliv. 9). The uncircumcised, in the sense of Ezekiel, are found among the Jews no less than among the heathen, because the sign loses all significance, and is regarded as not existing, when the thing signified does not exist (Rom. ii. 25.; Jer. ix. 26).

In the second section (vers. 11-19) the lamentation over the king of Tyre. Ver. 11. And the word of the LORD came unto me, saying, 12. Son of man, take up a lamentation over the king of Tyre, and say unto him, Thus saith the Lord Jehovah, Thou sealest the archetype,[1] full of wisdom, and perfect in beauty. 13. In Eden the garden of God wast thou: every precious stone covered thee, sardius, topaz, and diamond; tarshish, onyx, and jasper; sapphire, carbuncle, and smaragd, and gold: the work of thy drums and thy pipes was in thee; in the day when thou wast created they were prepared. 14. Thou wast the anointed cherub that covereth; and so I made thee: upon the holy mountain of God wast thou; amidst the stones of fire thou didst walk. 15. Thou wast innocent in thy ways from the day when thou wast created, until iniquity was found in thee. 16. In the abundance of thy merchandise they filled the midst of thee with violence, and thou sinnedst: and I will profane thee from the mountain of God, and destroy thee, O covering cherub, from the midst of the stones of fire. 17. Thy heart was high because of thy beauty; thou didst corrupt thy wisdom by reason of thy brightness: I will cast thee to the ground; before kings will I set thee for a spectacle. 18. By the abundance of thy iniquities, in the perversity of thy traffic, thou didst defile thy sanctuaries; and I will bring forth a fire from the midst of thee, this shall devour thee; and

---

[1] Luther, "thou art a fine seal," as if it were חותם.

I will bring thee to ashes upon the earth in the eyes of all that see thee. 19. All who know thee among the nations shall be amazed at thee; thou shalt be a terror,[1] and thou shalt not be for ever.

A sealer of the archetype[2] is one who has a right to lay aside the idea of his being, because he himself completely represents it; because he is a personified idea, a corporate ideal, completely represented in life, which he, and in general man, may be. Quite in harmony with this stands the following, where the king of Tyre is described as "full of wisdom and perfect in beauty." "In Eden the garden of God wast thou" (ver. 13): in the first book of Moses, ch. ii. 8, the garden of God is in the region called Eden; comp. here, ch. xxxvi. 35. But in our passage the name of the whole is transferred to the most eminent part. We have here an abridged comparison. The thought is, Thou didst enjoy as it were a paradisaic existence— a glory like that of the first man in Paradise. A like abridged comparison is found, for ex., in naming a cloister paradise. The precious stones with which the king is bedecked bring the glory of his rank to outward view. Of the precious stones, there are in all ten, including the gold, which is here the more readily added to the precious stones, because they are usually set in gold. The nine precious stones, which have been supposed, without any reason, to be related to the precious stones in the breastplate of the high priest, with which they have no real connection, fall into three times three; being respectively limited in this way, that *and* always stands before the third. The gold then completes the decade. "The work of thy drums and pipes was in thee:"[3] with this is to be compared the enumeration of the instruments in Dan. iii. 5. Music appears there as a necessary element of the royal grandeur, which it is even to the present day. With the king of Babylon goes (Isa. xiv. 11) also

---

[1] Luther, "that thou art so suddenly overthrown." בלהה in the still even now often assumed but not ascertained meaning, sudden downfall.

[2] תכנית signifies, ch. xliii. 10, outline, model. The meaning ornament, beauty, is assumed without ground. To seal never stands in the meaning of completing, often in the sense of setting aside; because we are wont to seal up things which we have locked up or put aside for greater security. Comp. *Christol.* on Dan. ix. 24.

[3] נקב, the perforated, signifies in general the wind instrument, in contrast with those which are struck.

the "noise of his viols" down to the grave. The *work* of thy drums and pipes denotes the artistic workmanship of them; comp. ch. xxvii. 16. "In the day of thy birth were they prepared:" this intimates that the Tyrian monarchy from its very origin was surrounded with this music, that it came into existence, as it were, amid drums and trumpets, as according to Job xxxviii. 7 the earth was ushered into existence amid the songs of the morning stars, and the shouting of the sons of God. For the king, who is here an ideal person, the Tyrian monarchy, the day of being created is that of his accession to the throne; comp. Ps. ii. 7. "Thou wast an anointed cherub that covereth" (ver. 14): the cherub is the ideal combination of all living creatures on the earth. The king of Tyre resembles it, in so far as he represents the earthly creature-life in its highest stage and in its utmost perfection. The anointed[1] cherub is the holy one, with reference to the statement of the books of Moses, that all the vessels of the temple were anointed, to impress on them the character of holiness (Ex. xxx. 22–33). The anointing, the consecration from God, is common to the king of Tyre with the cherub; comp. the phrase "thy sanctuaries," ver. 18, and also vers. 7, 9. He is *res sacra*, because God has imparted to him of His grandeur, and kept him in the possession of it. All earthly majesty is holy, and remains holy, until it desecrates itself. "That covereth:" this points to Ex. xxv. 20. The cherubs in the sanctuary cover and protect the ark of the covenant; the covenant, the people of the covenant. So the king of Tyre covers his people so long as the favour of God is with him. Instead of "And so I made thee," it is literally, "And so I gave thee"—in such a situation I placed thee. This situation is then denoted by two figures, which are as well independent of one another as of the preceding figure of the cherub. Many false expositions have been occasioned by this, that men are confused by the sudden change of the figures in Scripture, and seek to bring unity into the figure by force, instead of resting simply in the unity of the thought. First, the king of Tyre was on the holy mountain of God. It is not said, On *a* mountain of *gods*, so as to be compared with Isa. xiv. 14, but on the mountain of *God;* nor does it refer to a pretence or imagination, but to one actually certified by God.

---

[1] משח, in Hebrew only to anoint.

Every earthly dignity is an elevation on the holy mountain of
God, a participation in the divine dignity. On the mount of
God is God Himself enthroned, as David is enthroned in the
mount of David (Ps. xxx. 8). It is a figure for His exalted
position, which is elsewhere expressed by sitting in heaven.
The mountain of God stands, as we have said, in as little connection with the cherub as with " the walking amidst the stones
of fire " that follows. We have in the verse three designations of the glory of Tyre quite independent of one another.
" Amidst the stones of fire thou didst walk :" to the fiery stones
here correspond the fiery wall in Zech. ii. 5, comp. ix. 8. Both
denote the divine protection, which makes him that stands
under it inaccessible to all his foes. Whosoever will assail him
must first pass through the fiery stones and consume himself,
before he approaches him. The innocence which is ascribed
in ver. 15 to the king of Tyre in his beginnings, is naturally
such as may take place on the ground of Gen. iii., especially
among a people to which God has not made Himself known,
that stands out of connection with His arrangements for salvation, which present the right remedy against sin, and render a
sincere walk with God possible. Our passage, which is in harmony with Gen. xv. 16, according to which in the time of
Abraham the iniquity of the Amorites was not yet full, as well
as with that which Jesus says of the (relative) innocence of
children, is in favour of caution in the definition of natural
corruption, and implies that there are important differences
among those who have not yet by God's grace attained to regeneration, so important as to condition the awarding of the
judgments of God, and the communication of His grace. A
sound experience is in harmony with this. It shows that on
the common ground of hereditary corruption there are yet in
the life of individuals and of nations very important diversi-
ties, times of comparative innocence and of deep declension
provoking the judgments of God. As a rule, youth is the
better time: the rule holds in nations as in individuals, who
have not given way to grace; the older, the worse. Sin not
vigorously resisted in its beginnings, grows from step to step.
In harmony with our passage are the experiences which the
missionaries to the heathen have now to obtain, compared with
the earlier ages. " They (thy inhabitants) filled the midst of

thee:" those filling belonged to the king of Tyre, who is, so to speak, an ideal person; comp. on ver. 8. The city also belongs to him, the representative of the collective Tyrian state. Hence we may speak of his midst. The expression sets forth the dangers of trade for whole nations and for individuals.[1] In accordance with this, Jesus of Sirach says in ch. xxvi. 18, " A merchant can hardly keep himself from doing wrong, or a huckster from sin;" and in ch. xxvii. 2, " As a nail in the wall sticketh between two stones, so also doth sin stick between buyer and seller." The constant excitement of selfishness and covetousness connected with trade can only be effectually counteracted by the grace of God. Where this does not prevail, trade, no less than influential position, brings deep confusion with it, as history also clearly shows in the daughter city of Tyre, Carthage; the proofs of which Münter gives with abundant fulness in the treatise, *The Religion of the Carthaginians*. In ver. 17 a second cause of corruption. The soul, entangled in the bonds of self-interest and covetousness, and thereby deeply degraded, is now also led captive in other respects by sin; in particular, it is a sport of pride which is the immediate forerunner of the divine judgments, because God will be alone great, and gives His honour to no other. " Thou didst corrupt thy wisdom by reason of thy brightness :" the brightness is the cause on which the effect depends. The foundation of wisdom is humility, which sees things as they are, has an open eye for its own weaknesses and the excellences of others, and is on its guard against dangerous undertakings, as David says in Ps. cxxxi. 1: " O Lord, my heart is not haughty, nor mine eyes lofty; neither do I walk in great matters, and too wonderful for me." The " brightness " received into the heart blinds the eye, so that one regards himself alone as great, and everything else as small, and rushes wantonly into dangers for which he is not prepared, and enters on paths which lead to perdition; as, for ex., Tyre undertook the combat against the flourishing Chaldee monarchy. God does not need to appear as a *deus ex machina* in the judgment upon the proud, who wantonly brings himself to ruin. There is here a weighty lesson for all nations, and for individuals: if thy safety is dear

---

[1] Comp. viii. 17, xxx. 11. The verb is followed by a double accusative of the space and the material filling it.

to thee, withstand the beginnings of pride. The only effectual resistance, however, is fellowship with God, walking with Him after the example of Enoch and Noah, from whom alone can flow the living power to overcome the living lusts and passions, which appear of themselves with the "brightness," and defy all mere good resolutions, and all morality severed from God. This is the rock on which all the heathen powers of the old world were shattered. "Will I set thee for a spectacle:" formerly in its brightness a spectacle of wonder and envy for kings, Tyre is now become for them a spectacle of astonishment and spiteful joy[1] in its terrible downfall. In ver. 18 the prophet returns to the sin of avarice as the cause of its downfall. "Thou didst defile thy sanctuaries:" any greatness consecrated by God, any glory imparted by Him, may be regarded as a sanctuary, the desecration of which by the feoffee is followed by desecration by the feudal lord. The idea of the sanctuary is that of separation from the world, which exerts all its destructive powers in vain against the gift imparted by God, so long as the possessor remains in the right position towards God. "I will bring forth a fire from the midst of thee:" the destructive catastrophe has its starting-point in that which is thereby destroyed; comp. in ver. 17, "Thou didst corrupt thy wisdom." "From the midst of thee:" this is explained by the fact that the king comprehends in himself the city and the people. The ashes are the mournful remnant of the process of combustion. A terror (ver. 19) is he at whose sight one trembles.[2] The cause of this trembling and becoming a terror is the total destruction, "and thou shalt not be for ever,"—a destruction like that of Sodom in ancient times, in which the sin-root of Canaan first came to full development—the sentence, "Sin, when it is finished, bringeth forth death" (Jas. i. 14), first verified itself; while the judgment on Tyre forms the close of the long series of judgments on the Canaanites.

Ch. xxviii. 20-26. Here follows the prophecy concerning Zidon. After Tyre, Zidon was the most important among the Phœnician cities. It appears in the books of Moses, in which

---

[1] Comp. xxvii. 36. ראה with ב signifies the impassioned regard, and especially that with joyful interest.

[2] The ordinary meaning terror corresponds with amazement.

Tyre is not yet mentioned, as the oldest and most prominent settlement of the Canaanites (Gen. x. 15), as the representative of the whole Canaanitish trade (Gen. xlix. 13). It had formerly had the leadership, but had long lost it in favour of Tyre. That it was dependent on the latter, appears among other places from ch. xxvii. 8, where the inhabitants of Zidon, along with those of Aradus, appear as rowers in the Tyrian state-ship. Yet it must have retained a certain independence. This appears from Jer. xxvii. 3, where messengers (or a messenger) of the king of Zidon appear in Jerusalem along with the messengers of the king of Tyre. This explains why a special prophecy is here devoted to Zidon apart from Tyre. The fulfilment of this prophecy appears in ch. xxxii. 30, where in an announcement which belongs to the end of the twelfth year, the Zidonians appear in the list of the nations who have already experienced the judicial activity of God, and have fallen by the sword of Nebuchadnezzar. Our prophecy was, as the want of a new date shows, contemporary with that relating to Tyre, of which it forms an appendix. The latter belongs, according to ch. xxvi. 1, to the beginning of the tenth month, in the eleventh year, so that the fulfilment followed very close upon the prophecy. The visitation of Zidon followed soon after the beginning of the siege of Tyre, which, favoured by its situation, was able to present a longer and more vigorous resistance to the hostile power.[1]

Ver. 20. And the word of the LORD came unto me, saying, 21. Son of man, set thy face against Zidon, and prophesy against it, 22. And say, Thus saith the Lord Jehovah; Behold, I am against thee, O Zidon; and I will be glorified in the midst of thee: and they shall know that I am the LORD, when I execute judgments on it, and am sanctified in it. 23. And I will send into it pestilence and blood in its streets;[2] and the slain shall fall in the midst of it by the sword upon it round about; and they shall know that I am the LORD. Ver. 24. And there shall be no more to the house of Israel a pricking thorn nor a grieving sting from all round about

[1] Niebuhr, p. 213.
[2] Luther, "and I shall send pestilence and bloodshed among them in their streets," so that the pestilence is imparted even to the streets, contrary to Deut. xxxii. 25.

them that despised them; and they shall know that I am the Lord Jehovah. 25. Thus saith the Lord Jehovah, When I gather the house of Israel from the nations among whom they are scattered, then I will be sanctified in them in the eyes of the heathen, and they shall dwell in their land that I have given to my servant Jacob. 26. And they shall dwell therein securely, and build houses and plant vineyards, and dwell securely, when I execute judgments upon all that despised them round about; and they shall know that I am the LORD their God.

The God of Israel, so despised by the inhabitants of Zidon, comes upon them (ver. 22) in judgment; and they must recognise or experience Him in His operations, whom they obstinately refused to recognise willingly. How consoling it is, however, for the people of God, when lying in the dust, that their God is above, and in the very time of their deepest humiliation interposes for their exaltation! That the operations here ascribed to Him belong to Him in fact, they can the less doubt, as He has proclaimed them as His work by His servants the prophets (Jeremiah in ch. xlvii. 7, and Ezekiel here). "And am sanctified, or sanctify myself in it:" to be sanctified is the same as to be glorified or to glorify Himself, as surely as the holy God is separate from all creatures, sublime and glorious. To be sanctified is to be active in this absoluteness or infinity. Both pestilence and blood are sent against it (ver. 23), but the blood only belongs to the streets.¹ Ver. 24 already turns into the path of a general consideration, embracing Zidon in a greater whole, which applies no less to the other bordering states than to the Zidonians. The point of view here opened is a consolatory one. While the Lord chastises His own people with an unsparing rod, He visits the neighbouring heathen nations for the wrong which they have done to His people, as if it were directed against Himself, and verifies in them His word, "He that toucheth you, toucheth the apple of His eye" (Zech. ii. 8). Vers. 25, 26 give the close of the prophecies against the smaller bordering nations, and mark them off from the prophecies concerning Egypt, the chief power in the coalition, which formed the starting-point for the prophetic activity of Ezekiel. Here Zion in her

² Instead of the *Pilel* of נפל stands in xxx. 4, xxxii. 20, the *Kal*.

glorious restoration is contrasted with the annihilating judgments which pass over the heathen world. It was needful here to meet the despondency, which was now, after the opening of the siege of Jerusalem, the most dangerous foe. Thus, with the one-sidedness which so commonly adheres to prophecy when it enters on definite periods and determinations, only the bright side of the future of the covenant people is presented to the eye. That along with this also in the future a shady side, and that a terrible one, will appear, that which Jerusalem had even now to suffer will not permit us to doubt. The deep corruption of the people, which provoked the catastrophe of the present, will also manifest itself in the future, so that along with grace wrath must intervene. With respect to this side, here intentionally concealed, the successors of Ezekiel, Zechariah and Malachi, provide an essential supplement to him. They enter fully into the shady side, the existence of which Ezekiel also clearly and sharply recognises, as in particular ch. v. 1–4 shows. A great national judgment is there expressly announced, which is to follow after the Chaldean.

CHAPTERS XXIX.–XXXII.

The prophecies against Egypt now follow, in which the prophet turns from the members of the coalition to its head.

Of the prophecies against Egypt there are in all six, each with a date,—properly only five, as the second (ch. xxix. 17–xxx. 19) proves itself to be an appendix to the first by this, that it departs from the otherwise so strictly observed chronological order: it does not lie, as most of the other prophecies against foreign nations, between the date given in ch. xxiv. 1 and that in ch. xxxiii. 21; it departs from the chronological order even within the collection of prophecies against Egypt. Its object is to point out that the fulfilment of the first prophecy is fast approaching, to which it is in part verbally attached, to show most emphatically that it has no independent import, but is merely a supplement. Thus there remain only the prophecies, ch. xxix. 1–16, xxx. 20–26, xxxi., xxxii. 1–16, and 17–32. The number seven can only be carried through by forcibly separating what is united. There is in the whole collection of Ezekiel no single independent discourse which is not dated.

The first prophecy (ch. xxix. 1-16) belongs to the twelfth day in the tenth month of the tenth year after the captivity of Jehoiachin, and thus lies between the last prophecy against Judah, of the tenth day of the tenth month in the ninth year (ch. xxiv. 1); and the prophecy against Tyre of the first day of the tenth month in the eleventh year, in ch. xxvi. The prophecy was delivered, as ch. xxiv. 1 shows, during the siege of Jerusalem. The occasion is the hope of recovery through Pharaoh. The practical point of view, which it is of so great import to recognise in the exposition, is presented in vers. 6, 7, 16. The prophet predicts concerning Egypt, not for Egypt— what are things outside to Him?—but for Judah. The prophecy is to oppose the foolish hopes which were again placed in Egypt, to which Israel had so often resigned itself to its injury with idolatrous reliance; comp. ch. xvi. 26, xxiii. 8, 19. How foolish to trust in the land which already stands itself on the brink of a precipice, which must so soon experience the judicial strokes of God! Who would bind himself to a corpse?

The prophet is, according to ver. 2, to prophesy against Pharaoh, and against all Egypt. Accordingly he turns to the king, vers. 3-7; to the land, vers. 8-12. In the third section, vers. 13-16, a mitigation, which, however, makes no change in the chief point: Egypt will, after the fall of the Chaldean empire, recover itself in some measure, but never again attain to such a state that Israel could be led to make it the object of its reliance.

Ver. 1. In the tenth year, the tenth month, on the twelfth day of the month, the word of the LORD came unto me, saying, 2. Son of man, set thy face against Pharaoh king of Egypt, and prophesy against him, and against all Egypt. 3. Speak, and say, Thus saith the Lord Jehovah, Behold, I am against thee, Pharaoh king of Egypt, the great dragon that lieth in the midst of his Niles, which says, My Nile is mine, and I have made myself. 4. And I will put a double ring in thy jaws, and hang the fish of thy Nile in thy scales, and bring thee up out of the midst of thy Niles, and all the fish of thy Niles shall stick in thy scales. 5. And I will leave in the wilderness thee and all the fish of thy Niles; upon the field thou shalt fall;

thou shalt not be gathered nor heaped up: to the beast of the earth and to the fowl of the heaven I have given thee for food. 6. And all the inhabitants of Egypt shall know that I am the LORD; because they were a staff of reed to the house of Israel. 7. When they take hold of thee by thy hand, thou breakest and splittest all their shoulder; and when they lean upon thee, thou breakest and stayest all their loins.

The dragon (ver. 3) denotes, according to Gen. i. 21, the great sea animals in general, the monsters of the deep. That the prophet has the crocodile chiefly in view, which belongs to the remarkable peculiarities of Egypt, follows from the mention of the scales in ver. 4. Already in Isa. xxvii. the crocodile is named, the leviathan along with the dragon. The sea, in the symbolic language of Scripture, denotes the world. The dragon appears often as the king of the sea and head of the sea animals (comp. Ps. lxxiv. 13, 14). In the sea of the world its natural counterpart is thus the great king, or the great power; comp. Isa. xxvii. 1, where it is said in reference to the world power: "In that day will the Lord visit with His hard, great, and strong sword leviathan, the flying serpent, and leviathan the wreathed serpent, and will slay the dragon which is in the sea." Of Nebuchadnezzar it is said, Jer. li. 24: "He has swallowed us like the dragon." In the Apocalypse the prince of this world appears as the great dragon, whose servants and instruments only the earthly despots are.[1] As the dragon is the symbol of the king, so are the Niles (the Nile in its several branches) the symbol of the land of Egypt in its riches and its power, which have the Nile for their source. In this sense the Nile occurs already in Isa. xix., where in an extended delineation the destruction of the prosperity of Egypt appears under the figure of the drying up of the Nile. "I have made myself:" the Nile belongs to him. First, in connection with the Nile, is he what he is. There is an

[1] The form תנים is found only here. It is a *pluralis majestatis* from תן = תנין, the more suitable here as a variation for this, as this dragon puffs himself up so much, presents himself as the ideal of all dragons. It appears that תן and תנין are originally the same word, and that only in the ordinary speech usage the first form was generally used of monsters on land, the second of monsters in water; an assumption the more natural, as תן never occurs in prose, and is a term not of natural history, but of poetry. As תן occurs here of the water animals, so תנין in Lam. iv. 3 of jackals.

accordance in the thought with ver. 9, where, in opposition to the sentence, "Let him do and rule," he asserts that he has made all himself. By the rings, fastened in the softest and tenderest parts of the head (ver. 4), are the monsters tamed. The double ring is a ring that consists of two halves joined together in the middle, which are fastened on both sides, so that the joining middle comes into the mouth.¹ If the Nile denotes the prosperity of Egypt, the fish are its inhabitants living in prosperity, that feel themselves indeed as fish in the water, but now are placed on the dry ground. They are drawn out with the dragon; the subjects fall with the king, and in consequence of his fall. The wilderness (ver. 5), in contrast with the Nile, denotes the state of weakness without help or means. The contrast is taken from the natural conditions of Egypt, where the waste, awful wilderness borders on the fertile banks of the Nile. "I will leave thee into the wilderness" is the concise expression for, "I will bring thee into the wilderness, and leave thee there." The field is the open field, in contrast with the splendid mausoleums in which the Egyptian Pharaohs were buried in the times of their glory. He comes down so low, that he does not even receive an honourable burial. Who would trust in a deliverer, and make him an idol, who cannot provide this for himself, who is destined to feed the raven, and will very soon be carrion! The king is, so to speak, an ideal person, who comprises in himself a great numerical multiplicity. Thus the statement is appropriate: "Thou shalt not be gathered nor heaped up." Each of his deceased subjects was, as it were, a part of Pharaoh, as in the retreat from Moscow Napoleon was seen in every dead Frenchman. "They shall know that I am the Lord" (ver. 6): they have put themselves in Jehovah's place, offered themselves as deliverers in scorn of Israel; so they must learn that they are men, and the God of Israel alone God, whereby it is not considered whether they recognise the effect proceeding from the God of Israel as proceeding from Him: it suffices that it really proceeds from Him, and is recognised by His believing people as proceeding from Him. A staff of reed can yield no firm support. There is an allusion to Isa. xxxvi. 6, where Rabshakeh, the general of Sennacherib, says to Hezekiah: "Lo,

¹ The reading in the text, חתים, is the dual, in accordance with לחיים.

thou trustest in the staff of this broken reed, in Egypt, which if a man lean on it, goes into his hand and pierces it: so is Pharaoh to all that trust in him." So long has this miserable staff of reed already betrayed the people of God; even in the Assyrian times it was manifestly such; and yet men seek even at the present to lean upon it, and it makes every effort to delude into such folly. But soon is the miserable business to be arrested. "When they take hold of thee by thy hand, thou breakest" (ver. 7): the Jewish intended amendment of the text, "by the hand," which Luther follows, arises from a material conception of the figure. They thought that a reed-staff could have no hand; but the king of Egypt has one, and yet is a reed-staff. We have an abridged comparison: when they take thee by the hand, thou wilt be like a breaking reed-staff. The king of Egypt not merely helped them not; he injured them, because he had led them to rebel in reliance on his aid, and prevented them from capitulating. "And stayest all their loins:" the staying is put sarcastically. He had promised to stay, and what he afforded to them was all he could do in the way of staying—was the staying in his sense and according to his lexicon; so that thus the staying is provided, as it were, with a note of quotation. A pretty staying, which is, in fact, a casting down.[1]

From the king the prophet now turns in the second section to the land. Ver. 8. Therefore thus saith the Lord Jehovah, Behold, I will bring a sword upon thee, and cut off from thee man and beast. 9. And the land of Egypt shall be desolate and waste, and they shall know that I am the LORD; because he said, The Nile is mine, and I have made. 10. Therefore, behold, I am against thee and thy Niles, and I will make the land of Egypt an utterly desolate waste from Migdol to Syene, and to the border of Kush.[2] 11. No foot of man shall pass through it, nor foot of beast shall pass through it; and it shall not sit[3] forty years. 12. And I will make the land of Egypt

---

[1] Allusion to הַמְעַד, Ps. lxix. 24.

[2] Luther, "from the tower at Syene even to the border of the Moorish land," which, as Egypt lies even on the border of the Moorish land, has no meaning whatever.

[3] Luther has, in place of "sitting," "be inhabited," against the usage of speech, although even Hitzig renders, "it shall remain uninhabited."

desolate amidst the desolate lands, and its cities shall be desolate among the waste cities forty years; and I will scatter Egypt among the nations, and sprinkle them in the lands.

"Because he said, The Nile is mine, and I have made" (ver. 9)—namely, all that was to be made, so that no place remains for God: Luther rightly, " I am he who does it." Isa. x. 13 shows that we may not explain, I have made it, the Nile. Yet the Nile is of all things the department in which the making of the king appears, and from which the supernatural causality is excluded. The land must suffer for what the king has committed, because the spirit of the people rules only in the king; Pharaoh was the Egyptian. "I am against thee, Pharaoh, and thy Niles" (ver. 10): the judgments of God against the foreign nations consist, with Ezekiel generally, only in hostile invasions, especially in the visitation by the Chaldeans. On the height of the usually so-called Nile, the enemy had as little influence as Pharaoh, who could in regard to it utter the proud speech, I have made. The Nile must thus also here stand in a symbolic sense, as a designation of the prosperity and power of Egypt—of its resources. As in this sense Pharaoh regarded himself as the creator of the Nile, so the king of Assyria says in Isa. x. 13, " By the strength of my hand I have done it, and by my wisdom; for I am prudent." Migdol appears also in Jer. xliv. 1, xlvi. 14, as the border city of Egypt towards Judah, and thus in the north. It there stands at the head of the cities in which the Jews had sought refuge from Nebuchadnezzar. Syene is the southern border city of Egypt: it is distinguished as such by the addition, " and to the border of Kush;" Kush, Ethiopia, the south border land of Egypt. Thus the whole land shall be wasted, and nowhere a tenable point remain for Pharaoh. Ver. 11 is naturally to be understood with the limitations arising from that which generally happens in a hostile occupation, which never involves the complete cessation of all intercourse, least of all in a great kingdom. " It shall not sit :" the opposite of sitting is here also the lying down. The time that Egypt is to lie waste is here fixed at forty years. That the Chaldeans must be regarded as the authors of this desolation, appears not only from the historical starting-point of the prophecy, which was uttered when Nebuchadnezzar's army had already reached Judea, the border land of Egypt, and from the analogy of all other prophecies of Ezekiel against foreign nations; comp. especially ch. xxvi. 7, but also from the passage in Jer. xlvi. 26, where it is said of the Egyptians: " And I will deliver them into the hand of those that seek their lives, and into the hand of Nebuchadnezzar and his servants; and afterwards it shall dwell as in the day of old, saith the Lord." The time that the nations, and among others the Egyptians, will be subject to the Chaldeans, is fixed in Jer. xxv. and xxix. at seventy years. The beginning of these seventy years is the fourth year of Jehoiakim. In this year was fought the great battle at Karkemish or Circesium, on the Euphrates, in which the power of Egypt was for ever broken, which in the struggle between the African and the Asiatic world-powers decided in favour of the latter; comp. ch. xxx. 21. The desolation of Egypt, here fixed at forty years, is different from the servitude of seventy years, as in Judah also the desolation of the city and the temple was separated by an interval of eighteen years from the beginning of the servitude. Thirty years it lasted, until the war passed from the confederate nations or dependencies of Egypt to the proper head-land of the anti-Chaldaic coalition, and wasted it from end to end. The analogy of the seventy years, of which the forty here are merely a branch, shows clearly, that even the latter have a historical import,—not, as has been asserted, " a purely theological," as a supposed antitype of the forty years' march of Israel through the wilderness, with which the forty years here have nothing whatever to do. Yet we may suppose that the period of time here, as most of the periods in the book of Judges, is a round number, which in general better suits the nature of prophecy, which reckons in the gross, and is the more probable, as the desolation is not so precise a fact as the supremacy, which was decided by a single battle. It is sufficient if the beginning of the desolation took place within the fourth decennium before its end. The end of the forty years, at all events, coincides with that of the seventy years. The beginning of the forty years was not yet immediately in view. Of the seventy years of Jeremiah, seventeen had elapsed at the time when our prophecy was published, of which seven fall in the eleven years of the reign of Jehoiakim, and ten, according to ver. 1, in the reign of Zedekiah. Thus at least thirteen years must still have expired before the beginning of the forty years. Before the main blow could have been given to Egypt, the great and difficult work of the conquest of Tyre must have been completed, the maritime power of which might have been very dangerous in a premature march against Egypt, the chief enemy. Niebuhr (p. 217) places the war, " which was decided most unfortunately for Egypt," in the thirty-fourth year of Nebuchadnezzar. The prophet has himself afterwards, in ch. xxix. 17, expressly determined the beginning of the four decenniums. He places it in the twenty-seventh year of Jehoiachin, which was the thirty-fourth of the seventy years of Jeremiah. " Amidst the desolate lands" (ver. 12) : the desolate lands are those of the anti-Chaldaic coalition, the desolation of which the prophet had announced in the preceding prophecies.

Vers. 13-16. In the foregoing the duration of the desolation of Egypt was limited to forty years. This announcement is here confirmed by the express announcement of its cessation after forty years. That this cessation is in connection with the cessation of the Chaldean sovereignty, we must already expect from Jer. xxv., where, after the end of the seventy years of the Chaldean servitude, the judgment on Babylon is published ; as also from Isa. xxiii. 15, where the seventy years of the prostration of Tyre are designated as the years of " one king" of a reigning dynasty, after the fall of which Tyre again rises to power. The cessation of the desolation of Egypt is not, however, the chief thought of the section. It is rather, that even after this cessation takes place, Egypt will still continue in a feeble state, and never recover her ancient greatness. This served the practical object of the prophet, which was to warn against trusting in Egypt.

Ver. 13. For thus saith the Lord Jehovah, At the end of forty years will I gather Egypt from the nations whither they were scattered. 14. And I will return to the captivity of Egypt, and bring them back to the land of Pathros, to the land of their birth ; and they shall be there a low kingdom. 15. It shall be lower than the kingdoms, and shall not exalt itself above the nations ; and I will diminish them, that they shall no more rule over the nations. 16. And it shall no more be the confidence of the house of Israel, bringing iniquity to remembrance, when they turn after them: and they shall know that I am the Lord Jehovah.

"I will return to the captivity of Egypt" (ver. 14), is the same as, I again take pity on their misery.[1] The return to Pathros, South or Upper Egypt, is specially mentioned, because this was the proper kernel of the land—their birth-land: the restoration was thus only then complete, when this came again into their power. The passage is of historical interest, because according to it the original seat of the Egyptian kingdom must have been in the Thebaid; which leads us up beyond the Mosaic period, in which the capital Zoan or Tanis was in Lower Egypt.[2] "They shall be there a low kingdom:" this is, as already remarked, no mere prediction, but has an immediate practical import, that of an indirect advice, as Isaiah, in ch. xli. 28, terms the utterances of the prophet. It serves the object of the whole prophecy, to dissuade from a foolish confidence in Egypt. Even after its restoration, Egypt will not again return to its ancient greatness: its power is for ever broken. The weakness of the old Pharaonic monarchy after the time of Nebuchadnezzar, here so clearly and definitely announced, is fully attested by history. Never has it again pointedly affected the progress of history. Great catastrophes must have befallen Egypt in the time of Nebuchadnezzar, otherwise the consequence in the world's history could not have been so thorough and enduring. How radical it was, is manifest from the single fact, that Cambyses seeks the daughter of Amasis of Egypt, not for a wife, but for a concubine, in which condition that of her people reflects itself; and that Amasis, who knows beforehand what is in agitation, although the Persian monarch had not expressly mentioned it, does not venture to refuse his request (Herod. iii. 1). The words, "And they shall be there a low kingdom," refer, besides, to ch. xvii. 14. "A low kingdom:" the condition that Pharaoh had formerly prepared for the Israelitish kings, is now imposed upon himself, and that for ever; while the kingdom of Israel rises from its deep humiliation to the highest pre-eminence (ch. xvii. 22 f.). Thus the

[1] Comp. on xvi. 53. שׁוּב, to return, is here obviously different from the following הֵשִׁיב, to bring back. The returning is the root of the bringing back.

[2] Comp. my treatise on *Egypt and the Books of Moses*, p. 41 f.

places are changed. Whosoever beguiles into iniquity brings iniquity to remembrance (ver. 16), or to the knowledge of him to whom the iniquity refers. For existing iniquity cannot remain unmarked or unpunished by the " Judge of all the earth."

Ch. xxix. 17-xxx. 19. We have here an appendix to the preceding prophecy,—an announcement from the twenty-seventh year of Jehoiachin, above sixteen years later than that in vers. 1-16; later also than the concluding prophecy of this altogether chronologically arranged book, the vision of the new temple. For this belongs, according to ch. xl. 1, to the twenty-fifth year of Jehoiachin. The appendix that, as already remarked, proves itself to be such by departing from the chronological order, goes on to the following new superscription, and so embraces not merely ch. xxix. 17-21, but also ch. xxx. 1-19. The resumption of vers. 1-16 must, if it had taken place, have been more distinctly marked in ch. xxx.; and we cannot think of an independent discourse there, because all independent discourses are dated in Ezekiel. We have seen already that the prophecy in ch. xxix. 1-16 was not designed to go immediately into fulfilment. At the time when this fulfilment was to take place, and the course of instruction for Egypt during four decenniums was to begin, the prophet takes up again his earlier announcement, and enlarges it. The hindrance to the immediate fulfilment of the former prophecy, the resistance of Tyre, is now removed. The siege of Tyre began, according to ch. xxvi. 1, towards the end of the eleventh year of the deportation of Jehoiachin. It lasted, according to Menander, extracting from the Tyrian annals (Joseph. *c. Ap.* i. 21) and Philostratus (Joseph. *Arch.* x. 10, 1), thirteen years. Some time of rest must have been granted to the army, which, according to ch. xxix. 18, was completely exhausted. The blow also which was to shake the foundations of Egypt required much preparation. Two years after the conquest of Tyre, at the beginning of the twenty-seventh year of Jehoiachin, began the expedition against Egypt, the principal foe; and simultaneous with this beginning is our prophecy, which, with a clearness and certainty that can only be given by the Spirit of God, declares the end from the beginning (Isa. xlvi. 10). There is much probability that we have before us, in the chronological date at the beginning of our prophecy, at the same time that of the present collection of the prophecies of Ezekiel, and that on the occasion of this collection he added this supplement. The collection was prepared in connection with the great conclusion, which was accomplished by the expedition of Nebuchadnezzar to Egypt. The whole prophetic activity of Ezekiel moves around the great anti-Chaldaic coalition. His first appearance was contemporary with its formation. With its close, the expedition of Nebuchadnezzar to Egypt, the mission of Ezekiel is completed; and as soon as it is completed, he brings together the documents relating to it.

First, the introduction (ch. xxix. 17-21). Ver. 17. And it came to pass in the twenty-seventh year, in the first month, in the first of the month, the word of the LORD came unto me, saying, 18. Son of man, Nebuchadnezzar king of Babylon caused his army to serve a great service at Tyre: every head was made bald, and every shoulder peeled; and there was no reward for him or his army from Tyre, for the service that he served against it: 19. Therefore thus saith the Lord Jehovah, Behold, I will give Nebuchadnezzar the king of Babylon the land of Egypt: and he shall take its tumult, and seize its spoil; and it shall be a reward for his army. 20. As his hire, for which he has served, I give him the land of Egypt, because they wrought for me, saith the Lord Jehovah. 21. In that day will I cause a horn to bud forth for the house of Israel, and I will give thee the opening of the mouth in the midst of them; and they shall know that I am the LORD.

In the statement in ver. 18, that the Chaldeans had laboured in God's service against Tyre, it is involved that the taking of the city was actually accomplished: for where God gives a special mission, He causes it to attain its object; and the mission in regard to Tyre, according to all the announcements of Ezekiel, is not directed to the siege, which comes into view only as the means to the end, but to the conquest. That they attained the object of their mission is as good as expressly said, inasmuch as they obtain a reward for their severe labour. If they had not executed their task, there could have been no talk of a reward. For the work concerns God not in itself, but only in its result. The failure here intimated of a reward in Tyre for their labour there, says nothing against the conquest.

For the prophet speaks of a reward which was suitable to a grand and decisive result obtained by immense efforts; and it will be expected beforehand, that after a siege of so many years, not much was to be found in Tyre, as the best was partly consumed, partly destroyed, and partly carried away. Moreover, we must distinguish between the thought and its form. The thought is, that Nebuchadnezzar, by God's appointment, will find in Egypt abundant satisfaction for his expectations in Tyre that were not quite satisfied. The form is taken from human relations, where to one who has executed a task that does not repay him, another is committed in which he finds a recompense. It is impossible, in truth, to speak of reward, as Nebuchadnezzar acted not in obedience to the command of God, but in the service of his own lusts and passions. "Every head is made bald, and every shoulder peeled:" the labours in which this took place—the erecting of besieging towers, and especially the raising of a mound against Tyre—are described in ch. xxvi. 8. To the impending humiliation of Egypt, the prophet in ver. 21 opposes the impending exaltation of Zion, as he had done in regard to the other nations of the coalition at the close of the prophecy against them in ch. xxviii. 25, 26. "In that day"—when Egypt is thus humbled. The whole period of the humiliation of Egypt is viewed under the figure of an ideal day. The horn is an emblem of power and ability for self-defence,[1] in contrast with the weakness which befalls Egypt, which can no longer push the nations (Deut. xxxiii. 17), but only be pushed by them. The real fulfilment is, according to the other indications of the prophet himself—for ex., ch. xvii. 22 f.—to be sought in Christ, in whom Israel obtains the absolute power of defence against the heathen world (comp. Luke i. 69, Rev. v. 6), yet so that even earlier the prophecy several times prelusively verifies itself. "And I will give thee the opening of the mouth in the midst of them:" the prophet speaks, even after he is dead, lives still among his people, in his book still to be found at the close, on which, after the analogy of the *monumentum exegi aere perennius*, he here impresses as it were the seal. When all is finished that he has announced in this book, in salvation for Israel as well as in punishment for his foes and betrayers, then may he as it were joyfully open

[1] Comp. on Ps. cxlviii. 14.

his mouth and say, "You have heard it, see it now all" (Isa. xlviii' 6): ye see now that the son of man is no mere son of me., that the sentence, "And the word of the Lord came unto me, saying," is true, that I do not fall under the judgment of Deut. xviii. 20. If his prophecy were not fulfilled, then must he, surviving in his book, have been dumb, and not have gone out of the door (Job xxxi. 34). The expectation that his prophecy of the horn being caused to bud forth for Israel would be fulfilled in his lifetime, Ezekiel could not entertain. For he was thirty years old in the fifth year of Jehoiachin (ch. i. 1), when twelve only of the seventy years of the Chaldean servitude had elapsed; and according to ch. xxix. 12, 13, the Chaldean supremacy was to endure forty years after the desolation of Egypt here announced as impending, which absolutely excluded the budding forth of the horn for Israel.

Ch. xxx. 1–5. The naked thought, expressed in the introduction of the prophecy (ch. xxix. 17–21), of the great catastrophe hanging over Egypt, assumes flesh and blood in the main bulk of the prophecy (ch. xxx. 1–19). In four paragraphs the prophet brings the destruction of Egypt to view in a pictorial way, as a substitute for sight to those to whom not seeing and yet believing is so difficult. Ch. xxix. 17–21 as introduction, and ch. xxx. as completion, are inseparably connected. We have no complete prophecy in Ezekiel that is so general as ch. xxix. 17–21, none that blunders out so awkwardly as ch. xxx. Vers. 2 and 3 especially require that the party to be judged should be mentioned before. That ch. xxx. 1–19 also belongs to the prophecy, which announces the speedy fulfilment of the earlier prophecy in ch. xxix. 1–16, the intentionally verbal repetition of passages of this prophecy leaves no room to doubt.

Ver. 1. And the word of the LORD came unto me, saying, 2. Son of man, prophesy and say, Thus saith the Lord Jehovah, Howl ye, Alas the day! 3. For near is the day, and near the day of the LORD, a day of cloud; a time of the heathen will it be.[1] 4. And a sword shall come upon Egypt, and trembling shall be in Kush, when the slain shall fall in Egypt,

[1] Luther, "The time is present that the heathen shall come," contrary to Jer. xxvii. 7 and the other parallel passages.

and they shall take away her tumult, and her foundations shall be pulled down. 5. Kush, and Phut, and Lud, and all the throng, and Kub, and the sons of the land of the covenant, shall fall with them by the sword.

"A time of the heathen will it be" (ver. 3) : the time of the heathen here is identical with the day of Egypt in ver. 9. These are the heathen, who, according to the introduction (ch. xxix. 17 f.), here come into view. The general designation is explained by the contrast with the people of the covenant, whose time had come earlier. The heathen are judged in Egypt, one of their chief representatives, after the judgment on the house of God had already begun. We have here the fundamental passage for the often misunderstood word of the Lord, Luke xxi. 24 : "And Jerusalem shall be trodden down of the Gentiles, until the times of the Gentiles be fulfilled"—that is, arrive (Gen. xxv. 24). The times of the heathen are, according to the fundamental passage here, the times of judgment; comp. Isa. xiii. 22. The judgment begins with unbelieving Jerusalem, and passes, after it has there consumed all its fuel, over to the heathen, who were the instruments of the judgment on Jerusalem : being the fall of the Roman empire elsewhere also often foretold by Jesus, of the mountain that shall be cast into the sea after the barren fig-tree of the Jewish people is dried up (Matt. xxi. 21), of the sycamore-tree that is to be rooted out and cast into the sea in Luke xvii. 6. Kush trembles at the fall of the slain in Egypt (ver. 4): this shows that Ethiopia had made common cause with Egypt, and thus behoved to be afraid of being involved in its fall; comp. on ch. xxiii. 42. "Their tumult:" this is here the prosperity of Egypt bringing active life with it. "Her foundations shall be pulled down :" the state under the figure of a house that is destroyed from the foundation, after the example of Isa. xix. 10, where it is said of Egypt, "Its foundations shall be broken." The enumeration of the foreign auxiliaries of Egypt that suffer with it (ver. 5), begins with Kush, which was already (ver. 4) mentioned as closely connected with it. Then follow Phut and Lud, that already occur, ch. xxvii. 10, among the mercenary troops of the Tyrians. The Phutæans appear, Jer. xlvi. 9, along with Kush and Lud as mercenaries of Egypt. The three names are followed by a collective term, "and all the throng"—the whole remaining motley company of mercenaries. Two others besides are then made prominent. First, Kub. This seems to correspond with the Persians named in ch. xxvii. 10 along with Phut and Lud, and indeed at their head, who, as was remarked, had probably entered in consequence of the coalition into the service of Tyre; so that it cannot surprise us if we meet them here also. As the name Kub does not occur elsewhere in the Old Testament, we must antecedently expect that those who are thereby designated, and here occupy so important a place, may appear under other names—that the name Kub may be a native one, that first became known in anterior Asia in the time of Ezekiel, in consequence of the nearer political contact with this country. In old Persian Kufa means mountain. Kufa occurs in the Egyptian monuments as a mighty Asiatic power with which the Egyptians had relations.[1] It has been already indicated that the coalition had formed a connection with Medo-Persia. Among those who must drink of the Chaldean cup are named (Jer. xxv. 25) all the kings of Elam and all the kings of Media. Elam had then, at the time designated in ch. xxix. 17, already suffered a severe defeat from the Chaldeans (ch. xxxii. 24). It was natural that they should seek to avenge this defeat, as they were a strong, pushing people, destined to succeed the Chaldeans in the supremacy. Wherever the battle against the tyrants burned, in Tyre and in Egypt, their mercenaries appeared. Along with Kub are the "sons of the land of covenant" specially signalized. The pre-eminently so-called covenant land of Egypt can only be Kush. This appears everywhere as such in the Assyrian and Babylonian times. The close returns to the beginning, and explains that there the beginning was made with Kush. Kush appears in vers. 4, 9 as partaking next in the fall of Egypt. The "sons of the land of covenant" that, according to ch. xxiii. 42, entered into direct relation with Israel, the confederate of Egypt (for the Sabeans there mentioned belong to Kush), are before all led to the help of Egypt, and along with them the volunteers from farther Asia, and others from the African confines.

Vers. 6-9. Desolation strikes Egypt, after it has fallen with

[1] Wilkinson's *Manners and Customs of Ancient Egypt*, i. 1, p. 375 f.

all its auxiliaries, from end to end. Ver. 6. Thus saith the Lord Jehovah, And they that uphold Egypt shall fall, and its mighty pride shall come down: from Migdol to Syene they shall fall in it by the sword, saith the Lord Jehovah. 7. And they shall be desolate among the desolate countries, and their cities shall be among the wasted cities. 8. And they shall know that I am the LORD, when I set a fire in Egypt, and all her helpers are broken. 9. In that day shall messengers go forth from me in ships to frighten Kush the secure, and trembling shall come upon them in the day of Egypt:[1] for, lo, it cometh.

After the new break, "Thus saith the Lord" (ver. 6), the *and* connects this paragraph, and shows that only new touches are to be given to the picture. This beginning with *and* is common to all new sections after the first (vers. 1-5). They thereby show themselves to be parts of a whole. The defeat of the helpers of Egypt is taken over from the foregoing, and includes what was said in vers. 4, 5. This is followed by the defeat and desolation of Egypt itself, which in this and the following verse is intentionally depicted, in almost literal agreement with ch. xxix. 10, 12, to show that already the term for the fulfilment of that earlier prophecy is come, which in the continued prosperity of Egypt might have been a mockery to many. The "mighty pride" appeared in ch. xxiv. 21 in reference to Jerusalem; now comes the succession of humiliation on the heathen people. The "knowing" in ver. 8 is an actual experience, in which it does not appear whether they in their thoughts refer to the Lord that which they must suffer from Him. So much the worse for them if they do not. The fire is the fire of war (comp. Rev. viii. 7, ix. 17), which often also comes to view in material fire. The point of comparison is the consuming power. The messengers sent from the Lord in ver. 9, who, ascending[2] the Nile in ships, bring the news of

---

[1] Luther, "as it happened to Egypt when her time came." He took כ, which here, as in the fundamental passage, Isa. xxiii. 5, serves as a definition of time, as a particle of comparison.

[2] Of the difficulties which the navigation on this river from Egypt to Ethiopia presents, Ezekiel has taken as little account as Isaiah in the fundamental passage. The papyrus boats, of course, ply on the Nile (Isa. xviii. 2).

the fall of Egypt effected by the Lord to the covenant land of Ethiopia, belong to the poetic conception. The real import is, that the alarming news will soon reach Ethiopia. The sending of the messengers is ascribed to the Lord, because the act which forms the substance of the message proceeds from Him. The messengers here form a contrast to the messengers with joyful tidings for Ethiopia in Isa. xviii. 1–3. Then the Lord, by the defeat of Sennacherib, graciously turned away the danger from Jerusalem which threatened, as Judea, so also Egypt and Ethiopia, from Assyria. Now it is otherwise. To Babylon is given power, as over Judea, so also over Egypt and Ethiopia. Sons of the latter fall in Egypt (ver. 5), and it is threatened in its own borders by the Chaldeans. A second allusion to Isaiah is found in the words, " And trembling shall come upon them in the day of Egypt." In Isa. xxiii. 5 it is said in the prophecy against Tyre: " They (the Egyptians) shall tremble at the report of Tyre." Tyre, Egypt, Ethiopia, stood together in the battle formerly against Assyria, afterwards against Babylon. When the one of these powers, the bulwark, falls, the next following trembles in expectation of a like fate. " It comes "—the threatened misfortune.

The peculiarity in vers. 10–12 is the naming of the conqueror—the same man who is engaged in the *invasion* of Egypt. Ver. 10. Thus saith the Lord Jehovah, And I shall make the tumult of Egypt to cease by Nebuchadnezzar king of Babylon. 11. He and his people with him, the violent of the heathen, shall be brought to destroy the land : and they shall draw their swords against Egypt, and fill the land with the slain. 12. And I will make the Niles dry, and sell the land into the hand of the wicked ; and I will desolate the land and the fulness thereof by the hand of strangers : I the LORD have spoken it.

" The tumult" (ver. 10)—as it is heard in a land rich in men and goods, full of life and movement. The word comprises what is afterwards enumerated in detail. It refers not merely to the multitude, but to the prosperity of Egypt. Ch. xxix. 19 is also against the limitation of it to the multitude. " The violent of the heathen" (ver. 11)—those who are counted as violent even among the heathen, who are generally addicted to violence—occurred before in ch. xxviii. 7 as a designation of the Chaldeans. " Shall be brought :" they come not of themselves, but the Almighty brings them, and hence they are irresistible; he to whom they come is irretrievably lost. The drying up of the Nile in ver. 12 denotes, as in Isa. xix., the destruction of prosperity. The Nile in the strict sense—the foundation of this prosperity—is as good as dried up for Egypt, for strangers consume its produce. "And sell the land into the hand of the wicked:" this presupposes that the Egyptians also are wicked, yet in another sense than that in which (Matt. vii. 11) all men are so called : the *accomplished* sin first bringeth forth death (Jas. i. 15). God punishes one knave by the other, who does not escape His judgment, but is only reserved for the same; as in Jer. xxv. the king of Babylon has no other advantage over those punished by him but this, that he drinks *last*. "Into the hand of the wicked:" this shows that the want of a prophecy against Babylon in Ezekiel can only be referred to external grounds. Wickedness and judgment go hand in hand. Power can only be given to the wicked for a short time. The announcement, so often repeated in Ezekiel, of the restoration of Israel has the annihilating judgment on Babylon, the despot, for its presupposition.

Vers. 13-19. In the specification of the ruin hanging over Egypt, those points are made prominent which have special import in any respect. No, Thebes, occurs thrice ; Noph, Memphis, twice, to give special prominence to their importance as the two capitals of the country—No of Upper, and Noph of Lower Egypt. Along with these, Zoan, Tanis, situated also in Lower Egypt, which appears in Isa. xix. 11, 13, and previously in Num. xiii. 22, as the capital of Egypt. Besides are named Daphne and Sin as frontier fortresses. The latter, Pelusium, is designated by Hirtius the Lock of Egypt—*claustrum Ægypti.* Then On, the city of the sun—Heliopolis, as it is called by the Greeks—as the religious centre, the spiritual capital. Even in Genesis it appears as such, where Joseph marries the daughter of the high priest of On : this was the most distinguished alliance, that by which he could be most effectually freed from the disgrace of his origin. Pathros, not a city, but a country, is, according to ch. xxix. 14, named as the mother country—as it were, the birthplace of the people. Thus is the land robbed of all its ornaments (ch. xxv. 9).

Ver. 13. Thus saith the Lord Jehovah, And I will destroy

the detestable things, and make the vanities to cease out of Noph; and there shall no more be a prince of the land of Egypt: and I will put fear in the land of Egypt. 14. And I will make Pathros desolate, and set a fire in Zoan, and execute judgments in No. 15. And I will pour out my fury upon Sin, the stronghold of Egypt, and cut off the tumult of No. 16. And I will put a fire in Egypt: Sin shall writhe, and No shall be broken, and Noph shall have foes by day. 17. The young men of Aven and Pi-beseth shall fall by the sword; and these shall go into captivity. 18. And in Tehaphnehes the day shall spare, when I break there the yokes of Egypt; and her mighty pride shall cease in her: a cloud shall cover *her*, and her daughters shall go into captivity. 19. And I will execute judgments on Egypt; and they shall know that I am the LORD.

The idols and the princes are in ver. 13 connected, because they were the two chief objects of the pride and worship of the Egyptians. What still remains to Egypt after the catastrophe in the way of princes, in comparison with her former proud monarchs, deserves no more the name of princes: they are, in fact, miserable slaves. "The tumult"—Hamon of No. There is an allusion to the surname Amon, which No received from its god (comp. Nah. iii. 8, Jer. xlvi. 25). Amon is unable to preserve for the city its Hamon. The fire in ver. 16 is the fire of war, or of the annihilating catastrophe. "Noph shall have foes by day:" this denotes, as "the spoilers at noonday" (Jer. xv. 8; Zeph. ii. 4), a state of deep humiliation, in which the enemy disdains to surprise the city by night (Obad. 5), and rather, in consciousness of his absolute superiority, marches in broad daylight against the unresisting. "Foes by day" stands briefly for one that has to deal with foes by day. On, in Jer. xliii. 13 called Bethshemesh, sun-house, as the chief place of the Egyptian sun-worship, appears in ver. 17 with a slight alteration under the name of Aven, to indicate by this change the cause of the divine judgments coming upon it. These cannot fail where men commit the iniquity of worshipping the creature rather than the Creator. In like manner had the older prophets put in place of the name Bethel, house of God, that had become a lie from the time of Jeroboam, the real name Bethaven, house of iniquity (Hos. iv. 15, x. 5). The name On still more easily admits of this change. Pi-beseth is Bubastis, which is also regarded as a chief place of idolatry by its collocation with On, and by its name, which refers to the cat-worship there established. To the "young men," the men fit for service, as also in the New Testament young men without any addition stand for soldiers (Mark xiv. 51), are opposed the cities themselves, to the military the civil population,—a contrast explained by this, that in Egypt the soldiers formed a separate caste; for which reason the young men of On cannot here be all the young men in it, but only the soldiers who form its garrison. Tehaphnehes, in ver. 18, Daphne, is also mentioned in Jer. xliii. 7 as a frontier stronghold of Egypt. There, where a decisive combat with the invading Chaldean power was to be expected, the day is dark, as the sun no longer shines for the unfortunate: for him the luminaries of heaven are as good as extinguished. "The day shall spare"—withhold as a miser: this stands by choice for, It is dark, and as a variation from it. On the words, "When I break there the yokes of Egypt," we should compare ch. xxix. 15, "And I will diminish them (or bring them down), that they shall no more rule over the heathen;" and also here, ver. 13, "There shall no more be a prince of the land of Egypt." The yoke of Egypt, which in former times pressed heavily on Israel, and afterwards on other nations (comp. ch. xxxii. 2), will now be broken for ever, while the once enslaved Zion rises to universal dominion. The "mighty pride" refers not to Tehaphnehes, but to Egypt (comp. ver. 6 and ch. xxxii. 12), whose pride is broken in the battle at the frontier fort. The "daughters" of Daphne are the minor cities in its neighbourhood. In ver. 19 is the object of the judgment passed upon Egypt. The true God, whom they do not mean to worship willingly, must come to His rights in the punishment inflicted on them. This is not merely an alarming, but also a comforting point of view. The most comfortless of all thoughts is to have no part in God. How many transgressors have joyfully devoted themselves to the sword, in the conviction that by the punishment they come to have a part in God!

Ch. xxx. 20-26. We have here the second prophecy against Egypt, delivered on the seventh day of the first month in the eleventh year, and thus separated from the first (ch. xxix. 1) by the interval of almost a quarter of a year. In the fourth month of the eleventh year, almost three months after our prophecy, the conquest of Jerusalem took place (Jer. xxxix. 2). The practical point of view is here the same as in ch. xxix. 1-16. It is designed to annihilate the hope of aid from Egypt; by the relentless destruction of all earthly expectations in the exiles, to direct the eye to God alone. The earthly hope had probably then received new vigour from the circumstances of the times. We see from the thirty-seventh chapter of Jeremiah, that during the siege of Jerusalem Pharaoh had marched with an army from Egypt to drive the Chaldeans from Palestine, and that the latter, in consequence of this, raised the siege and went to meet him. The first prophecy referred to this hope. Already had it, as it appears, attained to full bloom through the departure of the Chaldeans.

Ver. 20. And it came to pass in the eleventh year, in the first month, in the seventh of the month, the word of the LORD came unto me, saying, 21. Son of man, the arm of Pharaoh king of Egypt I have broken; and, lo, it is not bound up to apply healings, to put a roller to bind it, that it may be strong to hold the sword. 22. Therefore thus saith the Lord Jehovah, Behold, I am against Pharaoh king of Egypt, and will break his arms, the strong and the broken; and I will make the sword fall out of his hand. 23. And I will scatter Egypt among the heathen, and sprinkle it through the lands. 24. And I will strengthen the arms of the king of Babylon, and put my sword in his hand: and I will break the arms of Pharaoh, and he shall groan with the groans of a wounded man before him. 25. And I will seize the arms of the king of Babylon,[1] and the arms of Pharaoh shall fall; and they shall know that I am the LORD, when I put my sword into the hand of the king of Babylon, and he shall stretch it out against the land of Egypt. 26. And I will scatter Egypt among the heathen,[2] and sprinkle it through the lands; and they shall know that I am the LORD.

The breaking of the Pharaoh in ver. 21 refers to a great defeat. This can only be that at Karkemish or Circesium, in

[1] Luther's translation, "I will *strengthen* the arms of the king of Babylon," overlooks the distinction of the *Hiphil* here from the *Piel* in ver. 25.

[2] Luther, "And I scatter the Egyptians among the heathen," mistaking the independent character of the verse in which the *object* is stated.

the very beginning of the career of Nebuchadnezzar (Niebuhr, p. 205 f., 369), in the fourth year of Jehoiakim, and thus seventeen years before our prophecy. By this battle the fate of Egypt was decided for ever, and from this it has never recovered. Already Jeremiah, in ch. xlvi., sees in this battle the beginning of the end of Egypt, and regards it as having inflicted an *incurable* wound on Egypt; comp. especially ver. 11, a passage which leaves no doubt of the reference of our author to the defeat at Karkemish: " Go up to Gilead, and fetch balm, O virgin daughter of Egypt: in vain dost thou multiply medicines; there is no cure for thee." Of a defeat which the Egyptians suffered in the attempt to come to the aid of Judah, history knows nothing. The retreat of the Egyptians without crossing swords cannot have ensued at the time of the composition of our prophecy. After it, it would have been unnecessary. Our prophecy must have been delivered at a time when, humanly speaking, there was hope from the Egyptians. The "healings," or cures, which might be applied, consist chiefly in the bandage itself. The arm comes into view as the seat of power. The broken arm in ver. 22, that is to be broken a second time, denotes the already weakened power of the Egyptian kingdom; the strong, what still remained of unbroken power. "Before him" (ver. 24)—the Babylonian conqueror. The Lord seizes the arms of the king of Babylon (ver. 25), and they are thereby kept strong, as it is said of Joseph in Gen. xlix. 24, " Strong are the arms of his hands by the hands of the Mighty One of Jacob;" while, on the contrary, the arms of the king of Egypt, left to his own weakness, hang down powerless. In ver. 26 the scattering is once more repeated, to connect with it the statement of the object, in which the whole suitably issues. The true God, despised by Egypt from ancient times, is thereby to come to His rights regarding them. If He be the true Jehovah, the personal Being, the absolute Essence, He must necessarily be glorified, if not by their action, yet by their passion.

Ch. xxxi. This prophecy belongs to the time shortly before the taking of Jerusalem, which was in the fourth month of the same year on the ninth day, and so about a month and eight days later. The practical point of view is the same as in the foregoing prophecies. That the hope in Egypt still continued even at this last moment, we see from this, that they still held out. With the full extinction of the hope in Egypt, the resolution to surrender must have gone hand in hand. The peculiarity here is, that the already accomplished fall of Assyria is held before the eyes of the king of Egypt as a mirror of his future, precisely as the prophet in ch. xix. had employed the history of Jehoahaz and Jehoiachin as a prophecy of the fate of the then reigning king Zedekiah. A future in a historical dress—this is the pervading character of the chapter. The imposing grandeur that still remained to Egypt exercised on the minds that sought a support on earth, a safe embankment against the overflow of the Asiatic empire, a magic influence. This influence vanished when Egypt was chained to the already overwhelmed Assyria. The prophecy falls into three sections. First, vers. 1-9. Ver. 1. And it came to pass in the eleventh year, in the third month, on the first of the month, the word of the LORD came unto me, saying, 2. Son of man, say to Pharaoh king of Egypt, and his tumult, Whom resemblest thou [1] in thy greatness? 3. Behold, Assyria was a cedar in Lebanon, fair in leaves, and shading the wood, and tall in growth; and its top was among the clouds. 4. The waters made him great, the flood raised him up, with its streams going round his plant-ground, and it sent its channels to all the trees of the field. 5. Therefore his growth was high above all the trees of the field, and his branches were great, and his boughs were long, from the many waters, when he shot forth. 6. In his branches all the fowls of heaven nested, and under his boughs all the beasts of the field brought forth, and in his shadow all the many nations. 7. And he was fair in his greatness, in the length of his shoots: for his root was by great waters. 8. The cedars in the garden of God darkened him not: cypresses resembled not his branches, and the plane-trees were not like his boughs; all the trees in the garden of God resembled him not in his beauty.[2] 9. I had made him fair in

---

[1] Luther, "Whom thinkest thou, then, that thou art like?" But the question is not about an opinion, but about an actual likeness.

[2] Luther, "Yea, he was as fair as a tree in the garden of God." He understood by the garden of God, Paradise, in the usual sense, and consequently changed the subordination into a mere comparison.

the multitude of his shoots; and all the trees of Eden, that were in the garden of God, envied him.

"Whom resemblest thou in thy greatness?" (ver. 2),—as much as to say, Shall I tell thee whom thou art like in thy greatness? Thou art like Assyria. The greatness of Egypt: this was the point by which the urgent warnings of the prophet against relying on it, the announcements of its downfall, were rebutted. The prophet shows, from the example of Assyria, that greatness does not secure from a fall—that no greatness on earth can withstand the strokes of God. The words, "Behold Assyria," etc., in ver. 3, are the answer to the question, Whom art thou like? that is, Thou art like Assyria, who was a cedar in Lebanon. This, the queen of trees, is a figurative designation of that which was prominent above all others in the human world. The flood in ver. 4 denotes the subterranean waters coming up in springs (Gen. xlix. 25; Deut. viii. 7). In reality, water and flood denote that which the world calls good fortune, —the divine blessing that accompanied the undertakings of Assyria, the flow of favour which gave it prosperity.[1] "Round his plant-ground:" it is properly *her* plant-ground, the feminine referring to Assyria as a tree. The trees of the field, to which the flood nourishing Assyria sends its channels, denote his subjects in contrast with the king of Assyria, the cedar on Lebanon. The limitation to the territory of Assyria is given by the foregoing. To name it expressly was not suitable, as Assyria is to be represented as the world-power. "From the many waters when he shot forth" (ver. 5); that is, because he had many waters in his time of shooting (xvii. 6, 7). To the fowls of heaven and the beasts of the field, the wild in contradistinction to the domestic animals, correspond in the spiritual tree of Assyria the nations; comp. xvii. 23. The last words give an explanation of the figurative expression, which includes in it a comparison. The grandees of the earth appear in ver. 8 as stately trees, according to an oft-recurring figure; as for ex. in Isa. x. 18, 19, the trees of Assyria, in contrast with his underwood (ver. 17), are his grandees. The chief seat of this figurative representation is in the Old Testament in Daniel and Ezekiel, in the New Testament in Revelation; comp. on Rev. vii. 1. The total of the great men of the earth Ezekiel

---

[1] The masculine הֹלֵךְ is the more suitable, as מַיִם precedes.

denotes as the garden of God, in which he regards them as the counterpart of the garden which God once planted in Eden—of Paradise with its glorious trees. The comparison is the more suitable, because, as Paradise was planted by God (Gen. ii. 8), so all human greatness has its origin from God. The envy of the remaining trees in the counterpart of the garden of God in Eden, and so of the remaining grandees on the earth (ver. 9), comes into view only so far as it places in a clear light the greatness of the gifts bestowed upon the king. Envy has an aspect in which it may be regarded as a good for him whom it affects. Let us only reflect on the proverb, Better envied than pitied.

In vers. 3–9, the glory bestowed by God on Assyria; in vers. 10–14, the judgment which for the warning of Pharaoh he brought on himself by its abuse. In the face of the judgment, the greatness of Pharaoh can no longer impose. Ver. 10. Therefore thus saith the Lord Jehovah, Because thou art high in growth, and he hath set his top among the clouds, and his heart was lofty in his height; 11. Therefore I give him into the hand of the mighty one of the heathen; he shall deal with him: for his wickedness I drove him out. 12. And strangers, the violent of the *nations*, cut him off, and left him: on the mountains and in all the valleys his shoots fell, and his boughs were broken in all the plains of the earth; and all the peoples of the earth went down from his shadow, and left him. 13. On his ruins shall all the fowls of heaven dwell, and all the beasts of the field shall be upon his boughs: 14. To the end that none of the trees by the waters exult in their growth, nor set their top among the clouds, nor any drinkers of water stand up by themselves in their height; for they are all delivered unto death in the nether earth, among the sons of men, to those who go down to the pit.

"Therefore" (ver. 10)—because I made him fair (ver. 9). The greatness bestowed by God, being abused, is the cause of his fall. The first two members come into their full light by the third. That the king of Assyria became high in growth in ver. 5, and that his top shot up among the clouds in ver. 3, were described as the gift of God. But greatness itself becomes a sin and a cause of the divine judgment, if it is not as it were expiated and sanctified by humble submission to God. Ver. 14 shows that the first two members denote an offence, that the expression of this does not appear first in the third, which rather affords the explanation of the others. "Therefore I give him" (ver. 11): the fact, already belonging to the past, is transferred to the present, that it may happen as it were before the eyes of the reader; which was the more suitable, as the like in Egypt was shortly to be repeated. At the close the discourse is calmer, and the past appears in the form of the past: "I drove him out." "The mighty one of the heathen," among the heathen, who in regard to him appear as powerless: so is Nebuchadnezzar, the world-conqueror, named. For this mighty one of the nations the lot of Assyria was no less an actual prophecy than for Pharaoh. Yet the question was not about him: not on him, but on Pharaoh, rested the foolish hopes which the prophet wishes to destroy; and he had also other grounds for leaving to his readers the application to him. "He shall deal with him:" properly, do to him. What he will do to him is not more particularly defined. It is enough that the action is on his side: to Pharaoh is left nothing but to suffer. Pharaoh had also a time of activity. Where this is abused, the period of pure passivity breaks forth with violence. In place of the hammer comes the anvil. "For his wickedness:" the wickedness denotes the pride, and the conduct flowing from it. Where pride has first occupied the heart, there all divine and human rights are trampled under foot. The tender respect for them roots in the consciousness of being under God. All righteousness and goodness flow from humble submission to God. "I drove him out:" this points to the driving of the first man out of Paradise, that was also a consequence of pride, with reference to vers. 8 and 9, according to which the king of Assyria was also in a garden of God. The allusion is the less to be mistaken, because the driving out proper is less suitable to the tree. "All the peoples of the earth went down from his shadow:" they had formerly, like birds, perched upon the branches of the tree in its shade (ver. 5). The ruin in ver. 13 (ver. 16 shows that it must be so translated) stands for the fallen tree, that is as it were a living ruin. The fowls of heaven and the beasts of the field, the wild beasts that formerly sought protection under this tree, assemble now for another object beside the fallen—to peck, and gnaw, and take what they please of its fruits. In great catastrophes every one seeks to draw advantage from the misfortune. In ver. 14 the object of the catastrophe ordained for the king of Assyria: it is to be a lesson for all the high things of the earth, to place before their eyes the dangers of pride. High in his growth, in the sense here meant, is he only who gives himself over with all his heart to his height. Genuine humility brings to elevation its only corrective. It fixes the eye on the lowliness, which in all human greatness is present with the greatness. The trees of the water and the water-drinkers are the great of the earth, to whom God gives joyful prosperity. "Nor any drinkers of water stand up by themselves," assuming to themselves what belongs to God. As water-drinkers, they have nothing but what they receive: to stand by themselves, is to steal what belongs to God; and to seize upon the property of God is a wholly wicked procedure. "For they are all delivered unto death,"—namely, those proud trees, the grandees of the earth, who were tempted to haughtiness by their greatness. Haughtiness comes before a fall, and in this fall they must learn humility; for they go down into the kingdom of the dead, where they are nothing else than ordinary sons of men: comp. Job iii. 19, "Small and great are there."

The third and last section of the discourse now follows. Ver. 15. Thus saith the Lord Jehovah, In the day when he went down to the grave I caused a mourning; I spread over him the deep, and held back its rivers, and the many waters were stayed; and I made Lebanon black over him, and all the trees of the field sank in weakness over him. 16. At the sound of his fall I make the heathen quake, when I cast him down to the grave with those that go down to the pit; and all the trees of Eden, the choice and best of Lebanon, all that drink water, sighed in the nether earth. 17. They also went down to the grave with him, to those slain by the sword; and they who were his arm sat in his shadow among the heathen. 18. Whom dost thou thus resemble in glory and in greatness among the trees of Eden? and thou shalt be cast down with the trees of Eden unto the nether earth: thou shalt lie among the uncircumcised, with those slain by the sword. This is Pharaoh and all his tumult, saith the LORD.

The flood (ver. 15), the subterranean store of water that supplies the springs (comp. ver. 4, Gen. vii. 11), mourns because it cannot flow farther into the wonted, well-loved paths. Lebanon, denoting the kingdom of the heathen (comp. ver. 3, and on xvii. 3), mourns over the fall of its greatness, which forebodes evil to all other world-powers. In deep pain sink the trees of the field, the great ones of the earth (ver. 8). "I caused a mourning, I spread over;" that is, I spread over him for mourning. The king of Assyria is here also an ideal person, the Assyrian empire; and we are not to think of a reference to Sennacherib slain by his servants, nor even to the personal fate of the last Assyrian king. The trees of Eden in ver. 16, and the water-drinkers, are parallel phrases. The trees of Eden are the former high ones of the earth, who resembled the trees of Paradise in glory, and in whom these were represented, as it were, anew; the water-drinkers are those who formerly enjoyed a glorious prosperity. In the fall of Assyria they went through their own sorrow, as it were, a second time.[1] The lamentation obeys the general law, which was fulfilled in the king of Assyria, as it had been exhibited before in them; *sic transit gloria mundi.* We have here a variation of Isa. xiv. 9, 10, where the king of Babylon is received in the kingdom of the dead by those who had gone down before him. "With him" (ver. 17), that is, no less than he, denotes not simultaneousness—for they are on his arrival already in Sheol —but similarity. The vassals of the king have gone before him in their fall. He comes to the close, and is received by his former associates in Sheol. Then at the close of the whole tragedy there is sung in chorus a lamentation over the vanity of worldly glory. "His arm"—his auxiliaries. "Whom dost thou thus resemble in glory and greatness?" (ver. 18): according to the foregoing, one in whom it was already obvious that glory and greatness cannot shield from a fall, but rather, if abused, involve in it. After removing the supposed hindrance, which consisted in the greatness of Pharaoh blinding the eyes, his downfall is announced to him. The uncircumcised stand here, as in xxviii. 10, for the impure and ungodly. "This is Pharaoh" —namely, in regard to the issue. "His tumult;" comp. ver. 2.

---

[1] נחם in the *Niphal*, sigh, be troubled, not be comforted. This meaning would be against ver. 15, where Lebanon *mourns*, and also against ver. 17, according to which those who received the king of Assyria in Sheol were those who had formerly been *friendly* to him.

Ch. xxxii. The work of God in His people is come to a close. A time of lamentations has arrived. Besides these lamentations, comes as a consolation the double lamentation of our chapter over Pharaoh and over Egypt. It reminded Israel that even in its deepest misery it had an infinite advantage over the world-power that was apparently far superior, which is here represented by Egypt. For all that the latter now possesses will soon be taken away; and while a joyful resurrection awaits Judah after it has endured the pains of death, the other remains in death, and beyond the darkness sees no light. The occasion of this lamentation was probably the circulation of the Lamentations of Jeremiah in the lands of the exile. It pleases Ezekiel in general to follow this his leader.

First, in vers. 1–16, the lamentation over Pharaoh, in two sections.

Ver. 1. And it came to pass in the twelfth year, in the twelfth month, in the first of the month, the word of the Lord came unto me, saying, 2. Son of man, take up a lamentation for Pharaoh king of Egypt, and say unto him, Lion of the heathen, thou art undone, and thou art like the dragon in the sea; and thou brokest forth with thy rivers,[1] and troubledst the water with thy feet, and didst tread in their rivers. 3. Thus saith the Lord Jehovah, And I will spread over thee my net in the congregation of many peoples; and they will bring thee up in my net. 4. And I will leave thee upon the land, and sling thee upon the field; and I will make all the fowls of heaven to dwell on thee, and satisfy all the beasts of the earth with thee. 5. And I will lay thy flesh upon the mountains, and fill the valleys with thy height. 6. And I will water the land of thy overflowing with thy blood, even to the mountains; and the plains shall be full of thee. 7. And when I put thee out, I will cover the heavens, and darken the stars thereof; the sun I will cover with a cloud, and the moon shall not give her light. 8. All luminaries of light in the heaven I will make dark for thee, and set darkness upon thy land, saith the Lord Jehovah. 9. And I will vex the heart of many peoples, when I bring thy breach among the heathen into the countries which thou knewest not. 10. And I will astonish many peoples at

---

[1] Luther, "and leapest forth in thy rivers," against the meaning of the verb, which means to break forth only, and against ver. 6.

thee, and their kings shall quake greatly for thee, when I brandish my sword in their face; and they shall tremble every moment, each man for his own soul, in the day of thy fall.

"Lion of the heathen, thou art undone"[1] (ver. 2): we have here a short outline, which is afterwards filled up; the lion receives its explanation even in this verse, the undoing in ver. 3. The figure of the dragon at the side of that of the lion is explanatory, to bring to view the demeanour of Pharaoh among the nations. The sea is the sea of nations. The mischief which the crocodile commits in the waters presents a figure of the mischief which Pharaoh commits among the nations. The words, "Thou brokest forth with thy rivers," have respect, as it appears, to this, that the natural crocodile pours out water in breathing. Bartram, in Oedmann in the *Miscellaneous Collections from Physiology for the Illustration of Holy Scripture*, part vi., says, in the description of the North American crocodile, p. 59: "Before I had got half the way, I was assailed on all sides by a great number of crocodiles, some of which attempted to upset my canoe. Two especially attacked me, one on each side, raised at once their heads and a part of their bodies above the water, and, amidst the most horrible roaring, squirted a great quantity of water on me." P. 63: "I went on thence; but scarcely had I rowed a few strokes, when an enormous crocodile rushed from the reed-bank, darted like an arrow under my boat, came up on the lee side, opened its horrible jaws, and poured over me a stream of smoke and water like a torrent in a hurricane." P. 67: "The weaker crocodiles must content themselves with roaring and puffing in the smaller pools. But an old champion, who is become absolute master of a sea, pushing into the river, proceeds in a direct line on the surface of the water from the reed-covered strand. At first his course is rapid as the lightning, but it becomes gradually slower until he reaches the centre, where he takes his place. He then puffs himself up by drawing in air and water through his mouth, which for a minute occasions a clear rustling in his throat. But presently after he spirts out the air through his mouth and nostrils with a loud noise, swings his strong tail, and spouts out through the holes of the nose a vapour which looks like a smoke. Sometimes he is wont, after his belly has

---

[1] נדמה never means to be made like, always to be silent, undone.

been so stretched out that he is ready to burst, to raise up his head and tail, and swing himself round in this position above the water like a wheel." The water of rivers and wells is a frequent symbol in Scripture of resources, prosperity, means (comp. on Rev. xvii. 1). That the rivers here also are to be taken in this sense, appears from this, that only thus do the rivers here come under *one* point of view with the waters and rivers in the following passage. As the natural crocodile overflows all around him with water, so Pharaoh the nations with his troops. The counterpart to the rivers here which are poured upon others, consists in the streams of Pharaoh's own blood, with which he must water the earth. "Troubledst the water with thy feet:" because Pharaoh makes use of his resources, he disturbs the welfare of the nations. "And didst tread in their rivers"—the rivers of the heathen. But the rivers could not be rivers of water. The sense is the same in either case. For the rivers of water would also belong to the nations whom Egypt subdued, and denote their prosperity. The *nations* in ver. 3 are not mere onlookers, but at the same time instruments of the judgment. "*They* will bring thee up." Jehovah spreads His net in the congregation of many nations, and gives it over to them, that they may draw it out. The thought in ver. 4 is, that it will fare no better with thee than with a fish, which must perish miserably, because it is taken out of its element. To the fowls of heaven, and the wild beasts which fall upon the dragon flung on the land, correspond the nations in the case of Pharaoh. Mountains and valleys in ver. 5 denote together the whole of the places in which the fish out of its element lies. The height forms the contrast to the valleys, properly hollows. They are filled with the proud carcase. "The land of thy overflowing"¹ (ver. 6)—the land which thou didst formerly overflow with thy rivers (ver. 2). "When I put thee out" (ver. 7): Pharaoh in his glory is a bright shining light. In the quenching of this light the heavenly luminaries lose their splendour: in great political catastrophes, and the endless woe connected with them, the heavenly luminaries appear, as it were, to be extinguished (Isa. xiii. 10; Amos viii. 9, 10; comm. on Rev. vi. 12). They shine truly only for the happy; the sun is only present when the eye is

¹ The verb צוף in the sense overflow, see in Lam. iii. 54.

for the sun. The nations are troubled at the fate of Pharaoh (ver. 9), because they see in his fall the proof of the vanity of all human grandeur, the threat of their own downfall (comp. ver. 10). Jehovah brings his fall among the heathen, in so far as He by means of it gives occasion to the news of it pervading the countries; and also when He scatters the Egyptians through all lands, and thereby causes them to bring the news thither (comp. ch. xxx. 9). "When I brandish my sword in their face" (ver. 10): the sword is brandished immediately over Pharaoh, but so that the other high ones of the earth shall see it, and take example by him for themselves (comp. xxxi. 14 and Deut. xiii. 11), according to which the evil-doers are to be judged, that "all Israel may hear and fear, and do no more such wickedness in thy midst."

In vers. 11–16, the second part of the lamentation over Pharaoh. Ver. 11. For thus saith the Lord Jehovah, The sword of the king of Babylon shall come upon thee. 12. By the swords of the heroes will I bring down thy tumult: the violent of the heathen are they all; and they shall lay waste the pride of Egypt, and all its tumult shall be desolated. 13. And I will destroy all its cattle from the many waters; and the foot of man shall trouble them no more, neither shall the foot of cattle trouble them. 14. Then will I deepen their waters, and cause their rivers to run like oil, saith the Lord Jehovah. 15. When I make the land of Egypt a desert, and the country desolate from its fulness, when I smite all that dwell therein, then shall they know [1] that I am the Lord. 16. This is a lamentation, and they shall sing it: the daughters of the heathen shall sing it; over Egypt and over all her tumult shall they sing it, saith the Lord Jehovah.

The peculiarity in ver. 11 is the express naming of the instrument of the divine judgment: the man, in fact, already lifts the sword to brandish it against Egypt. The pride of Egypt in ver. 12 is, according to ch. xxx. 6, 18, its greatness and glory. By the many waters in ver. 13 is meant the Nile. No foot any more troubles the waters, because man and beast are gone.

---

[1] Luther, "that they may learn." Thereby is the verse brought into a wrong connection with the foregoing; and the thought that all shall tend only to make the Egyptians feel the true deity of the living God, is brought down from its dominant position: comp. xxxiii. 29.

The Nile is also a symbol of the prosperity of Egypt, as in Isa. xix. In ver. 14 this symbolic import of the waters comes into the foreground. The thought is, that Egypt's prosperity and power will sink. The comparison with the oil turns solely on the easy flowing. In this new stage of its existence Egypt will be a low kingdom (xxix. 14)—no longer, as in former times, partly dangerous (it can no more overflow, vers. 2 and 6), partly seductive to the other nations. "Saith the Lord Jehovah," who, as the possessor of omnipotence, can with easy effort make a gentle brook out of the proud river. The lamentation is (ver. 16) not the vain show of a lamentation, but the type of one which will be actually sung. The nations will strike it up yet over Egypt, and then will the difference between a poet and a prophet be obvious. We may compare ch. xix. 14, where the same is said of the lamentation over Judah. In reference to the latter, the lamentation has now actually become a lamentation. So will it also be in reference to Egypt. The daughters of the nations are, as ver. 18 shows, the nations themselves, as daughters or virgins. They here appear under this figure, because the lamentation bears a feminine character, and because it was the custom in common life that the laments should be sung by women; comp. Jer. ix. 16.

In ch. xxxii. 17–32, the wail over Pharaoh is followed by the wail over Egypt. The prophet in this funeral song brings Egypt into connection with the congeries of nations on which the Chaldean judgment fell. In the announcement of this in Jer. xxv., are named, along with Egypt, Edom, Zidon, Elam, and the kings of the north. There are wanting in Jeremiah only Assyria, which had already fallen when he made his announcement, and Meshech and Tubal, which were probably conquered with the Assyrians (Niebuhr, p. 201). As Jeremiah uttered his prophecy when the Chaldean empire had already begun its career and dealt out heavy blows, while Ezekiel referred to the whole Chaldean judgment on the nations, some names must occur here which are wanting in Jeremiah. On the other hand, Tyre, mentioned by Jeremiah, is wanting here. It was still standing when the prophet struck up this dirge. But only in Egypt does he anticipate the future. Of the remainder he only names those who had already fallen. That which still belonged to the future in Egypt, should have its ground in that which had already taken place. The practical aim is expressed in the words of the Psalmist, "Trust not in oppression and fraud; if riches increase, set not your heart on them." The prophecy is fitted to call forth a deep feeling of the vanity of earthly things, to warn against carnal confidence in earthly power, and its abuse by violence and wrong, and, what comes specially into account here, to guard against envying those who enjoy such power for the moment. Human nature, what is it? In an hour it falls to the ground!

Ver. 17. And it came to pass in the twelfth year, on the fifteenth of the month, the word of the LORD came unto me, saying, 18. Son of man, wail for the tumult of Egypt, and cast it down, her, and the daughter of the glorious nations, into the land of the depths, with those that go down to the pit. 19. Beyond whom art thou lovely? go down, and be laid among the uncircumcised. 20. They shall fall among those slain by the sword: the sword is given; they drag her and all her tumult. 21. The strong heroes from the midst of hell shall speak to him with his helpers: the uncircumcised are gone down, they lie slain by the sword. 22. There is Asshur and all his company: around him are his graves: all of them slain, fallen by the sword: 23. Whose graves are put in the depths of the pit; and his company is around his grave: all of them slain, fallen by the sword, who caused terror in the land of the living. 24. There is Elam, and all his tumult around his grave; all of them slain, fallen by the sword, who are gone down uncircumcised into the land of depths, who gave their terror in the land of the living; and they bear (now) their shame with those that go down to the pit. 25. Among the slain they set him a bed with his tumult: around him are his graves; all of them uncircumcised, slain by the sword: for their terror went forth in the land of the living, and they (now) bear their shame with those who go down to the pit; among the slain he is laid. 26. There is Meshech, Tubal, and all his tumult: around him are his graves: all of them uncircumcised, slain by the sword; for they gave their terror in the land of the living. 27. And should they not lie with the heroes, the fallen of the uncircumcised, who are gone down to hell with their weapons of war? And they laid their swords under their heads, and their iniquities were upon their bones; for a terror were the heroes in the land of the living. 28. And thou shalt be broken among the uncircumcised, and shalt lie with those slain by the sword. 29. There is Edom, his kings and all his princes, who are joined in their might with those slain by the sword: they lie with the uncircumcised, and with those that go down to the pit. 30. There are the princes of the north, all of them, and all the Zidonians who are gone down with the slain, ashamed in their terror (proceeding) from their might; and they lie uncircumcised with those slain by the sword, and bear their shame with those that go down to the pit. 31. Pharaoh will see them, and will sigh over all his tumult; Pharaoh and all his host are slain by the sword, saith the Lord Jehovah. 32. For I gave him to be a terror in the land of the living:[1] and Pharaoh and all his tumult shall be laid among the uncircumcised, with those slain by the sword, saith the Lord Jehovah.

The month is not named in ver. 17; it is to be taken from ver. 1: comp. on ch. xxvi. 1, where we have quite an analogous case. The lamentation over the land falls in the same month with that over the king, and being closely connected with it, is separated from it only by fourteen days. The remaining nations (ver. 18) are already in Sheol. The prophecy belongs to a time when, of the opponents of the Chaldeans, only Tyre and Egypt were on the stage, and all the rest were gone. But the prophet will send down, as it were, a second time those already sent down with Egypt, the first to be sent down, since he goes over the whole process anew. Even in respect to Egypt the sending down has only a representative character. As the prophet in respect to it represents what the Lord will do, foreshadows the future process, he repeats, in respect to the other nations, that which has taken place, and thus unites that which is internally connected into a grand whole—the great judgment of the nations by Nebuchadnezzar the servant of the Lord. The "daughters of the glorious nations" are the glorious nations themselves, as virgins or daughters, once

[1] Luther, "for all the world shall also yet fear before me." He follows the Masoretic conjecture חתיתי for חתיתו, the reading attested by manuscript.

splendid in the bloom of youth, lovely to behold; comp. ver. 19. "Beyond whom art thou lovely?" (ver. 19): thou hast no advantage over one of these glorious nations; they were no less lovely than thou, and yet must go down to Sheol. Thus their fate is the prophecy of thine. *The* Egyptian is addressed, the ideal unity of the Egyptians, who appear in ver. 20 in the place of the Egyptian. In ver. 18 also, the nations were presented in the unity of the daughters. "Go down and be laid among the uncircumcised:" the uncircumcised are, in the usage of Ezekiel, the unclean; comp. on ch. xxviii. 10. As Egypt is like the other fallen nations in its sinful uncleanness, so must it share their fate also. From the mention of the unclean, the words "Beyond whom art thou lovely?" receive their more exact import. Hence we perceive that the advantage of loveliness, if it existed, must have consisted chiefly in freedom from the blemish of sin. The expression in our verse applies also to those who with uncircumcised hearts are found in the external community of the people of God. The outward circumcision loses all significance where the state of the heart indicated by it is wanting. No less, also, baptism under the New Testament. "The sword is given" (ver. 20)— namely, into the hands of the earthly executors of the divine wrath, the Chaldeans. These are the subject in the words "They drag her"[1]—like a criminal who is dragged to the place of execution, or like a corpse to the pit. The helpers of Egypt (ver. 21) are those who remained with him to the last; comp. the enumeration in ch. xxx. 5. The "strong heroes" are preeminently of the nations that are afterwards enumerated, and were already sent down by the avenging hand of God. The address of the strong heroes to the king of Egypt and his helpers is not given; for the words "are gone down," etc., do not suit in the mouth of the heathen. Even because the address is not given, we can only think of the obvious and self-evident thought. They greet him as a colleague. That which is here only indicated is unfolded in the fundamental passage, Isa. xiv. 10, 11, where the departed receive the king of Babylon in Sheol with the words, "Thou also art become weak as we: thou art become like unto us." The words "are gone down," etc., give the closer description of the strong heroes—

[1] משכו is 3d præterite, as נתנו, ver. 25.

denote them as those who have already gone down into Sheol before the Egyptians. With this agrees the description in ver. 22 f. of this subterranean company by individual persons. Asshur (ver. 22) stands at the head as the brightest example of human greatness going to destruction. In this respect he was already (ch. xxxi.) presented to Pharaoh as a mirror of his future. "Around him are his graves:" Asshur, the ideal person of the people, bodily represented by the king, has all his graves, the graves of his people, around him.[1] The graves here and in ver. 23 are distinguished from Sheol, as generally in the Old Testament, even in Isa. xiv., Sheol and the grave are separated, although here, in ver. 27, indeed the grave appears, so to speak, as a station on the way to Sheol. The depth in ver. 23 is that of the grave. The grave is deep even if, materially taken, it be only a few feet, as a stream is very deep if it be only six feet. The grave is deep enough to cover all glory. A terrible contrast, in which they who formerly spread terror over the earth, now in death lie so impotent beneath. How have they raged in vain! (Ps. xxxix. 7.) After Asshur follows, in ver. 24, Elam. To him, in Jer. xlix. 34 f., "in the beginning of the reign of Zedekiah," a great defeat is predicted, doubtless in consequence of taking part in the anti-Chaldaic coalition then forming; comp. on viii. 16 f., xxx. 5. Here the defeat has already taken place. Concerning Meshech and Tubal (ver. 26), the Moschi and Tibareni on the Pontic mountains, comp. xxvii. 13. "For they caused their terror in the land of the living:" this appears here otherwise than before as the *cause* of the slaying with the sword, in accordance with the rule not merely of human, but *principaliter* of divine judgment, " Whosoever sheddeth man's blood, by man shall his blood be shed" (Gen. ix. 6), and, "They that take the sword shall perish by the sword" (Matt. xxvi. 52). This thought is further expanded in ver. 27. What is there said immediately of Meshech and Tubal, holds in fact of all other nations lusting after war and victory. The ground on which the thought is expressed immediately in regard to Meshech and Tubal is probably this, that the custom regarded as significant by the prophet prevailed among them, to bury the fallen war-

---

[1] Asshur is here treated as masculine; in the foregoing, and also in ver. 23, as feminine,—a frequent variation.

riors with their death-weapons, in which they have, as it were, their misdeeds with them, so that guilt and punishment are united in the grave. "And should they not lie:" the question without the interrogatory particle is especially frequent in Ezekiel. "They laid their swords:" to the dead is ascribed what took place by their order, and that in which they placed their highest honour, like the race of Cain, that counted the fratricide of their ancestor as bravery. Edom also appears in ver. 29 among the number of those already judged. He had shown a malicious joy at the downfall of Judah; but immediately after, the Chaldean storm must have swept over him also. Only the beginning indeed of the judgment can be regarded as having already taken place. The threatening in ch. xxxv. shows this. "In their might:" in the exercise and encounter of it, or even notwithstanding their might, as Luther translates, "although they were mighty." To the "princes of the north" (ver. 30) correspond in Jer. xxv. "all the kings of the north near and far," who there appear among those who must drink the cup of the Chaldean catastrophe. Here they have already drunk it. There are the Aramæans. To them belong Arpad, Hamath, and Damascus, to whom Jeremiah in ch. xlix. 23-27 predicts destruction.[1] To the Aramæans are joined the neighbouring Zidonians, who were subdued at the time when Nebuchadnezzar placed his army before Tyre. In ch. xxviii. 30 f. they are, in a prophecy of the tenth month of the eleventh year, still the object of threatening; here, in a prophecy of the twelfth month of the twelfth year, this threatening has been carried into effect. Tyre is here not found in the company which greeted Pharaoh on his entrance into Sheol. At the time when this prophecy was uttered Tyre was still standing, though the siege was already begun. The prophet might certainly have anticipated its clearly foreseen fall, and mingled it in the company. But he omits it to prevent mistake. But the fact that Tyre is not named, shows clearly that all those named have already received their doom. Pharaoh sighs (ver. 31): others explain, he comforts himself.[2] But Pharaoh could so much the less derive comfort from the

---

[1] Comp. on the enterprises of Nebuchadnezzar in Syria, Niebuhr, p. 208 f.

[2] Comp. on נחם, not to comfort oneself, but to sigh, be troubled, at xxxi. 16.

view of the others, as they had been not his foes, but his confederates on earth, and their defeat was at the same time his own. The Lord gave the terror of Pharaoh in the land of the living (ver. 32): he was for a long time terrible on the earth, not by his own power, but by the operation of God, who made use of him as His instrument. Used up, he is now destroyed by the same power which employed him before for its ends. He has, in the time of the power vouchsafed to him, proved himself unclean and uncircumcised, and hence he must share the fate of the uncircumcised.

Ch. xxxiii. 1–20. We have here the author's conclusion to ch. i.–xxxii. No other view is admissible. According to ch. xxiv. and ver. 22, here a prophecy delivered among the people before the arrival of the fugitives from Jerusalem is impossible. The contents, which only resume throughout, and in part almost verbally repeat, what has been already said, are decisive against the hypothesis of an introduction to the following passage. Then there is the want of a date. Before the prophet passes to a new epoch of his prophetic activity, he lays down, in relation to his prophetic past, as it is given in ch. i.–xxxii., three fundamental thoughts, which are deeply important for all times of the church.

The first section (vers. 1–9) accords in thought, and partly also in expression, with ch. iii. 16–21, where Ezekiel, in his call, receives the office of a watchman. The end returns to the beginning. The section falls into two parts: first in vers. 1–6, the comparison of a watchman, whom a people appoints at a time of approaching war; then the application in vers. 7–9. In the comparison the watchman is appointed by men; in the application by God. The lesson is, that the relation between the prophet (and in general the servant of God in His kingdom) and the people is one full of responsibility. As the prophet has in the foregoing fulfilled his duty, the response falls upon the people. Let every one take heed how he hears, among the contemporaries of the prophets and among their successors, to whom he commits his book. The neglect of the faithful admonitions of the servants of God, has in the past brought down the divine judgments, against which none ought to murmur, as they have their root and justification in culpable

CHAP. XXXIII. 1-9. 289

disobedience to the word of God (Zech. vii. 11 f.). The neglect of the admonitions of the prophet will also in future bring down the judgments of God.

Ver. 1. And the word of the LORD came unto me, saying, 2. Son of man, speak to the sons of thy people, and say unto them, When I bring a sword upon a land, and the people of the land take a man from their midst,[1] and set him for their watchman; 3. And he sees the sword coming upon the land, and blows the trumpet, and warns the people; 4. And any one hears the sound of the trumpet, and takes not warning, and the sword comes and takes him away, his blood shall be upon his own head. 5. He heard the sound of the trumpet, and took not warning, his blood shall be upon him; and he took warning,[2] he delivered his soul. 6. And if the watchman see the sword come, and blow not the trumpet, and the people be not warned, and the sword come and take a soul of them, he is taken away in his iniquity; but his blood will I require at the watchman's hand. 7. And thou, son of man, I gave thee to be a watchman to the house of Israel; and thou shalt hear a word from my mouth, and warn them from me. 8. When I say unto the wicked, O wicked, thou shalt die; and thou speakest not to warn the wicked from his way, he, the wicked, shall die in his iniquity; but his blood will I require at thy hand. 9. But when thou warnest a wicked man of his way, that he turn from it, and he turn not from his way, he shall die in his iniquity, and thou hast delivered thy soul.

"His blood shall be upon his own head" (ver. 4): he will be to blame for his own fall. The head is named, from the custom of carrying on the head. Blood often stands for bloodguilt. "He is taken away in his iniquity" (ver. 6): mishap befalls no one undeserved, even if under the circumstances he might have been delivered. For the unwarned it is decreed as the deserved punishment of his other sins, that warning should

[1] Properly, from their end, that is, of their number. The end includes in itself that which is before the end, or that which lies between the ends (on both sides). In form the word is singular, but it may also be plural, as in 1 Kings xii. 31, where Jeroboam takes priests from the ends of the people, from their number—laymen instead of Levites.

[2] Luther, "But whosoever takes warning." But the thought is, If he had taken warning, he would have delivered his soul; so that he is thus to blame for his own fall.

T

not be given him, as Joseph's brethren, innocent in the particular case, cry out, " God hath found out the iniquity of thy servants" (Gen. xliv. 16). But the unfaithful watchman is punished for his neglect.

In vers. 10, 11 is the second thought. The prophet has had to punish and to threaten very much. The effect of his address might easily be depressing and disheartening. At the close, therefore, once more he gives prominence to a thought which he had already expressed in ch. xviii. 23, 30, 32, and which by this repetition he secures against being overlooked: Say not I have been too severe. The sinner should not despair: the merciful God accepts sinners. Repentance is the way to salvation. To invite to this is the proper object. To afford more tranquillity is not the aim of the prophet. He combats despair only so far as it is a hindrance to repentance. Ver. 10. And thou, son of man, say to the house of Israel, Thus ye say, If our transgressions and our sins be upon us, and we pine away in them, how should we then live? 11. Say unto them, As I live, saith the Lord Jehovah, I have no pleasure in the death of the wicked, but that the wicked turn from his way and live. Turn ye, turn ye from your evil ways; and why will ye die, O house of Israel? "And we pine away in them" (ver. 10): as thou thyself hast said (ch. xxiv. 23), and also the lawgiver has said in Lev. xxvi. 39.

The third thought (vers. 12–20) is comprehended in the one word theodicy. The greatest danger that can arise out of suffering, is that a man should misunderstand his Maker: one of the hardest problems of the servants of God is to bring reason to bear on suffering. God, the prophet proceeds, is righteous in all His ways: every one murmurs for his sins (Lam. iii. 39). Whosoever fails of salvation, let him not—as Israel, sighing under his distress, is so prone to do—accuse God, who always bestows salvation on the righteous, and on him who turns from his sin. Evil only befalls the formerly righteous, who has turned away from righteousness, and the wicked, who will not repent. Thoughts are also here repeated from ch. xviii.; comp. especially vers. 20, 21, 24, 25, 29. They are of extreme importance; for the heart that in distress misunderstands its God, will not tread the path of repentance, which determines the return of salvation; and man is quite prone to mitigate his guilt, and to think that God has dealt too hardly with him. It may easily be the same persons, who think in vers. 10, 11 that they have been severely treated, and here that God has done too much for them. In such times of suffering, the one wave relieves the other.

Ver. 12. And thou, son of man, say unto the sons of thy people, The righteousness of the righteous shall not deliver him in the day of his transgression; and by the wickedness of the wicked he shall not fall in the day that he turns from his wickedness; and the righteous shall not be able to live thereby in the day of his sin. 13. When I say to the righteous that he shall live, and he trusts in his righteousness, and commits iniquity, all his righteousness shall not be remembered, and by his iniquity that he has done he shall die. 14. And when I say to the wicked, Thou shalt die, and he turns from his sin, and does judgment and righteousness; 15. If the wicked restore the pledge, repay that which is robbed, walk in the statutes of life, so that he do no iniquity, he shall live, not die. 16. All his sins wherein he sinned shall not be remembered to him: he has done judgment and righteousness, he shall live. 17. And the sons of thy people say, The way of the Lord is not right; but *their* way is not right. 18. When the righteous turns from his righteousness, and commits iniquity, then he shall die thereby. 19. And when the wicked turns from his wickedness, and does judgment and righteousness, he shall live thereby. 20. And ye say, The way of the Lord is not right: I will judge you, O house of Israel, every one after his ways.

" *Thereby*" (ver. 12): that he has been righteous formerly, or until now. " He trusts in his righteousness" (ver. 13): it was a widespread delusion among the Jews, that they possessed a hereditary righteousness; that whatever they might themselves be, yet the righteousness of their pious fathers, from Abraham down, would avail them; and if they experienced the contrary in their misfortunes, they held themselves justified in murmuring against God. The prophet teaches, on the contrary, that the fate of every generation is determined by its own relation to God. "If the wicked restore the pledge" (ver. 15); comp. xviii. 7. "The way of the Lord is not right" (ver. 17): properly, not weighed; comp. xviii. 25, 29.

WORDS OF COMFORT.

CHAPTERS XXXIII. 21–XXXIX.

CHAPTER XXXIII. 21, 22.

THE book of Ezekiel has only two chief parts—prophecies before and after the destruction of Jerusalem—threatening and promise. If this be mistaken, and the prophecies against foreign nations be made a separate part beside the other two, the position of ch. xxxiii. 1–20 is inconceivable, as in that case it must have followed ch. xxiv. This follows also from the fact that the beginning of the prophecy against foreign nations in ch. xxv. is connected with that relating to home affairs in ch. xxiv. The prophecies against foreign nations are merely an appendix to the first part, designed to throw a stronger light on the judgments pronounced against Judah, by unfolding to the view the judgment impending over the heathen. This subordinate place is already assigned to the prophecies against foreign nations by this, that the prophet (ch. xxiv. 27) at the opening of the siege of Jerusalem is dumb, and (on the main subject) does not speak again until the fugitive comes. Accordingly, what he says between ch. xxiv. 27 and xxxiii. 23 cannot be co-ordinate with the rest; it can only have a subsidiary importance.

Our two verses give, in accordance with the end of ch. xxiv., the historical introduction to the discourses of the second epoch.

Ver. 21. *And it came to pass in the twelfth year of our captivity, in the tenth month, on the fifth of the month, the fugitive from Jerusalem came unto me, saying, The city is smitten.* 22. *And the hand of the* LORD *was upon me in the evening before the fugitive came; and He opened my mouth,* until he came to me in the morning; and my mouth was opened, and I was no longer dumb.

This cannot refer to the first news of the taking of Jerusalem. This took place nearly one and a half year sooner, on the ninth day of the fourth month in the eleventh year; and the news of such events spreads with amazing rapidity. The intelligence arrived no doubt in eight, or at the most fourteen, days at the abode of Ezekiel; so that the difficulty is not removed by assuming most arbitrarily an error in the text, and putting the eleventh in place of the twelfth year. It refers rather to the first account of an eye-witness, who had himself passed through the terrors of the catastrophe, and was in his miserable plight a living proclamation of it. The "fugitive" is here, as in Gen. xiv. 13, an ideal person, or according to the usual designation, a *collectivum*—not a single individual, but a transport. Ezekiel had already said, in ch. xiv. 22, 23, that a whole host of such fugitives would come to the exiles; comp. also ch. vi. 9. There we have the commentary on the fugitive here. These sufferers were by their very appearance a testimony to the fearfulness of the divine judgments: in them the smitten city presented itself as it were bodily. Their narratives gave only the commentary on their appearance: they said, The city is smitten, even before they opened the mouth. Analogous to this is the deep impression, which, according to Neh. i., the description of the desolate condition of Jerusalem by eye-witnesses made on Nehemiah, although this condition had existed for a century. Here the impression must have been still deeper. On the night before the arrival of the transport, which was doubtless announced the day before, took place the opening of the prophet's mouth, that had been closed since ch. xxiv. 27—as it were the removal of the seal from it. The impulse to speak to the people again asserted itself. The prophetic activity itself first commenced after the transport appeared, the arrival of which was to form the ground for the assumption of new hopes. Only after the complete death, the annihilation of all earthly hopes, had passed before their eyes, could the announcement of the joyful resurrection be made. Already in ch. xxiv. 27 it was said that God would open the prophet's mouth to the fugitive. Accordingly the actual arrival of the ruined people, in whom the ruined city was represented, was the prerequisite of the discourse.

Ch. xxxiii. 23-29. The new discourse here first takes up again the former threatening, and meets those who, still giving themselves up to illusions, thought that the judgment would not inexorably run its course. That there were such people, was proved by the revolt in which Gedaliah the Chaldean governor was slain. The new discourse is essentially comforting. But before the seed of divine hope could be sown, the last thorns and thistles of false human hopes, and of the efforts that grew out of them, had to be destroyed, which even now, although against all appearances, were convulsively grasped by those who avoided the passage through the strait gate of repentance, which is the condition of participating in the divine hope, and did not wish to put off the spotted garment of the flesh.

Ver. 23. And the word of the LORD came unto me, saying, 24. Son of man, the inhabitants of those ruins in the land of Israel say, Abraham was one, and he inherited the land: and we are many; the land is given to us for a possession. 25. Therefore say unto them, Thus saith the Lord Jehovah, Ye eat with the blood, and lift up your eyes to your detestable things, and ye shed blood: and shall ye possess the land? 26. Ye stand upon your sword, ye work abomination, and defile every one his neighbour's wife: and shall ye possess the land? 27. Say thus unto them, Thus saith the Lord Jehovah, As I live, they that are in the ruins shall fall by the sword; and him that is in the field I will give to the beast for food; and they that are in the forts and the caves shall die of the pestilence. 28. And I will lay the land desolate and waste, and her mighty pride shall cease; and the mountains of Israel shall be desolate, without any passing through. 29. And they shall know that I am the LORD, when I lay the land desolate and waste, for all their abominations which they have done.

"The inhabitants of these ruins" (ver. 24): according to ver. 27, the ruins are those of the places destroyed. The whole land was a land of ruins, and therefore ground enough to let go at length the hopes of a deluded heart. They still cherish these hopes, and connect them with Abraham. He was childless, and yet has inherited the land in his posterity. Why shall they, who are still numerous in reference to him, not receive again the possession of the land? They believe that they must approach the nearer to Abraham, as they hold themselves to be the true continuation of Abraham's being—the holders of the promise given to him—but overlook the wide gulf that stands between them and him. If they were Abraham's children, they would do his works. " Ye eat with the blood ! " The eating of blood was forbidden in Gen. ix. 4 as the first step to the prohibition of murder : in the blood of animals was to be seen a type of the blood of man. The prescription had a didactic end. It was to call forth an abhorrence of shedding human blood. Whosoever disregarded this prohibition showed, under the Old Testament, after the law had made the *horror* of animal blood national, that the germ of the murderous spirit was in him. " Ye work abomination " (ver. 26) : the feminine form of the verb is surprising : Your wives work. This goes hand in hand with the fact that in ch. xiii. 17 f. the false prophets appear as women. The feminine character of the sinner is already indicated in Gen. iv. 7. There it appears unmanly to let sin conquer, instead of ruling over it. In reference to sin, the men are not to be womanly, but the women manly. The abomination is afterwards more exactly defined. It is adultery. The man who defiles his neighbour's wife is, in truth, himself a woman. In the foregoing we have the transgression of the first commandment of the first table, and of the first of the second : the eating of blood is only mentioned by way of introduction. Here we have the transgression of the first two commandments of the second table. The pestilence is in ver. 27 the companion of the famine, which pursues those who have fled from the Chaldeans to the inaccessible hills, and to the caves.

Ch. xxxiii. 30-33. This second part of the introductory discourse, which proves itself to be such by this, that the sentence, " And the word of the Lord came unto me, saying," first recurs in ch. xxxiv. 1, endeavours in another respect to prepare the mind for the chief contents of the new message. The prophet had, otherwise than Jeremiah, a well-affected audience, especially now, after the violent catastrophe had gone over Jerusalem, and confirmed his former predictions : as the power of the opposition which had formerly risen against him (ch. ii. 6, iii. 7) was broken. But many were still wanting in real earnestness: they listened to his fair speech; but the heart was still addicted to worldly things—the word bore no good fruit. With a view to such, the prophet warns men against hearing him for the tickling of the ears. The word of God is a very serious matter. Let every one take heed how he hears, that he be not a hearer only, but a doer. What the prophet announces comes to pass; and if the fulfilment takes place, the mere hearer will be the loser: he is overtaken by the threatened punishments, and excluded from the promised blessings. He has not to deal with an excellent orator; but behind the son of man stands the Lord, mighty to punish and to save.

Ver. 30. And thou, son of man, the sons of thy people talk[1] concerning thee by the walls and in the doors of the houses, and speak with one another, each with his brother, saying, Come now, and hear what is the word that cometh from the LORD. 31. And they come unto thee as a people comes, and sit before thee as my people, and hear thy words, and do them not; for they deal tenderly with their mouth, their heart goeth after their covetousness. 32. And, lo, thou art to them as a song of love, pleasant in voice, and playing well; and they hear thy words, and do them not. 33. And when it comes, lo, it is come; and they shall know that a prophet hath been in the midst of them.

The talking in ver. 30, as the following shows, is not hostile,[2] but well-meaning: amidst the national impoverishment they amuse themselves with the surpassing rhetorical gifts of the new classic. "By the walls"—on the divan. This is the place for household talk. "As a people comes" (ver. 31): the prophet has not merely several followers, but he is become popular among the exiles—has a quite different position from that of Jeremiah in Jerusalem, who had to cry, Woe is me, against whom every man contended in the land. "As my people:" so respectful, attentive, and apparently earnest and

---

[1] Literally, "who talk." They are, as it were, placed before the prophet that he may have them clearly in his eye—be aware of their character. A "behold" might have been prefixed.

[2] ב need not lead to this supposition. The person *concerning* whom often stands elsewhere with ב.

willing. "They deal tenderly with their mouth" (ver. 31): properly, they show ardour[1]—affect in words an ardent love to God and His word, while the real inclination of their heart goes quite another way—is turned to mammon, the god of the Jewish old man. The essence of the *dealing* desired by the prophet is sincere conversion to God, the turning of the heart from covetousness to Him. As a person can only be compared with a person, so "as a song of love" (ver. 32) means, as one who sings and plays a love-song.[2] "A prophet" (ver. 32)—no mere orator. The difference they discover in painful experience when it is too late: the threatened punishment has already overtaken them; they are already excluded from the promised salvation, which can be gained only by true repentance. "Lo, it is come, and they shall know:" they shall know even by its coming.

Ch. xxxiv. The prophet now comes to the chief calling which he had to fulfil in the present circumstances: his discourse assumes a consolatory character. As he was before only a threatener, so he is now only a promiser. Those who failed to infer the restoration from former prophecies of threatening import, that must always return under similar circumstances, might easily fall into grave misconceptions. But the prophet was not bound to obviate these misconceptions by cautionary hints, and thereby make his discourse less palatable to troubled souls by presenting a handle for their anxiety. The misconceptions of those whose heart is not right with God are not to be removed—they form a part of their judgment: this is one of the many stones cast in their way to cause them to stumble. The trouble which the prophet here encounters arises from the loss of civil government. The seeming loss, he contends, is a real gain, as the present government was so bad (vers. 1-10); and then God makes ample amends for it when He Himself undertakes the pastoral care of the people (vers. 11-22), and in this pastoral care raises up David for their shepherd, under whose government the fulness of salvation will be imparted to them (vers. 23-31). If thus they need

[1] The meanings loveliness and delight are not well founded.
[2] Jerome: *Tales sunt usque hodie multi in ecclesia, qui aiunt; venite audiamus illum et istum, mira eloquentia prædicationis suæ verba volventem, plurimique plausus commovent et vociferantur et jactant manus.*

not look in despairing grief to the past, they must look in joyful hope to the future.

Ver. 1. And the word of the LORD came unto me, saying, 2. Son of man, prophesy against the shepherds of Israel, prophesy, and say unto them, the shepherds, Thus saith the Lord Jehovah, Woe to the shepherds of Israel, who have fed themselves! shall not the shepherds feed the flock? 3. Ye eat the fat and clothe you with the wool, ye kill the fed: ye feed not the flock. 4. The weak ye strengthened not, nor healed the sick, nor bound up that which was broken, nor brought back that which was driven away, nor sought that which was lost; and with force ye ruled over them, and with rigour. 5. And they were scattered without a shepherd, and they became food to all the beasts of the field, and were scattered. 6. My flock wander on all the mountains, and on every high hill: and my flock was scattered on the whole face of the earth, and there is none to search and none to inquire. 7. Therefore, ye shepherds, hear the word of the LORD. 8. As I live, saith the Lord Jehovah, Because my flock is become a prey, and my flock is become food to every beast of the field without a shepherd, and my shepherds searched not after my flock, and the shepherds fed themselves, and fed not my flock: 9. Therefore, ye shepherds, hear the word of the LORD; 10. Thus saith the Lord Jehovah, Behold, I am against the shepherds, and will require my flock at their hand, and cause them to cease from feeding the flock; and the shepherds shall no more feed themselves: and I will deliver my flock from their mouth, and they shall not be food for them.

What the prophet announces in vers. 1-10 had already actually taken place. It is an explanation of the judgment in the form of an announcement of it. Yet it is not to be overlooked, that two of the dethroned kings, Jehoiachin and Zedekiah, were still alive, and also many of the chiefs who had been formerly at the helm. In this respect the announcement actually extends into the future. It is certain that nothing can be said of a restoration, of a return to the former state, of which many then still dreamed; comp. ch. xxxiii. 21-29.

The shepherds of Israel in ver. 2 are the kings; these, however, not as individuals, but as inclusive of the whole then ruling order. That the nobles partly were still worse than the kings, is shown by Jeremiah (xxxviii. 5): "Behold, he is in your hand; for the king can do nothing against you." That the shepherds are only the civil rulers, not including the priests and prophets, as many old expositors thought, appears from the fundamental passage, Jer. xxiii. (*Christol.* ii. p. 447, comp. 423); and also from this, that in ver. 23 the Messiah is opposed to them under the name of *Shepherd* and *Prince;* no less, moreover, from the whole description of their conduct, in which nothing at all is said of false doctrine, but only of that which comports with bad civil rulers—tyranny, violence, wrong. That in the New Testament what is here said of the bad shepherds is applied to the Pharisees (comp. especially John x. 8, 10), affords the less warrant here to go beyond the civil rulers, because in these times the pharisaically disposed hierarchy also occupied the place of the domestic civil government. "The shepherds:" this is emphatically repeated, to indicate the contrast of the idea and the office to the reality. The high office of rulers of the people serves them (ver. 3) only as a means of satisfying their selfish desires. Instead of the *fat,* some, after the example of the LXX. and Jerome, wish to place the *milk;* appealing to this, that the eating of the fat presupposes the killing of the sheep, which is mentioned only in the third place. Only in the figurative sense of the sheep can a man eat the fat without killing them. The eating of the fat is, as the clothing with the wool, the draining of the subjects. Killing, the culminating act, denotes the murder of the subjects in order to seize on their goods. But milk does not suit, as it is a right of the shepherds to eat the milk of the flock (1 Cor. ix. 7). The eating of the *fat* follows also from the conclusion in ver. 10, "I will deliver my flock from their mouth, and they shall not be food for them." To the three sins of commission is opposed, in the words "Ye feed not the flock," the one great sin of omission. "With rigour" (ver. 4) points to that which the Egyptians once did to the Israelites (Ex. i. 13, 14)— the native shepherds are no better than the heathen despots were in the olden time — and also to Lev. xxv. 43, "Thou shalt not rule over him *with rigour,* but shalt fear thy God." The first "and they were scattered" in ver. 5 points to the internal dissolution of the people. In consequence of this, the neglected people unlearned the power of resisting the external foe. The beasts of the field are here, without doubt, the heathen nations, the wild stock. By being scattered, in the second place, the exile is meant; comp. vers. 12, 13.

In the place of those bad shepherds, whose removal is in truth a benefit, God Himself will in the future appear with His pastoral care. Ver. 11. For thus saith the Lord Jehovah, Behold, it is I; and I will search after my flock, and seek them out. As a shepherd seeks out his flock, in the day that he is among his flock that is scattered; so will I seek out my flock, and deliver them out of all the places where they have been scattered in the day of cloud and fog. 13. And I will bring them out of the peoples, and gather them from the lands, and bring them to their own land, and feed them on the mountains of Israel, in the valleys, and in all the dwellings of the land. 14. I will feed them in good pasture, and on the mountains of Israel shall their walk be; there shall they lie in a good walk, and on a fat pasture shall they feed on the mountains of Israel. 15. I will feed my flock, and cause them to lie down, saith the Lord Jehovah. 16. I will seek the perishing, and bring back the scattered, and bind up the broken, and strengthen the sick: and the fat and the strong will I destroy; I will feed it with judgment. 17. And ye, my flock, thus saith the Lord Jehovah, Behold, I judge between sheep and sheep, the rams and the bucks. 18. Is it too little for you to feed on the good pasture, that ye tread down the residue of your pasture with your feet; and to drink the settled water, that ye foul the residue with your feet? 19. And my flock must feed on that which your feet have trodden, and drink what your feet have fouled. 20. Therefore thus saith the Lord Jehovah unto them, Behold, it is I; and I will judge between the fat and the lean sheep. 21. Because ye push with side and with shoulder, and thrust with your horns the sickly, till ye have scattered them abroad. 22. And I will save my flock, and they shall no longer be a prey; and I will judge between sheep and sheep.

"Behold, it is I" (ver. 11): this found its most glorious fulfilment in the appearance of Christ, as vers. 23, 24 expressly announce that God will execute His pastoral office specially by the Messiah. Yet even before the appearance of Christ the pastoral care of God was active in the restoration from the exile and the other gracious gifts and benefits, which, however, all point forward to the true fulfilment, and call forth the desire for it. The day of cloud and fog, in ver. 12, is from Joel ii. 2. Here, as there, this day denotes the dark, afflictive time of the people of God, the time of being visited by their foes—not the day of judgment on the heathen, with which Joel deals only in ch. iv. The fat and the strong, in ver. 16, are the new robber-knights, who will appear among the people when the old are set aside by the Chaldean catastrophe. Even among the people of God such pests spring forth; but they differ in this respect from the heathen, that against these pests, which have their root in Gen. iii., an internal reaction always arises, so that they cannot maintain a perpetual dominion. By the fat and the strong are designated here not all the mighty, but those whose essence is exhausted in possession and might. David designates himself, even on the throne, as wretched and poor. A rich man in Scripture is not one who has many goods, but whose heart is in this possession, so that it ceases to be for him something accidental; while a poor man is only one who knows and feels himself poor, who is so not merely externally, but also in *spirit*—in his consciousness. To *feeding* belongs also judgment on the part of the flock committing trespass: the tending must in this case be with a rod of iron (Rev. ii. 27). The care announced in the first part of the verse for the suffering part of the flock can only be realized by a powerful interference with those who commit trespass. The thought, here first coming out, of the reaction of God against the return of the wicked state before the exile, is carried out further to the end of the section. In ver. 17 the rams and bucks are in apposition with the sheep in the second place. God procures for the one part of the sheep, the sufferers, justice against the other part, the evil-doers. The rams and the bucks are identical with the fat and the strong in ver. 16. The quality of the bucks, which comes here into account, is the pushing, and in general the violent dealing. The address in ver. 18 is to the tyrants of the future. But what has been already seen in the tyrants who have retired, forms the ground of the picture. " Settled water " is water in which a settling has taken place, and the impurities have gone to the bottom. They themselves drink the pure water, and thereon wantonly stir up the impurities. "Till ye have scattered them abroad" (ver. 21): the condition of the people, disturbed by the bad internal administration, had at length brought on the exile; comp. ver. 5. Similar relations will return in future; but God will check them powerfully. "I will judge between sheep and sheep" (ver. 22): the work begun in exile will be continued in the course of time, and find its completion at length in the judgments announced in Matt. xxv. The connection with what follows shows that the chief fulfilment is here also to be sought in Christ, whose government and secret but powerful sway permits no tyranny or injustice to endure, and brings back the right and the normal into the place of the fallen state. A chief phase in the judgment between sheep and sheep was decision given by God in the conflict between the synagogue and the rising Christian church. But that this judgment between sheep and sheep pervades the whole history, that we have here to do with a true prophecy and not with a patriotic fancy, is shown by the comparison of the present Christian world with the heathen and Mohammedan powers, and also with the state of justice that appears in the Old Testament. We invariably see that, since the coming of Christ, a new judicial power is busy among the people of God, which quietly and noiselessly removes the abnormal,—a reforming power which the old covenant did not yet possess.

According to vers. 23-31, the pastoral care of God is specially shown in this, that He raises up David as the shepherd of His people. The peace and happiness under his government are depicted in a series of figures that are mostly taken from the books of Moses, especially from Lev. xxvi.[1]

Ver. 23. And I will raise up one shepherd over them, and he shall feed them, my servant David; he shall feed them, and he shall be their shepherd. 24. And I the LORD will be their God, and my servant David prince among them: I the Lord have spoken it. 25. And I will make with them a covenant of peace, and cause the evil beast to cease out of the land; and they shall sit safely in the wilderness, and sleep in the woods. 26. And I will make them, and the environs of my hill, a blessing; and send down the rain in its season: there shall be showers of blessing. 27. And the tree of the field shall yield

[1] Comp. the copious treatment of this section, *Christol.* ii. p. 571.

its fruit, and the land yield its increase; and they shall be safe in the land, and know that I am the LORD, when I break the bars of their yoke, and deliver them from the hand of those whom they served. 28. And they shall no more be a prey to the heathen, and the beast of the field shall not devour them: and they shall sit safely, and none shall make them afraid. 29. And I will raise up for them a plantation for a name, and they shall no more be swept away by famine, and no more take upon them the reproach of the heathen. 30. And they shall know that I the LORD their God am with them; and they are my people, the house of Israel, saith the Lord Jehovah. 31. And ye are my flock, sheep of my pasture; ye are men : I am your God, saith the Lord Jehovah.

The unity of the shepherd in ver. 23 can only refer, as the comparison of ch. xxxvii. 24 shows, to the separation of the kingdom caused by the revolt from the Davidic dynasty. As *one* God, so is there now again *one* king. With the unity is connected the glory of the king and his kingdom, as the decline was connected with the multiplicity of the shepherds. The words "one fold and one shepherd" in Isa. x. 16 are an extension of this sentence. With the coming of that great Shepherd ceases not only the division of Israel, but also the separation between Israel and the heathen. The more explicit announcement in the earlier prophets—for ex. Isa. ix. and xi., and other passages of the same prophet—leaves no doubt that by David here is meant the true David, the Messiah, in whom the stem of David is to culminate. No one who was at home in the language of Scripture could think of a personal reappearance of David, any more than in Mal. iii. 23 of a personal reappearance of Elias. The Messiah, the glorious offspring of David—this had long been in the times of the prophets a lesson of the catechism. It is also not a resurrection of David that is spoken of, but a sending of a David who has not yet been present. "I the Lord have spoken it" (ver. 24): this strikes down the doubt of the announcement that appears incredible under present circumstances. However deep was the present humiliation of the people and their kingdom, he who promises is the man to perform. "Is anything too wonderful for the Lord?" The peace in ver. 25 is the security against hostile powers. The "evil beasts," according to vers. 5 and 28 especially, appear in human form. Through Christ the people of God are predominant. The heathen world is forced from the dominant place which it had hitherto taken, and sinks to the servile. "Them and the environs of my hill" (ver. 26): Israel dwells spiritually on Zion (Isa. x. 24), which is the well-spring of blessing (xvii. 23). This blessing is so mighty, that it extends even to the environs of the hill—the heathen joining themselves in the time of salvation to the old covenant people. Comp. xvii. 23, according to which all the fowls dwell under the tall cedar of the Davidic race, attaining to its glory in Christ; xvi. 61, according to which her sisters become daughters to Zion; and especially xlvii. 8, according to which the waters flowing from the sanctuary heal the dead sea of the world. That the blessing overflows to the heathen, attests the super-abundant fulness of it, and is therefore full of comfort even for Zion. The explanation, "they who dwell around my hill," would, contrary to the view of Zion as the dwelling-place of Israel, which pervades the whole Old Testament, exclude them from Zion itself, change the temple merely into a dwelling-place of God; whereas it appears throughout as the place where God dwells with His people, and even the tabernacle is called the tent of meeting. Moreover, the environs of Zion or Jerusalem are always in Ezekiel the heathen. The words, "And I will raise up for them a plantation for a name" (ver. 29), point to Gen. ii. 8, 9, "And the Lord God *planted* a garden eastward in Eden, and made to grow out of the ground every tree pleasant to behold and good to eat." The reference to this passage appears more explicitly in ch. xxxvi. 35, "This desolate land is become like the garden of Eden." On the other hand, ch. xxxvi. 29, 30 shows that the renovation of the paradisaic plantation here announced consists in the distribution of rich harvest blessings. This serves them for a name, inasmuch as they are thereby represented as the people of the blessed of the Lord. Corn cannot be at once directly described as a plantation. It can be so called only as an antitype of the paradisaic plantation. The house of Israel in ver. 29 has an emphatic meaning. It denotes the people of God and of covenant in a true and proper sense. Israel is the *holy* name of the head of the race. "Sheep of my pasture, ye are men" (ver. 31). What grace, when the God of heaven condescends to men, who are taken from the earth and return to it! comp. Ps. viii., xxxvi. 8.

CHAPTER XXXV.

This contains the desolation of Edom. The light of Israel is set off by the shadow of Edom. There is a prophecy against Edom already in ch. xxv. 12-14. A special occasion for resuming it was here presented by the account of the fugitive, concerning the injustice committed by them in the destruction of Jerusalem, and particularly concerning the denial of the future of Israel by the Edomites; comp., besides that which is contained in our prophecy itself, ch. xxxvi. 2. We need not assume that Edom here represents the whole heathen world. That the heathen world universally is to be admitted to a participation in the salvation destined for Israel in the future, is affirmed in ver. 14; comp. also ch. xxxiv. 26. In a like relation with Edom stand only the other small bordering nations, who correspond with it in intensity of hate (xxxvi. 4). Edom appears here as a people corrupted to the root, that is to have no part in the Messianic salvation. In accordance with the present prophecy, not a trace of it is left on the earth.

Ver. 1. And the word of the LORD came unto me, saying, 2. Son of man, set thy face against Mount Seir, and prophesy against it, 3. And say to it, Thus saith the Lord Jehovah, Behold, I am against thee, O mount Seir, and I will stretch out my hand over thee, and make thee desolate and waste. 4. Thy cities I will make a ruin, and thou shalt be desolate; and thou shalt know that I am the LORD. 5. Because thou hadst a perpetual hatred, and gavest over the sons of Israel to the hands of the sword in the time of their calamity, in the time of the iniquity of the end: 6. Therefore, as I live, saith the Lord Jehovah, I will make thee into blood, and blood shall pursue thee: forsooth thou hast hated blood, and blood shall pursue thee. 7. And I will make mount Seir desolate and waste, and cut off from him the passer and the returner. 8. And I will fill his mountains with his slain: in thy hills, and thy valleys, and all thy dales, the slain by the sword shall fall. 9. Perpetual desolations will I make thee, and thy cities shall not sit; and ye shall know that I am the LORD. 10. Because thou saidst of the two nations and the two lands, They shall be mine, and we shall possess them; and the LORD was there: 11. Therefore, as I live, saith the Lord Jehovah, I will do according to thy anger and thy jealousy, as thou hast done in thy hatred against them; and I will make myself known among them, as I judge thee. 12. And thou shalt know that I the LORD have heard all thy blasphemies which thou hast spoken against the mountains of Israel, saying, It is desolate, they are given to us for food. 13. And ye boasted against me with your mouth, and heaped up your words against me: I have heard it. 14. Thus saith the Lord Jehovah, When the whole earth rejoiceth, I will bring desolation on thee. 15. As thou didst rejoice over the inheritance of the house of Israel, because it was desolate, so will I do to thee; thou shalt be desolate, O mount Seir, and all Edom, all of it; and they shall know that I am the LORD.

Mount Seir, so called from a chieftain of the primeval Canaanitish inhabitants of the country, who were driven out by the posterity of Esau, appears as the dwelling-place of Edom in Gen. xxxvi. 9. The words, "And I will stretch out my hand against thee, and make thee desolate and waste," are significantly repeated in ver. 3 from ch. vi. 14, where they occur in reference to Israel, to indicate that the judgment begins certainly at the house of God, yet never ends there, but infallibly passes to its foes and persecutors; so that these have never occasion to rejoice or triumph; much more must they say, This is done in the green tree, what shall be done in the dry? The confession in ver. 4 is, as usual with Ezekiel in this formula, not voluntary, but constrained. That Jehovah, whom they have despised, is really God, they learn from their destruction. In ver. 5, the announcement of the catastrophe is followed by the indication of its *cause*. The "time of the iniquity of the end," that is, which brings on the end, the catastrophe, is taken from ch. xxi. 30, 34. The words point to the divine causality, concealed behind the human, in the fall of Judah. "Thou hast hated blood" (ver. 6): the murderer hates the blood which he sheds. If he hates the man with such an energy of hate that he attempts his life, he hates the blood, in which is the man's soul. "And cut off from him the passer and the returner," so that all intercourse ceases, and the land becomes a silent desolation, as it is at this day. The words refer to ch. xxxiii. 28, where this is threatened to the land of Israel. To-day to me, to-morrow to thee; so says the woe-begone church to the triumphant world. " Thy cities will not sit" (ver. 9), but lie prostrate; comp. xxvi. 20.¹ In ver. 10 the *second* cause of the catastrophe. The two nations and lands can only be Judah and Israel. For they are designated as those in which the Lord was. After the removal of the ten tribes, Judah was successor to their rights, and in Judah Israel continued to exist,—a conception often found elsewhere in Ezekiel; comp. on ch. xxiii. 44. From ch. xxxvi. 3 we see that Edom wished to put himself in possession of the previous inheritance of Israel, not alone, but in conjunction with other bordering nations. For our passage, it is indifferent whether he had associates in his plan or not. This only is of consequence, that this plan proceeded from him, and that the aim was directed to the complete exclusion of Israel. The plan had humanly taken much likelihood of success. The present clear and correct acknowledgment that it did not succeed—that Edom, so far from extending, will itself fall under the annihilating judgment—shows that the prophet spoke by another spirit than his own. The words, " And the Lord was there," belong not to the Edomites, but to the prophet. They point to a great flaw in the otherwise correct reckoning of the Edomites. Whosoever will appropriate God's portion to himself, will always be the loser. Where God is in the midst, there Edom cannot possibly gain a footing, though he give over His people even for a long time to the foe. It is not said, " The Lord is there," but " *was* there." For a moment He had withdrawn Himself (comp. ch. xi. 23); but that He was there, secures that He will be there, since He has not yet definitely given up His inheritance, as happened after the rejection of the good Shepherd. " As thou hast done" (ver. 11); that is, as thou hast practised and wrought. " And I will make myself known among them" (the children of Israel, of whom the immediately preceding passage speaks). " As I judge thee:" both the becoming known to Israel and the judgment on Edom go hand in hand,

---

¹ The marginal reading תשבנה, they will return, has arisen only from a misunderstanding. To return cannot, without addition, mean to be restored.

and have like proportion. The becoming known, which according to ch. xxxiv. has its central point in the raising up of David, is as glorious as the judgment is terrible. The salvation of Israel was also, in ch. xxviii. 25, 26, placed in contrast with the downfall of the neighbouring nations. A quite brief and as here allusive contra-position is also found in ch. xxvi. 20. The inhabitants are, as it were, eaten up (ver. 12), when the land, which formed the basis of their existence, is appropriated.[1] In vers. 14, 15, the close. "When the whole earth rejoiceth"—over the great salvation which falls to Zion. This is an object of joy to the whole earth, because it bears witness to the glory of God, whose deeds for the part are always prophecies for the whole, and who can only bless His people, that in them all nations may be blessed. Already, Deut. xxxii. 43 f. calls upon the heathen to rejoice at that which the Lord does in the end of the penal period to His people. According to Isa. xlii. 10 f., the isles, the inhabitants of the wilderness and the mountains, are to rejoice over the great deeds which the Lord does first for His people. In Ps. xcvii. 1 it is said, "The Lord reigneth" (that is, He will in the future enter upon His reign, and prove Himself to be governor by the deliverance of His people); "let the earth rejoice, let the many isles be glad." "The joy of the whole earth" is Zion designated in Ps. xlviii. 3, Lam. ii. 15, on account of the unfolding of the glory of God in it.

CHAPTER XXXVI. 1–15.

The prophet's third word of comfort obviates the grief for the desolation of the holy land. It shall cease in no long time. The sentence, "Thus saith the Lord Jehovah," constantly recurring in this prophecy, shows how little hold the consolation of the prophet, justified by history, had in visible things.

Ver. 1. And thou, son of man, prophesy to the mountains of Israel, and say, Ye mountains of Israel, hear the word of the Lord. 2. Thus saith the Lord Jehovah, Because the

---

[1] The reading of the text, שְׁמָמָה, 3d fem. sing., refers to the land hidden behind the mountains of Israel, as יִרְשָׁנוּה (ver. 10). The Masoretes wish to read שְׁמֵמוּ, on account of the following plural; but this refers to the men: comp. the lands and the nations, ver. 10.

enemy saith against you, Aha, and the perpetual heights are become our possession: 3. Therefore prophesy and say, Thus saith the Lord Jehovah, Because and since ye are desolated, and they long after you round about, that ye may become a possession to the residue of the heathen, and ye are taken up in the word of the tongue, and for a reproach of the people: 4. Therefore, ye mountains of Israel, hear the word of the Lord Jehovah, Thus saith the Lord Jehovah to the mountains and to the hills, to the dales and to the valleys, and to the desolate ruins, and to the forsaken cities, which are become a prey and a derision to the residue of the heathen that are round about; 5. Therefore thus saith the Lord Jehovah, Surely in the fire of my jealousy have I spoken against the residue of the heathen, and against all Edom, who have given themselves my land for a possession, in the joy of all their heart, in contempt of soul, that their suburbs should be a prey. 6. Therefore prophesy concerning the land of Israel, and say to the mountains and to the hills, to the dales and to the valleys, Thus saith the Lord Jehovah, Behold, I have spoken in my jealousy and in my fury, because ye have borne the reproach of the heathen: 7. Therefore thus saith the Lord Jehovah, I have lifted up my hand; surely the heathen that are about you, they shall bear their shame. 8. And ye mountains of Israel shall shoot forth your leaves, and yield your fruit to my people Israel; for it is nigh to come. 9. For, behold, I am for you, and will turn unto you, and ye shall be tilled and sown. 10. And I will multiply upon you men, the whole house of Israel, all of it; and the cities shall be inhabited, and the wastes builded. 11. And I will multiply upon you man and beast, and they shall multiply and bear fruit; and I will make you to sit as in your foretime, and will do unto you better than in your past; and ye shall know that I am the Lord. 12. And I will bring upon you men, my people Israel; and they shall possess thee, and thou shalt be their inheritance, and thou shalt no more make them childless. 13. Thus saith the Lord Jehovah, Because they say unto you, Thou land devourest men, and makest thy people childless; 14. Therefore shalt thou no more devour men, and no more make thy people stumble, saith the Lord Jehovah. 15. And I will no more cause to be heard in you the shame of the heathen, and ye shall no more take upon you the reproach of the nations, and thou shalt no more make thy people stumble, saith the Lord Jehovah.

By the mountains, in ver. 1, as the most prominent part, the whole land is represented. What is flat appears as an appendage to the mountains, which are to the land the same as the king and his nobles to the people. The "perpetual heights" (ver. 2) are the natural mountains as a figure of the unchangeable grandeur of which Israel boasted, because it had the Eternal for its protector, and in Him the security of its own perpetuity; comp. Ps. cxxv. 2. The words are to be regarded as marked with inverted commas. The revilers take them from the mouth of Israel, who opposed His "perpetual mountains" to all their pretences and boasts. The *desolation*, in ver. 3, is the cause of the striving and longing. It is wasted on a good that is apparently without a master.[1] The *residue* of the heathen is spoken of because they had themselves already suffered severe losses by the Chaldean invasion, and greater still awaited them. The consideration of their own condition might have kept the neighbouring nations from striving after an increase of possessions. "Because and since" (comp. xiii. 10) points out that there was abundant reason for this address of God, and for His actual procedure. "In contempt of soul" (ver. 5); comp. xxv. 6. The "suburbs" of the land is all that lies round the central point, the capital.[2] The whole land is represented as the border of Zion, which appears often in the Psalms and prophets as the spiritual dwelling-place of the whole people. The lifting up of the hand (ver. 7) is the gesture of swearing; comp. xx. 5. Leaves and branches (ver. 8, comp. xvii. 8, 23) come into view as food for cattle, while the fruit is for man. The use of the young branches for fodder is still very common in southern countries. "It is nigh to come;" properly, "they are nigh to come:" the old and legitimate possessors of the land *soon* come back. Ezekiel

---

[1] On account of desolation: so we must explain, as שמם usually, and especially in Ezekiel, occurs in a passive sense. שמות is a verbal noun.

[2] Michaelis after Coccieus, *suburbana terræ sunt, quæ extra metropolin sunt*. The words literally mean, on account of their fields for a prey. The whole striving of the neighbours was that Zion's fields might be their prey. מגרש stands always, and especially in Ezekiel, for the parks of the towns.

knows that the exile will last only a short time,—a knowledge which he also avows in ch. xi. 16. This is in accordance with Jeremiah, according to whom the Chaldean servitude, beginning in the fourth year of Jehoiakim, is to last seventy years, and then the return of the people into their own country is to take place. Of these seventy years, according to ch. xxxiii. 21, twenty had already elapsed, so that many of those still living might yet see the joyful day. The sitting (ver. 11) forms the contrast to the lying low. "Better than in your past:" this was fulfilled when He appeared in the holy land, who could say of Himself, "Come unto me, all ye that labour and are heavy laden," and who far outshone Solomon in all his glory. "Thou shalt no more make them childless" (ver. 12): the self-evident condition is, if they do not fill up anew the measure of their sins. To those who would not there is no privilege. Our promise gives only the security that the former guilt is to be removed, and at the same time that all is to be done to guard against incurring more. This is done in the most glorious manner: God Himself came, in His Son, to His inheritance; but when His own received Him not, the promise expired, and the former threatenings revived. The supplement we have in Ezekiel himself, in ch. v. 3, 4. In vers. 13–15, the conclusion. "Thou devourest men" (ver. 13). The land of Israel had a dangerous position. It was a land of transit (Zech. ix. 8), an apple of discord for the Asiatic and African powers, and exposed to oppression by the surrounding nations of the wilderness, who always went to it for barter. On account of this dangerous position, it is designated even in Num. xiii. 32 as a land that devours its inhabitants. Precisely such a land had God chosen for His people. They should always have occasion to look up to Him; and when they fell away, the rods were also laid up. Peaceful seclusion would have produced a stagnant condition, the worst that can befall the people of God. It is essential to the church in this world to be militant. "Thou shalt no more make thy people stumble" (ver. 15); that is, no more make them unfortunate. Moral stumbling is not to be thought of in this connection.[1] The land had no part in this. The covenant people stumbled

[1] הכשׁיל must in substance be equivalent to שׁכל, which the *Keri* would unadvisedly substitute for it.

afterwards indeed (Rom. xi. 11; 1 Pet. ii. 8); but God's gift and grace remained the same, even when they were ungratefully despised. The rock on which they stumbled was the rock of salvation!

CHAPTER XXXVI. 16-38.

Here is the fourth word of comfort. Israel has found misery in the way of his sins; but God will, for His name's sake, bring salvation, and certainly a salvation of infinite fulness,—restoration to the holy land, sprinkling with the water of forgiveness, the bestowment of a new heart, the outpouring of the Spirit, the adoption to be the true people of God, and the consequent fulness of all other blessings. The very kernel of this comfort is, that God will redeem Israel, not for anything in their own nature, but only for His own name's sake. This was certainly very humiliating, but at the same time very consoling; and the consolatory aspect comes absolutely into the foreground, when the prophet spake to a people who sighed under the judgments of God, and by them had attained to the knowledge of their own sinfulness. With the consolatory import is also joined the hortatory. If Israel has found misery in the way of his sins, real conversion is the means of partaking in the coming salvation. The section consists of the introduction (vers. 16-21), the main subject (vers. 22-36), and the conclusion.

Vers. 16. And the word of the LORD came unto me, saying, 17. Son of man, the house of Israel sat in their own land, and defiled it by their way and by their doings; like the uncleanness of the removed woman was their way before me. 18. Wherefore I poured out my fury upon them, for the blood that they had shed upon the land, and by their detestable things they polluted it. 19. And I scattered them among the heathen, and they were sprinkled through the lands: according to their way and according to their doings I judged them. 20. And it came to the heathen whither they came, and they profaned my holy name, when they said of them, These are the people of the LORD, and are gone forth out of his land. 21. And I had pity for my holy name, which the house of Israel profaned among the heathen whither they went. 22. Therefore say unto the house of Israel, Thus saith the Lord Jehovah, Not for your sake do I this, O house of Israel, but for my holy name's sake, which ye profaned among the heathen, whither ye went. 23. And I will sanctify my great name, which was profaned among the heathen, which ye profaned among them: and the heathen shall know that I am the Lord, saith the Lord Jehovah, when I sanctify myself in you before your eyes. 24. And I will take you out of the heathen, and gather you out of all lands, and bring you to your own land. 25. And I will sprinkle clean water upon you, and ye shall be clean from all your filthiness, and from all your detestable things will I cleanse you. 26. And I will give you a new heart, and a new spirit I will put within you; and I will remove the heart of stone out of your flesh, and give you a heart of flesh. 27. And I will put my Spirit within you, and cause you to walk in my statutes, and keep my judgments, and do them. 28. And ye shall sit in the land that I gave to your fathers; and ye shall be my people, and I will be your God. 29. And I will save you from all your defilements; and I will call for the corn, and multiply it, and not lay famine upon you. 30. And I will multiply the fruit of the tree, and the increase of the field, that ye may not receive the reproach of famine among the heathen. 31. And ye shall remember your evil ways, and your doings that were not good; and ye shall loathe your own face for your iniquities and your abominations. 32. Not for your sake do I this, saith the Lord Jehovah, be it known unto you: be ashamed and confounded for your ways, O house of Israel. 33. Thus saith the Lord Jehovah, In the day that I cleanse you from all your iniquities, I will cause the cities to sit, and the ruins shall be builded. 34. And the desolate land shall be tilled, instead of being desolate in the eyes of every passer. 35. And they shall say, This desolated land is become like the garden of Eden; and the waste, and desolate, and ruined cities, sit fortified. 36. And the heathen that are left around you shall know that I the Lord builded the ruined places, planted the desolate: I the LORD speak and do. 37. Thus saith the Lord Jehovah, I will yet for this be inquired of by the house of Israel, to do it for them: I will multiply them with men like a flock. 38. As the holy flock, as the flock of Jerusalem in her festivals, so shall the waste cities be full of the flock of men; and they shall know that I am the LORD.

The blood and the detestable things (ver. 18), murder and idolatry—with reference to the first commandment of the first table, and the first of the second. " It came" (ver. 20), namely the fate which was spoken of in ver. 19, the news of the calamity into which they had fallen. This came at the same time with themselves: it came whither they came: they were the embodied intelligence. " They profaned my holy name :" according to the connection with the immediately foregoing, as well as with the next following, when this came to the heathen, they of the house of Israel even thereby profaned my holy name, not by their doing (Rom. ii. 12), but by their suffering, from which the unfaithfulness or weakness of their God was inferred, who would not or could not help His people. But it is the profanation to which they gave occasion by their fate, ascribed to them as a deed, because they had brought it on by their active profanation. " When they said of them, These are the people of the Lord, and are gone forth out of His land :" a *forced* departure, a carrying forth into exile, is here spoken of. This appears to the heathen a striking proof that the God of this people, the Jehovah about whom they formerly made so much ado, whom they triumphantly opposed to the heathen world, does not signify much. They judged thus, because, first, they did not recognise the righteous judgment of God upon His rebellious people; and next, they looked upon their banishment from their land as permanent. If it bore this character, it would certainly be in contradiction with the word and nature of God, as He had guaranteed to His people the possession of the land, and in general a future of salvation, while temporary interruptions of gracious relations were expressly designed by God Himself, and accorded with His nature. Hence there is a point where God appears for His name's sake. He must, by acting, remove the delusion of perpetual abandonment. " I had pity for my holy name" (ver. 21): the main body of the discourse shows[1] what measures resulted from this care of God for His name, which must dwell in Him as surely as He is God. " Not for your sake do I this" (ver. 22): here we have the action in general; in the following the sphere in which it

[1] On vers. 22–36, comp. *Christol.* ii. p. 579 f.

moves is more exactly defined. The holiness of the name of God denotes His incomparable and absolute glory.[1] God sanctifies His name (ver. 23) when He glorifies it, and removes everything that drags it down to the dust of the earth and of the finite. "Great:" this shows why God must resist the profanation of His name. "Before your eyes:" we might expect "before their eyes;" but the thought of the manifest salvation is better so expressed, that those immediately concerned are the same whose eyes have beheld the misery, and are thus immediate spectators; comp. Job xix. 27, "Mine eyes behold, and not a stranger." "Before their eyes" is the necessary consequence of "before your eyes." If it hold of Israel that "they shall see eye to eye when the Lord returns to Zion" (Isa. lii. 8), it holds also of the heathen. The saving gifts of God to His people, by which the sanctification or glorification of His name is effected, are more exactly described in ver. 24 f. The first is the restoration from exile, ver. 24; the second is the sprinkling with clean water, ver. 25. This is, on the ground of Num. xix. 17-19, the symbolic expression for the forgiveness of sins, the exposition of the Mosaic rite in which it was incorporated. The beginning of this benefit, the root and presupposition of all others (Jer. xxxi. 34), must have preceded the restoration from exile, which holds the first place. Its various degrees are subjectively conditioned by the various degrees of acknowledgment of sin, faith in forgiving mercy, endeavour after a godly life, desire to do the will of God,—in one word, repentance. Regarded in this subjective way, the fulfilment, which precedes the return, might be only very imperfect. Repentance was then only superficial. The practical testimony for the low degree of forgiveness of sins was the indigent circumstances of those restored. Had the sprinkling with clean water been complete, their peace would have been like the river, and their righteousness like the waves of the sea. But the true fulfilment might also for this reason begin in the time of Christ, because then, first, by the propitiation of Christ, the proper foundation was gained for justification: comp. Isa. liii. 11, "My righteous Servant shall justify many;" and in general that whole prophecy, in which the propitiating act of Christ is presented as the neces-

[1] Comp. my comment. on Ps. xxii. 4, Rev. iv. 8.

sary foundation of the sprinkling or absolution. The sentence here, "I will sprinkle clean water upon you," only resumes the "He shall sprinkle" of the older prophecy, ch. lii. 15. Thus, in substance, the return from the exile precedes the sprinkling with clean water; comp. Heb. x. 23, where having the body washed with pure water is represented as a characteristic of the believers of the New Testament. On the forgiveness of sins follows, in ver. 26, as the third main benefit, the bestowment of a new heart, which is also in Ps. li. immediately connected with the forgiveness of sins. Here is again taken up what was already promised in ch. xi. 19. This promise also is essentially Messianic. The stony heart could not be entirely overcome through the means available in the old covenant. The elevation of the Son of man on the cross, and the more complete forgiveness of sins therein rooted, formed, according to John iii. 14, 15, the foundation of this conquest. From the bestowment of the new heart flows, according to ver. 27, the altered position toward the law of God. On Israel, thus become the true people of God, is the fulness of all other blessings poured. "Ye shall loathe your own face" (ver. 31) : ye shall be loathsome to yourselves; comp. vi. 9. "I will cause the cities to sit" (ver. 33)—raise them up again. In ver. 35 the passers-by say, "This land is become like the garden of Eden." We have here the clear counterpart of the night-piece, Joel ii. 3, where it is said of the time of the judgment which was to befall the people of God through the heathen world, "The land was as the garden of Eden before it (the heathen horde represented by the figure of locusts), and behind it a desolate wilderness." The comparison of this fundamental passage, according to which the figure of the land of Eden can only signify a prosperous state in general, shows how erroneous it is to find in our passage the restoration of Canaan to a really paradisaic glory, and to charge those who cannot find this in it with a spiritualizing evaporation. Even Gen. xiii. 10 might have warned them against this. Through the guilt of the people the land afterwards still once more became a desolate wilderness ; but the election has obtained a better inheritance, in possession of which it looks down on the old land of Canaan, on which now still to lay a weight is a miserable anachronism,—namely, the earth from end to end, and the heavenly glory. " The cities sit fortified ." the sitting here also forms the contrast to lying prostrate. A fortified city sits as such, while a city whose wall is broken lies on the ground. "I the Lord speak and do" (ver. 36): I Jehovah, whose name and nature afford a security that between speaking and doing no gulf can be fixed. In vers. 37 and 38, the conclusion. " I will be inquired of by the house of Israel "—will give an answer to his prayer or grant his request; comp. xiv. 3. In ver. 38, formal mention is made of the festivals in general. But the limitation lies here, as in Mark xv. 6, in the connection. The passover was the only one among the festivals in which there was a great accumulation of sheep, with which the fulness of men in restored Israel is compared. But the *consecrated* sheep are meant here, not any other gathering of sheep, because the people that is compared with the sheep is the people of the saints of the Lord. The fulfilment is to be sought in the church of Christ still more than in the times between the exile and Christ.

CHAPTER XXXVII.

This contains a twofold prophetical word of comfort, the second separated from the first by the new beginning, " And the word of the Lord came unto me, saying;" by the form—in the first a vision, in the second a symbolic action; and by the contents. Yet both stand in an inner connection, and present themselves as a pair. In the first (vers. 1-14), the restoration of Israel as a covenant people; in the second, the restoration of Israel as a brotherhood. The peculiarity of the first discourse [1] lies not in the dogmatic thought, but in this, that the restoration of Israel appears under the figure of the resurrection. Under this figure the removal of the afflictive condition is already presented in Hos. vi. 2, where Israel, fallen into calamity, says, " After two days He will revive us, on the third day He will raise us up;" and even in Deut. xxxii. 39 we read, " I kill, and I make alive;" comp. 1 Sam. ii. 6, Ps. xxx. 4. But the peculiarity here is the unfolding of what appears there only in germ.

Our passage has often been referred to the real resurrection. But this discourse is thereby severed from the con-

[1] Comp. on this, *Christol.* ii. p. 587 f.

nection with all the other comforting words of the prophet, which are occupied with that which belongs to this world, and was soon to take its beginning (ch. xxxvi. 8), and in particular from the connection with the discourse in ver. 15 f., which is united with it in one pair. The persons risen are those who are thus *united.* But the union is an event of this world. But decidedly against this view is ver. 11. The dead are there introduced speaking: they lament that their bones are dried, and confess their despair of a restoration. Accordingly the passage cannot refer to the really dead, who cannot appear speaking, but to the living dead. The misery of Israel, which forms the starting-point for the prophetic discourse, refers, according to this verse, to the state of the people in exile. "Our bones are dried:" this is there explained by "Our hope is lost, we are cut off." If death accordingly be a figurative designation of evil, of a sinful state,[1] the resurrection may also be only a figurative designation of the return to salvation. The same appears also from ver. 12. According to this, the "slain" of ver. 9 are in exile. The slaying can therefore only denote the national dissolution. The slain, in a literal sense, were in Canaan. That death is the state of exile, follows also from ver. 14, according to which those raised from the graves are to be brought to Canaan. On the whole, the resurrection of Israel is three times put in connection with the return to his own land. This does not comport with a bodily resurrection.

That the doctrine of the proper resurrection was already known in the time of the prophet, forms the presupposition of the so expanded figurative representation, and is attested by Isa. xxv. 8, xxvi. 19, and especially by ch. xii. 2 of Daniel, who was almost contemporary with our prophet. But not merely does the prophet set out from this doctrine, and use it as a means of representation: his figurative representation, and the historical confirmation which it received, must also have powerfully awakened the belief in the resurrection. If God proves Himself the master of death in a figurative sense, and delivers His people from eternal and spiritual misery, into which they had fallen by the exile, how should the death of the body set limits to His grace? Yet there is a still closer

[1] Venema: *Israelitas hic repræsentari non naturaliter, sed* civiliter *et* religiose *mortui.*

reference to the bodily resurrection. While we need not think immediately and exclusively of this, against which even this decides, that the dry bones—which according to this view, just as they are, would form the basis of the resurrection body, and only receive a new clothing of sinews and flesh—comport very badly with 1 Cor. xv., the salvation here announced under the figure of the resurrection is completed in the resurrection; and if we look away from this, and rest merely in the region of the present, yet the word of the apostle in 1 Cor. xv. 19 will hold good.

The discourse falls into two parts: the symbol, vers. 1–10; and the interpretation, vers. 11–14. Whosoever feels himself constrained to conceive vers. 11–14 not as an interpretation, even thereby expresses judgment concerning his view of vers. 1–10. All analogies, especially in the prophets Daniel and Zechariah, standing so near the time of Ezekiel, and even in Ezekiel himself, lead to such a relation: it is a rule that the prophetic discourse, which follows the description of a vision, gives the interpretation of it, in accordance with the vocation of the prophets, who were not poets, but preachers for the people, and thus bound to furnish throughout the key to the meaning. But it is the less possible to conceive the relation otherwise, because in ver. 11 it is expressly said that it is to be explained what "these bones," of which it was spoken in vers. 1–10, are to signify: they denote not the corporeally dead, but the house of Israel in its present desperate condition. "These bones:" this brings the two parts of the sections into the closest connection with one another. It is an unessential difference, that the prophet in the description of the scene (ver. 1) represents the bones as exposed to view; while, on the contrary, in ver. 12, the graves are opened, and the slain brought from their graves. It is a vain effort to bring these two representations into accordance. The first representation belongs to the vision, as the survey of the condition of the people was to be afforded to the prophet. The interpretation is not an ordinary exegesis; it moves more freely. It introduces the new figure of the grave, in order to place in a clearer light the real state of the people. All the expositions in Scripture are of this kind: they always mingle new elements in the explanation.

Ver. 1. *The hand of the Lord was upon me, and he carried me out in the Spirit of the Lord, and set me down in the midst* of the valley,[1] and it was full of bones. 2. And he led me by them round about: and, behold, they were very many on the face of the valley; and, lo, they were very dry. 3. And he said to me, Son of man, will these bones live? And I said, O Lord Jehovah, thou knowest. 4. And he said to me, Prophesy over these bones, and say unto them, Ye dry bones, hear the word of the LORD. 5. Thus saith the Lord Jehovah unto these bones, Behold, I will send spirit into you, and ye shall live. 6. And I will lay sinews upon you, and bring up flesh upon you, and cover you with skin, and put spirit in you, and ye shall live: and ye shall know that I am the LORD. 7. And I prophesied as I was commanded: and there was a voice as I prophesied, and behold a noise,[2] and the bones approached, bone to his bone. 8. And I looked, and lo, sinews and flesh came up, and skin covered them above: and there was no spirit in them. 9. And he said unto me, Prophesy to the wind: prophesy, son of man, and say to the wind, Thus saith the Lord Jehovah, Come from the four winds, O wind, and blow upon these slain, and they shall live. And I prophesied as he commanded me, and the spirit came into them, and they lived, and stood up on their feet, an exceeding great army. 11. And he said unto me, Son of man, these bones are the whole house of Israel: behold, they say, Our bones are dried, and our hope is lost; we are cut off for us. 12. Therefore prophesy, and say unto them, Thus saith the Lord Jehovah, Behold, I will open your graves, and raise you out of your graves, O my people, and bring you into the land of Israel: 13. And ye shall know that I am the LORD, when I open your graves, and when I bring you up out of your graves, O my people. 14. And I will put my Spirit in you, and ye shall live; and I will place you in your land: and ye shall know that I the Lord have spoken and done it,[3] saith the LORD.

[1] Luther, "a wide field." But the valley is not characterized by its width, but by its depression.

[2] Luther, "And behold there was a rustling as I prophesied, and behold a moving." He makes the voice as well as the rustling proceed from the bones, whereas the voice is that of God, and the rustling of the bones its consequence.

[3] Luther, "And ye shall know that I am the Lord, I speak it and do it also;" against xxxvi. 36, xvii. 24, xxii. 14, according to which "I the Lord" is connected with what follows.

The detached section, without *and*, in ver. 1, points out that the fact here related is extraordinary, and out of connection with the usual prophetic activity. The hand of the Lord denotes the overruling divine influence. "In the Spirit:" this points to the communication being a vision.[1] *The* valley, in opposition to the mountain, is simply *a* valley. The valley denotes depression of state; comp. xvii. 22, where the mountain, high and eminent, denotes the state of exaltation. The valley here has nothing to do with the valley in ch. iii. 22 f. The dry bones denote the collective misery of the state of exile, not merely the political, but also, and pre-eminently, the spiritual. This appears clearly from the following. The life which is there imparted to the bones is the spiritual life. The external restoration appears there only as the preliminary to reanimation. They were very dry (ver. 2): this denotes not so much the long duration of the condition, as rather the depth of the misery into which Israel had fallen. All is vanished that even only reminds of a former life. The question of the Lord, in ver. 3, is only to call forth the answer of the prophet, and then append to this the revelation. The address as son of man is significant: as such, Ezekiel knows nothing of the matter; the secrets belong only to God, and to those to whom He will reveal them. In vers. 5 and 6 the Lord gives, in the form of an address to the bones, the reason of the summons to be addressed to them by the prophet; or He imparts beforehand to the prophet what He will Himself afterwards say to the bones: comp. Amos iii. 7, "The Lord will do nothing, but He revealeth His secret to His servants the prophets." In fact, the two verses are connected with ver. 4 by a *for*. "Thus saith the Lord Jehovah:" that is, Thus say I who am the Lord Jehovah. The noun is put instead of the pronoun, because in it lies the security for the reality of that which is to be revealed. The order in ver. 5 is other than in the execution in ver. 7 f. Here the quickening by the Spirit appears at the head as the chief thing, without which the remainder, the merely corporeal resurrection, is of no importance. There, on

---

[1] The second Jehovah is not the genitive, but the nominative, as the accents rightly indicate. The mere ברוח corresponds to the ברוח אלהים in xi. 24; comp. ἐν πνεύματι, Matt. xxii. 43. The contrast is ἐν σώματι, 2 Cor. xii. 2.

the other hand, the corporeal resurrection is the beginning, and the quickening by the Spirit follows. The same sequence presents itself also in ver. 6. Yet it does not appear even there, as it is determined in vers. 7-10 that the corporeal resurrection and the quickening by the Spirit are two different elements: we might suppose that both go immediately hand in hand with one another, and that the quickening refers only to the natural life—in fact, to the political restoration. Such a supposition is distinctly forbidden first by ver. 7 f.—" I prophesied as I was commanded." The prophesying limits itself to the summons, " Ye dry bones, hear the word of the Lord." All that the prophet as such has to speak in the ecstasy bears the character of prophecy. To prophesy is to speak in the Spirit. " And there was a voice :" the voice proceeds here, as in ch. i. 25, from God; comp. John v. 28. It expresses that which, designed for the bones, was already imparted to the prophet in vers. 5, 6. The noise (ch. iii. 12), which immediately follows the voice that brings the announcement with it, can only proceed from the bones. It is thereby effected that they get into movement, and seek one another. " And there was no spirit in them :" this shows that the restoration was first pre-eminently an external, political one. There is a reference to the first creation of man. There also the lower element comes first into being, then the higher; or the difference of these two elements is represented under the form of a difference of time. For man created after the image of God, for the people of God, whose essence in connection with God consists in this, that His image is living in them, that they partake of His Spirit, the mere external restoration cannot suffice. The prophet is penetrated with the thought that the real misery of the people is the moral ruin, the revolt from God and His holy word, the dominion of sin. In the political disorder he sees only the reflection and the righteous punishment of sin. The remedy, therefore, cannot stop at the restoration of the civic state: were it so, the gift would be only a mockery, as the thing must have been instantly resumed. The main thing is a renewed outpouring of the Spirit, and the restoration of union with God thereby effected, which was originally accomplished by God breathing into man the breath of life. This outpouring of the Spirit had its prelude already in the return from the exile: that a spirit of awakening then ruled among the people is shown, for ex., by the prophecies of Haggai and Zechariah, and the Psalms belonging to this period. The proper fulfilment is to be sought in Christ; comp. John vii. 39, "The Holy Spirit was not yet present, because Jesus was not yet glorified," which points back to our passage. The detailed account in ver. 9 points to the high importance and the decided significance of the fact which is here treated of. That the address is formally to the wind, and not to the Spirit, denoted in Hebrew by the same word, is shown by the phrase " from the four winds," in place of which it is impossible to put the four spirits. Yet in point of fact the wind is identical with the Spirit: it comes into view only as a symbol of the Spirit, which is spoken of before and after, and which alone can evoke the effect here mentioned—the making alive; or the Spirit presents itself here under the symbol of the wind: comp. John xx. 22, where Jesus breathed on the disciples, and thereby imparted to them the Holy Ghost. That the wind is to come from the four winds, from the four quarters from which the wind comes, indicates the fulness and force of the Spirit's operations. Parallel is the phrase, "as of a rushing mighty wind" (Acts ii. 2). " Blow upon the slain:" this means not the individuals killed in the Chaldean catastrophe, but the whole people slain, robbed of their life by external violence. This follows from vers. 11, 12. According to these the slain are in exile, not in Canaan, where those slain in the literal sense are buried. The slain are further, according to ver. 11, the whole house of Israel, not a separate part of it. Now, as all Israel had not submitted to death, we can only think of walking bodies. That the quickening of the slain by the Spirit refers to the higher life, the life in God, is shown by the distinction from the political restitution denoted by the corporeal restoration; and then the parallel passages, ch. xxxvi. 26, 27, and xi. 19, where the bestowment of a new heart is spoken of, and the Spirit produces a walking in the commandments of God. To the symbol is annexed, in vers. 11–14, the interpretation. "The whole house of Israel" (ver. 11): not merely Judah, but the people of the ten tribes, which had yielded to death long before Judah. " We are cut off for us:" the *for us* points out how grievous the sad fact is for those concerned, how painfully they were affected by it. "My people" (ver. 12); that is, because ye are my people. Even in the interpretation the political and the spiritual restoration are clearly distinguished from each other. The words, "And I will put my Spirit in you, and ye shall live" (ver. 14), even if their prelude was to be acknowledged before the restoration to their country—which, according to the whole tenor of Scripture, presupposes a certain quickening by the Spirit, whence it is also explained that here, otherwise than before, the restoration follows the quickening by the Spirit; still more, however, in the time soon *after* the return—yet found their true fulfilment only in the saving presentation of the gifts of the Holy Spirit to the whole people by Christ, and in the appropriation of this Spirit by the election, which formed the stock of the Christian church. Wherever within it a new state of death arises, there this prophecy always comes again into force, until at the end of days death be fully overcome. The rejection of the gift of the Spirit by the majority of the covenant people, and their continuance in the state of death, belong to the chapter "Ye would not," and cannot diminish the glory of the gift of God. We need not extend our prophecy to the unbelieving Jewish people and their future conversion. It applies, as is expressly said in vers. 12, 13, only to Israel as the people of God, and the dispensation of grace grows out of this relation. Only in view of Rom. xi. 28 can we admit a certain by-reference to the Jews shut up in unbelief.

Ch. xxxvii. 15-28. This sixth word of comfort is occupied with the union of the people, and the other benefits which are annexed to this under the great King of the future. The proper object of the prediction is, however, only the union—the removal of the former separation of Israel and Judah. This appears from the fact that to this only the opening symbolical action refers. Besides, in the remainder, only that which was already predicted is repeated, which receives a new significance only by the connection in which it stands with the union. The partial reference to the old covenant people is explained by the fact that this was at that time the suffering part. But the conclusion contains a reference to the participation of the heathen in the promised salvation. If the reality do not perfectly correspond with the image of the future, which the prophet here presents; if, in place of the separation, the removal of which the prophet here announces, after the coming of Christ a still worse took place, the separation between believers and unbelievers, this does not arrest the grace and gift of God, which the prophet here, where his mission was to comfort, is alone to paint. But, according to the New Testament, we may expect a time when the difference between the image of the future and the reality will stand out less sharply. But those of Israel who believe have no less, but receive more, than is here promised them. The church of which they were the stock, has by the calling of the heathen received a rich compensation for the unbelieving Jews; and instead of the possession of Canaan, has entered upon the lordship of the earth, which the Lord (Matt. v. 5) has guaranteed to the meek.

Ver. 15. And the word of the Lord came unto me, saying, 16. And thou, son of man, take to thee a stick, and write on it, For Judah, and for the sons of Israel and his companions; and take another stick, and write on it, For Joseph, the stick of Ephraim, and of the whole house of Israel his companions. 17. And join them one to another for thee into one stick; and they shall be one in thy hand. 18. And when the sons of thy people shall say to thee thus, Wilt thou not show us what these are to thee? 19. Say to them, Thus saith the Lord Jehovah, Behold, I will take the stick of Joseph, which is in the hand of Ephraim, and the tribes of Israel his companions, and lay them on it, the stick of Judah, and make them one stick, and they shall be one in my hand. 20. And the sticks on which thou writest shall be in thy hand in their eyes. 21. And say to them, Thus saith the Lord Jehovah, Behold, I will take the sons of Israel from among the heathen, whither they are gone, and gather them from around, and bring them to their land: 22. And I will make them one nation in the land on the mountains of Israel, and one king shall be king to them all; and they shall be no more two nations, and shall be no more divided into two kingdoms. 23. And they shall no more defile themselves with their abominations, and their detestable things, and all their transgressions; and I will save them out of all their dwellings where they have sinned, and cleanse them: and they shall be my people, and I will be their God. 24. And my servant David shall be king over them, and one shepherd shall be to them all; and they shall walk in my judgments, and keep my statutes, and do them. 25. And they shall sit in the land which I have given to my servant Jacob, in which your fathers sat; and they shall sit in it, they and their sons, and their sons' sons, for ever; and David my servant shall be their prince for ever. 26. And I will make for them a covenant of peace; it shall be a perpetual covenant with them: and I will give them, and multiply them, and set my sanctuary in the midst of them for ever. 27. And my tent shall be over them; and I will be their God, and they shall be my people. 28. And the heathen shall know that I the LORD sanctify Israel, when my sanctuary shall be in the midst of them for ever.

The beginning with *and* in ver. 6 points to the connection of the symbolic action *here* with the vision in ver. 1 f. The companions[1] of Judah are a small part of Benjamin, Simeon, and Levi, and the members of the former ten tribes, who had already attached themselves to Judah. Joseph is prefixed, because the honourable position of Ephraim, and his equality with Judah, rested on him. We see from the blessing of Jacob that this took its rise in Egypt. The stick is, however, ascribed to Ephraim, because he stood in reality at the head of the ten tribes. These sticks must have been so formed as to present a unity when combined, and therefore planed. Round staves, which some wish to take from Num. xvii. 17 f., will scarcely suit the purpose. The stick belongs, according to ver. 19, properly to Joseph, who was "crowned among his brethren" (Gen. xlix.); but it is in the hand of Ephraim, who actually stood at the head. It is said, "on it the stick Judah" (properly, "the stick of Judah," I think), not simply, on the stick of Judah, to indicate that Judah is the proper stem of the people of God; and the rest is only of accessory importance. What is here announced was already prepared in the times before Christ. Judah was the central point for the whole people, and the temple in Jerusalem his spiritual abode. The confirmation of this preliminary unity, the prevention of new and mischievous divisions, was to take effect in Christ,

---

[1] The reading attested by MSS.; the *Kethib* is the singular, his companion, the combination of the companions into an ideal unity, the companion for the company. Such combinations are quite frequent in Ezekiel.

who is introduced in the later development as the centre of the unity. But here the election only as yet has attained what is here held out to view. The great mass has by its guilt forfeited the gift of God. By the sad "Ye would not" the schism is not removed, but only increased; comp. Matt. x. 35. This takes place according to the rule which Ezekiel himself lays down in ch. xxxiii. 13. The promise is in itself not conditioned: the promised blessings must have been offered, and were offered to the whole people; but the participation of individuals in these blessings is of course connected with conditions; and where these conditions are not fulfilled, in the place of the blessing comes a deeper curse. Ezekiel himself has in ch. xxxiii. 23-29 intentionally prefixed to the announcement of salvation, a severe threatening against those who do not fulfil the conditions of salvation, and announced to them that the judgment on them will complete its course begun in the destruction of Jerusalem. In this threatening the announcement of salvation has its limits: the two run parallel; they have in the same way found their full realization. It was not the prophet's fault, if those who stood under the threatening appropriated the promise.

After the symbolic action, and its interpretation, follows in vers. 20-28 an explanation, in which the chief benefit of which the section treats—the union of the people—is connected with the other gifts which God will bestow on His people, especially with the already given promise of the one Shepherd and King of the family of David, and by this arrangement receives new light. On the one king, in ver. 22, comp. xxxiv. 23. The statement, "They shall no more defile themselves with their abominations" (ver. 23), furnishes only the warrant for the rich offer of the means against sin to the whole people, and the use of these means by an election; but it does not offer, in contradiction to the spirit and letter of the whole Scripture from Gen. ii. down, a security to the whole mass against a relapse into sin, which would be a denial of the divine image created in man, wherewith the free moral decision is given. "I will save them out of all their dwellings, where they have sinned:" the dwellings are those of the exile, in which the people were at the starting-point, the time of the announcement. The former sins in Canaan do not come into account. They leave, as it were, their sins in the foreign land; they are presented with an opportunity, in quite new relations, of beginning a new life in righteousness, and leaving behind the old defilement. The phrase "for ever," in ver. 25, needs not be either weakened, or referred to a future possession of the land of Canaan, of which the whole New Testament knows and can know nothing, as blessings of this kind are nowhere presented in it. If the fulfilment be sought in the latter, the interruption of two thousand years is inconceivable, as a *constant* possession is here contemplated. With respect to the perpetual possession, we must rather look to Matt. xxiii. 37: "How often would I have gathered thy children together, . . . and ye would not." Already Moses lays it down as an inviolable rule: If ye are fit for nothing, the land will spue you, as it spued out the former inhabitants. That they are excluded from the holy land by their own guilt, the Jews themselves acknowledge, although their eyes are blinded so that they do not recognise the nature of their guilt—the rejection of the good Shepherd, who appears in Ezekiel as the channel of all divine blessings. As a supplement to Ezekiel, we have here Zechariah, one of his immediate successors, who soon after the return from the exile predicts (ch. xi.) a desolation of the land in consequence of the rejection of the good Shepherd. The *covenant of peace*, ver. 26, guarantees security against all hostile powers. As the basis of this covenant of peace, appears in ver. 24 the walking in the commandments of God, to which this especially belongs, that they hearken to the great Prophet whom God will hereafter raise up (Deut. xviii.). The expression "I will give them" denotes the removal to a certain condition, and of course an agreeable one; "and multiply them" gives a more exact description of this condition. It is not simply, I will make them more. The independent prefix, "I will give them," intimates that the multiplying is not *the*, but *a* gift of God along with others; comp. ver. 25, and the conclusion here. That the essence of the *sanctuary* is the presence of God among them, is shown by ch. xi. 16, where the sanctuary stands in a purely spiritual sense. Whether this sanctuary will appear continually, as was of course soon to be the case, in the form of an external temple, is a question which Ezekiel leaves undecided. This depends on the conduct of the people. At all events, this promise is gloriously fulfilled to the election, which is the stem of the Christian church. It is again taken up in the words of Christ, " Lo, I am with you alway, even to the end of the world." " Over them" (ver. 27) refers to the protecting power which is afforded in the house of God; comp. Ps. lxviii. 30. The heathen know that the Lord sanctifies Israel (ver. 28): this separation and preference, this marking off from the profane world, which constitutes the idea of sanctification, follows from this, that God's sanctuary is in Israel, that He dwells among them with all the fulness of His blessings and gifts. The natural consequence of this recognition compelled by facts is, that they seek for admittance among this people; comp. Isa. xliv. 5.

CHAPTERS XXXVIII. XXXIX.

We have here the seventh and last in the series of consolatory prophecies, which Ezekiel pronounced soon after the arrival of the fugitive—the full-toned conclusion of the whole.

The dogmatic idea of the prophecy is very simple. The community of God, renewed by His grace, will victoriously resist all the assaults of the world. This idea the prophet has here clothed with flesh and blood: he brings it before us in a grand finished picture, in which he unites what is realized in the course of time in a long series of successive events. The applications to a single historical event are all at the same time true and false: true, so far as the idea governing the prophecy is certainly realized in these several events; false, in their exclusiveness,—in mistaking the fact that all that here appears to lead to a single event belongs to the form.

The starting-point is the fear which penetrates the sick heart. What avails it, is the question that meets the prophet, even if we recover, according to thy announcement, from the present catastrophe? The predominance of the heathen still remains. Soon shall we sink under another attack into permanent ruin. Against such desponding thoughts the prophet here offers comfort. He unites all the battles which the restored community has hereafter to fight in one great battle, and lets this be decided by one glorious victory of the Lord and His people.

The comprehensive character of the prophecy appears especially in vers. 5, 6, 13. Nations from the most diverse countries, without national connection, unite in an expedition against Israel. The attempt at a historical explanation here at once proves itself to be vain. The description has a utopian character. The prophet fetches from all ends of the earth whatever can be raised of formidable heathen powers, of hitherto unknown terror. He sets aside all bounds and limits in which all historically understood events are included.

The freedom with which the prophet forms from the land Magog, which Gen. x. 2 alone knows, a king Gog, who appears only in him and those dependent on him, shows that we are here in respect of detail in the region of holy fancy, and must beware of taking the garb for the man. The Apocalypse, in the resumption of this announcement, goes a step further, and casts, by the freedom it assumes, light on the poetical freedom of the original. It makes out of the king Gog a land and people of Gog beside Magog. It destroys also the appearance of a historical character, inasmuch as it at once identifies Gog and Magog with the heathen in the four ends of the earth. Its knowledge of the comprehensive character of the prophecy appears in this, that it recognises the fulfilment of the prophecy in different historical events (xix. 17 and xx. 7–16).

How clearly the prophet was conscious that everything special serves only for individualizing and poetical delineation, appears from the following facts. The older prophets know nothing of Gog and Magog; and yet the prophet says that these older prophets, who speak only in general of the enemies of the kingdom, have prophesied of him (ch. xxxviii. 17). Further, according to ch. xxxviii. 3, 12, the future expedition of Gog and Magog against the people of God was only a renewal of an earlier enterprise from the same quarter. This is explained only when under Gog and Magog are concealed the enemies of the community of God in general, so that the Assyrian and Chaldean catastrophe may be regarded as the prelude of that here announced. From Magog and all other nations here named, Israel had suffered nothing in the past.

Ch. xxxix. contains descriptions which give the cold sweat to the historical expositors,—as we may see, for example, in Venema. Seven years they leave the wood untouched, and burn only the weapons of the enemy, etc. Who can be ignorant that we are here in the region of painting, and not in that of prediction?

We have here a good preparation for the exposition of the vision of the new temple. Our prophecy shows clearly how wide a space is given to painting in Ezekiel, how attentive he is to fill the imagination with holy figures, how carefully we must distinguish in him between the idea and its garb, how ill-applied is in him the so-called "biblical realism," to which it often happens to take the garb for the man. He who should carry it out here, would fall into a labyrinth of impossibilities. To seek the fulfilment in the dark region of the end of the days is the less possible, because most of the nations named either no longer exist, or are no longer heathen. Magog, Gomer, Meshech and Tubal, Phut, Sheba, and Dedan, are no more to be found. Kush is a Christian people, and according to recent experience will scarcely again attain to world-wide influence.

In accordance with the prophecy of Joel, where the outpouring of the Spirit upon the covenant people, who are first thereby brought into the normal relation with God, is followed by the judgment on their enemies, as it is described from ch. iii. 3 to the end of the book, the prophet also designates the outpouring of the Spirit in ch. xxxix. 29 as the ground of the judgment of the nations which he announces,—the ideal concentration of that which history discloses in a whole series of events. As the outpouring of the Spirit, according to the earlier announcements of the prophet himself and his predecessors, bears an essentially Messianic character, and is connected with the coming of the good Shepherd of David's line, on whom (Isa. xi. 1) the fulness of the Spirit rests; so is the accomplishment of these movements, presupposing this outpouring, to be regarded as of the first importance in the Messianic time. The phrase "at the end of the days" (ch. xxxviii. 16, comp. ver. 8) speaks for this, which is employed in the prophets only of the Messianic time. So does the resumption in the Apocalypse. But as beginnings of the outpouring of the Spirit already occur in the time before Christ, so has our prophecy found a prelude to its conclusive fulfilment in the battles which the Jews had to fight with the Greek empire. But one of the most glorious fulfilments was the victory of the true community of God over the Roman empire,— the same empire which had enslaved Israel after the flesh, the mere seeming Israel, destroyed its capital, scattered it in all the world, and by all this withdrawn from it the mask: all which was the necessary preparative to the victory of the true Israel, the legitimate continuation of the Old Testament covenant people. But the fulfilment did not rest here. It is going forward even now. Even the breaking up of the Mohammedan empire, which we now see before our eyes, is included under it. The glorious consummation belongs, according to the Apocalypse, to the end of the days.

Ch. xxxviii. 1-9 states the fact in its general outlines. The details are then added.

Ver. 1. And the word of the LORD came unto me, saying, 2. Son of man, set thy face against Gog, the land of Magog, the chief prince of Meshech and Tubal, and prophesy against him, 3. And say, Thus saith the Lord Jehovah, Behold, I am against thee, Gog, chief prince of Meshech and Tubal; 4. And I will lead thee back, and put rings in thy jaws, and bring forth thee, and all thy army, horses and riders, clothed all in splendour, a great gathering with targe and shield, all handling swords: 5. Persia, Kush, and Phut with them; all of them with shield and helmet: 6. Gomer, and all his squadrons; the house of Togarmah in the farthest north, and all his squadrons; many nations with thee. 7. Prepare thyself, and prepare for thee, thou and all thy gatherings that are gathered unto thee, and are obedient to thee. 8. After many days thou shalt be visited: at the end of the years thou shalt come into a land recovered from the sword, gathered from many nations, upon the mountains of Israel, which have become a perpetual waste: and it is brought forth out of the nations, and they shall sit all in safety. 9. And thou shalt go up, like a ruin shalt thou come; thou shalt be like a cloud to cover the land, thou and all thy squadrons, and many nations with thee.

The land of Magog (ver. 2) stands for "in the land of Magog," as the connective word is often omitted where the connection is clear of itself. This takes place among ourselves, for ex., in addressing letters. Magog, the nation of the Scythians, occurs already in Gen. x. 2 among the descendants of Japheth. Of Gog Ezekiel only knows. He has doubtless formed the name of the king from that of the country, as if one were to give a bishop Erm to the diocese of Ermeland. The Apocalypse goes further in this direction, and without scruple changes the king Gog of Ezekiel into a people Gog beside Magog. Both have intentionally adopted this freedom, to guard beforehand against all historicizing interpretations. Gog is prince over Magog, moreover *chief* prince, king of the kings over Meshech and Tubal, the Moschi and Tibareni (ch. xxvii. 13, xxxii. 26), who had their own kings, but appear here as vassals of Gog. Many expositors render, instead of chief prince, prince of Rosh, Meshech, and Tubal. But the poor Russians have been here very unjustly arranged among the enemies of God's people. Rosh, as the name of a people, does not occur in all the Old Testament. The mere prince would not suit. It would not accord with the relation of Gog to his immediate subjects. This appears particularly in ver. 3, where the native land of Gog is not named; and so all reference to his native sovereignty is wanting, if it is not contained in this, that he is styled chief prince of Meshech and Tubal, which leaves us to infer a direct native sovereignty. It must at least have been "who was *also* prince." Meshech and Tubal are besides always, and particularly in the already quoted passages of Ezekiel, independent nations, that cannot be without more ado subjected to the king of Magog. Only as *chief* prince can he have the very warlike nations of ch. xxxii. 26 in his train. The distinction between Magog and Meshech and Tubal is that of subjects and subordinate allies. To the chief prince here corresponds the supreme authority, which is ascribed in ver. 7 to the king of Magog in reference to the "nations with him." Besides, Meshech and Tubal are here only selected out of the whole number of allied nations as the most powerful and warlike. The fuller enumeration follows in vers. 5, 6. "I will lead thee back" (ver. 4): in Gog the earlier foes of God's people, namely the Chaldeans, reappear.[1] It is significant that the irruption of Gog is here, and in what follows, referred to Jehovah. He means to march against Jehovah,

---

[1] The historicizing expositors wish to give other meanings to the verb here and in ch. xxxix. 2; but with the meaning to turn back it recurs in ver. 8, and also in ch. xxxix. 27. The bringing back of enemies is also spoken of in ver. 12; and with the return of the former foes in Gog here

but the latter has him in tow—he must march whither He will to his own destruction, as in former times Pharaoh did not thwart the God of Israel when he refused to let His people go, but acted so because Jehovah Himself had hardened his heart to plunge him into destruction. "Put rings in thy jaws:" the rings which are put in the most tender parts of intractable animals, on which to fasten the bridle or reins; comp. xix. 4, xxix. 4. The "great gathering" is in apposition with the riders, and indicates that they are numerous. To understand this, with many, of the foot-soldiers does not agree with ver. 15, according to which the whole expedition consists of cavalry, which suits best to the march from a distant land. Only in regard to cavalry also is the description complete—the array of the riders, their multitude, their armour. "Clothed in splendour:" this is designedly transferred from the description of the troopers of Assyria in ch. xxiii. 12, in accordance with the words, "I will lead thee back." The Persians, in ver. 5, represent the far east; the Kushites or Ethiopians, the far south. With these appear in ver. 6, as representatives of the farthest north, Togarmah or Armenia, and Gomer or Cimmeria. Phut occurs before in xxvii. 10, xxx. 5; in the latter place, as here, connected with Kush. There is no impossibility in the connection of nations so distant from one another. The anti-Chaldaic coalition, which the prophet himself had witnessed, actually extended from Ethiopia to Persia. The impossible lies rather in this, that all these nations are to cooperate at a definite time against the petty Palestine; which must be assumed, according to the historicizing conception. The spoil of so petty a territory could have no charm for such a mass of nations. What would it be among so many? "Prepare thyself, and prepare for thee" (all that is necessary for such an expedition): the form of the summons, in which the prediction here appears, points to this, that the expedition comes, quite according to the wish of the God of Israel, against whom it is directed. In the words, "and are obedient to thee," or, thou art their authority, the prediction appears as such. "After many days thou shalt be visited" (ver. 8): the

it goes hand in hand, that in the invasion of Gog (ver. 17, ch. xxix. 8) the fulfilment of earlier prophecies is recognised, in which Gog is not expressly mentioned.

fundamental passage is Isa. xxiv. 22. It is there said of the ungodly world-power, "After many days (a long period of impunity) they shall be visited." Gog meant to visit the people of God, but in reality he is himself visited. It was God who led him, in order to prepare for his downfall. It is very consolatory to the church, that God not merely conquers its enemies, that even their hostile undertaking is under His guidance, that they move not hand nor foot but at His command. "At the end of the years:" this indicates that the catastrophe belongs to a quite new order of things. As the corresponding phrase "at the end of the days," so this denotes the Messianic epoch. The land has reference to its inhabitants. In so far it may be said that it dwells on the mountains of Israel. "Like a ruin shalt thou come" (ver. 9): Gog is, as it were, the incarnate desolation.[1]

In the filling up of this outline, the detailed account of the enterprise is first given in vers. 10-16, connected with the general announcement of its failure, which contains the germ of the following amplification.

Ver. 10. Thus saith the Lord Jehovah, And it shall come to pass in that day, words will come upon thy heart, and thou shalt think an evil thought, 11. And say, I will go up against a land of villages; I will come upon the quiet that sit securely, all of them sitting without a wall, and they have no bar nor gate, 12. To take a spoil and seize a prey; to turn thy hand again on the inhabited ruins, and to a people gathered from the heathen, acquiring cattle and goods, sitting on the navel of the land. 13. Sheba, and Dedan, and the merchants of Tarshish, and all their wild lions, will say to thee, Comest thou to take a spoil? Hast thou gathered thy gathering to seize a prey? to bear off silver and gold, to take cattle and goods, to take a great spoil? 14. Therefore prophesy, son of man, and say to Gog, Thus saith the Lord Jehovah, In that day when my people Israel dwell securely, shalt thou not know it? 15. And thou shalt come from thy place out of the farthest north, thou, and many nations with thee, riding all on horses, a great gathering, and a numerous army. 16. And go up against my people Israel as a cloud to cover the land; in the latter days it shall be, and I will bring thee against my

[1] The meaning "storm" is not ascertained.

land, that the heathen may know me, when I am sanctified in thee before their eyes, O Gog.

Ver. 11 depicts the community of God, in its want of earthly defence or help. It appears as a peaceful people, a people of quietness in the land, that in reliance on its God looks for no earthly defence, in regard to which it must always be at a disadvantage against the world, while God has reserved to Himself its defence. The perception of this defenceless state offers the occasion for the undertaking of the enemy. They have no conception, that among this defenceless people dwells One who is mighty in their weakness—against whom their might is mere impotence. To turn the hand again upon any one (ver. 12), means always, to make him again the object of action. In Gog, the world-power, that had before caused desolation, appears anew. "Acquiring cattle and goods :" the land of villages (ver. 11) is adapted to the possession of flocks. Goods are the general to the special, the genus to the prominent species. They acquire with their hands what is requisite for daily need, according to the rule, He who does not work shall not eat. The words refer to the first book of Moses (xxxiv. 23), to the peaceful patriarchal state. "Sitting on the navel of the land :" the navel stands for the middle, and this for the best; comp. v. 5. The *height* does not suit. That only is meant which gives a charm to the land in the eyes of the enemy. Those named in ver. 13 are simply commercial nations, —the Arabian nations Sheba and Dedan as representatives of the land trade, and Tarshish of the sea trade. Where the carrion is, the eagles gather ; where there is spoil, the traders. The Sabeans occur before as traders in ch. xxvii. 22, 23. The great men of Tarshish are designated as wild lions, on account of their relentless ferocity, that goes hand in hand with the spirit of trade; comp. xix. 3. The *question*, in case of affirmation, implies joyful participation. This did not need to be more definitely expressed, as it was understood from the character of the speakers. "Therefore" (ver. 14) : because Gog will undertake it. The address is not to the Gog of the future; but it tells the Gog of the present what will happen, if he meddle in future with the people of God. "Shalt thou not know ?"—even this, that my people dwell securely. That he knew this, was the inducement to his undertaking ; comp. ver.

11. God is sanctified in Gog, when He displays His incomparable glory in his punishment.

In carrying out the brief intimation of ver. 16, the defeat of the hostile enterprise—which formed the theme of the previous section—by the intervention of Jehovah is depicted in vers. 17-23, and certainly in great strong outlines, to which is subjoined the further finishing in the following sections.

Ver. 17. Thus saith the Lord Jehovah, Art thou he of whom I spoke in former days by my servants the prophets of Israel, who prophesied in those days during years,[1] that I would bring thee upon them ? 18. And it shall come to pass in that day, the day when Gog comes to the land of Israel, saith the Lord Jehovah, my fury shall come up in my nose. 19. And in my jealousy, in the fire of my wrath, have I spoken, Surely in that day there will be a great earthquake in the land of Israel; 20. And the fishes of the sea, and the fowl of heaven, and the beast of the field,[2] and every creeper that creepeth on the ground, and all men that are upon the face of the earth, shall quake at my presence; and the mountains shall be thrown down, and the cliffs[3] shall fall, and every wall shall fall to the earth. 21. And I will call a sword upon him on all my mountains, saith the Lord Jehovah : a man's sword will be against his brother. 22. And I will plead with him by pestilence and by blood; and a pouring rain and hailstones, fire and brimstone, will I rain on him, and on his squadrons, and on the many nations that are with him. 23. And I will be magnified and sanctified, and made known in the eyes of many heathen; and they shall know that I am the LORD.

The predictions of the earlier prophets are mentioned (ver. 17), in so far as in them the victory of the kingdom of God over the heathen world is announced, as well as the judgment which the Lord will execute on it. Only when this is known does the reference to these predictions accord with the remaining contents of the section. Among these predictions, that of

---

[1] שנים is omitted by Luther.

[2] Luther, "the cattle on the field," against the usage, according to which the living creature of the field is the wild animal, in opposition to the tame.

[3] Luther, "the walls," contrary to Song ii. 14, where the word stands in parallelism with סלע.

Joel, in ch. iii. 3-5, takes the first place. This follows especially from the fact that here, in ch. xxxix. 29, as there, the judgment of the Lord on the raging heathen power is closely connected with the outpouring of the Spirit on the house of Israel, which is thereby raised to the full dignity of the covenant people. Even the picture of Joel, as well as the present announcement, is comprehensive in its character. As in the first part of Joel all judgments upon the covenant people, so in the last part all assaults of the heathen world on the community who have part in the " teacher of righteousness," and the outpouring of the Holy Spirit, are combined into one grand figure. Along with Joel, we have specially to consider the prophecy in Isa. xxiv.-xxvii., to which the prophet referred verbally in ver. 8. Isa. xxxiv. comes also into consideration, as indeed Deut. xxxii., where the announcement of the visitation of Israel by the heathen world is followed by that of the glorious deliverance from it. But we need not pause for a moment at the predictions in which the impending inundation of Israel by the heathen power, and the judgment upon the latter, are announced in a general way. Special announcements also concerning the invasion and defeat of several empires, especially Assyria and Babylon, may be added. For all these rest on a common ground, which revived them again after the latest fulfilment has taken place, as soon as a new heathen power entered on the scene. Venema rightly remarks on this, that the question, " Art thou he?" presupposes that the oldest prophets did not speak of Gog under this name. The phrase " during years" indicates that the prophecy of the victory over the heathen power went through the whole course of time. As in ver. 18, so already in Deut. xxxii. 22, the divine wrath is ascribed to the nose, by which it manifests itself to men, snorting with anger; comp. also Ps. xviii. 9, 16. The earthquake in ver. 19, as the storm in Ps. xviii., is a figure of a great annihilating catastrophe in the human world (comp. on Rev. vi. 12), in which all has the feeling as if the earth were dissolving. The catastrophe affects only the enemies of God's people—comp. 22 (in the whole prophecy, ch. xxxviii. and xxxix., all that is heavy and destructive is aimed only at Magog); but it is so dreadful, that the whole world seems to come to an end—that all that lives on earth is felt to be affected by it: every high thing is cast to the ground, without discriminating whether it belongs to the enemy or not. All terrible particular judgments in their operations come upon the sense, like a universal judgment. The earth appears in them to go out of joint. " One man's sword shall be against his brother" (ver. 21): one great means by which God sweeps away the enemies of the king, is the internal discord, for which He presents the natural occasions. The community of hatred can scarcely offer successful resistance to these. At the ground of this lies perhaps the historical example of the event recorded in 2 Chron. xx., where, under Jehoshaphat, the nations of the wilderness, combined for the destruction of Judah, destroy one another, so that Judah is delivered without a blow, and the name of the king, " the Lord hath judged," is realized. The colours of the picture in ver. 22 are partly taken from the Egyptian plagues (the pestilence, the blood, the hail), and from the destruction of Sodom and Gomorrah.

In ch. xxxix. 1-16 the description of the fall of Gog is continued. In powerful terms the vastness of the overthrow is presented to the view. Seven years the weapons of the slain enemies serve the whole people for fuel. Seven months are they employed with the burial of the dead, and even then the labour is not completed. We have here the main thing in the description of the catastrophe, as appears from this, that we go back to the beginning of the undertaking, and do not begin at the point we had reached at the close of the preceding section. This is to be regarded as the introduction, the remainder as the conclusion.

Ver. 1. And thou, son of man, prophesy against Gog, and say, Thus saith the Lord Jehovah, Behold, I am against thee, O Gog, chief prince of Meshech and Tubal: 2. And I will lead thee back, and six thee, and raise thee up from the farthest north, and bring thee upon the mountains of Israel: 3. And I will smite thy bow out of thy left hand, and cast thy arrows out of thy right hand. 4. On the mountains of Israel shalt thou fall, thou and all thy squadrons, and the nations that are with thee: I give thee to the ravenous birds of every wing, and the beasts of the field for food. 5. Upon the face of the field shalt thou fall; for I have spoken it, saith the Lord Jehovah. 6. And I will send a fire on Magog, and on those that dwell securely in the isles; and they shall know that I am the LORD. 7. And I will make my holy name known among my people Israel: and the heathen shall know that I the LORD am holy in Israel. 8. Behold, it is come, and it is done, saith the Lord Jehovah: this is the day whereof I have spoken. 9. And the dwellers of the cities of Israel shall go out and kindle and burn armour, and shield, and targe, bow and arrows, and hand-staff and spear; and they shall burn with them a fire seven years. 10. And they shall not fetch wood from the field, nor hew it from the forests: for they shall burn a fire with the armour, and spoil those who spoiled them, and rob those who robbed them, saith the Lord Jehovah. 11. And it shall be in that day, I will give to Gog a place there of burial in Israel, the valley of the passengers east of the sea;[1] and it hinders the passengers: and there shall they bury Gog, and all his tumult, and shall call it The valley of the tumult of Gog. 12. And the house of Israel shall bury them to cleanse the land seven months. 13. And all the people of the land shall bury: and it shall be to them a name, the day when I am glorified, saith the Lord Jehovah. 14. And they shall set apart appointed men passing through the land, burying with the passengers[2] those that remain on the face of the land to cleanse it; from the end of seven months shall they search. 15. And the passengers shall pass through the land, and one shall see a man's bone, and set up by it a sign, till the buriers have buried it in the valley of the tumult of Gog. 16. And also the name of the city shall be Tumult; and they shall cleanse the land.

"I will lead thee back, and six thee" (ver. 2): we have here the outline that is afterwards unfolded. "Six thee," that is, afflict thee with six plagues, which are named in ch. xxxviii. 22. That the plagues there are precisely six, leaves no doubt of the correctness of this interpretation.[3] "Ravenous birds of every wing" (ver. 4)—as many as have wings (comp. xvii. 23). "On those that dwell securely in the isles" (ver. 6):

[1] Luther, "the valley as they go by the sea to the east." All that is characteristic in the designation of the locality is thus left out.
[2] Luther, "And with them the buriers." But the appointed men are themselves the buriers.
[3] The meaning "to six" is determined by xlv. 13.

the word denotes the islands and coasts. In the usual sense it includes only Tarshish of all the partners in the expedition above mentioned, which is the less satisfactory, as it held only a secondary place, and was counted as a trading people. It is natural to suppose that the prophet uses the word for states and countries in general, islands in the sea of the world. In this sense islands often occur in the Old and New Testament (comp. on Rev. vi. 14). One reason for so taking them here is that the expedition belongs to the land, as the whole army consists of riders, and not a trace appears of ships. The proud " security" which the inhabitants of the islands enjoy at home, has led them to the expedition against the people of God. Pride in the world goes hand in hand with prosperity. The punishment is directed against this expedition. Nothing is said of a punishment that falls upon the nations engaged in it in their own homes. With the fire here goes hand in hand the making known of God's name among Israel. The fire must also kindle on Israelitish soil. The holy name of God (ver. 7) is His character, arising from His former historical manifestations, as God in the full sense, the absolute, the transcendently glorious, unconditionally separate from all untruth and impotence. God makes known His name among His people when He verifies His historical character anew, when He gives His people the victory over the heathen world that rages against them. He would profane His name if He were to abandon His people continually to the heathen world, as He had done in the time of the prophet on account of their apostasy, comp. xxxvi. 20, though only by the way xxxvi. 22. "It is come, and it is done" (ver. 8)—the defeat of the enemy announced in the previous passage. The predicted events come so vividly before the mind of the prophet, that he sets it down as already past, as it is the nature of faith to see that which is not as if it already were. The words, in fact, indicate that we have to do not with a patriotic fancy, but with a word of Him who speaks and it is done. "This is the day whereof I have spoken" in this very prophecy; comp. especially ch. xxxviii. 19. In ver. 9 f. it is evident that we have a picture of the scene of destruction, not an idle play of the fancy, but a stay which is presented to weak faith, which has to wage war with the visible in all its terrible urgency. In the face of this, the future also is clothed in the form of sight. The word on which faith has to live, puts on, as it were, flesh and blood, to gain an influence over the fancy, in which frightful forms so readily take their seat. It would be against the evidence to ascribe a real import to the specialities, which are so obviously means of representation. In ver. 9, first the general armour (comp. ver. 10), then the enumeration of particulars. Of the armour, only that which is combustible comes naturally into view. Gog meant to bury the people of God, and appropriate their land; but it falls out quite otherwise—he is buried by the people of God, and receives only so much of the land as suffices for a grave (ver. 11). The place of his burial is designated as the "valley of the passengers," because it lay on the great commercial and military road. The valley of Megiddo is no doubt meant, to which this description eminently applies. Hergt (*Palæstina*, p. 77) says; "The old main road of commerce between Egypt and the Euphrates . . . passes over Karmel at Megiddo (Lejun)." Megiddo, the very name of which points to battles,[1] is celebrated in history as a battle-field. Josiah fell there in battle against Pharaoh-Necho, whose way he hoped here most successfully to oppose; and this explains why he first encountered him here so far to the north. "East of the sea:" as the whole country lay east of the sea, the Mediterranean, the designation means nothing, unless a known and celebrated valley pretty near the sea is intended. This also suits Megiddo. "And it hinders the passengers:"[2] it is a narrow pass, or glenny region, similar to the Preussengrab, so called by the Austrians. Such passes are found at Megiddo. Hergt, p. 69, says: "Beyond the above described northern part not much more is now known of Karmel than the two passes that lead farther east by Megiddo or Lejun over the hills. It is only known that the range, abounding in springs, and covered with trees and thick underwood, is pierced by a hundred great and small defiles, and is almost impassable." In this dangerous locality the prophet makes Gog be overtaken by the divine judgment. All the three marks which the prophet gives suit Megiddo. In all probability, Legio, now Lejun, the modern

[1] *Locus turmarum incursantium;* so it is explained by Simonis in the *Onomasticon*, and by Gesenius after him.
[2] חסם, "stop" (Deut. xxv. 4), and then in general, "hinder."

name of Megiddo, is derived from our passage. Legio corresponds to the great multitude here. (The "tumult" here and further on is the noisy crowd, the *strepera multitudo*.) To suppose that the name Legio arises from our passage is the more natural, as in ver. 16 it is expressly said, not merely that the valley is named from the noisy throng, but also the adjacent city will receive the name of Hamonah, a great multitude. Men were more inclined to call the city Legio in reference to our prophecy, because in the times of the Roman empire they certainly applied the prophecy concerning Gog pre-eminently to it, and eagerly anticipated the time when the great heathen grave at Megiddo would receive the Roman legions.[1] "And it shall be to them a name" (ver. 13) : that the house of Israel should bury the foe, not the reverse, serves them for fame, which has its root, however, not in themselves, but in their God. Their fame is, that they have a God that can deliver from death, and send destruction on their foes. Throughout seven months the whole people are to be employed with the burial of the foe. This time, however, suffices only to bury the foes lying by one another in a heap in the chief place of the defeat. Even at the end of the seven months the labour continues. They now choose buriers, who go through the whole country to inter the bodies, or rather bones, still to be found. "Appointed men" (ver. 14); properly men of continuance, who have a permanent office in opposition to a passing function. These buriers go through the country "with the passengers :" ver. 15 shows what part the latter have in the burial. They, the proper searchers, mark the places where bodies or bones lie; then come the proper buriers, and do their work. These bury the bodies, but not in the places where they are found, but transfer them all to the great heathen grave at Megiddo.

In the new section of the description of Gog's overthrow (vers. 17-24), is detailed that which was briefly touched upon in ver. 4, that the flesh of the foes, with whose bones the foregoing section was so fully occupied, serves for food to the beasts and

---

[1] From המן גיא in ver. 11 the Κυάμων of Judith vii. 3 is formed, where the camp of Holofernes extends from Bethulia ἕως Κυάμωνος, ἥ ἐστιν ἀπέναντι 'Εσδραηλώμ. So the name of the place, Καμμωνά, according to the *Onom.* of Eusebius, six Roman miles from Legio.

birds of prey. Then follow some general concluding observations on the import of the event.

Ver. 17. And thou, son of man, thus saith the Lord Jehovah, Say to the fowls of every wing, and to every beast of the field, Assemble and come; gather around to my sacrifice that I kill for you, a great sacrifice on the mountains of Israel, and eat flesh and drink blood. 18. Ye shall eat the flesh of heroes, and drink the blood of princes of the earth: rams, lambs and bucks, bullocks, fatlings of Bashan, all of them. 19. And ye shall eat fat to sating, and drink to drunkenness of my sacrifice which I have killed for you. 20. And ye shall be sated at my table with horse and chariot, hero and all men of war, saith the Lord Jehovah. 21. And I will set my glory among the heathen, and all the heathen shall see my judgment which I have executed, and my hand that I have laid upon them. 22. And the house of Israel shall know that I am the LORD their God from that day and forward. 23. And the heathen shall know that the house of Israel went into captivity for their iniquity: because they trespassed against me, and I hid my face from them, and gave them into the hand of their adversaries; and they all fell by the sword. 24. After their uncleanness and after their transgressions have I done unto them, and hid my face from them.

The defeat of the foes appears in ver. 17 under the figure of a sacrifice, after the example of Isa. xxxiv. 6, Jer. xlvi. 10, because the Lord as it were pays Himself by the downfall of those who refused Him His own, and obtains for Himself the sacrifice refused. God must come to His rights from every creature formed after His image, either so that it gives it to Him, which is the sacrifice, or that He takes it. This is the proper *cherem*, the contrast of the sacrifice, and yet closely related to it, so that it may be figuratively designated as a sacrifice. The sacrifice by blood is here specially intended, because with this a sacrificial meal, a communion, is connected. The communicants are here the wild beasts and birds. In ver. 18 the heroes and princes are first named. Then the whole mixed multitude is denoted by rams, lambs, bucks, and bullocks. The general idea of enjoyment is to be taken from the previous words, "Ye shall eat the flesh and drink the blood." The words "fatlings of Bashan, all of them," refer merely to the bullocks. There is an allusion to Ps. xxii. 13, where the righteous man complains, " Strong ones of Bashan beset me round." The fat oxen of Bashan correspond to the heroes and princes. The chariots in ver. 20 come naturally after their occupants. As here horse and chariot, so elsewhere horse and rider, or chariot-warrior, are connected (Ex. xv. 1). The knowledge that the Lord is his God, Israel gains from the operations of His grace in the battle against Gog and otherwise. The heathen know that the house of Israel was formerly led captive for its iniquity, according to ver. 23, from the present glorious proof of the omnipotence, love, and truth of the God of Israel, which leaves no other explanation of its former suffering.

In vers. 25-29, at the close of the prophecy against Magog as contained in the previous section, follows the close of the whole system of prophecies of a predominantly comforting character, from ch. xxxiii. 21 onwards. Thus the prophet had already closed large sections with a like finale: ch. xxxiii. 1-20 appears as the close of the whole first part; in ch. xxviii. 25, 26, the denunciation against the neighbouring nations is separated by a brief close from that concerning Egypt. That *here* the close refers not merely to the denunciation against Gog, appears from this, that the prophet has here to do mainly with the restoration from exile, which is presupposed in the prophecy against Gog. That this appears at the close of the whole, rather than the victory over Gog, is explained by the fact, that the longing eye of the people languishing in exile must have been directed at once to this primary benefit.

Ver. 25. Therefore thus saith the Lord Jehovah, Now will I bring again the captivity of Jacob, and have mercy on the whole house of Israel, and be jealous for my holy name. 26. And they shall take upon them[1] their shame, and all their trespass which they have committed against me, when they dwell[2] securely in their land, and none makes them afraid. 27. When I bring them back from the nations, and gather

---

[1] Luther, " they bear," which, however, נשא never signifies.

[2] That this must be so rendered, not " dwelt," appears from ch. xxix. 25, 26. The former state also was no such undisturbed security as is here indicated.

them from their enemies' lands, and am sanctified on them [1] in the eyes of many heathen. 28. And they shall know that I the LORD am their God, when I led them captive to the heathen and now gather them into their land, and leave no more of them there. 29. And I will no more hide my face from them, because I have poured out my Spirit upon the house of Israel, saith the Lord Jehovah.

Therefore (ver. 25) rests on the whole system of previous prophecies, and intimates that here their sum is to be given. " Now"—under the present relations, when my righteousness has been satisfied by punishment. The captive state, or the captivity, denotes the misery or sad condition, as ch. xvi. 53, Job xlii. 10. The original passage is Deut. xxx. 3, "And the Lord thy God will return to thy captivity." "They take upon them" (ver. 26): the former misery is proved by the present salvation to have been merited punishment, and its origin from the impotence or malice of God is refuted. Considered in itself, the misery was a former punishment, but it becomes what it is in itself when it is displayed before the world in this character. "And leave no more of them there" (ver. 28): after the fall of the Chaldean monarchy, access to their native land was free to all Israel; and those who voluntarily remained had yet in Canaan their home, and in the temple at Jerusalem their spiritual dwelling-place.

[1] Luther, "in them." But this does not come before the eyes of the heathen. Comp. ch. xxxvi. 23, 24, xx. 41.

RESTORATION.

CHAPTERS XL.-XLVIII.

FOURTEEN years after the conquest of Jerusalem, the destruction of the temple, the desolation of the land, the deportation of its inhabitants, Ezekiel describes in this section the restoration of all that was lost, and gives at the same time, in ch. xlvii. 1-12, a glance into the distant future, in which from the restored Israel salvation for the whole world goes forth in fulfilment of the ancient prediction, "In thee and in thy seed shall all the families of the earth be blessed."

After the introduction (ch. xl. 1-4) follows the description of the temple of the future, its enclosing walls and its gates, ch. xl. 5-16; the outer court, vers. 17-27; the inner, vers. 28-47; the proper temple, ch. xl. 48-xli. 4. In ch. xli. 5-11, the proportion of the lateral buildings to the temple; in vers. 12-14, that of the rear buildings; in vers. 15-26, whatever else is to be said of these structures. In ch. xlii. 1-14, the offices for the priests. In vers. 15-20, after the description of the several parts of the sanctuary, the proportions of the whole. In ch. xliii. 1-9, the entrance of the Lord into the finished temple. In vers. 10-12, why the revelation of the second temple is given. In vers. 13-17, the proportions of the altar of burnt-offering; in vers. 18-27, its consecration. In ch. xliv. the prophet turns from the temple to the priests of the future, to whom the description of the place leads, which formed the central point of their ministry, the altar of burnt-offering. In ch. xlv. 1-17, the environs of the temple, the glebe land for the priests, the Levites, and the princes of the future. In ch. xlv. 18-xlvi. 15, the sacred seasons and the sacred actions of the future. In ch. xlvi. 16–24, supplements to the foregoing. In ch. xlvii. 1–12, an entirely new subject: the waters of the Dead Sea are made wholesome, and filled with life by the stream from the sanctuary. At the close the prophet returns from the distant to the nearer future. After the temple here follow the land and the city of the future. The prophet describes, in ch. xlvii. 13–23, the borders of the land; then in ch. xlviii. the distribution among the several tribes, and how they are grouped around the temple, and the city adjoining it. Thus all that was lost is restored, and a broad foundation for the hopes of the future is given to the people languishing in misery, to the worm Jacob creeping on the ground.

This great picture of the future belongs to the end of the literary activity of the prophet. The only prediction of a later date to be found in the collection, that in ch. xxix. 17–xxx. 19, which belongs to the twenty-seventh year of Jehoiachin, while the present belongs to the twenty-fifth, bears no independent character, but is only the resumption of an earlier one at a time when its fulfilment was approaching. It was probably inserted in the collection of prophecies occasioned by the circumstances of those times. Our prophecy simply forms the conclusion of the second consolatory part of ch. xxxiii. 21. But, at the same time, it forms the counterpart to the first great description of the destruction in ch. i.–vii., as it is introduced by the majestic vision of the cherubim in ch. i. The cherubim and the new temple, the introduction and conclusion,—this is what every one thinks of when the name of Ezekiel is mentioned.

When our prophecy is usually designated as Ezekiel's vision of the second temple, there is nothing to find fault with, if it is only understood that the designation refers to its most prominent part. Along with the temple, Ezekiel is concerned in everything else that seemed to be for ever lost in the Chaldean catastrophe.

With the exception of the Messianic section in ch. xlvii. 1–12, the fulfilment of all the rest of the prophecy belongs to the times immediately after the return from the Chaldean exile. So must every one of its first hearers and readers have understood it. Jeremiah the prophet, whom Ezekiel follows throughout, with whom the very *and* with which he begins the collection of his prophecies connects him, had prophesied that the city and temple should be restored seventy years after the date of the Chaldean servitude, falling in the fourth year of Jehoiakim. Of these seventy years, thirty-two had already elapsed at the time when our prophecy was delivered. Ezekiel himself had announced, in ch. xxix. 13, that forty years after the desolation of Egypt, the nations visited by the Chaldeans would return to their former state. And what is more obvious, according to ch. xi. 16, the restoration is to follow in a brief space after the destruction of the temple. Accordingly the first hearers and readers could not but expect that, with respect to the restoration of the temple and city, the word holds good which Habakkuk once uttered (ch. i. 5) with regard to the destruction, " I do a deed in your days;" and we enter upon the interpretation with the presupposition that here also the word of the Lord applies, " Verily I say unto you, This generation shall not pass till all these things be fulfilled."

What can be maintained against this assumption rests on mere appearance. We have before us not a foreboding, which represents the future in its accidental and indifferent circumstances, but a prophecy, for which it is essential to give truth and poetry, which contains a kernel of real thoughts, but does not present them naked—how would the holy Scripture shrivel up if we should reduce it to its matter of thought!—but clothed with flesh and blood, that they may be a counterpoise to the sad reality, because they fill the fancy, that fruitful workshop of despair, with bright images, and thus by the word alleviate life at a time when all that is visible cries aloud, Where is now thy God? If we mistake this characteristic of the prophecy, that comes out more strikingly in Ezekiel than in any other prophet; if we ascribe a real import to everything without discrimination, an incongruity will certainly appear between the prophecy and the state of things after the exile. But it vanishes at once, if we can distinguish between the thought and its clothing; and this distinction will be easy, if we place before our eyes the first hearers and readers of Ezekiel, figure to ourselves the wounds for which the remedy is here proposed, and at the same time the mental world of Ezekiel the priest, the circumstances in which he grew up, and the materials within him for clothing the divine verities which he had to announce to the people of God. But we must regard this distinction as the chief problem of the expositor in the present section. Exactly in proportion to the fitness of the solution will be the value of the exegetical result. A double danger here lies before us, — to ascribe to forms what belongs to thought, and to thought that which belongs to mere form.

Let us take a glance at the views deviating from that now given. According to some, we have here " a model, according to which, on the return of the people, the temple should have been rebuilt,"—a building specification by divine authority. But this opinion forgets that we have here to do not with an architect, but with a prophet—with one whose department is not the hands, but the hearts, which he has to awaken to faith and hope, and walking in the ways of God. It cannot produce a single analogy from the prophetic region : nowhere have the prophets intruded into the department of legislation, for which under the old covenant other organs were provided. Especially all the other prophecies of Ezekiel of the time after the destruction bear not a legislative, but a hortatory character. In particular, the adjoining prophecy concerning Gog and Magog leads us to expect that here also much will belong to mere pictorial description, which is excluded if we ascribe a legislative import to the section. To this is added the obvious impossibility of erecting a building according to the specifications given. These suffice only to give play to the imagination. For a practical end, the most necessary things are wanting. We have in particular almost nothing of materials, to which so much space is devoted in the description of Solomon's temple. As a rule, the specifications are confined to the mere measures and distances; whence those who, like Villalpandus, have undertaken to give literal plans of Ezekiel's temple, have been obliged to draw much from their own fancy. Lastly, in the building of the second temple, it is manifest that no reference is made to Ezekiel's temple. As the reason of this cannot be sought in any doubt of the divine mission of Ezekiel, whose prophecies were admitted into the canon, it can only be found in this, that men saw in this prophecy something else than a building specification.

In the older theology, it was customary to regard not merely ch. xlvii. 1-12, but the whole section (ch. xl.–xlviii.), as a prophecy of the Christian church.[1] There is truth at the foundation of this view. Although the restoration of the city and the temple is first predicted, as it took place on the return from the Chaldean exile, yet this special announcement rests on the general ground of the firm conviction of the living power and indestructibility of the kingdom of God, the symbol of which was the temple, according to a view pervading the whole of the Old and New Testament. And as the prophecy reaches beyond its first fulfilment, it guarantees that within the kingdom of God life shall arise out of every death, —that the old covenant cannot go down without rising again gloriously in the new. But the fault in the older exposition, as it has been lately revived by Dr. Kliefoth, with the addition that the prophecy here describes not merely the development and operation of the Christian church in this world, but its consummation in the next, was this, that it referred the prophecy *directly* and *exclusively* to the Christian church, and excluded the fulfilment in the time of Zerubbabel. It is against this opinion so stated, that it is unnatural to suppose that the prophet has left out all consideration of the nearer deliverance; that, with the exception of ch. xlvii., there is not the slightest reference to the peculiarities of the church of the New Testament, and all that is advanced as such is only imported; that the statement, " The new theocracy which he depicts is more intellectual and spiritual than the old," is nowhere verified; and that in this way we lose the whole substance of the prophecy, and are compelled to fill up the vacuum thus occasioned with our own thoughts. It is, for ex., obviously to import and not to expound, if we are to find in the close of the prophecy, from xlvii. 13 onwards, " the introduction of the people of God, gathered by Christ from Jew and Gentile, as a new manhood, into the perpetual Canaan of the new earth at the consummation." None of the first readers of Ezekiel could find this in it. They must have understood by the Jordan simply the Jordan, by the sea the Mediterranean, by the tribes themselves those who still bore the yoke of banishment. The

---

[1] But the older theologians were not without a sense of the difficulties which pressed upon the view, and awaited fuller light in the future. Starck, for ex., says, *Precor Deum, ut aliis Ezechielis revelationem meditantibus majorem affundat lucem, majora dicendi et nodos solvendi.*

return of the people to the old home, the restoration of the temple, of the priestly service to be performed by the sons of Zadok, of the sacrifices in the Old Testament form,—these are obvious realities; and nothing leads us to suppose that they are to be regarded as figures belonging to the action of the prophetic scene of the future. If so interpreted, the prophecy would be altogether vain. The people might then reject the former threatenings of the prophet also, because they referred them to a people of the future, and explained all that cried aloud, " Thou art the man," as mere figures. Had the prophet wished all these things to be regarded as mere figures, he must have explained this in the clearest manner. The apagogical argument for this view, drawn from the fact that there is much that is not found in the times soon after the exile, so that we must be perplexed about the divine mission of the prophet if we cling to these times, loses its force as soon as it is admitted that a distinction must be made between the thought and its clothing. But we do not see how this argument can be maintained by those who themselves extend the domain of form much further, and in fact draw upon themselves the charge of arbitrary spiritualizing unjustly brought against others.

Finally, most unfortunate is the interpretation, according to which that "national order" is here described, "in which at the end of the times converted Israel, with the church engrafted into it from the heathen, shall live in the millennial kingdom." There is not the least ground to refer to the last time a prophecy which, rightly understood, has found its fulfilment a few decenniums after it was delivered. It is manifest on the clearest grounds, that the delineations of the prophet have something intentionally utopian, and much belongs only to the pictorial. If we neglect this, and are led by a literal interpretation to overstep the bounds of the Old Testament, we arrive at very doubtful dogmatic results. The restoration of the temple, the Old Testament festivals, the bloody sacrifices, the priesthood of the sons of Zadok, can only be expected *within* the bounds of the New Testament by a misunderstanding of the nature of Christ and His church. But if we shrink from these consequences, if at this point we distinguish between the thought and its form, if we cease to cling to the literal interpretation, we do not see why the fulfilment is to be sought in so cloudy a distance. Dr. v. Hofmann says justly in the *Scriptural Proof:* "In the face of the fall of the Israelitish community, the desolation of the holy land, the destruction of God's house, the people needed a promise which assured them of the restoration of all that seemed lost." All this is actually bestowed again upon the people through God's grace under Zerubbabel and Joshua, Ezra and Nehemiah; and with what gratitude this grace is acknowledged, Ps. cvii. for ex. shows. It would be unreasonable to ignore this restoration, rather than be led by so manifest a fulfilment of the promise contradicting all natural reason, to the hope of the deliverance of the church from all the troubles and sorrows which it now suffers.

THE INTRODUCTION—CHAPTER XL. 1-4.

Ver. 1. In the five and twentieth year of our carrying away, in the beginning of the year, on the tenth of the month, in the fourteenth year after the city was smitten, in the self-same day the hand of the LORD was upon me, and he brought me thither. 2. In the visions of God brought he me into the land of Israel, and set me on a very high mountain, and on it was as the frame of a city in the south. 3. And he brought me thither, and behold a man, whose appearance was like the appearance of brass, and a line of flax in his hand, and a measuring-rod; and he stood in the gate. 4. And the man spake to me, Son of man, see with thine eyes, and hear with thine ears, and set thy heart on all that I show thee; for thou art brought hither that I might show them to thee: declare all that thou seest to the house of Israel.

There is a far-reaching import in that which is given in ver. 1 simply as a date. The removal into exile, and the destruction of the city, with its centre the temple, are the points around which the thoughts of Ezekiel and the people move, the difficulties which the following vision happily removes. Both had already lasted some time: the exile, which Ezekiel always reckons from the deportation of Jehoiachin, in which he himself was carried away, twenty-five years;[1] the destruction of the city, between which and Jehoiachin's deportation the eleven

[1] The Chaldean servitude had begun seven years before, in the fourth year of Jehoiakim, in which Daniel with his companions was carried

years of Zedekiah's reign lay, fourteen years; so that it was now high time that a new and strong staff should be offered to the people of God waxing faint in their hopes. "In the beginning of the year, in the tenth of the month:" the month did not need to be more exactly defined. It follows from the words "In the beginning of the year," that the first month only can be intended. In the words, "In the beginning of the year, in the tenth of the month," we have an abbreviation from Ex. xii. 2, 3, where the Lord says to Moses and Aaron in the land of Egypt, "This month shall be to you the *beginning* of months: it shall be the first of the months *of the year* to you. Speak ye to all the assembly of Israel, *In the tenth of the month* they shall take to them every man a lamb for a family, a lamb for the house." That every word is taken from this original passage, is equivalent to an express quotation. That the day is significant for the thing, appears even from this reference, and is confirmed by the prominence given to the day in the words "in the self-same day." It is not difficult to determine in what the significance consists. On the day when the passover was instituted in Egypt, and the people were brought, as it were, within the sacred precincts of the approaching redemption, the day on which after so many centuries the impending new sealing of the redeeming grace of God was solemnly proclaimed, the pain of the captivity of the people, and the destruction of the city and the temple, with which the cessation of the festivals celebrated in the temple was connected, must have been greatly enhanced; but at the same time, the hope of deliverance in the believing mind must have been more strongly awakened than ever, because the ancient God still lived, who in this deliverance of the olden time had given His people a pledge of deliverance from all future calamities. This day was therefore specially fitted for the new assurance of saving grace which Ezekiel was now to impart to the people. The day is significant in other respects. On the tenth day of the first month were the people led in a miraculous manner across the Jordan (Josh. iv. 19). Then followed on the fourteenth the solemnity of the passover, suspended for thirty-eight years, —the renewed assurance of the saving grace, which the people

away. Of the seventy years of the Chaldean servitude in Jeremiah, thirty-two had already elapsed.

so urgently needed in the approaching conflict. On the same day also took place the solemn entrance of Christ into Jerusalem—the inauguration of His kingdom, which He wished to earn, by bleeding and dying. The day was thus as significant here as the day on which John received the Apocalypse—"I was in the Spirit on the Lord's day" (ch. i. 10); the day of the resurrection was a fitting day for the reception of the revelation, the fundamental thought of which is, that Christ will come to deliver His church from death. So also was the day of the institution of the passover a fitting day for a revelation which set forth the healing of the wounds which were inflicted on the people by the captivity, and the destruction of the city and temple. That even in later times the popular hope of deliverance from the oppression of the world was connected with the passover, appears from the right of the release of a prisoner at the passover, which had been obtained from the Romans. The prisoner represented in the eyes of the Jews the people enslaved by the Romans.

There can be no doubt that the introduction here stands in relation to that of the first vision in ch. i. 1–3. Common to both are the fulness in the date, and the mention of the hand of the Lord, and of the visions of God. The internal connection of the two visions, to which the relation of the introduction points, is, that the first vision sets forth anger and judgment, the last the healing of the wounds thereby occasioned. There the prophet encounters the dreams of a God gracious to sinners, and an immediately approaching future of salvation. Here at the end, after that announcement has been made, he deals a last powerful blow against the second dangerous enemy of God's people that now advances into the foreground,—the despair, which averts from treading the divinely appointed way of repentance as effectually as the former false security. But the germ of this last prophecy appears even in the first, in the rainbow which surrounds the appearance of the offended Deity, and presents to view the grace returning after wrath. The present prophecy is not the last in point of time. The prophecy in ch. xxix. 27 f. belongs to the twenty-seventh year of Jehoiachin, and is therefore two years later than it. But the prophet has subjoined it as an appendix to an older prophecy, in order to close with this great vision of the restoration, in opposition to the great introductory vision of the destruction. The God appearing above the cherubim for the work of destruction, and the description of the new temple, are obviously the two grand pieces in the prophecies of Ezekiel, which are in their place only at the opening and the close of the whole.

"In the self-same day the hand of the Lord was upon me:" herein verifies itself anew the name of the prophet, "God is strong:" he in regard to whom God is strong (p. 5). He records here that which flesh and blood have not revealed to him, which cry in him as in all others, Gone is gone, lost is lost, but the Father in heaven who alone can teach to hope where is nothing to hope. Isaiah (ch. viii. 11) was already enabled, by the strong hand of the Lord upon him, to proclaim to the people the vanity of all attempts against the kingdom of God.

"And He brought me thither:" the *thither* floats in the air if we do not apply it to the smitten city. In the place where this once stood is now already a new building, but the locality is essentially the same; and besides, the new building is present only for the higher view: for the lower, the smitten city still remains.

Visions of God (ver. 2) are visions that proceed from God, and clearly have divine things for their object; comp. on i. 1.

The very high mountain is mount Zion, but not in its present form, the state of humiliation, but in glorious exaltation. The height is here in fact moral, though, in accordance with the nature of the vision, it presents itself in a physical form. It existed already in the times before the destruction of the temple (Ps. xlviii. 3, lxviii. 17). It now returns, because the Lord is present again among His people with His help and grace. The new exaltation had its beginning in the return from the exile; it found its consummation in the coming of Christ (ch. xvii. 22, 23).

"And on it was as the frame of a city:" the *as* points, as Ezekiel so often and so designedly does, to the distinction between the visionary sphere and the reality, and gives to expositors the so often unregarded warning not to transfer their inborn prose to the prophets. Instead of the city there is the less need to substitute anything else without warrant from the usage, because the building which the prophet here sees is evidently the substitute for the smitten city in ver. 1. And we do not need to say that he has first seen a temple on the mountain, and then beside it a city: for there is not the slightest trace of the temple beside the city, as also in Heb. xii. 22 the city and nothing else is on the heavenly Zion; and that the temple is here included in the city (in the wider sense) we must expect from ver. 1, where the temple obviously forms the central point of the city. But the reason which has led to these false assumptions, that the prophet gives the description of the temple immediately after the introduction, and that the gate in ver. 3 appears to belong to the temple, is removed by the remark that the temple forms the proper essence of the city, and the city in the stricter sense is only accessory, and all the more because the temple was regarded as the spiritual residence of the whole people. The earlier temple also in ch. viii. held this absolutely central position.

The prophet sees the form of a city southward, or in the south. The mountain and the building are southward to one coming from Babylonia. He lands, as it were, in the most northern part of the mountain. Ch. xxi. 2 forms the key, where all Canaan appears to the prophet as a southern land. The north is in Jeremiah and Ezekiel the usual designation of the Chaldean land; comp. on i. 4.

The words, "And he brought me thither" (ver. 3), give no new event, but only resume that which has been already said, to attach to it a new event—the meeting with the angel of the Lord.

He who is here a man, is in ch. xliv. 2, 5 called Jehovah. In Zechariah (ch. ii. 5-17), the angel who measures the future compass of Jerusalem is the angel of the Lord, the godlike revealer of God; comp. *Christol.* iii. p. 265. It is quite in order that the Lord and architect of the church (with the words " and He made" here in ver. 14, comp. Matt. xvi. 18) sets before the eyes of the prophet and the people the glory of His future building; and all the more suitable, because the angel of the Lord in ch. ix. 10 had appeared to judge the city and to destroy it, and at the same time, by reserving to himself the preservation of the pious, while the work of destruction was executed by him in common with the ministering angels, had intimated that he had rather deliver than destroy, build up than pull down.

The comparison of the appearance of the angel of the Lord with brass can only refer to the property of which every one thinks in brass,—the solidity, the durability, the counterpart of all softness and weakness—the power of resisting all impressions and influences: comp. the tubes of brass, Job xl. 18; the gates of brass, Isa. xlv. 2; and the question of Job, Is my flesh of brass?—a question to which no man, whatever the angel of the Lord may do, can answer Yes. The passages Dan. x. 6, where it is said of Michael, under which name the angel of the Lord appears in Daniel, " His arms and his feet were like glowing brass ; " Rev. i. 15, where to Christ, the angel of the Lord manifest in the flesh, are ascribed " feet like unto clear brass heated in a furnace,"—differ from our passage only so far as the brass there, because its annihilating effect on the enemy comes into view, appears as glowing, which would not suit the present purpose. " His appearance as brass :" this is quite consolatory to the church of God, and all the more because its earthly representatives have so little of this brass-nature in them, and resemble not brass, or iron, or steel, but rather soft wax. But when they grow into communion with their heavenly Leader, his brass nature comes more and more upon them.

The line of flax and the measuring-rod are emblems of the building activity, and indicate that the angel of the Lord has here to do with a building. That they appear here in this sense, and not with a view to a special practical application, is manifest from this, that the line of flax occurs no more in the sequel, while the measuring-rod is often applied. There are circumstances in which the measuring-line must be applied—for ex., when the circumference of a round pillar is to be measured—but these do not come into consideration here. It is perhaps not without significance that *a* line of flax is spoken of, and *the* measuring-rod. The angel in Rev. xxi. 15 has " a golden reed to measure the city, and its gates, and its wall." The line is not mentioned, although the dimensions are very great. The opinion that the great dimensions are to be measured with the line, has here also the subsequent context against it, where all dimensions, great or small, are measured with the rod. Thus the implements only draw the prophet's attention to the fact that the following revelation relates to a building.

They form the counterpart to "the instruments of destruction," which in ch. ix. 1 the heavenly ministers of righteousness have in their hands. The activity which the angel of the Lord is to put forth is, besides, not properly a building one. According to ver. 2, the frame of the city already existed. He has the function of an architect who is to introduce a person interested in the building into his finished work, and show him its bearings. "And he stood in the gate:" as the prophet comes from the north, the gate can only be the north one. There stands the angel of the Lord awaiting "the son of man," whom he is to introduce in the building.

The threefold summons to attention in ver. 4 intimates that a matter is here treated of which is of the greatest importance to the community of God. To this it is essential that faith in the indestructibility of the kingdom of God, and in its resurrection from every death, live in it in full power. It is this alone which is here treated of, however dense may be the veil of architectural details behind which it is concealed. The address, Son of man (comp. on ch. ii. 1), reminds the prophet of his weakness and his low estate, that he may grasp the more eagerly that which is presented to him from above to raise him to a higher; and reminds the community that they remain not with the son of man, but ascend to Him who is mighty in their weakness.

CHAPTER XL. 5-16.

The description of the new temple begins in vers. 5-16 with the encompassing wall and its gates. The description goes so much into detail to furnish a stay for the imagination against the visible, which drew the eye to it with so much force, and pronounced all hope to be foolish. The terrible impression of the "smitten" city was to be overcome by the animating image of the restored city, which is painted in all its details, to be able to cope with the smitten city. Further on (ch. xlvii. 1-12) are intermingled traces which characterize the nature of the kingdom of God before the catastrophe, and show that the resurrection will be at the same time a glorification, or rather will end in the glorification. But in this section such traces are wanting; and the object is simply and solely that already indicated, to impress upon the mind the restoration of the kingdom of God lying on the ground in dust and ashes. That in the greater cubit a reference has been sought without ground to the surpassing glory of the kingdom of God in its new epoch, and that a cubit different from that of the earlier temple is chosen merely because it was current in the prophet's time, will appear hereafter. If the cubit had then been smaller than the former one, the prophet would have chosen it nevertheless. Besides, the dimensions of the wall and of the gates are by no means colossal, so that there could be found in them any reference to the surpassing glory of the future state of the kingdom of God. And a compensation for that which is otherwise wanting is vainly sought in the numbers. The theological significance of the numbers is throughout the Old Testament much less than is presupposed in this attempt, and then some artifice must be applied here to obtain significant numbers. The preponderance of the insignificant number six, by which the measuring-rod is regulated, shows that nothing is to be gained in this way. The change of the six into the seven is only gained by reverting to the old cubit, which however, according to the prophet, comes into account only so far that he states the proportion of the measure used by him that was current in his time, to that former one, to which he makes no further allusion.

The commentary of Dr. Kliefoth has rendered an essential service in regard to the architectonic details in the description of Ezekiel, and has its special weight in this department. Many hitherto dark points are here cleared up for the first time. Even where we cannot agree—and this is certainly very often the case—we acknowledge in this work an essential progress and a help.

The arrangement in vers. 5-16 is systematic. First, the wall in general; then the most notable part of it, the gates, the relation of which to the most prominent of them, the east gate, is presented to view. First the dimensions of the several parts of the gateway are laid down in order, from the out- to the inside, the threshold or step, in ver. 6; the guard-rooms with their partition-walls and the inner threshold, ver. 7; the porch bordering on the temple court, and opening into it, which finishes the gate-buildings, vers. 8, 9. After the gateway follows (in ver. 11) the measuring of the gate in the proper sense, the gate-door, after a supplementary remark has been made on the guard-rooms, at the end of which are the gate-doors, the situation of which is fixed by that remark: the doors open to those who have undergone the threefold inspection, and they now step on the inner threshold, then into the porch, and thence into the court. Ver. 12 refers to a contrivance which is applied for the decisive inspection, at the guard-rooms. After laying down the measurements of the several parts, comes the statement of the relations of the structure as a whole: in ver. 13 the greatest breadth of the structure, in ver. 14 the greatest height, in ver. 15 the length. At the close, in ver 16, is a statement concerning the arrangement for light in the gate-buildings, which was so important for decisive inspection; and in the last words an allusion to Him to whom the gate, with all to which it gave admission, was consecrated—the Creator and Lord of nature.

Ver. 5. And behold a wall outside the house round about, and in the man's hand the measuring-reed of six cubits, by the cubit and hand-breadth :[1] and he measured the breadth of the building, one reed; and the height, one reed. 6. And he came to the gate which looketh towards the east, and went up its steps, and measured the threshold of the gate, one reed in breadth, and the *one* threshold, one reed broad. 7. And the guard-room one reed long, and one reed broad; and between the guard-rooms, five cubits; and the threshold of the gate, by the porch of the gate within, one reed. 8. And he measured the porch of the gate within, one reed. 9. And he measured the porch of the gate, eight cubits; and its pillars, two cubits; and (this is) the porch of the gate within. 10. And the guard-rooms of the gate eastward were three on this side, and three on that; they had all three *one* measure: and the pillars had one measure on this side and on that. 11. And he measured the breadth of the doors of the gate, ten cubits; the length of the gate, thirteen cubits. 12. And a border before the guard-rooms one cubit, and one cubit the border on that side; and

---

[1] Luther, "every cubit was a hand-breadth longer than a common cubit;" whereas Ezekiel's cubit was then the common one, in contrast with one then out of use, by which the measurements in the ruined sanctuary were made.

the guard-rooms six cubits on this side, and six cubits on that. 13. And he measured the gate from the roof of the guard-room to its roof: a breadth of twenty and five cubits, door against door. 14. And he made the pillars sixty cubits, and at the pillar the court which is around the gate.[1] 15. And from the entrance-gate to the place before the porch of the inner gate, fifty cubits. 16. And closed windows in the guard-rooms, and in their pillars within the gate round about, and likewise in the parting-walls;[2] and the windows round about inwards; and at each pillar palms.

The object of the wall (ver. 5) is, according to ch. xlii. 20, to draw the boundary between the sacred and the profane. This boundary had a double meaning. To the community it was a warning not to draw near the sanctuary with unrenewed hearts; comp. Ps. xv. With respect to God, it guaranteed that He would eventually separate His people from the world. Because the people of God had neglected the warning implied in the boundary, as a just punishment the boundary was also in the latter respect destroyed. To the desecration as guilt, succeeded the desecration as punishment. In the pierced wall, the smitten city lay an image of the abandonment of the people of God to the world. That this relation will be altered again in the future, that God will again raise His reformed people to independence, this is figured by the erection of the new wall, which in this respect is an embodiment of God's help and grace, that are to be imparted to the covenant people renewed in spirit. The description of the wall as such is very brief; while that of the gates, which present a resting-place for the eye in the uniformity of the wall, is full. "Outside the house:" this indicates that the wall is a ring, enclosing all buildings and areas which belong to the house—the temple in the widest sense. Before the statement of the first measurement the measuring-rod is defined. It is six cubits long, each containing one cubit and a hand-breadth. The length of the

---

[1] Luther, "and before every projection a court at the gate round about;" whereas here the court of the temple is spoken of, within which lay the whole structure of the gate.

[2] Luther, "in the porches;" but these received their light through the passage, and also needed less the light, which was specially required for inspection.

cubit is here defined by reference to a measure formerly current. The cubit with which the prophet measures is a hand-breadth longer than the former one. The relation to this it was the more needful to give, because it had been used in the former temple. In accordance with our passage, Chronicles (2 Chron. iii. 3) speaks of a cubit " after the former measure." The dimensions of Solomon's temple are given according to this, because it was current at the time of the building. Since the greater cubit meets us first in Ezekiel, it is probable that it was borrowed in the exile from the Chaldeans. The distinction of a sacred and a common cubit, which many expositors make here, is a mere fiction. Scripture knows nothing of a sacred cubit. Moses declares, in Deut. iii. 11, that he measures with the customary " cubit of a man." On Rev. xxi. 17, " And he measured the wall of it, an hundred and forty and four cubits, the measure of a man, which is that of the angel," it was remarked in my Comm.: " When an angel measures, we might expect him to do so with a measure unknown to us. The remark opposes this thought. Because angels, when they measure, only measure for men, the man's measure is at the same time the angel's measure, and the 144 cubits are ordinary cubits." To the question of Bertheau, " How came the prophet to borrow a measure for the erection of so peculiarly sacred a building from the Babylonians, who stood in his time so sharply defined over against the Israelites?" it may be answered that the prophet wrote first for his contemporaries, and wished to make the measurements clear to them. For this purpose the then current, the ordinary measure, only was suitable; and it would have been a useless piece of antiquarianism if the prophet had chosen to adhere to the old one. The building is the wall itself, which deserves the name the more as the gate-structures also belong to it. The height of the wall is not important, but the thickness is, which is equal to the height.

The prophet has met the angel at the north gate, the one which he must have reached first coming from the north (ver. 3). The angel, that he may describe to the prophet the gates of the wall, proceeds thence to the east gate. At this, as the chief gate, the relations of all the gates were to be explained to the prophet. The east side, that of the rising sun, is always the chief side. To this one turns the face in taking the bearings.

By the east gate, according to ch. xliii. 1, the Lord enters. At the gate is first presented the stair, which cannot be wanting, as the sanctuary, into the environs of which we now enter, must rise as the higher above the profane. The church is always τὰ ἄνω, the things above (Col. iii. 1). This stair lies, as it appears, within the wall, which is a rod broad. The gate-structure from the threshold on lies within the court. After the stair comes the threshold in the wider sense, or the gate-step. This has the by no means extravagant breadth of a rod: the step is as great in many an ordinary dwelling-house. The words at the end, "one threshold (measured he), one reed broad," do not imply that this breadth was extraordinary, but prepare us for hearing afterwards of another threshold or another step at the passage of the gate-door, before the porch into which the whole gate-structure runs, and from which we enter at once into the court.

From the threshold at the entrance of the gate-structure, the description passes to the guard-rooms, from these to the outgoing threshold, then to the porch. The guard-rooms are, according to ch. xliv. 11, 14, occupied by the Levites, who exclude all the profane. The idea here implied is expressed in Rev. xxii. 15: "Without are dogs, and sorcerers, and whoremongers, and murderers, and idolaters, and all who love and make a lie." Then also in Ps. xxiv.: "Who shall ascend into the hill of the Lord? He that hath clean hands and a pure heart." But in reality only a very limited consequence can be given to this idea, as the church does not judge of the heart. Here only the size of each chamber is stated, and its distance from the next. The details concerning them, their number and their barriers, come afterwards. The interval between the guard-rooms cannot have been open, otherwise the gateway would have been no gateway: every one who wished to avoid inspection might have entered the court by the side. The interval was filled by a wall, which is afterwards expressly mentioned. Such side-walls were, as is also afterwards mentioned, at the front threshold also. They went from the front threshold to the gate, where there were no guard-rooms. In the steps lying within the wall it took their place. Beyond the door that was behind the three guard-rooms at the back threshold they were no longer necessary. The inspection was there completed. "The guard-room:" the article stands generically, to indicate what belongs to the class, and is common to each. The measurement is here also very moderate, and there appears no intention to impress by colossal magnitude. Six cubits long and six broad—this goes not beyond a monk's cell.[1]

In vers. 8, 9, the last part of the gateway, the porch. The measurements may refer only to the length of the porch from east to west. The porch is first measured in the narrower sense, so to speak—the space in it for company; for this is the first question: How much space it afforded for those who, before they went into the open air, wished to stand for shelter against storm and rain. Then in ver. 9 is the measurement of the porch given in the wider sense. To the six cubits are added three cubits as an area, which must have been separated in some way from the principal space; then also two cubits as the thickness of the main pillars terminating the porch and the whole gate-structure, which formed the majestic egress and ingress on both sides, so that the whole had a length of ten cubits. With the words, "And this is the porch of the gate within," is the way prepared for returning to the parts lying farther towards the front entrance.

After the description of the gateway follows that of the gate in the strict sense, the proper door. To arrive at this, the prophet goes back once more in ver. 10 to the guard-rooms, at the end of which the door was, and which were inseparably connected with the door: those who stayed in the guard-rooms were properly the gatekeepers. The guard-rooms are three on each side. All the guard-rooms are of the same size, already stated in ver. 7. The pillars also on both sides of the guard-rooms are equal in compass. What this compass was in each pillar, is not expressly stated. For this very reason must they be equal to the thickness of the pillars of the porch, which are fixed in ver. 9 at a cubit. The pillars are to be regarded as standing in the inner space all round before the wall. For the

---

[1] מהבית may either mean inwards, or at the side of the house, the temple structure. Both come, in fact, to the same thing. At all events, the מהבית forms the contrast to the wall outside the house in ver. 5. According to ver. 8, it is better to refer the מהבית to the porch than the threshold. Indirectly it leads in any case to that which immediately adjoins the porch, and places it in contrast with the entering threshold.

gate has its significance only for those who go through; and the prophet is within the gate, and can only see what is there present. The object of the pillars appears afterwards in ver. 16. In ver. 11, in immediate connection with the guard-rooms, are the statements concerning the gate in the strict sense, the proper gate-door, which obviously adjoins the last guard-room, so that the back threshold and the porch were beyond the door. The work of inspection must have been ended before the entrance was possible; and when it was ended, there was no more reason to refuse entrance. The second threshold has no meaning, if it lay not at the egress of the gate-door. The gate-door can the less be placed in the porch, because the porch is elsewhere in Scripture the place before the gate; comp. Matt. xxvi. 71, "he went *out* into the porch." Besides, on that supposition, the whole arrangement of the section is incomprehensible. The breadth of the door is fixed at ten cubits, the length at thirteen. As in a door we cannot speak of length in the usual sense, by the length, as the old writers observed— for ex. Starck—must here be denoted the height. This may be explained by the supposition that the gate was lying when measured. In a door the height must be more important than the breadth. Thus, to the last number of perfection—the ten derives its name in Greek from taking in the other numbers— is added the first number of perfection, three, which often meets us as such in the Old Testament: for ex. in the Aaronic blessing, and in the thrice holy in Isa. vi., in Ezekiel in ch. xxi. 32, and in our section itself in the guard-rooms. The number thirteen must have a definite ground, otherwise a round number would be put in its stead. Before every guard-room, according to ver. 12, is a border or barrier, a cubit broad, so that the guards may step out of the guard-rooms and control the passengers, without these having access to the guard-rooms, by the back-doors of which they might penetrate into the court. The arrangement presumes that there are impudent people among the entrants, who are willing to force an entrance not allowed to them; comp. Luke xiii. 24. The statement of the dimensions of these borders forms the transition to ver. 13, where the measures of the borders are to be included in the collective measure of the breadth.

After the statement of the dimensions of the several parts,

follows now, in ver. 13, the statement of the breadth of the whole gate-buildings. The measure is taken where this breadth is greatest, not at the partition-walls or side-parapets, but at the guard-rooms. It is measured "from the roof of the guard-room to its roof," that is, from the end of the roof of the guard-room on one side, to the end of the roof on the other side. The writer does not speak of different roofs of the guard-rooms on both sides. One roof covers the guard-rooms on both sides, and at the same time the intervening gateway. That this is to be considered covered, is evident from this, that there are windows in the building. These would be unnecessary if the light fell from above. The somewhat obscure expression, "from the roof of the guard-room to its roof," is elucidated by the addition, "door against door." The doors of the guard-rooms are where they go out into the court: towards the gateway they were open, and the barriers occupied the place of the door. The doors would have been useless, as the guards must have been at their posts. If the roof was measured from the point where the door was under it, the extreme end only of the roof on both sides can be meant. We see here also how the measurement was obtained. Beforehand it is not natural to suppose that the angel mounted on the roof, as this would be so much out of the way that it must have been mentioned. There was no occasion for this. He obtained the measure from roof to roof, when he measured beneath from door to door. For the door was on both sides under the end of the roof. That the angel takes the measure with perfect ease, appears indeed from ver. 15, where he does not measure the pillars sixty cubits high. Of the twenty-five cubits, ten fall to the passage (comp. ver. 11), twelve to the guard-rooms on both sides, two to the borders on both sides (ver. 12), so that one remains over for the outer wall on both sides. If this be thought insufficient, it is open to us to place the barriers in the gateway. Yet it appears that their measures are stated for the purpose of being included in the total measure.

After the statement of the breadth of the structure where it is broadest, follows in ver. 14 the statement of the height where it appears highest: the usual height might have been taken from the statement of the height of the gate-door in ver. 11. The pillars form this point of height, in which the whole structure ends towards the court, and thus at the end of the porch. They are, as it were, the head of the whole, that which the tower is in our churches, striving and pointing towards heaven. It is said, not he measured as elsewhere, but he made. The height of sixty cubits was too great to be conveniently measured. So the prophet goes back to the time when he who here explains the building to him prepared it. In fact, though not literally, "he made" is "he had made." We are to think of the angel stating the measure to the prophet; yet this is not to be imported into the word. It is not said "he fixed," but "he made." This, according to all usage, can only refer to the construction. To the statement that the pillars here referred to immediately adjoin the court, in contrast with the pillars that were spoken of in ver. 9, is attached the notice, that the gate in the wider sense, or the whole gate erection, was surrounded by the court, which could not be otherwise, because it began at the wall surrounding the court, and so was entirely built into it.

In ver. 15, on the statement of the greatest breadth and height of the gate-buildings follows that of its length. Of the fifty cubits that begin from the end of the breadth of the wall, into which the stair is built, twelve go to the two thresholds, eighteen to the three guard-rooms on each side, ten to the intervening walls, and ten to the porch. The door-opening in the entrance is marked out as the starting-point of the measurement.[1] A gate in the usual sense, a door (comp. ver. 11), was neither at the entrance nor at the end of the whole structure. We speak also of a rock-gate. The end is the end of the porch, and the door-opening given with it towards the court.[2]

In ver. 16 is explained how the gateway receives its light,—an important matter, as light is requisite for the sharp inspection of the passengers. The gateway obtains its light by closed windows in the guard-rooms and in the side-walls. The win-

---

[1] יאתן, the reading attested by MSS., is an adjective formed from the future of the verb אתה, to come,—a formation from the 3d fut. which is very common. The Masoretes were puzzled by such a form, and substituted at their own hand the new form איתן.

[2] In the definitions of the egress and the end the prepositions *from* and *to* are omitted, as is often the case with the relative word when the relation is clear.

dows could not be quite open. This would contradict the nature of a gateway, which must have no other passable opening but the door watched by the guards. On the other hand, that the closing can only be partial, only extend so far as to prevent leaping through, lies in the design which the windows serve. Windows completely closed would not be windows at all. The admission of light must not be hindered by the closing. In Solomon's temple, according to 1 Kings vi. 4, the windows were closed by beams. How the closing is here effected, is shown by the words " and in their pillars." These, which were already mentioned in ver. 10, and here first receive their definition, stood before the windows, so that only a small, not passable, opening remained on both sides.[1] The windows closed by the pillars were not merely in the guard-rooms, in which we are to suppose the open windows lying beyond the cognizance of the prophet towards the court, through which light entered, but also in the side-walls between the guard-rooms (and next the thresholds, vers. 22, 25), which are, in fact, already mentioned in ver. 7, but which are here first denoted by a term of art, the meaning of which, after vers. 7, 22, 25, cannot be doubtful. By these the light came direct from the court. It is further mentioned that palms stood by the pillars. That whole palms besides the pillars are meant, and not ornaments of palm-leaf work on the pillars themselves, appears from ver. 26. What these palms signify, is manifest from the discussions in Append. Part ii. They indicate that the gate leads to a building which is consecrated to the Lord of creation. It corresponds with the merely introductory character of the gate, that the creation is here represented not by the animal world, but by the lower region of the vegetable kingdom, of which the palm is king. All other explanations of the palms sever them from connection with the other passages in the description of the temple, where the palms are inseparably connected with the cherubim.

[1] Balmer-Rinck (*Vision of the Temple by the Prophet Ezekiel*, Basel, 58) says, "Of the arrangement of pillars, by means of which the windows are as it were latticed, an alabaster plate from Kuyunjik (Fergusson's *Handbook of Architecture*, p. 180) gives a surprising example." It is conjectured by Fergusson that the sculpture represents a palace of Samaria, Jerusalem, or Van.

CHAPTER XL. 17–27.

Having arrived in the outer court through the east gate built into it, the prophet here states what was further to be said of it. He speaks in vers. 17, 18 of its chambers and its pavement; gives in ver. 19 the distance from the east gate of the outer court to the east gate of the inner court, and thus indirectly the measurements of the whole court; then turns in vers. 20–23 to the north gate, and describes its relations as corresponding to those of the east gate, and likewise in vers. 24–27 to the south gate. The description of the outer court by its gates is thus completed. For on the west side, for reasons hereafter appearing, there was no gate.

Ver. 17. And he brought me into the outer court, and behold chambers, and a pavement made for the court round about: thirty chambers by the pavement. 18. And the pavement was by the side of the gates, over against the length of the gates, the lower pavement. 19. And he measured the breadth from the point of the gate of the lower (court) to the front of the inner court without, a hundred cubits the east and the north. 20. And the gate which was toward the north of the outer court, he measured in its length and in its breadth. 21. And its guard-rooms, three on this side and three on that; and its pillars and its side-walls were after the measure of the first gate: its length was fifty cubits, and the breadth five and twenty cubits. 22. And its windows, and its side-walls, and its palms, after the measure of the gate that is towards the east; and they went up into it by seven steps, and its side-walls were before them. 23. And the inner court had a gate over against the gate to the north and to the east; and he measured from gate to gate a hundred cubits. 24. And he brought me toward the south, and behold a gate toward the south: and he measured its pillars and its side-walls by those measures. 25. And there were windows to it, and to its side-walls round about, like those windows; the length fifty cubits, and the breadth five and twenty cubits. 26. And its ascent had seven steps, and its side-walls were before them; and it had palms, one on this side and one on that side, by its pillars. 27. And the inner court had a gate toward the south; and he measured from (this) gate to the gate toward the south a hundred cubits.

The prophet sees (ver. 17) in the court, chambers and a stone pavement. The chambers go before, and we thence conclude that they lay near the surrounding wall which forms the natural starting-point for the examination. It is to be supposed that the chambers were attached immediately to the wall behind, like the churches in many old towns; or the wall formed their back-wall, as in the house of Rahab. Of both the chambers and the stone pavement it is said that they were round about the court.[1] This is to be understood with a limitation. In the relation in which the chambers and pavement stand to the gates, the west side, which had no gate, cannot come into account. The number of the chambers is fixed at thirty, and it is to be supposed that these are to be equably distributed among the three gates, and that they, as far as they extended, occupied the whole space from one gate to another. That the chambers might be very spacious, is shown by 1 Sam. ix. 22, where thirty persons sit at table in such a chamber. The court was the abode of the whole people; and as it was uncovered, there must have been considerable apartments for refuge from storm and rain (Isa. iv. 6; Ezra x. 9; John x. 23), in which respect the pavement with the chambers come under one point of view: when it was dirty they retired to the pavement, but especially to be able to respond to the command to rejoice before the Lord (Deut. xii.), and to eat and drink before Him (Luke xiii. 26). The chambers stand in relation with the sacrificial kitchens afterwards mentioned. In them were prepared the sacrificial feasts, to which, according to the above passage of Deuteronomy, a considerable number of persons were often invited,—sons, daughters, men-servants, maid-servants, the poor Levites, and other *personæ miserabiles*. They were the *agapæ* of the Old Testament, the type of the *agapæ* in the Christian church. Jeremiah wishes, according to ch. xxxv., to entertain the whole house of the Rechabites with wine in such a chamber of the temple. We have so little reason to limit the chambers in point of space, that the question is rather whether they did not consist of several stories, which

---

[1] עשׂוי, the partic. masc. sing., does not agree with רצפה, and is to be referred to the whole of the chambers and the stone pavement.

is the more probable, as it is expressly affirmed of the priests' chambers. That every chamber was a separate building, although they joined one another, appears from this, that the prophet could not otherwise have observed their number from the outside. The chambers were beside the stone pavement; they stood not upon it, but they opened on it. This is shown by the preposition, which cannot have been put here negligently, and by the nature of the thing: we only pave under the open air (2 Chron. vii. 3 and Esth. i. 6); and the prophet could not see what was under the chambers, but only what was before them. The pavement, according to ver. 18, was by the side of the gates, over against the length of the gates: it filled the whole space from where the chambers terminated to the end of the gates; so that if we give a depth of twenty-five cubits to the chambers, twenty-five cubits were occupied by the stone pavement. The lower pavement is so designated in reference to the court of the priests, which was higher. The *elegans et pretiosum* has been ascribed to this pavement by the expositors of their own fancy. Ezekiel's whole description is averse to such things. His whole view is to present a support to weak faith despairing of the kingdom of God, to oppose to the sorrowful "judged" a joyful "delivered."

The starting-point for the measurement in ver. 19 is the end of the gate of the lower or outer court,[1]—the end, the boundary, of the inner court: the "without" belongs in reality to the starting-point as well as to the end. The determination here receives a necessary supplement in vers. 23 and 27. It is there expressly said that the end was not the court itself, but its gate, which is indeed evident of itself, as the door of the inner court, which extended fifty cubits into the outer, already formed an integral part of the inner; and the angel would not remain outside of the inner court when he had measured its gate. The distance between the two gates is a hundred cubits. To get the breadth of the whole court, the fifty cubits of the outer gate and the fifty cubits of the inner gate must be added.

---

[1] The fem. התחתונה cannot refer to the gate, but only to the omitted חצר. It is characteristic for the priest Ezekiel, that "the lower" is with him at once the lower court; comp. on ch. viii. 3, where "the inner" likewise stands for the inner court, according to a breviloquence usual in sacerdotal speech.

Thus we have two hundred cubits, still a very moderate extent. The remark, "the east and the north"—that is, such measure applies not merely to the gate in the east, but also to the gate in the north, so that there also the distance from the end of the outer court gate to the beginning of the inner court gate was a hundred cubits—leads to a description of the north gate. In this, as in the following description of the south gate, is observed the method which we usually find in the Old Testament, and particularly in the first chapters of Genesis—for ex. in ch. ii. 19, ix. 10—in repetitions. These are never literal and mechanical: several parts are omitted, as here the porch is wanting; in the south gate also the guard-rooms. In the arrangement there is less completeness than in the fundamental passage, which is thus not made superfluous, to which rather the reader will have occasion to refer. Some new traits are added, to give the charm of novelty to the repetition, and to prevent dulness in the reader.

That the side-walls mentioned in ver. 21 are noticed a second time in ver. 22, has its ground in this, that in the close of this verse side-walls are spoken of to complete the description of the east gate, which are not there expressly mentioned. That description mentioned only those side-walls which were between the guard-rooms. Here we see that the entrance threshold also was provided with side-walls, which we must expect beforehand, because it was within the court, and thus could not be open, unless the whole design of the gate-structure were to be defeated. After the remark, presenting also a new trait, that the stair had seven steps, it is said, "and its side-walls were before them:" before the stair, which was built into the wall, was the threshold or step; there, according to this remark, the side-walls took their beginning. For it lies obviously in this remark, that the side-walls began equally with the end of the stair. "Over against the gate" (ver. 23): the gate is that of the outer court, with which the prophet has to do. This gate at its end was separated from the beginning of the gate to the inner court, as in the east gate, by a hundred cubits.

In vers. 24-27 the south gate. "By those measures"—those given at the east gate and the north gate. "Windows to it and to its side-walls" (ver. 25): the chief place of the windows, according to the measured description of the east gate, was the guard-rooms, whose occupants needed the light for the discharge of their function. The side-walls also had windows. Ver. 26 gives a new trait. In ver. 6 it was said with surprising brevity, pointing to a fuller explanation to be expected afterwards, " and by the pillar palms." This explanation we now receive. We learn that by every pillar stood two artificial palms, which put it between them. Whether this applies to all the pillars, or to the two main pillars in ver. 14, which formed the completion of the whole structure, and immediately adjoined the court, is not clear; but the latter is most probable.

CHAPTER XL. 28-37.

After the description of the outer court follows that of the inner. First, the gates. As these are built in the main like those of the outer court, all that is necessary is to bring out this likeness. Yet still even here some elements are touched upon for the first time that were passed over there; for ex. ver. 30; and a variation from the gates of the outer court is discovered at least in the number of the steps.

Ver. 28. And he brought me to the inner court by the south gate: and he measured the south gate by those measures; 29. And its guard-rooms, and its pillars, and its side-walls, according to those measures: and there were windows to it, and to its side-walls round about: the length fifty cubits, and breadth twenty and five cubits. 30. And side-walls round about, the length five and twenty cubits, and the breadth five cubits. 31. And its side-walls were toward the outer court, and palms by its pillars; and its ascent had eight steps. 32. And he brought me to the inner court toward the east: and he measured the gate according to those measures. 33. And its guard-rooms, and its pillars, and its side-walls, according to those measures; and there were windows to it, and to its side-walls round about: the length fifty cubits, and the breadth five and twenty cubits. 34. And its side-walls were toward the outer court, and palms by its pillars, on this side and on that: and its ascent was eight steps. 35. And he brought me to the north gate, and measured according to those measures; 36. It had its guard-rooms, its pillars, and its side-walls, and windows round about: the length fifty cubits, and the breadth five and twenty cubits. 37. And its pillars toward the outer court, and palms by its pillars, on this side and on that: and its ascent was eight steps.

In the outer court the prophet had at length inspected the south gate. This is the reason that in the inner court he makes the beginning with the south gate, which was next the south gate of the outer court, although the east gate here, as in the outer court, was the principal one.

Ver. 30 gives the length and breadth of the side-walls, and thus completes the former description. The length round about the gate, or the gateway, so far as the side-walls reached in their whole extent, is fixed at twenty-five cubits, the half of the total length of the gateway amounting to fifty cubits. This measurement is in harmony with the former statements. The side-walls are expressly mentioned at the intervals between the guard-rooms (comp. ver. 7 and ver. 16), the length of which was fixed at ten cubits; then at the thresholds (vers. 22, 26), which together make twelve cubits; then there must have been side-walls also at the porch, which, as such, must not have been open at the sides. Yet the side-walls will have belonged to the porch only in the strict sense, not to the space before the terminating pillars, which, as such, was separated from the proper porch by this, as it seems, that it was open at the sides. Thus of the porch only the six cubits in ver. 8 come into account. From the twenty-eight cubits thus obtained is deducted the space which the walls of the guard-rooms occupied. Such walls there must have been specially for the guard-rooms, as they were broader than our side-walls, which therefore could not take the place of side-walls of the guard-rooms. These side-walls of the guard-rooms must be reckoned into the five cubits, which, according to ver. 7, were between the guard-rooms, and into the six cubits of the threshold. If we reckon these walls of the guard-rooms at three cubits on the whole, we have our twenty-five cubits. The breadth is stated at five cubits. They could not be narrower, not to contrast too much with the guard-rooms. The breadth of the guard-rooms was six and a half or seven and a half cubits, so that they projected one and a half or two and a half cubits before the side parapets; comp. on ver. 13. As a bulwark of five cubits must have been useless, we may suppose a wall on both sides towards the gateway and the court, and a dark space within, if we wish to draw the thread further where the prophet does not decide.

Ver. 31 states further, in reference to the side-walls, that they went into the outer court, into which all the gates to the inner court were built. Then he touches on the end toward the inner court, the pillars with their palms, which in the inner gate as in the outer enclosed the porch, and between which they went forth into the inner court, and on the commencement of the gateway, which reached farthest into the outer court, the stair. To this are given eight steps, in contrast with the seven in the outer gate. As the number eight has no import elsewhere in the Old Testament, it is here to be regarded merely as an advance on the number seven,—a hint of the superior dignity of the inner court, which, with its altar of burnt-offering, rises still higher above the outer court than this does above the profane exterior.

In vers. 32-34 the east gate. "And he brought me to the inner court towards the east." A comparison with ver. 28 shows that this means where the east gate was. The gates of the inner court belonged to it, although they lay without it in the outer court. Hence the meaning is, he brought me from the south gate of the inner court to its east gate. That such is the explanation appears from ver. 35: he brought me to the north gate.

The north gate, in vers. 35-37, forms the close. To this the prophet is brought last, because to it alone belonged the notabilities of the inner court, to be described in the following section, the arrangements for the slaughter of the victims, and the preparation of their flesh. Ver. 37, as ver. 31, places the pillars at the one end, and the stair at the other, over against it. That the pillars in which the whole structure ended belonged to the outer court (they occupied the two last of the fifty cubits, which the gate-structure of the inner court reached into the outer), it was the more suitable to remark, because they passed immediately from these into the inner court. As the stair rose eight steps above the outer court, the whole gateway naturally must have been raised so far in regard to the outer court, so that they entered at the end on a level into the inner court, which was higher by the extent of the eight steps above the outer court. All gets into confusion, if we forget that the order of the several parts in the gates of the inner court was exactly the same as in the gates of the outer court—stair, first threshold, guard-rooms, second threshold, porch. There is not the least tenable ground to depart from this order. If there was to be a variation, the prophet must have set it forth in the clearest and most indubitable terms.

CHAPTER XL. 38–47.

In these verses we have what is noteworthy in the inner court besides the gates: the arrangements regarding the victims (vers. 38–43); the chambers for the singers (vers. 44–46); the size of the court; and lastly, its crown, the altar of burnt-offering (ver. 47).

Ver. 38. And a chamber, whose door was at the pillars of the gates: there they wash the burnt-offering. 39. And in the porch of the gate two tables on this side, and two tables on that, on which to slay the burnt-offering, and the sin-offering, and the guilt-offering. 40. And at the side without, for him that goeth up the way of the gate to the north, two tables; and on the other side of the porch of the gate, two tables. 41. Four tables on this side, and four tables on that, by the side of the gate; eight tables on which they slaughtered. 42. And four tables for the burnt-offering of hewn stones,[1] a cubit and a half long, and a cubit and a half broad, and one cubit high, on which they lay the instruments with which they slay the burnt-offering and the slain-offering. 43. And the ledges of a hand-breadth are fastened within[2] round about; and on the tables was the flesh of the offering. 44. And outside the inner

---

[1] Luther, "*were* of hewn stones;" afterwards, "on which they laid;" mistaking the import of the ו in ויניחו, which serves to put the object of this table in contrast with that of the table in ver. 41. Böttcher, "With ו as for a new sentence after a pause of thought, thereupon—they shall now," etc.

[2] Luther, "bent inwards;" whereas בבית refers to *the* tables which stood within the gate-structure, in the porch itself, in opposition to the tables without, *beside* the porch.

gates the chambers of the singers in the inner court, which was at the side of the north gate, and their front towards the south: one at the side of the east gate, fronting towards the north. 45. And he spake to me, This chamber, whose front is toward the south, is for the priests, who keep the charge of the house. 46. And the chamber whose front is toward the north, is for the priests who keep the charge of the altar: these are the sons of Zadok, who of the sons of Levi come near the Lord to minister to him. 47. And he measured the court, a hundred cubits long and a hundred cubits broad, squared; and the altar was before the house.

The description of the arrangements concerning the offering, as they were placed in and by the north gate, begins in ver. 38, with the chamber for washing the flesh, because this lay most in advance. The prophet had already, in ver. 37, reached the extreme end of the north gate, the two pillars which closed. To these he had opposed the stair, which formed the beginning of the whole doorway. Here he returns to the pillars occupying the place of the tower. Hard by these lay the chamber for cleansing the flesh, the last stage which the sacrifice had to pass through before it was laid on the altar. The pillars are spoken of as a whole, although the door of the chamber could only adjoin one of them. It was not designed to determine more exactly the situation of the chamber. The pillars are characterized as gate-pillars, as distinguished from other pillars in the interior of the gateway, by which the windows were closed; comp. ver. 16. By the gate is here designated the gate-opening, as in ver. 15.[1] A proper gate could not be in the porch, the nature of which was to be open, to form a space before the gate. The burnt-offering, as the most excellent kind, here represents the whole class of offerings: in ver. 39, the sin-offering and the guilt-offering are named along with it; in ver. 42 the slain-offering; and in ver. 43 stands the general name for all offering. According to many, arrangements are described here, and in what follows, that were found alike at all the gates. But there is no reason

---

[1] השערים, the gates, stands, with omission of the preposition, for *at* the gates, as they were at the gates. The pillars only of a definite gate, the north gate, are spoken of. But these are denoted in a generic way as gate-pillars, to distinguish them from those in the interior.

for this assumption, as here the north gate only is spoken of: the gate in ver. 39 refers to the expression, "And he brought me to the north gate," in ver. 35; and in vers. 40 and 44 the north gate is expressly mentioned. According to the old prescription of Moses, the offerings were to be slain "on the side of the altar northward" (Lev. i. 11); and there, according to the statements of the Talmud (Böttcher), the arrangements for slaughtering continued in the later temple.

From the pillars at the end of the porch, beside which was the chamber for cleansing the flesh, the consideration of the arrangements for offering turns to the porch itself, in which four tables stand for slaughtering—two on each side. The slaughtering is here to be taken in a wide sense, so as to include the whole preparation of the flesh for offering. According to ver. 43, the flesh lay on these tables, and they were provided with ledges, that in the separation nothing might fall off. It appears that the proper slaughtering was performed outside the porch; and the proper slaughtering-tables were those standing there, according to ver. 40. The communication out and in was the easier, because the porches at their ends had no side-walls. We have to suppose the tables placed at the end, close to the egress into the inner court.

Four other tables stood, according to ver. 40, without, in regard to him who went up to the door of the north gate. He that passes the whole gateway is thus designated, because the door was, for every one that entered the way, the chief point. Thus it is meant that these tables lay outside of a position taken in the interior of the gateway. The tables stand without the porch, on both sides of it,—thus in the outer court, hard by the boundary of the inner. This is the place where the slaughtering was done.

Ver. 41 sums up the tables named, for greater clearness: there are eight of them in all—four on the one side of the gate, two of them within and two without, and four on the other. Besides these eight slaughter-tables, the prophet sees, according to ver. 42, four other tables for the burnt-offering, so designated because they also stand in relation, though more distant, to the sacrifice, for depositing thereon the instruments used in slaughtering—knives, etc. That the burnt-offering stands here as a representative of offerings in general, is clearly shown by the close of the verse, where burnt-offerings and slain-offerings are named, which so often together denote all kinds of offering; on which it is to be remarked, that to the burnt-offering in a wide sense the sin-offering and guilt-offering are reckoned, that have this in common with the burnt-offering in a strict sense, that the offerer does not partake of them, no communion is connected with them, as is the case in the slain-offering. Those who have put in place of the *burnt-offering* the *stair*, neglect the usage, and bring all into confusion. The whole apparatus for the offering is found at the egress of the inner gateway, near its opening into the inner court, in which the offerings were made. If we take away the stair, the position of the four tables designed for the instruments is not precisely marked: but this is not necessary; it follows at once of itself from their design. They must have stood close by the proper slaughter-tables, that the instruments might be at hand, one by each pair. These tables are of stone, while the proper slaughter-tables were of wood, which was suitable for cutting up the flesh. There are twelve tables in all, according to the number of the tribes of Israel, and in harmony with the number of the victims in Ezra vi. 17 and viii. 35,—"twelve he-goats" and "twelve bullocks," after the number of the tribes of Israel. In ver. 43 we have the borders or ledges, with which the tables standing "within," inside the porch, in contradistinction to those without (ver. 40), were provided; and certainly round about, so that the ledges went round the tables, to keep the pieces when cut up from falling off. It has been asked, "How was the ledge enclosure worth so many words?" But the very going into details apparently so minute showed how clearly and sharply the prophet in faith looked into the not-being as being, and was well fitted to draw away the minds of the people from the fixed look at the smitten city. We must indeed always keep in view the object of the prophet, to set up an interim temple for the imagination, in which they might expatiate as long as the real temple, and with it the kingdom of God, lay in ruins. "And on the tables was the flesh of the offering:" here, intentionally, at the end the generic name of the offering, Korban, is placed, that we may not be led into error by the designation of the whole of the offerings by their prominent kinds in the preceding passage.

That the cells (ver. 44) in the inner court, destined for the priests, are different from those already described in the outer court, destined for the use of the people, is understood of itself. That the singers are here so prominent, is explained by this, that in the exalted position of the community of God more ample material was given them for new songs, so that the singing in the worship of the new temple must play a chief part, as indeed the multiplication of the singers and musicians under David stood connected with the advance which the people of God had then made. According to Ps. lxxxvii., when the future of salvation is come, the singers with the dancers say, "All my springs are in Thee," that is, We praise Thee, O Lord, as the Author of the great deliverance which we enjoy. The second part of Isaiah, and its lyric echo in Ps. xci.-c., are full of the thought, that in the time of salvation all shall sing and play. Even in the times soon after the return from the exile, singing revived in a degree that had not been since David. In a long series of Psalms, from Ps. cvii. onwards, the people thank their God for the blessing of restoration. Hallelujah—this was then the word. The chambers of the singers are generally faced toward the south. There was the entrance of the temple-house, the chief place where the singers had to perform (1 Chron. xvi. 37). The singers had this entrance always before their eyes, to be able to observe it on the occasion of their office. But a portion of the cells of the singers[1] lay at the side of the east gate, with the front toward the north: there in the court stood the altar of burnt-offering, where the singers had to perform at the offering of the great national sacrifices (1 Chron. xvi. 41). The chamber in ver. 45 denotes a series of chambers. Of what kind the service was which the priests had to perform in the temple, appears from ver. 44, according to which the singers are here singly and solely concerned.[2] "These are the sons of Zadok," etc. (ver. 46): this refers not merely to the singers, who had the charge at the

---

[1] The masc. אחד shows that we are not to think of a single cell, but a set of cells.

[2] Concerning the import of שמר משמרת, comp. *Christol.* iii. p. 629. To keep the keeping of any one, or of his business, is to take care of him or it. To keep the keeping of the house, is thus to take care or be studious of his service in the house, to perform it. If any one, against the usage,

altar of burnt-offering, but also to those who had the charge as singers in the temple. With the entire holy service, the sons of Zadok had also the service of holy singing, whereby they are not excluded, however, from calling in the aid of such Levites as could sing. The prophet afterwards (ver. 44 f.) gives a fuller explanation concerning the sons of Zadok.

In ver. 47, the matter of the inner court is completed by the statement of its dimensions. It was a square a hundred cubits long and a hundred broad, in contrast with the three hundred cubits of the outer court. To this is added the remark, that in the inner court before the temple stood the altar of burnt-offering, to be fully described in xliii. 13 f., which formed the radiant point of the inner court.

After the consideration of the court, the prophet turns to the description of the proper temple. This is remarkably distinguished by its brevity from that of the court. In the description of the temple of Solomon in our historical books, the reverse is the case. Bähr, in *The Temple of Solomon*, p. 147, says: "For the character of the court in contrast with the temple, the brevity, abruptness, and indefiniteness with which both narratives, the books of Kings as well as those of Chronicles, describe it, are very significant. While in the temple the description goes partly into the minutest detail, and states precisely even things apparently the most indifferent, as the quality of the building-stone, the proportion of the several entrances, the wood and the ornaments of the doors, in the court most things are left undefined, the compass and size are not fixed, and that which is necessary to form an idea of this second chief part of the whole building is scarcely mentioned." The problem has been explained in various ways. The simplest explanation is this: The annals of Judah, from which our historical books are here drawn, pass rapidly over the courts, because they were known to every Israelite from childhood by personal inspection. On the other hand, they were copious in the description of the parts of the sanctuary inaccessible to the

explains the phrase of a supervision of the temple or keeping watch in it, he is in conflict with ver. 44, according to which we have here to do only with the holy singers. Hence the phrase refers here only to the service which the priests had as singers in the temple, and in ver. 46 to the service at the altar of burnt-offering.

people. Ezekiel, who wrote for the people in exile, might reckon, in regard to the proper temple, that the hints which he gave regarding the sanctuary to be restored, would find an ample supplement in the existing historical sources. On the contrary, in the courts he was obliged to go more into detail, if the hope of restoration was to make a deep impression on the minds of his readers, who had not, like himself, seen these courts with their own eyes. That the reason of his method is to be sought here, is evident from this, that in the description of the proper temple, Ezekiel coincides often verbally with the accounts derived from the annals of Judah in our historical books, and by the merely allusive nature of his accounts, which receive and are only to receive their meaning by comparison with the historical books, almost expressly refers to them. Let us compare, for ex. the close of ch. xli. 7. The obviously intentional obscurity of the expression there can only be regarded as an indirect reference. First, in

Ch. xl. 48, 49, *The porch of the temple.*—Ver. 48. And he brought me to the porch of the house, and measured the pillar of the porch, five cubits on this side, and five cubits on that; and the breadth of the gate was three cubits on this side, and three cubits on that. 49. And the length of the porch twenty cubits, and the breadth eleven cubits; and (such was the breadth) at the steps by which they go up to it; and there were columns by the pillars, one on this side, and one on that.

The corner pillars of the porch had, according to ver. 48, on both sides a thickness of five cubits. The gate had three cubits on the one side, and three cubits on the other. It was of the nature of the porch to be open, being an open approach to a space that is or may be closed, which shelters from the inclemency of the weather those who must wait for the opening. A door is not mentioned here, as otherwise generally in the closed rooms of the temple. The words " three cubits on this side, and three cubits on that," indicate that an open space was left in the midst. We are to conceive the matter thus: In the porches of the court, that had a large thoroughfare, the whole space within must have been open. It was otherwise in the porch of the sanctuary, which the officiating priests only had to enter. There the inaccessibility for the multitude, the *odi profanum vulgus et arceo*, was figured by this, that the greater space on both sides was cut off by a certain contrivance, probably a grating, and in the midst only a free passage five cubits wide, the half of that in the porches of the courts, was left. The grating probably did not take in the whole height any more than the whole breadth, so that it did not hinder the free view into the whole porch.

The length of the porch in ver. 49 corresponds to that of the porch in Solomon's temple (1 Kings vi. 3), where expositors, against the clear letter of the text, have often put the breadth instead of the length, and then adopted the incongruity that the porch was as broad as the house itself. The breadth of the porch is here fixed at eleven cubits. This refers to the open space. The whole breadth, inclusive of the corner pillars, each five cubits broad, amounted to twenty-one cubits. The breadth of eleven cubits here is not in contradiction to that of ten cubits in the porch of Solomon's temple. According to ch. xli. 2, the door of the sanctuary, to which the porch led, was also ten cubits broad. The eleventh cubit here affords only the space for the posts of the door on both sides, so that in fact the porch is here only ten cubits broad. The eleventh cubit here is not essential, but serves another purpose,—is purely accessory,[1] as we must expect beforehand that the eleven will return to a round number. The breadth of eleven cubits applied to the stair that went up to it, no less than to the porch itself. The number of steps in this stair is not given, as it was in those of the outer and inner courts. But, according to ch. xli. 8, the height must have come to six cubits. Accordingly we may have fourteen steps in contrast with the seven steps of porch of the outer court. As in the porch of the outer and inner court, here also the corner pillars on both sides of the porch are mentioned. This, however, is done quite in passing, and it must be surprising that here the height of these pillars is not mentioned, as is done in ver. 4 in the case of the corner pillars of the porch of the court. We expect to find what is wanting in the historical books. For in the account of Chronicles, derived from the annals of Judah, we are presented

[1] So already Sturm: *undecim cubitorum, vel ab initio postis decem, nam ab initio postis præcipue latitudo numeranda.*

(2 Chron. iii. 4) with the statement that the porch (at its highest point) was 120 cubits high, with which the statement of Josephus (*Arch.* viii. 3, 2) is in harmony. This statement suits well with the height of sixty cubits of the corner pillars of the court in Ezekiel. The proportion in height agrees with the thickness of the corner pillars, which in the court amounts only to two cubits, here to five. The objections which have been raised against the statement of Chronicles must vanish when it is considered that art in the old Orient, and particularly in Solomon's temple, is only the minister of religion. That which Bähr (p. 198) says with respect to the two pillars Jachin and Boaz, applies here also: "Their form has arisen from their meaning: they are not lank, soaring, slender, but very thick, enormously strong pillars, that measure twelve cubits in compass with only eighteen in height,—a form that can by no means be called beautiful, but yet shows that art was here wholly in the service of symbolism, and the beautiful was made subordinate to the expression of the religious idea." In a building which was consecrated to the Lord of heaven, and was to effect a connection between heaven and earth, the most emphatic reference to heaven could not be wanting: as far as it was possible for man, the head of the building must point to heaven: humility, no less than pride, has need of a tower whose top is in heaven (Gen. xi.). On both sides of the corner pillars, that are connected architecturally with the porch itself, stand, without external connection with the building, and quite free, two columns, which are mentioned in so brief and significant a manner, that we perceive an almost express reference to what is already otherwise known: if we disregard this, we can make nothing of the two columns, and the prophet might have left them altogether unmentioned. Every Israelite knew that the two columns in such a place can only be the two celebrated columns Jachin and Boaz in Solomon's temple raised from ruin (1 Kings vii. 15 f.), which, as Bähr (p. 36 f.) has shown, also received a free place beside the porch. These columns, which the prophet himself had seen in their place, on which his youthful fancy had no doubt dwelt with delight, were removed by the Chaldeans (Jer. lii. 20 f.). Again in the spirit he sees them in their old place. The import of these columns cannot be doubtful. They were, as it were, the stone program

of the temple, and of the kingdom of God signified by it. They signified what the people of God have in their God. Their name shows this, in which, as usual, their nature is exhibited: Jachin, " He (God) establishes (me);" and Boaz, " In Him (am I) strong." In harmony with their form, " cast of brass (comp. on ver. 3), round, very thick, uniform to the top," they are a figure of the unchangeable stability and strength of the kingdom of God, which was practically refuted only in appearance by the Chaldean catastrophe. By the restoration, seen in vision, this fact enters into its true light: it is shown that only He has taken away stability and strength who bestowed them, because the people had made themselves unworthy of His aid; it is shown that the Chaldeans were only instruments in His hand. In the porch are described only the entrance, the stair, the corner pillars, the outstanding pillars on both sides. Where the corner pillars terminate the side-walls probably came in, as in the porch of the court.

After the porch of the house, the proper temple building, follows now the house itself. First the measurements of the entrance of the holy place; then, in the second half of ch. xli. 2, the length and breadth of itself.

Ch. xli. 1. And he brought me to the temple, and measured the pillars six cubits broad on this side, and six cubits broad on that, the breadth of the tent. 2. And the breadth of the door ten cubits, and the sides of the door five cubits on this side, and five cubits on that: and he measured the length of the temple forty cubits, and the breadth twenty cubits.

The temple denotes in ver. 1, as in 1 Kings vi. 5 and elsewhere, not, as frequently, the whole of the temple building, but the chief room, the nave of it, the holy place in contradistinction from the most holy, to which the prophet passes in ver. 3. The corner pillars of the entrance are on each side six cubits, in contrast with the five cubits of the corner pillars of the court. The strength (and corresponding height) of the corner pillars is, according to Starck, to remind the entrants what the King is who dwells in this temple. The words " (this is) the breadth of the tent," do not mean that the twelve cubits which the pillars occupy make the whole breadth of the temple, which would be in contradiction with what immediately follows, according to which the free space of the house alone had a breadth of twenty cubits. The words point out rather that the two pillars form the ends of the breadth of the temple, so that we have the whole breadth, if we measure from the end of the one to the end of the other, in which measurement the twenty cubits of the free space in ver. 2 are included. The temple-house, holy and most holy together, is designated antiquely as "the tent," because the sanctuary originally, and for a series of centuries from Moses to Solomon, had had the form of a tent. In commemoration of the very brief sojourn of the people in tents, that came to an end with the conquest of Canaan, the houses of the Israelites were several times designated as tents (Josh. xxii. 8; 1 Kings xii. 16). But the prophet had here a definite reason for speaking of the breadth of the tent, and not of the temple. He had before briefly put the tent in a strict sense for the holy place. But here the breadth of the whole building was to be given, inclusive of the most holy places to which the same breadth is ascribed in ver. 4, while the length in the holy and the most holy place is different. The breadth of the door of the house is in ver. 2 fixed at ten cubits. Adding to this the two side-walls of the door, five cubits each, of which half a cubit on each side is destined for the door-posts (comp. on xl. 49), we have a total breadth of twenty cubits, the half of the forty cubits' length of the holy place. As the length and breadth agree with the temple of Solomon, the statement of its height, thirty cubits (1 Kings vi. 2), will also apply to the temple of Ezekiel. The breadth is, besides, only that of the open space. The total breadth, including the pillars on both sides, amounted to thirty-two cubits. The agreement of the temple of Ezekiel with that of Solomon, where we have materials for the comparison of the two, points out to us that essential agreement will also be found where, as in the courts, the comparison cannot be instituted, because the descriptions of the temple of Solomon are incomplete. But that the prophet in his measurements retains the number of cubits in the temple of Solomon, although his cubit was different from that employed in Solomon's temple, being a hand-breadth greater, that he does not think of reducing the number of cubits to the former standard, proves how little the description of the new temple was meant to be realistic. If it concerned him only to give a firm hold to the future hopes of the people; if he wrote not for the architects of the future, but for the believers of the present; if it concerned him only, at a time when the stone temple was fallen, to erect an interim temple for the imagination, he must have reckoned in whole numbers, and a reduction of the proportion would have been paltry and confusing. The design to represent the temple of the future as greater than that of the past, need not be ascribed to the prophet. For this purpose the difference is too slight. A sixth part more or less is nothing in such matters.

In vers. 3, 4, the inmost part of the temple, or the most holy place. Ver. 3. And he went inward, and measured the pillar of the door, two cubits; and the door, six cubits; and the breadth of the door, seven cubits. 4. And he measured its length, twenty cubits; and the breadth, twenty cubits, before the temple: and he said unto me, This is the most holy place.

"And he went" (ver. 3): Ezekiel might as priest follow the measuring angel into the holy place, but not into the most holy, which was accessible only to the high priest. Here, therefore, he beholds the taking of the measure only from without. The whole breadth of the door is seven cubits, because one cubit for the posts is added to the six cubits for the door. The opinion that the six cubits are the height of the door, has been already refuted by Villalpandus. The pillars on both sides, with the door-posts and the door, include a breadth of eleven cubits. It is not said how the most holy was separated from the holy place in the remaining nine cubits. But it lies in the nature of the thing that it was separated. For otherwise, wherefore the door? Probably the separation was by a curtain. It is a question whether the pillars, each at two cubits, stood beside the door-posts, or at both sides of the enclosing wall, so that on each side the half of the nine cubits was between them and the door-posts. At all events here, as in ch. xl. 16, pillars in the interior of the building are spoken of, such as stood within "the wall of the house" (ver. 5). The measurements given in ver. 4 agree again with those of Solomon's temple. The *temple* denotes here also the holy place. The most holy lay before the holy in its whole breadth.

In vers. 5-11, the sheds of the temple, or the sacristies for the sojourn of the priests before they entered upon their functions (Luke i. 8, 9), for keeping all holy things, vessels, dresses, antiquities (1 Kings vii. 51, viii. 4; 2 Kings xi. 10); then the open spaces on this side and on that side of the enclosing wall.

Ver. 5. And he measured the wall of the house, six cubits; and the breadth of the side-chamber, four cubits round about the whole house. 6. And the side-chambers were chamber on chamber three, and thirty times; and they came to the wall, which was to the house for the side-chambers round about, that they might have hold, and they had not hold in the wall of the house. 7. And it was broader, and wound about still upward round about the house; for the winding of the house was still upward round about the house: therefore there was breadth to the house upwards, and from the lowest they went up on the highest by the middle. 8. And I saw the height of the house round about: the foundations of the side-chambers were a full reed, six cubits its story. 9. The breadth of the wall, which was for the side-chamber without, was five cubits, and the place that was left free. This is the side-building of the house. 10. And between the chambers was a breadth of twenty cubits round about the whole house. 11. And the door of the side-building was toward the free place, one door toward the north and one door to the south: and the breadth of the free place was five cubits round about.

The thickness of the wall of the temple is stated in ver. 5 to be six cubits, the breadth of the side-building, which surrounded the temple on all three sides,[1] four cubits. Thus we obtain as the breadth of the whole building, including the side-building, which serves to give greater fulness to the building, and make it more respectable, 40 cubits: 20 cubits for the open room, 12 for the walls, and 8 for the side-buildings. Ver. 6 says that the side-chambers had three stories, one above the other.[2] It is added that the side-chambers adjoined the wall of the temple,

[1] That of the four sides only three come into account, and the fourth is for obvious reasons omitted, is intimated by the threefold repetition of the סביב.

[2] It is literally chamber on chamber. But that they are to be not one beside, but one above another, is manifest from what follows, and could not

which enclosed the side-chambers, so that the beginning of the breadth of the side-chambers coincided with the end of the wall; and further, that they were connected with this wall, and by this connection had their hold, yet so that they were not inserted in the wall of the house itself. 1 Kings vi. 6 gives the requisite commentary. It is there said in reference to the temple of Solomon and its side-chambers: " He had made rebates to the house around without, that they might not be fastened in the walls of the house." On this Keil observes: In the temple wall, when the joists of the several stories were to be applied, ledges were made, so that the ends of these joists rested on the ledges, and did not enter the proper wall of the house. 1 Kings vi. 10 is also to be compared, " And it (the chamber) rested on the house with joists of cedars ;" on which Keil says, " By the cedar-joists of the several stories, which rested on the ledges of the temple-wall, the side-building took hold of the house: it was firmly connected with the temple-house, without interfering injuriously with the sanctuary." In the exposition of ver. 7, it must be laid down as the first rule, that we do not get into contradiction with the description of the side-building in Solomon's temple. For all clear and certain statements of Ezekiel essentially agree with those given there; and the more subordinate the side-chambers are, the more improbable it is that Ezekiel has here given a quite new construction,—the more obvious is the assumption that the side-chambers, with which were probably connected the fondest associations of his youth (we have only to think of Samuel, who, as well as Eli, had his sleeping apartment in such a chamber in the tabernacle), appeared to him in vision in their early form. Now, according to 1 Kings vi. 6, the breadth of the under story was five cubits, that of the middle six, and that of the highest seven; and this difference arose from the thickness of the temple-wall, which was six cubits below, and diminished first one and then two cubits.[1] Now the words

antecedently be doubtful to any one acquainted with the former temple. The remark of Böttcher, "אל for על here, where the rise of one story above another is concerned, would be more than negligent," does not apply, because the very inexactness is an indirect reference to the existing description of Solomon's temple, which was accessible to the reader.

[1] Starck on our passage: *Murus sex cubitos habuit, sed quo altior ascen-*

here agree quite well with this, if they were scarcely intelligible without this commentary. In ascending, a continual change took place in the stories,[1] which consisted indeed in the increasing breadth of the chambers.[2] The last words of the verse, "And from the lowest they went up on the highest by the middle," have the key to their meaning in 1 Kings vi. 8, "And by a winding stair they went up to the middle, and from the middle to the third."[3] The winding stair here is not expressly mentioned. It must be transferred from the former description. This therefore presupposes the stair. Hence it is plain that, by the breadth increasing above, space was gained for the stair. In ver. 8, the height of the house here spoken of, the side-building, is given. The *socle* has a height of a whole reed—whole, this is here added, because the elevation above the ground might easily be supposed less. If this be the elevation of the side-building, it must also be that of the proper temple, the entrance of which, it is self-evident, was not on level ground. With the statement of the size, here corresponds the mention of the stair in ch. xl. 49. Then follow three stories (in the original it is properly joints, xiii. 18), each of six cubits. According to 1 Kings vi. 10, every story in Solomon's temple had a height of five cubits. There is no

debat, tenuior fiebat, et cubicula in illis spatiis spatium lucrabatur, ut hæc æquali linea essent exterius, sed interius tamen latiores uno altero, quia nempe murus illis locum ampliorem concedebat.

[1] סבב, to turn, Zech. xiv. 10; *Piel*, change, alter, 2 Sam. xiv. 20; *Hiphil*, change, 2 Kings xxiii. 22.

[2] Böttcher: רחבה refers not to קיר, ver. 6, where this was not the subject, but, from 1 Kings vi. 6, necessarily to the internal enlargement of the side-chambers, of which it is said impersonally, "and it widened." So ונסבה. He further remarks: למעלה is pictorially reduplicated in that which is continued upwards; and so the farther up, the more enlargement and alteration.

[3] The defectiveness of the expression is intentional, and is an indirect reference to the earlier description, from which the meaning is to be learned. In the under story the preposition is quite wanting, which, according to the whole style of this local section in Ezekiel, creates not the least difficulty. In לתיכונה it is quite generally expressed, that the middle story also comes into account, instead of saying definitely, that the way from the lowest to the highest lay through it. And we only arrive at the certain understanding of the יעלה, one goes up, when we refer to the יעלו in the book of Kings.

difference, as here probably the floor and the roof are included. If, in the statement of the height of the temple in 1 Kings vi. 3, the *socle* and the upper chambers (1 Chron. xxviii. 11; 2 Chron. iii. 8) were to be included, for which 1 Kings vi. 20 speaks, according to which the most holy place, in harmony with its length and breadth, had only a height of twenty cubits, the side-building reached the height of the temple; if, on the contrary, the thirty cubits in 1 Kings vi. 2 be exclusive of the *socle* and the upper chambers, the temple exceeded the side-building by twelve cubits. We prefer the former view. Ver. 9 gives five cubits for the breadth of the outer wall of the side-building, and remarks that beyond this breadth that of the free place comes into account, which extended along the side-building, made it accessible, and gave it light. After this brief allusion to the free space, of which the prophet speaks more fully in ver. 11, but to which reference had to be made here, lest the breadth, in which the free space should have been included, might be too hastily summed up, the description of the side-building itself is closed with the words, "(This is) the side-building of the house," as it is the manner of Ezekiel to give such limiting conclusions (comp. for ex. i. 11); and he now still turns in vers. 10 and 11 to the free spaces which were connected with the side-buildings.[1] First in ver. 10 the *greater* free space, twenty cubits broad, that lies between the outer wall of the side-stories and the chambers to be described first in ch. xlii. 1 f., and indeed on all the three sides of the temple: "between the chambers" stands for between the side-building spoken of at the end of ver. 9, and the chambers. Then in ver. 11 the smaller free space, five cubits broad, between the side-building and the outer wall enclosing it. If we add to the already obtained breadth of forty cubits for the temple and the side-building, the five

[1] The name מֻנָּח, left free, is borne only by the relatively narrow free space between the wall of the side-building and the enclosing wall. In this narrow lane (five cubits broad) the idea of the space left open comes out more sharply by the opposition to the building on both sides. That the two free spaces, the narrow and the wide, cannot immediately border on one another, but must be separated by the enclosing wall, is understood of itself, and is also implied in the way in which the narrow free space is spoken of in ver. 9, but still more definitely in ver. 11, according to which the doors of the side-building open into the free space.

cubits of the inner free space on both sides, and therefore ten cubits, the five cubits of wall thickness on both sides, making also ten more, and the twenty cubits of free space on both sides, making forty more, we have 100 cubits for the total breadth, in harmony with ver. 14.

In vers. 12–14 the prophet gives the measurements of a new building, which rises to the west of the temple, and connects therewith the statement of the total length and total breadth of the temple-house, which results from summing up the former statements regarding the measurements of the several parts. The outer court encloses on three sides—east, south, and north— a space 300 cubits long and 100 cubits broad, that falls into three parts, each 100 cubits long. The inner court forms the eastern part, the temple-house the middle, and the building here described, which abuts on the western enclosure of the outer court.

Ver. 12. And the building which was before the gizrah (off-space), on the side of the west, was seventy cubits broad; and the wall of the building was five cubits thick round about, and its length ninety cubits. 13. And he measured the house, a hundred cubits long; and the gizrah, and the building, and its walls, a hundred cubits long; 14. And the breadth of the front of the house, and of the gizrah toward the east, a hundred cubits.

The space on which the building to be measured in ver. 12 stands, is designated the gizrah. In this name the design and import of the building are given. Gizrah means the cut-off, separate, the separate place, the off-place or off-room.[1] The place and the building thereon serve negatively the same purpose which the temple serves positively. If this is to retain its dignity and sanctity, a place must be assigned whither all uncleanness is removed; which was the more necessary, as in the holy areas, especially on festivals, many thousands, yea myriads of men, remained the whole day (Ps. lxxxiv. 11), held their intercourse and their meals, and rejoiced " before the

---

[1] LXX. τὸ ἀπόλοιπον; Aq. and Sym. *separatum*. The corresponding גזרה stands in Lev. xvi., of the place to which the buck consecrated to Azazel is sent away—the wilderness, in opposition to the cultivated land. The line of cultivation forms a sharp boundary.

Lord."[1] Already in the books of Moses is found the order for setting apart a place for such a purpose outside the camp, which corresponded to the temple with its courts, and the injunction that this place is to be kept clean, which is laid down as a religious duty (Deut. xxiii. 13, 14). That there was a building for this purpose near the temple of Solomon, appears from 2 Kings xxiii. 11, according to which the stabling of the horses, which the idolatrous king had consecrated to the sun, were in this building. According to 1 Chron. xxvi. 18, this building lay quite, as here, to the west of the temple. According to 1 Chron. xxvi. 16, the gate which led to this building was called the refuse-gate; and from this gate a street led to the city on the west, which probably served for carrying away.[2] Even now in the East, in the churches and mosques, are found the most extensive arrangements for this purpose, to concentrate the impurities in a place assigned to them, and separate them from the holy cities. The building is described as lying to the west side, in opposition to the temple, which lay east of the boundary line. The building formed the close westward. There it extended to the outer enclosing wall of the court, and by a gate built in this had its egress into the city. The breadth of the building is fixed at seventy cubits. The walls contain five cubits on both sides. Twenty cubits therefore remain, ten on each side for the entrances and the galleries (ver. 15). In length, and therefore from east to west, the building filled the whole extent of the gizrah. This amounted to 100 cubits. Of these, the building filled ninety cubits, and the walls at both ends ten cubits. The gizrah was equal in length and breadth to the temple-house. We have already shown that the latter was 100 cubits broad. The

---

[1] The gizrah must have had access to the outer court, by which it was bounded on the south and north. The arrangements are too extensive for the priests alone.

[2] The name פרור, which this building bears in 2 Kings xxiii. 11, or פרבר, as it is called with hardened form in Chronicles, is derived from פרר, to split, rend (Ps. lxxiv. 13; Isa. xxiv. 19), and denotes, quite like gizrah, localities that are separated from others by a sharply defined boundary line. In the Targums and the Talmud occurs פרורין, *de suburbiis locisque urbis vicinis*, of all that is separated by the boundary line of the wall from the towns, then of islands which are severed from the mainland by the boundary line of the sea.

length of 100 cubits amounts thus: six cubits the thickness of the walls of the sanctuary (ver. 5); sixty cubits the holy place and the most holy; four cubits the side-building in the west; five cubits the free space between the side-building and the surrounding wall; five cubits this surrounding wall; twenty cubits the free space bordering this surrounding wall; and therefore 100 cubits from the end of the court to the gizrah.

After stating the measurements of the buildings, the prophet in vers. 15-26 gives a series of observations which he made upon them.

Ver. 15. And he measured the length of the building in front of the gizrah which was behind it, and its galleries, on this side and on that, a hundred cubits, and the inner temple, and the porches of the court; 16. The thresholds, and the closed windows, and the galleries round about for all three, over against the threshold a boarding of wood round about, and from the ground to the windows, and the windows were covered; 17. On that which was above the door, and to the inner house and outside, and on the whole wall round about, within and without, were measures. 18. And there were made cherubim and palms, and a palm between a cherub and a cherub; and the cherub had two faces; 19. And the face of a man was toward the palm on this side, and the face of a lion toward the palm on that side, made on the whole house round about. 20. From the ground to above the door were cherubim and palms made: and (this is) the wall of the temple. 21. The temple had a square post, and in the front of the temple the view was as the view. 22. The altar of wood was three cubits high, and its length two cubits; and it had its corners, and its length and its walls were of wood: and he said unto me, This is the table that is before the LORD. 23. And the temple and the sanctuary had two doors. 24. And the doors had two leaves, two turning leaves; the one door had two, and the other had two leaves. 25. And on them, on the doors of the temple, were made cherubim and palms, as they were made on the walls; and a step of wood was in front of the porch without. 26. And closed windows and palms were on this hand and on that, on the sides of the porch, and on the sidechambers of the house, and the steps.

Ver. 15 recapitulates. Beginning from the building which was last measured, the erection in the gizrah, and proceeding thence to the porches of the court, with which the description had commenced, he repeats that the angel has measured all the buildings, to connect therewith the supplementary notices to be given. Yet we have no mere repetition. The prophet here inserts something that serves to define more exactly what goes before. First, in elucidation of what is said in ver. 12, he gives once more the situation of the building in the gizrah. It lay in front of the gizrah; but this front was the back front, in harmony with ver. 12, according to which the building lay before the gizrah on the west side, which was the hinder side: in the forefront of the gizrah on the east lay the temple, between which and the western building the gizrah formed the boundary line. Then he intimates that the building in the gizrah had on both sides passages or galleries.[1] This statement fits into that which is said in vers. 12, 14. Accordingly, of the 100 cubits in the breadth of the gizrah from south to north, only eighty cubits were occupied by the proper building, so that on both sides, south and north, ten cubits remained over. Here we learn that these ten cubits were not an open street, but were occupied with a passage or gallery. By the inner temple is designated the whole temple-building, the holy place and the most holy, in opposition to the doubled outwork of the building in the gizrah and the courts, the whole of which are called "the court." In ver. 16 the verb "he measured" is to be supplied from ver. 15. All that is mentioned in this verse is new, except the closed windows (xl. 16), which, however, are explained at the close of the verse by a more intelligible expression: the passages were previously mentioned only in reference to the building in the gizrah. It is common to all that is mentioned in this verse, that it is viewed from without, although in the wainscoting the glance penetrates into the interior. The sills are naturally door-sills: window-sills are

---

[1] The LXX. rendered the word אתיקים—occurring only here in vers. 15, 16, and in ch. xlii. 3, 4—in the latter place by περίστυλον, colonnade; the Vulg. by *porticus*. The meaning passage, gallery, is demanded by ch. xlii. Here also the circumstance that the object spoken of is measurable in the same way as the building itself, and also the correspondence between the statement here, and that in vers. 12, 14, lead to the same conclusion.

not known to the Old Testament. We must the rather expect the thresholds to be mentioned here, as the posts are spoken of in ver. 21. Of the passages it is said that all three had them, —namely, the three buildings named in ver. 15, the building in the gizrah, the temple, and the porches of the courts. We have already seen when they were applied in the gizrah. In the temple their place cannot be doubtful — the space of twenty cubits, that according to ver. 10 went round the temple on all sides except the east, where the porch was. That this space was no bare street we must expect beforehand, as it is considered an appendage of the temple, and included in its dimensions; and this is the more natural, as the designation of the "free" or unbuilt "space" (in ver. 11) is restricted to the street before the side-building, and not extended to this space. The passages in the porches of the courts we conceive most simply as covered galleries, that led from the porch of the outer court to the gate of the inner court, and from the porch of the inner court to the altar of burnt-offering and the temple, perhaps also from the one outer gate to the other. That there were such passages in Solomon's temple, appears from John x. 23, and Josephus, *Arch.* xx. 9, 7. " Over against the threshold a boarding of wood : " this can refer only to the ground floor, which was seen when one looked over the threshold into the sanctuary. In Solomon's temple also the ground floor was boarded, as were also the walls (Bühr, *Solomon's Temple*, p. 24). To the latter refers the expression, " and (the wooden boarding was) from the ground to the windows." [1] As the wooden boarding obviously covered the whole walls in Solomon's temple, we must assume that the windows above were fitted in the roof, as in the ark, according to Gen. vi. 16. Thus we escape the difficulty, that the wing-building was, at the sides, probably equal in height to the temple. If any one insists that the windows were in the sides, he must either

[1] The omission of the preposition before הארץ has not the least difficulty, according to the general style of the prophet, and especially in these topographical sections that abbreviate as much as possible. Obviously corresponding is מהארץ in ver. 20. If we deny the omission of the preposition, the sense is that the windows reached to the ground; which is very improbable, and does not agree with the words, as nobody wishing to express such a sense will say that the ground reached to the windows.

suppose that the temple was higher than the wing, and the windows were quite above it, or that the windows opened into the wings, and received their light through corresponding windows in the outer wall of these. Both assumptions have something perplexing. The *covering* of the windows can only have been partial. How it was effected is not explained, as it was in the windows of the porch (ch. xl. 16). But 1 Kings vi. 4 gives the supplement, according to which it was effected by bars laid across. The upper chambers of Solomon's temple are perhaps connected with the windows. Ver. 17 says that wherever one turned in the sacred edifice, from one end to the other, within and without, all was arranged according to measure, although it would lead too far to give these measures in detail: it was a house worthy of God, who has wisely arranged all things in His creation (Ps. civ. 24), and nothing is left to caprice or chance. The space over the door, not the door itself, forms the starting-point, because the measures of this were already given. The inner house, the house in the interior from end to end, forms the contrast to the space over the door of the sanctuary. To this again is opposed the outer, the outside of the building. The walls come into account on their two sides, the inner and the outer.

In vers. 18–20 the decoration of the walls of the temple with cherubim and palms. These were found also in the temple of Solomon (1 Kings vi. 29; Bähr, p. 24). There are carved works in the temple, the destruction of which by the Chaldeans is lamented in Ps. lxxiv. 6; and now they are here again. They indicate that the house is dedicated to the God of the whole terrestrial creation, to Him to whom the whole work belongs which is described in Gen. i.; not to a national god of limited power, but to Him who spake and it was done. The faces of the cherub look to the palms, to indicate that all creation, animate and inanimate, is a whole—a harmonious work of the creative power of God. Of the four faces of the cherub only two could appear here, as we have to do not with statues, but with figures, that can only present one side. If the whole animal world were to be denoted by one representative, the lion would be the most suitable. The wild beast denoted by the lion bears pre-eminently the name of the living thing, in distinction from the cattle, in which a lower energy of life appears. The cherubim and the palms, according to ver. 20, extended from the ground to the space above the door; this represents the upper part of the wall of the house. If they were applied above the entrance-door, they would naturally, where no door was, fill the whole space from the ground or the floor to the roof. The words "and (this is) the wall of the temple" finish the subject of the wall of the temple and its decoration, and lead to other matters: comp. on the close of ver. 9.

Of the front of the temple, the prophet in ver 21 describes only the door-posts,—an ideal unity which includes under it a material duality. This is described as squared,[1] the chief form, which meets us everywhere in the temple of Ezekiel, as in that of Solomon (Bähr, p. 97). All the rest—the door itself, the threshold (ver. 16), the wall, the porch at the entrance—was already mentioned, so that the prophet only saw on review what he had seen before. That the words " and the front of the house" (omitting the preposition for " *in* the front) (was) "the view as the view," compare a new view with a former one, which the prophet had had, is the simplest sense, and is put beyond a doubt by the corresponding parallel in ch. xliii. 3.

In ver. 22 the altar of incense. It is described as the altar (of) wood, in opposition to the brazen altar of burnt-offering, which is to be described later still. The gold plating is not mentioned here, as in Solomon's temple (1 Kings vi. 20), as a deep silence is generally observed by Ezekiel concerning gold, which plays so great a part in the description of Solomon's temple. In the floor also, and the walls, mention is only made of the wooden boarding, not of the gold with which it was overlaid in Solomon's temple. Temple and city should be built again in " troublous times" (Dan. ix. 25),—a remarkable parallel between the two prophets. Zechariah, who prophesied after the return, joins these as a third, in whom the Lord in ch. iv. 10 admonishes not to despise the day of small things. The dimensions of the altar of Solomon are not given. Those here given are without doubt borrowed from it. They suit the enlargement of the measurements, as they are found in the temple of Solomon, compared with the tabernacle. There the

---

[1] " A post of the square" is a square post. The square is, like many adjectives, made independent.

altar of incense was two cubits high and one cubit broad. "Its length and its walls of wood:" the length can only be that of the top of the altar. The corners of the altar are the elsewhere so-called horns of it, into which it ran at the corners, and which formed as it were its head. The altar is designated as the table or board before the Lord, because that which is set on it—the incense, denoting the prayers of the saints (Ps. cxli. 2; Rev. v. 8, viii. 3)—is regarded as a spiritual food, which the people present to their heavenly King.[1] The altar appears as the table of the Lord also in ch. xliv. 16. The offering appears as the food of God, Mal. i. 7. Not without cause is the altar in 1 Kings vii. 48 compared with the table of shewbread: the bread laid on the latter denoted the spiritual nourishment which the people are to present to their heavenly King, which is good works. In Matt. xxi. 18, 19, Jesus hungers after the fruit of the fig-tree, which signifies the Jewish people. From the altar of incense the supplementary description, which is bound to no systematic order, turns to the doors. It is first said in ver. 23, that the holy place and the most holy had each a door of two doors, that is, a door with two leaves. The most holy cannot in itself be denoted by the holy place; but it may, after the temple in the strict sense, the great room of the temple, has gone before. Of the entire holy space, only the most holy then remains; and this might be the rather designated the holy, as it is in respect of the great room pre-eminently the holy. Ver. 24 says that the two doorleaves of the two entrances were again divided into two parts, that the whole, or some part, might be opened as occasion required: in a door ten cubits wide, such a division was very suitable to facilitate the opening. The two parts of the doorleaves are described as turning or revolving,[2] because they could be folded or unfolded. According to ver. 25, there were cherubim and palms in the great room of the temple, on the doors no less than on the walls. It is also said that the porch had a wooden step.[3] Ver. 26 dwells still further on the *porch*.

---

[1] Comp. on John xxi. 5, 10, and my treatise on *The Day of the Lord*, p. 52.

[2] Comp. מוסב in ver. 7.

[3] עב is in 1 Kings vii. 6, " a threshold-like piece, a step or perron;" comp. Thenius and Keil. Ezekiel here first uses the older form. Then for explanation he puts the form current in his time at the end of ver. 26.

CHAP. XLII. 1–9.   401

It had closed windows, like the guard-rooms of the gate at the outer court (xl. 16), and like the temple itself (xli. 26). The porch, and likewise the wings, take the character of the subordinate from this, that only palms are figured on them, and not cherubim also (comp. on ch. xl. 16). In the creation, proceeding from the lower to the higher, the vegetable kingdom, represented by the palm, was in existence before the animal kingdom, represented by the cherubim. The words at the close, " and the steps," as much as to say, " and besides, the steps also are to be noticed in the porch" (comp. ver. 25), place the extreme end to the east, over against the extreme end to the west, the gizrah, with which the section in ver. 15 began.

In ch. xlii. 1-9, the description of a building destined for the priests in the outer court, that immediately adjoins the gizrah on the north, and runs parallel with its whole length. We must beforehand expect that a description of buildings destined for so numerous a priesthood will follow. For the chambers, which according to ch. xl. 17 adjoined the enclosing wall in the outer court, were destined for the people. The chambers in the inner court, mentioned in ch. xl. 44, belong only to the priestly singers. The cells in the wings of the temple, however, afforded, if they come here at all into account, at all events only a temporary sojourn for the officiating priests. There is as yet altogether wanting a proper dwelling-place for the priests, a great number of whom must have remained the whole day in the temple.

Ver. 1. And he brought me forth into the outer court, the way toward the north, and took me into the chamber which is over against the gizrah, and which was before the building toward the north. 2. Before the length of a hundred cubits the door toward the north, and the breadth fifty cubits. 3. Over against the twenty of the inner court, and over against the pavement of the outer court, passage was against passage, in the chambers of the third story. 4. And before the chambers a walk ten cubits broad inward, by a way of one cubit, and their doors toward the north. 5. And the upper chambers are shortened; for the passages consumed building space from them, from the lowest and the middle. 6. For they are three-storied, and have no pillars, as the pillars of the courts: therefore is (space) taken away from the lowest and from the middle, from the ground. 7. And the fence-wall which is outside, next the chambers, toward the outer court, in the face of the chambers, its length was fifty cubits. 8. For the length of the chambers which are toward the outer court was fifty cubits; and, lo, before the temple a hundred cubits. 9. And under it (the fence-wall) are these cells: the entrance on the east, in going into them from the outer court.

The prophet had to be led into the outer court (ver. 1), because the building lay in it. He is led the way toward the north, because the building was not on the south side of the area in which he had last been, of the inner area, consisting of the inner court, the temple, and the gizrah, but on the north side. It serves to designate the situation of the building more exactly, that it lay north over against the gizrah and the building. The building here can only be that on the gizrah, which is denoted in ch. xli. 12-14 by the same word: any other building must have been more precisely determined. In ver. 13 the gizrah merely is named instead of the gizrah and the building,—a proof that there was no local difference between the gizrah and the building. To understand the temple by the building is inadmissible, for this reason, that it should not be even partially obstructed by building; whereas it was quite consistent with the design of the gizrah and its building, to withdraw it from the view, by an additional structure immediately adjacent on both sides. To point directly to this, the words "and before the building" may have been added. But it was also fitting, in the mere interest of the local description, to point out that the gizrah, on which the building to be described bordered, was built upon. Nay, if this building lay on the north side of the gizrah, it must have occupied the most westerly part of the north side of the outer court. For the gizrah occupied in the inner area the last 100 cubits, and ended on the west at the enclosing wall. The after-mentioned priests' kitchen need not be regarded as a separate building, which lay more westerly than this building, but as an integral part of it, as indeed kitchens are not generally separate buildings. The building bears the name of the chamber in the sense of a system of chambers.

In ver. 2 the measurements of the building are given. The length is not directly stated; but it is said that the building lay in the face of or along "the length of a hundred cubits,"— the definite length, that which was before ascribed to the gizrah and its building in the direction from east to west; so that thus the building began in the east, where the gizrah began, and ended in the west, where the gizrah ended. These words are quite unambiguous. The breadth, on the contrary, which is peculiar to this building, is directly given. It amounted to fifty cubits. As, according to what follows, a building for priests of equal breadth lay on the other side of the gizrah, the 100 cubits breadth of the gizrah were enclosed, and set in the middle, by the fifty cubits breadth of the priestly court. But according to the following, this breadth applies only to the lower story. In the two upper there was a diminution, so that the building was in the form of a terrace. Between the statements regarding the length and breadth of the building, it is remarked that the doors (the door stands collectively) opened toward the north. This statement is fitly appended to that of the length, because the doors were in the long side. If there, they must be on the north side, as the gizrah lay on the south. The south opposite of the building, the gizrah, on the north of which it was placed, and likewise the west, the enclosing wall, had been already mentioned in vers. 1 and 2. Thus the doubled *over against* in ver. 3 can refer only to the east and the north. " Over against the twenty of the inner court:" this points to a definite space in the inner area, which in the foregoing was characterized by the number twenty. The pointing would be a mispointing, if in the foregoing there were several such spaces. But there is, in fact, only one passage, twenty cubits broad, provided, according to ch. xli. 16, with galleries round the temple; and to this we must refer all the more, because in ch. xli. 10 it has been intimated that it extended to the chambers here described. As this space extended on the west side of the temple by the gizrah, while the building here was of the same length with the gizrah, and the fence-wall, which, according to what follows, enclosed the priests' court on the east, belonged to it, being about twenty cubits distant from the building proper, as well as the passage which led thence to the gate of the inner court; so the east side of the building, at its end, lay over against this space. The building proper came in contact with the end of the twenty on the west; the fence-wall with the end of the twenty on the east. That the twenty are here applied to the inner court, whereas they formed a constituent part of the temple, need not surprise or mislead. The word is properly not court, but enclosed space. The prophet here divides the whole sanctuary into two spaces, the inner and the outer. First within the inner area there was a distinction between the temple and that which was merely inner area in general, the remaining inner area not specially characterized. For our passage this distinction does not come into account. There remains now still that which is over against on the north side. The pavement of the outer court is thus designated. This occupied on the west side of the court probably the whole breadth of fifty cubits, the half of which was taken up on the remaining sides by the chambers for the people (comp. xl. 17, 18). The words, "passage (comp. on xli. 15) was against passage in the chambers of the third story," imply that one looked down from the passage before the chambers of the third story, to another passage that was before the chambers of the second story.¹ Before the chambers, according to ver. 4, was a street ten cubits wide, to afford entrance to them. It went on the long side from west to east, or north of the building. From it there was access to the interior of the chambers, which was only one cubit from the street, which was the thickness of the walls. That the doors led to the north, had been already said in ver. 2, but is here once more repeated, that no one may be in doubt where the way is to be sought,—namely, in the 100 cubits of the long side of the building. According to ver. 5, the upmost chambers, those of the third story, were narrowed, less in breadth than the rest. This narrowing is here applied only to the upmost chambers, because it was there most visible. But it found place, as appears more definitely in ver. 6, also in the middle, in relation to the lowest; so that the building had three stages: in the first story, fifty cubits; in the second, perhaps forty; in the third, thirty, if we measure the breadth of the passage by that of the street, which formed the entrance to the lowest

¹ שְׁלִשִׁים occurs quite as here in Gen. vi. 16, of the chambers of the third story (of the ark). The word cannot signify three stories.

chambers. The occasion of the narrowing is given in the words, " For the passage consumed building-space from them, from the lowest and the middle." " Consuming" stands in the sense of subtracting. The passages or galleries correspond in the upmost story (as also in the middle) to the access or the street in the lowest. They were necessary to obtain access to the several chambers. They served the purpose also of balconies or verandahs. " From them :" this refers to the chambers in general, which are more exactly defined in the words, " from the lowest and the middle (chambers) ;" in the latter, the half of the space, which was deducted from the lowest by the galleries of the highest. " Building," or building-space—space that might otherwise have been built upon—is that which is as it were consumed in the upper chambers by the galleries. The space is taken from the upper stories. But the prophet says, from the middle and the lowest, because he gives an ideal prolongation to the end-line of the breadth of these. It means, in fact, from the space which the middle and the lowest took. Ver. 6 explains why the passages or galleries, which deducted from the building-space, were necessary. Had the chambers had a colonnade before, with a threefold floor in the first, second, and third stories, no galleries diminishing the breadth of the building itself would have been necessary: the object which they served would have been answered by the front. Such a colonnade was found elsewhere in the courts, but not here. No express mention has yet been made of pillars in the courts, which are here spoken of in the plural number. But we shall have to seek them there, where they are here wanting, in " the chambers,"—those for the use of the people in the outer court, and those for the singers in the inner court: only the similarity can invite comparison. We learn from our passage, what we already found probable, that these chambers also had several stories. The words, " Therefore is space taken away from the lowest and from the middle, from the ground," indicate that in the middle chambers a diminution of the given ground was effected with respect to the lowest, and in the upmost a still greater diminution in reference to the lowest and the middle. " From the ground :" this points out that the diminution of space refers to the normal breadth of fifty cubits which the building had in the ground floor. The *earth* denotes here the bottom or ground floor. Near the building, according to ver. 7, a fence-wall, to withdraw what was within it from the curious gaze: according to ch. xliv. 17-19, these chambers, and others abutting on the outer court, served for the dressing and undressing of the priests. The screen-wall needed to be only so high as to protect the chambers of the lowest story. It must have stood at some distance from the building, otherwise it would have interfered with its air and light.[1] On what side it is to be sought, is shown by the statement that it was in the face of the chambers: in local designations in the Old Testament, the face is always to be conceived as turned to the *east*. The length of the wall of fifty cubits leads also to the east side: this, according to ver. 2, is the breadth of the building; so that, as the west side, abutting on the enclosing wall of the court, cannot come into account, the east side must needs be meant. According to ver. 8, the chambers had on the east side, over against the fence-wall, a length of fifty cubits. These chambers are distinguished as those which belonged to the outer court. The whole building lay in the outer court. But these chambers on the east side belonged to the outer court in a special sense, inasmuch as they opened into it, received their light from it, and had their windows and galleries towards it. This was the case only with the chambers on the east side. That it was not so with the chambers on the north side, appears from this, that there was no fence-wall there, as on the east side. The chambers that had their entrance there had their look-out on the gallery of the gizrah. The gizrah is the part of the temple, in the wider sense, which comes here into account; for that the building lay only before the gizrah, and was conterminous with it, appears from vers. 1 and 2. According to ver. 9, the chambers were under the wall mentioned in ver. 7: the wall—this was its design—rose above

---

[1] If we assume that the distance of the wall from the building was twenty cubits, it lay on a line with the west end of the wing-building in the temple; and the twenty cubits, which according to ch. xli. 20 were between the wing-building and the chambers, are those to be measured from the wall. If we suppose the wall nearer the building, the twenty cubits there must refer to an ideal prolongation of the building here—its building range.

and covered them.¹ The entrance to the chambers was on the east side, "from the east," where the fence-wall must have had a door; not, as it might have been, from the north, where the interval between the wall and the chambers terminates northwards.

In vers. 10-12, the two priestly courts in the east and in the south. As these are perfectly similar to the fully described priestly courts in the north, the description confines itself to the exhibition of this similarity, and is carried out quite briefly and allusively. Yet a little is given here that was passed over in the measurements of the priestly court in the north.

Ver. 10. In the breadth of the fence-wall of the court toward the east, in the face of the gizrah, and in the face of the building, were chambers. 11. And a way before them was as the look of the chambers which were toward the north, as their length so their breadth; and all their outgoings after their fashions and their doors. 12. And like the doors of the chambers which were toward the south, was a door at the head of the way: the way before the fence-wall was convenient toward the east in entering them.

The fence-wall mentioned in ver. 10 can only correspond to that in vers. 7 and 12. The indefinite description, the fence-wall of the court, is more exactly defined by ver. 7 as the fence-wall of the eastern priestly court situated in the court, which corresponds to the before-mentioned wall of the northern priestly court. As that fence-wall, so this also is on the broad side of the priestly court, or set of priestly cells, the side from north to south, and indeed at the end of it toward the outer court; whereas the beginning of the priestly court lies on the enclosing wall of the inner court. The fence-wall has there an extent of fifty cubits. The priestly court lies on the breadth of this fence, that is, it extends to the same breadth with it—is, no less than the fence-wall which closes it on the east, fifty cubits broad. These fifty cubits begin at the south or north side of the gate to the inner court, but go beyond this side, as of the 100 cubits breadth of the inner court, twenty-five cubits go to the gate, so that for each of the two sides only

¹ We must read מִתַּחְתָּה. The vowels here belong to the wrong conjecture of the Masoretes, which removes the ה to the following word.

thirty-seven and a half remain. The priestly court lay in the face of the gizrah, that is, east of it, whereas the two other priestly courts lay north and south. That the site is determined by reference to the gizrah, with which the priestly court has no inner connection, is explained by the circumstance that the two other priestly courts north and south lie close by the gizrah. Hence the gizrah was the natural bearing in regard to the site of the priestly courts. With the determination of the relation of this court to the gizrah, was determined at the same time its relation to the other two priestly courts. The expression "in the face of" was the more suitable, because the view from the gizrah to this eastern priestly court, separated from it by 200 cubits, was prevented by nothing: on the free space, 100 cubits long by twenty broad, at the south side of the temple-building, followed the 100 cubits of the inner court, unbuilt upon; so that on the south side of the gizrah this eastern priestly court was the proper *point de vue* on which the eye rested. The "building" is here also the erection on the gizrah. The way before the chambers (ver. 11) is the passage between the fence-wall and the chambers on the east end of the eastern priestly court, which is here intentionally mentioned, because this way was only presupposed in the northern priestly court. This way was "as the look of the chambers in the north," looked as the way in these, or as these looked in regard to the way. No less had also the priestly court in the east a similar appearance with those. "As their length, so their breadth:" it was like that in the north, 100 cubits long from east to west, and fifty cubits broad from south to north. Even so were they of like appearance, of like nature: "after their fashions and their doors;" that is, their fashions in general, and especially their doors. These are specially mentioned in connection with the following, where in the south priestly court, in regard to the doors, a supplement to the former description of the priestly court is to be given; even as in the east priestly court the description receives a completeness by the express mention of the way. In ver. 12 the south priestly court, which is separated by the gizrah 100 cubits broad from the north, and with the latter encloses the gizrah in the middle. That the doors of this south court agree with those of the east and the north, only particularizes the idea of the agreement in all arrangements. But the doors are specially brought out, in order to introduce a supplement which concerns a particular door. In ver. 9 was wanting the distinct statement, that the fence-wall, which went along the west end of the priestly court, had a door. The way is here, as is afterwards expressly affirmed, the way on the outside of the fence-wall. At the end of this way was a door. The words, "The way before the fence-wall was convenient toward the east, in entering them," agree in substance with the close of ver. 9. The word convenient shows that the access in the east was serviceable, as the east side of the south priestly court lay next the temple, in which the priests had to perform their function.

In vers. 13, 14, the design of the three priestly courts is stated to the prophet. Ver. 13. And he said to me, The chambers of the north, the chambers of the south, which are in face of the gizrah,[1] these are the holy chambers, where the priests who approach the LORD shall eat the most holy things: there shall they lay the most holy things, and the meat-offering, and the sin-offering, and the guilt-offering; for the place is holy. 14. When they, the priests, come in, they shall not go out of the holy place into the outer court, and shall there lay their garments wherein they minister; for they are holy: they shall put on other garments, and approach to that which belongs to the people.

According to ver. 13, the priests' portions of the offerings are to be taken to the priestly courts, that they may there be prepared in the priests' kitchens, to be afterwards mentioned, and then consumed. The most holy is the genus: meat-offerings, etc., are the several species. Only the meat-offerings, the sin and the guilt offerings, are mentioned, not the slain or peace offering, because only in the former were the portions falling to the priests most holy, and as such to be consumed by the priests

[1] Luther puts two instead of the three chambers, "and the chambers toward the south, toward the temple," misled by the want of the conjunction, which, however, occurs in the second priestly court, and so several times in ver. 17 f. The brevity of the expression, which meets us so often in the topographical sections of Ezekiel—for ex. even in this, that in ver. 16 f., רוח, wind, stands simply for the quarter whence the wind comes—should the less have given rise to misunderstandings here, as the local designation is taken word for word from ver. 10.

alone, in their official function; whereas in the peace-offerings the priestly portion was consumed by the priests with their whole family, including even the females (Lev. x. 14). Bähr (*Symbolism of the Mosaic Worship*, ii. p. 372) says of the sin-offering: "It was a proper priestly eating: rejoicing and festivity were altogether wanting. The priests appear therein as priests, that is, in their office, in their proper dignity." Of the meat-offering, Kurtz (*The Old Testament Sacrificial Worship*) says: "The remainder of the meat-offering, after removing the azkarah, fell in all its forms (Lev. ii. 3, 10), as most holy, to Aaron and his sons, who are to consume it in a holy place" (Lev. vi. 9, 10, 12, 13). The reference even to this passage of the law, shows that we must render "the holy chambers," not the chambers of the sanctuary. The holy chambers here correspond to the holy place there. In ver. 14, the second design of the chambers, as places of undressing for the priests. These, when they come from the discharge of their duty (not when they go into the sanctuary to minister), shall not at once go out of the sanctuary, the inner room, into the outer court, and there mingle among the people, but shall first in these chambers—which, though situate in the outer court, are to be regarded as an appendage to the inner—put off their official garments, and deposit them there, because they are holy: they shall then put on their usual garments, and in them enter into intercourse with the people.

In vers. 15-20, after the description of the several parts of the sanctuary, and the statement of their measures, the measurements of the whole are given. Ver. 15. And when he had finished the measures of the inner house, he brought me forth by the gate, whose face is toward the east, and measured it (the house) round about. 16. He measured the east side with the measuring-reed, five hundred cubits in reeds, with the measuring-reed around. 17. He measured the north side, five hundred in reeds, with the measuring-reed around. 18. He measured the south side, five hundred in reeds, with the measuring-reed. 19. He turned to the west side; he measured five hundred in reeds with the measuring-reed. 20. On the four sides he measured it; it had a wall round about, the length five hundred, and the breadth five hundred, to separate between the holy and the profane.

The inner house in ver. 15 is the whole sanctuary, including the outer court in its inner side. The work, whose completion is here announced, had in ch. xl. 5, 6, begun with this, that the angel had gone from the wall outside around the house into the east gate of the outer court. To obtain the measurements of the whole, the angel was obliged to leave the inner house, and betake himself to the outside of the wall. For this wall itself belongs to the circumference of that which was to be measured. The total measure could not be taken in the interior of the house, because the walls were not accessible throughout; on the contrary, they were interrupted by the gates and the chambers. "And measured it:" this can only refer to the house, the whole of the sacred building. That we have to abstract it from the adjective *inner*, lies clearly in the connection. In ver. 20, where "he measured it" recurs, there is added in explanation the wall round about. This "he measured it," according to which the measuring here refers to the same space with which the former was concerned, prepares a quite insurmountable hindrance to those who wish to refer the measuring to a space different from the house. The statement of the results of measurement begins with the east and ends with the west. It is thus independent of the way which the angel took. If the prophet had followed him, the order would have been east, north, west, south. But the prophet wished to set the south side opposite the corresponding north side. On the east side it is expressly said that there are five hundred *cubits*.[1] Then on the remaining sides the mere number suffices. It is then added, still in harmony with ch. xl. 5, how the measure was obtained not by cubits, but by reed, with the already described reed containing six cubits. The measures here, on all sides 500 cubits, agree exactly with the earlier

[1] אֵמוֹת is a blending of אַמּוֹת and מֵאוֹת. The vowels belong to the Masoretic conjecture מֵאוֹת. Yet we are to conceive the word as thus originally vocalized. The א belongs to the אַמָּה, but in the vowel the second word comes to its rights. The incorrect view of this word—the impossible assumption, supported by no tenable parallel, that it stands at once for a hundred—is the common starting-point of the different erroneous assumptions in our section. The one party wish to efface the reeds altogether, the mention of which would indeed be inadmissible, if the mention of cubits excluding all doubt had not gone before. The others rightly declare the setting aside of the cubits to be purely arbitrary, but then

details. If we measure from east to west, we have 50 cubits the length of the outer east gate, 50 cubits the length of the inner, 100 cubits the length of the outer court between both (xl. 23), then 100 cubits the length of the inner court, 100 cubits of the temple, and 100 cubits of the gizrah. If we reckon from north to south, we have again 50 cubits of the outer north gate, and 50 of the inner; 100 cubits between, 100 cubits the breadth of the inner court, 50 cubits of the inner south gate, and 50 of the outer, and 100 between. The exact correspondence of the total here with the several measurements of the house formerly given, leaves no doubt that the measurements of the house are here given, and not of a space different from it. We must also, according to the whole procedure of Ezekiel in this topographical section, antecedently expect that he will give a general summary of the space relations of the sanctuary, and not leave the reader to arrive at them by summing up the separate statements. Such a general summary we should here miss. On the contrary, we should be surprised with the measurements of a space which wants alike all definition and all occupation, which would be nothing but a bare space; " nothing but space," as the Hungarian said when he was introduced to a bad prospect. A bare space of five hundred reeds on each of the four sides, designed to separate between the holy and the profane, without having the character of holiness impressed upon it, would indeed be intolerable. We can the less imagine this, because in the temple of Solomon, the form of which is perpetually before the prophet's eyes, there is nothing corresponding to this. On the other hand, the department of the holy terminates with the enclosing wall of the court, because farther the measures elsewhere confine themselves to very modest limits, but here at

labour in vain to show that the space in question had actually five hundred reeds on each side. Hävernick, against evidence, wishes to force such a compass on the sanctuary itself. With Kliefoth, on the other hand, the measurement is to be applied to an empty space on all sides of the enclosing wall of the court. Besides that which we shall remark in the text against this view, it is fairly urged that all the greater measures in Ezekiel elsewhere are given in cubits, and not in reeds. Besides, the Hebrews were fond of such abbreviations; they occur especially in proper names—1 Sam. i. 20 (Ewald, *Gr.* pp. 767-74). We have a quite analogous case in ch. xliii. 13.

once they pass into the region of the enormous; because a glaring contradiction arises between the narrowness of the important space and the broadness of the unimportant; finally, because, according to the express statement of ch. xlii. 20, the region of the profane began immediately beyond the enclosing wall of the sanctuary. The words in ver. 20, "to separate between the holy and the profane," state the object which the wall just measured served; comp. xlii. 20.

In ch. xliii. 1–9, the entrance of the Lord into the completed temple. We have here the parallel to the description of the entrance of the Lord into the tabernacle in Ex. xl. 34 f., and into the temple of Solomon, 1 Kings viii. 10, 11, and the counterpart to ch. xi., where the Lord in the face of the Chaldean catastrophe leaves the temple, and indeed by the very gate by which He here again makes His entrance. The peculiarities by which this appearance of the Lord is to be distinguished from all others, have been only dwelt upon by the expositors, who wish to limit the temple of Ezekiel to the Messianic times, or even to the final completion of the Messianic salvation. The prophet himself describes in ver. 3 this appearance of God as essentially similar to the former one which he had himself seen. On the assertion that the glory of the Lord, when entering the temple of Solomon, appears in a veil of cloud, while here it beams forth in clear light, it is to be remarked that the cloud in 1 Kings viii. 10, 11 is also to be regarded as shining ($\nu\epsilon\phi\epsilon\lambda\eta$ $\phi\omega\tau\epsilon\iota\nu\eta$, Matt. xvii. 5): it conceals in itself the brightness of flaming fire (Ex. xl. 38; Isa. iv. 5). All that is here related is implied in this, that the glory of the Lord appeared; nothing serves to set off this appearance against the others. The Lord is again present in His mercy and grace. "They shall see eye to eye when the Lord returns to Zion" (Isa. lii. 8): this is that which must have been said to comfort the minds that were vexed with the thought, Where is now thy God? We have nothing which surpasses the divine appearance in Ps. l. or in Isa. vi.; nothing which would not be a simple carrying out of the words, "The glory of the God of Israel came," and is included in them. If God appears, He can only present Himself in His glory, which is His eternal essence.

Ver. 1. And he brought me to the gate, the gate that looketh towards the east: 2. And, behold, the glory of the God of Israel came from the east; and his voice was like the voice of many waters: and the earth shone with his glory. 3. And it was as the sight of the appearance which I saw, as the appearance which I saw when I came to destroy the city: and sights like the appearance which I saw by the river Chebar;[1] and I fell upon my face. 4. And the glory of the Lord came to the house, by the way of the gate whose face was toward the east. 5. And the spirit took me up, and brought me to the inner court; and, behold, the glory of the Lord filled the house. 6. And I heard one speaking to me from the house; and a man stood by me. 7. And he said unto me, Son of man, the place of my throne, and the place of the soles of my feet, where I dwell in the midst of the children of Israel for ever, and the house of Israel shall no more defile my holy name, they and their kings, by their whoredom, and by the corpses of their kings in their high places. 8. When they set their threshold by my threshold, and their post by my post, and the wall (only) was between me and them, and they defiled my holy name by their abominations which they did: and I consumed them in my anger. 9. Now they shall put away their whoredom, and the corpses of their kings, from me, and I will dwell in the midst of them for ever.

To behold the entrance of the Lord, the prophet is brought (ver. 1) to the outer east gate of the temple, at which the angel, according to ch. xl. 5, had begun, in order to introduce him to the relations of the new temple. By the east gate the Lord behoved to enter, because it was the chief gate: from the east also He behoved to come as the rising Sun of righteousness, under whose wings His people should have salvation (Mal. iii. 20), the day-spring from on high (Luke i. 78). It is first said, "He brought me to the gate," the gate merely, the chief gate; then this gate is more exactly defined. The voice of God was (ver. 2) like the voice of many waters. In ch. i. 24 the voice of the wings of the cherubim is compared with the voice of many waters. The relation of our passage to this is

[1] Luther, "And it was like the vision which I had seen at the water of Chebar, whither I came, that the city might be destroyed." He combines into one the two former visions with which Ezekiel compares this.

clear to us from Ps. xciii. 3, 4: " The floods lift up, O Lord, the floods lift up their voice; the floods lift up their roar. The Lord on high is mightier than the voices of many waters, than the mighty waves of the sea." The creature has its voice only from the Creator, and therefore must His voice sound above its voice, loud though it be. What is here said of Jehovah is in Dan. x. 6, " And the voice of his words like the voice of a tumult," said of Michael, the uncreated angel and revealer of God; in Rev. i. 15, " And His voice as the sound of many waters," of Christ, the brightness of His Father's glory. How the prophet had occasion to hear the voice of the God of Israel, we learn from ch. i. 25, " There was a voice from the vault," which gave command to the cherubim. Here also the voice determines the direction which the procession is to take. With the words, " The earth shone with His glory," is to be compared Ps. l. 2, " Out of Zion, the perfect in beauty, God shineth," and also Deut. xxxiii. 2. He who said, " Let there be light," shines forth when He appears in the clearest light, as He who dwells in inaccessible light (1 Tim. vi. 16), the Father of lights (Jas. i. 17). As here of Jehovah, so it is said in Rev. xviii. 1 of Christ, " And the earth was lightened with His glory." In ver. 3 the prophet describes this appearance as corresponding to that which was imparted to him before, when the destruction of the city was to be foreshadowed, in ch. x., and still earlier, at the Chebar in ch. i., which first appearance was already in ch. x. 20 compared with that later one. The comparison naturally refers only to that which belongs in that first appearance to the unchangeable essence of God, not to that which bears specially on the then existing relations to the work of wrath, which was then to be executed on the corrupt people (comp. App. p. 537); as indeed in the recurrence of the description of the cherubim in the Apocalypse all is set aside which refers to anger and destruction. This would here, as there, produce an utterly confusing impression, because the appearance is a gracious one. Instead of " When I came to destroy the city," we might expect " When He came." But the prophet speaks thus on good grounds; for the Lord came not first of all in outward reality, but in the spirit of the prophet, in visions of which he was the bearer. Parallel is Jer. i. 10, where the prophet is sent to destroy and to throw down, and to build and to plant; because the ideal world is contemplated in which he moves, and in which is foreshadowed what is afterwards to come into reality. So long as the matter is confined to the region of the internal, there is an interchange of the prophet, and of God who works in him, which meets us already in Gen. xlix. 7, where Jacob says of Simeon and Levi, "I will divide them in Jacob, and scatter them in Israel." The prophet here, no less than in ch. i. 28, falls down on his face, there before the majesty of the angry God, here before that of God appearing in His grace; comp. Rev. i. 17. At the east gate the prophet had seen the entrance of the Lord. When the Lord entered into the house, the prophet is brought so near to Him, that this is possible from his position. He is removed to the inner court, which was accessible to him as priest (ver. 5), and beholds there through the opened door of the house which was filled with the brightness of the glory of the Lord. That we must render, "The spirit (not wind) lifted me up," appears from that which was remarked on ch. iii. 12; comp. xi. 1 and 24. The prophet might have made the short passage on foot, as he had already done in company with the angel. But the reason why the spirit lifts him up we learn from ver. 3. Overcome by the impression of the vision, he lies powerless on the ground. The prophet hears one who spoke to him from the house; and aroused by the voice, and looking toward it, he beholds a man standing by him. He stands in the inner court, as near to the vision to be observed as is requisite for verification, hard by the door of the sanctuary; and the man has entered the door to speak to him. What he said to him follows in ver. 7. Between the statement that one spake, and the speech which was made, stands the account concerning the person of the speaker, to which the prophet is first turned by the speech. The seeing was first occasioned by the hearing. The relations here only indicated are more fully unfolded in Rev. i. 10–13. There the prophet hears first behind him a voice as of a great trumpet. Looking after the voice, he beholds Christ. The speaker is designated as a man, and yet in ver. 7 he speaks as God, and applies to himself that which can belong only to Jehovah. We have thus without doubt the angel of God before us, the only one in whom the opposition of God and man is mediated and removed. The man here is no other than the man whose appearance was like brass in ch. xl. 3. The prophet intentionally perhaps does not expressly set forth the identity, because the reader should find it out by his own judgment. The angel of the Lord in ver. 7 designates the temple as His throne, and the place of His feet. The ark of the covenant, with which the presence of the Lord is elsewhere usually connected, is not here referred to. It perished in the Chaldean destruction; and that it was not to be restored after this downfall, Jeremiah had already announced before it was accomplished (ch. iii. 16). A more essential loss was not therewith connected. It was a mere symbol of the presence of God, which was not inseparable from it. "For ever:" this might also have been said of the temple of Solomon, with the same right with which in Ex. xxxii. 13 and elsewhere Canaan is promised to the Jews for a perpetual possession. Such promises are conditional, and terminate when the condition ceases. They secure only that the blessing will never be withdrawn on the part of God. This condition is expressly made, for ex., in Deut. v. 29: "Oh that there were such a heart in them, that they would fear me, and keep my commandments: always then would it be well with them, and with their children for ever!" Isa. xlviii. 18: "Oh that thou hadst hearkened to my commandments! Then had thy peace been as the river, and thy righteousness as the waves of the sea." Even here there is a reference to this condition in the words, " And the house of Israel shall no more defile my holy name." These words certainly imply as much as the words of Christ (John x. 28), "No man shall pluck them out of my hand." They have essentially the force of a promise. They present before the children of Israel a help against themselves, whereby they may succeed in conquering the enemy, that makes the dwelling of God among them impossible. They go hand in hand with the promise elsewhere expressed of a new spirit and a heart of flesh (ch. xi. 19). But this is here clearly expressed, that if they go on as before, they will also come to an end " for ever." And it is the uniform doctrine of Scripture, that all internal helps from God are free from compulsion, that the not willing (Matt. xxiii. 37) is not thereby excluded, and that to this not willing there is in human nature, and especially in the character of the man Judah, a desperately strong inclination (Deut. xxix. 3, xxxi. 29). That the Roman destruction of the temple is not at variance with the term "for ever" here, is shown by John ii. 19, where Jesus declares the Jews to be the destroyers of the temple. That Jesus aimed at the preservation of the temple, is shown by the cleansing of the temple, undertaken by Him, according to John, in the beginning of His ministry, whereby He evinced His design to accomplish a salutary reformation. Only after this reformation was decidedly rejected, He effected at the end of His ministry a second cleansing of the temple, which is the symbolic announcement of its destruction: The reformation ye have refused, the *revolution* must come upon you. The sentence, "Behold, your house is left unto you desolate," immediately follows the exclamation, "How often would I have gathered thy children together," etc. Had they been gathered together, their house would not have been destroyed; it would have become "a house of prayer for all people" (Isa. lvi. 7). The words, "There shall not be left here one stone upon another that shall not be thrown down" (Matt. xxiv. 2), Jesus utters immediately before His passion, when the stiff-necked obstinacy of the people was fully revealed to Him. Had the Jews hearkened to Jesus and His disciples, had they not reduced them to silence, the stones of the temple would not have cried out (Luke xix. 40; comp. Hab. ii. 11). Only after they stopped the mouth of the true witnesses did the stone sermon sound forth. But while the abolition of the form was occasioned by the conduct of the mass of the people, who once more in the most culpable manner thrust from them their Creator, and despised the rock of their salvation (Deut. xxxii. 15), the elect, far from being robbed of the blessing due to them, found a glorious recompense for the loss of the temple in the church of Christ, which He Himself in John ii. 19 declared to be the legitimate continuation of the temple. It is cast as a reproach on the children of Israel, that they formerly defiled the holy name of God. This defilement coincides with the defilement of the sanctuary, reproved in ch. v. 11, xxiii. 28, by idolatry both within and without it. Whosoever placed these doleful forms, these miserable nothings, beside God, whosoever by an accommodation theology bridged over the gulf between the God of revelation and the gods of the world, insulted the sublime name of the God who revealed Himself by His deeds among His people. They have committed such impiety " by their whoredom, and by the corpses of their kings, their high places ; " that is, while they commit idolatry, whoredom in a spiritual sense, and transgress in the corpses of their kings and their high places. The enigmatical expression, " and by the corpses of their kings," which, in its connection with the preceding *whoredom* and the following *high places*, can only be referred to idolatry, points by its very mystery to the existence of a fundamental passage, which serves the purpose of a key. From the whole relation in which Ezekiel stands to the books of Moses, we must seek the passage first in these. And there is in fact such a passage in Lev. xxvi. 30, where we recover not merely the corpses, but also the high places : " And I will destroy your high places, and cut down your sun-pillars, and cast your corpses upon the corpses of your idols." In this expression, to which the prophet had already referred in ch. vi. 3, 4, the idols are figuratively designated as corpses, because they have no life and no power, as they are on like grounds called carcases by Jeremiah (ch. xvi. 18), and the dead by Isaiah (ch. viii. 19), " Shall one ask the dead for the living ? " The fundamental passage speaks of the corpses of the idols, this of the corpses of the kings. The kings here can only so far come into account as they have to do with the corpses, which were to be avoided, according to the law, as unclean and defiling. The ungodly kings, as Manasseh and Amon, were the proper patrons of idolatry. The high places, corresponding to the corpses, include in themselves the idols there worshipped, and forming their essence. The eighth verse [1] refers to the idols in connection with the corpses and the high places. In this we have to think not merely of the idolatry that was practised externally in the temple, where places of idolatry were erected in the outer court, in the immediate neighbourhood of the sanctuary, and wall to wall with it. Every form of idolatry which was practised in Israel was in fact a desecration of the temple, in which ideally it was performed ; comp. ch. v. 11 and ch. viii. " And I consumed them in my anger : " this points to Ex. xxxii. 10, where, in the first beginnings of the people, this consuming activity of God is immediately visible.

[1] The suffix in חתם refers to the kings, that in בםם to the idols.

In vers. 10–12 is stated to the prophet the point of view from which the revelation concerning the second temple is to be regarded—the purpose which it serves. It is to lead the people to repentance; and when this is accomplished, to give them comfort and warning.

Ver. 10. Thou son of man, show to the house of Israel the house, that they may be ashamed of their iniquities; and they shall measure the plan.[1] 11. And if they be ashamed of all that they have done, show them the form of the house, and its fashion,[2] and its out-goings, and its in-comings, and all its form, and all its ordinances, and all its form, and all its law: and write it in their sight, that they may keep all its form and all its ordinances, and do them. 12. This is the law of the house; On the top of the mountain all its border round about is most holy. Behold, this is the law of the house.

The announcement concerning the new temple is, according to ver. 10, to lead the house of Israel to " be ashamed of their iniquities" in the presence of the mercy of God, which will hereafter reveal itself to them, when they will be seized with a deeper shame on account of their former sins against this loving God, who, notwithstanding their sins, is not wearied of doing them good, and restores to them the pledge of His presence. Through the goodness of God they are led to repentance (Rom. ii. 4). When this fruit of repentance has been matured in them, and they have thus gained the authority in the house of the future, they "shall measure the plan," not as architects, but as Abraham went through the length and breadth of the promised land (Gen. xiii. 17), with the interest of the family in the house to be inhabited. Meditating, and loving, and thanking, they shall follow the measures announced in the preceding passage, and by this process receive a foretaste of that which is to be realized by them in no distant time (xi. 16), immediately after the lapse of the seventy years of Jeremiah, the half of which has already run. When they are brought to repentance,

---

[1] Luther, "And let them take a clean copy of it." תכנית is, according to ch. xxviii. 12, plan, model.

[2] תבונה is here, as in Job xxiii. 3, Neh. ii. 10 (comp. 1 Chron. xxii. 14, xxix. 3), derived from כון, and signifies arrangement, establishment. There is no proof of a תבונה derived from תבן. תבונה has thus nothing to do with תכנית.

the prophet (ver. 11) is to introduce them still further to the nature of the new building, which is the more important, as with the building relations there, quite otherwise than in ordinary buildings, precepts and laws go hand in hand; so that all here has a practical import, and implies what the apostle in 2 Tim. iii. 16 says in general of the holy Scripture. The high mountain, for ex., on which the house rests, proclaims "the hearts in the high places." The wall, which surrounds the whole (ch. xlii. 20), to separate between the holy and the profane, was the law presented in stone, " Ye shall be holy, for I am holy." In the guard-rooms of the gates is embodied the word, " Without are dogs, and adulterers, and murderers, and idolaters." The chambers for the people in the outer court preached, " Rejoice in the Lord alway," and, " Be ye thankful." The arrangements for the priests reminded of sin, and demanded that each should consecrate himself to God in the burnt-offering, present to Him always the thank-offering and the meat-offering of good works. The altar of incense proclaimed to all, " Pray without ceasing." The inner connection in which the architectural stands with the moral, is expressed by the words, " All its form,[1] and all its ordinances," and the emphatic repetition, " And all its form, and all its law." On account of this connection, this intertwining of the architectural and the moral in the last words of the verse, the former are also taken into the circle of that which is to be kept and to be done. Architectural arrangement and law do not lie parallel, but are only different sides of the same thing. The words " Write in their sight" are not to be referred to a draught traced by the prophet, but to this, that he shall not merely represent orally the description of the new temple, but also commit the same to writing. In ver. 12 is given the sum of the precepts indirectly contained in the building proportions of the temple, as it were the first and best of the commands expressed in the new building, of which, as even now, every church worthy of the name is to be a sermon in stone. The whole, as far as it is enclosed by the outer wall, is a holy of holies, or most holy. This was figured by the situation of the

---

[1] The vowels in צוּרָתוֹ belong in both cases to Masoretic conjecture, and also the vowels in תּוֹרֹתָו. We must read צֻוָּרָתָיו and תּוֹרֹתָיו.

whole. "On the top of the mountain," and also by the wall, which formed a sharp boundary between it and the profane world (ch. xlii. 20). The law here laid down has its import not in the future only. The new temple was already extant ideally; and all behoved, in view of it, to strive to be holy in all their conversation (1 Pet. i. 15), as we have to regard ourselves even now as citizens of the new Jerusalem, and in this character to walk. If they did not do this, their part would be taken away from the holy city. Quite perversely has a preference been here discovered of the new sanctuary above the old; and the sense has been thus defined: the holiness which formerly belonged only to the most holy place, is now to be transferred to the whole sanctuary, including the court. The same words might much rather be spoken of the tabernacle and the temple of Solomon. The most holy is most widely used of all that is eminently holy. It stands in general for a most holy place also in Num. xviii. 10. The question here is not concerning the relation of the parts of the sanctuary to one another (only where this is the case does the most holy stand in the stricter sense), but concerning the relation of the sanctuary to the surrounding world. The point of view is thoroughly practical. The sentence serves as the foundation for the confident expectation expressed in vers. 7-9, that the people will hereafter lay aside all unholy dispositions. The prophet has already said that within the house the old degrees of holiness shall continue. How could the most holy continue to subsist in a building, if degrees of holiness no longer existed?

In vers. 13-17, the measurements of the altar of burnt-offering. This was already mentioned by the way in ch. xl. 47; but on account of its pre-eminent importance, the prophet has reserved the proper description for this place, where it does not lose itself in the multiplicity of details. Of what import the altar is, appears from ver. 27, where the divine acceptance is made to depend on the service at the altar; further, from ch. ix. 2, where the ministers of the divine vengeance stand by the altar; as also in Amos ix. 1 the altar appears as the place where blessing and curse are earned. According to ch. iii. of the book of Ezra, the altar of burnt-offering was restored before all other things by those returned from the exile, because its existence was regarded as the condition of the success of the temple-building. The altar is decisive for the whole relation of the people to their God; but it was proper to give the description of the altar here only even for this reason, that the prescriptions concerning the service at the altar are properly connected with it. The description gives first the breadth, or thickness, of the outer wall of the altar (ver. 13), quite as the description of the sanctuary had begun with the wall and its thickness; then it turns, in vers. 14, 15, to the altitude; and lastly, in vers. 16, 17, is the statement of the breadth and length, which refers indeed only to the upper surface of the altar, but at the same time belongs to the whole, as it was equally broad and long from the ground up. If it had been otherwise, the measurements of the lower parts must also have been given.

Ver. 13. And these are the measures of the altar in cubits: The cubit is a cubit and a hand-breadth.; and the bosom was a cubit, and a cubit the breadth, and its border in its edge around a span; and this is the ridge of the altar. 14. And from the bosom of the ground to the lower closing, two cubits, and the breadth one cubit; and from the smaller closing to the greater closing, four cubits, and the breadth one cubit. 15. And the mountain of God four cubits; and from the ram-lion and upward, the four horns. 16. And the ram-lion twelve long by twelve broad, square in all its four sides. 17. And the closing fourteen long by fourteen broad in its four sides; and the border about it half a cubit, and its bosom a cubit around; and its (the altar's) steps towards the east.

In ver. 13, the statement regarding the length of the cubit is repeated from ch. xl. 5. We have in this verse the description of the bosom of the altar and its ridge, both of which denote only the same thing in different aspects. The inside of the altar, according to Ex. xx. 24, 25, should consist of earth or unhewn stone. Hence an enclosure was necessary to give support to the whole. This consisted, in the tabernacle and the temple of Solomon, of brass; and hence the altar received the name of the brazen altar. Now this enclosure is here called the bosom, because it embraced and grasped the heart. The bosom has its name in Hebrew from this grasping: it is properly grasp, and encloses the breast with the grasping arms.¹ This enclosure is called ridge, because it forms the outside, the periphery of the altar, as in ch. i. 18 the felloes of the wheels are called ridges. The bosom measures one cubit of the designated length, according to the old measure a cubit and a hand-breadth,² and measures it indeed in breadth; or the lining of the altar is throughout a cubit thick, which is afterwards repeated in the several parts, and from which the difference of the twelve cubits in ver. 16, and the fourteen cubits in ver. 17, is explained. The border or the rim at the end of this enclosure measures a span.³ This border recurs in ver. 17. Of the identity we cannot doubt, as, according to ver. 20, the altar had only one span, and indeed quite above, next the horns. Both passages, vers. 17 and 20, agree with the statement here, that the border was at the rim of the bosom, on its extreme end. The measure here also, a span, and in ver. 20 half a cubit, agree. For the span contains three hand-breadths, each of four fingers, excluding the thumb; and these are reckoned equal to half a cubit.⁴ As the statement "in the bosom" refers to the breadth, the statement "in the border" must go to the breadth, in accordance with which the half-cubit in ver. 17 is found among the statements that refer to length and breadth. Thus the rim stood not in the height, but extended in breadth half a cubit beyond the enclosure. In ver. 14, "the bosom of the ground" is the enclosure where it touches the ground. The earth denotes the ground also in ch. xli. 16, "from the ground to the windows," and ver. 20. "Closing:"⁵ this is the third designation for the wall of the altar, which held together the kernel of earth and stones, which is distinguished from the two others by this, that it specially denotes the external wall of the enclosure, which was two cubits thick, so that the bosom is its appurtenance (ver. 17); in another respect the whole, to which the closing belongs as a part. The

¹ The other explanations of the חיק are wrecked on ver. 17, where the חיק of the altar extends from bottom to top.
² The article points to this definite cubit.
³ אחד is treated as a noun, the one, the unity; a span of the unity stands for *one* span.
⁴ Comp. Gousset, *Lex. s. v.*
⁵ עזרה occurs of the court as the closing of the sanctuary, 2 Chron. iv. 9, vi. 13. If we assume that it is weakened from עצרה, it denotes the locking or closing. If it be referred to אזר (Cocc.), it denotes a girdle.

under closing is that part of the external wall which is lower in respect of that presently to be mentioned, as indeed the designations of the smaller and the greater refer to the relation of these parts to one another. The under or smaller closing, and likewise in the following the greater, is to be regarded in its totality, and in reference to its end. The breadth in the under and in the upper closing applies only to the several parts, what in ver. 13 was said of the thickness of the whole enclosure of the altar. That the first given measures in the under and the upper closing are measures of height, did not need to be expressly mentioned, because the statement of the breadth went before in ver. 13, and is here once more repeated; but no one could think of the length. In ver. 15 the height of the altar proper. This amounts to four cubits, which, with the six cubits of the substructure, make together ten cubits, in accordance with the height of Solomon's altar of burnt-offering in 2 Chron. iv. 1. Those who explain ver. 13 incorrectly adopt eleven cubits,—a number inconvenient in itself, of which it is sought to get rid in vain by forced assumptions. The substructure is not expressly named or described as such; but it appears as such from this, that here the proper altar is distinguished from the space mentioned in the foregoing. The whole altar bears the name of God's mountain, to indicate that, small though its external height may be, an important ideal height belongs to it, in harmony with ch. xl. 2, where the externally low temple mountain is, on account of its ideal height, represented as a very high mountain. The mountain of God is, in fact, God's most holy altar. The " ram-lion"[1] is different from the mountain of God. The upper surface of the altar is so called, because it consumes the rams, which here represent all offerings: directly in the consecration of the altar prescribed in the following section, rams are presented. Be-

[1] For the explanation of the ariel, we may refer to the passages in which the same word occurs in the sense "lion of God" (2 Sam. xxiii. 20; Isa. xxix. 1, 2), at all events as far as they show that the first part of the compound is to be taken in the sense of lion. We have here, without doubt, an imitation of that word before us. Against the assumption that the second part here, as there, signifies God, is the *Jod*, which, removed by the Masoretes on the ground of mere conjecture, points to איל, ram. The vowels here and in ver. 16, as always where a *Keri* is noted, belong directly to the marginal reading. It is possible, however, that the form

ginning from the surface of the altar, and rising above it, the four horns of the altar appear, which form as it were its head, and in which its significance culminated. It is designedly not stated how high they are, lest their measure should be added to that before given. The altar was to be ten cubits high, as that of Solomon, in which also, without doubt, the horns are not included.

After the height follow in vers. 16 and 17 the length and breadth. These are taken only at the surface in which the altar terminates. But the statements apply to the whole, which was equally long and broad, from the bottom to the top. In ver. 16 the measures of the proper sacrificial hearth are given, the altar surface without the enclosure. Here we have twelve cubits in length and breadth. In ver. 17 the length and breadth of the enclosing wall are given, and thus at the same time of the whole altar. Then we have fourteen cubits, inasmuch as on both sides of the length and the breadth, a cubit the thickness of the enclosure is added. The one cubit added to the bosom here, as in ver. 13, explains the difference of the measures here from those in ver. 16. In the mention of the border and the bosom here, the end of the description of the altar reverts to its beginning in ver. 13. Those who feel bound to understand by the border and the bosom here something else than in ver. 13, thereby show that they have formed a false conception of ver. 13. At the close is mentioned quite briefly the stair of the altar lying towards the east,[1] which from its height of ten cubits could not be wanting. This stair, which no doubt existed in the temple of Solomon, could only be brought into harmony with Ex. xx. 26 by a special arrangement of the stair itself, or of the priest's dress, which obviated the ground on which the Mosaic prohibition of the stair unnecessary for the law altar of the tabernacle is based.

originally sounded אַרְאֵיל, not אֲרִיאֵל. Then would the prophet have in view, as אֵל does not elsewhere occur of the ram, a double sense—lion of God, and ram-lion, the lion that consumes the rams for God. The designation is, at all events, a purely priestly one, and was probably borrowed by Ezekiel from the priestly terminology.

[1] פְּנוֹת is the infinitive, properly to turn toward, with omission of the preposition, for "if one turn."

In vers. 18-27, the consecration of the altar of burnt-offering. While the prophet enters into the details of this, he draws away the eye of the believer from the mournful circumstances of the present, and soothingly combats his despondent thoughts. This is the point from which we have to regard the description, which is still highly edifying for us, as it teaches us to hope where nothing is to be hoped, and to see the non-existent as if it already were. In a few years, that enters into external reality which the prophet here announces against all human probability, against sound reason, which declared to be foolish all hope of the restoration of the ruined sacred buildings. The endeavour to find traces which go beyond the Old Testament standpoint has here also not been fortunate. In a simple point of view, nothing occurs here which might not have occurred in consecrating the altar of burnt-offering under Joshua and Zerubbabel, although they could not have thought of arranging the details of the consecration according to our section, which aims at quite a different object. In all essentials we find agreement with that which is said in Lev. viii. of the consecration of the Mosaic altar of burnt-offering. We must never forget that the prophet wrote for the present. To be or not to be, that was the question which then occupied the mind in reference to the altar. The prophet wishes to uphold and comfort troubled souls, not to afford satisfaction to a sickly eschatological curiosity by detailed explanations concerning the future.

Ver. 18. And he said unto me, Son of man, thus saith the Lord Jehovah, These are the ordinances of the altar in the day when it is made, to offer a burnt-offering on it, and to sprinkle blood upon it. 19. And thou shalt give to the priests the Levites, who are of the seed of Zadok, who are near unto me, saith the Lord Jehovah, a bullock of the herd for a sin-offering. 20. And thou shalt take of its blood, and put upon its four horns, and on the four corners of the closing, and on the border around, and thou shalt cleanse and purge it. 21. And thou shalt take the bullock of the sin-offering, and he shall burn it in the appointed place of the house, without the sanctuary. 22. And on the second day thou shalt offer a kid of the goats without blemish for a sin-offering, and they shall cleanse the altar as they cleansed with the bullock. 23. When thou hast made an end of cleansing it, thou shalt offer a bullock of the herd without blemish, and a ram of the flock without blemish. 24. And thou shalt offer them before the LORD, and the priests shall cast salt upon them, and offer them for a burnt-offering unto the LORD. 25. Seven days shalt thou prepare every day a goat for a sin-offering; and they shall prepare a bullock of the herd and a ram of the flock without blemish. 26. Seven days shall they purge the altar, and purify it, and fill its hand. 27. And they shall complete the days; and it shall be on the eighth day and onward the priests shall make upon the altars your burnt-offerings and your peace-offerings; and I will accept you, saith the Lord Jehovah.

In ver. 18 the ordinances of the altar receive their definite form in that which immediately follows. Accordingly it is treated of the rite of consecration, by which the altar is prepared for its purpose as the place of sacrifice and propitiation. The direction of the address in ver. 19 to the prophet is a mere form, to give greater life to the recital, realize that which belongs to the future, and bring it home to the mind. The prophet represents those whom the matter concerns. "Thou shalt give" is, in fact, the same as "one shall give;" to which the prophet himself points, when in the sequel he exchanges for the address directed to himself the form, "One does this and that." The particulars concerning the priests of the line of Zadok belong to xliv. 15 f. The bull is the most prominent among the animals used for the sin-offering; hence the series of sin-offerings is opened with it. From the second to the seventh day the smaller he-goat appears in its place. We have here a *minus* in regard to the consecration of this altar in the tabernacle. In Ex. xxix. 36 the sin-offering of the bullock continues through the whole seven days. It is a question whether this deviation is significant—whether it is not a variation of things in themselves indifferent. The *minus* may perhaps be explained by this, that that arrangement was the first—the ground and root of the later one. Sin and sin-offering properly fall only into the human department, and in fact the sin-offering here also belongs only to this, and likewise the burnt-offering mentioned in the sequel. The altar does not come down from heaven: it is made (ver. 18)—prepared—by sinful man, and presented for acceptance to God by a sinful people. That the sin goes back to the altar, is shown, for ex., by Ex. xx. 22 and Lev. xvi. 16. The sin, as it were, removes to the altar. The object here, as usual in sin-offerings, is to make remembrance of sins (Heb. x. 3), and point to the necessity of divine sin-forgiving mercy. The erection of the altar was in itself a good work; but even in works good in themselves it is especially necessary to show that they can never please God without the blood of atonement—that they also need forgiveness. As the sin-offering, so the burnt-offering, has its proper reference to man. The people atoned for on the altar present themselves in the burnt-offering to God for new obedience. The blood of the sin-offering (ver. 20) is sprinkled on all the prominent parts above, on the altar, on the horns terminating its height, the border limiting its breadth, and the corners. The appointed place of the house (ver. 21) can only be an appurtenance or dependence of the house *outside*, as the addition "without the sanctuary" shows: house and sanctuary coincide; a diversity between them must have been definitely stated. To this lead also the fundamental passages—Lev. viii. 16, according to which, in the consecration of the sacrificial altar in the tabernacle, the bullock of the sin-offering was burned without the camp; and Lev. iv. 11, 12, where the flesh of the sin-offering is to be carried without the camp to a clean place—the same place to which the sacrificial ashes were taken (Lev. vi. 4). We have here no complete account of what was to be done with the sin-offering, which indeed, from the design of the prophet, cannot antecedently be expected: he wishes not to prescribe what was to be done—for this the law provided—but only by a few striking traits to prepare a ground for faith in the future of the people. The burning of the fat is unnoticed, which took place in the sin-offering at the consecration of the altar in the tabernacle (Lev. viii. 16), and in all other sin-offerings (Lev. iv. 10). Without the burning of the fat a sin-offering could not be thought of; it is precisely that which makes it an offering at all. That here it is said of the whole bullock that it shall be burned, cannot serve to prove that the prophet did not think of the burning of the fat, because in Lev. iv. 11, 12 the whole bullock is burnt, though, according to ver. 10, the fat had been offered on the altar. From the sin-offering the ordinance turns in ver. 23 to the burnt-offering.

We perceive from ver. 25 that this was to be presented on all the seven days of the consecration. Accordingly the words, "When thou hast made an end of cleansing it," are to be understood thus: on each of these two days and onwards, when thou hast presented the sin-offering, and therewith laid the necessary foundation, thou shalt offer burnt-offerings. Sin-offerings and burnt-offerings are inseparably connected. By the sin-offering is obtained the forgiveness of sins, that whosoever receives it may, by the burnt-offering, dedicate himself anew to God. But the prophet wished, before he spoke of the burnt-offering, to place fully before the eyes the material of the sin-offering. The salt which the priests (ver. 24) are to add to the burnt-offering points, in harmony with Lev. ii. 13, according to which no meat-offering was to be presented without salt, to the unsalted quality of human nature, which may not enter into relation with God. Ver. 25 receives from ver. 20 the supplement, that on the first of the seven days the sin-offering consists of a bullock. The words determine only the rule: every intelligent reader might add the exception. After the seven days' duration of the Mosaic solemnity forming the basis, and especially after the express declaration in ver. 26, that the whole ceremony lasted only seven days, the prophet certainly could not think that it would occur to any one that the seven days here were to be reckoned only from the second day in ver. 22. The filling of the hand in ver. 26 properly applies only to the conferring of office upon persons in whose hand is laid what they have forthwith to offer, and what they have to handle, but is here transferred to the altar, which henceforth enters, as it were, into office.

CHAP. XLIV.

In ch. xliv. the prophet turns from the holy places to the holy persons in the new order of things—from the temple to the priests, from the altar to those who attend the altar. He has here a twofold object. First, he wishes to draw away the view from the dreary present, the ruins of the priesthood, the priests without office or prospect of office, which now alone were exhibited to the eye. He presents, on the contrary, priests in office and honour before the eye, in whom the Mosaic ordinances are again in full exercise and authority, which in the natural view of things had become purposeless for all time. Secondly, he wishes to labour for the regeneration of the priesthood, the removal of the deep calamities into which the priesthood, involved in the apostasy of the people, had fallen in the period before the exile. The latter of these two objects meets us especially in vers. 1–16; the former in vers. 17–31. Yet the former section also serves this purpose. For the restoration of the priesthood is here the foundation and presupposition.

Vers. 1–5 are so far preparatory, as they exhibit the glory of the impending revelation of God, the immediate consequence of which is, first the restoration of the priesthood, and next its reformation. In the latter respect is to be compared Ps. xxiv., where, on the occasion of bringing in the ark, David expresses the high demands arising from the coming of the Lord of glory, the necessity to prepare worthily for His coming. Then also Isa. xl. 3–5, where the theme is handled: " Repent, for the kingdom of heaven is at hand." The glory of the coming Lord is exhibited in this, that the prophet finds the gate by which he entered shut (vers. 1–3), and that he sees the house filled with the glory of the Lord (ver. 4), which had been recorded in ch. xliii. 5, and to which new reference can here only be made, in so far as it affords the ground for that which immediately follows. Into the house of such a God access may only be permitted to the *worthy* (ver. 5), the old degeneracy of the priests with heathen hearts, of the Canaanites in the house of the Lord, must wholly cease in the new sanctuary (vers. 6–9); the unfaithful must be removed from office (vers. 10–14); only the faithful shall officiate in the new sanctuary (vers. 15, 16). The decisions of the law of God regarding the priesthood shall, in consequence of the new revelation of God, come again into living use: if He show Himself in His dignity, the dignity of His servants must also revive (vers. 17–31).

Ver. 1. And he brought me back to the outer gate of the sanctuary, that looketh toward the east; and it was shut. 2. And the LORD said unto me, This gate shall be shut;[1] it shall

---

[1] Luther, " shall remain locked." But it is here said what shall take place, if once the gate, here only foreshadowed, be made (ch. xliii. 18), and the Lord have made His entrance by it.

not be opened, and no man shall go through it, because the
LORD, the God of Israel, went through it, and it shall be shut.
3. As to the prince, the prince shall sit in it to eat food before
the LORD; from the porch of the gate he will come in, and
from it he will go out. 4. And he brought me through the
north gate before the house: and I looked, and behold the
glory of the LORD filled the house of the LORD: and I fell
upon my face. 5. And the LORD said unto me, Son of man,
set thy heart, and behold with thine eyes, and hear with thine
ears, all that I say unto thee, all the ordinances of the house
of the Lord, and all its law :[1] and set thy heart to the entrance
of the house, with all the outgoings of the sanctuary. 6. And
say to the rebellion, to the house of Israel, Thus saith the Lord
Jehovah, There is enough of all your abominations, O house
of Israel. 7. When ye brought sons of the outland, uncircumcised in heart and uncircumcised in flesh, to be in my
sanctuary, to profane it, even my house: when ye offered my
food, the fat and the blood, and they broke my covenant, for
all your abominations. 8. And ye have not kept the charge
of my holy things, and ye set keepers of my charge in my
sanctuary for you. 9. Thus saith the Lord Jehovah, No son
of the outland, uncircumcised in heart and uncircumcised in
flesh, shall come into my sanctuary, (say I) to every son of the
outland that is among the children of Israel. 10. But the
Levites who went far from me, when Israel went astray, who
went astray from me after their detestable things, they shall
take their iniquity on them. 11. And they shall be ministers
in my sanctuary, keepers at the doors of my house, and ministering to the house: they shall slay the burnt-offering and the
sacrifice for the people, and they shall stand before them to
minister to them. 12. Because they ministered to them before
their detestable idols, and became to the house of Israel a
stumbling-block of iniquity; therefore I lifted up my hand
upon them, saith the Lord Jehovah, and they shall take their
iniquity upon them. 13. And they shall not draw near me, to
be priests to me, and to draw near for all my holy things to the
most holy place; and they shall take on them their shame and

[1] Luther, "laws," according to the marginal reading, which is here
conformed to the foregoing חֻקָּה, without observing the difference between
them.

their abominations which they have done. 14. And I will make them keepers of the charge of the house, for all its service, and for all that is to be done in it.

The prophet was last found in the inner court for the consideration of the altar of burnt-offering (ch. xliii. 5): thence he is brought back (ver. 1) through the north or south gate, to the place where he had been in ch. xliii. 1, before the east gate. The object is no other than to see that the gate was shut. We are not to suppose that the prophet, in vers. 1 and 2, wishes to give a direction which is to be carried out in the new temple. This did not belong to his office; and in such things are found, along with the ideal, material causes which often decide the question. Here it depends simply and solely on the thought of the glory of the impending revelation of the Lord, which, in conformity with the nature of the vision, embodies itself in the door being shut through which the entrance had been made. It is also decisive against the realistic view, that the visible entrance of the glory of the Lord through the east gate belongs itself only to the vision, not to the reality. The thought is, that the Lord will again be among His people with His help and grace. This appears also from this, that the entrance forms the counterpart to the egress of the glory of the Lord at the Chaldean destruction, in ch. xi. If this egress did not take place visibly, the visibility in the entrance only belongs to the form of the contemplation. But if in the cause the visibility belong only to the region of the spirit, the consequence also will belong to the same. If the Lord did not actually enter by the east gate, this gate is not to be actually shut. The prophet himself is not slow to declare that he speaks in figure and enigma, to demand that we distinguish between form and matter. Ver. 3 forms no exception to what is said in ver. 2. For the prince comes, as is expressly said, from the porch to the gate, and goes back through the porch.[1]

[1] The assertion, that "the shut gate lay directly in the door of the porch adjacent to the outer court," is refuted even by our passage, according to which the porch, and a farther part of the gate-building, in which the king took his meal, lay out in the court, on this side of the shut gate. Our former investigation, according to which the gate lay directly at the end of the guard-rooms, is hereby confirmed. The inner threshold immediately adjoining the porch is specially fitted to be the place for the prince's meal.

He does not pass the gate-door, which was at the end of the guard-rooms, but comes from the outer court, into which he had entered by the north or south gate, and takes his seat in the east gate, on this side of the door which remains shut. The prophet here lets the agreeable state of the prince pass in splendour before the people, with which he will afterwards occupy himself more fully. The ceasing of the magistracy, of which only a feeble remnant was to be found in the exile, was a chief cause of trouble. The mention of it here must have been the more striking, as it was incidental. The prince is not announced, but his presence presupposed. The prince is here an ideal person, which enters into life in a multiplicity of historical appearances. It is quite intentional in the description of the new temple, to speak of the *prince* in general, and not of the king, that all these forms may be included. The prince finds his closing appearance in the Messiah, according to ch. xxxiv. 24, xxxvii. 25; but in the centuries which lay between him and the prophet, the prince appeared in various forms as well as in the kingly. First he appeared in the prefiguration of the last fulfilment, in the person of Zerubbabel, the descendant of David. The prophecy of Zechariah in ch. iv. 14 is related to this. The two sons of oil, who stand before the Lord of the whole earth, are the bearers of the priestly and kingly office, which the Lord maintains through centuries in His restored community, till both find their full truth in Christ. Along with the spiritual authority shall, according to this announcement, the civil also be the medium by which the Lord, as in the time before the exile, so in the time after it, impart His grace to His people. The sons of oil are there, as the prince here, ideal persons, who are represented at the time by Zerubbabel and Joshua. Then is to be compared also Zech. x. 4, " Out of him a corner, out of him a nail, out of him the battle-bow, out of him will go forth every ruler," where rulers and officers of themselves, and an independent military, are promised to the people,—an announcement which received its verification before Christ, especially in the times of the Maccabees. In Zech. xi., the sovereign power, the prince, is one of the three shepherds. The prefixed words, " As to the prince," fasten the attention on this remarkable person. To " eat food (not bread) before the Lord" refers to the partaking of the festivals, at the communion which was connected with the peace-offerings. The place here assigned to the prince for his sacrificial meal is not honourable in itself. The people kept these festivals in the court itself, in chambers built for the purpose. The gates cannot be in themselves more prominent than the court to which they admit: the *outer* east gate is here spoken of. The character of the place of honour, in connection with vers. 1 and 2, lies simply and solely in this, that by this gate the Lord entered; and to place the glory of the Lord who enters before the eyes, this is, in harmony with vers. 1 and 2, not less, nay, we say much more the object, than to indicate the high position of the prince. How glorious must the Lord be, when the prince cannot be more highly honoured than by a place in the gate by which He entered! It needs no further proof that men have without any ground sought, in eating before the Lord, a pre-eminence of the future prince over the former rulers. To eat before the Lord was common to all Israelites, as it is now common to all Christians (Luke xiii. 26).

That the prophet, in ver. 4, is brought through the outer and inner north gates into the immediate neighbourhood of the temple, appears not only from the phrase " before the house," but still more distinctly from ch. xliii. 5, to which our verse stands as the brief repetition to the fundamental passage: " And he brought me to the inner court, and behold the glory of the Lord filled the house." It is also quite natural that the prophet, if he was to behold the glory of the Lord, should be brought to the door of the sanctuary, where he had it immediately before him. "The Lord said unto me" (ver. 5): to this is to be added, from ch. xliii. 6, that the Lord spake to the prophet by His angel. The threefold demand for attention, which points back to the like demand by the man of brass in ch. xl. 4, has its ground in the glory of the Lord, just seen by the prophet. Who should not attend to that which such a God commanded? The entrance of the house, with all the outgoings of the sanctuary, is designated as the most direct object of the carefully to be observed "ordinances of the Lord's house." It is first to be settled who may go in and out of the house of the Lord, be present and have his being therein. As the house here can only be the house in the strict sense, the proper temple-building, this being the inference from ver. 4, according to which "the house" is filled with the glory of the Lord, those who are here referred to can only be the priests, the only persons who have access to the house. The question is, whether mere priestly descent is entitled to be present in the new sanctuary, or whether other qualifications are requisite? This question is answered in the following passage. The rebellion in ver. 6 is the house of Israel, as the embodied rebellion (comp. ch. ii. 8). "There is enough:" on this is to be compared 1 Pet. iv. 3.[1] The reproach in ver. 6 f. falls justly on the people, who should not have tolerated the degeneracy of heathenishly inclined priests, and indeed would not have tolerated them, had they not been themselves under the sway of a heathenish will. It is objected to them in ver. 7, that going beyond their own abominations, and as it were putting the crown upon them, they had proceeded to admit men of uncircumcised heart and flesh to the priesthood. This cannot refer to the externally uncircumcised, the heathen. The prophet himself declares in ver. 9, that he means not ordinary foreigners, but foreigners who are "among the children of Israel;" that is, Jewish heathen. The discourse here is not of the courts, but of the house and the sanctuary, the priestly places; indeed, the reproach refers still more definitely to this, that they have by such men presented to God His food, the fat and the blood; which cannot be said of the heathen in the ordinary sense. In ver. 8 also it is said, that they have entrusted to these men the ministry in the sanctuary. Not the slightest trace in the documents before the exiles implies that they had admitted actual heathens to the priesthood. Of decisive significance is the *but* in ver. 10, which is only explained if the Levites, who have there removed far from the Lord, are identical with the uncircumcised foreigners in ver. 9. In ver. 9 it was said that the delinquents shall not come into my sanctuary, that is, in fact, shall not discharge the priestly office; for the priests only had access to the sanctuary. In ver. 10 it is added: But they shall take their iniquity upon them. The thing stands thus. In the time of the apostasy, and of the giddy spirit poured out on the whole people, some of the

---

[1] Starck: *En novum templum instauro, jam novam vitam inchoate, en nova sacra doceo, nova corda præparate.*

priests also had taken part in idolatry—had indeed been leaders in it (ver. 12). They had thereby put themselves on a level with foreigners, as surely as the service of Jehovah is the proper Israelitish principle: the worldly wisdom, of which it is characteristic not to take its starting-point from Jehovah, appears in Proverbs as the stranger, the foreigner. They had also proved themselves to be uncircumcised in heart; for the essence of the circumcision of the heart, according to Deut. xxx. 6, consists in loving the Lord their God with all their heart and soul. But where circumcision of the heart fails, circumcision of the flesh also loses its import (Rom. ii. 25); for if that which remains is to be called circumcision, then it might be communicated even to a brute. It was from the beginning proper to circumcision not to be a mere corporeal quality. It had the import of a covenant seal; and this import it retained only so long as the state signified by the outward act was really present. Ishmael ceased to be circumcised in the flesh when he departed from communion with the house of Abraham, and ran wild. The Egyptian priests had externally that which was called circumcision; but the men of the Old Testament would never have acknowledged that they had circumcision. There is the less reason to carry out the realistic, more correctly the literal interpretation, by force in our section, inasmuch as in a whole series of other passages of the Old Testament rebellious Israelites are at once designated as heathen or uncircumcised. Isaiah, in ch. i. 10, addresses the princes of Israel as princes of Sodom, the people as the people of Gomorrah. Jeremiah, in ch. ix. 25, designates the rebellious Jews of his time as uncircumcised in heart. Zechariah proclaims, in ch. xiv. 21, "And in that day there shall be no more the Canaanite in the house of the Lord;" and thus presupposes that in his time Canaanites were in the house of the Lord; and in particular, a Canaanite was hidden under many a priestly gown. In the apocryphal history of Susanna, a worthless Jew is thus addressed: "Thou seed of Canaan, and not Juda." Ezekiel himself says, in ch. xvi. 3, to his degenerate people: "Thy descent and thy birth is of the land of the Canaanite: thy father the Amorite, and thy mother the Hittite." A parallel for the abridged comparison, which is found in our passage as in that, is presented in Ps. cxx., where those who hate peace are designated as Meshech and Kedar, the names of the wildest and most intractable nations. Similar forms of speech occur among ourselves. We call infidels Jews, heathens, Turks. In the ancient polemics, the designation of those who denied the faith by Mamelukes was endenizened. "To profane it, my house:" this is stronger than if it stood simply, to profane my house. The attention is fixed on this, what it is to profane *God's* house. The fat and the blood are the parts of the sacrifice which serve God as it were for food. How impious it is to set God's food before Him with defiled hands, that have been polluted with the "dirty!" (ver. 12.) "They broke my covenant:" these men broke the covenant of God, whom they were not ashamed to employ as priests, by this participation in idolatry (comp. Lev. xxvi. 15), according to which the covenant is broken by the transgression of the commandments, at whose head the prohibition of idolatry stands. The people themselves have ignominiously neglected the service in the sanctuary[1] (ver. 8), because they admitted to it as their representatives these men, the uncircumcised circumcision, heathenish Israelites. After the accusation follows, in ver. 9 f., the penal sentence. The godless priests shall lose their dignity, and be degraded to common Levites, the worst that can befall them; for they cannot go beyond the limits of the tribe. We are not to take the sentence in a judicial sense. The prophet is not appointed a judge over the priests. He wishes to awaken among the priests and the people a true abhorrence of the rebellious temper among the priests. In the spirit of Ezekiel, Nehemiah proceeds (ch. xiii. 28, 29) against a priest thus heathenishly inclined. "They shall take their iniquity on them" (ver. 10): this shows in general that they shall not go unpunished, as would be the case if they might officiate after as before in the sanctuary. In what follows, the punishment is more precisely stated. The whole context shows, that by Levites are here meant those who had hitherto been Levitical priests. Such are evidently spoken of as come into the sanctuary, offer the food of God, and do the service in the house. What follows is unintelligible if we think of the Levites in general. Levites cannot be degraded to the rank of Levites. In view of this degradation, the Levitical priests

---

[1] For שמר משמרת, comp. on ch. xl. 45.

are here by anticipation designated as Levites. The prophet, himself a priest, may not grant the honourable name of priest to these scandals of their order, as our lips will not permit us to call a rationalist a pastor. To " stand before them to minister to them :" this appears in Num. xvi. 9, in accordance with ver. 11 here, as the calling of the ordinary Levites. " Stumbling-block of iniquity" (ver. 12), for which Luther has " a scandal for sin." " For all my holy things" (ver. 13) : as for ex. the sacrifices. The reason why they may not enter is given in what is added, " to the most holy place," or the holy of holies. What is consecrated to the Lord of hosts is not merely holy, but most holy, and must therefore be withdrawn from men uncircumcised and unrenewed in heart. If they formerly served the Lord (ver. 8), for their unfaithfulness in this service they are now (ver. 14) degraded to be mere domestics, who do service outside of the house. The mere Levites might not enter even the holy place. The several acts enumerated in ver. 11 are only such as were performed in the courts. Menial servants with us also are not wont to enter into the inmost rooms. Mere sextons were made out of the bad priests, as were to be wished also of the bad pastors. That bad priests are of no use as Levites, the prophet knew ; but how shall he dispose of them ?

After the exclusion of the unworthy, follows in vers. 15, 16 the promise to the priests who remained true : they shall perform the priestly service in the new sanctuary; God rejects not the whole for the unworthiness of the part (Isa. lxv. 8). To this is subjoined, in vers. 17–31, a series of regulations regarding the priesthood in the new era. These are taken collectively from the Mosaic law. The attempt to point out new elements not yet exhibited there, must be regarded as a failure. There is no ground for a progress to deeper views of the priesthood in the New Testament, than those to be found elsewhere in the Old Testament; for ex. in Zech. vi. 13, where the Messiah appears as the true High Priest; Isa. lxvi. 21, according to which Levitical priests are to be taken from the heathen also ; Jer. xxxiii. 14–26, where the whole people of the Lord are invested with priestly dignity; and thus Ex. xix. 6 attains to its verification. Of these high things nothing is found here.

We remain quite on the ordinary priestly ground. The prospect of the New Testament relations remains completely closed. This must land those in helpless perplexity who ascribe a Messianic import to the whole prophecy of the new temple, or refer it altogether to the last time of the New Testament. But it will appear natural, if we reflect that it was the first problem of Ezekiel to announce the deliverance which the Lord was to accomplish in a brief period, according to the fundamental prophecy by Jeremiah of the seventy years of the Babylonish servitude. The recovery of that which was to human view for ever lost (our prophecy belongs to the reign of Nebuchadnezzar, the time of the power and bloom of the Chaldean monarchy), this it was which is primarily intended, which occupied all minds: the progress stood in a second line, with which the prophet occupies himself in ch. xlvii. How consolatory it must have been to the people, that the Mosaic regulations concerning the priesthood, which had apparently become antiquated, here once more enter into life! And in harmony with the announcement of the prophet, they actually entered again into life. They have been practised anew for half a millennium, and then, because the priesthood had again wholly degenerated, because the law must have been realized in it which Ezekiel had already proclaimed concerning the part then rebellious, they only perished as the seed-corn in the stalk, only perished to rise again in glory. How absurd it is to set aside this immediate fulfilment, which at the same time furnishes the security that God also in all later epochs will bring forth for His people life out of death, and by forced interpretations to introduce another thing, which could be neither intelligible nor edifying to the immediate hearers and readers! If we keep in view the object of the regulations here, we shall not expect them to be very complete. The only aim was by a few well-chosen strokes to bring out the thought of the restoration of the Mosaic priesthood in its customs and its rights. The rest is to be sought in Moses. Ezekiel is a prophet, not a lawgiver. His eye is not directed to the priests; he wishes only to uphold the desponding people, who in their officiating priests had lost the mediators of the grace of God.

Ver. 15. And the Levitical priests, the sons of Zadok who kept the charge of my sanctuary, when the sons of Israel went astray from me, they shall come near me to minister unto me, and shall stand before me to offer unto me fat and blood, saith the Lord Jehovah: 16. They shall come into my sanctuary, and they shall draw nigh to my table to minister unto me, and shall keep my charge. 17. And it shall be, when they enter the gates of the inner court, they shall put on linen garments; and wool shall not come upon them when they minister in the gates of the inner court, and in the house. 18. Bonnets of linen shall be on their heads, and breeches of linen shall be on their loins; they shall not gird themselves in sweat. 19. And when they go forth to the outer court, to the outer court to the people, they shall put off their garments wherein they minister, and lay them in the holy chambers, and put on other garments; and they shall not sanctify the people with their garments. 20. And their head they shall not shave, nor leave their locks to grow long; they shall poll their heads. 21. And no priest shall drink wine when they go into the inner court. 22. And they shall not take to them for wives a widow or a divorced woman; but they shall take maidens of the seed of the house of Israel, or a widow who is a priest's widow. 23. And they shall teach my people the difference between the holy and the profane, and make them discern between unclean and clean. 24. And in a strife they shall stand to judge according to my judgments, and shall judge him: and my laws and my statutes in all my festivals they shall keep; and they shall hallow my Sabbaths. 25. And to a dead man they shall not come to be defiled: but for father, and for mother, and for son, and for daughter, for brother, and for sister that hath no husband, they may defile themselves. 26. And after his cleansing, they shall count to him seven days. 27. And in the day of his coming into the sanctuary, to the inner court, to minister in the sanctuary, he shall offer his sin-offering, saith the Lord Jehovah. 28. And it shall be unto them an inheritance; I am their inheritance: and ye shall give them no possession in Israel; I am their possession. 29. The meat-offering, the sin-offering, and the guilt-offering, they shall eat them; and every devoted thing in Israel shall be theirs. 30. And the first of all the firstlings of all, and every oblation of all, out of all your oblations, shall be to the priests: and the first of your dough ye shall give to the priest, to bring down a blessing on thy house. 31. The priests shall not eat of carrion, or that which is torn, of fowl or beast.

In ver. 15 all is brought into confusion by the opinion that the prophet here assigns the priesthood in the new era to the sons of Zadok, exclusive of all who are not sons of Zadok. The truth is, all priests are sons of Zadok, even the unfaithful who were excluded in the foregoing passage. The priesthood is not here adjudged to the sons of Zadok in general, but to those of them who abode in the truth. These are in ch. xlviii. 11 described as "the sanctified of the sons of Zadok," the sanctified part of them as distinguished from the unsanctified. From the time of 1 Kings ii. 35, where Solomon, setting aside Abiathar, placed Zadok in the high-priesthood, all priests are sons of Zadok who survived in his posterity. The fatherhood is the primeval relation of authority, whence father and mother appear in the decalogue as the representatives of all superiors. Hence the name father is often employed in the Old Testament to designate the superior. The leading personages among the prophets bore the name of fathers; the subordinate, that of sons. The high priest appears as the father of the whole people in Isa. xliii. 27, in accordance with the names handed down even to the present day, *abbuna* among the Ethiopians, holy father, pope. Different from the sons of Zadok here and in ch. xl. 46, as a designation of the priests as a body, are the priests who are of the seed of Zadok in ch. xliii. 19, who officiate at the consecration of the altar of burnt-offering, where the heads of the high-priesthood are meant, the high priests, and those who stand next them who are of the high priest's kindred (Acts iv. 6).[1] That the apostasy here is limited only to a part of the priests, while the praise of fidelity is awarded to another and no inconsiderable part, shows that on ch. viii. 16 we rightly protested against the view that the twenty-five apostates there are the presidents of the twenty-four classes, with the high

---

[1] The assertion is incorrect, that in the whole vision of the new temple the high priest does not meet us. The opposite is shown by the fact that all priests are designated as sons of Zadok, who survives in his high-priestly descendants. Ch. xliii. 11 speaks of a special activity reserved for the house of the high priest. Prophecy is here in accordance with history. The high-priesthood of Zadok lasted centuries after the return from the exile till the time of the Maccabees.

priest at their head. The table of God is His altar; comp. what was remarked on ch. xli. 22 and ver. 7 here, where fat and blood, which were offered on the altar of burnt-offering, are designated as the food of God. The spiritual offering embodied in the outward offering is the spiritual nourishment, which the people are to present to their heavenly King. In vers. 17-19, first the raiment of the priests. This is to consist (vers. 17, 18) wholly of linen, not of wool, in accordance with Ex. xxviii. 42, Lev. vi. 3, xvi. 4. The reason is to be sought in cleanliness and the oriental sweat-producing climate. This appears distinctly in the words, "They shall not gird themselves in sweat," so that they fall into a sweat; which refer first indeed only to the girdle (it is said, gird themselves, comp. Lev. viii. 7, 13, xiii. 6, xvi. 4, not clothe themselves), but in fact apply also to the other pieces of raiment. The fundamental passage is Lev. xvi. 4, "A coat of linen he shall put on, and breeches of linen shall be upon his flesh, and with a linen girdle shall he be girded, and a mitre of linen he shall bind on." To the words there, "with a girdle of linen," correspond here, "not in sweat." The girdle of linen is that which does not produce sweat. "In the gates of the inner court" (ver. 17) means within it. The ministry at the altar of burnt-offering is intended; comp. xl. 46. Even in the Pentateuch, "in the gates" stands often of the space which is bounded by the gates. In ver. 19 the regulation that the priest's garments are to be only the official dress, and are to be laid aside as soon as his ministry is accomplished (Lev. vi. 3, 4), here forms the foundation. Where the change of garments is to take place, is not determined in the Mosaic law. From Solomon's time this took place no doubt in the priests' courts, which the prophet in the foregoing passage only sees revived. The reason why the priests, before they mingle with the people, are to put on other garments, is stated in the words, "And they shall not sanctify the people with their garments." In Lev. vi. 11, vi. 18, it is said, in reference to the portion of the meat-offering which was not consumed on the altar, "Every one that toucheth them is holy." "The same effect," Knobel remarks, "results from touching the sin-offering (ver. 20), the altar of burnt-offering, and the vessels of the tabernacle, which were also most holy" (Ex. xxx. 29). The priestly garments stand in quite the same relation with the holy vessels, so that here also the prophet gives nothing new. Only a holiness of the ceremonial law is here in question, that has nothing to do with holiness of heart and conversation, and was instituted to secure respect for the holy vessels, and for Him to whose services they were consecrated. This kind of holiness could not have clung to the ceremonially unclean persons who came into contact with it; it must have been separated from them. How this is to be done, has not been prescribed in the law, probably on the presumption that every one will keep himself from contact; and it is enough to pronounce the *noli me tangere*. The first thing is the presenting of a sin-offering, by which the guilt of the incautious approach to the holy thing was expiated. But if the priests in the holy garments had mingled in the throng of the courts, the guilt of profanation would have fallen upon themselves.

In ver. 20 it is arranged how the priests are to manage their hair: they are not to shave, according to a heathenish custom, already repudiated in Lev. xix. 27, xxi. 5, because this would be to find fault with the Creator, and reject the ornament bestowed by Him; and they are not to let the hair grow long, which is the sign of a wild, disorderly man, who leaves nature to its free course. The Nazarite might in consequence of a vow, undertaken for a time, let the hair grow long (Num. vi. 5), to signify his separation from the world;[1] but not the priests, whose duty it was to converse with the world, and adapt themselves to society, which even in Joseph's time was wont to go with the hair polled. This regulation is, in fact, contained in Neh. vi. 5. In the case of the Nazarite, *separation* is declared to be the reason for allowing the hair to grow. But the priest was not to be separate. In ver. 21 is the prohibition to drink wine before entering upon duty, taken from Lev. x. 9. The rules also concerning the marriage relations of the priests, in ver. 22, do not go beyond the Mosaic law. The ordinary priest in Lev. xxi. 5, no less than the high priest in vers. 13 and 14, is forbidden to marry any but a virgin. No restrictions are in this respect laid on the high priest which did not apply to other priests.[2] The permission here to marry a priest's

---

[1] *Religiosum quendam squalorem præ se tulit.*—LIGHTFOOT.
[2] This mistake could only be made by a false interpretation of the חללה,

widow is new. But this Ezekiel certainly did not fix of himself. It was a consequence drawn in current practice from the law. The priestly dignity of the deceased compensated, as it were, for the want of virginity. In vers. 23, 24, we have what the priests are to do. The vocation here assigned to them, to separate between the holy and the unholy, rests on Lev. x. 10 : comp. on xxii. 20, the share in the administration of justice which is assigned to the priests; on Deut. xvii. 8–12 and xxi. 5, according to which, in cases where the local court did not venture to decide, the right was granted to obtain the decision of the most esteemed priests as expositors of the law. The order of the festival and the Sabbath is maintained by the priests *doing* and *teaching*. In vers. 25-27, where directions are given how the priest is to act in cases of death, Lev. xxi. 1–3 is resumed. We have here the same six cases in which the priest is to take uncleanness on him. Those named are the nearest blood relations. The wife and her relatives are wanting here no less than there, where in ver. 4 by the correct interpretation they are expressly excluded; in which it is to be observed that the question is not about the feeling of the heart, but about bodily contact. The "cleansing" in ver. 21 begins with the beginning of the ceremony, lasting, according to Num. xix., seven days.[1] We have only one heptade of days, not two, as it would be if we put having been cleansed instead of cleansing. Seven days are the longest period which any uncleanness lasts. In vers. 28–30 we have the reward which the priest is to receive. The general proposition, that the Lord is the portion of the priests, that their sustenance is incumbent on Him, and is to be provided from that which is offered to the Lord, is taken from Num. xviii. 20, Deut. x. 9. That which is devoted (ver. 29) is awarded to the priests, on the ground of Lev. xxvii. 21, xxviii. 29 ; the offering of the firstlings of meal (ver. 30) was ordered in Num. xv. 20. It is indicated as an object of the gifts to the priests, and a motive to present them joyfully, " to bring down a blessing on thy house," in accordance with the decalogue, where the divine

---

forming the counterpart to the virgin, *perforata*, in Lev. xxi. 7, which includes under it the harlot, the divorced, and the widow.

[1] In Lev. xiv. 7 also טִהֲרָה is used of cleansing, as distinguished from having been cleansed.

blessing is made dependent on the honour to superiors, which is to be shown by a willing bestowment of all dues (Matt. xv. 4, 5). To the statement of the means of sustenance for the priests is appended, in ver. 31, the prohibition to eat of carrion, or that which is torn, according to Lev. xxii. 8.

CHAPTER XLV. 1–17.

From the sanctuary, with its ministers, the prophet turns to its immediate environs, for which the special occasion is that the Lord has declared in ch. xliv. 18 that He will be the possession of the priests. Of an investiture of the priests with lands ch. xliv. does not yet speak; we expect, therefore, that it will be mentioned in this, the next following section. This begins in vers. 1–4 with the ordinance, that in the approaching division of the land a portion, 25,000 cubits long and 10,000 cubits broad, shall be set apart as a heave-offering (oblation) to the Lord. The already described sanctuary of 500 cubits square shall form the middle of this; the remainder shall fall to the household of the Lord, the priests, who, as those "who are near the Lord," have by right their dwellings around Him. Along with the priests, the ministers of the house, the Levites, receive a portion of land of like extent (ver. 5). Then follows the district of the holy *city*, with the same length and a breadth of 5000 cubits; so that the whole first portion for priests, Levites, and city, is in breadth as in length 25,000 cubits. The whole of this ground is enclosed on both sides by the grounds assigned to the prince (ver. 7). The reason why he is to be provided with such a domain is stated in vers. 8, 9; the princes will then no more be tempted, as formerly, to seize a possession for themselves at the cost of their subjects. To the requirement to abolish this ancient interference with private rights, is annexed, in vers. 10–12, the admonition to enforce right in the new order of things, and to leave no room for lust. Then follows, in vers. 13–17, the requirement of the willing payment of a tax to the prince, whereby he and others are enabled to defray the costs of public worship.

The practical point of view in this section is twofold. First the prophet wishes to strengthen the faith of the people; and hence, in contrast with the dreary present, in which priests and Levites, city and civil authority are fallen, he paints before their eyes a future full of hope. Next he wishes to indicate the necessity of a moral reformation, to penetrate the mind with a zeal for the removal of old evils, and to awaken the sense of righteousness and free-will in offering. Self-interest and avarice, that have hitherto wrought so perniciously, shall no longer prevail among the people of the future, but rather righteousness (vers. 8-12), a spirit of willing sacrifice (vers. 13-17).

We should quite mistake the import of the section, if we sought to find in it special revelations concerning the relations of the future, and statutes which should then have the power of law. What appears to favour this is only colouring, the clothing of the thought with flesh and blood. The local determinations must be conceived in connection with those which afterwards occur in reference to the tribes. If we survey the whole, it is evident that the specifications are too mathematical, too much at variance with the relations of the ground and the number of persons to be sustained, to be intended as real. The seal of the utopian is intentionally impressed on them, that no one may entertain the idea that the prophet wishes to forestall the historical development, to which Moses had given the freest scope. The prophet cannot have meant the placing of the Levites in barracks to be real, because he would thereby contradict the Mosaic law, which distributes the Levites through all Israel. From the local specifications, light falls on the arrangements concerning the tax in ver. 13 f. to be paid to the prince. If we regard this as an actual prescription of law, the most surprising defects are found in it. How, for ex., could a statement of the way in which it applies to black cattle be wanting? We find not the smallest trace of these specifications of Ezekiel being adopted in the arrangement of the relations after the return from the exile. It is quite otherwise with the Mosaic law, which has been the determining power in the minutest details through all times.

Ver. 1. And when ye allot[1] the land for inheritance, ye

[1] Luther, "divide by lot." But casting the lot is not spoken of in what follows; indeed, it is excluded by that which the prophet says concerning the situation of the tribe-land. It is literally, when ye let fall (Ps. xvi. 6).

shall make an oblation to the LORD, holy from the land: the length five and twenty thousand, and the breadth ten thousand. It shall be holy in all its border round. 2. Of this shall be for the sanctuary five hundred (cubits) by five hundred square around; and fifty cubits a free space for it around. 3. And from this measure thou shalt measure a length of five and twenty thousand, and a breadth of ten thousand: and in it shall be the sanctuary, the holy of holies. 4. This holy portion of the land shall be for the priests, the ministers of the sanctuary, who are near to minister unto the LORD; and it shall be a place for their houses, and a holy place for the sanctuary. 5. And five and twenty thousand in length, and ten thousand in breadth, shall be to the Levites, the ministers of the house, to them for a possession twenty chambers. 6. And as a possession for the city ye shall give five thousand in breadth, and in length five and twenty thousand, by the holy oblation: it shall be for the whole house of Israel. 7. And for the prince on both sides of the holy oblation, and of the possession of the city, over against the holy oblation, and over against the possession of the city, from the west side westward, and from the east side eastward; and the length by one of the tribe shares shall be from the west border to the east border. 8. In the land shall it be to him for a possession in Israel: and my princes shall no more oppress my people; and the land shall they give to the house of Israel according to their tribes. 9. Thus saith the Lord Jehovah, It is enough for you, O princes of Judah: remove violence and rapine, and do judgment and justice, take away your expulsions from my people, saith the Lord Jehovah. 10. Ye shall have just balances, and a just ephah, and a just bath. 11. The ephah and the bath shall be of one measure, that the bath hold the tenth of the homer, and the ephah a tenth of the homer; the measure of it shall be after the homer. 12. And the shekel shall be twenty gerahs: twenty shekels, five and twenty shekels, fifteen shekels, shall be your maneh. 13. This is the oblation that ye shall make; a sixth of the ephah from a homer of wheat, and ye shall give a sixth of the ephah from a homer of barley. 14. And the statute of the oil, the bath (is for) the oil, is a tenth of the bath out of the kor, a homer of ten baths; for ten baths make a homer. 15. And one sheep out of the flock, from two hundred, out of the watered land of Israel, for the meat-offering, and for the burnt-offering, and for peace-offerings, to atone for them, saith the Lord Jehovah. 16. And all the people of the land shall give this oblation to the prince in Israel. 17. And upon the prince shall fall the burnt-offerings, and the meat-offering, and the drink-offering, in the feasts, and in the new moons, and in the Sabbaths, in all the solemnities of the house of Israel: he will make the sin-offering, and the meat-offering, and the burnt-offering, and the peace-offerings, to atone for the house of Israel.

The oblation (heave-offering) in ver. 1 is the part of the land which is heaved up to God, who dwells on high—is consecrated to Him. The oblation is here applied only to the priests' part, with the sanctuary in its midst. But in a wider sense it includes the portion of the Levites and the circuit of the city; even the portion of the prince might be reckoned to it, as he acts as the minister of God. The length is the extent from east to west, the breadth that from north to south. That the 25,000 and the 10,000 are cubits, and not reeds, is clear from this, that in ch. xl.–xlviii. throughout, all greater measures are reckoned by cubits, even in ch. xlii. 16 f.; and that in ver. 2 cubits are expressly named; and so *here* reeds must needs have been named, if the prophet wished them to be understood. The cubits expressly mentioned in ver. 2 apply also to the rest. The reason why they are only there expressly mentioned is, that the measure is there unexpectedly small, so that one might easily think of a larger scale. Besides, if we take the reed, we arrive at colossal magnitudes, which do not at all suit the otherwise very moderate statements in ch. xl.–xlviii., particularly the measurements of the new temple, which is only 500 cubits square. With perfect right Böttcher remarks: "If all the numbers were reeds, the holy oblation, for ex. ch. xlv. 1, must have been 150,000 cubits = 225,000 feet = 10 geographical (about 42 English) miles in length, and 60,000 cubits = 90,000 feet = 4 (17 Eng.) miles in breadth, and thus 40 (740 Eng.) square miles, almost a tenth of the whole land; the capital (xlviii. 16 f.) must have been four times 27,000 cubits = 108,000 cubits = 7 (30 Eng.) miles in circuit, more than seven times that of the later Jerusalem" (Joseph. *B. J.* v. 4, 3; *c. Ap.* i. 22) Such colossal proportions are the less suitable, because the limits of the land are, according to what follows, the old ones: the remark, "he finds the land of Palestine greater," finds no verification in him. Then, too, if we here take the reed as measure throughout, the inheritance lying west and east of the district already set apart would be so confined, that the object of the grant of land mentioned by the prophet would not be attained. There would remain for him only a very small strip on both sides, whereas we expect that his portion will be nearly equal to that of one of the tribes, and will suffer no material loss by the land previously set apart. By ch. xlvi. 16–18 it is presupposed that the domain of the prince is of considerable extent. The lot is also much too great for the priests and Levites, who are debarred from agriculture, if we take the reed as measure. What are the priests to do with a region of forty (740 Eng.) square miles? It is also important that, with such an extent of ground, the Levites, the ministers of the house, must have undertaken a formal journey every time they went to the house. The free space of 50 cubits round the sanctuary (ver. 2) shows very clearly that the 500 of the sanctuary are not reeds, but cubits. A free space of 50 cubits to a sanctuary of 500 reeds would be too small. And if we suppose that of the 500 reeds only 500 cubits were built upon, and the rest was vacant, the free space loses its meaning. It was obviously intended to be an interval between the house of God and the houses of the priests. That the measure of the whole heave-offering shall take its rise from the measures of the sanctuary (ver. 3), points to the central import of this, to the fact that the rest only exists on its account. The hallowed part of the land (ver. 4, comp. ver. 1) falls into a twofold division: the one for the priests, whose land is holy, because they are the ministers of the sanctuary; the other, the holy space for the sanctuary itself. After the priests, in ver. 5 follow the Levites. The salutary Mosaic ordinance, by which these are to be scattered through the whole land, the prophet cannot intend to abrogate. If he therefore here concentrates them all in one place near the sanctuary, this can only be the means of representing an idea, the exhibition of their relation to the sanctuary. The prophet nowhere speaks of the tithe to be paid to the Levites; yet it is presupposed, as without it the tribe would have no means of subsistence. Instead of the

Levitical cities arranged by Moses, appear here twenty chambers or courts, corresponding to the already mentioned priestly courts, barracks for the Levites, the inhabitants of which use the twentieth part of the land assigned to them as pasturage. The chambers or courts here include the land as an appurtenance. To the part of the priests and Levites is annexed in ver. 6 the possession of the city. This is to be distinguished from the city itself. The latter, according to ch. xlviii. 16, is square, the length being equal to the breadth, so that essentially it has the circuit which Josephus in the passages already quoted, and also Hecatæus Abderita, ascribe to the later Jerusalem. In ver. 7 the domain of the prince. This encloses on the east and west sides the holy oblation, by which the land of the priests and Levites is here designated, and the territory of the city, so that it takes into the midst and protects the two districts: it extends on both sides, east and west, as far as each of the tribe allotments. The prince obtains, as Jerome has remarked, as much as every tribe, with the exception of the square for the priests, Levites, and city. But in the portion of the princes, says Ch. B. Michaelis, lay the sanctuary, because it is the part of pious princes to make room for the church. In vers. 8, 9 it is stated why the prince in the new order of things is so richly endowed with lands. He is thus to be freed from the temptation to provide himself with land at the cost of his subjects. "My princes:" this shows clearly that under the ideal unity of the prince in Ezekiel a numerical plurality is included. Those who understand by the prince merely the Messiah, must here do violence to the text. The address in ver. 9 shows that representatives or descendants of the princes who formerly committed injustice, were also in exile. The political parties especially gave occasion for the "expulsions" or confiscations. But the history of Ahab's seizure of the vineyard shows that occasion was taken for these even without a cause. Already Samuel, in 1 Sam. viii. 14, points out that the king will take the best field and vineyard, and give them for pay to his servants. Righteousness shall in future govern the popular life: this is the thought in vers. 10-12. Ver. 10 only resumes Lev. xix. 35, 36, and Deut. xxv. 13-16,—regulations the frivolous violation of which had had a material part in the curse which fell upon the people. Moses had already given the motive for this command, "that thou mayest live long in the land which the Lord thy God giveth thee. For all that do these things, all that do wrong, are an abomination to the Lord thy God." The determinations in vers. 11, 12 are not designed to fix for ever the current weights and coins, but to show how exact men ought to be in measures and coins. Whosoever, for ex., takes one from the twenty gerahs of a shekel, either by clipping the coin or giving too little of the commodity, sins against God's ordinance. We have here thus only a particularizing of the general principle in ver. 10. What the ephah is for dry goods, the bath is for liquids. Both have the same content. The homer, which is common to dry goods and to liquids, affords the standard, of which both the ephah and the bath are a tenth. That the shekel contains twenty gerahs, is repeatedly stated in the Pentateuch (Ex. xxx. 13, etc.). The *maneh*, probably of external origin, which explains its rare and late occurrence, is stated at a threefold value, which coincides with its foreign origin: it had in the different countries whence it came a different valuation. The prophet places first, as the normal mina, that which contains twenty shekels: this corresponds to the twenty gerahs of the shekel. On this follows a mina which has five shekels more than the normal mina; and lastly, a mina which has five less. The prophet allows all three kinds of mina; but whosoever reckons, for ex., by a mina of fifteen shekels, must not diminish a shekel from it, either in money or in goods. The middle mina agrees with the Attic. This contains 100 drachmæ. But the shekel, according to Joseph. *Arch.* iii. 8, 2, contains four Attic drachmæ. Not "the shekel is equal to a didrachmon, a double drachma," but the half-shekel (Matt. xvii. 24). The stater there, the double of the didrachmon, corresponds to the shekel. There is no valid proof[1] for a Hebrew mina of 100 shekels, nor for one of fifty shekels. The oblation in vers. 13-17 is offered to God, and paid to His servant and plenipotentiary the prince, who has therewith to defray the cost of the public worship; though, as it appears, not that alone—for the amount is much too great for this purpose, and no barley was used in worship—but also the

---

[1] For מנים in 1 Kings x. 17 is to be read מאות, according to ver. 16 and 2 Chron. ix. 16.

other expenses for the general good, so that here we have the Old Testament foundation for Rom. xiii. 6, 7. Willingness to pay dues belongs still to the marks of a true church member. This is also the general doctrine, that the magistrate shall take first of all from the taxes levied the means for the proper observance of divine worship. In determining the amount of the tax, the prophet does not mean to trench upon the office of statesmen: what he states is only exemplification and outline. Of grain the sixtieth part shall be paid, of oil the hundredth, of sheep the two-hundredth: the oxen are not mentioned,—a proof that the determinations here have not the character of an actual regulation of taxes. The tax of wheat and barley is the same, with a difference only in the expression. The proper *sixthing* here—that is, taking a sixth part—occurred already in xxxix. 2. The kor in ver. 14 is only another name for the homer. The last is without doubt the native name. The kor, occurring only in books written in or after the exile, is transferred from the Aramaic. " Out of the watered land of Israel" (ver. 15): this points to Gen. xiii. 8, the only other place where watered land occurs. It stands then of the Jordan valley before the destruction of Sodom and Gomorrah. The reference is a significant one. Whosoever makes " pride and all fulness" (ch. xvi. 49) his watchword, whosoever shuns to give God His part of the blessing bestowed by Him, he is punished by the withdrawal of this blessing.

CHAPTER XLV. 18–XLVI. 15.

From the holy places and the holy persons, the prophet turns to the holy times and the holy acts. He directs his view to those who were grieved " for the festival" (Zeph. iii. 18), to the banished, who complained that " the ways of Zion lie waste, because none come to the feasts: all her gates are desolate, her priests sigh" (Lam. i. 4): " her adversaries look on her, and mock at her Sabbaths" (i. 7). " The Lord hath caused the feast and Sabbath to be forgotten in Zion" (ii. 6). He presents before their eyes the figure of the restored worship and the restored festival. He begins with the consecration of the house (ch. xlv. 18-20); then turns to the yearly festivals, of which the first and the last are made prominent (vers. 21-25); passes to the Sabbath and the new moon (ch. xlvi. 1-7); returns to the yearly festivals (vers. 9-11); states the manner of the free-will offering of the prince (ver. 12); and closes with the daily sacrifice (vers. 13-15). Restoration of the worship, removal of the intolerable void, which since its abolition pressed upon God-fearing minds: this is the thought which the prophet does not present naked, but paints before the eyes, to prepare a powerful counterpoise to the pain of the dreary present. We move here also quite on Old Testament ground; and the fulfilment of the rightly understood prophecy, in which the details are only means of representation, lies wholly in Ezra iii. The supposed contrast to the Mosaic law, in a series of particular determinations, does not in fact exist. The Mosaic ordinances concerning the number of victims are only to be regarded as general rules, from which under circumstances deviations are allowable; just as Solomon, in the building of the temple, was not deterred by the measurements of the sanctuary from adapting himself to the altered circumstances. The Mosaic law makes in the details concessions to poverty: instead of the paschal lamb, a kid might be taken; the poor lying-in woman might present (Lev. xii. 8), instead of the lamb and the dove, two turtle-doves; whosoever had no sheep for a guilt-offering, was accepted (Lev. v.) with two turtle-doves; and whosoever had not even these, with a little meal. So also, without doubt, in the public offering, were the people accepted according to that which they had, not according to that which they had not. In times of hard necessity, of deep poverty, a reduction of the victims and other services might take place. But still less was it forbidden on occasion to introduce a multiplication of the victims and other services, and thus give expression to the heart filled with thankfulness by a new and great benefit. The law says expressly and repeatedly, that it will set no limit to free and thankful love. In Num. vi. 21 it is said, " and besides what his hand affords"— what he may do of free-will. In the feast of Pentecost, according to Deut. xvi. 10, the feast is kept " according to the free-will offering of thy hand which thou givest;" as Knobel explains, according to that which thou mayest freely do after the blessing granted by Jehovah: comp. Lev. xxiii. 37, 38; Num. xxix. 30. But the deviations from the Mosaic law consist here almost always in increase and advance. This is shown in the most striking manner in the victims of the passover and in the meat-offering. In the daily sacrifice, this, in Num. xxviii. 5, amounts to a tenth of an ephah of flour, a fourth of a hin of oil; *here* to a sixth of an ephah and a third of a hin. On the Sabbath two-tenths of an ephah, in Num. xxviii. 9; *here* a whole ephah for every victim. On the new moon, by the law, three-tenths of an ephah to one bullock, two-tenths to one ram, and one to a lamb (Num. xxviii. 12); *here* a whole ephah to the bullock, and an ephah to the ram. In the passover by the law as in the new moon; *here* an ephah for the bullock, an ephah for the ram, and in the lambs the quantity is left to the free-will. The meat-offering signifies good works. Zeal in these, as the advance denotes, is to be mightily enhanced by the impending new exhibition of the grace of God. But a deviation from the law of Moses is here so much the less meant, as the prophet does not give legal prescriptions concerning that which it was the part of the prince and the people to determine; but as all details are for him only means of representation, his mission is confined to the impression which he is to make on minds assailed by despair; to which is only to be added, the aim to impress on them the thought: When salvation will have come, be ye abundantly thankful. Those who here wish to overleap the half millennium of the restored temple, and refer all to the times of the New Testament, or even to its millennial kingdom, unnaturally sever the announcement from the state of mind, the cares and anxieties of the first readers, and have ch. xi. 16 against them, according to which a restoration of the outward temple shall follow in a brief period. No less against them also is the analogy of the other prophets, who in great afflictions of the people first place before their eyes the lower deliverance, and then further direct their attention to the Messianic salvation, as the prophet does here in ch. xlvii. 1–12. Isaiah, for ex., in the Assyrian oppression, places first, in ch. x., deliverance from this before their eyes; then in ch. xi. lifts the view to the great Ruler of David's line, who makes an end of all the affliction of His people, and in whom they rule the world. But we move here quite on the ground of the Old Testament worship; and there is not the slightest indication that, by the sacrifice of bulls, lambs, and goats, other forms of worship are denoted. Though the details were only means of representation and colouring, yet such an intimation regarding the whole should not be wanting, if the announcement were to go to a time when, by the offered sacrifice of Christ, a total revolution in the worship was introduced. This is certainly correct: though the prophecy refers first to the restoration of the Old Testament worship, and in this respect has long found its fulfilment, and indeed a fulfilment that has long disappeared—the downfall was proclaimed by the word of Christ, "Behold, your house is left unto you desolate,"—yet at the same time it conceals in the details the kernel of a general truth, the imperishability of the worship in the community of God on earth, which is demonstrated, among other things, by this, that as the here predicted worship was overthrown by the Roman destruction, the worship of the Christian church rose again in glory.

Ver. 18. Thus saith the Lord Jehovah, In the first month, on the first of the month, thou shalt take a bullock of the herd without blemish, and cleanse the sanctuary. 19. And the priest shall take of the blood of the sin-offering, and put it upon the posts of the house, and upon the four corners of the enclosure of the altar, and upon the posts of the gate of the inner court. 20. And so shalt thou do on the seventh of the month for the erring man and for the simple, and ye shall atone for the house. 21. In the first month, on the fourteenth day of the month, ye shall have the passover, a feast of seven days: unleavened bread shall be eaten. 22. And on that day the prince shall offer for himself, and for all the people of the land, a bullock for a sin-offering. 23. And the seven days of the feast he shall offer for a burnt-offering to the LORD, seven bullocks and seven rams without blemish every day for the seven days; and for a sin-offering a kid of the goats daily. 24. And he shall offer for a meat-offering an ephah for a bullock, and an ephah for a ram, and a hin of oil for the ephah. 25. In the seventh month, on the fifteenth day of the month, in the feast, he shall do the like seven days, as the sin-offering, as the burnt-offering, and as the meat-offering, and as the oil.

Ch. xlvi. 1. Thus saith the Lord Jehovah, The gate of the inner court, that looketh toward the east, shall be shut the six days of work; and on the Sabbath-day it shall be opened, and on the day of the new moon it shall be opened. 2. And the prince shall enter the way of the porch of the gate without, and stand at the post of the gate; and the priests shall offer his burnt-offering and his peace-offering, and he shall worship at the threshold of the gate, and go out; and the gate shall not be shut until the evening. 3. And the people of the land shall worship at the door of this gate in the Sabbaths and in the new moons before the LORD. 4. And the burnt-offering that the prince shall offer unto the LORD on the Sabbath-day shall be six lambs without blemish, and a ram without blemish. 5. And the meat-offering an ephah for the ram, and for the lambs the meat-offering shall be the gift of his hand, and of oil a hin to the ephah. 6. And in the day of the new moon a bullock of the herd without blemish; and six lambs and a ram, they shall be without blemish. 7. And an ephah for the bullock, and an ephah for the ram, he shall offer for a meat-offering; and for the lambs what his hand affords, and of oil a hin to the ephah. 8. And when the prince enters, he shall enter the way of the porch of the gate, and by its way shall he go out. 9. And when the people of the land come before the LORD in the festivals, he that entereth the way of the north gate shall go out the way of the south gate, and he that entereth the way of the south gate shall go out the way of the north gate: he shall not return the way of the gate whereby he came in, but straight before him they shall go out. 10. And the prince shall go in among them when they go in; and when they go out they shall go out. 11. And in the feasts and in the solemnities the meat-offering shall be an ephah for the bullock, and an ephah for the ram; and for the lambs the gift of his hand, and of oil a hin for the ephah. 12. And when the prince shall offer a free gift, a burnt-offering or peace-offering, a free gift to the LORD, then one shall open to him the gate that looketh toward the east, and he shall offer his burnt-offering and his peace-offering as he offers on the Sabbath-day; and he shall go out, and one shall shut the gate after he goeth out. 13. And a lamb of the first year without blemish thou shalt offer for a burnt-offering in the day to the LORD: every morning thou shalt offer it. 14. And for a meat-offering thou shalt offer with it every morning the sixth of an ephah, and of oil the third part of a hin, to moisten the wheat flour, a meat-offering to the LORD, an ordinance of continual standing. 15. And they shall offer[1] the lamb, and the meat-offering, and the oil, every morning, for a continual burnt-offering.

First, in ch. xlv. 18-20, the consecration of the sanctuary. This corresponds to the consecration of the altar of burnt-offering in ch. xliii. 20; and after the analogy of this, we shall have to regard the solemnity as occurring only once, corresponding to the seven days' solemnity on the consecration of the temple of Solomon (2 Chron. vii. 8), and to the new consecration of the temple under Hezekiah by the offering of burnt-offerings (2 Chron. xxix. 18-30), but especially to the consecration of the tabernacle, which, according to Ex. xl., took place also on the first day of the first month. But even if it were treated of a yearly recurring solemnity, the institution of it would not be contrary to the law of Moses. That men did not think of seeing in the Mosaic festival ordinances an insurmountable barrier for all time, is shown, for ex., by 2 Chron. xxx. 23, and also by the feast of Purim, but particularly by the feast of dedication. It would only be inadmissible if the prophet himself wished to ordain such a festival, which was not at all in his power, and lay beyond the range of his vocation. But this cannot be intended. All details serve the one object, to express the assurance with which the prophet looked forward to the restoration of the Mosaic worship. The " post" and " the door" stand collectively. All the doors of the inner court are meant. The cleansing of the house took place after ver. 3. " For the erring man and for the simple:" he alone, the well-disposed in heart, but weak, easily tempted, is by the law (Num. xv. 27-31) made partaker of the forgiveness of sins effected by the sacrifice. Those who sin boldly and wantonly, who daringly break the covenant of God, are to be wholly disregarded: they stand beyond forgiveness, and belong not to Israel; they are souls who are cut off from their people. But even if we disregard these, the sanctuary is ever built by poor sinners, and presented by them to God: with its

[1] The reading of the text is the præt. with *Vau;* the marginal reading is the future. The vowels belong to the latter; and of an imperative there is no trace.

erection no merit is connected, but the building is only acceptable through the atonement.

After the consecration of the building, the chief and fundamental festival, the passover, is celebrated in it (vers. 21-24). In this festival the enhancing of the offerings appears quite prominent, which is explained by this, that the grace of redemption sealed by this festival was to receive so rich an accession by the events of the future. The law requires for each of the seven days two bullocks and one ram for the burnt-offering. Here we have, on the whole, forty-nine bullocks and forty-nine rams for it. The passover is called " a feast of the seven of days," because it lasted seven days every time it occurred.[1] That the prince must offer the bullock as a sin-offering, not merely for the people, but also for himself, shows quite clearly that we should understand by him neither exclusively nor immediately the Messiah. Princes in Israel between Ezekiel and Christ are presented to us among other things by the coins, which bear the superscription, " Simon the prince of Israel." It could not come into the mind of Ezekiel, with the end he had in view, to transcribe the whole Mosaic catalogue of festivals. If one and another revived, it is evident of itself that the others also revived. Hence in ver. 25 only the feast of tabernacles is mentioned along with the passover. That this forms the end of the Mosaic cycle of feasts, as the passover forms the beginning, shows at once that we are to understand all that lies between. Ch. xlvi. 11 decides for this still more definitely. A multiplicity of feasts and solemnities to be celebrated in the future is there mentioned. The distinction between the two indicates that there are solemnities which are not seasons of joy. This leads us to the continuance of the great day of atonement, on the supposed disappearance of which so far-reaching conclusions have been founded. The brevity also with which the feast of tabernacles is mentioned points back to the Mosaic law, from which is to be taken the regulation concerning the number of victims; only that here the meat-offering receives an increase (comp. xlvi. 11). The

---

[1] שבע stands in the original meaning of a heptade, in which it also occurs in Daniel, where it denotes a heptade of years. Other interpretations are refuted by the fundamental passage, Num. xxviii. 17, "The feast of seven days, unleavened bread shall be eaten."

similarity to the passover here intimated refers, as is expressly said, only to the kinds of offering, not to the number of the victims. Similarity of the latter in the passover and the feast of tabernacles would mar the individual physiognomy of both. "In the feast"—the feast which, according to the law, falls on the day named. Neither here nor elsewhere in Scripture is the feast of tabernacles designated merely as the feast. This was a distinction which applied only to the passover, as the root of all feasts.

On the yearly festivals follow, in ch. xlvi. 1–7, the weekly and monthly festivals. First, in vers. 1–3, the place where prince and people are to worship. The inner east gate of the temple, otherwise shut, shall be opened on the Sabbath and new moon. This rule does not interfere with ch. xliv. 1. There the *outer* gate is expressly named. This also here remains shut, as indeed ch. xlvii. 2 presupposes that it is shut once for all; otherwise it would have been opened for the prince. That the inner east gate is shut on ordinary days, we learn first from our passage. His sacrificial feast the prince eats, according to ch. xliv. 3, in the outer east gate, which remains shut from without. On the contrary, in making the offering, he is to advance to the end of the inner gate opening in the inner court upon the altar of burnt-offering. He enters the outer court by the north or south gate, and then passes through the open door of the inner east gate, to the threshold and post of it. He does not pass the porch, but remains on this side of it,[1] beyond the open gate, but close by it, on the threshold, which lies between the open gate and the porch (comp. xl. 7). The right here granted to the prince does not extend at all to the position of the kings before the exile. In the consecration of the temple, Solomon (2 Chron. vi. 13) stood on a scaffold *within* the inner court before the altar of burnt-offering (comp. 1 Kings viii. 22). A raised stand in the inner court for the king is mentioned elsewhere also (2 Kings xi. 14, xxiii. 3; 2 Chron. xxiii. 13). The matter in hand is not merely about "a subordination of the prince under God:" there is in regard to the worship a sharp line drawn between prince and priest, which does not at all permit us to understand the prince of Christ exclusively, or even primarily. In harmony with the limit here

[1] מחוץ is not from without, but without, beyond.

drawn is ch. xlv. 22, according to which the prince must offer a sin-offering for himself. Plainly incompatible with it is the assertion, resting on quite a loose ground, "The prophet assigns to him also priestly rights and functions." The *people* may not enter the inner gate; they worship at the opened door, through which they catch a glimpse of the altar of burnt-offering, which the prince—that is the only difference—sees better from a nearer point. In vers. 4, 5, the offering of the Sabbath. The increase of grace shows itself here also in the augmentation of the victims. In lambs we have here threefold (Num. xxviii. 9), and the ram is a new addition. The meat-offering also, with the ram, appears enhanced above the minimum appointed by the law. In the lambs, the amount of the meat-offering is left to the free-will of the prince, only that naturally it should not fall short of the determination of the law, which is a very small quantity. "The gift of his hand" here, and "what his hand affords" in ver. 7, show that, according to the view of the prophet, there is in the offerings a range of freedom along with the obligation, and cast light also on his apparent deviations from the Mosaic law. The number of bullocks at the new moon (ver. 6) is apparently left to the free judgment; only it should not fall short of the two required by the law[1] (Num. xxviii. 11). In vers. 8–11 the prophet returns to the yearly festivals. He states first how prince and people are to go in and out at the festivals. Ver. 8 is quite general: it applies not merely to the Sabbaths and new moons (comp. ver. 2), but also to the festivals: in these also the prince takes the place of honour before the porch of the inner gate. That which is peculiar to the festivals is contained only in ver. 10. There the prince, so far as the common ground, the outer court, extended, is not to separate himself from the people, but to come and go among them. This was formerly the manner of the pious princes in Israel, to walk in the festivals among the multitude keeping the holy day. David, in banishment, says in Ps. xlii. 5: "These things I remember, and pour out my soul

---

[1] That the unity of the bullock is ideal, while the word is used collectively, is shown by the plural תמימם. It appears unsuitable to explain this plural of the return of the festival; it is used in no other way than in the second half of the verse. A *minus* in relation to the Mosaic law is beforehand scarcely conceivable, and contrary to analogy.

in me: for I went in the crowd; I walked to the house of God, with the voice of joy and praise, in the multitude keeping the holy day." The reason of the regulation in ver. 9, that no one at the festival is to go out by the same gate by which he came in, cannot be sought in the endeavour to avoid a throng: in that case it must have ordained that all should go in by the same gate, and go out by the opposite one. The reason can only be a theological one, to signify that each should go out of the sanctuary another man than he came in; or what the apostle also says, Phil. iii. 13, "I forget that which is behind, and reach forth to that which is before." In ver. 11 the amount of the meat-offering and the oil, which in ch. xlv. 24 was specially required for the passover, is fixed as the general rate for all festivals. The distinction between feasts and solemnities here (the latter are the genus, the former the species) is illustrated by Lev. xxiii. 27 f. The regulation concerning the mode of presenting the free-will offering of the prince (ver. 12) is distinguished from that regarding the Sabbath offering in ver. 2 by this, that *here* the inner east gate is closed after the prince has made his offering, whereas there it remains open till the evening. The distinction is explained by this, that in the free-will offering the prince appears as an individual, in the Sabbath offering as the representative of the people. In vers. 13-15, the ordinance concerning the daily sacrifice. This is limited to the morning sacrifice, which suffices for the object of the prophet. The evening sacrifice is unnoticed. From the circumstance that here the people are addressed, whereas in the other offerings the prince appears as the offerer, it appears all the more to follow that the prince had not to provide the material for the daily sacrifice, while in ch. xlv. 17 the providing of the offering on the Sabbaths, new moons, and solemn feasts, is assigned to the prince alone. Yet the conclusion is not certain. The transition from the prince to the people is an easy one, as in the foregoing passage the prince represents the people. The section also in ch. xlv. 18-20 had begun with the address to the people, and there is scarcely a doubt that the close here corresponds to the beginning there: the prince is enclosed on both sides by the people. But in ch. xlv. 17 the daily sacrifice may be passed over, because, according to the material side there alone coming into account, it was relatively unimportant. The whole section is for us of transcendent importance, as it teaches us to live in the word, if the grace of God does not make itself known to us in the visible. What the prophet here announces appeared to the natural reason to be mere fancy; but of those to whom he addressed his words, not a few lived to see his announcement forcing its way into reality. They took part in the solemn sacrificial worship, in which the 116th Psalm was sung after the return from the exile. This begins with the words, "It is dear to me that the Lord heareth my voice and my supplication;" and ends thus, "I will offer to Thee the sacrifice of thanksgiving, and call upon the name of the Lord. I will pay my vows to the Lord before all His people: in the courts of the Lord's house, in the midst of thee, O Jerusalem. Hallelujah." "Thus saith the Lord Jehovah:" so begins the whole section with all right. The prophet announces in it that which flesh and blood had not revealed unto him, but the Father in heaven, who alone can teach to hope where there is nothing to hope. The formula refers not merely to the matter, but also to the form. The means of representation are such as were best adapted to bring home the truth to the people pining in exile, and impress it deeply on their minds.

CHAPTER XLVI. 16-24.

Before passing to an entirely new subject, the prophet gives some additions to the foregoing. The first of these additions is connected with ch. xlv. 7-9, where the prophet had presented to view the separation of an estate for the prince. The second, in vers. 19, 20, gives, in continuation of the description of the chambers of the priests in ch. xlii. 1 f., an account of the sacrificial kitchens for the priests, forming the termination of them toward the west. To this is then annexed, in vers. 21-24, an account of the sacrificial kitchens for the people. The practical point in the first of these additions is to warn against the recurrence of the former despotic spirit in the government. The second and third additions are intended to teach the people to rise from the visible to their God, who is so plenteous in redemption. The energy of the prophet's faith is shown in this, that he enters into the minutest architectural details of the temple of the future. As, moreover, the section concerning the princes takes its rise from the relations of the past, so the sacrificial kitchens of the future are doubtless portrayed with reference to that which the prophet had seen with the bodily eye in the past. Such apartments could not be wanting in the temple of Solomon. Where it belongs properly to the priestly calling to eat parts of the sacrifices, where the piety of laymen is to employ itself in the preparation of sacrificial feasts "before the Lord," there must have been cooking-places within the bounds of the sanctuary.

Ver. 16. Thus saith the Lord Jehovah, When the prince gives a gift to any of his sons, this shall be his inheritance to his sons: it shall be their possession by inheritance. 17. And if he give a gift of his inheritance to one of his servants, then it shall be his to the year of freedom, and it shall return to the prince; only his inheritance to his sons shall belong to them. 18. And the prince shall not take of the people's inheritance, to force them out of their possession: out of his own possession he shall endow his sons, that my people be not scattered every man from his possession. 19. And he brought me through the entry, which was at the side of the gate, to the holy chambers to the priests, that look toward the north: and, behold, there a place on their side westward. 20. And he said unto me, This is the place where the priests shall boil the guilt-offering and the sin-offering, where they shall bake the meat-offering, so as not to bring it forth to the outer court to sanctify the people. 21. And he brought me forth to the outer court, and led me to the four corners of the court; and, behold, a court in the corner of the court, and a court in the corner of the court. 22. In the four corners of the court were smoking courts forty long and thirty broad; one measure was to the four corner rooms. 23. And there was a range around in them around the four, and cooking-places were made under the ranges around. 24. And he said to me, These are the house of the cooks, where the ministers of the house boil the sacrifice of the people.

That we have in vers. 16–18 not an attempt of the prophet to set up for a lawgiver, but a clear representation of the thought that the princes of the future are to be no despots, are to beware of the unjust absolutism of those of the past, is manifest from that which we have already remarked concerning the purely ideal character of the partition of the land. The prince here cannot be Christ. He is one who may have several sons of his own body, who disposes of his property in the prospect of his death, who stands not beyond the region of sin, else he should not need to be warned against it. We have here, in fact, not two commands, but one concession,—namely, that the prince may bequeath of his own proper and hereditary lands to his later born sons; and one command,—namely, that he may not give away thereof to his servants, because he who gives much is forced to take from others their own. The danger against which the prophet here provides, Samuel has pointed out in 1 Sam. viii. 14. The regulation that the gifts of land to the prince's servants shall revert to him in the jubilee, points to Lev. xxv. 10, 13, where the jubilee is also called the year of freedom.

The "holy chambers" mentioned in ver. 19 are the chambers of the priests described in ch. xlii. 1 f. "To the priests:" this is added, because the chambers are regarded as a perquisite of the priests,—a usage for which many analogies are to be found in Catholic countries—"to the Carmelites," etc. The entry is that mentioned in ch. xlii. 9. It leads to the inner court gate west of the eastern gate of the fence-wall of the priestly cells. *There:* thus the kitchens are in the cell-building, not by or outside it. It formed, as we have already shown, the western part of it.[1] The priests must have their separate kitchens, lest, if they carry the food through the throng of the court, the people be sanctified: this is explained by the remarks on ch. xliv. 19.

The repetition of the words, "a court in the corner of the court," in ver. 21, points out that the same observation is repeated several times. Ver. 22 then says more definitely, that in each of the four corners of the court was such a kitchen for the people, which we must regard as an offshoot of the chambers of the people in the sides of the court. "Smoking courts" (ver. 22): the rising smoke is the characteristic mark of these

---

[1] The singular יְרֵכָתָם is to be read as in Gen. xlix. 13. The suff. refers, in fact, to the chambers, formally to the priests, including the chambers under them.

buildings.¹ Not without reason are the slain-offerings only mentioned in ver. 24, as distinguished from the sin and guilt offerings to be prepared in the kitchens of the priests. Only with the slain-offerings, such as are akin to common slaughtering, was a communion connected. The greatest part fell to the offerers, and was consumed in the sacrificial meals. But the sacrifice of the people might not be prepared by the people, but only by the Levites, who were designated in ch. xliv. 11 the ministers of the people.

CHAPTER XLVII. 1–12.

Here suddenly the view becomes wider and freer. It enters into the Messianic times. From the restored temple at length salvation goes forth for the whole world: this is the naked thought. We shall have to regard as the Mediator of this salvation the exalted descendant of David, who, according to ch. xvii. 23, grows from a feeble sapling to a glorious cedar under which all fowls dwell: to the fowls of every wing there, correspond here the fish of every kind (ver. 10). In harmony with our prophecy the salvation here announced took its beginning at the time of the second temple, and flowed thence, where Jesus had the chief seat of His activity (comp. on John vii. 3, 4), over the nations of the earth.

The relations of the New Testament to our section are very rich and manifold. In reference to it the Lord in Matt. iv. 18, 19 says to Peter and Andrew, "I will make you fishers of men." On it rests the miraculous draught of fishes by Peter at the beginning of the ministry of Jesus (Luke v.), and also the

---

¹ The verb קטר, with all its derivatives, has in Hebrew only the meaning, to exhale, steam, smoke; and to abandon this in favour of another far-fetched meaning there is the less occasion, where *kitchens* are in question. That the proper name Keturah, written as our word, means the fragrant, is admitted. The Talmud (*Middoth* ii. § 8) has rendered מהקצעות here *atria fumum exhalantia*, with which the Masoretes were perplexed, as the points over it show; and which is probably a kind of priestly proper name for those rooms, which Ezekiel here brings forward as a fond reminiscence. It is properly the part. *Hoph.*, and signifies not, as מקצע, corner, but cornered, a corner room.

² The name referring to the form is here intentionally used; formerly *Shelamim*, the name expressing the nature.

draught after the resurrection in John xxi. Jesus designedly embodies, at the commencement and the close, the contents of our prophecy in a symbolic act. No less allusive to our prophecy is the parable of the net, which gathered of every kind, in Matt. xiii. 47. Finally, in Rev. xxii. 1, 2 is announced the last and most glorious fulfilment of our prophecy. Our section is the only one in the whole cycle of ch. xl.-xlviii., the fulfilment of which is represented in the New Testament as belonging to the time of Christ. It should have set aside the old application of the whole prophecy concerning the new temple to the Christian church, that the New Testament affords no support for this interpretation. On this side of the Apocalypse the references are limited to ch. xlvii. 1-12; all the rest is ignored, which would be inconceivable if it referred to the times of the New Testament. But the new Jerusalem in the Apocalypse, far from establishing the interpretation of the whole prophecy by the Christian church, stands to the restored Jerusalem of Ezekiel in an antithetic relation. In Ezekiel all is earthly; there all is above the earthly. The measures are quite different. In Ezekiel the whole city has the moderate circuit of about a mile and a half (about 7 Eng.), which agrees with its extent after the exile. On the contrary, in Rev. xxi. 16 the city is 12,000 stadia long, broad, and high. It measures on every side 300 geographical miles (above 1200 Eng.). In the Apocalypse all is of gold, precious stones, and pearls, while here the most moderate relations are presented. The temple that forms here the absolute centre is wanting altogether in the Apocalypse.

It is not otherwise with the closing prophecy of Ezekiel than in the prophecy in the first book of Moses. There the announcement concerning the blessing coming upon all the families of the earth through Abraham, and of the Shiloh, to whom the people cleave (Gen. xlix. 10), only penetrates into the Messianic region. Irrespective of this, the prophetic announcement—as Gen. xii. 1-3, and particularly the blessing of Jacob in Gen. xlix., clearly show—refers to the deliverance of the nearer future, to the people springing from the descendants of the patriarchs, the release from the land of pilgrimage, the possession of Canaan. So, in Ezekiel, the lower but nearer deliverance preëminently draws his attention to itself, as indeed is the case in all other prophets; as, for ex., Habakkuk opposes to the Chaldean catastrophe first the release from the Chaldean bondage. Such a course is evidently wise and natural. The plain, obvious matter of fact could only be mistaken in a time when the mind was not alive to historical apprehension. It is an anachronism to attempt to revive such an interpretation. We certainly need not therefore mistake the fact, that in a certain sense the whole description of the new temple bears a Messianic character. The restoration of the temple here announced is not exhausted by the immediate fulfilment. It assures us that even in the church of Christ life will ever issue from death. But there it stops: ch. xlvii. 1-12 alone is directly and exclusively Messianic.

The order in this section, which runs parallel with ch. liii. of Isaiah, ch. xxx. and xxxi. of Jeremiah, and ch. xi. of Zechariah, is very simple : first, the description, the water from the sanctuary, vers. 1-6; the trees on its banks, ver. 7; then the statement of the purpose served by that which is described—the water, vers. 8-11; the trees, ver. 12.

Ver. 1. And he brought me back to the door of the house; and, behold, waters issued from under the threshold of the house eastward: for the front of the house was toward the east, and the waters came down from under the right side of the house south of the altar. 2. And he brought me forth the way of the gate northward, and led me round without to the outer gate that looketh eastward; and, behold, waters gushed from the right side. 3. And when the man went forth to the east, and the line in his hand, he measured a thousand cubits, and brought me through the waters, waters of the ankles. 4. And he measured a thousand, and brought me through the waters, waters to the knees. And he measured a thousand, and brought me through waters of the loins. 5. And he measured a thousand; and it was a river that I could not wade: for the waters were high, waters of swimming, a river that could not be passed. 6. And he said unto me, Seest thou, son of man? And he led me, and brought me back to the brink of the river. 7. When I returned, behold, at the brink of the river were very many trees on this side and on that. 8. And he said unto me, These waters go out to the west circuit, and go down to the waste, and enter the sea; brought forth they fall into the sea, and the waters are healed.

9. And it shall be, that every living being that creepeth, to which the two rivers come, shall live; and the fish shall be very many : for these waters shall come thither, and they shall be healed ; and every thing shall live to which the river cometh. 10. And it shall be, that fishers shall stand on it, from En-gedi even to En-eglaim ; they shall be a spreading place for nets : their fish shall be of all kinds, as the fish of the great sea, very many. 11. Its mire and its marshes that are not healed are given to salt. 12. And on the river, on its brink, on this side and on that, shall grow all trees for food : its leaf shall not fade, nor its fruit cease ; it shall ripen every month, for its waters flow forth from the sanctuary ; and its fruit shall be for food, and its leaf for healing.

Under the figure of water salvation is often presented in Scripture, which appears even in paradise in the shape of water ; comp. Gen. xiii. 10. In Ps. xlvi. 5, " The river, its streams gladden the city of God," the blessings of the kingdom of God, His royal graces, appear as a river that conveys its saving waters by a series of channels to the community of God. The saving waters that there belong first only to Zion are here led out also to the heathen. In Ps. lxxxvii. 7, when the Messianic salvation is come which quickens the thirsty soul and the dry land, Israel sings, " All my springs are in Thee." Isaiah prophesies in ch. xxx. 25 of this time : " And there shall be on every high mountain, and on every lofty hill, rivers, waterbrooks, in the day of the great slaughter, when the towers fall." While the judgment on the world proceeds, and in it annihilates all pride and abases all haughtiness, Zion is quickened by the waters of salvation. The figure is directly explained in several places. In Ps. xxxvi. 9, " And of the river of thy pleasure thou makest them drink," the river denotes the fulness of delight which the Lord pours upon His own. Isaiah says in ch. xii. 3 of the Messianic times, " And with joy shall ye draw water out of the wells of salvation." In Rev. vii. 17 it is said, " The Lamb in the midst of the throne shall feed them, and lead them to living fountains of waters." Accordingly water signifies life, a powerful happy life disturbed by no hindrance. So also in Rev. xxii. 1. Ezekiel expands here what Joel has indicated in ch. iv. 18, " And a fountain goes forth from the house of the Lord, and waters the acacia dale," the symbol of human need; and Zechariah again in ch. xiv. 8 points back to Ezekiel. The water comes out under the threshold of the house. The house is the proper temple, the holy place, and the holy of holies. The proper fountain is in the latter. According to the Apocalypse, the water goes out from the throne of God. The prophet has in ch. xliii. 1 f. seen the new entrance of the Lord into the sanctuary forsaken by Him. In this entrance, from which the city again receives the name "Jehovah thither" (ch. xlviii. 35), not only the appearance of Christ announced elsewhere by the prophet, but the issue of the waters consequent upon it, has its ground. But Ezekiel, held fast by the Old Testament limits, cannot advance to the fountain of waters. The entrance into the holy of holies was allowed only to the high priest. The words, "For the face or front of the house was toward the east," explain the foregoing passage, where the threshold toward the east was spoken of. The front side is, as such, at the same time the door side. But the front of the temple is toward the east. That the descent of the water is spoken of is explained by this, that to depict its internal elevation the temple was higher than the court. The water comes down under the right or south side of the house, that is, to the south-east; for from what goes before, the south side can only be the south part of the east side. The water flows to the south end of the threshold. The reason why it came forth there, and not in the middle of the threshold, is given in the words "south of the altar." The altar of burnt-offering lay immediately before the east door of the sanctuary (ch. xl. 47): the water must therefore issue not from the middle of the threshold, if it was not to meet with an immediate hindrance; it must first come forth where the altar did not stand in the way. The prophet has, so far as he was allowed, seen the origin of the water. Now he is to observe its further course. For this purpose he must leave the temple. The most natural way out was the east gate of the court, where the water flowed toward the east. But as, according to ch. xliv. 1, 2, the outer east gate was always shut, he must go round through the north gate, and outside the temple make his way to the east gate. There, according to ver. 2, he sees water gushing out[1] on the

---

[1] פכה, to roll, is connected with בקק, both formed after the sound, " of the sound which the emptying bottle makes," in Arab. to break forth,

right side. The right, or the south side, is here also, from the connection, the south-east. The south side of the east gate is first meant. But the water comes forth on the south side of the east gate, only because it has taken its rise on the south-east side of the temple. It goes forth thence in a straight course. The measuring in vers. 3-5 is fourfold. The thought is, that the Messianic salvation, at first small in appearance, will unfold itself in ever richer fulness and glory, *crescit eundo*, while the streams of worldly enterprise after a brief course dry up— are streams whose waters lie (Isa. lviii. 11; Job vi. 15-20). To be compared is ch. xvii. 22, 23, where the tender sapling grows to a cedar, in whose shadow all the fowls of heaven, all the nations of the earth, dwell,—a passage that affords the necessary supplement to ours, as in it the person of the Mediator appears; and also in the New Testament the parables of the mustard seed and the leaven. The same progress which is exhibited in the real world among the nations, appears also in the life of individuals. The wonderful power working in secret brings by degrees great out of small, fathers in God out of children. That it was not possible to walk through the water (ver. 5), the prophet ascertained by his own experience as he waded in to the neck (Isa. viii. 8). In ver. 6 the prophet is brought back from the stream to its brink. He cannot therefore have been satisfied with observing the state of the water from the brink, which has also all antecedent analogy against it. The words, " Seest thou, son of man" (ver. 6), point out the high significance of what precedes, and form at the same time the close and the transition. The words, " and brought me back to the brink of the river," indicate that the attention is now to be turned to this, whereas hitherto it was directed to the bed of the river, in which the prophet had to go hither and thither. It is said literally in ver. 7, " when he turned me back." [1] This is one of the verbal peculiarities which occur, in the whole of the Old and New Testament, only in Ezekiel. *Me:* this shows that the return was a passive act determined by a foreign influence. It is indeed preceded by, " He led me, and *brought me*

gush forth. Very unsuitable is the comparison with בכה, weep, then trickle. The water must in its very origin bear the character of fulness and life.

[1] In the infinitive, ינ— regularly and without exception denotes the accus. *me*, י— the genitive of the subject, *my* (Böttcher, *Gram.*).

back to the brink of the river." The need of salvation is denoted by hungering as well as thirsting. Accordingly life or salvation is here represented in the shape of the fruit-tree, as before by the water; comp. Isa. lv. 1, 2, where, in describing the future times of quickening, along with water for the thirsty, is named bread for the hungry. The trees have here no independent import. They come into account only for their fruit. If, by an unseasonable comparison of Ps. i. 3, Jer. xvii. 8, we understand by trees, men—the righteous of the Messianic time—by fruits their virtues, we violently sever our prophecy from the connection with Gen. ii. 9, iii. 22, on the one side, and with Rev. xxii. 2 on the other. That in the latter place persons are not spoken of, and the trees as in paradise come into account only for their fruits, is shown by the parallel passage, ch. ii. 7, "To him that overcometh will I give to eat of the tree of life, which is in the midst of the paradise of God." Here the righteous are not themselves the tree of life, but they eat of the tree of life. With ver. 8 begins the statement of the aim. First, we learn in vers. 8–11 what the water means. The words, "These waters go out to the east circuit," determine the region in which the waters are to prove effectual. The details then follow in the words, "And go down to the waste, and enter the sea." The waste, the Arabah, denotes in general the valley of the Jordan. In this connection, however, with the east region on the one side and the sea on the other, the Arabah can only come into account in its south end by the Dead Sea. There, in preparation for the Dead Sea, and as a fitter entrance to this, it is a horrid wilderness—" a solitary plain full of salt clay." The wilderness is in Scripture a figure of ungodliness—thus a suitable emblem of the world estranged from God and excluded from His kingdom, to which applies the words in Ps. cvii. 5, " Hungry and thirsty, their soul fainted in them." In the fundamental passage of Joel corresponds to the Arabah here, "The vale of the acacias, the wilderness tree;" and in Isa. xxxv. 6, the Arabah is in parallelism with the wilderness: " In the wilderness shall waters break out, and streams in the waste." The figure of the wilderness transferred from Joel, the prophet only indicates. He turns immediately to a second more striking figure of ungodliness, and gives this at full length. " The sea" is from the whole context the *east* sea (ver. 18), the Dead Sea, of which Von Raumer says, p. 61, " The sea is called Dead, because there is in it no green plant, no water-fowl—in it no fish, no shell. If the Jordan carry fish into it, they die." Gadow relates : " Some herons had taken their stand on the miry delta (of the entering Jordan), and sought the little fishes washed into the sea, that died instantly in the sharp lye. I remarked some struggling with death." This explains the passage of Ezek. xlvii. 8–10. Sea-fishes, which Marshal Marmont at Alexandria cast into the water taken from the Dead Sea, died in two or three minutes. As a symbol of the corrupt world lying in wickedness (1 John v. 19), the Dead Sea is the more appropriate, as it owes its *origin* to a judgment on the corrupt world, and the spiritual eye discerns under its waves the figure of Sodom and Gomorrah. The prophet has already, in ch. xvi., presented Sodom as a type of the world dead in sins ; comp. above, p. 144. " Into the sea" is a repetition, in order to attach to it the statement of the aim and the import. All before this was purely geographical. For the statement of the aim the phrase " brought forth" prepares, which points to the higher hand, which by deliberate counsel executes the plan of salvation. " And it shall be" (ver. 9) directs the attention to the remarkable change. As there is in the Dead Sea no other " living being" than those who wrestle with death, or have yielded to it, so also its counterpart the world is a great charnel-house. " Living beings :" they merit this name first after the waters from the sanctuary have overcome the substances hostile to life. The " two rivers" stand for the strong river, as in Jer. l. 21 the double revolt means the strong revolt. The first oppressor of Israel in the time of the Judges bears, on account of his great wickedness, the name Rishathaim, double wickedness.[1] In a certain respect the foregoing passage speaks of a doubled water—the source as it first comes from the sanctuary, and the increase which it afterwards receives. Only after they receive this reinforcement they effect the here mentioned miraculous change in the Dead Sea. " And the fish

---

[1] Perhaps עֲגָלִים in ver. 10 is also such a dual, the double calf in parallelism with the goat. Springs are named after the discoverers. The calf had signalized itself by the discovery. The doubled stands often for the distinguished : thus כְּפָלַיִם, Job xi. 6 ; מִשְׁנֶה, Isa. lxi. 7.

shall be very many:" the sea appears in Scripture as the symbol of the world. Accordingly men appear as the living creatures in the sea, and in particular as the fishes; comp. on Rev. viii. 9. In the Dead Sea of the world there were hitherto only dead fish, that are not reckoned as fish, but only unspiritual, unsaved men. If the meaning of the fish be settled, that of the fishers cannot be doubtful. If the fish be the men who have attained to life by the Messianic salvation, the fishers can only be the messengers of this salvation, who gather those who are quickened into the kingdom of God—introduce them into the communion of the church. So also has our Lord repeatedly and emphatically expounded this trait of our prophecy; thus in the words directed in the apostles to all the ministers of the church: "I will make you fishers of men; fear not, henceforth thou shalt catch men" (Luke v. 11; in Matt. xiii. 47, etc.). The question is not of fishers who will divide the fish caught after their kind, but only of those who catch fish of different kinds. The forced transference of the prophecy to the last time of the kingdom of God has nothing for, everything against it: the gradual growth of the river of life; the authority of Christ, who sets out from this, that the fishing of men predicted by Ezekiel begins immediately; and the nature of the thing, as it would be absurd to ignore the beginning and contemplate the end alone or even chiefly, since it is already contained in the beginning. The fishers will stand from En-gedi to En-eglaim. Both places are combined, because they are both named from a fountain. En-gedi is known. It lies on the west side of the sea, pretty far toward the south, though by no means on the south end. Jerome places En-eglaim at the north end of the sea, where the Jordan flows into it. But as obviously the whole compass of the sea is intended, it is much better to look for En-eglaim on the east side of the sea. Now En-gedi is in fact obliquely over against the Eglaim mentioned in Isa. xv. 8; according to the *Onom. s. v. Agallim* 8 *m. p.*, south of the old Moabite city Ar, probably identical with *Agalla*, a city which Alexander Jannæus had wrested from the Arabs (Joseph. *Arch.* xiv. 1, 4).[1] " They shall be a spreading place for nets;"

---

[1] That Eglaim in Isaiah is written with א is not decisive, as ע and א are not seldom exchanged; comp. Gesen. *Thes.* under א. אגלים affords no suitable derivation.

literally, they shall be a place for the spreading of the nets. The subject is the places from En-gedi to En-eglaim, thus the whole compass of the Dead Sea, on which hitherto no spread nets, as it were the symbol of the fish kingdom, were seen. The nets are spread after fishing to dry, in preparation for new work, new success. "Their fish shall be of all kinds:" this refers to Gen. i. 21. In the Dead Sea of the world arises such a joyful swarm of those who are made partakers of life from God, as once at the creation in the natural sea of ordinary fish. The salvation is for all, without distinction of nation, rank, or age.[1] "Its mire[2] and its marshes that are not healed" (ver. 11): the height of the water in the Dead Sea is different at different times. If the water subsides, salt morasses and marshes arise here and there, that are cut off from connection with the main sea (Robinson, Part ii. pp. 434, 459). In the Dead Sea of the world, the swamp and marshes are originally of the same nature as the main sea: the only difference is, that they cut themselves off from the healing waters that come from the sanctuary: comp. the sayings, "and ye would not;" and, "No man can come unto me, except the Father, who hath sent me, draw him"—whose drawing the longing of the soul must meet (John vi. 44). "Are given to salt:" the salt comes into account here not as seasoning, as often, but as the foe of fruitfulness, life, and prosperity. The salt land denotes, in Job xxxix. 6, the desert, barren steppe. To be given to salt forms the contrast to deliverance from the corrosive power of salt, which would be effected by the water from the sanctuary, if access were afforded to it; the waters remain given over to the salt: "He that believeth not the Son of God shall not see life, but the wrath of God abideth on him" (John iii. 36). It is punishment enough for the world lying in wickedness, that it abides as it is. That the trees bring forth new fruit every month (ver. 12), indicates the uninterrupted enjoyment of

[1] Jerome: *Omnia capta sunt ab apostolis, nihil mansit incaptum, dum nobiles et ignobiles, divites et pauperes et omne genus hominum de mari hujus seculi extrahitur ad salutem.* The great multiplicity of kinds has since then become infinitely more manifest.

[2] The singular stands in the text. The *Keri*, to which the vowels belong, substitutes the plural on account of the following plural. But בצה occurs elsewhere only in the sing. (Job viii. 11, xl. 21); and also בץ, mire, Jer. xxxviii. 22.

salvation. The salvation must present itself for the deadly sick heathen world, before all in the form of saving grace. Besides the nourishing fruits, therefore, are named also the healing leaves.

CHAPTER XLVII. 13–23.

From the far future the prophet returns to the near, from the higher salvation to the lower, which formed its presupposition. He has already painted the temple and city of the future. It remains to show how Israel is reinstated in the possession of the land. In this section the boundary of the land is given. In ch. xlviii. then follows the partition among the several tribes.

In Num. xxxiv. and in Josh. xv. the statement of the boundaries proceeds from the south; here, on the contrary, it begins in the north, and the tribes also in ch. xlviii. follow from north to south. The distinction arises from this, that in ancient times Israel came from the south into the land, but here the return takes place from the land of the north.

Everything also in our section depends on this, that we rightly conceive the aim of the prophet. His problem is this, to give a hold and a ground for believing hope in the restoration to the land of their fathers as it existed for the people affected by the Chaldean catastrophe (to those affected by the Roman conquest such a hope is nowhere held out in the Old or New Testament, and could not be held out according to the nature of the New Testament). Questions of detail—whether the Phœnicians and the Philistines shall keep their coast-land, whether the transjordanic region shall, as formerly, come into possession of Israel as a frontier of the proper Canaan—interest him not. He deals only in the general. He knows that the Mosaic boundary is not completely covered by the later actual boundary—that circumstances have changed the state of things. He adheres closely to this Mosaic boundary as it is presented in Num. xxxiv., as in the description of the temple he does to the pattern of that of Solomon. In conclusion, he declares that the strangers who have been incorporated with Israel during the exile, shall be made equal with the natives in the partition of the land. We have here a remarkable monument of faith—a parallel to the blessing of Jacob, who, far from the land of promise, contemplated its future possession as present. The exposition that would transfer all to the times of the New Testament, is in this section also involved in perplexity. It asserts that all is to be spiritually understood here, but cannot give the spiritual sense more precisely. It is true our section contains "truth and poetry;" but if we do not understand that the truth in it is the restoration from the Chaldean exile, which even in Jeremiah, for ex. in ch. xxx. 31, presents itself as the chief source of comfort, all floats in the air.

Ver. 13. Thus saith the Lord Jehovah, The inside of the border by which ye shall inherit the land, for the twelve tribes of Israel: for Joseph two portions. 14. And ye shall inherit it, every one as his brother; which I lifted up my hand to give to your fathers: and this land shall fall to you for inheritance. 15. And this is the border of the land on the north side, from the great sea towards Hethlon, and thence to Zedad; 16. Hamath, Berathah, Sibraim, which is between the border of Damascus and the border of Hamath; Hazer the middle, which is on the border of Hauran. 17. And the border from the sea shall be Hazar-enon, the border of Damascus, and the north northward, and the border of Hamath. And this is the north side. 18. And the east side, from between Hauran, and Damascus, and Gilead, and the land of Israel, is the Jordan; from the border to the east sea ye shall measure. And this is the east side. 19. And the south side southward, from Tamar to the waters of Meriboth Kadesh the inheritance reaches to the great sea. And this is the south side southward. 20. And the west side is the great sea, from the border over against the way to Hamath. This is the west side. 21. And ye shall divide the land for you unto the tribes of Israel. 22. And it shall be, that ye shall allot it for an inheritance to you, and to the strangers that sojourn among you, who have begotten children among you; and they shall be unto you as the natives among the children of Israel; with you shall they share in the inheritance among the tribes of Israel. 23. And it shall be, that in the tribe with which the stranger dwells, there ye shall give him his inheritance, saith the Lord Jehovah.

The inside of the border (ver. 13) is the land enclosed

within the border.¹ The following "by which"—in what relation, to what extent—"ye shall inherit the land" serves for explanation. "Joseph parts;" that is, wherein Joseph shall receive two parts. The allusive brevity, which shows itself particularly in this, that a multiplicity of parts is spoken of instead of a definite duality, arises from this, that the proportion is generally known. Jacob, in Gen. xlviii. 5, makes the two sons of Joseph equal in respect of the share in the land of Canaan—raises these grandsons to the rank of sons. In the statement of the north boundary in vers. 15-17, the direction is first defined in ver. 15 by a prominent point. It commences at the Mediterranean, and proceeds thence over Hethlon to Zedad. This, the present Zadad or Sudud, four hours from Hasya on the west edge of the desert, was named in Num. xxxiv. 8 as the north-eastern point of the territory of Israel. In ver. 16 are then named some of the most important places lying on the north border; at the head Hamath, as the most considerable of the border lands. Then in ver. 17 the sea is designated as the western point of the north border; Hazar-enon as the eastern, which appeared in Num. xxxiv. 9 as the eastern point of the north border; and Hamath as the northern,² which often presents itself, after the example of Num. xxxiv. 8, as the northern limit of Canaan. Solomon assembles all Israel to the dedication of the temple, from Hamath to the river of Egypt (1 Kings viii. 65).³ As the east border, by which the land of

¹ גה is no "old mechanically perpetuated clerical error for זה." Had this been so, no writer would have put גה for it. Any one must have attentively considered the letters before he wrote גה. It seems almost that Ezekiel wished to teaze scribes and critics, and put them to the test with the גה. גה is of like import with גֵהָה, Prov. xvii. 22, "A merry heart doeth good to *the inwards*, and a broken spirit drieth the bone." The stem is נהה or גוה. Cognate is גֵּו, middle—in Chald. גֵּו; גִּיא, valley, the interior enclosed by mountains; גּוֹי, people, the interior, the centre, in opposition to the individuals as the periphery. The Syr. renders גה rightly by נַחֲלָה. It is not the border that is afterwards spoken of, but the territory. גה is here also the fitting word, as זה in ver. 15.

² צפון, north, without the preposition, denotes the north border, to which all the places named belong. צפונה, toward the north, gives the special in the general. The north border was no straight line, but had its more and less northern points. The most northern was Hamath.

³ "This is the north side." את may also here be regarded as a sign of the accus. We may supply "ye see," or the like. We have here in the local

Israel is separated from Hauran, Damascus, and Gilead, appears in ver. 18 the Jordan. The transjordanic region is thus not reckoned to the land of Israel. A reversal of relations has thence been wrongly inferred. Even in Num. xxxii. 30, xxxiii. 51, the land of Canaan is the land west of the Jordan. In Josh. xxii. 9, Canaan and Gilead are set over against one another quite as here. But when the prophet here excludes Gilead from the proper land of Israel, he does not in the remotest degree say that they shall not have it as a frontier in the future, as formerly. If he asserted this, he would be at variance with Ps. lx., with Mic. vii. 14, where it is said of the people delivered from the Babylonian catastrophe (ch. iv. 9, 7), "They shall feed in Bashan and Gilead as in the days of old;" with Jer. l. 19, where, along with Karmel and Mount Ephraim, Bashan and Gilead appear as the possession of the people restored from Babylon; with Zech. x. 10, and not less with history. "From the border to the east sea ye shall measure :" the border on the north has been already defined in vers. 15-17; and then again in our verse, where Hauran stands at the head as the northern point of the east border, the east sea is named as the southern point of the east border—the Dead Sea, so called in contrast with the Mediterranean, which lay to the west. The starting-point of the south border, Tamar, in ver. 19, occurs not elsewhere in the Old Testament. As the west sea is given as the end of the south border, we must look for Tamar at the extreme south-east, at the end of the east sea, which appears in ver. 18 as the southern part of the east border. To this also point Num. xxxiv. 4 and Josh. xv. 2, according to which the south border begins at the end of the salt sea, the tongue that looketh southward from the southern end of the Dead Sea, on which Tamar must have stood.[1] The

descriptions of Ezekiel a style which closely resembles our telegram. In such a style it is quite perverse to wish, by critical alteration and verbal exposition, to force that which is so easily explained by the assumption of omissions.

[1] Robinson (*Travels*, iii. 1, pp. 179, 186), whom several have inadvertently followed, looked for Tamar on the site of the present Kurnub. But the positive grounds are wholly uncertain. The situation of the Thamara mentioned in the *Onom.* is determined by a change of text—a mere conjecture! But Robinson's hypothesis leads to the unnatural assumption that the description of the border begins at a point in the middle, and then

second point, the strife-waters of Kadesh, is made prominent on account of the theological monitory significance which it has in the history of the old time.¹ The great sea is designated as the western point of the south border.² The west border in ver. 20, the Mediterranean, begins with the western point of the south border mentioned in ver. 19, and goes in the north, "over against the way to Hamath," to the point where the way from the sea to Hamath, that lay inland in the extreme north, begins, ver. 17. The land so designated by its boundary is to be divided (ver. 21) among the tribes of Israel; yet so, it is added in vers. 22, 23, that the strangers who have been naturalized in Israel in the times of affliction (strangers in general are not intended; but the more exact definition is added, "who have begotten children among you") are considered in the partition, and indeed each in the tribe to which he has attached himself. Some have wished to find here a New Testament trait; but they have not reflected that the boundaries of the land confined between the Jordan and the Mediterranean render it impossible to think of the hosts of heathen who were then received into Israel, and still less that

turns first to the east, and then to the west, against which all analogy speaks.

¹ The designation is taken from Num. xxvii. 14; only, instead of the singular there, the plural מריבות is put, which points to this, that the strife there involves a whole fulness of rebellion,—a solemn *N.B.* for those who bore in themselves the nature of their fathers, who were still to the present day a " house of rebellion."

² Instead of " the inheritance goes to the great sea," it is now usually said, by the river to the great sea, with reference to Num. xxxiv. 5, Josh. xv. 4, where, in the definition of the south border, mention is made of the river which falls into the Mediterranean at the old Rhinokorura, the modern Arish. But this river is nowhere else briefly called the river, or river without the article—always the river of Egypt, even in Isa. xxvii. 12 —and could least of all here be so designated by mistake in a section that treats so strictly of the נחלה, the inheritance of Israel. The assumption connected with this interpretation of the incorrectness of the vocalization and accentuation—the word must then have been written as in Num. xxxiv. 5—has not a single analogy in the whole so carefully elaborated text of Ezekiel. The oldest translators, LXX.—who have here παρεκτείνον, in the repetition (ch. xlviii. 28) κληρονομίας—Jonathan, the Syriac, are against this explanation. The *inheritance* here corresponds to the border of the land in the first two places. That there is an allusion to the river in Num. xxxiv. we may certainly assume.

only the strangers already naturalized in Israel are here spoken of. The general principle which lies at the root of this regulation is already expressed by Moses in Lev. xix. 34 : "The stranger that dwelleth with you shall be as the home-born among you, and thou shalt love him as thyself." Thus, according to the Mosaic law, heathens by birth might be received into the community of God. The exception that in this respect is made regarding the Ammonites and the Moabites (Deut. xxiii. 3–5), serves only to confirm the rule (Deut. xxiii. 7, 8). Already in the condition of the people, as Moses discovered, was found a considerable foreign element—the whole posterity of the servants who went to Egypt with Jacob.[1] A new accession took place in Egypt at the time of the exodus. We find of those in the train of Israel a great swarm of Egyptians (Ex. xii. 38; Num. xi. 4). In 1 Chron. ii. 34, 35 we have an example[2] that these Egyptian strangers were considered in the partition of the land, and indeed in the territory of the tribe to which they were attached. Further, Moses gives the friendly invitation to his Midianitish brother-in-law, according to Num. x. 29 f., to share with his tribe the lot of Israel : " What good the Lord does to us, we will do to you." "Hobab," says Knobel, "shall have equal rights with them; thus, for ex., a share in the land. As no further refusal, but immediately after the departure of Israel, is recorded, Hobab consented. In fact, we find his family afterwards in the Hebrew land." We may compare Judg. i. 16, iv. 11; Jer. xxxv. Only apparently at variance with Ezekiel is the conduct of Ezra towards the heathen wives (Ezra ix. 10), and that of Nehemiah in ch. xiii. toward the heathen men who had settled among the Israelites. Ezekiel speaks of those who had attached themselves by inner inclination to Israel at a time when he had no form nor comeliness, and when there was nothing in him to desire but the true God ; Ezra and Nehemiah are zealous against the attempt to make heathendom of equal right with Israel, and to break down the partition wall so necessary in the times before Christ. Both the attraction which Ezekiel commends, and the repulsion for which Ezra and Nehemiah are zealous, arise rather from

---

[1] Compare my essay, "Moses and Colenso," *Ev. K. Z.* lxiv. p. 195.
[2] Compare on this the essay above quoted.

the same principle. It is the true God who here binds and there severs.

CHAPTER XLVIII.

This chapter falls into three parts. It describes the order of the tribes in the recovered land from north to south, vers. 1–7 and vers. 23–29. Then the oblation situated in the midst of the tribe territory, between the seven northern and the five southern, which was already spoken of in detail, but must still be here introduced in its order in vers. 8–22; in which vers. 8, 9, and 20 treat of the oblation in general; vers. 10–12, of the priests' part with the sanctuary; vers. 13, 14, of the Levites' part; vers. 15, 16, of the city; ver. 17, of the free space; ver. 18, of its guard; vers. 21, 22 of the land of the prince. The third part, vers. 30–35, treats of the boundary of the city and its gates, and gives at the close the significant name of the city.

Everything leads to the conclusion that this plan of the situation of restored Israel is designed only to give a provisional support to hope, to withdraw the view from the comfortless present, and afford an image for the fancy. Against the realistic interpretation are the equality of the tribe allotments, without reference to the numerical proportions of the tribes expressly enjoined in the Mosaic law, the complete neglect of the nature of the ground, and the grouping of the tribes on a theological principle. Yet we must not extend the department of figure too far. The real thought is, that the same covenant people who were carried into exile, are to be restored in a brief space to their native land. Against those who find here a prophecy of the church of the new covenant, it is decisive that there is not the slightest trace that by the tribes anything else is to be understood than Judah, Ephraim, etc., as they lived in the time of the prophet; that the region is the old country between the Jordan and the Mediterranean, whereas the bounds of the Messianic kingdom, according to Ps. lxxii. and Zech. ix. 10, " and He shall reign from sea to sea, from the river (the Euphrates) to the ends of the earth," coincide with the bounds of the earth; and that Jerusalem, in its very limited compass of 18,000 cubits, nearly 50 stadia, which Hecatæus ascribes to it in the early times of the Greek empire, presents itself not as the centre of the world, but as the capital of a small territory.

In regard to the succession and grouping of the tribes, the prophet has acted on a threefold point of view. First came into account the situation of the old Jerusalem, nearly in the centre, but yet more to the south. With a view to this he could not divide the twelve tribes into the double six, but he distributed them into seven and five,—a division of twelve which also occurs often in the grouping of the Psalms, where the sacred number seven is always the chief number, and five appears as its supplement. Then it behoved him to represent Judah and Benjamin, of which at least a part remained true to David's line in the separation of the kingdom, as the kernel of the whole, as it presented itself in the later history: the whole of the people, indeed, afterwards received their name from Judah. Hence the prophet makes Judah the close of the number seven, which also receives its import by running out in Judah, and bringing him up immediately to the oblation. Benjamin opens, on the other side, the supplementary five. Three pairs go before Judah, two after Benjamin. A third point of view for the prophet is the essential equality of all the tribes—the prominence of the thought that they are all equal members in the body of the people of God. In this interest the prophet has in the two enumerations of the tribes, at the tribe allotments and at the gates, intentionally and artfully mingled the sons of the maidens and of the wives, and those of the latter again among one another, as is shown in details in my comment. on Rev. vii. 5-8. From the thought that with God is no respect of persons, it arises also that Dan, the son of a handmaid, is placed at the head, and opens the series of tribe allotments, in accordance with the prominence given to the equality of Dan with the sons of the wives already in Gen. xlix. 16. Israel is a fraternal people, in which no member may raise itself above another.

Ver. 1. And these are the names of the tribes. From the north end to the part of the way of Hethlon, towards Hamath, Hazar-enan, the border of Damascus northwards, to the part of Hamath, and they shall be to him the east side the sea; Dan one. 2. And on the border of Dan, from the east side to the west side, Asher one. 3. And on the border of Asher, from the east side to the west side, Naphtali one. 4. And on the border of Naphtali, from the east side to the west side, Manasseh one. 5. And on the border of Manasseh, from the east side to the west side, Ephraim one. 6. And on the border of Ephraim, from the east side to the west side, Reuben one. 7. And on the border of Reuben, from the east side to the west side, Judah one. 8. And on the border of Judah, from the east side to the west side, shall be the oblation which ye shall offer, five and twenty thousand the breadth, and the length as one of the tribe-shares, from the east side to the west side, and the sanctuary in the midst of it. 9. The oblation which ye shall offer to the Lord shall be in length five and twenty thousand, and in breadth ten thousand. 10. And to these shall be the holy oblation to the priests, northward five and twenty thousand, and westward in breadth ten thousand, and eastward in breadth ten thousand, and southward in length five and twenty thousand: and the sanctuary of the Lord shall be in the midst of it. 11. To the priests, to him who is sanctified of the sons of Zadok,[1] who kept my charge, who went not astray, when the children of Israel went astray, as the Levites went astray. 12. And they shall have a heave-portion of the oblation of the land most holy, by the border of the Levites. 13. And the Levites over against the border of the priests, shall have five and twenty thousand in length, and in breadth ten thousand; the whole length five and twenty thousand, and the breadth ten thousand. 14. And they shall not sell of it, nor exchange, nor alienate the first-fruits of the land: for it is holy unto the Lord. 15. And five thousand that are left in the breadth, before the five and twenty thousand, shall be profane for the city, for dwelling, and for suburbs: and the city shall be in the midst of it. 16. And these are the measures of it; the north side five hundred and four thousand, and the south side again five hundred and four thousand, and on the east side five hundred and four thousand, and the west side five hundred and four thousand. 17. And there shall be a suburb to the city northward fifty and two hundred, and southward fifty and two hundred, and eastward fifty and two hundred, and westward fifty and two hundred.

---

[1] Luther, "that shall be consecrated to the priests the children of Zadok," contrary to 2 Chron. xxvi. 18.

18. And the residue in length, over against the holy oblation, shall be ten thousand eastward, and ten thousand westward; and it shall be over against the holy oblation : and the produce of it shall be for food for those who serve the city. 19. And they that serve the city shall serve it out of all the tribes of Israel. 20. All the oblation shall be five and twenty thousand by five and twenty thousand : a fourth part ye shall offer the holy oblation, for a possession of the city. 21. And the residue shall be to the prince, on this side and on that side of the holy oblation, and the possession of the city, before the five and twenty thousand of the oblation toward the east border, and westward before the five and twenty thousand toward the west border, over against the portions for the prince : and the holy oblation and the sanctuary of the house shall be in the midst of it. 22. And from the possession of the Levites, and from the possession of the city, in the midst of which is the prince's, between the border of Judah and between the border of Benjamin, shall be the prince's. 23. And the rest of the tribes, from the east side to the west side, Benjamin one. 24. And on the border of Benjamin, from the east side to the west side, Simeon one. 25. And on the border of Simeon, from the east side to the west side, Issachar one. 26. And on the border of Issachar, from the east side to the west side, Zebulon one. 27. And on the border of Zebulon, from the east side to the west side, Gad one. 28. And on the border of Gad, from the east side to the west side, and the border shall be from Tamar over the strife-waters of Kadesh, the inheritance to the great sea. 29. This is the land which ye shall allot of the inheritance to the tribes of Israel, and these are their portions, saith the Lord Jehovah. 30. And these are the outgoings of the city on the north side, five hundred and four thousand by measure. 31. And the gates of the city shall be after the names of the tribes of Israel : three gates northward ; the gate of Reuben one, the gate of Judah one, the gate of Levi one. 32. And on the east side five hundred and four thousand : and three gates ; the gate of Joseph one, the gate of Benjamin one, the gate of Dan one. 33. And the south side five hundred and four thousand in measure : and three gates ; the gate of Simeon one, the gate of Issachar one, the gate of Zebulon one. 34. The west side five hundred and four thousand :

and three gates; the gate of Gad one, the gate of Asher one, the gate of Naphtali one. 35. Around are eighteen thousand: and the name of the city from that day is Jehovah thither.

The north border, with which the tribe-land begins, is briefly transferred to ver. 1 from ch. xlvii. 15-17. First, as in ch. xlvii. 15, the course of the north border from west to east; then, as in ch. xlvii. 17, the eastern point, Hazar-enan, and the most northern, Hamath. "To the part of the way:" this shows that the border runs along this way. The words, "And they shall be to him the east side the sea," assert that all the tribe-lands fill the whole breadth of the land of Canaan. What is here said in general of all the tribes is in the following applied to every single tribe except the first, Dan, which the prophet had specially in his eye in the preliminary general statement. "To him:" this can only refer to the whole of the tribes previously named, which are combined into an ideal unity. The reference to Dan, who is first named afterwards, is impossible. A general expression for that which is afterwards applied to the several tribes we expect beforehand; and the deviation from the standing formula, which is afterwards used in the several tribes, is obviously designed to prevent the application to Dan.[1] The oblation stands in ver. 8 in the widest sense, including even the land of the prince. Only when the portion of the prince is taken in, has the oblation the given dimensions. Oblation is all that is not included in the partition, but is antecedently set apart for God. The prince is no less than the priests and Levites the servant of God, and as such is endowed with lands. The breadth is here throughout the extent from north to south, the length from east to west. The reason why the length of the oblation is not given, as the breadth, is that the prophet by such statements would go out of his proper sphere. The length is determined by the boundaries of nature, the Jordan on the one side and the Mediterranean on the other; and to fix them must be left to the geometers. In regard to the length of the oblation, the prophet contents himself with remarking that it is equal to that of the tribe portion, in which he also does not fix the length. Von Raumer (p. 25) reckons the middle breadth of the land at 15 (about 68 Eng.) miles. This

---

[1] The LXX. are correct: Καὶ ἔσται αὐτοῖς τὰ πρὸς ἀνατολὰς ἕως πρὸς θάλασσαν.

whole breadth (or, according to our passage, length) belonged to the prince, with the exception of 25,000 cubits for priests, Levites, and city. "And the sanctuary shall be in the midst of it"—of the whole oblation. The sanctuary lies in the midst of the priests' part. This is enclosed on the east and west by the portion of the prince. On the north and south it lies in the midst of the Levites' part, south of the tribe-land of Judah and of the city territory, and north of the tribe-land of Benjamin. The oblation that is to be specially set apart for the Lord (ver. 9), the holy oblation in ver. 10, as distinguished from the oblation in general (ver. 8), is the priests' part, with the sanctuary in the midst. The prophet begins with this, because he has in view not the situation, but the dignity. The length, the extent from east to west, is the same in the portion of the priests, Levites, and city—25,000 cubits; the breadth, the extent from north to south, is peculiar to each—the priests' part 10,000 cubits, the Levites' part also 10,000, and the city's part 5000. In the north (ver. 10), as also in the south, the border of the priests' part measures from east to west 25,000 cubits; in the west and the east, the border from north to south or the broad side, 10,000 cubits. As the receivers of the priests' part are named in ver. 11 the sons of Zadok, who remained faithful to the Lord in the time of the apostasy, excluding the rebellious, comp. ch. xliv. 10, 15. They are sanctified by their fidelity, by which their election is made sure. The others are in punishment desecrated, degraded, reduced to mere Levites.[1] "As the Levites went astray," those who defiled themselves by the service of idols are no longer honoured with the priestly name; comp. ch. xliv. 10 f. Here also it is clear that the range in which the prophet moves is the time immediately after the exile. The relations and persons with which he is concerned had long disappeared in the times of the New Testament. The heave-portion,[2] which fell to the priests, is described in ver. 12 as *most holy*, because it has God's sanctuary in the midst of it, and belongs to His most eminent

---

[1] The singular המקדש denotes the hallowed part, as distinct from that which is not hallowed. The plur. would attribute the consecration to the collective priestly class; comp. 2 Chron. xxvi. 18.

[2] תרומיה, different from תרומה, the י denoting descent, is a terumah-part.

ministers, in contrast with the part of the Levites, which had only the second degree of holiness, and with that of the city, which had only the third. "By the border of the Levites:" this forms the transition to that which follows, where the Levites' part is spoken of. But it was, even apart from this, proper to make it prominent that the Levites' part bordered on that of the priests. In the description of the oblation, for theological reasons, the prophet had begun with the middle portion, the priests' part. It is necessary now to guard against the thought that the Levites' part was separated by the city, or the city by the Levites' part from the sanctuary. The servants of the house, the Levites, and also the inhabitants of the city, who in the divine services were to form the holy assembly, behoved to have the sanctuary as near as possible. The "whole length" in ver. 13 is explained by ver. 10 : the length from east to west, not merely on the south border, which was spoken of in the beginning of the verse, where the Levites' part adjoined the priests' part, but also on the north border, where the Levites' part bordered on the tribe of Judah.

The ordinance in ver. 14 transfers to this new Levitical land what was said in Lev. xxv. 34 regarding the lands of the Levitical cities. The ordinance applies naturally also to the priests' land; but it is expressly given only for the Levites' part, because its holiness is less, so that the thought of its being saleable might more readily arise. The "first-fruits of the land" is thus the oblation, to which the Levites' part belonged, denoted by an abridged comparison, to indicate that of this first part, as of the first-fruits, nothing may be given over to common use. Barter is excluded where God is the landowner and the Levites are only the usufructuaries.[1] In ver. 15 follows the third part of the oblation, the city, with its environs situated in the south part of it. Here the breadth of the city lands, its extent from north to south, is first given. It takes in 5000 cubits which remain over of the total breadth of 25,000. In regard to the length, it is only stated that the city ground, so far as it reaches, lies before the 25,000 cubits, the total length of the oblation, which are common to the priests' part and the Levites' part. The particulars of the length, the extent from

---

[1] The *Keri* יעביר, *Hiph.* instead of *Kal*, rests on a perverse assimilation to ימר.

east to west, appear first in ver. 16. The city has the 25,000 cubits over against it, but the 25,000 have the city opposite only for 5000 cubits; for the city quarter extends so far in length. The city lies in the midst of the whole city quarter: it is surrounded on all sides by an open space, which serves the inhabitants for many purposes.[1] The district of the city is designated as *profane*, in comparison with the holier district of the Levites, and the most holy of the priests. In a general sense, the city also is holy. The city is indeed a part of the oblation, and oblation and holy coincide. The former Jerusalem is commonly called the holy city. The restored Jerusalem itself is called Kadytis, the holy city, in Herodotus. In vers. 16 and 17 are given the complete measures of the city in the strict sense, and of the free space. To the already known 5000 of the north side are here added those of the other sides. We learn here that the city part, which according to ver. 15 has half the breadth of each of the other two parts of the oblation, includes in the length from east to west only a fifth part of it. The city itself is 4500 cubits on each side.[2] The free space has (ver. 17) 250 cubits on each side, so that the whole city district contains 5000 cubits in length and 5000 in breadth. The small compass of the city district wholly excludes the inhabitants from agriculture. Vers. 18 and 19 now dispose of the 20,000 cubits, which still remain in the extent from east to west of the 25,000 cubits of the oblation. These 20,000 cubits, which no less than the 5000 of the city lie beside the holy oblation, the priests' part—which is here once more emphatically repeated, that no one may mistake the situation, or in particular shove in the Levitical part between, by which the holy oblation would be separated from its guardians—are divided into two parts of 10,000 cubits each, which take the city in the midst and enclose it east and west. The produce of these two districts is destined for those who "serve the city."

[1] The suff. in בתוכה refers to the city in the wider sense—to לעיר; the city in the strict sense lies within the city in the wide sense. The Masoretes could not understand this, and appended the masc. suff.

[2] The Masoretes could make nothing of the second חמש. They have left it without vowels, to indicate that it is to be omitted in reading. But it points to this, that the south side *equally* with the north side has 4500 cubits. Five stands, by an abbreviation usual with Ezekiel in local statements, for on the five, or to the five, etc.

We can only understand by this a militia, who take the city in the midst—military service is the only rude service which can be rendered to a city—and, as is so emphatically stated, are encamped as a guard by the holy oblation with the temple. On the north side of the holy oblation are the Levites as the *militia sacra* (Num. iv. 23, viii. 24); on the south side the ministers of the secular arm, which is to protect the church. Adjoining the provision made for these servants on both sides is the domain of the prince, who is to be considered the commander of these guards.[1] Among others, Egypt afforded an example of such military colonies endowed with land. The militia is to be out of all the tribes of Israel; not a hired host gathered out of the lands of other lords, as formerly the Kerethi and Pelethi, but consisting of those who will also serve their Lord in this lower sphere.[2] In ver. 20 is the closing remark on the whole oblation thus far described. The holy oblation in the wider sense has without the city 20,000 cubits in breadth: 5000 cubits in the breadth—that is, the fourth part of 20,000 cubits—fall to the district of the city, this being taken in the wider sense, so that it includes the land of "the servants of the city."[3] The parts of the priests and the Levites are together four times greater than that of the city. The city is here also included in the holy oblation. In vers. 21, 22 the part of the prince. This contains on both sides of the holy oblation, extending 25,000 cubits from east to west, which is included in the midst of his department, the land eastward to the Jordan and westward to the sea. On the north, like the holy oblation, particularly the Levitical part, it abuts on Judah; and on the south, as the city portion, on Benjamin. From north to south it has on the east and west sides, first the Levitical part, then the priestly part, then the city part, specially the land of "the servants of the city."[4] In ver. 22, "the possession of the Levites" either includes at the same time the part of

[1] עבד occurs of military service also in ch. xxix. 20. עבדים for soldiers is quite common.

[2] The fem. suff. in תבואתה the Masoretes could not understand, because the residue means the remaining land, and here the produce of land is to be spoken of.

[3] רביעית means only the fourth part, which refutes the other explanation.

[4] The suff. in בתוכה, ver. 21, refers to the domain of the prince.

the priests who were also Levites, or the two ends only of the oblation, the northern and the southern, are given. In vers. 23–28 follow the five remaining tribe territories. On ver. 28, comp. xlvi. 17. In ver. 29, the closing formula to the account of the partition among the tribes. It is said of, not to, the inheritance, because a part of the whole was not to be distributed, but set apart first as holy ground. In vers. 30–35 follow now the "outgoings" of the city. These comprise, as the following details show, two things,—first the boundary lines marked out by walls on the four sides, and next the gates. Both together are that in which the city terminates. The boundary line measures on each side 4500 cubits: the gates on each side are three, each denoted by one of the names of the tribes of Israel, only for honour, not with reference to the situation of the tribe-land; whence Levi, omitted in the statement of the tribe allotments, must also be mentioned, while the two tribes Ephraim and Manasseh are comprised under the name Joseph, so that the number twelve, which has become the signature of the covenant people, remains to the tribes. At the close of the whole is given the name of the city in its new state. It is henceforth called[1] "Jehovah thither." This name is explained by Deut. xi. 12. There the land, which Israel prepared to occupy, is designated as "a land which the Lord thy God seeks, on which the eyes of the Lord thy God are continually from the beginning of the year to the end of it." "Jehovah thither" accordingly means the city to which Jehovah continually turns His heart and eye. This "Jehovah thither" showed itself in the most glorious manner in the coming of Christ, in the many attempts which He made to gather the children of Jerusalem, in the tears which the Son of God shed over the fruitlessness of these attempts. When, however, they would

[1] After מיום, from the day, usually follows the definition of the day: for ex. Deut. ix. 24, "from the day that I knew you;" Ex. x. 6, "from the day that they were in the land." *Here* this definition is not expressly stated; but it is to be derived from the context, from the day that it is restored, that it appears in the state so fully described. מיום stands thus elliptically in Isa. xliii. 13: "from the day" means from the time when the prophecy will be fulfilled; comp. xlviii. 16. מיום never means, and cannot mean, "always," and just as little "from to-day." שמה never means "there," always "thither," and there is no reason here to abandon this meaning; comp. *Christol.* on Hos. ii. 17.

not, when His own received not Him that came to His own, the highest grace was turned into a curse—Jerusalem was destroyed; and the "Jehovah thither," which had availed the restored city for five hundred years, now passed to the new people of God gathered out of Jews and Gentiles, the legitimate continuation of Israel and Jerusalem (Matt. xxi. 43), to which Jesus has promised, "Lo, I am with you alway, unto the end of the world." The material Jerusalem has thenceforth and for ever lost its significance. The fig-tree of the Jewish people, as the people of God, has been torn up with the root (Mark xi. 20); and Jerusalem has not merely for a time, but for ever, ceased to be a privileged city for the worship of God and the revelation of His grace (John iv. 21–24).

RETROSPECT.

EZEKIEL, carried into exile in the captivity of Jehoiachin, seven years after the beginning of the Chaldean bondage, eleven years before the destruction of the city, appeared there as prophet in the fifth year after his captivity, in the thirtieth year of his life (ch. i. 1). The latest date which we find in the superscriptions of his prophecies is the twenty-seventh year of the captivity of Jehoiachin (ch. xxix. 17), so that the historically ascertained period of the prophet's activity embraced twenty-two years. It was shown that the prophet had precisely in that period a definite occasion for the collection of his prophecies.

The prophecies contained in the present collection, like those of the contemporary Daniel, are all provided with chronological superscriptions. These are in all twelve, of which six belong to native prophecies, and six to prophecies against foreign nations,—xxvi. 1, xxix. 1, xxix. 17, xxxi. 1, xxxii. 1, xxxii. 17.

The collection falls into two main parts,—prophecies before and prophecies after the destruction of Jerusalem. That we may not, with some, make the prophecies against foreign nations in ch. xxv.-xxxii. a special main part, that they are rather to be considered an appendix to the prophecies before the destruction, is manifest: 1. Because the beginning of these predictions in ch. xxv. is connected with the last native prophecy before the destruction in one chronologically determined section; 2. Because the section ch. xxxiii. 1-20 forms the literary close to ch. i.-xxxii.; and with special reference to the main portion, ch. i.-xxiv., gives some *nota benes* concerning the whole previous literary activity of Ezekiel.

The essential character of the first part is threatening; that of the second, promise.

The starting-point of the first main part is a great anti-

Chaldaic coalition, and the danger connected with it of the people failing to discern the signs of the times.

The first main part contains four groups of native prophecies—ch. i.-vii., viii.-xix., xx.-xxiii., and xxiv.—in regular chronological sequence. The first dates from the fifth year of Jehoiachin, a time when the formation of the coalition began to fill men's minds with joyful hopes; the last from the tenth day of the tenth month in the ninth year of Jehoiachin,—the fatal day of the opening of the siege of Jerusalem, which put an end to the hopes founded on the coalition.

The mission of the prophet in these four groups is to make clear to the people the import of the great Chaldean catastrophe, and to bring them to understand the day of their visitation, and escape the miserable fate of those who are severely afflicted, without gaining the peaceable fruit of righteousness. To the book of the works no less than to the book of the words of God we may apply the saying, "Understandest thou what thou readest?" It was the great privilege of the people of God, that such an interpretation always went along with the doings of God. The prophet leads the people to discover in the coming event a long reckoning of God,—the visitation of a guilt that goes back to the very origin of the people. He makes every effort to bring the people to acknowledge the depth of their corruption, which alone could account for their sufferings, and thus not send them far from their God, but connect them closely with Him. The destined event, thus recognised in its necessity, had to be represented as inevitable. The prophet is inexhaustible in the denunciation of the foolish hopes of the people, before whose eyes he portrays the future calamity as if it were already present, as indeed the roots of it in reality were; inexhaustible also in the destruction of the false views concerning the source of the approaching suffering, and the beating down of the craftiness of the natural man, who in the deep indwelling antipathy to repentance makes every effort to cast the blame on God. He deals annihilating blows to those who led the people away from the way of repentance, and flattered them with foolish hopes. The radiant point in these discourses is the grand survey of the whole past development of Israel in ch. xxiii., which places before our eyes the figure of a people such as they ought not to be, and the result of which is, that the judgment is inevitable. Few sections of Scripture call so powerfully as these for earnest self-examination.

At the close of ch. xxiv. the prophet announces that native predictions will now be silent, until with the execution of the judgment a new beginning for the prophetic activity be given. The servant is silent in the beginning of the practical discourse of the Master Himself, for the understanding of which sufficient provision has been made. But with the previous ending of native prophecy is connected the beginning of the prophet's activity in regard to foreign nations. This connection is shown by this, that the beginning of this activity is included in the same section with the closing prophecy concerning Judah. The prophecies against foreign nations have the special aim to shed a fuller light on the judgment on Judah announced in the native prophecies, and already beginning its course. They give the answer to the natural question, Lord, but what of these? (John xxi. 21.) They are all directed against the nations of the anti-Chaldaic coalition, and the executors of the judgments are in them all the Chaldean monarchy. Judah was first to drink the cup (ch. xxi. 18 f.). God sanctified Himself first on those who were near Him (Lev. x. 3); the judgment began at the house of God. It appeared as if the people of the covenant must alone suffer among all the members of the coalition. The scorn of these confederates themselves was poured out on the people of Jehovah (ch. xxv. 3, 6, xxvi. 2); indeed, they made common cause in part with the Chaldeans, and sought to derive advantage from the misfortune of Judah (ch. xxxv. 10). The prophet portrays before the eyes the judgment which in his time will fall upon them. He turns the heart of the people to their God when he points out that for the heathen the judgment has an annihilating character; whereas Israel rises from it to a more glorious state. Thus these predictions against foreign nations appear as the transition from the first part to the second —the comforting and promising part.

Of the foreign nations there are seven, divided into four and three—four neighbouring nations and three world-powers, the last Egypt, which had formed the centre of the coalition; so that there is thus a progress from the less to the greater.

On this side and on that side of the prophecies against foreign nations the arrangement is strictly chronological. There occurs no prophecy which is not chronologically determined; and all prophecies so determined stand in regular order. In the external predictions also the chronological prevails. But a certain deviation must be allowed, otherwise things intimately connected must have been separated. The prophecies are here arranged according to the nations, so that, for ex., all those referring to Egypt come together. Among the prophecies referring to Egypt, that in ch. xxix. 17 goes before the one in ch. xxxi. 1, which belongs to an earlier period, because it stands in a close relation with the foregoing (ch. xxix. 1), and resumes it at a time when its fulfilment was close at hand. Although the main body of the external prophecies belong to the time before the term, given in ch. xxxiii. 21, of the recommencement of the home prophecies, yet the date of some external prophecies precedes that in ch. xxxiii. 21 (ch. xxxii. 1, 17), because the external prophecies forming a connected cycle should not be separated from one another, and because the following cycle of home prophecies also should meet with no interruption.

The first part contains in all a decade of prophecies—four native and six foreign. At the close of the first part in ch. xxxiii. 1–20 follows, in vers. 21, 22, the historical introduction to the discourses of the second period; in vers. 23–33, the warning and admonishing preparation for the new message,—the mediation, as it were, between it and the first part. With ch. xxxiv. begins the communication of the comforting message. From this forward the prophet is as inexhaustible in comforting as he was before in threatening. The dangerous foe was now despair, as it was before false confidence. Common to the comforting and to the threatening discourses is the pictorial character; the viewing of that which is not as if it were, a result of dependence on God, in whose nature salvation as well as judgment is founded. The comfort is in this first group unfolded in seven paragraphs. In the first discourse (ch. xxxiv.) the prophet meets in a soothing manner the grief for the loss of civil government, and places before the eyes of his hearers and readers the bright form of the glorified David, in whom the civil government of the future will culminate. In the second (ch. xxxv.) he portrays the desolation of Seir. The light of Israel is relieved by the shade of Edom, who here represents the nations, who, in their hatred of the kingdom of

God, are not fit for it, but are ripe for destruction. The third discourse (ch. xxxvi. 1–15) relieves the pain occasioned by the desolation of the holy land. The fourth (ch. xxxvi. 16–38) lays down the name of God as the pledge of salvation. The fifth announces the restoration of Israel as a covenant people (ch. xxxvii. 1–14); the sixth, as a brotherly people (vers. 15–28). The seventh (ch. xxxviii. xxxix.) represents the renovated people as victorious in every conflict.

The second principal part has only two dates (ch. xxxiii. 21 and ch. xl. 1), and thus presents only two sections, which increase the ten of the first part to twelve. In the great closing picture in ch. xl.–xlviii. the prophet portrays in detail the recovery of all that was lost, in fulfilment of the words of the psalmist, "He keepeth all his bones: not one of them is broken;" and points in the midst of it, in ch. xlvii. 1–12, to the great progress of the kingdom of God in the future.

In the picture of the future drawn by the prophet, the following are the principal traits. Vain is every attempt of the people to avert the threatening misfortune. They must drain to the bottom the cup of the divine wrath (ch. xxi. 26). Egypt, the power on which their hopes chiefly rest, proves a broken reed: the time of its political importance is for ever gone. But what earth denies, heaven will grant in its own time. After the people have attained to repentance, wrath is followed by grace; all that is lost—the temple, with its priests and worship, the city, the land—is restored. Yet not this alone: the future brings an enhancement of salvation. The people receive a rich treasure of forgiveness of sins (ch. xxxvi. 25, xxxvii. 23); the Lord takes away the heart of stone, and gives them a heart of flesh (xi. 19); He awakens them by His quickening breath from spiritual death (ch. xxxvii.). The centre of all graces is an exalted descendant of David, who will spring from His family when reduced and wholly deprived of the sovereignty, and connect the high-priestly with the kingly office (ch. xxi. 27, xxxiv. 11–31). The blessing is so potent that it extends also to the heathen, who will join themselves to Israel in the time of salvation. According to ch. xxxiv. 26, "the environs of his hill" will be partakers of it with Israel; according to ch. xvii. 22–24, the descendant of David, at first small and inconsiderable, is raised to the sovereignty of the world; according to ch.

xlvii. 1–12, the waters of the Dead Sea of the world are healed by the stream from the sanctuary. This great revolution of things, however, will give the old covenant people no cause for self-exaltation; it will rather tend to their deep humiliation. They find salvation only through the redeeming mercy of God in common with the heathen world, sunk deep in sin, to whom they are become like, as in sin, so in punishment (ch. xvi. 53–63). And then in the future, along with grace, which is only for the willing, comes also judgment. The prophet announces in ch. v. 4 a second annihilating judgment, which after the Chaldean will come upon the people restored by the grace of God,—a fire which will devour the people as such, and leave only an election of them which participates in the blessings of salvation.

The name of the prophet denotes one in relation to whom God is strong (p. 5), who speaks not out of his own heart, but is moved and determined by a supernatural power. The verification of this name we have in the prophecies before us. That which the Lord said to Peter applies to him, " Flesh and blood hath not revealed it to thee, but the Father in heaven." None of His words have fallen to the ground. The whole course of history has verified His word in ch. xxxiii. 33 : " They shall know that a prophet was in the midst of them."

APPENDIX.

THE CHERUBIM.[1]

I.

WHAT Christian should not feel a desire to know the nature of the cherubim? When we sing the Ambrosian anthem, we dwell with special emotion of heart on the words: "The cherubim and seraphim, and all angels, serve Him." As long as the nature of the cherubim is concealed from us, a whole series of scriptural passages is inaccessible to us. The cherubim occur in the Old Testament no less than eighty-five times. They meet us in the very first pages of revelation: the cherubim and the flame of the blazing sword repel the parents of our race from the tree of life. In the tabernacle and in the temple of Solomon the cherubim receive an important place. The grand visions of Ezekiel in ch. i. and x., even on a superficial examination, awakening the anticipation of a glorious meaning, and presenting a fulness of earnest warning and comfort, are sealed to us, if we have not learned the nature of the cherubim. In the Psalms God appears enthroned on the cherubim, as the firm ground for the confidence of His people; and whosoever will be a partaker of this confidence, must before all know what the cherubim are to signify. Even in the New Testament the holy enigma of the cherubim meets us. John, in the Revelation, sees in the midst of the throne, and about the throne, four beasts full of eyes before and behind, that had no rest day and night, saying, Holy, holy, holy is the Lord God, the Almighty.

The right knowledge of the cherubim, however, has a

[1] From the *Ev. Kirchenzeitung* (*Evangelical Church Gazette*), 1866.

special interest for our own times. The opposition therein existing has its last root in the proper foundations of this knowledge. All questions that now move the heart most deeply go back to the *one*, whether the first article in our Confession of Faith be true or not. Whosoever is at home in this article, into which he has entered in heart and life, to him the other two give no trouble; and whosoever shrinks from these, thereby shows that he has not yet truly received the first article into his heart, even though he may have confessed it with his mouth. Janet, in his work *On the Materialism of our Time in Germany*,[1] says: " Two fundamentally different views of the world and of nature prevail at present. According to the one, the world is only a descending series of causes and effects: something exists from all eternity with certain original properties. From these properties spring phenomena; from the combination of these phenomena arise new phenomena, which on their part give existence to others, and so on without end. There are undesigned and unforeseen wild movements and leaps, which, thanks to the co-operation of a boundless term, have carried on the world as we now see it to-day. According to the other, the world is an organic and living being, that developes itself according to an idea, and raises itself gradually to the completion of a nature eternally inaccessible in its infinite perfection. Each of these steps is conditioned not only by that which precedes it, but also by that which follows it. Each step is designed for progress by the effect which it must introduce. Thus we see nature ascend from dead matter to life, and from life to feeling and thought. According to this view, nature is no longer a kind of play, in which all things are due to accident, whereby an effect is brought out somewhere: it has a plan, a reason, an idea. It is not a kind of improvisation, where each speaks, and thence arises an apparent discourse: it is a real poem, a drama directed by wisdom, where all the threads of the action, however intricate they may be, unite to a definite end. It is an ascending series of means and ends. A first thought has selected and directed. Among the endlessly varied tendencies in which the world was involved by the unconscious and irregular impulse of mechanical causes,

[1] Translated, with introduction and notes, by Fr. v. Reichlin-Meldegg, with a preface by Fichte, Leipzig 1866.

one tendency has prevailed over all. As a horse turned from his path, and urged by a blind rage into a bold course, may strike into a thousand different ways, but when held back and guided by a strong and wary hand, takes only the one which leads to the end; so blind nature, held fast from her origin under the yoke of an incomprehensible will, and guided by a concealed master, ever advances, step by step, with a movement full of grandeur and dignity, to the ideal whose influence rules and animates it. The idea guides the all: it is in the beginning, in the middle, at the end; and nothing arises that is devoid of the idea." In the chief conflict of our times, which, recognised in its significance, makes the oppositions of churches and confessions, important though they may be, ever appear as subordinate, the cherubim, understood in their true nature, give not only a firm hold for the thoughts, but at the same time fill the imagination with a holy image, which, once gained, ever enlightens anew, and precludes the opposite destructive views from all access to the mind.

It is, however, of the first importance to ascertain the true nature of the cherubim. That this is no easy matter, is manifest from the wide diversity of opinions on the subject. The sacred Scripture nowhere gives us a direct explanation of the nature of the cherubim. The key to this matter we have in Gen. iii. There the cherubim meets us in the history of the first man. We learn from this, that the revelation beginning with Abraham found them already existing,—that they do not originally belong to the department of revelation, but to that of natural religion,—that they are an image in which the piety of the primeval world represents the nature of surrounding things. As we have nowhere an intelligent account of the nature of the cherubim, and this is rather presupposed to be already known, we must endeavour to discover it from the scattered hints that have come down to us; and this is a difficult task.

That antiquity was not successful in determining the nature of the cherubim, that it diverged into all manner of conjectures, is explained mainly by the tendency of the older theology to conceive everything in a dogmatic and realistic way, from its incapacity to recognise a poetic element in Scripture,—its misunderstanding of the truth, that it is the problem of Scripture not merely to furnish the understanding with right thoughts, but also the imagination with holy images.

This error, which is the more difficult to remove, because many think to secure their faith by a crude literal apprehension, continues in many forms to the present day. It robs very many of an insight into that which is contained in Scripture, and deprives them, especially in the closing book of the Scripture, where the poetic imagery stands out in so bold relief, of the blessing of a deeper penetration into its meaning.

One thing must be held fast before all, if we go into the definition of the nature of the cherubim, that only that definition can be correct which equally suits all the passages of Scripture in which it occurs, from the first to the last book. Whoever has marked the wonderful unity of Scripture, must be antecedently certain that views which ascribe to the cherubim now this and now that import, thereby pass sentence on themselves. In the present state of scriptural knowledge, a view like that expressed by Herder in the *Spirit of Hebrew Poetry*—namely, "In the oldest legend it was an awe-inspiring, miraculous creature; in the tabernacle, a dead work of art; in the Psalms and poems, a figure; in the prophetic vision, finally, a heavenly creature, bearer of the glory of God"—would be an anachronism, a late birth from the time of rationalism, that had no conception of the unity of the spirit pervading holy Scripture. When Dr. Riehm, in his treatise on the cherubim, assumes that in the Revelation, in which the cherub appears as the combination of the creatures of God, the original and genuine meaning is obscured, he thereby gives us to understand that he has not been able to discover the original and genuine meaning. That he, with his preconceived opinion, has suffered shipwreck in the Revelation, might have induced him to retrace his steps.

Velthusen, in a small treatise on the cherubim, of the year 1764, first came on the right track in defining the nature of the cherubim, though still doubtful and uncertain. "Perhaps," says he (p. 21), "it is merely notified that there is no kind of living creature which the Most High does not employ for His purposes, as well as lifeless nature; and no animal, either rational or irrational, tame or wild, flying or walking on the earth, is excluded from His sway. The figure would then refer to the chief dogma of the Jewish religion, and would be directly opposed to all idolatry, especially to the Egyptian worship of irrational animals, and in particular to the worship of oxen or calves, to which the Israelites so soon showed a leaning."

The merit of having first fully established this view belongs to Bähr in the *Symbolism of the Mosaic Worship*, and in the treatise on the temple of Solomon. "The beings of whom the cherub is composed," says he, "belong to those creatures of the visible world that form the upmost and highest of its three kingdoms—the kingdom of organic life; and in this kingdom, again, they belong to the highest class, to that which has warm blood, and therefore the highest physical life; and in this class they are again the highest. The cherub is far from being a figure of God Himself; on the contrary, its essential character is to be a creature: it is a figure of the creature in its highest stage — an ideal creature. The living powers distributed in the visible creation to the highest creatures are combined and idealized in it." "The whole creation is combined in it as in a point in one being; it represents in so far also the whole creation, and stands naturally of all the creatures nearest to God: only God is above it. The cherub, as creation individualized, is at the same time the being in which the glory of God manifests itself. Hence it appears as the throne of God itself, or in the closest connection with the throne: where Jehovah in His majesty and glory reveals Himself, there the cherub also appears."

This view in the main is alone correct; only it is to be remarked, that the cherubim represent first not the creature in general, but only the animated creation on the earth. Yet this is regarded as the apex of all created things on earth, so that the remainder is in some measure represented by it, and is appended to the animated creation as an accessory, and all the more because it has been created for its sake. But we must not include the heavenly creature: He that sits on the cherubim, and the God of hosts, are co-ordinate expressions; by the hosts are meant the heavenly creatures.

The cherubim never occur alone—always in connection with God. The formation of the symbol has arisen not from the motive of the consideration of nature as such, but from the motive of piety. In the consideration of the multitude of visible creatures the mind may easily distract itself, and dwell on the individual—now on this, now on that. "Whilst they move and search among the works of God, they are caught by the sight, because that which is seen is beautiful," says the author of the Wisdom of Solomon (ch. xiii. 7). The pious mind, therefore, protesting against such distraction and such service of the creature (Rom. i. 15), comprehends all visible multiplicity in an ideal unity, and places this unity absolutely under God, who by His creative Spirit is the foundation of this unity. This representation has for piety a profound significance. If we look to God, who sits above the cherubim, we are filled with adoring reverence for Him, who is so wonderful in His works, with the heartfelt desire to do the will of this God, whose is the earth and the fulness thereof, the world and they that dwell therein (Ps. xxiv. 1), with the dread of calling down upon us the wrath of the God of the spirits of all flesh, with joyful courage in the face of the world, with an absolute refusal to make concessions to it, with a holy contempt for its foolish pursuits, with invincible strength under its persecutions, with the consciousness that it cannot move hand or foot without the influence of God; that in the last resort we have to do, not with it, but with God; that it concerns us to come to terms, not with it, but with God by true repentance; that He visits us through it; and that an endless fulness of means are at His command to help us, when His visitation has attained its end.

If we consider attentively the God who sits above the cherubim, we are filled with deep contempt, holy wrath, and strong pity at the sight of the theory, now so wide-spread, of a degraded, half-brutalized generation. "No power without matter," so runs the theory; "no matter without power. A power ruling over matter is a senseless thought. Power is the property of matter, and inseparable from it. The idea of an absolute creative power, which is distinct from matter, creates it, regulates it according to certain absolute laws, is a pure abstraction." We know, on the contrary, that power is the original principle; that the Spirit, who proceeds from Him who sits above the cherubim, gives to everything its existence; that in Him it lives, and moves, and is. Sabaoth and cherubim—that is our watchword in the face of such error.

The original generation of men with its cherubim, however, not merely raises a protest against the false science of our day, but turns with friendly consent to that which is found in it of true science. There are here two important points of agreement. First, that the living creature, as it is represented by the cherubim, forms a distinct department of the terrestrial creation. And next, that exactly in this department the creative power of God displays itself most gloriously; that of it in a special manner the word of the apostle holds good, " The invisible things of God, His eternal power and Godhead, we see and know in His works." Janet says in regard to this: " Let us hold by the chief facts, which hitherto have supported a distinction not to be effaced between dead or inorganic and living matter. The first and weightiest of these facts is the harmonious unity of the living and organic being; it is, to make use of an expression of Kant, the correlation of the parts to the whole." " Organic bodies," says the great physiologist Müller (Joh. Müller, *Physiol.* v. i. p. 17), " not only differ from inorganic in the mode in which their elements are combined; but the constant activity which works in the living organic matter, acts according to the laws of a rational plan in conformity with an end, because the parts are adapted to the end of the whole: and this it is exactly that marks the organism." Kant says: " The reason of the kind of existence in each part of a living body is contained in the whole, whereas in the dead mass each part bears it in itself." Joh. Müller, quoted by Janet, says further: " The harmony of the members necessary to the whole (in the organism) subsists not *without the influence of a power* (' the Spirit of the living' in Ezek. i. 20, 21), *that works also through the whole, and depends not on the several members, and this power exists before the harmonious members of the whole are joined together:* they are first formed in the development of the embryo by the power of the germ. In a piece of mechanism constructed for a given end—for example, a clock—the whole thus adjusted may exhibit an action proceeding from the co-operation of the several parts, which are set in motion by a cause; but organic beings subsist not merely by an accidental combination of these elements, but produce the organs necessary for the whole by their own power out of the organic matter. This *productive power, acting in conformity with reason*, displays itself in each animal according to strict laws, as the nature of each animal requires: it is already present in the germ, before the later parts of the whole are distinctly present; and it is that which actually produces the members that belong to the idea of the whole."

Even a Moleschott, constrained by the power of the truth, must acknowledge, in p. 57 of the *Treatise on the Unity of Life*, that "the unity of life arises from the deep and universal dependence that concatenates all functions with one another, from the internal and necessary co-operation of the several parts to a given end, which constantly affects all parts of the body from one point, from that most expressive bond operating by symmetry, by freedom, by inviolable and intrinsic utility, that has produced from the noun the ideal adjective "organic," by which we ascribe order, connection, harmony, freedom of movement—in short, capacity of life—to every creation of the human spirit, to languages, to laws, to art, and to every branch of science." On which Reichlin-Meldegg remarks: "The whole is certainly not derived from the favourite principle of material change." Moleschott himself is compelled to declare (p. 37), that "the secret animating the spirit of the naturalist" —the God who sits above the cherubim, and penetrates them with His Spirit—" has not vanished away."

The cherubim, the ideal combination of the multiplicity of living things—this assumption is antecedently the less doubtful, as the holy Scripture expressly intimates that we have here before us not simply realities—that we must distinguish between phenomenon and thing, between the thought and its dress, and thus decidedly opposes the realistic tendencies of those who deal with holy Scripture just as if they had a compend of theology before them. Ezekiel says, in ch. i. 5: "And out of the midst thereof (saw I) the *likeness* of four living creatures." On this Theodoret remarks: "He says not simply that he has seen four animals, but only a likeness of four animals; so that it is obvious that the divine prophets saw not the very essences of the invisible things, but only certain likenesses and patterns, which were shown to them according to the requirements of the great Giver."

II.

The time of mere assertion in the exposition of holy Scripture is past, although many are unwilling to observe this. It is necessary, therefore, in regard to the cherubim, to prove that they are the ideal concentration of the animal kingdom; and on this proof we will now enter.

In regard to the name cherubim, men have given way to manifold conjectures; and the end has been, that they have despaired of any interpretation. The cause of this despair lies in the incorrect definition of the nature of the cherubim. As soon as we recognise in the cherub the ideal unity of the animal creation, the interpretation follows of itself. It means, " as a multitude"—the concentration of all multiplicity on earth into a unity. We have the commentary in Ezek. i. 24: " And I heard the noise of their wings, like the noise of many waters, as the voice of the Almighty in their going, the voice of *a roaring like the voice of a host*. Here is developed before us the " like many."[1]

The designation, " the living," takes the place of a second proper name of the cherubim. The idea of the living creature

---

[1] Analogous is Kabul, " as nothing," the name of the district which Solomon gave to Hiram, 1 Kings ix. 13 (Ewald and Thenius). The כ enters into the composition of the proper name; and so this may stand in the plural, and with the article. By the origin of the proper name is explained the tendency to use the singular along with the plural, as Ps. xviii. 11, Ezek. ix. 3. That the כ belongs not to the root, is, as Abenezra says on Ex. xxv. 18, the old Jewish tradition, and has also remained, according to Abenezra, who combats this view, the usual Jewish assumption. " *Hanc traditionem*," says Buxtorf, *Exercitationes*, p. 100, "*fere omnes neoterici Judæi amplectuntur.*" In their conception of the second element of the proper name the Jewish expositors deviate from the correct view, which did not agree with their preconceived opinion that the cherubim are angels. They explain, " as *youths.*" But we can show, that even at an earlier period these two elements were conceived with at least verbal correctness. Theodoret often repeats the remark, that the word rendered into Greek signifies the *multitude* of knowledge—on Ezek. i. 22, x. 1, and at the close of ch. x.: πλῆθος and πλήρης always recur in him. We cannot pursue this explanation further. According to Philo, in the *Life of Moses*, b. iii. p. 668, the name of the cherubim signifies *much* knowledge and science. The word yields the *muchness:* the man infected with knowledge adds of himself the knowledge.

is already fixed by the first chapter of the first book of Moses. There the living creature is only on the earth, including the water and the sky. According to Gen. ii. 7, the living creature has a twofold source, the earthly material and the quickening breath of God. According to Gen. ix. 16, " every living creature, all flesh which is upon the earth," the idea of the living creature is covered by that of the (animated) flesh, which belongs only to the earth. Now, the circumstance that the cherubim are called living creatures, might in itself be only a designation of the genus to which they belong—only express that they, like many other things, are living creatures. Even according to this view, a series of hypotheses would be excluded by the fact that the cherubim are to be sought among the number of living creatures. To these the angels in particular do not belong, who have been reckoned among the cherubim, according to the assumption very widely spread among Jews and Christians, and first thoroughly contravened by Vitringa. The remark of Theodoret, " The angels are living creatures no less than men—the latter mortal, the former immortal;" and likewise that of Keil, " The cherubim, as living creatures, take the highest place in the realm of spirits,"—are contrary to the usage of speech, in which the living always denotes the animated earthly creation, in opposition to the lifeless. But we must not stop at this point. The fact that the designation of the cherubim as living creatures takes exactly the place of the proper name—as in Revelation the name cherubim does not occur, they are only designated as living creatures —shows that by this designation their nature must be fully expressed, that the genus does not exist beyond them, but is completely represented by them. All doubt, however, is removed by this, that the singular designation, " the living creature," alternates with that of the cherubim as living creatures (Ezek. i. 20, 21, " The spirit of the living creatures was in the wheels;" x. 15, " And the cherubim were lifted up;" x. 20, " This is the *living creature* that I saw by the river of Chebar"). This singular designation shows that in the cherubim the whole genus of the living on earth, man and beast, is represented.

On the cherubim, further, the signature of the *number four* is impressed in the strongest manner. Four animals appear in Ezekiel and in Revelation. In the former still further play is given to the number four: the four animals have each four faces and four wings. This number four in itself points to the earth. The number four always appears in the Old Testament as the signature of the earth. We have four classes of living creatures on the earth besides man, in Gen. vii. 21, 23: "All flesh, that moves upon the earth, in *fowl*, and in *cattle*, and in *wild beast*, and in *creeping thing*, that creepeth upon the earth." In Ps. cxlviii., the creatures who shall praise God on the earth are four times four. In particular is to be compared ver. 10, "wild beasts and all cattle, the creeping thing and winged fowl." The number four thus constrains us to remain on the earth, and does not at all permit us, for ex., to think of the angels belonging to heaven. We are led, however, still further, when we take a nearer view of the four animals of which the cherub is composed. Only on the assumption that the cherub is the concentration of all that lives on the earth, can this composition be referred to a rational ground. The four animals appear as the representatives of the four classes of the animal world. An old Jewish saying runs thus: "Four are the highest in the creation,—the lion among the beasts, the ox among the cattle, the eagle among the fowls, and man above all; but God is the highest of all." Here we have briefly and well the explanation of the phrase, He that sitteth above the cherubim. That the ox comes actually into consideration as the representative of the *cattle*, appears from this, that, on purpose to preclude other interpretations, the calf is twice put in its place, in which those properties of the ox, which the other interpretations have in view, are not at all present (Ezek. i. 7; Rev. iv. 7). And that the eagle is designed to represent the class of birds, appears from the same passage in Revelation, "And the fourth beast was like unto a flying eagle," where the epithet of the eagle can have no other end.

Of importance is also the position which *man* takes in the composition of the cherubim. It is quite that which we should antecedently expect, if the cherubim are the representation of all that lives on the earth. According to the position which is assigned to man among the living creatures in the Mosaic history of the creation, in the symbolic representation of the animal world, no mere co-ordination of man with the other kinds of living creatures could take place: the human type must preponderate in the representation of the living. Quite so we find it in the cherubim. In the cherubs in the tabernacle and the temple of Solomon all is human, as it appears, except the wings: all the rest of the animal world must be contented with this one symbolic representation, which is taken from that class which in the history of the creation opens the series of living things, as man closes it. In Ezekiel, ch. i., the human face is towards the *east*. This is, in the Old Testament, the front and chief quarter. Right and left are the lion and the ox; behind, the eagle, which, according to what has been remarked, takes also the last place in Genesis. The creation proceeds from the lower to the higher. First fish (which is here left out of account, as belonging to the lower stage of life), and fowl, and last man. According to Ezek. i. 5, the human form is further predominant in the cherubim, and this is very emphatically exhibited at the very beginning of their description. From man, who according to Gen. i. is the crown of the animal creation, as the only bearer of the divine likeness, the lord of the whole remaining creation, they have the upright walk, the hands, and other peculiarities.

That the cherubs represent the animal kingdom in a concentrated form appears also from this, that according to 1 Kings vii. 29, in the temple of Solomon, lions, kine, and cherubim were figured on the bases of the lavers for the purifying of the sacrificial flesh. This fact shows, on the one hand, that the cherubim of Solomon did not bear the faces of the lion and the ox, like those of Ezekiel. This is only explained then, when we find that in the cherubim of Solomon, externally viewed, only man, and the class of birds that are at the other extreme, were represented,—man in the whole figure, the birds only in the wings, the design of which to represent the flying clearly appears, especially from this passage. Josephus, who at his own hand adds the eagle, and Züllig, who thought that the eagle had only been left out " from inadvertence," overlooked the fact that the eagle could not be introduced, because the bird had its representation already in the very form of the cherubim. But on the other hand also, the addition of the lion and the ox, with which Dr. Riehm knows not what to do, to the cherubim, shows that they must stand to these in an internal relation; and such only finds place when the cherubim represent the animal world. Then the lions and oxen come in at their side, completing and explaining, inasmuch as they represent those classes of animals which had found no express representation in the cherubim themselves, though implied in them. Züllig rightly remarks, that the grouping together of the cherubs with the lions and the oxen presupposes the thought that the whole animal kingdom falls into those four classes designated by the noblest of every kind. Not merely on the ark and the walls of the temple, but on the other furniture of it, was the signature of the Almighty Lord of nature impressed. Israel was to be constantly reminded that his God is not *a* god, but God absolutely, possessed of infinite power to bless and to punish, the only One in the whole universe who is worthy to be feared and loved, and certainly with all the heart, with all the soul, and with all the powers. Hand in hand with the absoluteness of His power goes the requirement of absolute devotion to Him. The God of the spirits of all flesh desires an undivided heart. All other things depend absolutely on Him: it is therefore unreasonable to divide the heart between Him and these others; and because unreasonable, wicked; and because wicked, the object of the divine resentment.

Only when the cherub represents the animal world can we explain also the grouping of it with palms and flowers. According to 1 Kings vi. 29, all the walls in the temple of Solomon bore " round about in carved work, cherubim, and palms, and open flowers." It is clear as light that the cherubim must be placed under the same point of view with the palms and flowers. If we suppose, with Bähr, that the palms and flowers are in general symbols of salvation,—that the adorning with flowers denotes the state of the richest fulness of life, of prosperity and happiness,—we violently sever the flowers from the cherubim, with which they are inseparably connected. Ezekiel says, in the description of the new temple, in ch. xli. 18, 19, 25 : "And there were made cherubim and palms, and a palm between cherub and cherub; and the cherub had two faces. And the face of a man toward the palm on this side, and the face of a lion toward the palm on that side; they were made on the whole house round about. And there were made on the doors of the temple cherubim and palms, like as they were made on the walls." The inseparable connection between the cherubs and the palms appears here still more strongly than in the temple of Solomon,—namely in this, that the faces of the cherubs look towards the palms. We cannot therefore regard as correct the opinion of Dr. Kliefoth, that " the palms remind us of the feast of tabernacles, and the cherub-figures are signs of the presence of God, who has His dwelling here." Thus the cherubs and palms fall quite asunder. There is only *one* way of explaining the connection of the cherubs with the palms and flowers. The cherubs are first a representation of the living; but at the same time, as the living forms the crown of the whole earthly creation, this also is represented by it. The addition of the palms and flowers serves to indicate this more comprehensive meaning, and to show that the living forms no counterpart to the rest of nature, but rather represents this also. Next to the animal creation, the vegetable kingdom is the most glorious revelation of the creative power of God. In modern science it is connected with the animal kingdom, under the head of the organic creation. But the vegetable kingdom cannot be better represented than by the palms and flowers. According to Celsius, the palm is called by the Arabs " the blessed tree." Libanius says of it: " The palm raises itself on high, and removes itself as far as possible from the earth. It hastens as it were towards heaven, and cannot bear to remain on earth, though sprung from it." Celsius carries out the thought: " Palms and men are similar in many respects." Linné called the palms " the princes of the vegetable kingdom ;" Humboldt, " the noblest of plants, to which the nations ever assign the prize of beauty." As the animal life culminates in man, lion, ox, and eagle, so the vegetable life in the palms and flowers. Herbs and trees are the two halves of the vegetable kingdom in the history of the creation: the tripartition of the vegetable kingdom, which some expositors have there assumed, rests on a false explanation. The herb culminates in the flower; the king of the trees is the palm. We have a commentary on the grouping of the palms with the cherubim in Ps. cxlviii. In this psalm, the design of which is to raise the children of God to gladness, by pointing to the supremacy of the Almighty God over nature, " mountains and all hills, fruit-trees and all cedars" (ver. 9), praise the Lord; " beasts and all cattle, creeping things and winged fowl" (ver. 10); and men with kings at the head, in ver. 11 f.; and thence down to the smallest, praise Him. As the objects quoted in ver. 10 f., as speaking proofs of the omnipotence of God, correspond to the cherubim, so do the fruit-trees and all cedars to the palms and flowers. The cedars and palms contend for the rank of being " the trees of God" (Ps. civ. 16, lxxx. 11).

That the cherubs represent the living creatures on earth, and in general the terrestrial creation, is borne out by the relation in which they stand in Ezekiel to the "vault." It is said, Ezek. i. 22, " And there was a likeness over the heads of the living creature as a vault, as the look of the crystal the terrible (the awe-inspiring, imposing, glorious), stretched out over their heads above." This vault is the place of the throne of God. In ver. 26 it is said, " And above the vault that was over their head, in appearance as a sapphire-stone, the likeness of a throne, and upon the likeness of a throne one like the appearance of a man." There can be no doubt that the vault is a type of the heavens; for in the representation of the universe, as it is given in this majestic vision, the heavens cannot be wanting, and so much the less as it appears in the scriptures of the Old and New Testament as absolutely the most important part of creation, while the earth in reference to it occupies a lower place. The *vault* is, moreover, according to Gen. i., the vault of heaven. The heaven appears as *the place of the throne of God* elsewhere in a great number of passages; for ex. Isa. lxvi. 1, " The heaven is my throne, and the earth is my footstool." " Stretched out :" this is the usual designation of the relation in which the heaven stands to the earth; as, for instance, Isaiah (in ch. xl. 22) says, " Who sitteth upon the circle of the earth, and its inhabitants are as grasshoppers; that *stretcheth out* the heavens as a curtain, and spreadeth them out as a tent to dwell in." To the comparison with "the crystal the terrible" corresponds that which Daniel (ch. xii. 3) says of the sublime splendour of the vault of heaven. If it is certain on these grounds that the vault means the heavens, the cherubim under the vault can only represent the terrestrial creation; for heaven and earth are usually joined together in the Old Testament as the two spheres of the glorification of God. On that which is here presented to the prophet in a figure—above all, the Lord, under Him the vault, and under the vault the cherubim—Isaiah in ch. xlii. 5 gives the commentary: "Thus saith the Lord, who created the heavens and stretched them out, that spread forth the *earth* and its products, that giveth breath unto the people upon it, and spirit to them that walk therein." As Ezekiel presents Him who sits above the vault and the cherubim as a terror to the secure sinners, who expected to be able to attain salvation without repentance, and shows them that there is no refuge for them in the whole universe; so Isaiah points out Him who stretches out the heavens and spreads forth the earth, as the security for the poor worm Jacob, that he shall not abide in death, but be raised to a glorious life, and attain to the supremacy of the world. In the whole universe is no power that can injure him, and all powers that rule in the universe stand absolutely at the disposal of Him who will achieve the salvation of Zion.

It is also of decisive import, that He who sits on the cherubim is often joined with the God of *hosts*, the God whom sun, moon, and stars obey, which appear in holy Scripture not as mere flickering luminaries, but as the "powers of heaven," that far surpass the earth in glory. The whole earthly sphere only stands worthily beside the heavenly sphere of God's omnipotence, being represented by the cherubim, the concentration of the living, in which the whole earthly creation culminates. The 80th Psalm, which expresses the grief of Judah for the captivity of the ten tribes, and entreats God to make an end of the desolation of His vine, begins with the words, "Thou Shepherd of Israel, give ear; Thou that leadest Joseph like a flock, that sittest above the cherubim, shine forth." He turns first to the love and pastoral faithfulness of God, and then to His omnipotence, to which the whole terrestrial creation, with all its power, is subject. The second strophe begins with the words, "O Lord God of *hosts*, how long wilt Thou burn against the prayer of Thy people?" Here the Lord of the heavenly powers appears beside the Lord of the earthly. In 1 Sam. iv. 4 it is said: "And the people sent to Shiloh, and brought thence the ark of the covenant of the Lord of *hosts*, who *sitteth on the cherubim*." The author has already in view the sad catastrophe which he has to relate in the sequel, the taking of the ark of the covenant by the Philistines. In view of this, he makes it prominent that the ark of the covenant is the sanctuary of the Almighty Lord of heaven and earth, so that the loss of it cannot arise from the impotence of the God of Israel, but from the sins of the people, whom God condemned by His righteous judgment to the loss of their sanctuary. According to 2 Sam. vi. 2, David goes with all the people to bring up the ark of God, on which is named the name of the Lord *of hosts, who sitteth on the cherubim.* The words imply that the undertaking was a sublime one, with which a new epoch began for the people of God. He who made His entrance anew among them was not one among the many, was the Almighty Lord of heaven and earth. We have the elucidation of the two names Jehovah Zebaoth and Sitting on the cherubim in Ps. cxlviii. There praise the Lord, first, from the heavens and the heights, all His angels, all His hosts, sun, and moon, and all the stars of light; then from the earth, beasts and all cattle, the creeping thing and all winged fowl, the kings of the earth and all peoples, young men and maidens, old men and children. The practical result is this: "He exalteth the horn of His people, the praise of all His saints, the children of Israel, a people near unto Him. Hallelujah." The church is preserved as sure as God Almighty reigns in heaven and on earth; no power there prevails that had not its origin in Him, and by Him is given and taken.

This also leads to the given interpretation, that He who sitteth on the cherubim is often joined with the name Elohim, which designates the God of Israel as the Deity absolutely, the possessor of all the fulness of the Godhead—for instance, in 1 Sam. iv. 4 and Ps. lxxx.—and also with other designations of true deity and absolute omnipotence. Hezekiah, when he was extremely oppressed by Assyria, at that time the concentration of the world-power, prays (2 Kings xix. 15), "O Lord God of Israel, who sittest on the cherubim, Thou art God alone over all the kingdoms of the earth; Thou hast made heaven and earth. Let all the kingdoms of the earth know that Thou, Lord, art God alone." The sitting of God over the cherubim appears as the immediate security that the world-power can have no advantage over the people of God, and as running parallel with God's being over all the kingdoms of the earth, and with the creating of heaven and earth, which is secondary to it, as well as with His being God alone. No other interpretation of the cherubim is sufficient to explain this fact. In none is the idea of omnipotence, and especially of sovereignty over the earth, given simply along with sitting above the cherubim; in none is the sitting above the cherubim absolutely equivalent to God alone, and the Creator of heaven and earth.

David says, in the description of the all-powerful interposition of God against his foes (Ps. xviii. 10), "He rode upon a cherub, and flew, and soared upon the wings of the wind." Elsewhere God usually sits on the cherubim, here He rides upon them. The explanation of this is, that the Almighty Sovereign of the earth, from whose hand no one can deliver, who is able to save whom He will save, even him that is sunk in the lowest depth of misery, and can destroy whom He will, even the mightiest, is here found in action. As sure as God sits, so surely He also rides. The sitting denotes the constant relation, the moving the particular operation of this relation. If God be the Lord of the whole earthly creation, He must also give practical effect to this lordship for the salvation of His own, and for the destruction of His foes. What principally concerns us, however, in this place, and forms an important contribution to the discovery of the nature of the cherubim, is the connection of the cherubim with the wind. This connection is explained only where we perceive in the cherubim the representation of that which lives. The wind represents the power of nature. The Lord of all that lives is at the same time He who "gives way, course, path to clouds, air, and winds." Whosoever has Him for a friend, need not despair though the bands of hell surround him, and the cords of death overpower him. His God sends out of the height, and fetches him, and draws him out of many waters.

Hand in hand with the grouping together of cherub and wind, in Ps. xviii., goes the fact that in Ezekiel under and along with the cherubim appear four *wheels*. By these wheels are the powers of nature designated, which serve God no less than the living creatures. The point of comparison is the weight. Joh. Heermann expresses the thought that finds its picturesque expression in the wheels in the song, "Ah, God, how dreadful is thy wrath," thus:

> "Thou art the Lord and God alone,
> Whom thunder, lightning, wind obey,
> Whom all things are compelled to own,
> And do His will without delay.
>
> Lord, where is any like to Thee,
> In heaven above or earth below?
> Who hath a realm so great and free,
> That all must reverence to Him show?"

The proof that the wheels are the powers of nature, in addition to the joining of the cherub with the wind in Ps. xviii., is found in Ezek. x. 13, where the prophet expressly declares concerning the import of the wheels, "The wheels, they were called the whirlwind in mine ear." With this Isa. v. 28 is to be compared. As there the wheels in the war-chariots of the world-power sent by God for the punishment of His rebellious people are compared with the whirlwind, so here inversely the whirlwind, representing the powers equal to it in weight, appears under the figure of the wheels. Ezek. x. 6 affords a further proof of this. There the *fire* with which the ungodly Jerusalem shall be burned is taken from between the wheels, and certainly from the cherub, who hands it to the angel. Jerusalem was to be burned by men, otherwise than Sodom and Gomorrah. But their activity is only subordinate, being directed by God. They take the fire from between the wheels; and the angel stands behind and above them, who performs the work of burning. These are quite clear and certain grounds, which leave no doubt concerning the import of the wheels. To the wheels of Ezekiel correspond in Ps. cxlviii. 8, fire, hail, snow, and vapour, stormy wind fulfilling His word, which there appear along with the living creatures on the earth as the practical praise of God, as the security of the victory of His church. How the powers of nature serve God along with the cherubim, the history of Job shows: of the four catastrophes there, two are effected by human instruments, so that they belong to the department of the cherubim, and two by the powers of nature—the fire of God and the wind. The word of the Psalmist also (Ps. civ.) serves to elucidate the symbol of the wheels: "Who maketh the clouds His chariot, who walketh upon the wings of the wind; who maketh the winds His angels, and a flaming fire His ministers." Here the clouds appear as the chariot of God, because He leads them whither He will; the winds are obedient to Him as their Master, as the horses to their earthly driver. The application to the relations of the people of God is this: He who gives a way, course, and path to the clouds, air, and winds, will also find a way where thy foot may go. "Whither the spirit was to go," it is said (Ezek. i. 20) of the cherubim, "thither they went, and the wheels lifted themselves equally with them; for the spirit of the living creatures was in the wheels." The creature and the powers of nature work equally for the end appointed by God, for salvation or for destruction, because both are equally dependent on the Spirit of God moving them; so that we have nowhere to do properly with man or beast, fire or storm, but always with their Lord, who summons and sets them in motion. The unity of the Spirit in the beasts and in the wheels points to this, that in consequence of their equal dependence on God, they both with one accord obey the will of God, be it for blessing or for punishment, as in the destruction of Jerusalem the Chaldeans and the fire co-operated.

Only, if the cherubim are the concentration of all that lives, can it be explained that they, as well as the wheels, are all covered with *eyes* in Ezekiel and in Revelation. In Ezek. i. 8 it is said that the felloes of the wheels connected with the cherubs were full of eyes. This is to show that the powers of nature, notwithstanding their apparent wild irregularity, are under the guidance of Divine Providence. The wind appears to go whither it will; but, in truth, it has no independent will: a secret hidden power binds all its movements according to a wise design. "The eyes," remarks Hitzig, "are on the outside of the felloes, not the inside: naturally, for they are to look outwards into the world and on the way, not turned inwards, to regard the spokes and the axle." The place in which the eyes are set shows that the powers of nature, in their action on the world and their relation to man, are not subject to a blind chance, but are guided by deliberate counsel—that reason is in them, because above them. While the passage now discussed refers only to the wheels, it is said in ch. x. 12 of the cherubim themselves, "And their whole flesh, and their backs, and their hands, were full of eyes round about." And in Rev. iv. 6 it is said, "And in the midst of the throne, and round about the throne, were four beasts, full of eyes before and behind." The thought expressed by the symbol of the eyes in the cherubim, the Psalmist enunciates in the words (Ps. civ. 24), " How *manifold* are thy works, O Lord!" (the cherub is the being that represents the *multiplicity* of the works of God;) "in *wisdom* hast Thou made them all." And this thought lies at the root of that which is said in Prov. viii. 22-31 concerning the constructive wisdom of God. In the living creation rules no chance, but everywhere law, order, design: it is not a *monstrum horrendum ingens cui lumen ademtum*, as the modern materialists teach, who place themselves on a parallel with the apes, from which they derive the origin of the human race; but all in it is guided by intelligence. This belongs not to the creatures, but to God, who has created them in wisdom, and in wisdom guides and directs them. The whole living creation is penetrated by the spirit; and where the spirit is, there is also reason, end, design. For the spirit is the spirit of the personal intelligence. The whole living creation has its origin in God, and therefore bears the seal of intelligence in its being and in its working. The worm in the dust has no less the signature of the eye than man. That this is the import of the eyes, is shown by Zech. iii. 9, according to which seven eyes are directed to the one foundation-stone of the temple that was then to be built anew: the thought can be nothing else than this, that the building of the temple was under the special guidance of Divine *Providence*. Further (Zech. iv. 10), the seven eyes of the Lord, which pervade the whole earth, preside over the building of the temple. The eyes here are the powers of God, which work not blindly, but are the radiations of His providence. These eyes penetrate the whole earth, to counteract the dangers from every quarter to the kingdom of God, and from all sides to gather help. According to Rev. v. 6, the Lamb has seven eyes as well as seven horns, which are the seven spirits of God sent into all the earth. Horns and eyes denote here the whole fulness of divine power and intelligence with which Christ is endowed for the destruction of His foes and the salvation of His own. If the eyes are so conceived as the symbol of intelligence, which does not perhaps dwell in the cherubim, but is developed in them, this explains also the connection in which (Rev. iv. 8) the eyes of the cherubim stand with their song of praise. This forms, accordingly, the *elucidation* to the eyes. It is there said, "And around and within they are full of eyes, and have no rest day and night, and say, Holy, holy, holy is God the Lord, the Almighty." The expression already employed, around (before) and within (behind) they are full of eyes, would be an *unnecessary* repetition, if it did not stand in close connection with the following; and because they are a living actual testimony to the wisdom and glory of God, they unceasingly proclaim by their very presence that which is holy.

The cherubim are full of eyes, in accordance with which modern science, so far as it really deserves the name of science, and is not a secretion of "evil beasts, slow bellies," acknowledges that nature appears throughout as a work of intellect—that the stamp of providence is impressed upon it. The celebrated naturalist of Petersburg, Karl von Baer, in the treatise, *What View of Animated Nature is the Correct One?* Berlin, 1862, calls "the processes of life" ideas of creation: he finds in the natural instinct of the insect-world "something original, not proceeding from the constitution of the body, but standing above it." Instinct is to him "an emanation from the universe, and not from the bodily relations. The intelligence, which lies at the root of it, is *not the intelligence of the beasts, but a necessity which a higher intelligence has laid upon them.*" He cites, among other examples, the life-process of the gnat, which begins its life in the water and closes it in the air. While it places itself on a leaf floating on the water, or an overhanging blade of grass, it lets its eggs fall into the water, because the newly-formed germ must begin its existence in the water. Here we cannot think of a prescience of the gnat, and yet it acts in the given case quite as if the future fate of the brood were known to it. It shuns the water as long as it has no need of it; it seeks it when it becomes necessary for the future germ. The sainted Schubert has already referred to many similar facts in the *Mirror of Nature*, which has not, we think, obtained the circulation it deserves. Professor Fichte says, in the preface to the German translation of Janet's

Treatise on Materialism, " The spirit of materialism and the spirit of natural philosophy are diametrically opposed; they stand essentially in irreconcilable contradiction. That which animates all natural philosophy, which fills it with ever new enthusiasm, is the never actually disappointed confidence, that there is *reason in things;* that an intrinsic harmony and an intelligent mutual adaptation embraces the whole as well as the parts of nature; in short, that that great principle never and nowhere denies itself, which speculation has designated as ' immanent teleology,' the internal design and *omnipresent reason* in things. And that which natural philosophy actually finds, which it most emphatically proves and brings to be admitted without question, is only the perpetual confirmation of this great thought. It is, according to its proper spirit, an *uninterrupted worship of God,* a rational and intelligent glorification of that inexhaustible wisdom which reveals itself in nature. The materialistic view is by no means a protest merely against a philosophical or religious theory, but against the whole finding of experience—against the constitution of the universe itself. The creation must have been different, if materialism was to be right. And so we say with confidence, if it should ever be accounted the true and all-sufficient conception of the world, then would the last memory of the great results of natural philosophy vanish, and scientific barbarism would make good its entrance." These are golden words; and if the author had spoken no other than these, he would deserve to have lived. He has thereby fulfilled the highest task assigned to science: " I will ascribe righteousness to my Maker" (Job xxxvi. 3). Hence may those learn to be ashamed of themselves, who, like C. Vogt, are full of eyes round about, and yet cannot see,—who thus divest themselves of the high privilege of men, to acknowledge Him whose seal is impressed upon all nature.

The cherub signifies that which lives on earth: only by acknowledging this is the joining of the cherub with the elders in Revelation explained. The elders are there the representatives of the church. If they are purely ideal beings, an ideal element will also be present in the cherubs that are joined with them; and those will be astray who simply see in them real beings. In ch. xiv. 3, the community of the completed saints on the heavenly Zion sing the new song " before the throne, and before the four beasts and the elders." The ground on which the four beasts are here joined with the elders we learn from ver. 4, where it is said of the elect in their heavenly perfection, " These are bought out of men, to be first-fruits unto God and the Lamb." The four beasts, or more exactly, the " four living creatures," have their culminating point in man; and the glorification of the human race is here solemnized in the glory of the elect. In the similar scene, ch. vii. 9–17, in which the believers in Christ are brought before us in the heavenly glory which awaits them, the elders go before the four beasts, after whom they were placed in ch. iv. Where the elders stand before, they come into view as the party immediately concerned. On the contrary, the four beasts have a claim to the first place, because they represent the genus, while the elders form only a species of that genus. There the one condition is satisfied, here the other. No less clear and transparent, according to our view, is the connection of the elders and the four beasts in ch. xix. 4. Here the twenty-four elders and the four beasts fall down and worship God, who sits on the throne, saying, Amen; Hallelujah. The starting-point, the great deed of God, which calls forth the worship and praise, is the overthrow of the great whore. Along with the representatives of the church, over which the bloody persecution of the Roman empire, represented by the adulterous woman, has passed, the representatives also of the animal creation on earth offer their thanks for the redemption of the earth, which, according to ver. 2, it had corrupted by its whoredom, its crafty hypocritical policy. Not merely the church, but all mankind, trodden under foot, is interested in the overthrow of imperial Rome.

Only if the cherubs are the combination of that which lives on earth, is explained their interest in the judgments on the earth in Revelation. On the opening of the first four seals, in ch. vi., the seer each time hears one of the four say, with a voice of thunder, " Come and see." The beasts announce the different phenomena of the judgment, because they are the representatives of the living on the earth, on which the judgments shall fall. In ch. vi. 6 it is further said : " And I heard a voice in the midst of the four beasts say, A measure of wheat for a penny, and three measures of barley for a penny, and hurt not the oil and the wine." The voice sounds "in the midst of the four beasts," because this news concerns them. The cherubim accordingly represent beings who are concerned in the thriving of wheat and barley, oil and wine—who must suffer want in years of famine. On this must all other views of the cherubim suffer shipwreck; for ex., that of the creative powers of God, of the angels, of the four evangelists, of the officers in the church. In ch. xv. 7, one of the four beasts gives to the seven angels seven golden cups full of the wrath of God, who liveth for ever and ever. The earthly creature of God on whom the judgments fall, by this act acknowledges their righteousness. It says with downcast head, We receive what we have deserved.

Only by the view in question is explained also the fact, that the cherubim appear so regularly under the throne of God, and indeed in circumstances where it is either intended to give comfort to the church in the face of the seemingly omnipotent world, and to assure it of the certainty of the victory over the world, as in Rev. iv., or where it is designed to oppose the blindness of the degenerate sons of the church, who expected to be able to escape the vengeance of their angry God, as in Ezekiel. The cherubim under the throne, which indicate that God is the God of the spirits of all flesh, equally oppose the despair and the security of the church.

Finally, the only plausible one among the other various conceptions of the cherubim—the only one, also, which possesses a wide popularity, and an existence so tenacious, that it is ever turning up anew, that which takes them to be angels—suffers shipwreck on Rev. v. 11, "And I beheld, and I heard the voice of many angels round about the throne, and the beasts, and the elders: and their number was ten thousand times ten thousand;" and on Rev. vii. 11, "And all the angels stood round about the throne, and the elders, and the four beasts, and fell before the throne on their face, and worshipped God." The diversity of the beasts from the angels is here clear as the sun. The myriads of angels, *all* angels, form the *environs* of the circle, in which, with the throne and the twenty-four elders, the four beasts also are found. Further, the department of the cherubim is always sharply defined by that of the angels. The cherubim never perform the part of messengers, of the " spirits who are sent to minister" (Heb. i. 14), of "the mighty in strength, who do the commandments of God, hearkening unto the voice of His word" (Ps. ciii. 20). Their business is only to be under the throne of God—to set forth His omnipotence—to thank and praise God, because their presence is the actual praise of God, in accordance with Ps. ciii. 22, " Bless the Lord, all His works, in all places of His dominion ;" as, according to Ps. xix., the heavens declare the glory of God, of which they are a speaking proof; and then, on account of His benefits, which He bestows upon His creatures on earth; finally, to be active in the representation of the judgments which fall upon the earth. On the whole, only few words are put into their mouth, in proof that speaking is not their proper business; that it is only granted them for the interpretation of the practical speech, which is implied in their very presence.

Our task, to demonstrate the correct interpretation of the symbol of the cherubim, is completed. It remains now to examine more particularly some of the principal passages in which the cherubim are mentioned.

III.

We turn our eye first to the properly fundamental passage, Gen. iii. 24, " And He drove out the man, and placed at the east of the garden of Eden the cherubim and the flame of the flashing sword, to keep the way to the tree of life."

The thought that most obviously meets us here, in accordance with the original state of the human race, that is pictured as it were before our eyes, is, that by the *wrathful omnipotence* of God men found themselves wholly excluded from the life which should have been the reward of their true obedience.

The wrath of God is figured by the flashing sword. We may not assign the sword to the cherubs. For it is not said, *with* the flame (Luther has freely translated, the cherubim *with* a naked hewing sword), but, *and* the flame. The sword appears as a second power along with the cherubim. A sword would not indeed suit the many cherubim. And then the cherubim have never and nowhere anything to do with the sword. They are in themselves quite unconcerned with the divine wrath, which is represented by the sword. Under other circumstances, if man were not fallen, they would appear themselves friendly in a friendly circle, as the cherubim on the ark of the covenant already show. As bearer of the sword we have, according to all parallel passages, much more to think of God or His angel, who carries on all His relations with the human race. In the books of Moses himself, it is God who says (Deut. xxxii. 41), " If I whet the flash of my sword, and my hand take hold on judgment, I will take vengeance on my adversaries, and requite them that hate me." With drawn sword the angel of the Lord appears to Balaam, and also to David when he sinned in numbering the people (1 Chron. xxi. 16). Also in Josh. v. 13, Isa. xxxiv. 5, the sword belongs to God and His angel. If, then, the sword is to be placed in the closest relation with God, the same holds good in regard to the cherubim. According to the analogy of all other passages, we shall have to think of God as sitting upon them, as appearing above them; and so much the more, because the cherubim are never employed on any mission like the angels. The seeming independence of the cherubim, as of the sword, is only put forward, in order that these points in the whole phenomenon might engage the attention of the first men—namely, the wrath of God and His omnipotence, which are sufficient to show that every attempt to reach that which is prohibited is foolish and vain. " He placed the cherubim and the sword," then, is as much as to say, He that sitteth on the cherubim, and beareth the sword, shut him out. " To place" occurs elsewhere in the sense of setting up (Josh. xviii. 1), and is of abiding significance. He set up, not without or beside Himself, but Himself appearing over them. In point of fact, the setting up of the cherubim still takes place after every sin. The conscience calls to the sinner, that he is wholly excluded by the wrath of God from access to salvation. A whole swarm of false views meets us in this passage. The cherubim are not " guardians of paradise" nor " executors of judgment:" they do not serve to exhibit " the majestic presence of God *in the attitude of wrath*," with which the cherubim have nothing whatever to do, and which is represented here by the *sword* alone. Much less still may we say that the garden is given to the cherubs for a *dwelling-place*: in that case the same must also hold good of the sword. We have here no " mythic being" before us, no " griffin," but the presentation of an eternally true thought in pictorial form, in the spirit of the olden time, in which the thought of itself took flesh and blood. This is the truth in one of the many unfortunate hypotheses concerning the second and third chapters of Genesis, which regarded the contents of this chapter as an attempt to translate a hieroglyphic picture into words.

Turn we now to the cherubim over the *ark of the covenant* in the tabernacle. The state of things as it is represented in Ex. xxvi. 16 f. is this. In the ark of the covenant is laid the " testimony," externally represented by the two tables of the law. Over the testimony is the " mercy-seat," externally represented by the lid of the ark. Over the mercy-seat rise two cherubim, in close connection with it, externally represented by this, that they are formed of the same mass of gold of which the mercy-seat is made, and, as it were, grow out of it. The cherubs stand on the two ends of the mercy-seat. The faces of the two are directed towards one another. They look down on the mercy-seat. The mercy-seat is covered by their outstretched *wings*. Over the cherubim sits the Lord, and thence communicates to Moses all His orders to the people.

The following is the exposition of these facts. The foundation of the covenant of God with Israel is the testimony, the revelation of the will of God to Israel. This is a great grace which the Lord has bestowed on His people, and in them on the church of all times, that they should possess in His word a light on their paths, as the Psalmist sings: " He showeth His word unto Jacob, His statutes and His judgments unto Israel. He hath not dealt so with any nation, and His judgments they have not known. Hallelujah." And as Moses himself says (Deut. iv. 8): " And what nation is so great, that hath statutes and judgments so righteous as all this law, which I set before you this day?" If with this boon they are true—if they endeavour with all their heart to fulfil His commands, they have in the mercy-seat the pledge of the forgiveness of their sins of infirmity, or as Philo expresses himself, of the " gracious power of God." This is the second great benefit. From the second arises a third: from the propitiation comes forth the protection of the cherubim, who with their faces cast a friendly look on the mercy-seat and the ransomed people, and cover it with their protecting wings. To those who love God, and are loved of Him, must all things work for the best: the creatures go with their Creator. If the people of God only have Him on their side, the whole creation stands in a friendly relation to them.

We have still some points to discuss more fully.

In reference to the *form* of the cherub, Züllig remarks: "According to Ex. xxv. 20, the faces of the two cherubs were directed to the lid of the ark of the covenant. Had they been the cherubs of Ezekiel, they could only have had one of their four faces in this direction, while the three other faces must have looked towards the three other opposite points. Hence each of these must have had only one face, while those had four." The cherubs of the ark of the covenant had human forms and faces; and the three other classes of living things must have been contented with the representation by the wings taken from the birds, which in the history of the creation form the beginning of the animal world, as man forms the close. These wings had the double purpose,— above, to form the throne of God; beneath, to overshadow the mercy-seat.

Why do the cherubim appear over the ark of the covenant? In general they belonged to it, because it was of the deepest moment to indicate that the God of Israel was at the same time God absolutely, which is so emphatically and designedly held forth in the books of Moses from the very first chapter, that the temple is dedicated to the God of the spirits of all flesh, who is almighty to save those who keep His commandments, and to destroy those who transgress them. For the same purpose, cherubim were to be woven in the inner curtains or hangings of the tabernacle, according to Ex. xxvi. 1. What special significance the cherubim had here in connection with the whole of the ark, we have already pointed out. This significance is in the first place comforting. In the background, however, stands along with this a warning and deterring one. If the church be not in earnest regarding the foundation of the whole—the testimony, the revelation of the divine will; if she turns the great grace, that she knows the will of her Lord, into lasciviousness; if she has in her mouth only the commandments, which are to be kept and obeyed, in order to boast of them, and judge others by them

(Rom. ii.),—the mercy-seat forthwith loses its significance; the protective power of the cherubim, which is inseparably connected with it, at the same time comes to an end; their friendly face turns into a terrible one; the majesty of the offended God sitting above them arms them for the punishment of His unfaithful people.

The further question, Why are the cherubim of one piece with the mercy-seat? is answered by that which has been already remarked. The fact points to this, that the protection which the cherubim secure comes from the propitiation.

That the faces of the cherubim are directed to one another, is indicative of the mutual harmony of the creatures, which rests on their common relation to the Lord, whose spirit rules in them.

That the face of the cherubim is directed to the mercy-seat, points to this, that grace is the most adorable secret. The passage in 1 Pet. i. 12, which refers to the angels who have nothing to do with the cherubim, has been without reason connected with this; but the face turned inwards is a sign of the friendly disposition which the creature entertains towards the community reconciled to God (Ps. xxxiv. 16), as the averted or concealed face is so often the sign of a hostile disposition. As the cherubs, and in them the Lord who sits above them, here look to the mercy-seat, so in Ps. lxxiv. 20, in a time of heavy oppression to the commonwealth, the Lord is entreated by it to "look unto the covenant." Thus regarded, the direction of the faces of the cherubim to the mercy-seat is in harmony with the fact that they cover it with their wings, and both facts come under the same point of view.

It cannot be doubted that this covering of the mercy-seat is a symbol of the protection which the cherubim secure to the redeemed community. The covering is often used of a protecting covert; for example, Ps. cxl. 8, "Thou *coverest* my head in the day of battle;" and the wings are often the figure of *protection*, as in Ps. xxxvi. 8, "How excellent is Thy goodness, O God! and the children of men trust in the shadow of Thy wings;" and Ps. lxi. 5, "I will abide in Thy tents for ever; I will trust in the covert of Thy wings." But it is quite decisive, that in Ezek. xxviii. 14, according to the connection, "the covering" must necessarily be the protecting cherub. Hence, so much the more light falls on the covering of the cherubs in the sanctuary, as the prophet has borrowed the figure from this, and expressly alludes to it. The thought which lies at the root of the symbolic representation, that the creature goes along with the Creator, that the community reconciled to its God enjoys the protection of the creature, we find often expressed in the Old Testament. Thus it is said, Lev. xxvi. 3 f., "If ye walk in my statutes (the right relation to the *testimony*, as the condition of sharing in the *propitiation*), . . . I will rid *evil beasts* out of the land, and the sword (of man, the apex of the animal world) shall not pass through your land." In contrast with this, it is said in vers. 22, 25, of those who violate the testimony, and thereby *exclude* themselves from a part in the propitiation: " And I will send against you the beast of the field; and it will rob you, and destroy your cattle, and diminish you; and your ways shall lie waste. And I will bring upon you a sword, *avenging the quarrel of my covenant*" (the *propitiation*, which can never be idle, acquires now a destructive import); " and ye shall be given into the hand of the enemy." In Hos. ii. 20 it is said of the people when awakened to repentance: "And in that day I will make a covenant for them with the beasts of the field, and with the fowls of heaven, and with the creeping thing of the ground; and bow, sword, and battle I will break out of the land." Here we have a fourfold array of the "living" creature, which the Lord makes friendly to His renewed people: from the irrational the prophet rises to man: Also in Ezek. xxxiv. 25 f. peace with the creatures follows peace with God: " And I will make with them a covenant of peace; and I will rid the evil beasts out of the land, and they shall dwell safely in the wilderness, and sleep in the woods. And they shall be no more a prey to the heathen, and the beasts of the land shall not devour them, and none shall make them afraid." The "beasts of the land" appear not seldom also in human form. By the lions, one of the faces of the cherubs in Ezekiel, are often designated the wickedness and tyranny of the heathen; for ex., in Isa. xxxv. 9. In Nebuchadnezzar, man, lion, and eagle are presented at the same time. The four world-powers appear in

Daniel not without design in the form of four beasts. And in Isa. lvi. 9 the beasts of the field are the heathen, whom the Lord sends over His degenerate people. Schiller also sings, " The women became hyenas." The limits which the original order of creation has placed between man and beast may be destroyed by the degeneracy of man.

The cherubs in the *temple of Solomon* demand, on the whole, no special treatment. The same applies to them as to the cherubs in the tabernacle. Solomon's formative activity was here confined within narrow limits. What was communicated to Moses by revelation, he was obliged in the main only to repeat. Only a few single points here claim our attention.

To the smaller cherubic figures immediately over the ark Solomon added (1 Kings vi. 23 f.) " in his temple two others ten cubits high, of olive tree, carved and overlaid with gold, which stood near the ark with outstretched wings. Their outstretched wings formed a second higher covering over the ark" (Züllig). That the wings of these cherubim extended from one wall of the most holy place to the other, signified the completeness of the protection which God secures to His people by means of His creatures.

According to 1 Chron. xxviii. 18, David gives to Solomon the gold " for the pattern of the chariot, the cherubim, that spread out their wings, and cover the ark of the covenant of the Lord." The cherubim do not here draw a chariot, but they are themselves the chariot; as also in Jesus Sirach, in ch. xlix. 8, the cherubim-chariot is the chariot that consists of the cherubim themselves; and in Ps. xviii. 11 God rides on the cherub. The relation of God to His living creatures resembles that of the driver to his chariot, which takes its direction absolutely from him. God is the absolutely guiding principle in His creatures and for His creatures: this is the thought which lies at the root of the designation of the cherubim by the chariot.

When once the figure of the chariot used by David in Ps. xviii. was naturalized, it was easy to add to the chariot also wheels. We have seen before, that these wheels, at the same time under and near or beside the cherubim, not absolutely subordinate to them, but co-ordinate with them, represent in Ezekiel the powers of nature, which are directed by the Lord of creation no less than the living creatures in harmony with them. The proper source of this sensible representation is not, however, to be sought in Ezekiel. Vitringa has clearly shown that it goes back to Solomon; and those who will now deny this are either ignorant of his argument, or have not duly appreciated it. In the place of the single laver for cleansing the sacrificial flesh, which Moses (Ex. xxx. 28) placed before the tabernacle, between it and the altar of burnt-offering, entered in the temple of Solomon, along with the brazen seas, ten lavers, which Hiram the artisan constructed by command of Solomon. The description of these lavers is extremely brief; it occupies only a single verse. On the other hand, no vessel of the temple has the author of the book of Kings described so fully as the bases of these lavers: he devotes to them no less than twelve verses (1 Kings vii. 28-39). This at once indicates to us, that these bases must have a deeper positive import; and it will not disturb us that these bases, together with the lavers resting on them, externally considered, had only a very subordinate position: for what was represented in the part belonged to the whole; and to represent it precisely here was natural, as only here, in these newly introduced vessels, was freer scope given for holy art, whereas in the more important vessels it was necessary to copy the patterns of Moses. Now on these bases were figured lions, oxen, cherubim, and palm trees. This indicates that the temple was dedicated to the Lord of the whole organic creation. "The figure," says Velthusen, "announced the presence of the only true supreme Lord of all nature, and thereby distinguished this building consecrated to Him, where He was worshipped, and had promised graciously to receive offering and prayer, from all idolatrous temples." Under the bases are four wheels. That these must have a symbolic meaning is clear, not only from the analogy of the significant figures on the bases, and from the comparison of Ezekiel, where even as here the wheels connected with the cherubim, and taking the lower place in relation to them, on clear and certain grounds, denote the powers of nature; but it lies in the nature of the thing, as there is here no practical end which the wheels might serve. It has been supposed that the wheels were to make the bases with the lavers easily moveable. But they occupied a fixed place, as is expressly said in 1 Kings vii. 39; and motion is not to be thought of.

We will conclude with the discussion of the grand vision of the cherubim in Ezekiel. But first, we will take a glance at the passing mention of the cherub in Ezek. xxviii. 14. The prophet, in the prediction against the king of Tyre, here says to him, "Thou art an anointed cherub, that covereth." As the cherub comprehends the multiplicity of the creatures in a unity, so the king the multiplicity of his people. The nature of the kingly office can scarcely be more aptly designated than by the name cherub. Jeremiah, in Lam. iv. 20, calls the king of Israel the life-breath of his people, so that they live and die with him. Further, the king, like the cherub, is a concentration of productive nature. Bähr rightly says: "The accompanying description of the wisdom, beauty, perfection, might, grandeur, and glory of this king, shows clearly that the designation of cherub was applied to him, because he was on the highest stage of created life. All that this creation has of grandeur and glory was united in him, as in the cherub." The king calls himself God. The prophet accords to Him a position similar to that of an anointed cherub; but because he went beyond this position which was granted him by God, who had anointed him and endowed him with gifts by His Spirit, it is wrested from him by God, and he sinks into absolute nullity. The cherub is more exactly described as "the covering." The article points to the well-known covering cherub in the sanctuary, and specially to Ex. xxv. 20. As the cherub in the sanctuary covers the ark, and in particular the mercy-seat, in token of the protection which, in consequence of the operation of God who rules over him, he secures to the covenant people, so is the king of Tyre the protector of his state, with all the nations that are subject to him. But as in the cherub the protective power only comes directly from him, but ultimately from the power of God that animates him, so also the king of Tyre has only by the grace of God the power to cover; and as he has made himself unworthy of this grace, the power has been lost. Much confusion is introduced by extending further the comparison with the cherub, which is limited singly and alone to the words quoted: thus, for example, B. Bähr remarks, "Here the king of Tyre is figuratively called a covering cherub; and it is said of him, In Eden, in the garden of God, thou didst dwell;" and Riehm, "The king of Tyre is compared with the cherub that dwells on the mount of God, and walks in the midst of the stones of fire." The expression, "In Eden, the garden of God, wast thou," in ver. 13—in a situation glorious like that of the first man in paradise—and also the following one on the comparison with the cherub, in ver. 14, " On the mount of God wast thou in the midst of the stones of fire," that formed around thee a protecting wall, so that thou, under the mighty protection of God, mightest protect thy subjects, stand in no near relation to the cherub, but depict the glory of the king of Tyre under another figure. He resembles in this his glory, (1) the first man in paradise, (2) the cherub, and (3) one who on a high hill is surrounded by walls of fire.

We now turn to the sublime vision of the cherubim, which opens the prophecies of Ezekiel.

The historical starting-point of this vision lies in the false hopes which had at that time seized the minds of those who remained in Jerusalem with Zedekiah at their head. A spirit of infatuation had fallen on the people. They cast the prophecies of Jeremiah to the wind, which announced the approaching completion of the judgment by the Chaldeans. Confiding in the confederacy with the Egyptian power, which must at that time have taken a lofty flight, they hoped soon to be able to free themselves altogether from the Chaldean supremacy. These hopes also were spread among the exiles, as the letter addressed to them by Jeremiah (ch. xxix.) shows. He therein warns them, "Let not the prophets that are among you deceive you, and hearken not to your dreams, for they prophesy falsely to you in my name." Soon, it was thought, will a return to their country be opened up; and to this thought was joined the other—namely, to work together for it. These illusions and excitements, which prevented the people from entering with sincerity on the path of repentance pointed out by God, Ezekiel was to oppose. This opposition was made first by the vision of the cherubim, the real import of which Grotius thus briefly and well defines: "After the long-suffering of God, all tended towards vengeance." The following discourses of the prophet are related to this opening vision as the commentary to the text.

Parallel with the vision of the cherubim in Ezekiel is the seething-pot coming from the north, which, according to Jer. i. 13, is shown to his senior colleague in office on his call, with the added elucidation, " Out of the north the evil will be opened upon all the inhabitants of the land. For, lo, I will call all the families of the kingdoms towards the north; and they shall come, and set every one his throne before the gates of Jerusalem, and against all the walls thereof round about, and against all the cities of Judah." The vision of Ezekiel serves to uphold and confirm that older vision against the assaults of the time. It opposes the wrath of the Almighty to all hopes of salvation. We have here at the same time the counterpart of that first appearance of the cherubim in paradise. As there, God appearing above the cherubim with the flaming sword excludes from the tree of life; so here, God appearing above the cherubim interposes between the people and salvation, and cuts off all access of the people to it.

The picture begins in ch. i. 4 with the words, " And I looked, and, behold, a whirlwind came out of the north, a great cloud, and enfolded fire, and a brightness about it, and out of the midst of it as the look of *chasmal*, out of the midst of the fire." That the appearance has a threatening character, appears from the connection of the three chief figures for wrath, judgment, and punishment,—the storm, the cloud, and the fire, the more precise description of which as *enfolded*, fire gathered into a ball, borrowed from Ex. ix. 24, indicates that the same energy of the punitive righteousness of God which was once in ancient times displayed on the Egyptians, will now once more direct itself against the chosen people of God, who have turned the grace of God into lasciviousness, of that God who in earnest warning has said to them, " The Lord thy God is a consuming fire, a jealous God." Out of the midst of the fire appears to the prophet, as the look of *chasmal*, the figure of God. *Chasmal* denotes here the essence of the personality of God, the holiness, that is, the infinite glory, the absolute pre-eminence above all creation, His incomparableness, His perfection. The "splendour" parallel to it in ch. viii. 2 leaves no doubt that it denotes something of the clearest brightness. "Out of the midst of the fire:" this makes the soul shake in its inmost depth. It is dreadful to have for a foe the fountain of all salvation. All hope is thereby cast down. There is no one in heaven or on earth who can deliver from His hand. And yet the matter has also a cheering side. It is better to fall into the hands of God than into those of man—better to have to do with God than with the terrible Chaldeans. If He is angry, and indeed with an anger "which burns unto the lowest hell, and consumes the land with its increase, and sets on fire the foundations of the mountains" (Deut. xxxii. 22), yet is there ever in Him a background of compassion, and indeed of a compassion that is as great as Himself, the infinity of which is an emanation of His holiness; and salvation will follow on repentance.

The further description of the vision, as it is given from ver. 5, presents the following points. First, under the high throne on which God sits in human form like a glorious king, appears the cloud, the type of the heavens, the incorporation of the name Zebaoth, with which the Lord is so often designated as the Almighty Ruler of heaven. The description of the cloud is very brief, because the powers of heaven are not immediately concerned in the present matter. So much the more full is the description of those points in the vision, which present God as the Lord of the works and powers of nature. For the Lord wished to summon these for the punishment of His unfaithful people. The Chaldeans, the representatives of the living creatures, composed of man, lion, ox, and eagle (Dan. vii. 4), were to take Jerusalem, and it was to be burned with fire. The living creatures are represented by the cherubim, which in this connection admit of only the one explanation—God sends the creature against His backsliding people. The powers of nature are denoted by the wheels. It is quite an irrelevant question, in what way the wheels were connected with the cherubim. It suffices for the figure of the chariot that the cherubim took the upper place, and the wheels, under which figure the powers of nature are represented, on account of their weight and energy, the lower. All is easy and obvious to thought. We have before us an inspired ideal form, much too ethereal for either painting or sculpture to master. "The appearance of the wheels and their work was as the look of the chrysolite:" this points to the glory of the powers of nature. "A wheel was in the middle of a wheel:" in every wheel a wheel was inserted. "To their four sides they went in going:" this indicates that the powers of nature are absolutely at the disposal of God—that He can use them where He will, and send them whither He will. That the felloes of the wheels are full of eyes, is a sign that the powers of nature do not work blindly, but are directed by Providence. That the spirit of the living creature is in the wheels, shows that one and the same divine power is active in the living creatures and in the powers of nature, so that they work harmoniously for the end appointed of God. In the repetition of the vision of the cherubim in ch. x., the cherub stretches forth its hand, takes the fire, with which Jerusalem is to be burned, out of the midst of the wheels, and hands it over to Him that is clothed in linen, the angel of the Lord, who has received from Him that sits on the throne the command to burn Jerusalem. By this it is indicated that the activity of the Chaldeans in the burning of the city, figured by the action of the cherub, is altogether subordinate; that the burning of Jerusalem in the main is to be no otherwise regarded than that of Sodom and Gomorrah, in which there was no human co-operation. The fire is found under the throne of God, is an element created by Him; and the cherub hands it only at the command of God to the angel from whom the proper action proceeds. In Ezek. xi. 22 it is said, "The cherubim flapped their wings, and the wheels moved beside them; and the glory of the God of Israel was over them." Kliefoth rightly observes that it is merely said "the wheels," whereas it is said "their wings." This proves that the wheels, although they followed the movement of the cherubim, do not belong to the cherubim. Those who do not wish in the cherubim to distinguish between the idea and its dress, are brought into a dilemma by the wheels. Velthusen rightly maintains, that "the wheels are so connected with the cherubim, and make with them so much one figure, that they stand, go, and rise with these animals, without being able to separate the one from the other; so that he who holds the cherubim to be not a mere figurative appearance, must regard the wheels and throne at the same time as things actually existing in nature, of which the Most High makes use in His advent. The Jews perceived this, and therefore regarded the wheels as a peculiar kind of angels."

It will be necessary to distinguish, in the grand representation of the universe in Ezekiel, between that which belongs to the constantly identical being, and that which specially refers to the present circumstances—to the work of wrath, which is now to be executed on the degenerate covenant people. This distinction makes itself known even in Him who sits upon the throne. According to ch. i. 27, the appearance of God below the loins was as the look of fire, which is enclosed around, a concentrated fire, and above as shining brass. The shining brass denotes the "wrathful glow of His judicial and vindictive function," which is now significant, though in general it has only subordinate importance. But the same distinction meets us also in the cherubim. Here there is special reference to present circumstances in "the feet sparkling as the look of glowing brass," in ch. i. 7, with which they will destroy everything that resists. Vers. 13, 14 likewise refer to the present mission, "And the likeness of the living creatures was as coals of fire: they burn like torches. The fire goes in between the living creatures, and the fire is bright, and out of the fire goes lightning. And the living creatures ran hither and thither, as the appearance of a flash." The animals can scarcely await the time when they are to fulfil their mission as the ministers of the divine vengeance. This is the temporary element in the delineation of the cherubim in Ezekiel; as in the first appearance of the cherubim in paradise, the connection with the flashing sword was only a temporary and separable one. In other circumstances all would bear a more serene and friendly aspect. In the repetition of the delineation of the cherubim in Revelation, where God appearing above the cherubim comes forward on behalf of His church, all that points to anger, punishment, and destruction is removed.

But though the appearance is so severe and threatening, yet the friendly element is not wanting here. According to ch. i. 27, 28, the whole of the appearance is surrounded with a brightness: "As the appearance of the bow that is in the cloud in the day of rain, so was the appearance of the brightness round about." Grotius has rightly perceived the real import of the figure: "The divine judgments, however severe, shall not obliterate the memory of the covenant made with Abraham, Isaac, and Jacob." The rainbow since Gen. ix. is unchangeably consecrated to be the symbol of mercy returning after wrath. Although in us there is much sin, in God there is much more grace: thus the lovely form of the rainbow exclaims to the church affrighted by the terrible cloud (ver. 4), and trembling on account of her sins. To her *alone* belong the sayings, "I kill, and I make alive;" and, "He woundeth and bindeth up; He smiteth, and His hands heal;" whereas the clouds are common to her with the world. The vision of the rainbow has been gloriously fulfilled, since after the Chaldean destruction, first the joyful return took place, and then the tidings were heard, "Behold, I announce to you great joy, for to you is born this day a Saviour." And it will be fulfilled even to the end of the days. "If it come to pass that I bring a cloud over the earth, my bow shall be seen in the cloud:" this is the perpetual privilege which is conferred on the church of God on the earth. If we lay this to heart, the clouds will not make us afraid, but fill us with joyful hope. The denser they are, the more gloriously will the rainbow shine.

www.ingramcontent.com/pod-product-compliance
Lightning Source LLC
Chambersburg PA
CBHW052045290426
44111CB00011B/1618